1991

John Dewey

The Later Works, 1925–1953

Volume 17: 1885–1953

EDITED BY JO ANN BOYDSTON

TEXTUAL EDITOR,

BARBARA LEVINE

ASSISTANT TEXTUAL EDITOR,

RICHARD W. FIELD

With an Introduction by Sidney Hook

Southern Illinois University Press

Carbondale and Edwardsville

COMMITTEE ON
SCHOLARLY EDITIONS

AN APPROVED TEXT

MODERN LANGUAGE
ASSOCIATION OF AMERICA

The text of this reprinting is a photo-offset reproduction of the original cloth
edition that contains the full apparatus for the volume awarded the seal of the
Committee on Scholarly Editions of the Modern Language Association.
Editorial expenses were met in part by a grant from the Editions Program of the
National Endowment for the Humanities, an independent Federal agency.

The paperbound edition has been made possible by a special subvention from
the John Dewey Foundation.

The Library of Congress catalogued the first printing of this work (in cloth) as
follows:

Dewey, John, 1859–1952.
    The later works, 1925–1953.

    Vol. 17 has introd. by Sidney Hook.
    Continues The middle works, 1899–1924.
    Includes bibliographies and indexes.

    CONTENTS: v. 1. 1925—[etc.]—v. 2. 1925–1927.—[etc.]—v. 17.
1885–1953.
    1. Philosophy—Collected works.   I. Boydston, Jo Ann, 1924–.   II. Title.
B945.D41 1981   191   80-27285
ISBN 0-8093-1661-7 (V. 17)

ISBN 0-8093-1683-8 (paperback)

Contents

ɔ

Foreword

This final volume in The Collected Works of John Dewey, 1882–1953, presents all Dewey's writings not published in earlier Works volumes. Although it is much more comprehensive than its "Later Works" label implies, it has been numbered Volume 17 of *The Later Works* for the convenience of both librarians and readers.

With this volume, we conclude the three series that comprise the thirty-seven volumes of John Dewey's works—*The Early Works, 1882–1898*, five volumes; *The Middle Works, 1899–1924*, fifteen volumes; *The Later Works, 1925–1953*, seventeen volumes. A comprehensive subject and short-title index to all the Works is to follow within the year.

The first volume of The Collected Works appeared in 1967; Volume 17 of *The Later Works*—the thirty-seventh volume of The Collected Works—is the culmination of a pioneering venture: it is the first edition of the collected writings of a classical American philosopher and the first edition of philosophical works to have used the editorial principles and procedures of modern textual criticism. The emblem of the Modern Language Association Center for Editions of American Authors and later Committee on Scholarly Editions in each volume of The Collected Works signifies that the volumes have met and fulfilled the highest standards of editing and publishing.

This venture began in 1961 at Southern Illinois University as a small research project entitled "Cooperative Research on Dewey Publications," with the goal of preparing a concordance of the terms in John Dewey's writings. In 1961, many of Dewey's writings were scattered, hard to find, and difficult of access; the only listing of those writings—Milton Halsey Thomas's 1939 bibliography—was incomplete (Thomas's *Centennial Bibliography*, scheduled for 1959, appeared in 1962). Locating and collecting copies of everything Dewey produced throughout his highly productive seventy-year publishing career was the obvious first step in such a project. However, even our preliminary investigation of the corpus revealed its size and inaccessibility, and it soon became clear that developing a concordance would not be possible in the absence of a uniform collected edition of Dewey's works. Further, it was apparent early on that a collected edition of Dewey's writings was urgently needed to preserve the rapidly disappearing copies of materials published in pamphlets, newspapers, and nineteenth-century journals.

To organize such an edition, different plans were entertained; one of them was a scheme to arrange Dewey's writings into several series based on topical categories, an approach eventually abandoned. Although the Works edition itself was finally organized chronologically, we met the need for a comprehensive topical survey of Dewey's writings in 1970 with the separate volume, *Guide to the Works of John Dewey.* When the chronological plan was firmly fixed, the question of dividing this large body of material into volumes had to be answered. Issues of permissions, copyrights, publication subvention, and continuity of editorial leadership necessarily took precedence over philosophical considerations: both the University and the Southern Illinois University Press believed that the five *Early Works* volumes represented a reasonable initial commitment by the Press and the University. Thus, even though all volumes were planned in detail at the outset, the division into "early," "middle," and "later" periods stemmed more from expediency than from philosophical significance in Dewey's work.

Decisions about organizing Dewey's writings into volumes and series were less difficult than those about the editorial approach for such an unprecedented collected edition. We chose to follow the standards of the newly formed Center for Editions of American Authors of the Modern Language Association, which established principles, suggested procedures, and reviewed printer's copy for the volumes before awarding the "Approved Edition" seal. The internationally renowned textual expert, Fredson Bowers, agreed to serve as textual consultant throughout the edition. Bowers's wise guidance and constant support are directly responsible for the editorial excellence of the Works.

When we started editing Dewey's writings, only a few editions of literary works had been undertaken under the auspices of the Modern Language Association. This was the first edition of philosophical works included under that umbrella. Although critical editing by the standards of the Center for Editions of American Authors was little known and less understood, Vernon Sternberg, director of the Southern Illinois University Press, became an early promoter of the CEAA and strongly supported the need to apply its standards in this edition. His conviction and confidence made it possible for us to plan The Collected Works completely, to finish *The Early Works,* to publish most of *The Middle Works,* and to publish Volume 1 of *The Later Works.* The continuing and unstinting help of his successor, Kenney Withers, enabled us to publish all the remaining *Middle Works* and *Later Works* volumes. The intelligent leadership and generous cooperation of the Southern Illinois University Press resulted in this edition's serving as a model for other editions of American philosophical works.

The standards of the Center for Editions of American Authors (and later of the Committee on Scholarly Editions), as developed and applied in a number of editions, helped to ground the Works in the principles and procedures of scholarly critical editing. Association with and approval by those bodies have reassured us of editorial peer acceptance at every step.

Gathering the research materials to edit the volumes properly—multiple copies of all versions and printings of the works, newspaper reports and advertisements, oral history interviews, publishers' correspondence, editorial and style manuals of publishers and journals, Dewey's correspondence, manuscripts, and typescripts, and published writings about Dewey—created the nucleus of a research center. In 1972, the John Dewey Foundation increased the potential of that center exponentially with a gift of the John Dewey Papers: eighty-seven warehouse boxes of personal and professional correspondence, Dewey's library, and memorabilia. With the help of Kenneth Duckett and David Koch in Morris Library's Special Collections, that gift attracted in turn many Dewey-related papers in American philosophy and education, so that in time, "Cooperative Research on Dewey Publications" became in name as well as in fact the "Center for Dewey

Studies." Although it grew up as an adjunct to the Works, this research center, along with Special Collections, will continue to serve Dewey scholarship after the edition is completed.

Our gratitude to all those who contributed to the early planning of the edition has been acknowledged in various places, particularly in the preface to each volume of the *Early Works*. But, because the basic plan and the editorial approach have continued from the first through the thirty-seventh volume, those early acknowledgments must be repeated for the entire edition. Starting with President Delyte Morris, Vice-Presidents John E. Grinnell, Charles Tenney, and Robert MacVicar, the administration of Southern Illinois University at Carbondale has been highly supportive of our work. Librarians around the world have been universally considerate, alert, and thoughtful; the contributions of the staff of Morris Library have been most important throughout the leadership of two deans of library affairs, Ralph E. McCoy and Kenneth G. Peterson.

We express our profound appreciation for the contributions of the first editorial advisory board to the project and its long-time chairman, Lewis Hahn, and to the many other scholars who wrote introductions, who found and contributed copies of Dewey items, correspondence, and Dewey-related materials, who advised and consulted on a range of philosophical and textual matters, who cheered and encouraged us, especially Dewey's leading protégé and spokesman, Sidney Hook.

Sidney Hook's role in completing The Collected Works of John Dewey transcends his direct participation through advice and writing volume introductions; as president of the John Dewey Foundation, he urged that we accelerate the pace of editing and publishing the volumes, then helped to make that acceleration possible with the Foundation's financial support of both the editing and publishing. His support took many forms; it was considerable and integral.

Six editors are responsible for most of the *Middle Works* and *Later Works* volumes. Although their names appear on the title pages of these volumes both as associate textual editors and as textual editors, their contributions to the success of this edition extend well beyond such published listing; their commitment and their extraordinary skills have been indispensable. They are Patricia R. Baysinger, Barbara Levine, Kathleen Poulos, Anne

Sharpe, Harriet F. Simon, and Bridget Walsh. Other editors and editorial assistants who have played an important role in producing these volumes are Polly V. Dunn, Elizabeth M. Evanson, Richard W. Field, Paul Kolojeski, and Diane Meierkort.

Both the editing and publishing of the Works have been generously supported by several institutions, agencies, and individual donors: Southern Illinois University, the Southern Illinois University Press, the National Endowment for the Humanities, the John Dewey Foundation through the presidencies of both Sidney Hook and Steven Cahn, the American Council of Learned Societies, and two private contributors. This edition—these thirty-seven volumes—will serve as a continuing testimonial to the vision and the intimate involvement of the many organizations, editors, scholars, librarians, researchers, and administrators who believed the edition could be done, done well, and done before the end of this century.

JO ANN BOYDSTON

Introduction

The Relevance of John Dewey's Thought
By Sidney Hook

The abuse of the term *relevance* by radical extremists might justifiably have set up an allergic reaction in the minds of critical readers to its use. Nonetheless, if we recall that *relevance* is a relational term, the question "Relevant to what?" is one whose legitimacy cannot reasonably be disputed.

When I speak of the relevance of John Dewey's thought I refer not to its bearing on crisis situations but to its bearing on the condition of man, his problems and predicaments in war *and* peace, good times *and* bad, whenever he reflectively examines alternatives of action in the course of choosing a desirable way of life. John Dewey wrote millions of words on the topical issues that arose during the three quarters of a century that spanned his adult life. But it is not for that reason that his ideas have relevance today. They are relevant to areas of thought and action in which our basic intellectual and practical interests are still involved—education and ethics, culture and politics, social philosophy in the broadest sense. In some of these areas his views are emerging once more; in others, events and institutional change are giving an *actualité* to positions that seemed Utopian if not unrealistic at the time he enunciated them.

As one familiar with the whole corpus of Dewey's writings would have expected, the basic educational ideas and ideals that pervade them have been foremost among the rediscoveries of his thought. Addressing the American Association for the Advancement of Science in 1909, Dewey affirmed the central importance of science in the curriculum of the schools long before his post-Sputnik critics sought to reconstruct the American school system to overtake Soviet technological achievements and developments. But by the study of science Dewey does not mean the acquisition of a miscellaneous store of information of facts, laws, theories, and interesting correlations that constitute the subject matter of so much of the science curriculum of the schools. He means the understanding of what it is that confers scientific validity upon a particular conclusion or the "knowledge of the ways by which anything is entitled to be called knowledge instead of being mere opinion or guess-work or dogma." It is this kind of knowledge which for him is of most worth. Long before the critics of "scientism" appeared on the scene Dewey warned against the view that any specific method in the particular sciences—whether it was physics, biology, or psychology—could define the pattern of rationality. When Dewey criticized the traditional humanistic education of his day, his analysis was directed against the formal study of languages and literature that gave a narrow training in certain techniques that constricted the imagination and emotions instead of liberating and humanizing them. For him the humanities were not merely subjects to be taught, they were the means of affecting liberal and humane minds, what he sometimes called "the production of a social and socialized sense." They were preeminently the field in which the qualities of value were revealed and their interrelations explored. A half century before C. P. Snow's superficial book on *The Two Cultures* appeared, Dewey had defined the problem facing reflective citizens concerned with education as "how we are to effect in this country a combination of a scientific and a humanistic education."

Dewey's conception of this combination was profound not superficial because he was aware of a third culture—the social or cultural—that embraced the "two cultures" and without reference to which humanistic training was in danger of becoming precious, if not snobbish, and scientific training harnessed to barbaric goals. The very distinction between the humanistic and scientific disciplines presupposes an overarching cultural or social dimension expressed in institutions, basic habits and some hierarchy of value choices that make up the quality of life or the distinctive character of civilization at any given time. An education that seeks to make its students imaginatively aware of those dynamic forces in society that ultimately affect the direction of both scientific and humanistic activity must stress the understanding of its basic social and economic structure, the problems and conflicts of the encompassing cultural milieu, and the alternatives of development or retrogression always open to it. That is why the abstract celebration of moral values—dignity, integrity, happiness, serenity—is insufficient to tell us what changes in social institutions are required to give them a concrete embodiment in the life of most human beings. Similarly, without the assessment of the effects of science and technology upon our social life and upon the quality of the resulting experience, we run the risk of adapting our ideals to the unplanned and unintended consequences of the applications of science rather than organizing its resources in the responsible service of man. Neither humanistic nor scientific education traditionally conceived, because of their failure to understand the encompassing third culture of social, economic, political, and historical studies, can tell us when to produce, what to produce, and why.

This suggests an even more fundamental area of thought in which Dewey, albeit much misunderstood, anticipated some very recent intellectual developments, namely, in the very conception of philosophy itself. Many have been the conceptions of philosophy that have prevailed in different societies, and these differences are present within our own. Dewey continuing the Greek tradition has maintained that philosophy is a quest for wisdom, but as distinct from ancient, medieval, and almost all other modern thinkers, he has rejected the attempt to identify or ground wisdom with or on some metaphysical or transcendental (ultimately religious) insight or with the purely descriptive knowledge of the natural sciences. Wisdom for Dewey is a moral term "and like every moral term refers not to the constitution of things already in existence, not even if that constitution be magnified into eternity and absoluteness. As a moral term it refers to a choice about something to be done, a preference for living this sort of life rather than that. It refers not to accomplished reality but to a desired future which our desires, when translated into articulate conviction, may help bring into existence." [1]

This makes philosophy a *normative analysis* of the basic value conflicts of the culture of which it is a part. It is a conception of philosophy which is both an historical interpretation of what philosophy has been and a proposal of what it should be and do.

1. John Dewey, "Philosophy and Democracy," *University* [of California] *Chronicle* 21 (1919): 43 [*The Middle Works of John Dewey, 1899–1924*, ed. Jo Ann Boydston (Carbondale and Edwardsville: Southern Illinois University Press, 1982), 11:44].

It makes the philosopher a moralist but not a moralizer or social reformer. It faces certain difficulties which I have attempted to meet elsewhere.[2] But what is significant for present purposes is that this conception (derided or ignored for many years by most American philosophers who have regarded philosophy either as a quest for a reality beyond the reach of scientific methods, or as an analytic explication of scientific methods, or as a linguistic analysis of basic concepts whose ordinary and peculiar uses, when not properly distinguished, gave rise to intellectual confusion) has now strongly emerged on the philosophical scene and is moving more and more to the center of current philosophical concern. Unfortunately not all who are now concerned with normative analysis of values in their social bearing have understood Dewey's conception of the vocation of the professional philosopher as distinct from the activity of the citizen. They seek to politicize philosophy by harnessing it to some specific controversial political program rather than to the analytic functions of clarifying the alternatives of social action and their consequences.

To some readers this will suggest that Dewey's thought has been an anticipation of certain of the themes in later-day existentialism. This would be more false than true. The existentialists were concerned like Dewey with moral choice, its phenomenology and psychology. But their irrationalism, their contention that no grounds can be given for our basic choices, that they are all on the same level, would raise doubts on Dewey's view whether they have a right to any theory of *moral* judgment. For the existentialists a moral choice is a passion. For Dewey it is more than a passion, it is a conviction for which rational grounds can be given, that is, it is "a passion that would exhibit itself as a reasonable persuasion." A persuasion can be reasonable even if it is not logically entailed by the facts of the problematic situation in which the judgment is made. For Dewey the usual objection to the view that values or ends can be rationally determined, namely, that rationality is a quality of *means* that are adapted to achieve specific ends but that the ends themselves

2. Sidney Hook, "Philosophy and Public Policy," *Journal of Philosophy* 67 (23 July 1970): 461–70; reprinted with revisions in *Philosophy and Public Policy* (Carbondale and Edwardsville: Southern Illinois University Press, 1980), pp. 3–15.

are a matter of arbitrary choice, does not hold. For he denies that there are any ultimate ends and contends that there is a plural means-end continuum in all problematic situations of moral choice. We never confront bare facts with pure ideals. The factual situation already includes some value commitments, not questioned in that particular context, and the pure ideal presupposes some assumption about the factual causal circumstances out of which it arose and the factual consequences to which it leads. That is why Dewey holds that "if ever we are to be governed by intelligence, not by things and by words, science must have something to say about *what* we do, and not merely about *how* we may do it most easily and economically."[3] The typical response of some philosophical intuitionistic critics to Dewey's view that moral virtue is intelligence is that this makes the economical use of means to the achievement of *any* given end moral. (For example, "then the person"—it is said—"who discovers that cyanide is the cheapest and quickest way of destroying the victims of a genocide program would be the most moral"!) But Dewey's point is that he is prepared to show that the choice of that given end in the determinate historical situation is unreasonable or unintelligent. Despite the denial by emotivists and existentialists that ends and goals are beyond rational evaluation, that it is unintelligible to speak of them as being "rational" or "irrational," "foolish" or "wise," the facts of ordinary experience, as well as of ordinary language, give this position the lie. We are continually discussing the reasonableness or unreasonableness of pursuing specific goals, ends, objectives, or ideals.

It is not enough to vindicate the cognitive validity of value judgments today. More important than the acceptance of beliefs about the good and the better is the way in which the beliefs are held. Despite widely held opinions to the contrary, it is not from ethical skepticism or even from subjectivistic relativism we suffer most. For at their worst they make for an indifferentism that the exigencies of practical choice often reveal as merely a conventional pose. And at their best they make for an initial tolerance toward expressions of difference that may broaden the spec-

3. Dewey, "Science as Subject-Matter and as Method," *Science*, n.s. 31 (28 January 1910): 127 [*Middle Works* 6:78–79].

trum of choice. The major threats to democratic political and social life stem not from relativism or skepticism but from fanaticism. We live in an age of true believers whose self-righteous absolutisms brook neither contradiction nor delay in bringing about the promised land of their faith. Disagreement is automatically attributed either to immeasurable stupidity or to unmitigated venality. Some of these fanaticisms are on the side of the angels, like absolute pacifism whose consequences often embolden aggressors like Hitler to believe that they can make armed moves and, ultimately, war with impunity. The fanatical social revolutionist equally with the fanatical reactionary or standpatter holds his beliefs in such a way that nothing that occurs can disconfirm them. The less fruitful and effective those beliefs are, the greater his impatience, the more intense his conviction of their truth. Only too often he ends up proclaiming that the evil system that defeats his demands—demands so clear, so obvious, so eminently reasonable—must be destroyed "by peaceful means if possible, by any means if necessary." In a few short strides the Utopian idealist becomes a bomb-throwing guerrilla warrior, an arsonist or an assassin—still self-righteous and full of moral indignation and completely unaware of the way in which the means he has used have corrupted both his ideals and his character.

In practice the fear of failure may curb fanaticisms except of the messianic varieties that border on the psychotic. But Dewey is interested not in the techniques of frustration or repression but in an intellectual approach that would prevent or at least hinder the emergence of fanaticism. To this end he believes that the cultivation of an historical sense is essential. Whether it is peace or justice or freedom or welfare that we have made the end-all and be-all of our social or political program, "the gist of rationality" in striving for them is "temporal perspective," for in human affairs, in contrast with pure logic and mathematics, our decisions are based on judgments of "more or less" rather than on judgments of "either-or."

This historical perspective on human affairs is wedded to a lively sense of the pluralism of values exhibited in such affairs. It is not that Dewey denies the validity of a moral stance that at some point stakes one's life, honor, and fortune on a position and digs in behind the declaration: "Hier stehe Ich. Ich kann nicht anders" (Here I stand. I can do no other). The question is, on what am I standing? On my conscience or on a platform of reason? For Dewey, conscience has no moral authority unless it is the result of a rational conscientiousness. And if it has moral authority, it necessarily requires taking note of the plural values of experience and their interrelatedness, and of rationally assessing the consequences of one's stand upon them. Especially today when "conscience" is often and sincerely invoked as an organ of ultimate and superior insight into one's moral duty—and not only as an easy pretext of avoidance of one's duty and responsibility, for betrayal of cause and country—it becomes necessary to point out that those who with a righteous pride affirm that they are prepared to take some action "in complete disregard of consequences" are immoral fanatics. For morality is always an affair of consequences. If we are prepared to say "let justice prevail though the heavens fall," well and good—provided we understand that the fall of heaven also means the death of love, the loss of freedom, the end of happiness, and the euthanasia of all other human values. And if these are rationally grasped as the true consequences of pursuing or realizing absolute justice, of what use or good would such justice be? We can ask the same questions of any other single value-term substituted for *justice*. The interrelatedness of values and the consequences of the means used to achieve one value, or the constellation of values of which it is a part, make the sharp disjunction between "merely" instrumental values and "pure" intrinsic values untenable.

Occasionally it is asserted that survival is the truly ultimate value which in cases of moral conflict always has an overriding validity. Reflective human behavior does not always square with the assertion. Sometimes the worst thing we can know of a human being is that he survived under the conditions laid down for survival—that he torture and destroy the innocent, betray friends, family, cause, and country.

For Dewey each situation has its own unique good discovered by intelligent analysis of the factual situation and of the competing value claims. No formula can guide our resolution. Sometimes we must give heed to the overriding imperatives of justice; sometimes we must subordinate the claims of justice to the overriding need of human welfare; sometimes both justice and welfare may temporarily be sacrificed to the requirements of security and survival. "This is opportunism," jeers the absolutist. To which one can legitimately retort that if opportunism means "the seeking of immediate advantage with little regard for principles or ultimate consequences," this is decidedly not opportunism, since regard for consequences is of the very essence of this approach. On the other hand, an absolutism that disregards fruits and consequences is the very quintessence of fanaticism, and often leaves no alternative where absolutes conflict except war, so that in the end sheer might determines what prevails in human affairs.

There is another generic sense of opportunism which stresses the intelligent application of principles to new occasions. In this sense, the social philosophy of Dewey is as opportunistic as scientific medicine. Those who issue the same prescription for all medical affairs are quacks. Social absolutism can be regarded as a kind of quackery in human affairs despite the high-mindedness and personal sincerity of its exponents. Sincerity is always a desirable trait in politics, but unless accompanied by intellectual humility, by a consciousness that one may be wrong in an area in which claims to certainty reveal a severe limitation of intelligence, it can express itself in monstrous form. Hitler did not lack sincerity.

Long before the misleading slogan of "participatory democracy" was sounded by the spokesmen of what was called the New Left, Dewey had developed the idea, expressed in germ in Jefferson's later writings, that democracy was not only a political form of government but a way of life, that it "must begin at home, and its home is the neighborly community."[4] The nature of community requires more than mere physical contiguity. It involves face-to-face relations and direct communication among citizens so that joint undertakings can be initiated. Individuals sharing ideas and emotions lose the feeling of being dwarfed by social forces moving behind their backs, of the impersonality of the political process and the anonymity of large numbers and organizations with their inescapable bureaucracies. This ex-

4. See Dewey, *The Public and Its Problems* (New York: Henry Holt and Co., 1927), pp. 212–13 [*The Later Works of John Dewey, 1925–1953*, ed. Jo Ann Boydston (Carbondale and Edwardsville: Southern Illinois University Press, 1984), 2:367–68].

plains why Dewey welcomed grass-roots movements and was quite critical of the functioning of purely formal mechanisms of political rule.

We must now confront a profound difficulty in Dewey's political philosophy which to the extent that he solves it requires the introduction of a faith that in the eyes of some may seem to transcend his commitment to the scientific attitude. The difficulty arises from the conjunction of a series of positions each of which appears to be well grounded. Dewey believes that our reflective behavior as well as the conclusions of analysis commits us to a cognitive theory of ethics according to which judgments of good and bad, right and wrong, can legitimately be called valid or invalid, true or false. He also is aware of the growth and complexity of government and that most of the tasks of government are administrative, requiring specialized and expert knowledge in the manifold technologies of the industrial arts and sciences. Why then, one asks, does not Dewey draw the conclusion that the likelihood of good government depends upon entrusting political rule to those who have the expert knowledge? Scientific judgment and truths do not depend upon the vote of majorities or even upon the participation of individual citizens in the scientific process. If scientific knowledge, as Dewey believes, is the only reliable method of reaching conclusions in human as well as in natural affairs, why not entrust the political destiny of the community to those who possess this scientific knowledge? And if we do, how can we still be loyal to the spirit and letter of democracy?

This is another way of asking Plato's question: If we do not elect the pilot of a ship to whom we entrust our lives and goods, why should we elect the pilot of the ship of state whose decisions may determine our collective lives and estates? We cannot make the easy answer of the emotivist: we elect pilots on the basis of their knowledge and craftsmanship to take us to our destinations, but the pilots have no authority to determine what our destination should be; for a choice is expressive of an attitude or wish or preference and not dependent upon any knowledge, scientific or other. Dewey cannot make that answer, for as we have seen, he believes that the relevant scientific knowledge can help "form the social and moral ideas of the sake of which it is used," and that "science must have something to say about *what* we do [and *where* to go], and not merely about *how* we may do it [and *how* to get there] most easily and economically."

Dewey is quite aware of the objections that can be made to the Platonic view, shared by Santayana and other honest totalitarians, that knowledge and knowledge only gives incontrovertible authority to rule. And in writings spanning his entire life he has voiced these objections incisively and vigorously— that history shows that the dictatorship of the wise becomes corrupted by its monopoly of power into the rule of vested interest, that it is not necessary to be an expert to judge or evaluate the recommendations of experts, that those who actually wear the shoes know best where they pinch and therefore have the right to change their political shoes in the light of their political experience.

But these rejoinders of Dewey are not enough to justify the democracy of a *self-governing* community. For they could be accepted by an elite to justify a nonparticipating democracy in which the electorate passively registers its approval or disapproval of executive or legislative decisions but does not engage in the multifarious activities of joint association that Dewey regards as the *sine qua non* of democratic health and vitality. Intelligent decisions in a democracy require extensive participation by the citizenry on all levels. Has the common man the capacity as well as the willingness to make intelligent decisions? And if he does not possess them now, can he be educated to acquire them? If his education isn't sufficient to enable him to acquire political sophistication and some expertise, has he the wit and gumption to learn from experience? Dewey answers all of these questions affirmatively, despite his awareness of the fact that the powerful mass media of press, radio, and television are hardly geared to the educational needs of an enlightened commonwealth. On what then do his beliefs rest? On the same faith that underlay Jefferson's faith in the success of the American experiment, namely, that most human beings who have access to relevant information can learn from their own experience, including their mistakes and defeats, and can discover what they really want, what they must do to achieve it, and what price must be paid for its achievement. They can learn this better than exalted rulers or leaders who claim to have superior knowledge of what is really good for those whom they rule or lead. It is a double-barreled faith—they *can* learn it, and they *will*.

It is interesting to observe that something like this faith was held by Marx, too, not about the people as an undifferentiated mass but about the idealized working class. At a time when democratic political institutions had not yet been introduced into Western Europe, when, since peaceful reforms were seemingly impossible, revolutionary action seemed necessary to those who experienced conditions as morally unendurable, Marx sought to assess the prospects of ultimate victory for the working class in the aftermath of a series of shattering defeats.

> The proletarian revolutions . . . criticize themselves constantly, interrupt themselves continually in their own course, come back to the apparently accomplished in order to begin it afresh, deride with unmerciful thoroughness the inadequacies, weaknesses and paltrinesses of their first attempts, seem to throw down their adversary only in order that he may draw new strength from the earth and rise again, more gigantic, before them, recoil ever and anon from the indefinite prodigiousness of their own aims, until a situation has been created which makes all turning back impossible, and the conditions themselves cry out: *Hic Rhodus, hic salta!*[5]

What is this but a colorful account of how the working class presumably learns from experience, suffused with an expectation and hope that it will eventually triumph? Dewey writes with much greater sobriety than Marx, not about the workers but about the public or organized citizenry, faced not by one task or challenge that is finally mastered but by a succession of them, working not under conditions of illegality and despotism but within an accepted tradition of change. Yet despite all these differences he, too, expresses the same faith in man and his ability to learn from experience that animated Marx's faith in the working class. Marx's faith turned out to be mistaken, for the workers in the Western world never espoused the cause of revo-

---

5. Karl Marx, *The Eighteenth Brumaire of Louis Bonaparte,* in *Karl Marx and Frederick Engels: Selected Works in Two Volumes* (Moscow: Foreign Languages Publishing House; London: Lawrence and Wishart, 1950), 1:228.

lution, and the workers elsewhere supported at best revolutions from above engineered by a small group of professional revolutionists. The workers of the Western world did learn from experience, however, but it was a lesson that Marx did not altogether anticipate, namely, that they could realize their demands for bread and freedom more effectively and in a less costly way by working within the democratic political process, and using the tax system and welfare state to redistribute wealth more nicely and justly, than they could by guillotine and firing squad.

Has Dewey any better reason for his faith that the masses will find their way to a participating democracy, a commonwealth in which institutions function to be helpful to all individuals seeking to achieve their maximum growth as persons—through "methods of consultation, persuasion, negotiation, communication, cooperative intelligence"?[6] This faith has been sorely tried by events in the United States since Dewey died, and by the growth and partial success of movements in many areas of public life that have relied not on the methods Dewey stressed as essential to a participating democracy but on force and violence or the threat of force and violence. It is true enough that it is very dubious that the genuine gains in civil rights, social welfare, education, and health are attributable to this violence, and a good case can be made for the contention that force and violence in behalf of good causes, by developing reactions and backlashes, have hindered them rather than helped further them.[7] It may even be true that if the democratic methods Dewey enumerates are not employed in the political process, the ideal of a self-governing participating democracy will remain a chimera. Nonetheless it remains true that despite these considerations Dewey has a right to hold this faith. Its invalidity has not been established. Like all faith it involves risk and gamble even if it be more reasonable than any other. It is a risk and gamble not only because it assumes that where fundamental interests collide men

6. Dewey, *Freedom and Culture* (New York: G. P. Putnam's Sons, 1939), p. 175 [*Later Works* 13:187].

7. I have discussed this in two related essays: "The Ideology of Violence," *Encounter* 34 (April 1970): 26–38; and "Reason and Violence—Some Truths and Myths about John Dewey," *Humanist* 29 (March–April 1969): 14–16, reprinted in *Education and the Taming of Power* (La Salle, Ill.: Open Court Publishing Co., 1973), pp. 131–43.

will use their intelligence to find the shared interests on the basis of which their differences can be composed, but because it also assumes that those who have the creative intelligence to discover ways of building on shared interests will have the moral courage to propound and defend them in the face of violent opposition. The behavior some years ago of the faculties of institutions of higher learning, not only in the United States but in most countries of the world, in meeting violent disruptions of the academic process showed lamentably that intelligence and moral courage do not go hand in hand, that they seem to be two independent variables in the life of the mind.

Among other reasons this is why it is still an open question whether Dewey's faith in intelligence will be vindicated. Or to put it in another and more paradoxical way, it is still an open question whether events will not make it more reasonable and intelligent, given existing human propensities and their institutional contexts, to use methods of social action that Dewey himself eschewed and condemned. Despite hysteria-mongers and apologists for one or another variety of totalitarianism, the history of politically democratic societies shows that more has been won by the methods of intelligence, of peaceful negotiation, persuasion, and reasonable compromise than by any other method. But the future in this respect is more problematic than in the past.

It remains briefly to discuss the relevance of some of Dewey's more technical philosophical ideas to the contemporary scene. This may be briefly summarized by the statement that Dewey's ideas are highly relevant to some of the present philosophical concerns of contemporary professional philosophers but that the latter are unembarrassedly unaware of it. Many of Dewey's positions are widely accepted but not in the form in which he developed them. Although a leading protagonist of a naturalistic and functional theory of mind and an arch-foe of psychophysical dualism, today a more materialistic or physicalistic theory largely prevails. This is a family of doctrines that accepts some version of the identity-thesis that "mental processes are purely physical processes in the central nervous system," to use the language of one of its systematic exponents. Those who have developed this theory have done so independently of any perceptible influence of Dewey. To the extent that they believe that the true relation between the mind and the brain depends upon the findings of science, Dewey would endorse their position. He would, however, contest their apparent isolation of the mental from the social and cultural, and maintain that the categories of the physical and mental are neither exclusive nor exhaustive. He would also assert that the dimension of the social, although it has necessary physical and biological correlates, is not reducible without remainder to them.

More surprising is the seeming evanescence of the philosophy of naturalism which received one of its most significant expressions in Dewey's *Experience and Nature*. To some, naturalism is a philosophy based upon the question-begging assumption that the methods of science are the only valid ways of acquiring knowledge and that, aside from commonsense knowledge which is continuous with science, there is no reliable knowledge except scientific knowledge. This conclusion has brought naturalism not only into conflict with all varieties of supernaturalism but also with those who believe in the existence of ontological or metaphysical truths (that are neither scientific nor logical) and more recently with those who on the basis of their introspective experience of intention and choice assert the existence of a freedom of action for man that scientific method cannot establish. The Kantian dualism has been reasserting itself according to which human life, especially man's moral life, cannot be accounted for in terms of scientific explanation. The doctrines of all these newer tendencies are incompatible with Dewey's clear-cut rejection of psychophysical dualism.

Dewey was unsympathetic to the doctrines of logical positivism or logical empiricism that flourished in the last two decades of his own lifetime not because of its absorption in the language and methodology of the natural sciences but because of its suspected atomism, its slighting of normative ethical and social propositions, and its emotive interpretation of their meaning. When this movement was eclipsed by the ordinary language analysis inspired by Wittgenstein, Dewey's initial neutrality turned to hostility on the ground that although it was true that *some* philosophical problems arose from errors in logical grammar, most of them arose from genuine *problems* in the extension of scientific categories from one domain to another. There is a haunting similarity between some pages of Wittgenstein and some pages of Dewey. Long before Wittgenstein, Dewey had established, by linguistic analysis of the way in which the question was posed, that the so-called problem of the external world was not a genuine problem and that the very use of mental or sensory predicates, without which the question could not be asked, already presupposed the world of physics and the environment of everyday things. Nonetheless, for most philosophical problems Dewey would deny that because they cannot be coherently stated in their own terms that therefore they are no more than mistakes in a logical grammar or false moves in a language game. He would maintain that they arise out of unclearly formulated scientific problems, and that philosophical analysis should go on to attempt to state the problem in such a way that we can see what would constitute relevant scientific and common-sense empirical evidence for its resolution.

Since Dewey believed that central to philosophic activity should be the normative analysis of value judgments, he is far from agreeing with Wittgenstein that philosophy leaves the world pretty much the same after it is through with its philosophizing. For Dewey all genuine knowledge is an implicit judgment of practice whose truth is established by some experimental activity that literally transforms part of the world. If there is genuine scientific knowledge of what is morally true or false, then philosophy, for better or worse, does not leave the world unaltered. This explains why for Dewey the social responsibility of science is not a problem which has emerged only in consequence of modern technology. For him all knowledge involves possible control and, when achieved, some actual change in the world.

Dewey himself set great store by his last great work, *Logic: The Theory of Inquiry*. This is a book not in formal logic but primarily in the methodology and philosophy of scientific investigation. As far as present-day logicians are concerned, it might as well not have been written; and few are the philosophers of science who are familiar with it. Ernest Nagel, who studied with Dewey, was the only outstanding philosopher of science who reflected its influence.

Although predictions in intellectual history are hazardous there is some reason to believe that in the future Dewey's purely technical philosophical work will be rediscovered, reassessed, and developed. If his educational and social views are taken seriously by professional philosophers, they will go on to explore the epistemological and logical views that Dewey thought were bound up with them. Although they may reject a great deal, they will also find that Dewey's philosophical writings are chock-full of fruitful insights, and that although they do not constitute a finished system, they hang together in a coherent way.

Dewey's philosophy remained in temporary eclipse until the phase of irrationalism and anti-intellectualism in American life ran its course, and reflective Americans once more sought a philosophic outlook consonant with an age in which a more adequate science of human nature serves the ideals and goals of an enlightened morality. The original inspiration of Dewey's philosophy was to find a rational basis of authority in morals comparable to the method by which claims and counterclaims in the natural sciences could be settled. This emphatically does not involve "the assimilation of human science to physical science" which represents only another insensitive form of absolutism, for it "might conceivably only multiply the agencies by which some human beings manipulate other human beings for their own advantage." This is the historical upshot of allegedly scientific Marxism in the Soviet Union and elsewhere that has betrayed both the spirit of scientific inquiry and the humanistic ideals of a responsible freedom. To the last, Dewey remained true to his original inspiration. His legacy to our age is a philosophy that would extend the area of desirable human freedoms by the arts of intelligence. Its most important corollary in social and political affairs is the interrelatedness and continuity of ends and means, of process and product.

Taken seriously this approach to human affairs puts us on guard against shortcuts and panaceas, empty revolutionary rhetoric, and the "reasons" of the heart, blood, or passion that have resulted in intellectual absurdities and often culminated in atrocities. At the same time it does not justify, out of fear of substituting new and greater evils for the old and familiar ones, a defense or glorification of the social *status quo*. For, according to Dewey, the cumulative effect of human knowledge and the consequences of human decisions make it impossible to preserve the *status quo*. Our choices, and even our refusal to choose on basic issues, make matters either better or worse. We must take our problems one at a time, admitting that some are related to others, and that some are larger than others, and therefore require large steps that in perspective may appear revolutionary. The health of society can be achieved like the health of the individual with which in many ways it is interrelated. As Dewey himself has put it:

> The human *ideal* is indeed comprehensive. As a standpoint from which to view existing conditions and judge the direction change should take, it cannot be too inclusive. But the problem of production of change is one of infinite attention to means; and means can be determined only by definite analysis of the conditions of each problem as it presents itself. Health is a comprehensive, a "sweeping" ideal. But progress toward it has been made in the degree in which recourse to panaceas has been abandoned and inquiry has been directed to determinate disturbances and means for dealing with them.[8]

This invites a program of unending social improvement inspired by visions of excellence. It is a program in which the political and cultural freedoms essential to a humane and democratic society, and on which other desirable social and economic freedoms must be built, come first. These freedoms can never be taken for granted. They can always be lost when men lose their nerve and intelligence.

To a willful romanticism that focuses only on goals, Dewey's melioristic outlook will seem prosaic. To a nearsighted realism that immerses itself only in efforts to preserve the familiar and customary, Dewey's vision of the consummatory experience that guides and tests institutional change will appear Utopian, if not fanciful, too optimistic in its estimate of human potentialities. But like William James, John Dewey would have defended his right to believe in the fruitful marriage of freedom and science as warranted by the nature of man and history.

Afterword

Sidney Hook had agreed several years ago to write the Introduction to this volume, which collects all Dewey's writings that do not appear in earlier volumes of The Collected Works

8. Dewey, *Freedom and Culture*, p. 170 [*Later Works* 13:183].

of John Dewey, 1882–1953. As John Dewey's most illustrious protégé, supporter, and interpreter, Hook was the ideal choice for this assignment: his views on the impact and importance of Dewey's career are indispensable in introducing a volume that spans Dewey's long publishing career.

Sidney Hook's final illness prevented him from writing a new assessment of John Dewey's continuing, now growing, influence. With the permission of Ernest B. Hook, Sidney's son and literary executor, we present here a slightly edited version of an essay that Sidney Hook wrote in 1972, "The Relevance of John Dewey's Thought," which was published in *The Chief Glory of Every People: Essays on Classic American Writers,* ed. Matthew J. Bruccoli (Carbondale and Edwardsville: Southern Illinois University Press, 1973), pp. 53–75.

The Chief Glory of Every People is a collection of essays about the first twelve authors whose works were edited by the standards of the Modern Language Association Center for Editions of American Authors: James Fenimore Cooper, Stephen Crane, John Dewey, Ralph Waldo Emerson, Nathaniel Hawthorne, William Dean Howells, Washington Irving, Herman Melville, William Gilmore Simms, Henry David Thoreau, Mark Twain, and Walt Whitman. As Dewey is the only systematic philosopher represented in this list of literary figures, it is appropriate that Hook's essay in this collection should serve as the Introduction to the last volume of The Collected Works, where it symbolizes the unique position of Dewey's writings in this group of critical editions.

"The Relevance of John Dewey's Thought" is also particularly appropriate for this volume because it is less well known than most of Hook's other writings on Dewey and because it is his most recent full treatment of Dewey's seventy-year publishing career. Here Hook evaluates and interprets the broad range of Dewey's thought from a lifelong informed and penetrating perspective.

JO ANN BOYDSTON

Essays

Doctor Martineau's Theory of Morals

The recent retirement of Dr. James Martineau from the principalship of the Manchester New College, with which institution his name has been inseparably connected since the first inception of the enterprise, marks an era in the history of liberal thought in England and calls attention afresh to the system of morals of which he has been a living and loved exponent to the successive classes that have enjoyed his magnetic instruction, and which, in his own setting, has just been given a wider hearing in England and America by the publication of his *Types of Ethical Theory*, reviewed at length elsewhere in the present issue of the *University*. In examining his own theory as it is there set forth among others that have been widely accepted, we must pass over the vast outgrowth of psychologic perception and ethical ripeness, the fruit of a long and varied contact with life, borne upon a stock of unwonted vigor and purity, and fix attention upon its head—the theory of conscience. Conscience is defined as the "critical perception we have of the relative authority of our several principles of action." And this includes evidently two elements: the objects of judgment and the mode of judgment. In pages of remarkable analysis, our author establishes the following positions regarding the objects upon which we pass our moral judgments. (1) It is persons exclusively that we so judge. The moral character of our actions goes forward with them out of our personality; it is not reflected back upon them from the effects which they produce. This leads to the statement (2) that what we judge is always the inner spring of action. Approbation is always turned to the purity of motive, not the magnitude of the result. (3) Moral consciousness is engaged primarily in self-estimation, and does not reach the judgment of its own actions

[First published in *University*, no. 206 (5 September 1885): 5.]

through prior observation of others. This principle he fixes upon as the most certain test by which to discriminate true from false theories of morals.

Between those who hold that our self-consciousness carries with it, of its own essence, the self-judgment in which the moral sentiment consists, and those who find conscience to be the product of observation of others, or of the action of others in society upon the self, no subsequent agreement is possible. "It is the inward consciousness which supplies the outward criticism, and not the outward critics that make us a present of the moral consciousness." Yet Dr. Martineau is careful to avoid that separation of one's self from the self of society which renders the solution of all concrete problems in ethics and in moral education forever impossible. He recognizes that the presence of others is indispensable to the development of this part of our nature; that the visible life of those about us not only reveals their inner nature, but develops our own. Without human persons about us, we should not recognize the *ego* of conscience, and so organic is the connection of self and society that it is idle to attempt to divide moral achievements between them. In time, "the 'individual' is the later product; and disengages himself into his independent wholeness as the ripe fruit of a collective development. *Humanity* first, as a plural organism; and *then, Personality,* in its singular force." "Spiritually man is not *himself* without others, and the major part of his individuality is relative to them. The social union is a concrete though spiritual form of life, penetrating and partly constituting all persons belonging to it, so that only as fractions of it do they become human integers themselves."

It is not our spontaneities (4) which we judge, but our volitions. The moral life is not in instinctive forces, but in the voluntary sphere. (5) The voluntary is distinguished from the spontaneous state, in that the latter contains one impulse, the former, at least, two. There can be no judgment without difference, without comparison, without *relation*. There is no moral judgment without a plurality of inner principles. (6) These principles must be present simultaneously, and both must be possibilities for us. If both are not present at once, there is no real conflict, no comparison, no deliberation, no preference, no decision—in short, no moral experience. And unless they are both possible to us, unless we can choose between them, and by that choice give either actuality, there is no personality involved; no meaning in approval or remorse. Either free will is a fact, or moral judgment a delusion. And moral freedom is a personal power of preference; the *ego* has a selecting power between two indeterminate possibilities, and in selecting renders one a determinate actuality. Moral experience dwells not in the region of the "is," but of the "ought to be."

What is said of the *mode* of moral judgment follows directly. Conscience is the perception upon the emergence of the two conflicting simultaneous principles of action that one is higher and worthier than the other. It is at once intuitive and relative. It is intuitive, for it is inherent in the experience of the principles themselves, a revelation inseparable from their simultaneous appearance. We cannot follow both, but we cannot doubt the rights and place of either. It is relative, for the moral quality arises only in the relation of two principles of action to each other. The moral quality is inherent only in the pair as a dual object. "We immediately perceive a graduated scale of worth or excellence among our natural principles, distinct from the order of their intensity and irrespective of the range of their external effects" in pleasure or pain. This is the meaning of moral experience.

The reader will doubtless agree with us that such a rehabilitation of the intuitive theory of morals is virtually a new creation. It is nearly allied to the ethics of Aristotle, and comes closer to the theory presented in Green's *Prolegomena* than the author seems to suspect. Such an agreement from the opposite methods ought to yield ethical investigation a rich crop for the future. In our attempt to present the reader the nut of this work, we have not only passed by the wealth of historic illustration that illuminates every page, and the side-lights of psychologic observation which flash into the obscure recesses of our nature; but the delicacy and grace of the whole, which give it wonderful fertility in stimulation and suggestion, have escaped our rough and dismembering treatment. But if education be in final resort the inspiration which comes to one's personality from another, through whatever medium, then this work is an educator. He who opening the book reads with awakening sympathy the introductory words which follow, will return, closing the book with deep gratitude, and almost personal affection. "I have always been a teacher; I have not ceased to be a learner; in the one capacity, I must tell the little that I know; in the other, I must strive after some glimpse of the immeasurable light beyond." And with pious hope he will read the closing words of the author, and desire that "the evening twilight of life shall linger a little longer, and leave the powers of industry still unspent," that he may redeem his promise, and in the sunset of his more than threescore years and ten illumine the heart and mind with his reflections upon the cords between the human spirit and the divine—the theory of religion.

The Health of Women and Higher Education

Since the publication of Doctor Clarke's work on sex in education, a decade ago, the fight regarding the relation of the healthy functional life of woman and her advanced education has raged hotly with now and then a lull. During the fight and during the lull of the controversy, however, the practical movement of things has been all in one direction—towards the opening of new and broader careers in scholastic matters for women. Wellesley and Smith both count the years of their life since the publication of Doctor Clarke's attack, for attack it is more than discussion. Almost the wealthiest of our colleges, and the most conservative in its social surroundings, has yielded to the pressure in the form of an annex, and only ecclesiastic influence and aristocratic pretension prevents Columbia from outdoing its Cambridge neighbor. In the state institutions of the west, coeducation has ceased to be an experiment or even a matter for discussion. It is an established fact, part of the institutional policy of the commonwealths. This constant extension of the sphere of woman's education has had one beneficial result even upon the theoretical discussion. It has tended to take it more and more from the *a priori* ground to that of experience. There is now an organized mass of results covering an average period of 15 years upon which to base generalizations. The man or the woman who neglects this and continues the discussion on the old line of possibilities, probabilities and self-asserted certainties stands condemned beforehand, and with no claim upon even public tolerance.

The most promising sign of the changed state of the discussion is found in a report printed in the Massachusetts labor bureau report for August, 1885, upon female health in colleges. The ma-

[First published in *University*, no. 208 (19 September 1885): 5.]

terial for this report was collected by the young "Association of Collegiate Alumnae" of the country, which thus at once amply justifies its formation, and gives hope of an influential future. The present report covers twelve colleges, coeducational and female only, embracing such representatives as Vassar, Smith and Wellesley; such state institutions as those of Michigan and Wisconsin, and such typical universities as Cornell and Syracuse. These colleges report about 1,300 women graduates, of whom over 50 per cent. give personal answers to the questions made. Concerning the questions themselves it can only be said that their summary statement would outrun the entire space allotted to this article. Suffice it to say that minute and exhaustive inquiries were made comprehending five features of the lives of those reporting. The first concerned the conditions of childhood; the second, individual health; the third, family health; the fourth, college conditions and environment; the fifth, life since graduation.

Colonel Wright, the head of the bureau, says of the result established by the inquiries that it shows conclusively that "the seeking of a college education on the part of women does not necessarily entail a loss of health or serious impairment of the vital forces." More specifically, he says that the inquiry does not "show any marked difference in general health from the average health likely to be reported by an equal number of women engaged in other kinds of work; or, in fact, of women generally without regard to occupation followed." There was, indeed, "a certain deterioration in health on the part of some of the graduates. But, on the other hand, an almost identical improvement in health for a like number was reported, showing very plainly that we must look elsewhere for the causes of the greater part of this decline in health during college life. If we attempt to trace the cause we find that this deterioration is largely due, not to the requirements of college life particularly, but to predisposing causes natural to the graduates themselves, and for which college life or study should not be made responsible."

By no means the least interesting portion of the report is the light thrown by it upon the subsidiary occasions of the failure in health. Enough is proved by the figures to give firm basis to the conviction that, even though the seeking of a college education is not in itself detrimental, much remains to be done in the investigation and improvement of the various conditions of college life. Severe study, lack of exercise, worry about study and personal affairs are responsible for too many disorders, and these disorders follow too much the line of nervous diseases and those peculiar to women. Bad sanitary conditions are too frequent; and the large percentage which report emotional strain as cause of disorders, show that the social and moral environment of young women in college life is by no means what it should be. The discussion upon the whole question of health and education should now be shifted from what has been regarded as the main issue, and settle upon the question how the conditions, physical and social, as well as intellectual, of college life can be improved. An intelligent discussion of this question and wise heeding of the results reached will result, we make no doubt, in a large and general improvement of health during college life, and in the years after graduation. There is no doubt that given no improper sanitary surroundings, good health will follow immediately upon natural relations. The fundamental cause of ill health, where no immediate bad sanitary conditions exist, is either improper, dwarfed or strained relations in life; and the opening of educational avenues to women so far as it corrects, extends and renders normal the relations of woman to life, must end in her improved health. We hope the association will continue their good work by a study of how the proper surroundings in college life are to be obtained. Meanwhile we can do our readers no greater favor than by commending to them the full report, which we have briefly discussed.

The Revival of the Soul

Some years ago a German announced a book with the somewhat startling title of the *Discovery of the Soul*. Those abnormal people who have been seeking all their lives to get their soul somewhere in a corner where they could have a little rational conversation with it, upon buying the book were somewhat disappointed to find that their soul was an odor. The learned German with equal profundity, obscurity and good faith had collected an immense number of psychological facts showing the importance of the sense of smell in psychical life. And having convinced himself that it was the fundamental fact in knowledge and in feeling, by a process not unusual with psychologists, diverted this fact into a gigantic substance. The soul was smell and the secret of the age was solved. Now, men may stand it to have their ancestors explained to be arboreal inhabitants with hairy skin and a tail, but to have themselves, together with their ancestors, resolved into a series of odors is too much. Herr Jaeger deserved to be made the patron saint, the god-father, as it were, of Cologne, but the rest of the world could only treat him with that silent ignoring which his rash theory—whether true or false—deserved. Now, this ambitious Columbus of the soul is unknown save to the casual inquirer into psychological curiosities.

But the present time witnesses a phenomenon equally striking and one which promises to be more enduring. It is the revival of the soul. For about a generation the soul has been most studiously ignored. Except having a soul yourself, nothing was so ill-bred as to suggest that your neighbor had one. The advanced scientific circle and polite society joined forces in putting the soul into the background. Not that it was certain that

[First published in *University*, no. 219 (5 December 1885): 6–7. For H. S. Swift's reply to this article, see this volume, Appendix 1. For Dewey's response to Swift, see pp. 15–18.]

man was all body. By no means. He might be something, a *soup-çon* of something at all events, which had served as the basis of the former belief in the soul, and this something served to keep alive an aesthetic interest in various peculiar phenomena of olden time, like art, poetry and religion, which the body of man seemed hardly able to account for. For it to have created them, would be a most erratic phenomenon and would make it necessary to put the body under the same ban which had abolished the soul. So there remained a lingering feeling that amid the depths of the unknowable there might be something, which, however, it would be vulgar to really know, and a profane impiety to designate by such a prosaic term as soul. It was in allowing the lingering of this feeling that our opponents of the soul made their mistake. They ought to have banished it entirely—by universal suicide if necessary. For, behold, the soul has been revived. It is getting omnipotent—except in morals; and omnipresent, except in English poetry and American fiction.

It does not fall within the scope of the present historian to discuss the causes of this new and greater renascence. He can but point out some of its characteristics as it actually exists. The causes must be studied by the laborious researches of some philosophic Symonds or Pater of the twenty-fifth century. Some superficial occasions he may note however. One seems to have been scientific. The farther men got into the body, the nearer they seemed to get to the soul. So Wundt, the physiologist who has devoted his life to studying the brain and nerves, declared a year or two ago, that the ordinary opinion of physiologists that the body was the cause of the soul must be reversed, and the soul be considered the cause of the body; so far as the latter has any advantage in complexity of structure and action over the substance of inorganic nature. And the late Professor Clifford, the iconoclast in English materialism, who began his career by asserting that he really didn't believe that there was any omnipotent spirit in the world, because he had examined space quite carefully and had not been able to discover that it bore any marks of brain structure, ended by declaring that the world was all made of mind stuff, whatever that is. Another reason for the revival of interest in the soul seems to be popular in its nature; it was the need of a new sensation. The present generation has been going about seeking to say and hear some new thing. It has explored heaven—or what used to be heaven—and earth that it may thrill with some new emotion, or expand with some new experience. But it grew jaded, all things seemed to repeat each other. And it occurred to some man wiser in his day to declare: "Say not lo here, nor lo there, for the great sensation, the absolute novelty is within you—it is your soul."

The prophet of the soul made a most decided hit. The tired searcher after new experience found a strange realm before him, and he has taken to inquiring into his soul with an avidity comparable only to the persistence with which he formerly neglected it. The soul has been annexed. There are societies for psychical research on every hand. Faith-cures, metaphysical healers, substantial mentalists and unsubstantial materialists, those who assert that the soul alone exists, and those that deny that the body exists, swarm in conventions, effervesce in public prints, and pre-empt the future. The old-time materialist realizes that he is under a cloud, and if he makes his appearance at all, it is to feebly mutter that this was what he meant all the time. Matter is only materialized soul, the old-fashioned spiritualist finds Othello's occupation gone. When everybody knew that he had no soul there was an adventuresome rashness, a titillating bravado in seeing how near he could come to beholding one, and still retain his certainty that there was none. But now that ghosts in the form of souls are the most authentic of phenomena, now that thought-transference and the action of mind on mind, and the appearance of phantasms are the most ordinary of occurrences, the old business of spirit-rapping, and low turned lights with waving of phosphorescent hands, and beating of heavenly cymbals and thrumming of earthly banjos, have become quite too stale. Every man his own ghost is the modern watchword.

But in all seriousness, there are some rather disheartening features in the whole thing. Perhaps it was not surprising that a New England woman of keen feeling, sharp intellect and miraculous faculty of introspection, who had previously seen the gates ajar, or even gone beyond the gates, should seize upon the movement and write the article which recently appeared in the *North American Review*. That, as all its readers will remember, took the ground that this re-discovery of the soul was the great opportunity of the nineteenth century if not of all time. It was only necessary to form enough societies of psychical research, observe carefully enough, collect extensively enough, weigh and sift thoroughly enough, generalize accurately and broadly enough, to settle the whole question of spiritual existence now and hereafter with the same thoroughness that Darwin and others have settled the question of physical life. This coming from its author was not perhaps surprising. But it is saddening to find that it reflects a widespread feeling, and utters a common hope. There could be no more significant token of the hopelessness and heartlessness of the skepticism of the age than this revival of the soul for scientific and spectacular purposes. Once for all, it should be said that it is absolutely impossible for science to settle any religious question. Religion would see the world as a whole, and would find that whole beating with love, pregnant with intelligence and vital with will. Science has nothing to do with wholes, nor with love, intelligence and will. It discovers only connections between facts. It establishes only certain relations of coexistence or sequence among phenomena, and to these relations it gives the name law. Beyond these phenomenal connections into the realm of absolute truth and reality it cannot pierce.

Could, however, scientific investigation and research establish all that Miss Phelps and others expect from it; either the question of the religious life would remain untouched, or the death knell of religion would be sounded. To connect the "other world" with this world as science connects one fact with another, would be to vulgarize the life of the soul in such manner that all the lowness and hopelessness of the life of this passing world would become an organic member of the eternal life. Spiritual life would become a more meaningless, paltry thing than that satirized by George Eliot under the name of "other-worldliness." But true religion would escape the snare set for it. It would declare that it knew nothing of the spirit, thus set as a fact before its senses, and had nothing to do with an immortal life which science had explored and connected with the earthly life, as it connects one planet with another. These may be facts, she would say, but they are as far outside the spiritual life as the name of the latest asteroid, or the structure of the newest beetle. She would refuse to be deceived by the Greeks, though they bore her the gifts of the soul discovered and labeled, and heaven explored and mapped. She would rise to her divine prerogative of life in things unseen, and faith in things yet unrevealed to sense. The soul a spectacular show, heaven known in all its recesses like our neighbor's drawing-room, this is not the essence of the religious life. It is as true now as ever it was that the just shall live by faith; and as the great poet of the nineteenth century sings:

> You must mix some uncertainty
> With faith, if you would have faith be.

The life of the spirit does not exist in a realm of things scientifically investigated and mathematically demonstrated. It is in the region of the will. Its root is not: I know that the soul and its eternal destiny exist, for I have been a member of a society for psychical research, and have seen with my eyes, and heard with my ears; but, I *will* that they be real, for without their reality I myself am not real. It is in this setting of the whole soul; upon this staking of the whole being; though this utterance of entire devotion be amid things not yet known, that the religious life exists.

The revival of the soul may lead to great increase in psychological knowledge. If not directed too exclusively to searching after ghost stories, and endeavoring to cure neuralgia by declaring that there is no body to have the neuralgia, it probably will. It may lead to the deepening of the impression that after all a man is as good as a bag, and psychology as much worth study as physics. The impression may gradually spread that a Greek is worth as much as a Glyptodon, and its study no more a fetich than geology. If this is not accompanied by the impression that the soul is not the life of man and history, but is a sort of "Black Crook" sprite, or "Midsummer Night's" Puck, whose activities are exhausted in miraculous appearances and spectacular performances, we may hope for this result. But that the revival of the soul either as a scientific phenomenon or a popular sensation has anything to add to religion,—forever no. The soul that religion has to do with always is, and needs no rediscovery or patronizing revival.

What Is the Demonstration of Man's Spiritual Nature?

To the Editor of the *University:*

I should be glad to have written what I did about the revival of the soul were it only to have called forth the eloquent and acute protest of Mr. Swift in a recent number of the *University.* Controversy is poor business, especially when you are inclined to suspect that there is more of sympathy than of difference between yourself and critic; but I willingly make use of the occasion thus offered me to say something more on one or two points.

I am inclined to suspect that there is more of sympathy than of difference between my critic and myself, because, if I understand him, he takes the position that the teaching and life of Jesus overcame the dualism of spirit and matter, and reconciled them in a perfect unity, and that this teaching is in complete conformity with reason. And in this position I fully concur, as also in the statement that all religious and philosophical systems must possess perfect rationality, must be tested by reason and must conform to it. That there is anything in this position inconsistent with the belief that the attempt to demonstrate the immortality of the soul and the possibility of miracles by psychical research and mind-cure is an evidence of skepticism. I do not see the question is as to the kind of demonstration called for. The teaching of Jesus is that the kingdom of God is within; that we are not to say, lo here, nor, lo there, nor to run about expecting to find it in this or that quarter. It is the teaching of Jesus that the kingdom of God is a spiritual kingdom, and its life one of the spirit. The sole requirement of Christianity is faith in the supreme reality of spirit, and complete devotion to it. That there is no dualism between spirit and nature, the soul and flesh, follows from this;

[First published in *University,* no. 226 (23 January 1886): 43–44. For H. S. Swift's article to which this is a response, see this volume, Appendix 1. For Dewey's original article, see pp. 10–14.]

for reality is one, not two. That the spirit will manifest itself in and through the workings of nature and of the flesh, follows also. Does it follow from this, that by a scientific study of nature, religious truth is to be established and skepticism done away with? Or does this attempt rather involve a failure to recognize the first principle of Jesus: that the spirit is truth and that the spirit is within; that its demonstration is all experience, not sensible exhibitions?

The idea that the religious life is to be built up through such scientific demonstration of any fact that there will be sufficient evidence for belief in it, seems to be an error of the same kind which Mr. Swift attributes to the teaching of the church—namely, that intellectual belief is a requisite for salvation. Mr. Swift seems to think that the church teaches that salvation is through intellectual belief—only without evidence; he would substitute intellectual belief, based on evidence, and evidence of the senses at that. As for myself, I cannot find that *intellectual* belief either with or without evidence has anything to do with the religious life, with salvation or condemnation—least of all, sensible evidence. It is demonstrated truth that fire burns; that water is a compound of oxygen and hydrogen; at least, there is sufficient sensible evidence of these facts. Suppose it demonstrated by the same sort of evidence that the soul is immortal, and that the soul can work changes in the body? What difference is there in the two classes of facts, as to their religious aspect? Is there any element that makes for salvation in the belief of the first set? Is there any element that makes for salvation in the same sort of belief upon evidence in the second class? My position was that, granted the equal demonstration of both classes of truth, the specifically religious life would still have to begin. It is the attitude which the *will* takes towards the facts, the vital personal setting of the soul which is faith. And it is this, and this only which constitutes the religious life, and which has aught to do with either salvation or condemnation.

Would Mr. Swift take the position that salvation (the religious life) depends on intellectual apprehension? He can hardly condemn the church for having adopted the position that condemnation (the lack of the religious life) depends upon the same. If this be the position of the church (I do not think that it is) the "indignation" which Mr. Swift attributes to me is not with those who are trying to find evidence for this intellectual apprehension; it is, rather, if one allow himself to indulge in what may be after all a superfluous emotion, with the church, for taking such a position. But why, it may be asked, is the attempt to demonstrate these truths by research an evidence of skepticism? Simply because it shows that spirit is not believed in upon its own evidence; that sensible evidence is required; spectacular appeal to eye or ear. It shows that what is believed in as ultimate reality is the things of sense; not the things of the spirit which is in a man; while the position of Christianity is that the ultimate reality is spirit, and that the things of sense are real indeed, but only because they partake of the reality of spirit. It shows, in other words, *practical* disbelief in spirit, disbelief in its living efficiency.

But it will be said that if the "scientific" demonstration of these truths may not help religious life, it may help theology, as the intellectual account of this life. Possibly, but much less than is supposed. Theology or philosophy has reflectively to show that the pre-suppositions of religion, namely of the reality of spirit and of the relations of the human spirit and the divine, are the ultimate truths of experience when experience is thoroughly interpreted. The demonstration of a continued existence of soul and of its power to heal bodily disease would be interesting additions enough to the store of facts to be interpreted; but they would still have to be interpreted. And their mere existence as demonstrated facts does not, in the least, ensure that their interpretation would strengthen the philosophical basis of religious truth. There would be just so many facts, and the materialist wouldn't wait a week to make them fit in some way into his scheme.

I am sure that I am entirely at one with my critic in the belief of the need of such a philosophical interpretation of religious truth as will show its thorough rationality; I do not believe that I differ from him much in the belief that the church has fallen short of its duty in this matter, and is so far responsible for some at least of the intellectual skepticism of the time. But I do not believe that the philosophy needed to meet the case is that of appeal to sense. I can only repeat, let the true interests of religion beware the Greeks though they come bearing the supposed gift of a demonstrated soul, if the demonstration is one of sense, and not of the complete interpretation of man's experience. Of that sort of demonstration, theology, and religion, so far as its interests are one with those of theology, can never have too much. Against the revival of the soul or the spiritual life of man, even working through nature and the flesh, I have, and have had nothing to say. Its revival as a ghost performing various pranks palpable to sense is another matter.

The Church and Society

To the Editor of the *University:*

Apropos of an editorial note in a recent number of the *University* regarding the question of capital and labor, may I call attention to a contribution towards the further definition of the problem by the inter-denominational congress at Cincinnati. The details of the discussion are, I suppose, more or less familiar to your readers. The topics were such questions as the modern city as a menace to civilization, socialism and atheism, the houses and homes of the poor, working men and the churches. Without going over the special points made, I wish to call attention to certain points clearly brought out at the meeting.

The first is that modern Christianity is getting itself alive to the fact that there is an industrial problem, and that the church has a duty in the matter. There can be no doubt that Protestant religion has tended to an extreme individualism, and in its reaction against political ecclesiasticism has largely abdicated its proper function as a social organization. All society is based on the development of the universal side of the individual, and has as its function the realization of this universal element. The church lays this subordination of the individual to the ultimate universal, God, upon each as an obligation, and thus merely consciously proclaims what is unconsciously involved in the very substance of all society. For the church to become individualistic is, therefore, for it to commit suicide. The function of the church is precisely to see that men are bound together by truly universal or social relations. This is the establishment of the kingdom of God. For the church not to interest itself actively in such questions as the industrial one, means not only loss to society, but

[First published in *University*, no. 222 (26 December 1885): 7.]

death to religion. The meeting of this congress is, accordingly, an exceedingly hopeful sign.

And, again, it is worth noticing that the interest shown was an intelligent and sympathetic one. So far as appears from the reports, there were no cranks present, with panaceas for every social ill; there was no patronizing of the working man, nor any assertion that if he would only "be good and go to church" there would be no conflict between capital and labor; the repetition of the statement that the present constitution of society is such as to secure an almost ideal distribution of wealth was left entirely to doctrinaires proceeding by a mathematical method in the construction of imaginary persons. Even socialism was recognized as having some lessons to teach the churches. The fact of the matter is, the question of capital and labor which your correspondent desired you to settle off-hand is the question of the age. The democratic movement has practically succeeded in the religious and political spheres. It must now be extended to the industrial realms.

War's Social Results

When Columbus discovered America, could any one have told what the discovery would mean? To the wise men of the time it meant a new route to the East. People's minds are governed by precedent. India was a fact in their minds, but there was no precedent for America. Naturally they couldn't conceive of the western civilization which was to follow.

Just now we are fighting for democracy. Democracy is a fact in the minds of most Americans. They think, at least, that they know what it means. It seems certain that the Allies will be victorious and I believe they will find democracy. But that democracy will be as different from the democracy of their concepts as the New World was different from the Orient which Columbus sought.

We are fighting to do away with the rule of kings and kaisers. When we have finished the job we may find that we have done away with the rule of money and trade. We are fighting for freedom to transact business; but this war may easily be the beginning of the end of business. In fifty years, it is altogether probable, the whole system which we know as "business" to-day will have vanished from the earth.

Business in the world we have known has consisted of the sale of goods and their manufacture for sale. For three years now the manufacture and distribution of goods in Europe have largely been conducted on a contrary principle. The change has already begun in America too. We are beginning to produce for use, not for sale; and the capitalist is not a capitalist in the sense that he was a capitalist before the war. His right to sell in the open market, according to the law of supply and demand, has been

[From interview by Charles W. Wood, first published in *New York World*, 29 July 1917, p. 1E.]

challenged. In France, Germany and England, his right to invest his capital has very largely been taken away. He must manufacture what the Government wants him to manufacture; he must sell the product at prices the Government sets; he must pay his help whatever the Government stipulates, and if there are any profits left over, the Government may appropriate them to pay the costs of war.

Doubtless the average business man is willing to make these sacrifices, and most of them are waiting patriotically for the end of the war when they may resume business on the old principle. But there is no reason to believe that the old principle will ever be resumed. A world once jarred so far from its orbit is not apt to return. It finds other attractions, another centre, another orbit. Unquestionably we are entering a different sort of civilization than the earth has ever known.

If New York can subscribe a billion to a Liberty Loan it can be taxed a billion for a Humanity Loan; and a billion dollars could be expended here to the great joy of the common people. I do not say that they will want to spend a billion dollars at a time, but if they do happen to want something that costs a billion they are quite apt to buy it. We never knew before how rich we were. When it came to spending money for the common good we thought we had to economize. The people who controlled money matters always impressed us with that necessity, but we have suddenly discovered that it wasn't necessary at all. I am not venturing to say what the people of the various nations are going to want; but, whatever it is, it is unthinkable to me that they will not be perfectly ruthless in going after it. Private property as a nominal institution will still go on, but it has already lost its sanctity.

Just glance at the situation in Russia. To most Americans the radical nature of that revolution must have seemed like insane anarchy. And yet the Russian revolution stands out as the great social phenomenon of the war. It was the sudden uprising of the submerged masses, not merely to overthrow the Czar and gain political recognition but to take the reins of government and industry itself into their own hands.

Germany will not stop with the overthrow of kaiserism. England, France and America will not rest when the world is made safe for political democracy. I do not expect the change to be so sudden here, but industrial democracy is on the way. The rule of the Workmen and Soldiers will not be confined to Russia, it will spread through Europe; and this means that the domination of all upper classes, even of what we have been knowing as "respectable · society," is at an end.

This revolution may burst upon the world in fury, coupled with a reign of terror and extravagant orgies of newfound power, or it may come through the gradual evolution of several decades. It is plain that it is coming, but it is not at all clear what the reign of the hitherto submerged classes will be like.

Has it occurred to you that the most sacred tradition of society may soon undergo a most radical change? Has it occurred to you that the family, as we have known it, may soon cease to exist; that the terms love, marriage and romance may come to express altogether different ideas to our minds than they express to-day?

Please understand two things at first. To begin with, I do not know what this change will be. In the second place, whatever it is, I do not advocate it. I do not advocate any change in the ideals of marriage as they exist. I do not advocate any revolution in our sex morality. I am speaking only as an observer of causes and effects, and from that standpoint it seems apparent that tremendous changes are due.

We must recognize that the family is now a very different institution from what it was a few hundred years ago. In the family of that time the father was supreme. In the family of to-day the father may play an inconspicuous role. The family tradition of obedience to parents has survived, but disobedience and disrespect are common. In the family of former times the father had jurisdiction over his children's lives; he educated them or not as he saw fit; he punished them as he saw fit; he supported them as he saw fit; he even picked out the partners they should marry. To-day he must send them to school as long as the State sees fit; he must support them according to standards set by the State; if he punishes them cruelly he is punished by the State, and he has nothing whatever to say about whom they shall marry.

What caused the change? Primarily a transition from one economic system to another, from feudalism to capitalism. Under feudalism the family was the economic unit, and an individual found his economic security in his relation to the family. Under capitalism the individual became the economic unit, and a person found his economic security in his individual job. It was in the natural course of cause and effect then that children threw off the yoke of patriarchal rule. Free selection in marriage was probably the most significant phenomenon of the new order, and the era of romance dawned upon the world. Instead of strengthening the family as an institution, however, the contrary result ensued. Divorce became common, separations even more common. In all countries where modern industry has developed the same change is noticeable. The family is no longer anything like the institution which it was.

And now we are entering upon another economic epoch. It has been approaching gradually for fifty years, but its progress has been accelerated inestimably by the war. And with the war have come three most startling changes in the social status of women.

In the first place, the sex balance has been decisively upset. Many millions of eligible young men have been killed. Other millions have been rendered unfit for the responsibilities of marriage. There won't be nearly husbands enough to go round, an important factor to be considered, but by no means the most important. Even more important, it seems to me, is the fact that women never had so little use for husbands as they have in France and Germany to-day.

For the world war has brought the economic independence of women to a degree which few people have ever dreamed of. Women have taken men's jobs by the million. In many they have proved more efficient than men. They are already in possession of economic power and are gaining political power fast. They might abdicate in favor of the men if they could get husbands in return, but they can't do that. Will they abdicate in favor of nothing at all?

There is still another factor to be considered, and that is the emphasis which has been placed upon child-bearing by all the nations at war. A child now has the right to be born, and his right to be fed is recognized as well as his right to be educated. The states are assuming the responsibility—taking it away from the individual father. Economically, husbands were never so little in demand.

But there has been no change in human impulses. Love and the love of children are as deeply implanted in human psychology as they ever were. They will continue, whatever form of expression they will take, and there will be no lowering of ideals. Ideals are born of circumstances, and only those with their eyes to the past are shocked when the ideals that no longer work give way to others. Our present code of morality, it seems certain to me, will not fit the new conditions. Shocking or not, there will be a change.

No, I can't say what it will be. Polygamy is unthinkable where women are free, but some shifting from our present ideals of marital monopoly seems sure. Not until peace is declared and the millions return from the trenches to resume their civil life can we safely speculate on what will happen. The war has done unspeakable things to them. They are not the same men who went to the front. They have developed strength and courage, perhaps, and a willingness to sacrifice for the common good, and they may inspire society with a new devotion. Or they have grown used to being cared for and their individual initiative may have waned. When they come back, it may be to build as men never built before. Or it may be to sit down brokenly, content to let their wives hold the jobs which they have taken in their absence. Whatever has happened to them will largely determine what will happen to society at large. One thing, however, seems evident. They will not submit to the old neglect again. Whatever they are, they are armed and powerful, and they are going to insist upon a different deal.

The Problem of Secondary Education after the War

The war has brought the question of secondary educa-tion to the forefront. Perhaps nothing but the war would have made us realize what a ghastly pretense is our "universal" educa-tion. We have been largely unconscious of what it meant even for children as individuals to have their schooling interrupted at or before the age of fourteen. We had hardly begun to consider what it meant for the community for our social life in general, that the great mass of the youth should have the school doors closed upon them at this age. Consider what it means. Consider boys and girls as they are from twelve to fourteen and as their regular instruction ceases. Even from the standpoint of learn-ing they are but children. Such special forms of skill as they may have acquired are generally obtained at the expense of learn-ing and of deeper attitudes, the basic dispositions which count socially and morally. They can read, but except where circum-stances are favorable or where native tastes are very strong they have next to no training to direct *what* they read. Their ability to read is far beyond their growth in intellectual and moral matu-rity; it is far beyond their initiation into history and science, as well as into life.

It is not the ability to put words and sentences together, the ability to pass in reading in school that decides *what* a person reads. The ability is a passport, but it does not decide into what port of knowledge and experience its possessor shall pass. It may be used upon trivial, superficial and sensational material as read-ily as upon what is worth while, namely what promotes further development. Nay, in view of the extent to which the technical ability called reading outruns at this stage knowledge of impor-tant things in the world and the creation of serious intellectual

[First published in *Sierra Educational News* 14 (December 1918): 571–72.]

tastes, the capacity to read is much more likely to go towards insignificant, if not evil, things than towards those which make for growth.

In short, it is not the deficiencies of knowledge and skill that exist when the mass of pupils leave school which are most important. These are but symptoms of an underlying lack, the immaturity of experience and tastes that characterize the great mass of boys and girls at the ages of from twelve to fourteen. So far we have tried as educators to remedy this state of things by improving elementary education. Much has been accomplished; much remains to be done. But the war has revealed what ought to have been clear to us before—that no conceivable improvement of elementary education can be a complete remedy. Our educational system has to get hold and keep hold of youth during the years of from fourteen to eighteen, eighteen at the least, and do it not sporadically and here and there, but for the great mass of pupils who now escape systematic educational influences.

It might seem at first sight as if the deficiencies revealed by the war in education with respect to social efficiency were connected with trade matters. Certainly almost pathetic efforts have had to be made both in England and this country to remedy the shortage in mechanical pursuits. But it is striking that with its greater experience, the educational reconstruction proposed in Great Britain while centering in secondary education is not primarily concerned with trade or narrow industrial training. It was not found, after all, that the greatest social need exists at this point. The real menace to the community well being was found to lie in the lack of intelligent initiative and adaptability, lack of *intellectual* rather than of technical efficiency. And the new educational bill aims first at providing educational facilities which will take care of this need.

There is danger, along with the complete military defeat of Prussia, of a subtle victory for Prussian ideals in education. There will be plenty who will urge upon us the technical and industrial shortcomings which the war has so plainly brought out, and who will proffer us schemes for secondary education aiming to turn out a larger number of skilled workers along lines required in competition for commercial superiority. They will, in short, try to play Providence by deciding just what are the niches to be filled in our industrial environment and how to go to work to turn out youth ready to fit into their predestined niches—this boy for this specific job, that girl for that. But we need a radically altered approach to the problem of secondary education.

We shall proceed amiss if we assume that for a few the present type of general education is to be continued, and that supplementary agencies of a specialized sort are to be created sufficient to take care of the mass who now drop out and who have no longing for the established type of general education. We must beware of every plan which unconsciously or consciously proceeds from this premise. The problem needs to be stated in this way: Let us assume that at least ninety per cent of those who now leave school at the end of the grades and before are to continue under the control of school influences till at least eighteen years of age. What *reorganization* of our present school secondary system in its curriculum, methods, school equipment will be required to adapt the system to this new school population? The problem is not one of adding things on to the present high school. It is a problem of thoroughgoing reconstruction. No one, certainly not the present writer, can offer any ready-made solution. But the first thing and the great thing is to get the right approach.

Impressions from Canton

It happened that a recent lecturing trip to the South brought us to Canton during the first week of May. That week was a period of anniversaries and celebrations. It began on Sunday with the labor demonstration of May first; then there followed in quick succession the anniversary of the May 4th movement (the students' revolt on Peking of two years ago), the inauguration of Sun Yat-sen as president, the dedication of the memorial monument to the seventy-two patriots who formed the vanguard of the revolution ten years ago, and the observance of the Day of National Shame—the signing of the Twenty-One Demands. It was a wonderful week from the tourists' point of view, moving and colorful in spite of rains. It also gave an unusual opportunity to witness the temper of the people. In addition, there were conversations with most of the leaders, political, administrative and intellectual, of the new movement. These conversations were not formal interviews and what was said was not intended for publication. But perhaps they gave all the better on that account a just view of the situation. At all events, the events and the conversations gave quite a different impression of the situation as a whole from that which was in the back of my head when I went to Canton, and I am glad to respond to the request of the editors of the *Weekly Review* for an account of my impressions.

The first noteworthy impression was that obtained from foreigners on the ground, such as were impartial and had good opportunities for knowledge. In my contact they were practically unanimous in feeling some resentment at the prevailing attitude in the North. They said we had the wrong dope and were being misled by interested parties; that the municipal and provincial governments were so far as their information went much the

[First published in *Weekly Review of the Far East* 17 (11 June 1921): 64–66.]

most promising in China, and many went so far as to say that in their judgment were the only governments in China which are considering the welfare of the people and not the power and pockets of officials and which are dominated by men who have not only good intentions but also a modern outlook and an intelligent training for the work of administration. This testimony was naturally impressive. It made one willing to revise the prejudice with which one had come to the situation based not so much on belief to the contrary as upon a feeling that Canton was furthering the division of China at a time when union was most needed.

Then one was led to consider the source of the information which had led to one's antecedent conviction or prejudice. And hence there was derived one impression which is more than an impression, a perception of a fact. A large portion of the present difficulty between the North and South is the product of scanty and distorted information. The English papers in Hongkong are devoted to local news and that of the home country. They have next to no general Chinese news and with one exception but little from neighboring Canton in spite of two trains and many boats each way every day. The paper published in English in Canton gives much more attention to Peking and has the Chung Mei service, but neither it nor the Chinese papers have direct telegraphic service. The news is two weeks old at least. It was not possible for example in Canton to get any accurate information about the status of the teachers' strike in Peking. In reflecting upon the news from the South which I had read in northern newspapers, I could not see that the situation was much better as regards *amount* of information while in quality it was worse; for while there were occasional telegraphic items, they were often distorted for propaganda purposes.

In general I should say that every reader in the North ought to be on his guard against "news" reports from Canton. For the most part, they are pure propaganda. This propaganda has two sources. One, of course, is the Peking government interests. The other source is British. Sun Yat-sen and his closest adherents have long been anti-British. The British authorities would perhaps be a little more than human if they were capable of taking a wholly disinterested view of political developments in Canton. But there is also a motive for discrediting the Canton provincial government in the Cassel Collieries Contract which was signed with the former Kwangsi militarists, and which the present government is too honest, too public spirited and too intelligent to recognize. Powerful Hongkong financial and political interests have a direct interest in the downfall of the present government and the restoration of the corrupt, inefficient and untrained old regime. This fact must be remembered in reading all "news" from Canton that comes via Hongkong sources.

For example, soon after my return I read in a fair minded English Peking paper an article directed against the local Canton government in which one of the leading arguments against Canton was the restoration of the gambling tax. Doubtless the writer believed what he wrote. But it would be difficult to find a statement wider of the facts. Not only is there no revenue from gambling but there is probably no town in China where the click of the Sparrow dominoes is so little heard. The old government had not only pocketed every available source of revenue but had collected and made away with taxes for eighteen months in advance. Finance is the crux of the whole situation, and assuredly most governments in China would have considered that, since their existence was at stake, the end justified the means. But the present provincial government heroically renounced an annual revenue of eight millions in order to save the people from the demoralization of the gambling industry and attendant corruption in administration. Nobody who knows Governor Ch'en Chiung-ming believes he will permit its re-establishment; foreigners who look with a lenient eye upon raising revenues from poppy growing on the ground that they enable tuchuns to pay their soldiers and thereby keep order, ought in justice to condone his act if he utilized gaming as a source of public funds.

Another example of misrepresentation came to my eye today. A newspaper report talked about the great labor unrest in Canton and the efforts of the mechanics of Canton to institute an eight hour day. In most countries the attempt of laborers to secure an eight hour day is looked upon as legitimate or even praiseworthy. But, after exaggerating the labor unrest in Canton, this news-propaganda item went on to connect this move with the "bolshevistic" tendencies of the Canton government. Such methods are clearly intended merely to create an emotional prejudice on the part of careless readers against the government. Governor

Ch'en's and Dr. Sun's administrations are both socialistic in the sense that they desire to retain governmental ownership of natural resources and of the basic industries that tend to become natural monopolies under private ownership. There is a double object, to preserve these things for the people and to procure revenue for the government. The attempt is just as bolshevistic as was Roosevelt's conservation movement in the United States. At the same time the authorities recognize the need for foreign capital in developing the province and would welcome foreign capitalists who have no political ends in view and who are willing to cooperate honestly on a basis of reasonable profit.

I have emphasized this matter of circulation of distorted news because it seems to me the key to the situation. Without a change in the character of the news reports it is impossible for those at a distance to have the basis for either an intelligent approval or disapproval of the new governments. I add, however, a brief enumeration of the reforms which the new provincial and municipal governments have got under way. The abolition of gambling and gambling revenue already mentioned; the continuation of the policy of modernizing the city and improving its transportation facilities; the creation of a municipal government on modern lines—in general, the American commission form—with trained administrators, the only one of the kind in China; definite and workable plans for popular participation in local government, partly through personal voting, partly by suffrage of guilds—the latter being the "soviet" plan heralded by the adverse press; the reform of the magistracies and magistrates throughout the province, including a plan for a school for the training of magistrates; the establishment of a department of public health and sanitation under the care of one of the very best trained men in public health in China; the formation of an educational commission of men trained in education who are working day and night for the improvement of the schools of the city and province, public education having steadily gone backward during the militaristic regime of the last five years. Definite plans are made for the establishment of universal primary education in Canton, girls as well as boys, to be completed in three stages, beginning with a district already selected where the plan can be tested out; in addition, there is a plan for a university and there are plans for the establishment of industrial schools throughout the province.

These reforms and others which might be mentioned are local and provincial. They touch the claims for sympathy and support of Governor Ch'en and his adherents rather than the claims of the new so-called national government under Dr. Sun. While the reports of active friction between the latter and Governor Ch'en are exaggerated, it is no secret that many of the supporters of the latter, even among those who are now giving loyal support to Dr. Sun, are not at all convinced of the wisdom of the step taken in establishing a new national government, many thinking the opportune time has not yet come. It is not necessary for a visitor to be more confident or more attached than the men who are on the ground, so I will only make one point about the new government.

Even those who are not heartily in favor of the move use one argument which it is hard to answer. They point out a striking inconsistency in the position of foreigners in the North and Chinese liberals who oppose the Southern national government on the ground that the Northern government represents the unity of China, while the Southern government introduces division. They point to the lack of unity in the North and through the country at large, and say that at most they are not creating division but merely acting upon the division that already exists. They point to the constant denunciations from foreign language newspapers in the North of the militaristic constitution of Peking and its servile subjection to the interference of provincial tuchuns, who meantime are quarrelling among themselves so that war among them is freely predicted even by supporters of the Peking government. They point to the fact that the sole hope of the Peking government in perpetuating itself, to say nothing of unifying the country, is through the use of the militaristic force which is so universally denounced. And then they ask: What is the consistency in coddling, supporting and idealizing from the standpoint of foreign relations the very government which is denounced as corrupt, inefficient and militaristic from the domestic point of view? I confess that I for one have no answer to this question. It is amusing to read in one issue of a newspaper a strong attack on the Peking government as hopeless, and then read in another issue an attack upon the Southern government for not abjectly giving the country over to the complete control of the Northern government for the sake of "unity."

In short, the local and provincial governments at Canton deserve the hearty support of every well-wisher of China. The "national" government merits at least a reasonably benevolent neutrality. By this I mean that the attempts of the Northern government to suppress it by military force should be frowned upon. Success would not mean unification. It would only mean that Kwangtung would come again under the rule of the brutal militarists of Kwangsi in comparison with whom the Anfuites were gentlemen and scholars. If the Sun government has no function in the present economy of China it will fall of its own weight. Let it alone and see what happens. If good provincial self-government is established in a number of Southern provinces following the lead of Kwangtung, there will in time be a federation which may serve as the nucleus of a real, and not a paper or a military, unification of China.

On Philosophical Synthesis

I think that the most important function your journal can perform in bringing about the ultimate objective of a "substantial synthesis of East and West" is to help break down the notion that there is such a thing as a "West" and "East" that have to be synthesized. There are great and fundamental differences in the East just as there are in the West. The cultural matrix of China, Indonesia, Japan, India, and Asiatic Russia is not a single "block" affair. Nor is the cultural matrix of the West. The differences between Latin and French and Germanic cultures on the continent of Europe, and the differences between these and the culture of England on the one hand and the culture of the United States on the other (not to mention Canadian and Latin American differences), are extremely important for an understanding of the West. Some of the elements in Western cultures and Eastern cultures are so closely allied that the problem of "synthesizing" them does not exist when they are taken in isolation. But the point is that none of these elements—in the East or the West—is in isolation. They are all interwoven in a vast variety of ways in the historico-cultural process. The basic prerequisite for any fruitful development of inter-cultural relations—of which philosophy is simply one constituent part—is an understanding and appreciation of the complexities, differences, and ramifying interrelationships both within any given country and among the countries, East and West, whether taken separately or together.

What I have just said might at other times and under other circumstances be considered so obvious as to be platitudinous. But at the present time and in the present circumstances, I venture to think that it is far from being such. Under the pressure of politi-

[First published in *Philosophy East and West* 1 (April 1951): 3.]

cal *blocs* that are now being formed East and West it is all too easy to think that there are cultural "blocks" of corresponding orientation. To adapt a phrase of William James, there are no "cultural block universes" and the hope of free men everywhere is to prevent any such "cultural block universes" from ever arising and fixing themselves upon all mankind or any portion of mankind. To the extent that your journal can keep the idea open and working that there are "*specific* philosophical relationships" to be explored in the West and in the East and between the West and East you will, I think, be contributing most fruitfully and dynamically to the enlightenment and betterment of the human estate.

Foreword, Introductions, Prefaces

Preface to *The Influence of Darwin on Philosophy*

An elaborate preface to a philosophic work usually impresses one as a last desperate effort on the part of its author to convey what he feels he has not quite managed to say in the body of his book. Nevertheless, a collection of essays on various topics written during a series of years may perhaps find room for an independent word to indicate the kind of unity they seem, to their writer, to possess. Probably every one acquainted with present philosophic thought—found, with some notable exceptions, in periodicals rather than in books—would term it a philosophy of transition and reconstruction. Its various representatives agree in what they oppose—the orthodox British empiricism of two generations ago and the orthodox Neo-Kantian idealism of the last generation—rather than in what they proffer.

The essays of this volume belong, I suppose, to what has come to be known (since the earlier of them were written) as the pragmatic phase of the newer movement. Now a recent German critic has described pragmatism as, "Epistemologically, nominalism; psychologically, voluntarism; cosmologically, energism; metaphysically, agnosticism; ethically, meliorism on the basis of the Bentham-Mill utilitarianism."[1] It may be that pragmatism will turn out to be all of this formidable array; but even should it, the one who thus defines it has hardly come within earshot of it. For whatever else pragmatism is or is not, the pragmatic spirit is primarily a revolt against that habit of mind which disposes of

1. The affair is even more portentous in the German with its capital letters and series of *muses:* "Gewiss ist der Pragmatismus erkenntnistheoretisch Nominalismus, psychologisch Voluntarismus, naturphilosophisch Energismus, metaphysisch Agnostizismus, ethisch Meliorismus auf Grundlage des Bentham-Millschen Utilitarismus."

[First published in *The Influence of Darwin on Philosophy and Other Essays in Contemporary Thought* (New York: Henry Holt and Co., 1910), pp. iii–iv.]

anything whatever—even so humble an affair as a new method in Philosophy—by tucking it away, after this fashion, in the pigeon holes of a filing cabinet. There are other vital phases of contemporary transition and revision; there are, for example, a new realism and naturalistic idealism. When I recall that I find myself more interested (even though their representatives might decline to reciprocate) in such phases than in the systems marked by the labels of our German critic, I am confirmed in a belief that after all it is better to view pragmatism quite vaguely as part and parcel of a general movement of intellectual reconstruction. For otherwise we seem to have no recourse save to define pragmatism—as does our German author—in terms of the very past systems against which it is a reaction; or, in escaping that alternative, to regard it as a fixed rival system making like claim to completeness and finality. And if, as I believe, one of the marked traits of the pragmatic movement is just the surrender of every such claim, how have we furthered our understanding of pragmatism?

Classic philosophies have to be revised because they must be squared up with the many social and intellectual tendencies that have revealed themselves since those philosophies matured. The conquest of the sciences by the experimental method of inquiry; the injection of evolutionary ideas into the study of life and society; the application of the historic method to religions and morals as well as to institutions; the creation of the sciences of "origins" and of the cultural development of mankind—how can such intellectual changes occur and leave philosophy what it was and where it was? Nor can philosophy remain an indifferent spectator of the rise of what may be termed the new individualism in art and letters, with its naturalistic method applied in a religious, almost mystic spirit to what is primitive, obscure, varied, inchoate, and growing in nature and human character. The age of Darwin, Helmholtz, Pasteur, Ibsen, Maeterlinck, Rodin, and Henry James must feel some uneasiness until it has liquidated its philosophic inheritance in current intellectual coin. And to accuse those who are concerned in this transaction of ignorant contempt for the classic past of philosophy is to overlook the inspiration the movement of translation draws from the fact that the history of philosophy has become only too well understood.

Any revision of customary notions with its elimination—instead of "solution"—of many traditionary problems cannot hope, however, for any unity save that of tendency and operation. Elaborate and imposing system, the regimenting and uniforming of thoughts, are, at present, evidence that we are assisting at a stage performance in which borrowed—or hired—figures are maneuvering. Tentatively and piecemeal must the reconstruction of our stock notions proceed. As a contribution to such a revision, the present collection of essays is submitted. With one or two exceptions, their order is that of a reversed chronology, the later essays coming first. The facts regarding the conditions of their first appearance are given in connection with each essay. I wish to thank the Editors of the *Philosophical Review,* of *Mind,* of the *Hibbert Journal,* of the *Journal of Philosophy, Psychology and Scientific Methods,* and of the *Popular Science Monthly,* and the Directors of the Press of Chicago and Columbia Universities, respectively, for permission to reprint such of the essays as appeared originally under their several auspices.

Introduction to *The Center, Function and Structure of Psychology*

It is a matter of common knowledge that psychology has become broken up into a large number of more or less independent interests and movements. What is even more serious is the fact that it has become an arena of contending schools, each of which assigns to psychology a different province and method. In some respects, this situation has been favorable to free growth; it marks an emancipation from swaddling clothes in which psychology has been confined. But as a permanent state of affairs, it is scientifically intolerable. It testifies to absence of an intellectual centre, a lack which in the end makes for confusion and uncertainty not only in the matter of interpretation but also in the conduct of detailed work.

Up to the present most attempts to introduce order and integration have been of a monopolistic character. The representatives of a particular tendency have sought to absorb the results of all other divisions of psychology, and when they resist incorporation have denied the validity of their methods. Some other attempts at unification are in reality only a mechanical compartmental division. The conception of psychology presented by Dr. Hughes in the following papers provides the science with a centre and axis; it also clearly indicates the reciprocal position and role of various methods and conclusions which are in the existing state of things incompatible rivals. These facts give his hypothesis an enormous propaedeutic value: it is not easy to see how it can be ignored by workers in the field. The idea of bios, of biotic career, and the assimilation, roughly speaking, of psychology to generalized biography, are like many revolution-

[First published in Percy Hughes, *The Center, Function and Structure of Psychology*, Lehigh University Publication, vol. 1, no. 6 (Bethlehem, Pa.: Lehigh University, [July 1927]), pp. 1–2.]

ary scientific ideas, extremely simple. Once the idea has been presented, it seems almost incredible that it has not occurred to any one before Dr. Hughes presented it. Like all genuinely simple ideas it is penetrating and far-reaching. I do not claim to grasp all its implications. Personally it seems to me by far the most promising point of view for integration of psychological material which has been offered. I am more concerned, however, to urge that it receive the serious cooperative attention which will ensure it the test that can come only through full development, than to plead for its acceptance.

Aside from its scientific value, its pedagogical significance is patent on its face. Students are easily repelled by psychology offered as a mass of specialized details connected by technical laws. Biographies, the dramatically developing careers of persons, make a direct appeal, and technical matter gets a vital meaning when it falls into place in these careers either directly or as affording their conditions and auxiliary supports. Because of my own limitations I write from the standpoint of philosophy rather than of psychology proper. In addition to the value of the standpoint for teachers, I am convinced of its importance in making possible a free alliance of philosophy and psychology. The liberation of psychology from submergence in philosophy was scientifically necessary. But I am sure that philosophy has suffered from the complete divorce which has taken place and I suspect that psychology has. The conception of biotic intuition goes far to remove what is almost a scandal in philosophy—the perception of selves. Some of the implications of the positions for logic and ethics are suggested by Dr. Hughes. More will develop. Physical science is moving in a direction where the narrative judgment, dealing with changes occupying a time span and presenting a series of phases, must assume importance. The hypothesis of a biotic career provides a direct empirical basis for such judgments. In short, the theory advanced by Dr. Hughes fulfills to an unusual extent the qualification of an illuminating, coordinating and fertile hypothesis.

Introduction to *Looking Forward: Discussion Outlines*

One of the topics suggested for study in the Discussion Outlines is "America, Land of Contrasts." One contrast is between our universal suffrage in theory and the fifty per cent who exercise it in practice; between the idea of general and active personal interest in politics and the fact that so many citizens are confused, almost paralyzed, by the complexity of the issues the country faces. Too often we give up the problems in despair and leave them to be handled by politicians and groups who make their living by keeping political machines going. Formal educational agencies have not as yet adequately met the need for information and for thought on the great issues. The L.I.D. is doing precisely this work in the Discussion Outlines which they have prepared and the lectures which are given in connection with them. The material is of the high quality that would be contained in any university extension course. It is focused on problems which the nation must meet and about which every citizen who wishes to take a stand based on intelligence must form a judgment. American political life will be on a higher plane if these Outlines stimulate discussion and receive the attention which they deserve.

[First published in Industrial Research Group, *Looking Forward: Discussion Outlines* (New York: League for Industrial Democracy, 1932), p. 3.]

Introduction to *Looking Forward,* 1933

One of the chief causes of the expansion of the American common school system almost a hundred years ago was the belief that literacy was necessary to insure the perpetuation of a republican form of government. Under present conditions, mere literacy only exposes citizens to an increased amount of sinister propaganda from interests which have something secret or private to gain. We are beginning to realize that the majority of voters leave school at so early an age that they have not been even introduced to the most important social needs and questions of the day. Adult education is as imperative now as was primary instruction a century ago. The Discussion Lectures prepared and sponsored by the L.I.D. meet the demand for continued education in economic and international problems in a most admirable way. The success of the courses in 1932 shows that there is a genuine popular hunger for the competent knowledge which these courses bring to the public. I can only repeat what I said of the earlier course: The material is of the high quality contained in well planned university extension courses. H. G. Wells has said that the whole world is taking part in a race between education and catastrophe. The kind of education given in the courses of the L.I.D. is a powerful force to hold back catastrophe.

[First published in Jean Benson and Industrial Research Group, *Looking Forward: Discussion Outlines, 1933* (New York: League for Industrial Democracy, 1933), p. 4.]

Introduction to *Looking Forward, 1934*

Every newspaper every day says that we are in a period of great social and economic change. The wiser ones also tell us that no one as yet knows where we are going, and that it is not certain whether those who are supposed to be directing the change have clear ideas of where they want to go, or whether they are improvising from day to day. Only one thing is sure. Not even the best laid plans can be successfully carried out without a spread of economic understanding among the mass of the people. There is grave danger that no plans or bad ones will rule the day unless an enlightened public opinion is developed on finance, money, industry and trade. Adult education in these things is not a luxury much less a fad. It is a necessity of democracy if it is to win the battle in which it is now engaged. The advance of Hitlerism in Germany proves that there are no depths to which a politically unenlightened community may not be degraded by use of modern methods of propaganda.

This is the third year in which the L.I.D. has carried on its campaign for a broader education of the American citizen. The standards are high, and the lecturers maintain the standards. The material presented for discussion comes home to the life of every American citizen in these days of uncertain transition. To take part in such discussions as these and to strive to answer the kind of questions that are raised is a necessity for American citizenship.

[First published in Mary W. Hillyer, *Looking Forward: Discussion Outlines, 1934* (New York: League for Industrial Democracy, 1934), p. 4.]

Introduction to *Looking Forward*, 1935

Is democracy in danger? In some countries, it is more than in danger; it is seriously wounded. Are attacks upon democracy likely to increase in our own country? No one can deny that they are already increasing. One cause of increasing doubt about the competency of political democracy to meet the existing situation is the complexity of present economic and social problems. The intelligent exercise of both the right of suffrage and the law-making function depend upon information and understanding that have been out of reach of the average voter and legislator, or else have not been thought necessary for him.

In these days of rapid change, of uncertainty, of promulgation of all sorts of policies, of charges and counter charges, of air darkened with controversy, authoritative knowledge is indispensable to an enlightened and effective public opinion. Adult education is a necessity both to save democracy and to fend off a constantly increasing confusion on all important social and political issues.

One of the most important means of meeting the pressing educational need is the lecture discussions offered, now for the fourth successive year, by the League for Industrial Democracy. The standards set for these lectures are high and they are maintained by a competent corps of expert speakers. The subjects contained in *Looking Forward* concern those matters foreign and domestic, that affect every American household and citizen. Those who are interested in maintaining the intelligent citizenship that is a necessity of American public life will lend support to this undertaking in every possible way.

[First published in Mary W. Hillyer, *Looking Forward: Discussion Outlines, 1935* (New York: League for Industrial Democracy, 1934), p. 6.]

Introduction to *Looking Forward, 1936*

The need for constructive thinking based on adequate knowledge was never greater than at the present time. It is imperative with respect to both domestic and international issues. Every passing day makes more evident the truth of the statement that "the world of which we are a part is engaged in a race between education and catastrophe." In international matters the world war ended the illusion that the United States is so isolated that it can go its own way without regard to what is happening in the rest of the world. As I write, the danger of a world war is imminent. The forces that involved us in the last war are still active. There is danger that the idea will grow that the way in which we can best cooperate with other nations is through war and direct political entanglement. Clear thinking as to the means by which we can cooperate in other ways for the cause of world order and peace is urgent.

There is no need to dwell upon the seriousness of our domestic problems. Politicians are ready to inflame public opinion for the sake of some party advantage and by methods that are fatal to clear and constructive thought and policies. The problems are so complex that it is comparatively easy to arouse emotion at the expense of intelligent insight and programs of action. Moreover, it is not enough that there be correct knowledge and sound ideas but there must be organization for action to put these ideas into effect.

The L.I.D. through its lectures and discussion as well as in other ways is doing, and doing upon a high level, necessary spade work in promoting knowledge, constructive thought, and orga-

[First published in Mary W. Hillyer, *Looking Forward: Discussion Outlines, 1936* (New York: League for Industrial Democracy, 1935), p. 6.]

nization. It is one of the chief forces making for a genuinely prepared citizenship. It is a personal satisfaction and an honor to commend to public attention its fifth annual course of lecture discussions given by men who treat their respective subjects with candor and insight based upon long study and authoritative knowledge.

Foreword to *Evolution and the Founders of Pragmatism*

There is an old English saying that good wine needs no bush. Dr. Wiener has provided for all who are interested in the development of the intellectual life of North America a generous supply of cultural wine, a wine with body and flavor. Being asked to write a brief Foreword, I gladly complied; not because the chapters forming the text are in need of any praise or recommendations, but because it is an honor to have even a remote connection with an authoritative study of the origin and early development of the intellectual and moral ferment generated in this country by the new scientific developments of the middle of the nineteenth century. For the work is more, very much more, than a study of the initiation of a particular philosophical Ism, and is also very much more than a well-documented and thoroughly informed presentation of material that completely annihilates the misstatements about the aim and tenor of the founders of the pragmatic movement that have flourished. Argument to refute the misrepresentations that were widely current a generation ago (and that are still put forth from some quarters) is not engaged in; Dr. Wiener's thorough familiarity with the facts, and his extraordinarily well-documented and penetrating recital of them, leave the misconceptions in the void of ignorance—not to say willful stupidity—in which they originated.

A British critic of the later period of the movement stated that pragmatism was an expression and organized reflection of American commercialism. Although years earlier he was not obsessed with anti-American prejudice, he had come within speaking distance of the movement by saying it was based on the inductive phase of modern science. But anyone who reads the first chapter

[First published in Philip Paul Wiener, *Evolution and the Founders of Pragmatism* (Cambridge: Harvard University Press, 1949), pp. xiii–xiv.]

of Philip Wiener's book will see how superficial is even that approach to understanding. In the last few years the work of Peirce has been receiving an attention long overdue. But if there is any account of the context which provided the soil, light, and atmosphere of his vital contribution that begins to compare with that of Dr. Wiener, it has missed my notice. One realizes the ineptitude of the method of pigeonholing classification of philosophical writings when one compares it with the method of placing them in the setting of a new and vital movement in culture which extends far beyond the confines of technical philosophy. This latter contribution Dr. Wiener makes; he has not merely contributed to the understanding of a significant distinctively American philosophical movement, but he has also provided a formation and exemplification of an enlightened and liberal method for dealing with the philosophical activity of *any* historical period.

His treatment of the "Foundations of Pragmatism" in terms of a deep, moving cultural current, takes us to a time when America was still a symbol of the dawn of a better day and was full of hope infused with courage. It will be a happy day for American philosophy if, after a period of loss of nerve, this stirring account of the initial period of a *movement* (not an Ism) recalls the wandering thoughts of American teachers of philosophy to the creative movement to which they belong as Americans, whatever school they belong to professionally.

Introduction to *William Heard Kilpatrick: Trail Blazer in Education*

In the best sense of the words, progressive education and the work of Dr. Kilpatrick are virtually synonymous. I say in the best sense because the phrase "progressive education" has been and is frequently used to signify almost any kind of school theory and practice that departs from previously established scholastic methods. Many of these procedures, when they are examined, are found to be innovations, but there seems to be no sound basis for regarding them as progressive. For progress is not identical with mere change, even when the changes may incidentally here and there involve some casual improvement over what previously existed. Still less is it identical with a happy-go-lucky process or flashy, spur-of-the-moment improvisations. "Progressive education" in the sense in which it properly applies to the work of Dr. Kilpatrick implies direction; and direction implies foresight and planning. And planning—as is surely obvious—implies taking-thought; the quality and depth of the thought depending upon how large and significant a field is taken for the exercise of direction, foresight and planning.

These remarks are, I believe, pertinent because what has often been criticised as constituting progressive education has taken progressive education to mean methods on the part of the teacher which are marked chiefly by following the immediate and spontaneous activities of children in the schoolroom.

Progressive education involves foresight and planning, which in turn requires some principles of organization. This does not mean that a fixed goal must be set up but that there must be a point of view from which to select materials and arrange them in

[First published in Samuel Tenenbaum, *William Heard Kilpatrick: Trail Blazer in Education* (New York: Harper and Brothers, 1951), pp. vii–x.]

some kind of order. Dr. Kilpatrick has amply met and fulfilled the conditions just stated, that is, of bringing together a wide and deep body of subject matter. That he has put the various parts of this material in orderly relations to one another is evident to anyone with even a superficial acquaintance with his work. In this connection, I have repeatedly been surprised, when there was discussion and perhaps controversy about some educational development in this country, even in regions quite distant from New York City, to find how complete and accurate was Dr. Kilpatrick's knowledge of what was actually taking place and of its significance, good or bad, for educational progress. Adequate information, as distinct from hasty improvisation, has always been the groundwork of Dr. Kilpatrick's educational contribution to progressive education.

The phrase "philosophy of education," while it is the opposite of mere improvisation, is often treated as a complete system of ready-made fixed principles which can be laid down by someone already acquainted with them and which can be accepted ready made by students. This is as deadening in effect as the other unorganized procedure mentioned.

In Dr. Kilpatrick's educational activities, philosophy has taken the form of a moving development. Organization has not been so rigid as to exclude modification and enrichment as new issues and new problems are presented by the actual course of events. It is coming to be a fairly common remark that teachers themselves do not practice the processes of learning that they recommend to their students. That good teaching involves continual learning on the part of the teacher is a fact that is exemplified in Dr. Kilpatrick's work. In this way, he has successfully avoided taking the position of a dogmatic authority. He has recognized in his own teaching the fact that good teaching involves participation on the part of teacher and learner, that it is a reciprocal and not a one-way process.

The foregoing generalities may take on more concrete form if it is noted that Dr. Kilpatrick has never fallen a victim to the one-sidedness of identifying progressive education with child-centered education. This does not mean that he has not given attention to the capacities, interests, and achievements and failures of those who are still students; but he has always balanced regard for the psychological conditions and processes of those who are learning with consideration of the social and cultural conditions in which as human beings the pupils are living.

The common habit of separating one body of subject matter called social psychology from psychology proper and then confining psychology to strictly individual activities is an illustration. That human beings are always and fundamentally social beings is thereby overlooked to the detriment of sound educational practice. Dr. Kilpatrick has consistently avoided the purely individualistic psychology approach by taking into account the differing capacities and interests that necessarily characterize children as learners. The state of the world in which children and youth live as human beings and the need of considering the kind of social relationships in which they will live in the future—the issues and problems with which they will have to deal—has always been a guiding consideration in Dr. Kilpatrick's educational philosophy.

The "project method" is identified on a world-wide scale with the educational contribution of Dr. Kilpatrick. As I learned on a visit to Russia during the early years of educational reform in that country, when there was still a considerable freedom, the guiding principle of their educational philosophy was the project method. Among the abler educators whom I met on that trip, the name of Dr. Kilpatrick was almost a household word. That these men were liquidated in the sense of either death or permanent exile is typical of the tragedy that has influenced every phase of life in the U.S.S.R. as personal freedom was suppressed, and then schools—and even the sciences and fine arts—became mere tools of a totalitarian regime. The earlier use of the project method is vital evidence of the balance that is maintained in Dr. Kilpatrick's philosophy and theory of education, namely, the development of individuality on one side and of social changes that are in the direction of betterment and human advance on the other side.

Specifically, the project method, as developed by Dr. Kilpatrick, involves the presence of a common purpose shared by teacher and learner, which extends over a considerable period of time, introducing thereby the continuity of development that is a prerequisite of genuine progress. The second main trait of the project method, I should say, is that it represents in terms of the attainments and capacities of the students some typical life situation in the world outside the schoolroom.

One of the soundest and most valuable features of the genuine progressive education movement has been that it strives to break down the walls erected to shut off the schoolroom from almost everything outside the school building. Under such conditions, learning for the great majority could have little direct bearing on the conduct of life outside the school building. Learning, when judged from the standpoint of actual practice, consisted largely in a passive reception of material which was already organized in books and in the teacher's mind from the standpoint of adults.

The adult standpoint was naturally so alien to the processes of those undergoing instruction that learning became passive and the standard for testing it tended to be accuracy of formal reproduction. The project method represented and—wherever intelligently adopted—brought about a repudiation of this kind of teaching and learning in favor of active, vital participation of students in real human situations which, if necessarily on a small scale, nevertheless was significant in the situation in which the student lived and was to live actively in the future. In short, it was completely faithful to that phase of progressive educational theory which was concerned with the breakdown of the walls that had been built up between the school and the life situations in which pupils as human beings lived but which they were not prepared by the school training to meet on account of the isolation of the school learning.

The traditional school against which progressive education reacted did not recognize in its practice that learning, of necessity, goes on in the years before the child goes to school and continues to go on the moment he arrives at home and shares again in family and neighborhood life activities. In consequence, of course, it had no concern with finding out how learning goes on most readily and most effectively. It had no interest consequently in learning about the way in which learning takes place as a necessary feature of the normal life of every human being.

I do not think it is a matter of accident that progressive education as represented in the project method originated in the United States. Although it is not as yet universally or sufficiently recognized that a democratic society means fundamentally the right of every human being to an environment in which his own personal activity will have an opportunity of full participation and development in social relationships, yet it can hardly be denied that democracy becomes an actual human fact only in the degree in which social customs and institutions are moving in this direction. Accordingly, a democratic school society operates as an agency for maintaining and developing a democracy only as it exhibits within itself the purposes and methods that a genuinely democratic life for the whole community must attempt to achieve. The aims and processes of learning, which have been so fully and concretely stated by Dr. Kilpatrick, form a notable and virtually unique contribution to the development of a school society that is an organic component of a living, growing democracy.

May I say in conclusion that it has been a great satisfaction to me personally to have been associated with Dr. Kilpatrick in the effort to develop a philosophy of education which will give direction to the promotion of the educational practices within a school society that will render education progressive from kindergarten through the university in the sense of promoting the progress of our common human life and of a society ever growing and ever more worthy, free, and just.

Preface to Japanese Translation of *Democracy and Education*

It is a pleasure to acknowledge the great pains the translator has taken to render my book accessible to the Japanese educational public. Unfortunately my ignorance of the Japanese language does not enable me to judge of the translation itself, but I have every confidence in the statement of friends who say that it is unusually clear, accurate, and fluent. That the translator was well prepared by previous study to understand both the language and the ideas of the book is well known to me personally, and also that he spared no time or labor. I am sincerely grateful to him for his kindness in introducing my educational writings to a new circle of readers. I am also indebted to him for the pains he has taken in preparing a summary of my general philosophical position.

[First published in *Minshu-shugi to Kyôiku* [*Democracy and Education*], trans. Riichirô Hoashi (Tokyo: Shunjû-sha, 1952), n.p.]

Introduction to *Selected Poems of Claude McKay*

When Claude McKay did me the honor of asking me to write some introductory words for his volume of poems, I gladly assented. When I read the poems I felt that there are occasions in the presence of which silence is the fitting response. I feel that this is one of those occasions; words of comment are idle, and even words of praise have something of the quality of impertinence about them. I shall, at all events, refrain from telling others what they ought to look for and find in this book of poems, and shall also, I hope, refrain from anything else that might seem to be assuming the seat of critic and judge. I shall be more than satisfied if I can tell where and how the poet's words have deeply touched me.

Were I to single out one line from the poems to convey what comes nearest to telling what the poems mean to me I think it would be from "North and South," reading

And wonder to life's commonplaces clings.

I realize that the eyes of insensitive readers may linger on "commonplaces" and less lightly over the wonder that clings to them. But that wonder which never fails or falters in the case of Claude McKay's vision is that in which commonplaces are identical with what is common in the life of all men since it cannot be escaped and yet is capable of being expressed only by one who has like McKay the eyes of a poet and the voice of a singer.

This poem in which the verse quoted is to be found is part of the first one of the five parts in which the poems are arranged. The part is entitled "Songs for Jamaica" where, it is evident, the poet spent his own childhood. Its immediate reference is to the

[First published in Claude McKay, *Selected Poems of Claude McKay,* ed. Max Eastman (New York: Bookman Associates, 1953), pp. 7–9.]

sense and feeling of life that belongs to childhood. All the poems of this part are filled with the most spontaneous manifestation that I have ever read of the ways in which a sensitive adult may recover and recreate the life of the child. It is spontaneous because it is fused with the material of which the poems are composed; it never stands out as a separate element.

I mention this for two reasons. One of them I have already mentioned. It is the extraordinary way in which almost every poem of the volume expresses that identity of the self with the ever fresh always renewed wonders of living which is the gift of childhood at its happiest. The other reason is that while the first section conveys this identification in the sense of childhood itself, each successive section unites its direct, straightforward quality, as free from artificiality and straining for effect as the spirit of childhood itself (when free from constraint from without) with that ever-increasing depth and intensity which should be the lot of all men as they mature but which is usually dulled into finding commonplace the deep things of common human life.

I shall make no attempt to follow this increment in its unfailing expression in the subsequent sections, "Americana," "Different Places," "Amoroso," and "Baptism." It is there in the poems in its own behalf and in its own terms. About the subject intervening between the first and the last sections I shall only say that the five poems of foreign cities and countries that are the Different Places reappearing in Claude McKay's vision, although they are by no means the most weighty of the volume, yet reveal with startling vividness his unspoiled and immediately sensitive response to scenes of the world in which the physical and the human blend into an indivisible yet distinctive unity.

The culmination of ever-increasing growth in depth and intensity constitutes the last section, "Baptism." The religious suggestion of the title is the very color and atmosphere of the poem composing it,

> And so to God I go to make my peace
> Where black nor white can follow to betray.
> My pent-up heart to Him I will release
> And surely He will show the perfect way.

It is in this section that the sense of being a black man in a white man's world, which is a recurring undertone of many poems in the previous parts of the book, comes to its full expression. I feel it decidedly out of place to refer to him as the voice of the Negro people; he is that, but he is so much more than that. "Baptism" is deeply dyed with hate, but with hate that is clean, never mean nor spiteful. No white man can do more than express his humiliated sympathy. For, in the words of the poet,

> There is no white man who could write my book
> Though many think the story can be told
> Of what the Negro people ought to brook.
> Our statesmen roam the world to set things right,
> This Negro laughs and prays to God for Light.

Addresses

Commencement Address: San Jose State Normal School

Wherever we take life the same facts confront us. Nothing appears absolute. It is all a matter of degrees, a matter of the scale. One man feels poverty pinching him because he cannot acquire a railway system; put him further down the scale and he will measure his possessions by the question of whether he can buy a yacht. Let him lose more of his wealth and it will be a question of whether he shall keep five or six servants; come down to a point lower still on the scale and it may be a question of whether he will purchase round or porterhouse steak; with still another, the pressing issue may be how many times in the year he can afford to eat meat at all. It is exactly the same sort of a question to each—a question of the margin or rates of expense and income. Each gets in his way the same sort of mental and moral discipline—quite possibly the same enrichment of life—through manfully facing and dealing with the problem upon the exact degree of the scale where it confronts him. So with a man's movements in life; to one it is a question of spending years of time in a journey which shall circumnavigate the globe in space; to another it is the question of spending the week or two of his vacation in journeying to a neighboring city or mountain, while to a third it is a matter of whether he can collect the pennies requisite to take his family upon a street car ride to enjoy an outing in the park.

It is not absolute possession that counts, nor is it absolute achievement. We are conscious in life only of those margins where our wants outrun our holdings; when our purposes and plans are sufficiently far ahead of our attainments and seeming resources that we must reckon up the latter and see what we can

[First published in *San Jose Daily Mercury*, 27 June 1901, p. 6, from address delivered 26 June 1901.]

best do with them. If the despairs and miseries of life have their origin here, so also do the bracing joys. If here we find our disappointments, so we find also here the fruition of hope that gives us the sense of power and expansion. All significance and helpful effort of every kind is concentrated upon just this margin of difference. To gloat over our present possessions, to rest satisfied with it, to be a miser in matters intellectual and moral, no less than monetary, to spend this carelessly with no thought of its application to covering the step that separates us from possible achievement ahead, is to be a spendthrift—it is to lead this indulgent life. On the other hand, to set up faraway and absolute ideals out of any ratio of our present achievement, is to lead the life of a dreamer and a doctrinaire. To attempt to realize Utopias and faraway goals unmindful of the great principle of margins, of the fact that effort is fruitful to the degree that it is directed at some definite ground that lies between what we are and what we would be, is to stamp one's self as a crank. The sane man is the man who neither lives within the range of his accomplishments and possessions, nor yet sets up vague ideals of our unattainable perfection, but who concentrates his mind and energy upon the step ahead. Here we find the great leveler—great in a positive way as death is the negative leveler. Whether a man have one problem or ten, his problem, his training are the same and the measure of his success or failure is the same: "Has he or has he not covered the margin of difference which lies next beyond him?" The absolute need of possession is nothing; the ratio which is set up by its effective use is everything. No man possesses so little that he cannot with that little unlock the door to more; no man has so much that he may rest in it and say there is nothing more beyond. As possession increases and the horizon expands, we may ascend the highest mountains on the face of the earth, but when we have done so we are not at the horizon line. It is simply further away from us than it was when we were on the flat plain.

Psychology shows this principle to be so deeply imbedded in our structure that we cannot escape it even if we would. The stars are in the heavens, day as well as night, but the light they shed does not offer a sufficient margin over and above the light of the sun so that we can bring them into our conscious experience. A man in a well is certainly not advantageously situated, but he can at least console himself with the thought that if it is darker above him he can still see the stars with his more fortunate fellows under the open sky of heaven.

Whatever is completely accomplished becomes a matter of habit, and whatever is purely habitual is if left to itself, mechanical and unconscious. The man who sets a goal of final achievement before himself, a goal in which he anticipates having overcome all defects, and exhausted all the possibilities, sets before himself a goal of extinction of conscious life.

It is the sense of the incomplete that stirs us to action; it is the stirring to action which makes us conscious of ourselves and of this world in which we live. It is through the effort to supply the want to overcome the obstacle, that we measure our powers and give ourselves a conscious station in the world about us.

Truth as a fundamental law of life gives significance to our modern interests in childhood in whatever is immature and undeveloped. For many centuries has mankind been impatient with the period of growth. Childhood has been but a time to get over as rapidly as possible; just an unavoidable delay in the full fruition of the meaning of life. We are beginning to recognize that it is growth, that it is the process itself which counts, and that consequently no step in infancy or childhood can be regarded simply as a preparation for the fullness of growth to be attained later on. Every step has its own problems, its own stimulus to growth, its richness of meaning, and its revelation of new possibility. To be impatient with this growth, to hurriedly slur it over in eagerness for the final fruit, is a defect of our aim. Growth comes through growing.

To-day in the world of politics, in the world of capital and labor, and in the world of education, we are confronted everywhere, with the man who will do nothing because he regards the ideal as essentially unpracticable, and also with the man who would wipe out the present, start afresh, and by some miracle usher in the ideal, the millennium.

In education for example we have the restless eagerness for change for change's sake, the law of novelty, the willingness to run after every new ideal, and every newly propounded method or device. Schools lose their centre of gravity; their stable equilibrium in their insistence. As a result reaction follows reaction. This school dissipates itself in meaningless oscillations and ineffective vibrations. On the other side stands the teacher who says: "Reform is desirable but it is so desirable as to be ideal, to be impracticable. I must deal with the conditions in which I find myself. The conditions of my community, of my school or of my room in the school, force me to a certain line of work. It may be well for these under different conditions to do something different, but I must be practical. I must meet conditions as they are."

Both types suffer from common error. Both destroy continuity and deny the principle of margins. One will have good all at once; the other will do nothing because he sees he cannot have it all at once. Both forget that any proposition of reform is not to be treated as defining a condition which is completely to displace and deface the present, but is rather a stimulus and a help in dealing more freely and effectively with the present. Neither to destroy present conditions nor to submit to them as final is the true ideal, rather in the light of a possibility just far enough ahead to give scope, to give room for energy, and just near enough to be free from vagueness and instability, to make use of the existing conditions to keep them moving.

The ideal hasn't virtue in life as some remote goal to be finally accomplished, but from what it does for us in enabling us to interpret and deal with our present circumstances. Save as we can transmute it from a fixed goal into a working method, from a remote end into a present resource, it were as well to have no ideal. It is the movement, the present activity, the next step, that counts, and to this the ideal must be made tributary. It is the servant, not the lord of life. Only in this way can we recognize success or failure.

My final wish for you all is that each of you may make the most of the margin of his own life, and may do something to enlarge the margin of his fellowmen.

The Educational Principles Involved

When your Executive Secretary, Mr. Fitzpatrick, asked me to speak on this subject I had a private understanding with him. I told him in the first place I was not going to speak of the question of giving credit, because that was an administrative question; and I knew nothing about the administrative side. I am not going to speak, therefore, about the matter of academic bookkeeping. Nor am I, of course, competent to speak as a specialist, as I am not at all in the field of public administration. It was arranged that I might speak from the standpoint of such general educational principles as may be involved.

I think the last speaker, Mr. McCarthy, brought out an educational principle as well as a practical one. We have to do with the general question of the relation of theoretical work, understanding and mastering of principles, and practical application. It goes without saying that there is in this matter an educational problem quite apart from the practical training of an administrator. There are many fields where the underlying principles or theories can neither be understood nor tested unless put to some practical application. The idea of the laboratory and its value, not merely in training a man for practical investigation but in training him to understand the subject-matter with which he is dealing, occurs to the minds of all of us. The question before us is not an isolated question. It is a question which has come up in all other forms of educational endeavor. The general history of professional education in this country has, I think, been something of this kind. In engineering, medical, and law schools we

[First published in *Universities and Public Service: Proceedings of the National Conference on Universities and Public Service* (Madison, Wis.: American Political Science Association, 1914), pp. 249–54, from address delivered at the Conference, New York City, 13 May 1914.]

set out to be very practical. The attempt was made to duplicate in college the technical operations of actual procedure. The same thing was done with practice work in connection with the training of teachers. The results were disappointing. It was found to be a matter of economy to make the college or professional course somewhat more theoretical, because the man could get his practical experience under actual practical conditions better than he could in the university work while the time given to practical details encroached upon the gaining of an understanding of fundamental principles. So certain things in the study of the law were relegated to the lawyer's office. Certain kinds of practical work in engineering were left for the man to acquire in his practical experience. The college could use its time better in giving insight into principles. In other words, however sound the general analogy of the laboratory, it is not self-applying.

At the present time there is, for example, a great deal of dissatisfaction about the training courses for nurses in hospitals. They seem to some physicians to have been in a sense overpractical in the way they kept nurses occupied with details, possibly because it was economical from the standpoint of the expenditure of funds to keep the nurses doing what was practical—house-cleaning work and floor scrubbing, so that they did not have enough scientific training in the principles of nursing. Just as Mr. McCarthy and a number of other speakers have said: *the question cannot be solved by giving a man a practical job of a somewhat routine kind and then giving him credit for it.* Some scientific men have even criticised what they regarded as a wrong use of laboratories in connection with the teaching of science. *Students sometimes master, they say, the mere technique of manipulating apparatus, but fail to see its bearing upon the problems of subject-matter.* So from an educational standpoint it does not follow that anything is to be gained by giving recognition to a man studying a theoretical course in the university, merely because he is taking some kind of practical work that involves some of the same processes that his theoretical work takes up. The practical work must be of a kind really to illuminate the theoretical instruction.

In the last page of the little program there is a quotation from the mayor, saying: "My own experience, both as commissioner of accounts and in my present office, has convinced me that the type of man qualified by training, experience, native ability and initiative to perform the work of even minor subordinate positions in the city government is so rare as to be practically unobtainable." Then he says, "Universities cannot fill the demand for this particular kind of training." Again, "With this training, the field work is absolutely necessary." I can illustrate, perhaps, what I have been saying by stating that the mere fact of taking some kind of a subordinate position in administrative work, whether in city, state or national government, even supposing it gave a man an experience valuable for practical purposes, would not necessarily be of any great educational or intellectual advantage to him. It is not enough, in other words, that a man should be carrying on theoretical work and practical work, either side by side or successively, either at the same time or one after he has done the other. What is wanted is that there should be some definite and active coordination between the theory and the practice. *Certainly one thing our administration needs is ideas, theories if you please, some kind of working hypothesis to get above the level of mere routine work.* Laboratory work in science consists of something which has possibilities besides washing bottles and running machines. Laboratory work is effective just in the degree in which it develops a sense of the great ideas that lie behind it, the practical work serving to make real the meaning of theories and to test their value.

The problem, it seems to me, is how to get some definite working coordination and correlation between the theoretical instruction and the field work, for merely having both of them does not insure their real interaction.

Mr. McCarthy made a suggestion that is fundamental to the situation, when he referred to the *survey of the situation* already made by the committee, and which I understand is still going on. And when this is supplemented by the active cooperation of educational institutions the result will certainly supply a method for the undertaking of field work that will be intellectually useful. *It is necessary to find both the particular institutions that are giving such combined work and the particular men in those institutions that are actively interested in bringing about this cross-fertilization between theory and practice.* So it is necessary to find the places and the particular administrative offices, municipal and otherwise, where there is somebody on the administrative side who is willing to see to it that these students shall get something intellectual out of their work, and not merely perform certain routine processes. There are doubtless some communities even now where there are people in governmental administration who are interested in the intellectual phase of their problems, but we cannot take it for granted that they are found everywhere, and then turn students in to sink or swim by finding their own way.

Dean Schneider pointed out this morning that when the work of cooperation is carried on under unusually good conditions, it is possible for a college to give even more theoretical work than under the old system; that it can relieve itself more completely than the professional and engineering schools have usually done of a kind of semi-practical activities which neither quite repeat the actual condition of business life nor are purely theoretical, and thereby devote themselves more definitely to the intellectual and scientific part of their work than at present.

And I think that the same thing applies also in this general field of the application of social science to practical work, provided always you have the men on the two sides who are actively interested in this possibility, and willing to cooperate with each other in seeing that connections are really made.

Mr. Cooke, in his speech this morning about the Philadelphia situation, pointed out the fact that quite aside from the matter of carrying on actual administrative work, whether in subordinate or routine positions, or in something higher, there is a very great demand for knowledge in certain constructive fields. We simply don't know enough about some practical matters to tackle them efficiently. He showed clearly that there is a great shortage of knowledge of the facts and ideas by which government officers might proceed. Wherever there are city administrations that feel the need of definite research in order to give them facts upon which to go, there is an opportunity, of the very first order, for universities to carry on a scientific and intellectual job of seminar work. In doing this work, students will get better training in methods of social research than if working in isolation upon mere artificial questions, while the result of their inquiries will actually help solve the problems which the administrators are actively engaged with.

There is one phase of public administration which has been

touched upon occasionally. I refer to the matter of public education itself. If we simply take it in the matter of figures in the
budget, this is one of the most important public functions. Before
closing I want to say just one word about this phase of the public
activity. Recognition of the problem of public education as a
political and sociological problem and not merely an intellectual
one is comparatively recent. It is only within the last generation,
largely within the last decade, that it has been seen that the leaders of school systems must have a certain sense of statesmanship
about the workings of the system—that they have to do not
solely, not mainly with what goes on inside the walls of the
school buildings, but have a very definite part to play in the
adjustment of the educational system to the civic and industrial
life of the community.

*The problem of university training for public service must take
account of the growing demand for a type of school officer—
principal and superintendent—who is thoroughly acquainted
with civic and political and economic problems, and whose
view goes beyond that of conventional pedagogical subject
matter and methods of teaching.* Already cities of the country
that have attempted school surveys have gone to the departments of universities in various colleges. The movement for a
wider utilization of the school plants has certainly received quite
as much stimulus from within the walls of the universities as
from without.

I don't want to stop without uttering a word in reference to
what Professor Howe said, although it has not to do directly
with my topic. I do not hold any particular brief for the defense
of democracy in universities, but I would like to say that the
intellectual atmosphere of the universities with which I personally have been associated, so far as general responsiveness to
social demands is concerned, so far as flexibility of curriculum is
concerned in willingness to change to meet changed conditions,
and so far as the freedom and intellectual initiative given to their
teachers is concerned, is far more democratic than that found,
for example, in the public school systems of the country.

Socializing the Schools

Mr. Chairman, Ladies and Gentlemen, and Fellow Teachers—I do not doubt that many here have read the sketch of autobiography written by our ex-president, Mr. Roosevelt. In that account of his life he said something about the sort of education he had or the sort of schooling that he had when he was a boy, a youth. I will not attempt to give his words, but the idea was that the motives that were appealed to when he was in school were entirely individualistic in character; that they were urged to be diligent, studious and regular at school because of the value of education in helping them to make their way in the world. Education was a necessary preliminary of success in the personal struggle and the personal achievement later in life. The motive for it, the great urging force back of the reason for schooling was the extent it would help the individual in making his way, in getting ahead in the world, and that meant, as he points out, that the social motive was not appealed to; he says that he does not remember that he ever heard anything said in all his school days about the importance of education as a preparation for social service, for usefulness to one's fellow-man in the world. The very idea of making preparation for social service, for doing one's part in the cooperative system of man, was passed over.

Now that does not mean, I think, that they were any worse in those days than we are now, or that we are any better than they were, but the change has come and it has meant that other conditions have changed, that the idea of education as related to individual achievement, making one's way in the world, getting on, was an idea that was natural and inevitable in the pioneer

[First published in *Proceedings of the Indiana State Teachers' Association,* Indianapolis, 25–28 October 1916, pp. 105–9, from address delivered 27 October 1916.]

conditions of our life. You have only to recall the conditions as they were a few generations ago, practically as they were in most parts of the country up to the time of the Civil War, to see how largely men were concerned with a struggle against nature, a struggle against the obstacles of a new country, and how there was plenty of land, plenty of opportunity and plenty of resources for all people. Men were engaged in subduing the wilderness, the forest and the prairies. They were more or less isolated from each other, for there was plenty of land and plenty of opportunity for everybody, and the great need was that every individual be trained to virility, to personal force and ambition, to a desire to make his own way and being equipped to make his own way, to get ahead. By doing that he was rendering upon the whole, under those conditions, the best service that he could render to other people.

Now I do not need to tell you that those pioneer days have passed away and that our conditions at the present, the conditions to which all our schooling has to be adapted, are very different. Instead of having a relatively sparse population with easy opportunity for all who are enterprising and courageous and ambitious, instead of having that sparse population with plenty of opportunity, we have a somewhat congested population and we have much less accessibility of natural resources, partly because in those earlier days we wasted so much of our patrimony; we failed to conserve it, thinking that our opportunities would remain boundless, and partly because of the growth of the population these natural opportunities have largely been occupied by others. The congestion is not merely the congestion of population in large cities, though this change in our population from a rural population to an urban population is one of the fundamental facts to which our education and our schools have to be adapted, but it is equally an industrial congestion, a congestion and a blocking of numbers, which has compelled men, in so much as they have not any longer to struggle against nature to get on, to struggle against one another. To get on, to get ahead, does not mean as it did once to get ahead of surroundings, to get ahead of the natural environment; to have one man to try, to struggle to get ahead of his neighbor, and while he was getting ahead to push his neighbor back; and that change is one that our schools have to take account of.

In the first place, I should say that our conception of the public school as an institution was undergoing a change. We used to think of it and we used to treat it essentially as the school, as a school building to which the children alone went, one by one, for a certain number of years of their life in order to master the ability to read, to write, to figure, to spell and to master a certain amount of information in subjects like geography and history, that would be useful or important to them in their later life. The school buildings, the school equipment, the school administration were all adapted to this idea of the school. The very physical picture of the school, of the schoolroom with its screwed down desks, its fixed seats, the mechanical rigidity and uniform absence of any equipment, excepting at the most a blackboard and chalk, and perhaps a few books, dictionaries, an atlas and encyclopaedia and a few little maps, gives us a kind of physical picture of that conception of the school as a place to which simply individuals went as individuals to acquire something for themselves; that the school building had any particular relation, or the school administration had any particular relation to the social activities, either of the children or of the adult, was a thing not dreamed of. Now we are coming to think of the public school as having a much larger purpose and function than that; essentially to serve as a clearing house, as a centre and a focus for all of the community activities, as related to the lives of those who have left school, the youths and even to the lives of the adults.

I notice that on your program in some of these meetings you are having a number of talks on the use of schools as community centres. That is an expression, one expression of this change of which I am speaking; that the school and those who are in charge of the administration of the school have a responsibility to the community life. It is not necessary that all of the libraries and all of the museums and art galleries and so on should be directly connected with the school, directly or physically connected with the school; it is not necessary that all the recreation facilities, facilities for public lectures and instruction to adults should be physically connected with the schoolroom; but it is necessary that the public school system should become more and more the harmonizing centre and clearing house, concentrating and unifying all these educational activities of the community, forcing them, stimulating them, and seeing to it that they are really made useful to the people. The use of the schools in the evening for recreation facilities, for social meetings, for getting people acquainted with each other is a part of this same thing. Unless I am mistaken there are already school buildings in this country and in this State where the number of adults that go into and use them in the course of a week or a month is equally as large as the number of children, yet this movement is hardly begun. Our imaginations are not yet awakened to what can be done by our educational system as a means of fostering the community spirit, and of giving to all of the individuals all of the best public resources of the community life. We are beginning to apply this principle more and more, not merely in the local school system, but in the State and even in the nation. We shall recognize that our whole educational system is a method that must be organized so as to become efficient in bringing to needy individuals, needy classes anywhere, the knowledge, the technical intellectual equipment which has been worked out by the more advanced and better trained members of the community, that it may help all alike.

We really can not make in the schools adequate preparation for social life, for instilling the social point of view into the pupils and furnishing them with a social motive and purpose, until the schools themselves are somewhat differently equipped. The social spirit and motive is the product of people living together and doing certain things in common, and sharing in each other's activities and in each other's experiences because they have common ends and purposes. It is because people have something to do which interests them and holds them all alike, and to the doing of which each makes his own contribution, that people become permeated with the real social spirit.

Now we have inherited certain conceptions of what it is to be an educated man. Those conceptions, I repeat, are for the most part aristocratic and feudal notions, notions derived from the time when learning was a badge and emblem of a class. I certainly believe that it is very important that there should be these learned specialists. I believe that there should be opportunity in our public school system for the selection of all those who have particular aptitude in every one of these lines. We have already made provision in our great public school system, with its state universities, for carrying on those who have this aptitude to higher ideals. I am saying nothing against that, but I am saying that our ideal, our notion, of what an educated man is must be based, not upon this relatively small learned class, but upon capacity to see into the meaning of the common social life, and that any man who understands the materials and the instruments and the equipment and the principles by which our modern complex social life is carried on is an educated man; and I do not care how much of technical learning he has, or whether it be Latin, Greek, mathematics, physics, chemistry or biology, the individual who can not see his own knowledge in its relation to the common and cooperative life of man, who can not see where that touches and comes home to the life of the community to which he belongs, is not really an educated man. He is merely a learned specialist.

Now it is the province of our schools to make educated men and women, educated boys and girls in this newer sense of the word "educated," to use the resources of the curriculum not as so many things to be studied, to be acquired for their own sake, but as so many things that have to be mastered and gained in order that pupils may see instead of being blind; that they may see into the realities and the meaning of the social life about them and be prepared then to do their own work effectively, to pull their own weight, to do their own jobs with effectiveness, and at the same time to be able to sympathize with the work and activities of others and to cooperate with them in the carrying on of the common life.

I repeat that our older ideas of education, our older methods, those which have come to us by tradition, which have found their way into our common schoolroom, have been very largely those fitted to a restricted community, a community where a few individuals have access to learning. We have widened the number of individuals who have access to this, but we have kept in mind the same old end. It is the public school, as the great organ in democracy of making social insight, insight into the social activities and resources, dominant in the minds of the public and in giving them a social purpose and motive in their work that I present to you under this idea of socializing the American public schools.

The Educational Balance, Efficiency and Thinking

There are two traits which have to go together and which have to be balanced with each other in order that we may get an adequate and rounded development of personality, and for that reason there are two factors which have to be constantly borne in mind in all teaching and borne in mind in such a way that we do not first tend to one and develop one, and then, forgetting that, develop the other, but that we keep the two balanced together all the time.

I call those two factors efficiency and thought.

Efficiency, or skill in execution and good, orderly, effective method and technique of doing things which is under control.

The other, thinking, or the recognition of the meaning of what we do, having a definite, well-thought-out and comprehensive plan or purpose in our actions.

Now, I do not care whether it is in school or out, in business, in politics, in science, or art, I find everywhere that these two factors are required for real, successful accomplishment. The business man has got to have his orderly habits of work. He has got to have his skill which belongs to his particular business, just as must the physician or the lawyer have a method of skillful operation which enables him to do promptly and without confusion in a regular, consecutive way, without waste, without constant faults and wasted moves, the things which he needs to do. So the scientific man in his laboratory has to have command of the technique of his particular method of inquiry. If he is a chemist, he has got to be able to handle and manipulate his materials and his tools in the way that they call for. If he is a mathematician, he

[First published in *Proceedings of the Indiana State Teachers' Association*, Indianapolis, 25–28 October 1916, pp. 188–93, from address delivered 27 October 1916.]

has got another set of tools and apparatus and another mode of skill. But he has to have that same definite control of materials. So with the housewife in the household; so on through all these undertakings. At the same time, just as the artist might have a fine technique with the instrument and yet the use of that instrument would not move people, would not affect them on any very deep level, because there was no feeling back of it or because there were no ideas expressed in it, so, of course, a business man might have a certain technique or skill but never rise above the level of a bookkeeper or accountant, never become able or competent really to take hold of the entire business and manage it for himself, because of the lack of ability intellectually to analyze situations, to see what the factors are and to form a broad plan, form a mental synthesis, that would bring these things together. So, I take it, while I have not any particular experience in that line, a housekeeper might know enough to handle a broom and the dishpan and the dishrag and all the other particular things where skill is needed in the household, and yet be a poor housekeeper for lack of ability to control these activities intellectually and make a plan, which would make the different details of the day's work and the day's duties that had to be attended to, fit into each other in some kind of harmonious and effective way.

Now, before we go on I want to generalize, in a way, what I have been saying. What elements of life is it that those two factors correspond to? Why do we need both this regular formed habit of action on the one hand, ability to do a thing with uniformity and promptness twice over, and on the other hand require this capacity to think? It is because there are two factors in every situation that we have to deal with. On the one hand there are certain factors that are stable, that are uniform, that are repeated from place to place, from time to time, from situation to situation. Now, if everything in life were fixed and uniform, habits, skilled habits, would answer every purpose and all that would ever be needed would be for teachers in the schoolroom to train for efficiency. They would drop the element of thought practically out of consideration. What we would get, of course, then, would be efficient machines. A well constructed machine will work as long as its structure remains uniform and constant and the conditions under which it is worked remain constant. If the conditions of life, if the conditions of our natural and social surroundings, were the same from hour to hour and day to day and year to year, all that would be necessary would be for a person to get stocked up with the right set of skilled habits, and having got started they would go on. But it is because beside these stable and constant elements in our lives there are changing elements, unexpectedly varying ones, that we cannot rely simply upon the element of habit to take care of ourselves. We have to have also the training and the variety in thinking to take care of these emergencies that come up because of the unexpected and changing elements in the situation. Wherever the conditions are routine conditions, I repeat, persons do not need to think. A horse in a treadmill would never have any particular occasion for thinking after he got his legs going and the treadmill going around; and persons that are engaged in these routine activities, all they need is a particular skill or habit in doing the particular thing that they have got started on. But when a machine breaks down the habits of the operator running that machine won't help him out. He will be perfectly helpless unless he can call science to his aid, unless he can call thought to his aid, unless he understands the operations of the machine; unless he understands, as we say, the theory of this machine and its workings, he will be helpless and he will have to call in somebody else who has this thought ability, this understanding, in order to help him out. We need these formed habits of skill and execution in so far as there are constant and regular elements in our surroundings and consequently things that can be dealt with two or three times or any number of times the same way, over and over, so when we have got the right habit formed we can dismiss that from further consideration and let that work. But we go through life in a world of variety and change and if we stop to think we know that the average person comes up against complex and varied circumstances in life. A few generations ago there was a time when society was pretty well stratified into classes, when it was known of a child at his birth in a general way what kind of thing he was going to do all his life, that he was going to follow the profession of his father, with the same social status. Under those conditions they could put the emphasis much more on forming the particular habits that would enable him to fit into his particular preordained niche in life. But our life today, and especially our American life, is very mobile and changeable. Things are flexible and fluid and elastic. A person meets one situation today and tomorrow another, and if he is following the same business calling, the changes under which that is done, or he has to drop behind and be abandoned or be able to understand things and think out and make his changes.

A man who employs labor, to whom it is a very important practical matter to be able to pick out people not in the factory but in another type of pursuit, told me that for his own protection he had evolved, as many men have nowadays under the stress of modern business conditions, certain ways of picking out young people particularly who were intellectually promising, that he could trust to take hold of a certain thing and go ahead with it and carry it out in a way that would be advantageous to themselves and to him. He said that one of his devices was to take one of these young men and tell him to go down and look up certain things in the files, look up a certain order and see what the date of the order was and the date upon which it had been filed. When he would come back he would ask him not only that, but ask him more questions about where the order came from and just what it was for, and so on. And he said there was always a certain percentage of people who could answer just the particular question they had been sent to get the information upon. Those were the people that he got rid of and found it profitable to get rid of as soon as possible. He would send him back again to get something else and he would come back again with just that one particular item of information he had been sent after. Then there were the various grades up to those who had sufficient intellectual interest, sufficient curiosity, that when they went down there to find out this one thing, would take in other things, too, or at least after they had been sent back a few times to get these other items of information, made it their business to find out all they could the first time and be ready to answer this variety of scope of questions the next time, and they were the people he found it profitable to take, people who could take intellectual responsibility later on and go ahead for themselves. That is one practical instance of what I mean about the ability to think as a very effective central factor in efficiency in action itself, because, as I said before, if our conditions were perfectly uniform and rigid then we could get efficiency from mere routine, mechanical method, but because we have to change conditions, because we have to readapt our habits that we have formed, we have to have this breadth of intellectual insight and foresight also to control.

The third point that I wish to make in this connection is that when our mere mechanical habits, our forms of skill and our thinking do fall out of balance with each other something happens also on the mental side. We not only become routine, mechanical and slavish in our outward activities, but our mental life becomes very irregular.

You cannot stop people's minds; you cannot stop people's thinking, if you mean by thinking their thoughts, their imaginations, their ideas in their head, not when they are awake. The only way to stop it is to go to sleep and to get into a deep sleep. What we can do, however, is to make a split, make a division, between our outward actions, our forms of skill and power of accomplishment, and our inner life. The extremely absentminded person is, of course, an example of a person who has had a split between two things, when his actions are going on in one direction and his thoughts and ideas are going in some other direction. So we have a story of a man who pulls out his watch to see if he has time to go back home and get his watch. He performs one action automatically and it has no connection with his thinking.

Now, there is a technique of teaching, a technique of the management of the schoolroom, keeping order, treating children, of asking questions, even of giving out, assigning lessons; assigning the different school work and so forth, is just as much a part of the art of teaching as the particular technique of the artist is a part of the calling of the artist, but over and above that is the need for that sense of the purpose and meaning of it that results in sympathy with a development of the life of the children, what is going on not in their more outward motions, in the things they do, but what is going on in their feelings, their imagination, what effect the schoolroom is having on the permanent disposition, the side of their emotions and imagination, without which the teacher cannot be an artist, no matter how complete and adequate the teacher's command is of the technique of teaching, that is, of the various forms of outward skill which are necessary to make the successful teacher. The teacher as an artist needs to be one who is engaged in getting the pupils as much as possible into the attitude of the artist in their relations in life, that is, to solve what is after all the great problem, the moral, the intellectual problem of everyone, to get habits of efficient action, so that the person won't be a mere day-dreamer or theorist, or a wasteful or incompetent person, but to get that unity with certain affections and desires and sympathies and with power to carry out intellectual plans. That can be got only when we give as much attention to the thinking side of the life of the pupils from the first day as we give to their forming these good outward habits. For this reason it seems to me that so far as the teaching is concerned the great problem of the teacher is the problem of keeping a balance between these two factors of efficiency in action and insight and foresight, ability to have the purpose to perform plans in thought.

Message to the American Federation of Teachers

I do not believe that any educational organization is more ready or better prepared to take a courageous view of the present situation than is the American Federation of Teachers. It has never been a body to take the cheap and easy way; it has never cultivated illusions about the seriousness of the work to be done. It has recognized that together with its larger organization, the American Federation of Labor, it has a cause that demands, and that has obtained and will continue to obtain, alertness of observation and planning, and solidarity in action. It knows from experience that these things bring their own reward with them. Confidence and courage grow with exercise. There are many fields of labor within the American Federation of Labor. There is none in which the need, the opportunity, and the reward are surer than in that of teaching.

I count it one of the satisfactions of my own teaching career that I have had from the first the opportunity to be a member of a local of the American Federation of Teachers. Today I prize this special opportunity to join in rejoicing in its past and in looking forward with confidence to its future.

May it continue to be steadfast in the great work in behalf of the schools of America, and thereby throughout our common America, in a world that must grow in common understanding if it is not to perish.

[First published in *American Teacher* 34 (October 1949): 16, from statement read for Dewey at Milwaukee, Wis., 24 August 1949.]

John Dewey Responds

I need hardly say that I am overwhelmed by what has been said and read on this occasion. I cannot express adequately my thanks to the Committee and to all who have come here this evening.

I am fortunate in one thing. It is not just that I have lived to complete fourscore and ten but that I have reached that age in 1949 instead of 1969 or what would have been even worse, 1979 or '89. Even now one can hardly pick up a periodical without finding an article on the social and psychological problems which are due to the increase in the span of life. If the span goes on increasing at its present rate, I can imagine that twenty or thirty years from this evening there will be no disposition to celebrate one's arriving at the age of ninety. The meeting would be more likely to be called to discuss what has become the serious social issue of longevity.

In any case, it is supposed to be the habit—if not the privilege—of old age to indulge in reminiscence. I have been reminded sufficiently of my years of late so that I have been almost forced to go back over my past and to consider how the years have been spent.

After due reflection, I have come to the conclusion that, for good or for evil, I have been first, last, and all the time, engaged in the vocation of philosophy; and that it is in the capacity of a philosopher that I am a Nonagenarian. Furthermore, strangely enough, this statement is not wrung from me as a reluctant admission, but is made as a boast—though I fear many of my confreres in that occupation may regard it as unjustified bragging.

[First published in *John Dewey at Ninety,* ed. Harry Wellington Laidler (New York: League for Industrial Democracy, 1950), pp. 32–35, from speech delivered at the Hotel Commodore, New York City, 20 October 1949.]

But as I look back over the years, I find that, while I seem to have spread myself out over a number of fields—education, politics, social problems, even the fine arts and religion—my interest in these issues has been specifically an outgrowth and manifestation of my primary interest in philosophy.

It has been an outgrowth in two respects—one negative and one positive. On the negative side, the demand of philosophy upon various forms of technical skill—one might say professional academic skill—are so taxing that excursions into outside areas are inviting on the old familiar principle that the berries on the other side of the fence are more numerous and brighter and bigger. The other and positive reason is that philosophy cannot flourish indefinitely nor vitally by ruminating on its own cud. Philosophers need fresh and first-hand materials. Otherwise the story of the ideas and beliefs of *past* philosophers will become an end-in-itself instead of a resource in dealing with the problems that are urgent in contemporary life.

It may well be that those engaged in the kind of inquiry that bears the name *philosophy* have exaggerated what philosophers can do in the way of solving problems. But there is a need that comes before that of solution. That is the need for getting a reasonably clear sense and statement of what the problems are that have to be met: what they arise from and where they are located. Here is a matter in which it is possible for philosophers to make good their claim that they go below the surface; go behind the ways in which things appear to be. It is quite possible for philosophers to become pretentious; but it is hardly possible to exaggerate the importance of obtaining a moderately clear and distinct idea of what the problems are that underlie the difficulties and evils which we experience *in fact;* that is to say, in *practical* life. Nor is it easily possible, I believe, to exaggerate the intellectual alertness and even excitement that could attend a systematic endeavor to convert our practical ills and troubles into intellectual terms, so that plans may be developed and subjected to intelligent inquiry as a condition of remedial action. For in the technological and the medical arts, we have learned that to plunge into action before we have located what is the matter is the way to make things worse than they were before. For apart from engaging systematically in search for the source of evils, the only alternatives we can employ are acting either mechanically on the basis of routine precedent and blind habit or impulsively from fear.

At the present time, tradition and custom are pretty well broken down as dependable resources in guiding our activity. Living as we now do in what is almost a chronic state of crisis, there is danger that fear and the sense of insecurity become the predominant motivation of our activities.

Of the various kindly and generous, often over-generous, things that have been said about my activities on the occasion of my ninetieth birthday, there is one thing in particular I should be peculiarly happy to believe. It is the statement of Alvin Johnson that I have helped to liberate my fellow-human beings from fear. For more than anything else, the fear that has no recognized and well-thought-out ground is what both holds us back and conducts us into aimless and spasmodic ways of action, personal and collective. When we allow ourselves to be fear-ridden and permit it to dictate how we act, it is because we have lost faith in our fellowmen—and that is the unforgivable sin against the spirit of democracy.

Many years ago I read something written by an astute politician. He said that majority rule is not the heart of democracy, but the processes by which a given group having a specific kind of policies in view becomes a majority. That saying has remained with me; in effect it embodies recognition that democracy is an educative process; that the act of voting is in a democratic regime a culmination of a continued process of open and public communication in which prejudices have the opportunity to erase each other; that continued interchange of facts and ideas exposes what is unsound and discloses what may make for human well-being.

This educational process is based upon faith in human good sense and human good will as it manifests itself in the long run when communication is progressively liberated from bondage to prejudice and ignorance. It constitutes a firm and continuous reminder that the process of living together, when it is emancipated from oppressions and suppressions, becomes one of increasing faith in the humaneness of human beings; so that it becomes a constant growth of that kind of understanding of our relations to one another that expels fear, suspicion, and distrust.

The friendliness that is radiated from this gathering is something to be sensed, not just talked about and hence, I take it, is a good omen for the causes I have had the privilege of sharing. For while it is, I am aware, the conventional thing to recognize such a tribute as one to cause, not to the person, I *know* in this case that such a manifestation of friendliness as I have experienced is a demonstration of sympathy for the things that make for the freedom and justice and for the kind of cooperative friendship that can flourish only where there is a freedom which we and untold multitudes possess in common: i.e., enjoy together.

I want to conclude with a reference to a letter from an old friend in Texas in which he said that while he should have liked to be here this evening, he does not regret his enforced absence so very greatly because the order of the day is not so much the commemoration of the past, as it is, "March Ahead into the future with resolution and courage."

I am happy to be able to believe that the significance of this celebration consists not in warming over of past years, even though they be fourscore and ten, but in dedication to the work that lies ahead. The order of the day is "Forward March."

The over-generous recognition that has been accorded me I take as a sign that faith in the will to realize the American dream through continued faith in democracy as a moral and human ideal remains firm and true even in a time when some people in their despair are tending to put their faith in force instead of in the cooperation that is the fruit of reciprocal good will and shared understanding:—and of nothing else.

Greetings to the Urbana Conference

To my friends of the College of Education, University of Illinois, Its Division of Social, Philosophical and Historical Foundations, and the American Education Fellowship:

In sending you through Dr. Benne my grateful appreciation of the honor conferred upon me by your gathering in commemoration of my Ninetieth Birthday Anniversary, it adds to my gratification that, as I allow my thoughts to travel back over the years, I find so many points of enjoyable and enjoyed connection between us during the past half century—the latest being pleasurable intellectual contacts had with Dr. Benne while he was at Teachers College, New York City. At the other end of the fifty years or so of the close and frequent associations I have enjoyed with members of the faculties of education and philosophy at the State University and at the State Normal University, are those had while I was teaching philosophy and education (pedagogics it was at first) at the University of Chicago. I owe more than I can express to the stimulation and intellectual assistance I derived from contacts at that time. I am afraid there are not many still living who have personal memory of the meetings of the Herbart Society during that period, and of the keen and friendly clashes and exchange of ideas between the McMurrys and De Garmo on one side and Dr. W. T. Harris on the other. I gratefully recall the contribution to my own education in educational matters that proceeded from those contacts in a formative period of my life. Among the outstanding events of intervening years the memory of the man McClure, later professor of Philosophy and

[First published as introduction to *Essays for John Dewey's Ninetieth Birthday,* ed. Kenneth Dean Benne and William Oliver Stanley (Urbana, Ill.: Bureau of Research and Service, College of Education, University of Illinois, 1950), pp. 3–4, from statement read for Dewey at the Conference on Education and Philosophy, University of Illinois, 21 October 1949.]

then dean at the University of Illinois, who came to Columbia for graduate work in philosophy is a bright spot.

Aside from personal gratification in recalling these contacts and associations, to which I may add that with one of your speakers of the day from the University of Wisconsin, through our joint indebtedness to and admiration of the work of Max Otto, there is the realization, peculiarly precious at a time of stress and strain such as we live in today, that we all are links in an ever-continuing and out-reaching chain of intellectual and moral continuity. In it each of us is able to give to those who follow because of what we have already received from others. Even in the most trying days there is ground for hope, and more than hope, for confidence, in this fact, to which Josiah Royce years ago gave the name "*The Great Community,*" and which it is an acute satisfaction to know is also *The Continuing Community.*

With gratitude and sincerely yours,

JOHN DEWEY

Reviews

Science and the Idea of God

The Idea of God as Affected by Modern Knowledge, by John Fiske. Boston and New York: Houghton, Mifflin and Co., 1885.

Mr. John Fiske has just given us an exceedingly interesting and suggestive sequel to his little brochure on the "Destiny of Man." As that was the outcome of the application of the theory of evolution to the nature and destiny of man in the discussion of the immortality of the soul, this is the application of the same theory to the subject of the relations of God to the universe. Mr. John Fiske has been ordinarily represented as an American popularizer of Herbert Spencer, and, as it seems to the present writer, has himself given cause for such an opinion in spite of an occasional divergence. But in the present work the divergence becomes marked, more marked, indeed, than Mr. Fiske seems willing to recognize. A brief summary, mostly in Mr. Fiske's own lucid and chosen speech, will reveal to the reader, acquainted with the voluminous reverberations of the English philosopher, the nature of the divergence.

The world of phenomena, according to Mr. Fiske, is intelligible only when regarded as the multiform manifestation of an omnipresent energy, that is in some way, quite above our finite comprehension, quasi-personal and quasi-psychical. It must therefore be conceived in an anthropomorphic way, though it be a purified anthropomorphism. In the universe there is an objective reasonableness; its events have an orderly progression, or manifest a dramatic tendency, an approach to a goal, although we can only inadequately recognize or describe just what the goal is. It is a theory which recognizes in and through the phenomena of the universe an omnipresent energy, which is none other than the living God. The final outcome of the theory of evolution is to make us regard the world as a complete organic

[First published in *University*, no. 223 (2 January 1886): 5–6.]

unity, all the manifestation of one and the same energy, a force which is teleological, has purpose and meaning, and hence can be more accurately, though still inadequately, expressed by the term spirit than by any other. Mr. Fiske, in short, holds that recent science has not invalidated the theistic argument, but has increased its force, by revealing more clearly the unity, continuity and rationality of the universe. On the other hand, he holds that the God made known by science is not to be conceived along the line of the anthropomorphic deism which he holds is the current theology of Christendom, but by the doctrine of a "cosmic theism," as the immanent life of the universe.

Mr. Fiske has made in this book, we repeat, a distinct advance upon the metaphysical theory of Spencer. There is no place in the philosophy of the latter for a psychical—even quasi-psychical—factor, nor for a dramatic tendency. His first principle is unknowable, that is to say out of all relation to intelligence, and of the nature and purpose of events nothing can be known by us. Mr. Fiske clearly recognizes that it is only by attributing an anthropomorphic element to the absolute that it can mean anything for our intelligence, and the attribution of this anthropomorphic element he considers justified by the results of modern science.

Yet Mr. Fiske speaks of himself as accepting, in a certain sense, Mr. Spencer's theory of the unknowable. Mr. Fiske thereby shows that he has fine thoughts, but has no philosophic basis. The unknowableness of the absolute means simply that the ultimate principle is out of all relation whatever to intelligence, that it has no rationality, no meaning, no purpose in it. Mr. Spencer, of course, when he comes to the constructive part of his philosophy finds no difficulty in attributing to it all sorts of qualities, until finally it is as well defined as the "Deity" of Paley. But one part of his philosophy contradicts the other, and Spencer finally straightens it out by declaring that the force all of whose ways and manners are formulated in his encyclopaedia of past and promised works, is as unknowable as the absolute with which he started. But it is not surprising that the average reader overlooks this statement of Mr. Spencer, considering that it would make all his writings nonsense. The ordinary mind is so constituted that it would rather believe that Spencer was still so involved in metaphysical mazes that his first principles contained a contradictory element, than that all his volumes are a collection of meaningless words about an unknowable.

The terms with which Mr. Fiske conceals this from himself are significant in that they are an unconscious revelation of the fact that his own fundamental principles are still those of a dualistic deism. He has never really got rid of the very principles against which he directs his best arguments. The term unknowable, he says, describes "*one aspect* of Deity." "Deity *per se*," he says, is "unknowable." It is "unknowable in so far as it is absolute and infinite, knowable in the order of its phenomenal manifestations." This metaphysical conception, and the conception of God as the universal life of the universe, made known to us by science, which is ever winning new conquests from the void of the unknown to the realm of the known, are in direct contradiction to each other. In the latter idea, there is absolutely no place whatever for an absolute unknowable God. God, according to it, has no two aspects, one of which is unknowable, while the other may be known to us in manifestations, which, as they are only appearances in finite consciousness, after all serve rather to conceal than to reveal the ultimate reality. According to the other conception, God is essentially the knowable; he is the truth, or the organic unity of all intelligible truths. He may be, in part, unknown; but that is because knowledge is still partial. To confuse the two ideas of the unknown and the unknowable is to make light darkness. To say that God is, in part, unknown, is simply to say that God (so far as philosophy is concerned) *is* completed knowledge or truth, and that the mind of man must ceaselessly press on to grasp more of knowledge. To say that God is unknowable means that he is out of all relation to intelligence and knowledge, and consequently out of all relation to the known universe. It results in an entire and complete shutting out of God from the known world of science, and relegation to an extra-mundane sphere, on the theory of Latin theology against which Mr. Fiske supposes that he is directing his arguments. More than this, it results from an ultimate metaphysical hypothesis, namely, that substance is separated from phenomenon, or the infinite from the finite, a supposition which Mr. Fiske imports into the argument as if it were the veriest commonplace of common sense, instead of, as it really is, the last and most dreary *caput mortuum* of an abstract metaphysical analysis. But above all it contradicts all the constructive portion of the book, that which, starting from the positive basis of science, or real knowledge, finds God to be "the immanent life of the universe." If such he be, why in the name of common sense, as well as of all historic philosophy, not leave him as such, the source, the process and the end of all knowledge, instead of returning to the mire of an outworn metaphysic which cuts reality into two pieces, one of which, the known, is only phenomenal, while the other, the absolute real, is unknown and unknowable?

Mr. Fiske's treatment of the end of the processes of the universe shows that his metaphysical presuppositions still revolve in the sphere of a mechanical dualism. The only reason for holding that the end toward which events are working is unknown, is the belief that this end is a last term, something, in short, which will not be reached until the entire process is over; something, in short, which is not organically connected with the known process. It is a theory of purpose which in its philosophical basis is one with that of the apologists of the 18th century; a theory which regards the end as external to the means. Between the teleology of the metaphysician who held that cork trees were created that stoppers for champagne bottles might exist, and the teleology of Mr. Fiske, who holds that it is "impossible to argue from the ways of Man to the ways of God," and that an infinite personality is inconceivable, the truth of the case is that if we could only find out what the real "ways of Man" are, we should know the ways of God, and that *all* personality is infinite, since it is at once the means and the end, the process and the result, the evolution and the goal of the universe. Mr. Fiske's sense for reality, when he can free himself from certain imported dogmatic metaphysics, leads him virtually to this conclusion. Organic evolution, he says, is tending toward the production of the highest and most perfect psychical life. Man is the crown and glory of the universe; all things work together for the evolution of the highest spiritual attributes of man. He who realizes these truths ought not to allow any inherited metaphysical obstructions to prevent him from recognizing that the universe must, therefore, be conceived as the outworking of psychical life; that it must be interpreted in terms of him who is its crown and glory, as, in short, the realization of spirit through spiritual attributes. If it is true that "the total elimination of anthropomorphism from the idea of God abolishes the idea itself," why not recognize that the thorough working out of the idea of anthropomorphism will complete the idea of God? For the evil is only in the partial or inadequate ideas of man; views which regard him as matter or as force, or as an abstract logical understanding, instead of living spirit, the consummation of the universe. Mr. Fiske's positive contributions all look in this direction; the greater the pity that he cannot wholly disenthrall himself from a worn out metaphysic, the last dowry of scholasticism to British thought.

Essays in the Law, by Sir Frederick Pollock.
London: Macmillan and Co., 1922.

It is quite unnecessary, especially for a layman, to commend the writings of Sir Frederick Pollock. The present volume has all the qualities of extraordinary learning combined with power of lucid summary and generalization which readers have learned to expect from him. In contents, it is varied. Some of the thirteen essays included are chiefly of technical interest to lawyers; some chiefly to historical scholars. Of the former class is that upon "Gift of Chattels without Delivery"; of the latter, "*Arabiniana.*" Many of them, such as that upon "Government by Committees in England," and the "Reformation and Modern Doctrine of Divorce" appeal to any student of contemporary society and politics. The more important appeal also although not exclusively to those interested in the philosophy of law as part of the general philosophy of human society. Such are "The History of Comparative Jurisprudence," "The History of the Law of Nature," "Locke's Theory of the State" and "Lay Fallacies in the Law"—the latter involving a clear exposition of what law is in actual operation, as distinct from what laymen often take it to be.

We select the essays on "The History of the Law of Nature" as typical of the merits of the book. The first traces the fortunes of the doctrine from Aristotle, through the Stoics and Roman lawyers, the medieval and renaissance doctrines, down to Protestant and Reformation influences, and then shows how under the name of "reason" the same ideas became incorporated in English common law—the "law of nature" having too much flavor of Roman law and of ecclesiastic courts to recommend itself to English lawyers. It is shown that amid all these historic vicissitudes, natural law has had a single common function: that of supplying

[First published in *Columbia Law Review* 23 (March 1923): 316–18.]

an ethical standard for legal ideas and practices, and that the application of the ethical criterion has been saved from becoming private and arbitrary by identifying natural law or the law of reason with custom in the degree of its generality or area of acceptance. The second essay on this subject traces the beneficial influence of the idea in English law, pointing out the indebtedness to it of national acknowledgment of international practices so that they become true law; of the incorporation of the Law Merchant into common law; of the development of the doctrine of quasi-contracts; of that of negligence; of the development of legal jurisdiction in cases where at first there seems to be no legal remedy available; of court review of the quasi-judicial decisions of administrative bodies; of private international law. It terminates with an account of the effect of the doctrine upon British administration of justice in India.

Everywhere Pollock carries an immense burden of historical knowledge. But he carries it lightly; so lightly that the reader is relieved of sharing the burden. There is no writer in any branch of learning who exceeds Sir Frederick in ability to convey to the reader the net result of long and exact research, together with clear indication of the nature of the evidence upon which conclusions rest. There are one or two points bearing upon matters of extra-legal thought where a layman in law may perhaps note an exception. Indications are not pronounced, but Sir Frederick Pollock appears to share the notion that the historical method, and the possibility of employing the comparative method in law, implies the notion of stages of evolution through which societies pass, some of course being more advanced than others. I think the tendency of present competent specialists is to hold that the doctrine of parallel stages is but a refined survival of the older tendency, rejected of course by Pollock, to draw comparisons without reference to the past histories of the things compared. According to these students we must study not only prior history but also the correlation of the practice under discussion with the whole complex of customs and beliefs which are locally characteristic—a method which puts the idea of uniform stages of development out of court.

Again Sir Frederick bears few grudges, or at least reveals but few. But he seems to "have it in for" utilitarianism, presumably because of its neglect of historic considerations. But while the utilitarians in law may have had personally all the dogmatic temper which Pollock finds in utilitarianism itself, he seems for once to miss the point when he says that "utilitarianism is just as much a system of natural law as any other dogmatic system of ethics or politics." In the sense in which utilitarianism signifies that an ethical criterion is to be applied to law this statement is of course quite true. But it fails to note that the ethical criterion of utilitarianism is prospective, future, based on foreseeable consequences, while that of other systems of natural law had been found in some antecedent state of affairs, in effect in custom. Their natural law tended therefore to consecrate the *status quo*, just the thing which the Benthamites were interested in questioning. The point throws some light perhaps upon (it certainly agrees with) the criticisms of purely historic jurisprudence with which Professor Roscoe Pound has familiarized students.

The Modern Idea of the State, by H. Krabbe.
Translated by G. H. Sabine and Walter
J. Shepard. New York: D. Appleton and
Co., 1922.

Both from the side of law and of politics there has been
of late years a growing revulsion against the theory of the state as
sovereign which ruled jurisprudence as well as political theory
from the seventeenth century. The problem of Krabbe's book is
to eliminate the concept of sovereignty from the theory of the
state and law, while at the same time reserving a distinctive and
indispensable sphere for the state. In other words, while adopt-
ing up to a certain point (although without using this terminology) the pluralistic theory of society which makes the state
only one among many forms of social organization, he aims also
at reserving and delimiting one definite and important province
for the state. This province is that of defining and adjusting
through law the various and oftentimes conflicting interests of
the community. The state is the legal order of the community and
a legal order is required in behalf of the non-legal concerns of the
community. Or, in a text frequently quoted from Laband, "The
state can command its subjects nothing and forbid them nothing
except on the basis of legal prescription." The state in giving and
administering law is still bound by law; it is not sovereign in the
old sense. But the statement as made by Laband and others only
raises the question: By *what* law is the state bound in its making
of rules of law? And Krabbe's answer is that it is bound by the
law of the welfare of the community as that is expressed in men's
moral judgments, beliefs and choices. Law and politics are in ultimate analysis branches of morals.

The strength of the book, it seems to me, is found in the application of this notion to various urgent problems. Its weakness
lies in the formulation and defense of the idea itself. The statement I have made above of Krabbe's position is gathered from

[First published in *Columbia Law Review* 23 (April 1923): 406–8.]

what he says in applying his notion. It is not the idea one gets from his own explicit formulations. In them he emphasizes not the community and its interests but the spiritual nature of man as evinced in his consciousness of right and duty—*Recht*. In other words he follows the German tradition of subjective and formalistic ethics. As a result the longest chapter in his book, that devoted to "The Basis of the Binding Force of Law," seems to me the least interesting and instructive. It moves almost wholly within a circle of notions hardly significant outside the boundary of those who have got tied up with the dialectical development of Kantian ethics.

The converse is true when he comes to specific issues where his formal concept drops into the background and that of adjusting conflicts of interests within the community comes to the foreground. He then shows how the political theory of the sovereign as the source of law led to a conceptual system of jurisprudence, what Professor Pound has called mechanical jurisprudence. The sovereign has not legislated *explicitly* on every subject; yet since the sovereign is the sole source of law, its explicit utterances must *logically* contain all law. So intellectual ingenuity was strained to the uttermost to deduce all possible law and decisions from a certain number of ready-made rules of law. The scheme was wholly intellectualistic and resulted in sacrificing material social interests to the formal exigencies of logic. The over-intellectualizing of law was also seen in the theory of the liberal school (in the continental sense of liberalism) that the *thinking* class of the community is the one to take part in law-making. But the unthinking part, the non-intellectual class, has its wants and interests, and to appreciate and understand these values, through close contact and sympathy, is quite as important as an abstract intellectual impartiality gained by aloofness. Recent tendencies toward social legislation are treated by Krabbe as evidence of the revolt of the moral factor in law-making against the over-intellectualization of the positive and historic schools.

The solution of the problem of right valuation through law of the interests of the community requires also a decentralization of law-making bodies and the development of quite new organs of law-making. Representative government has broken down not because it is a failure in principle but because of lack of adequate technique. The legislative bodies are too far away from the social interests with which they deal and represent them in too circuitous a fashion. Some method must be found by which all organized social interests shall become law-making bodies—such as labor unions and employers' associations. Only when law-making is decentralized and new organs are added will a share in voting and law-making become a significant and interesting opportunity.

While in principle the modern state is the legal or jural order of the community, in fact the realization of this principle is still hindered by the defects of international legal relations. Actually the interests of states have become intermingled but there is no legal method of evaluating and adjusting these interests. Hence the internal relationships which are tied up with the external ones cannot be accurately defined and maintained. There must be, so Krabbe thinks, an international political sovereign with police power to enforce its decisions. He is aware that this notion contradicts his own conception of the source of law and its binding authority, or at least that it marks a reversion to a form of state against which he has directed severe criticisms. But he is content to say that the phase of sovereignty is one which the international community must pass through, as did the national community.

I confess I cannot follow the logic here, unless it is that of an evolutionary fatalism. The whole burden of Krabbe's argument about the national state is that we have reached a point where the necessity for legal regulation of social relationships is perceived and supported by the moral convictions of the community. He also holds that the idea of the state as the community in its legal relations cannot be completely realized as long as international relations are what they are: the lawlessness of external relations reacts into the internal relations of the community. Why not then appeal directly to the moral consciousness upon which, according to his own view, all law rests for its source and binding force? Why go roundabout through a stage of dependence upon political force? The question, it may be added, is not a merely theoretical one. As this review is written, the United States Senate has before it two propositions concerning international law and its administration. One, that of Senator Borah, adopts the principle that the ultimate reliance must be upon the organized moral conscience of communities; that war should be excluded from recognition as legitimate, and that court decisions should be left to the public opinion of the world for enforcement. The proposal of Secretary Hughes goes much less far as regards change in international law, but it connects such law as there is with a distinctively political organization exercising the sanction of physically coercive force.

I hope that this inadequate summary indicates the interest of the volume. In spite of its occasional dialectical terminology and mode of approach, from which continental writers on jurisprudence have such difficulty in freeing themselves, its problems and points of view are distinctively modern. It represents what is most enlightened in existing European jural tendencies. As has been intimated, the argument for connecting law and lawmaking with the moral interests of the community (and thereby giving law its due while getting wholly away from that exaggeration of the political state which has proved so disastrous) seems unnecessarily tied up with a subjective view of morals. But in spite of this fact the book is a notable contribution to the movement to define the state as a legal organization of community interests instead of as an extra-legal political force, and to interpret concrete problems of law from this point of view.

Law and Morals: The McNair Lectures, by
Roscoe Pound. Chapel Hill, N.C.: University of
North Carolina Press, 1924.

It is fortunate for the general public that Professor Pound
is in so much demand for lectures on various foundations, since
by this means it becomes acquainted with his learning and his
ideas. Otherwise they might be available only to the professionally trained who read the law journals. The book before us
contains three lectures, and the only adverse criticism to be
passed is that it does not contain more. There is reason to hope,
however, that it will have a sequel, for in his preface Professor
Pound speaks of the need for supplementing his account of the
three great schools of the last century with a discussion of the
social-philosophical and sociological schools of today.

The three lectures are devoted, respectively, to the views of the
historical, the analytical and the philosophical schools of the
nineteenth century. In the first chapter, Professor Pound shows
how the discussion of the relation of morals and law arose in ancient Greece, when amid threatened social disintegration an attempt was made to discover an objective or "natural" basis for
both morals and state polities. In an interesting summary in his
concluding chapter, he points out that nineteenth century discussion has brought us back to the same general order of ideas. "If
we said that to the analytic jurist law is law by enactment, that to
the historical jurist it was law by convention, and that to the
philosophical jurist it was law by nature, we should do the car-
dinal juristic doctrines of the last century no injustice and should
be putting them in terms that would be entirely intelligible to a
Greek philosopher. Moreover he would perceive that we were
still debating the questions he debated and that at bottom we had
made little progress with them."

The lectures are themselves so packed with material that a fur-

[First published in *Columbia Law Review* 25 (February 1925): 245–46.]

ther summary is virtually out of the question. We may, however, select a sample. In his chapter on analytic jurisprudence, he points out that its theory of the lack of connection between law and morals broke down, even from its own standpoint, at four points, namely, the matter of judge-made law, the interpretation of legal precepts, the application of law, especially in the case of legal standards (such as "due care," etc.), and the exercise of judicial discretion. In each of these four cases, resort to ethical considerations, open or disguised, is inevitable. He gives the analytic school credit for making clear the fact that a legal rule always involves more than the mere formulation of an ethical principle; it is necessary to consider the means of making the moral principle effective in action, and to consider its relation to received legal materials and the existing legal technique. In this respect the analytic school may be said to have stood for a desirable "realistic" element in law.

While criticizing the historic school for their attempt to make historical facts take the place of recourse to moral principles, Professor Pound himself may be said to use the historical method in adjudicating the issue. That is, he shows the significance of alternating periods in legal history. During one period, there is need for revising and supplementing existing rules of law, and free rein, relatively speaking, is given to moral factors. This is the "creative" phase of natural law thinking. Then there are periods when these ethical loans are legally formulated and applied, until their ethical basis and import is lost from sight, and they are so rigidly applied that "justice" in the moral sense is subordinated. During these periods, natural law is often referred to, but merely as an apologetic justification for actual law.

In his final pages, he gives a condensed summary of the heterogeneous elements which have actually entered into present Anglo-American law, and makes this heterogeneity the basis of a plea for a more flexible and catholic intercourse between all the social sciences, law, economics, sociology, politics, ethics. A student approaching the topic of these lectures from the side of moral theory, as Professor Pound has approached it from that of law, would probably say that the deficiency he finds in the latter's treatment is failure to subject the topic of "morals" to the same kind of analysis as that to which he has subjected law; and that if this were done, present ethics, instead of being found to be simple and homogeneous, would be ascertained to be quite as heterogeneous in its constitution as law. And this conclusion would certainly reinforce the plea for more reciprocal incursions and an abandonment of the attempt to draw hard and fast lines between the various disciplines that deal with social relations.

It remains only to say that this little volume is enriched with numerous references in foot-notes and valuable bibliographies of each main topic at its close.

Human Conduct and the Law, by Mary
C. Love. Menasha, Wis.: George Banta
Publishing Co., 1925.

Miss Love had a happy idea in thinking of legal decisions as a rich field for the study of human nature in operation. Unfortunately, the execution is not equal to the idea. The reason is not in lack of care or industry; on the contrary, a significant body of material in the way of extracts from legal decisions or charges by courts has been compiled. The trouble lies with her psychology. She has uncritically adopted the notion of instincts as the fundamental thing in human conduct; and hence, after a brief account of the various instincts, has placed—one cannot say organized—the legal material under the heads of these instincts. Apart from the fact that the whole traditional theory of instincts is now under adverse critical consideration on the part of psychologists, the arbitrary nature of the pigeon-holing of cases is sufficient proof that, even if the existence of a lot of separate instincts as ultimate drives in conduct were much better established than it is, disputes about rights and obligations in human conduct are not of a character to lend themselves to being placed under instincts. Cases of arbitrary restriction of personal movement, dealt with legally under the title of "false imprisonment" appear under the instinct of locomotion; cases of free speech and war-time restrictions upon its exercise appear under "vocalization"—though the latter might just as well be put under the mythical entity of herd-instinct; not merely fraud and forgery appear under "unlawful devices of acquisitiveness," but murder and the keeping of bawdy houses. The latter figure also under the "protective instinct" where curiously enough appear cases of "police power" and "being affected with a public interest." Unlawful competition, the imitation of trade devices, etc., appear, however, under the instinct of self-assertion. And so it goes. Ad-

[First published in *Columbia Law Review* 26 (April 1926): 498–99.]

herents of the dogma of separate instincts as the sole motives of all conduct might, perhaps, be led to reconsider the value of their notion when they see how impotent it is for the intelligent analysis of such concrete specimens of human conduct as get before the courts. It is a pity that so much industry in such a significant body of material for psychological analysis should have been so misdirected. That cultural conditions and institutional habits should at the present day be thought capable of being ignored in a matter like rules of law is a curious commentary on the present state of knowledge. If such a work could have any practical influence it would towards the revival of a peculiarly naive idea of "natural rights" as expressive of instincts.

Universities: American, English, German, by
Abraham Flexner. New York: Oxford
University Press, 1930.

"No sound or consistent philosophy, thesis, or principle
lies beneath the American university today." This sentence does
not summarize Mr. Flexner's book, for it contains, among other
things, a vast amount of information. But it sets forth the conclusion reached. In the sense in which it is true, it holds good, as far
as I am aware, of universities in every country, at every time. In
another sense, universities have always exemplified—or tended
to do so—a fairly consistent, if not a sound, principle, and the
American is no exception. I mean that universities are always
upon the whole a reflection of some aspects of the contemporary
society in which they exist, and have the kind of consistency
which springs from that fact; from, that is to say, the kind and
amount of coherence there is in the social life contemporary to
them. This is true of the great vocational schools of the European
ages which are the prototype of our universities; of the fatuous
English universities of a large part of the eighteenth century; of
the German universities following the depression of Germany
after the Napoleonic wars. It is true of American universities to-
day. The strength of Mr. Flexner's report on the American university is the amount of information he gives which indicates this
relationship. The weakness of it is his failure to make the connection explicit, the failure to discuss the *ethos* of American life
which has determined the American institution which he depicts.

I do not think that anyone interested in the right development
of our universities should complain because more space is given
to adverse criticism than to favorable appreciation. The American people do not suffer from lack of self-appreciation; they do
suffer from lack of the detached and informed criticism which
Mr. Flexner gives. I can imagine no better omen for the future of

[First published in *International Journal of Ethics* 42 (April 1932): 331–32.]

higher education in this country than that the main criticisms of
Mr. Flexner should be taken to heart. When he speaks of the
splitting up of courses, with consequent attenuation and emacia-
tion; of the exaggeration of athletics; of surrender to the demand
for immediate and short-span time application; of domination
by units, points, and counts; of an excess emphasis upon giving
instruction which results in a practical assumption that no student will learn anything unless it is put in a course, in atomistic
training and multiplication of courses, and in a carrying of students as a dead load by teachers; of *ad hoc* courses; of the conception of the college as a place where a student may get a social
boost and make the right "connections," and so on, he says
things which need to be said. I think his book will do something
to halt the tendencies which he vividly describes.

What I seem to miss in the book is discrimination between the
absurdities, superficialities, and extravagances which he truth-
fully reports and the potential movement of which they are the
perversions. To all appearances, Mr. Flexner assumes that the
dualism between the cultural and the vocational is intrinsic and
eternal; he treats the defects of which he speaks as if they were
the necessary consequences of any attempt to break down this
dualism. Consequently I find myself agreeing with most of his
specific criticisms, and dissatisfied with the net outcome, because
conscious of a failure on the author's part to indicate the direction in which the American university might and should move.
We—the American people—are blindly trying to do something
new in the history of educational effort. We are trying to develop
universal education; in the process we are forced by facts to identify a universal education with an education in which the vocational quality is pervasive. Mr. Flexner's criticisms would have
been as truthful and as drastic if his criterion had been a recognition of what underlies both the excellencies and the defects
of our society and our education instead of one which looks,
however unconsciously, to the dualism of the past and of other
societies.

The Making of Citizens: A Comparative Study of Methods of Civic Training, by Charles Edward Merriam. Chicago: University of Chicago Press, 1931.

This important book is a summary survey of nine spe-cial studies which have been made of the procedures of various peoples in developing that kind of social cohesion which is re-quired for political organization and loyalty. To the student of politics, especially to one who approaches the problems of state and government from the side of sociology, the study of Dr. Mer-riam is significant in its assemblage of factual material. After reading the book I am inclined to doubt whether any other mode of approach would have brought out the complexity of political organization (and the consequent complexity of political prob-lems) together with so nearly an impartial survey of its pluralistic factors as does this approach from the side of the forces which produce (and which undermine) political loyalties.

For, the end sought in this particular problem requires first a survey of the chief factors which determine final social cohesion from the political point of view. There are groups within each of which cohesion rests on non-political grounds while political co-hesion requires their integration into a new loyalty. The chief of these groups are the economic (within which fall the agrarian, business, and labor groups, etc.), the ethnic, the regional, the re-ligious, and the intellectual—each one of which is diversified within itself, while in the different peoples studied there are all kinds of patterns formed by various combinations and permuta-tions. As I have already suggested, I doubt if a better approach could be found to a realistic study of political problems, even when that is made the chief aim.

Then the book takes up the various techniques employed to weld together the interests of the various constituent groups into a common loyalty. Of these, there are eight reported upon: the

[First published in *International Journal of Ethics* 42 (April 1932): 341–42.]

school system, governmental services (army and navy, nobility, parliaments, etc., as rallying centres), political parties, special patriotic organizations, the use of traditions, symbolism and rites, language and literature, organs of publicity (press, movie, and radio), and love of locality. Each of these reports is made concrete by study of the different methods by which each is used in different countries. The separate discussion of each technique is followed by an integrated picture in which are compared Great Britain, the United States, France, Germany, Russia, Italy, and Switzerland. A final summary discusses the general trend with respect to each of the main factors and techniques, raising, to cite a single example, such an interesting question as the probable effect of intercommunication, caused by scientific advances, upon the local and territorial bond.

The treatment is highly objective. But a number of general valuations are set forth, which raise definite problems of social ethics. The growing importance of the school system in the scheme of creating citizens, for example, raises the whole question of the possibility of reconciling organized social planning and control with the preservation of individual liberty as that has been prized in the social philosophies of the past.

In the present organization of the world, this problem runs of necessity into that of the value and proper status of nationalism. Another highly important question is the attitude to be taken by all the organs of education of discussion toward change and toward the conservation of the past. One of the points which stands out most clearly is, what Merriam happily calls, "the poverty of power." The heterogeneous plurality and complexity of the political state leave it in a condition of highly unstable equilibrium. The appearance of omnipotence and unassailability is a "false front." The problem of the relation of conservation to readaptation for the future cuts vitally into every practical problem. Speaking from the standpoint of education in the schools and out, I think it may fairly be said that the organs of education have not begun to face this problem. Much of our present confusion may be traced, unless I am mistaken, to the hiatus, the conflict, between forces which make education and propaganda an idealization of the status quo and the forces of invention and technology which are everywhere compelling readjustments in the entire practical field. Until we have faced these problems of the relation between social planning and control to freedom of individual thought, and of the attitude to be inculcated toward the past and toward the future, we shall make little headway, in my judgment, in solving the moral issues with which society today confronts us.

The Promise of American Politics, by T. V. Smith. Chicago: University of Chicago Press, 1936.

Let me say at the outset that Dr. Smith's book is an interpretation of the actualities and possibilities of American politics in moral terms, based upon sound psychology. But when I say moral, I do not mean moralistic—anything but that. He keeps his eye steadily upon human relations and associations and what they do and may do to make the lives of individuals who are caught up in these associations full and significant, for themselves and for others. This is the only meaning I can attach to "moral." The book displays imagination, but it is an imagination so based upon the realities of our common American life that imagination never degenerates into fantasy. The style in which the book is written accords with its substance; it is animated as well as lucid. The liveliness is not forced, but springs from a constant sense of the human conditions and forces that are playing for good and for ill in the American scene. It is not without significance, I think, that upon the title page Dr. Smith prefers to appear as Senator in the Illinois Senate rather than as a professor in the University of Chicago.

The first chapter is a tractate upon Individualism. The author is aware how ambiguous is the meaning of the term, and points out forcibly the necessity of arriving at clear ideas of "What kind of individualism, to whom applied, on what terms?" The answer is that individualism worth struggling for in American life is the development of individuality in all alike, without favoritism, and that it "has as its warp a pride and joy in cultural things, things which can be enjoyed the more because not monopolized." The promise held forth in American life is now hampered and more or less frustrated by the unequal distribution of power, due to inequality in the distribution of property and the attendant abil-

[First published in *Illinois Law Review* 31 (January 1937): 694–96.]

ity of the few to control the lives of the many. But it is a dominant, and to my mind genially cheerful, note of Dr. Smith's treatment that he does not make economic conditions and power ends in themselves. He sees them as means of that fullness and equality of the cultural development of individuals that is the deepest meaning of individualism.

I could wish that everyone interested in social and political affairs would read and study the second chapter on Liberalism, the would-be friends of liberalism as well as those to whom it has become a word of contempt because of appropriation by a group to designate the liberty that is restricted to operation in economic affairs in their pecuniary aspect. Upon the political side, he points out that socialism may be a species of liberalism when actual conditions require that individuals in order to live happily may have to depend upon governmental regulation and even ownership of property. "To safeguard the liberty of the few is the very essence of illiberalism." While government may own property consistently with liberalism, ownership of the thoughts and actions of individual human beings is contrary to its intrinsic significance. Hence the emphasis of liberalism upon liberty of speech and thought, and liberty of consent—not as mere phrases, but as things to be institutionally maintained at all costs. "Since a government cannot be liberal save with a liberal people, the important thing is to keep attention fixed upon society rather than the state." As an ideal, the principle that the best government is that which governs least is sound, for coercion is the opposite of the voluntary determination of belief and action that is the essence of government by consent. But the ideal cannot be realized until men and women in their social relations are genuinely able to direct their thoughts and actions by free agreement with one another. They are not so able as long as economic and legal institutions give the power of constraint and coercion to one group of human beings over others. To realize the ideal of minimum governmental action, government must intervene in order to secure the conditions of free and voluntary consensus of action among individuals and communities. Only a free society can breed free individuals.

The next two chapters discuss Fascism and Communism. While they are criticized upon the basis of principles that have emerged in the chapters on Individualism and Liberalism, an outstanding trait is the open mind displayed in apprehension of such values as they present. The discussion is taken out of the atmosphere of controversial attack and defense that so usually envelops them into the clear light of principles. The essential virtue of Fascism (Italian Fascism, not Naziism is discussed) is its emphasis upon the community. But in its moral aspect it rests upon the idea of power and coercion to maintain power to such an extent that it is, morally, "an ethical pretender of the lowest rank."

The discussion of Russian Communism is noteworthy for its recognition that the development of individuality for all is the end and goal. Its weakness is bound to be the emphasis it places, in common with Italian Fascism, upon coercive force as the means of attaining the end. At the same time full justice is done the arguments by which the Bolshevist communist justifies, realistically and idealistically, his plea for the use of violence as means. It is regarded as an evil but a necessary evil. Nevertheless, Russian Communism has a contradiction, which is practical as well as logical, as its root. It assumes, if I may say it in this way, that ends are good and only good since they answer our hearts' desire, and hence the consequences that will actually result are those which we would like them to be rather than the consequences that will surely result from the means used. The communists "believe what they want to believe, and then obscure their audacity by calling the result 'science.'" Lenin, in particular, holds a copy of theory of social knowledge, which theory implies that it cannot be creative of the future. Russian Communism involves the combination of use of immoral because strictly coercive means with a romantically impossible perfectionism of ends.

The next chapter discusses, under the head of Parliamentarianism, the political techniques for making government the instrument of development of a free society that will breed and nurse free individualities. The chapter does not gloss over the conditions that have brought Parliamentarism into increasing disrepute. The causes of its decline are summed up in the statement that the political world is "deserting intelligence at the very time when intelligence has reached its highest development in science." The problem of the future validity of this method of political action is, therefore, the problem of bringing available intelligence to bear more directly and weightily upon representative government. The problem involves such matters as functional versus territorial selection of representatives, proportional representation, and, perhaps above all, what is termed "creative deliberation among representatives." "Art is required to pool the high general intelligence of legislators into a wise social whole." As it is now, hearings before committees are meetings in which committee members do not hear. In consequence, the governor—and perhaps we may add the president—instead of confining himself to the art of skilled administration, usurps the function of determining policies. "In the states the civil service is usually the stepchild of politics; a label of skilled personnel to cover the patronage system at its worst." This fact prevents executives from being what they are supposed to be, while legislatures, on the other hand, waste "their energies in unconcerted talk."

For the final chapter upon Americanism, I must for the most part refer to the text itself, as my review has already grown too long. But I cannot abstain from calling attention to the noteworthy section upon the development in our politics of the doctrine and practice of judicial supremacy—especially as the journal in which this review is published is addressed to an audience of lawyers. The sections on the place of the middle-class and the function of women in politics are not to be neglected. I close by saying that I can imagine no happier omen for the realization of the promise of American politics than a very wide reading of this book by the citizens in general and politicians in particular.

Statements

Answer to "Do We Want Rifle Practice in the Public Schools?"

It would be a long step backward in the traditions of the American people and of American education to introduce rifle practice into our public schools. Aside from the general objections from the standpoint of civilization, humanity and moral progress, which ought to be absolutely final, the objections from the standpoint of school administration and discipline are most serious. It would introduce another distracting factor where high-school boys are already over-distracted and stimulated, and would increase the evil force of the exciting and distracting conditions that already, especially in our cities, are more than powerful enough. It is undemocratic, barbaric, and scholastically wholly unwise.

[First published in *Do We Want Rifle Practice in the Public Schools?* (Philadelphia: Peace Association of Friends, [n.d.]), p. 5.]

Opinion on "Military Training for American School Boys"

I am opposed to military training in our public schools for many reasons, among which are:

1. Experts in physical training are agreed that such exercises are far from the best form of physical training for youth of this age.

2. The usual experience of military schools (for pupils of this age) shows that the rigid discipline of this part of the training is accompanied by relaxed discipline in everything else, students not feeling full responsibility when not immediately under the direction of others.

3. The drill is not of sufficient importance to be a factor in any military sense. Germany never resorts to this method.

4. It puts an additional burden on education and a premium on release from schooling. If youths of from 14 to 18 are to have special training it should be given to those who have left school. They need looking after most, and this method does not penalize those who remain at school by imposing upon them from outside a non-educational activity bearing no relation to the rest of their school work.

[First published in *Educational Experts on Military Training for American School Boys* (Philadelphia: [n.p., n.d.]), p. 10.]

View on "What the War Means to America"

At the present juncture it is evident that what the war means to America is a thoroughgoing sacrifice and devotion—sacrifice and devotion on a larger scale than perhaps most Americans have contemplated up to the present time. It will aid in securing this spirit if we all realize that the war means to America the establishment in the world at large of the social and political ideals upon which this country has based its development, and that the failure to secure a decisive defeat of German autocracy will render the future of these ideals uncertain and precarious, not merely in Europe, but in this country.

[First published in *Columbia Alumni News* 9 (17 May 1918): 1002, as part of "Views of Members of the Faculty."]

On Military Training in Schools

Military training in schools cannot be defended on the ground of physical training. All authorities agree that so far as the health and development of the body are concerned, there are many better methods. From the military standpoint, it is entirely negligible. Its real purpose is to create a state of mind which is favorable to militarism and to war. It is a powerful agent in creating false standards. Now that war has been outlawed by agreement among the nations, it ought to be recognized that it is criminal to produce in the young, emotional habits that are favorable to war.

[First published in *Has Military Training Real Educational Value?* (New York: Committee on Education for International Goodwill, Teachers Union Auxiliary, [n.d.]), p. 5.]

Letter on *Encyclopaedia of the Social Sciences*

April 6, 1926

My dear Professor Seligman:

After a prolonged period of specialization there are many signs that we are approaching a period of much needed integration. I know of nothing which would contribute more to the realization of this need in the United States than the execution of the project regarding the cyclopaedia of the social sciences. From a study of the document which you were kind enough to send me I can see that the project has been thought out with great care; there is every assurance that the contemplated work will be carried out with accuracy, comprehensiveness and ability. I believe there is now the scholarship in this country to execute the scheme satisfactorily, and that when completed it will be a monument to the present state of learning in this country, as well as an indispensable book of reference to the great numbers interested in the social sciences.

Sincerely yours,
(Signed) JOHN DEWEY

[First published in *Memorandum on the Projected Encyclopaedia of the Social Sciences* (New York: Columbia University Press, [ca. 1929]), p. 14.]

On Immortality

I have no beliefs on the subject of personal immortality. It seems to be a subject, being one of continued existence, for science rather than philosophy or a matter of physical evidence. If it can be proved, it would have to be along the lines of the psychical researchers, and so far I haven't been much impressed with their results.

[First published in *New York Times*, 8 April 1928, sec. 9, p. 1.]

In Defense of Mary Ware Dennett's *The Sex Side of Life*

My dear Mr. Ernst:

I have read the pamphlet of Mrs. Mary Ware Dennett and it seems to me almost incredible that objection should be made to it.

Speaking from an educational point of view—including being a father in helping to bring up a large family of children (seven in all) as well as a teacher—the document is admirable. Instead of being suppressed its distribution to parents and to youth should be encouraged. It is the secrecy and nasty conditions under which sex information is obtained—or used to be—that creates the idea that there is anything obscene in the pamphlet. Instead of being indecent I should have been glad to have my own children receive such information as a protection against indecency. If such a pamphlet as this prepared under scientific auspices cannot be distributed without legal interference, the latter is equivalent in my judgment to putting a large premium on real indecency and obscenity of thought and action.

I am sorry that a minor accident prevented my attending the first meeting but assure that I shall be pleased to aid in the defense of this pamphlet.

Sincerely yours,

JOHN DEWEY

[First published in Mary Ware Dennett, *Who's Obscene?* (New York: Vanguard Press, 1930), p. 97.]

Report on "Forms of Art Exhibition" at the Pennsylvania Museum of Art

I found the "Forms of Art Exhibition" even more confused, both intellectually and esthetically, than the correspondence about it had led me to anticipate.

It was bad enough to call it, in the accompanying circular, a "fresh approach" when the leading idea of the circular is obviously borrowed from *The Art in Painting* without referring to that book. The exhibition itself not only fails to carry out the borrowed idea, as expressed in the circular, but so completely contradicts it as to show that Mr. Benson never got the idea, but only some verbal expressions of it.

(1) The very separation into three sections is a flat contradiction both of the idea and of statements (supposedly his own) that artists "speak essentially the same language," and of his reference to the "ageless continuities of the basic art forms." This alone is proof of Mr. Benson's confused state of mind.

(2) Esthetically his groupings of the works exhibited are based on common subject-matter and have nothing to do with similarity of artistic form. I noted at least three or four instances in which the actual grouping is based on a principle which exactly reverses his announced one. These groupings would have some artistic point if he had said their purpose was to show how common subject-matter receives radically *different* artistic treatment according to the individuality and different environments of the artists who created the works of art. Instead of making this point, which is obvious to anyone with personal esthetic understanding, the circular says they are grouped together as having a similar "procedure and attitude" and "approximating" one an-

[First published in Harry Fuiman, *The Progressive Decay of the Pennsylvania Museum of Art* (Philadelphia: Friends of Art and Education, 1938), p. 10. For E. M. Benson's circular, see this volume, Appendix 2.]

other "in form and feeling." Incidentally, the comment one acquainted with paintings would naturally make, is that some of the contemporary pictures exhibited "approximate" the surface appearances of the work of El Greco and Picasso, but only in an imitative sense. Numerous other paintings which Mr. Benson classes as "creative," are so clearly academic repetitions of antecedent painters' forms that they too prove that he does not know the difference between imitation and creation.

That Mr. Benson should be thus confused personally is not a matter of great importance. That a great public institution should lend itself to propagating the confusion is serious. Such exhibits ought to direct the efforts of students, both beginners and those more advanced. The present exhibit prevents this education, because of institutional prestige and its virtual endorsement of meaningless language.

Dewey Hails Editorial on United Command

To the Editor:

May I express my feeling of complete unity with the ideas expressed in your editorial upon "A United Command." The continued talk about a 'second front' is capable of doing great harm. We already have three or four "fronts." What is needed is unity of "fronts," and the adding of more fronts without unity of control of movements on ALL fronts may actually add to our weakness. It is for the authorities of the U.S.S.R., more than for those of any other country to decide whether or not we are to have real unity of command and effort.

[First published in *New Leader* 25 (25 July 1942): 8. For editorial to which this is a reply, see this volume, Appendix 3.]

What Kind of a World Are We Fighting to Create?

"There is nothing permanent except change," wrote that great Greek philosopher, Heraclitus, over two thousand years ago.

Today it seems to me, looking back over my fourscore years of work and study, that too few men have recently paid attention to this great truth.

Every day I hear people talking about the future in terms of "after the last war." But this is *another* war. What comes after this war will not be what came after the last one. Men have changed, living conditions have changed, ideas have changed.

Just as this is a new-style war, so the peace will be—must be—new-style, also. Military triumph, followed by truce, is not enough. Peace alone will not settle things permanently. Peace offers only an *opportunity* for building a better world.

We have been promised a *people's* world of security and opportunity after the war. But unless the peace is a *people's* peace, the promises may fail.

More than at any previous time in the world's history, *the future is up to the people.* They must see that the victory is a *true* victory for the democratic nations.

Of course, there will be no short cuts to our goal. The widespread plenty, the higher standards of life for all—these will come slowly and painfully, as they always have. But they will come surely, inevitably, if we keep our vision clear, and direct our energies into productive channels.

The opportunities for us, the people of the United States, will be tremendous. A means for widely distributing the world's goods among all nations must be provided. . . . A way of carrying

[First published in *American Aviation* 6 (15 August 1942): 28–29.]

health and education and a higher standard of life to the utmost corners of the earth must be assured.

The mechanical means have already been produced by science and invention. *Physically,* the world is now one and interdependent. Only human beings—interested that men everywhere have a society of peace, of security, of opportunity, of growth in cooperation—can assure its being made *morally* one.

A genuine democratic victory will be achieved only when it is made *by* democratic governments *for* the well-being of the common people of the earth.

Endorsement of Dean Alfange

I am voting for Dean Alfange and the American Labor Party ticket. The chief reason is to serve notice that the voters won't stand for reactionary measures after the war. Since powerful groups are already preparing these measures, the notice is needed.

[First published in *New Leader* 25 (31 October 1942): 3.]

John Dewey Hails the Liberal Party

Congratulations on the superb platform and the campaign of the Liberal Party. I believe that the formation of the Liberal Party will turn out to be an event of crucial importance in the political life of America. And I want to add that it is an honor to be associated with the men and women who are doing the fine and valiant work in which your party is now engaged.

[First published in *New Leader* 27 (4 November 1944): 7.]

Comment on "Religion at Harvard"

I have read with deep satisfaction the letter of Mr. Rafton and am writing to add my voice in favor of his suggestion that Harvard University, through its Divinity School, take the leadership in establishing courses that will, in connection with courses already given, prepare persons to serve in the conduct of Humanist Religious Societies. The reasons he advances are so cogent that there is little one can add. Moreover, the appropriateness of Harvard's taking the initiative in this step is as obvious as the reasons given are sound. The proposal is so thoroughly in line with its tradition of liberal leadership in higher education that it seems to me the Chair might well bear the name of its distinguished Alumnus, Emerson. For in spirit, if not in words, he is the Founder of Humanism in religion.

[First published in *Harvard Alumni Bulletin* 49 (8 March 1947): 450. For Harold R. Rafton's letter on which Dewey is commenting, see this volume, Appendix 4.]

Communists as Teachers

To the Editor of the *New York Times:*

Up to the present time I have hesitated to express the serious doubts I have felt about the view that no one who is known to be a member of the Communist party should be permitted to teach in any higher institution of learning. The ground of my qualms was not a belief that the issue is not serious; nor was the fear inspired by the idea that expression of doubt would result in my being regarded as a Communist sympathizer. It was due to my great respect for the university men who advocated the contrary view; and who are still actively engaged in educational affairs as I am not.

Moreover, I am bound to agree with them that membership in the Communist party explicitly and officially commits a member to placing his loyalty to the party and to a foreign nation above his loyalty to the country of which he is a citizen and subject. In the abstract, there can be no doubt that this fact unfits one for the office of teaching impressionable students.

Aversion, however, to deciding important matters on abstract grounds, without reference to concrete conditions and probable consequences, prevented me from giving ready assent to the proposition that this commitment is of itself alone, without evidence of bias in conduct of work, a sufficient ground for dismissal. In any case, it leaves the field open for more dangerous subversive action on the part of fellow-travelers and those who falsely deny they are members of the party.

In the case of fanatical Communists it even puts a premium on increased duplicity. It fails to take account of the fact that in all human probability there are members of the Communist party among the body of teachers who are not so fanatical as to have

[First published in *New York Times,* 21 June 1949, p. 24.]

engaged in subversive activity on the sly. It would not be strange if some of these teachers react to the proposed measures as a challenge to take their professed communism more seriously than they have done in the past.

The above reasons are technical, however, in comparison with the fact that action of the kind proposed is bound to have indirect consequences which will be much more harmful in the end than are the evils directly guarded against. Such a movement gets taken up into a larger movement where it goes far beyond the point that was intended by the scholarly leaders who proposed something which in abstract logic was justified. It acts as provocation to those who are much more emotional than scholarly; who are more given to following a crowd than to engaging in careful discrimination; it stimulates them to carry a campaign to the point where the university presidents and professors who endorsed a limited move will be the first to disapprove.

This consideration was the original ground of my doubts and dissent. I could not be sure, however, that in fact the proposed measure would add fuel to the flame of blind and emotional action. Recent events have now proved that the fear is warranted. It is enough in this connection to cite the action of the Committee on Un-American Activities, or at least of its chairman, in engaging in a hunt for passages in college textbooks that might be regarded as "dangerous," and in carrying on the hunt not by private collection of textbooks from publishers so as to have them examined by experts, but by publicly putting the heads of colleges and of universities in a position in which they are inevitably exposed to suspicion and to public resentment which has been needlessly and harmfully inflamed.

It is to be hoped that the public response to the very great error of the committee will check the hysterical wave. I do not see, however, how the original proposal, coming as it did from university leaders, did anything, to put it as mildly as possible, to discourage the sort of thing which has been going on. Probably some of these teachers were moved by a proper desire to protect institutions of learning from unjust and wholly needless suspicion and attack. The outcome, however, seems to teach quite a different lesson.

JOHN DEWEY

New York, June 18, 1949

A Statement to the Society

In congratulating The National Society of College Teachers of Education on its successful attainment of a half-century of useful activities, one's thoughts are naturally inclined to move to consideration of what the half-century we are now entering will bring forth and what demands will in consequence be made upon our educational institutions in general and our colleges in particular. It would be absurd to suppose that any foresight is possible which would enable the wisest among us to lay out specific plans for the conduct of the National Society during the coming years. But we do know that we are living in a time of crisis more serious than any falling within the memory of men now living and that its intensity may continue to grow. This fact is sufficient of itself to demand most serious consideration of the place and function of our schools in general and higher educational institutions in particular in connection with a time of widespread uncertainty, confusion, turmoil, and conflict. In our days of comparative calm, the attention of such a body as the National Society may quite properly go to matters that are in the main professional. But under existing conditions higher institutions of learning and teaching need to discover a positive and constructive direction for guidance of their specialized professional activities. The obligation weighs probably more deeply upon teachers of teachers than upon the teachers of any subject; not probably but assuredly if what we often say about the importance of right education be taken seriously.

It has been almost a commonplace in American life since the days of Thomas Jefferson and Horace Mann to say that education is the chief bulwark of democracy. As a statement of the end

[First published in *A History of the National Society of College Teachers of Education (1902–1950)* [n.p., n.d.], pp. 2–3.]

and aim of our American schools the saying is true and as significant as it ever was. In the measure in which the threats from without and within to genuine democracy are now particularly rife, recognition that the central and unifying purpose of public education is maintenance and development of democratic ways of life is perhaps as widespread as it ever was. But the issue of *how* the end is to be attained is more urgent than it ever was. It requires systematic and careful consideration of reconstructions that will be needed in old practices if the purpose is to animate our educational work. It demands critical consideration and weighing of every aspect of our institutions and social habits to see how they stand from the standpoint of democracy as a criterion. Only in the context of this re-consideration of common practices in the light of an informed idea of what democracy *is* can the theory and practice of education in our school system be properly judged; just as only on this basis can the schools be protected from the interests that would use the schools for their own one-sided purposes and be assured of constructive, not merely passive review of the democratic way of life.

Existing conditions do not render it any too easy for The National Society of College Teachers of Education to seek and find a vital centre for its activities in the endeavor to see to it that teaching of teachers throughout the country measures up to the purpose provided and standard set by the responsibility of our schools to be in fact the bulwark of democratic ideals and methods. But this very difficulty may provide stimulus for study and inspiration to practical activities. May the coming half-century extend and multiply the services rendered to American education by the National Society.

Mr. Acheson's Critics

To the Editor of the *New York Times*:

There must be many persons who are disturbed by the attacks made upon Secretary Acheson and who hope that, now the campaign is over and there is no immediate partisan advantage to be gained by continuing them, they will cease.

As a matter of calm observation and cool reflection, it would be hard to find a diplomatic achievement in the records of many countries for many years equaling in importance to the success achieved in handling the Korean affair by enlisting the support of the U.N. It has saved the U.N. from the paralysis that overtook the League of Nations because of its failure to act in the Manchurian affair. It also immensely increased respect for this nation among almost all the peoples of the world. In addition, it did much to relieve us from the charge of unjustified aggressive and imperialistic ambitions.

The largest aspect of the attack upon Secretary Acheson seems to have centered in the charge that the State Department is guilty of "coddling Communists." The charge perhaps paid off as a campaign cry; doubtless there have been cases that deserve public attention and criticism.

But the pitch to which the clamor was raised, together with the fact that many observers think it brought about the turning point in the campaign, is in substance a victory for the Communist cause that the rulers of the U.S.S.R. could not have obtained by any activity on their own part. Communist activities were immensely dignified by being treated as though they were of almost supreme importance in the domestic politics of this country instead of as a matter for vigilance on the part of citizens and particularly for continued attention on the part of the F.B.I.

[First published in *New York Times*, 19 November 1950, p. 14E.]

The fact that leaders in the campaign against Acheson are now engaged in denying that they are isolationists does not make up for the loss of confidence among the Western European democracies in our continued and energetic support. Repairing the damage that has been done is not of necessity a matter of political partisanship.

If those who control the policies of the Republican party are satisfied with having won an election and do not regard it as a "mandate" for maintaining the issues they put forward in the campaign, it is probably still possible to prevent our free gift to the Communist cause from doing the harm it has promised to do.

JOHN DEWEY

New York, Nov. 14, 1950

Tributes

Clarence J. Selby

Mr. J. A. Williams,

My Dear Sir:—I have met and conversed with Mr. Selby with great pleasure, and have become acquainted with his most interesting work. The cases of Laura Bridgman, Helen Keller and the more striking instances of the deaf-blind have familiarized the public with the great importance of the scientific and educational questions concerned. But there are other cases, not celebrated, but equally worthy of note for the degree of progress made, considering the opportunities, and equally worthy of encouragement for the force, bravery and intelligence with which this most discouraging situation has been met. Mr. Selby presents such a case.

Respectfully,

JOHN DEWEY

[First published in *Echoes from the Rainbow City* (Chicago: Travelers' Bureau, 1902), p. 13.]

Clifford Beers

February 16, 1933

Dear Dr. Welch:

I am extremely glad to hear that the work of Clifford Beers in connection with mental hygiene is to be commemorated. It has been given to few individuals to open the road to new and important movements as it has been to initiate an activity that combines social benefit, popular appeal, and scientific insight. To my mind there is something particularly encouraging, in this time of general discouragement, in the record of a man who emerged from a serious affliction with the energy and enthusiasm to make his experiences of value to other sufferers. The development of the Mental Hygiene Movement is in and of itself a lasting tribute to the heroism of Mr. Beers.

Respectfully yours,

JOHN DEWEY

[First published in *Twenty-Five Years After: Sidelights on the Mental Hygiene Movement and Its Founder,* ed. Wilbur L. Cross (Garden City and New York: Doubleday, Doran and Co., 1934), p. 115.]

Alvin Johnson

It is so easy to greet our friend Alvin Johnson as a scholar that I shall take that for granted and pass on to something more basic. Even though there are not many scholars whose range and accuracy of knowledge equal that of Alvin Johnson, to dwell on his learning apart from its source and the use to which he puts it would be so partial, so incomplete, as to be misleading.

Rather it is as a poet that I would greet the friend whose seventy-fifth anniversary we are celebrating here this evening for the celebration is more than just a performance of a stated rite no matter how justified and proper the latter may be. In naming our guest a poet I am going back to the primitive sense of the word: a maker, a creator,—which, I take it is of a different dimension from that conveyed by the words "doer" and "doing." For creation is the product of the rarest gift of man, imagination. His power of imbuing his fellow workers with his own ardor, is something that happens only in the case of the rare human beings who draw their inspiration from their creative look-ahead, the distinguishing trait of those who are pioneers in their own right, not just from the accident of circumstances.

In greeting our friend also as an encyclopedist, I do so in full recognition of the fact that there are those to whom compiling an encyclopedia is a job that has to do with organizing the knowledge and beliefs with what the past has provided the world, as if that were an end in itself. But Alvin Johnson is a humanist in the sense of the Enlightenment of the 18th century. As an encyclopedist his name belongs by the side of that of the French creator Diderot. Men as different as were Thomas Jefferson and

[First published in *New School Bulletin* 7 (26 December 1949): 2, from tribute delivered by Dewey, 18 December 1949, at the New School for Social Research, New York, N.Y.]

John Adams felt themselves to be offspring and the bearers of the Enlightenment of which Diderot was a representative figure in his time and which is today the mark of our guest Alvin Johnson as a creator or poet.

In the field which is often condescendingly referred to as practical and material we may apply to him the words of the Roman poet "if you seek his monument look around you." In the case of Alvin Johnson we have to look far beyond the physical structure. We have to look into the hearts and minds of the multitudes of men and women whose outlook on life is happier and freer because of the imaginative construction which Alvin Johnson has carried on in this physical building. One may have no finer desire for the future than that his imaginative spirit continue to guide the School and all who participate in its activities.

Emily Greene Balch

In honoring Emily Greene Balch, the Nobel Committee of Oslo has not only honored itself, it has given deserved and needed recognition to all those patient, hard-working pioneers of the peoples of the earth whose intelligent faith, courage and persistence is the sure guarantee as well as inspiration of the establishment of enduring peace among nations. As an outstanding representative of these unofficial citizens the world over, for more than thirty years the labors of Miss Balch for peace have been as unremitting as they have been free from self-seeking.

Emily Balch has always had the courage to follow and act upon her intelligence. She has never been afraid to speak out fearlessly in the face of public opinion, and, what is even harder, to speak out in the face of a differing opinion among those fellow-workers whom she held in greatest affection. She sacrificed her first career as teacher to oppose American entry into the World War in 1917. With unusual foresight and vision she has seen the real underlying issues long before most others. She was a pioneer in working for a League of Nations, and has given her realistic and not uncritical support to the United Nations organization, as one among many instruments through which habits of international cooperation on particular issues may become ingrained in practice. She worked out in detail a scheme for international colonial administration some years before the mandate system was set up at Versailles.

As one of the founders with Jane Addams of the Women's International League for Peace and Freedom in 1915, Emily Balch was among the first to enlist the organized intelligent cooperation of women in the cause of peace. She was instrumental in

[First published in *Emily Greene Balch, Nobel Prize Winner, 1946* (Philadelphia, Pa.: Women's International League for Peace and Freedom, [1946–47?]), p. 2.]

calling many international congresses of women at The Hague, Zurich, Vienna, Grenoble and elsewhere and in setting up international conferences on specific issues, such as opium control, scientific warfare, East European problems, statelessness and minorities.

What I should like to emphasize chiefly is her constructive statesmanship—her intellectual leadership in the understanding and solution of the complicated concrete problems of organizing the affairs of a dynamically peaceful world. She has a gift amounting to genius for discovering new approaches to political and economic problems of international importance. She can separate the underlying issues from all emotion and propaganda, and with an inventive statesmanship then work out a practicable and acceptable unifying formula.

The meaning of Miss Balch's international philosophy in practice is clearly illustrated in her treatment of the tragic problem of the refugees, especially of the Jews, into which she threw herself after 1933. She saw it not as primarily the occasion for compassion—which she felt in full measure—but as a challenge to realistic statesmanship. To her logical analysis, the problem raised by Nazi techniques was that of the status of minority groups in general. As such, it seemed to her a crucial test of democratic methods and procedures. She was early aware that the poison planted by the Nazis would outlast their military defeat. She saw that whatever the solution of the problem of Palestine, the only permanent settlement for all displaced peoples would be their full acceptance as citizens in the countries of their choice, and the freest possible right of immigration into every country.

With the accolade of the Nobel Committee, Emily Balch can well be hailed as one of the first private citizens of the world.

Syllabi

Introduction to Philosophy

Section I. Preliminary Statement

I. An invention arises out of the feeling of conflict, friction, or lack of harmony in a given activity. On one side, this conflict means waste, loss of utility, of power, lack of economy; that is, impeded or partial activity. Not to get the maximum result with the minimum means is to have a thwarted activity. On the other side, this is felt in pain, in dissatisfaction. Until elements in activity conflict with each other so much as to make the hindered activity felt in consciousness there can be no progress. There will be simply repetition of existing acts just as they are, with no idea of any need of improvement.

II. The felt discord leads to more or less conscious attempts at bettering matters. This improving consists in getting an adjustment of the various elements entering into an experience so that they constitute a *whole* instead of having value on their own account. It consists in substituting a harmonious activity for a divided or wasteful activity. Activities are related or coordinated. That is, activities which did not cooperate or work to a common end are so adjusted that they do work together. Physically considered, everything may be reduced to motion. If the movements are isolated, the resistance or distance between them has to be overcome so that they do move together. Every invention is this general process of coordinating movements previously independent of each other or opposed to each other.

III. The invention of the spear by the savage. The first sowing of seed, tilling of soil and harvesting of crops. Each is making a whole out of actions previously separated, and this, by coordi-

[First published by the Philosophical Department, University of Michigan, Ann Arbor, October 1892, 8 pp.]

nating movements, makes a saving and gives a greater net result of activity.

IV. This coordination of isolated and opposing activities by making them move together towards a common end, *frees* activity previously bound up. It allows more expression. It is progressive *manifestation*. Nothing is created but there is a change of direction, of distribution of movement, making it more effective, because more related, that is, more of a totality.

V. As each separate activity gets into a larger whole, it gets its *function*. Its full significance is brought out just in the degree in which it is related, that is, cooperates with other activities in constituting a more comprehensive one.

Questions: Is the invention artificial? How would you define a tool? Indicate the various elements coordinated in the railway. What is the freeing which has taken place here? How would you justify such a statement as that freedom is complete expression? What do you understand by realization?

N.B. The general course of development here. Beginning in an activity in which no conflict or opposition is felt; going through a period in which minor activities are isolated because of the friction between them, ending in a new whole in which the elements are readjusted, this new whole having for its content the activities previously isolated, but transformed so far as is necessary in order that they may work together. Compare this with Spencer's definition of evolution. The change from an indefinite, incoherent homogeneity to a heterogeneity, defined and coherent. Is there any analogy between the process of evolution and that of invention?

Section II. General Statement of Nature of Experience

I. Our experience is simply what we do. An infant is conscious only of the activity of his own organism, of his hand, eye, ear, legs. This activity is at first unconscious; not in the sense that the infant is totally sunk in unconsciousness as is a stone or a plant, but in the sense that it is not conscious of the various factors or conditions entering into its activity. It simply feels what it is doing as a vague whole, being conscious rather of the net result gained than of any "things." An apple, for example, is at first not something tasted, felt, seen; it is not a sweet, hard, yellow thing, but it is the tasting, touching, seeing. There is simply the experiencing. In experience at this stage there is no distinction of a me and not-me. We are at root *practical* beings, beings engaged in exercise. This practice constitutes at first both self and world of reality. There is no distinction.

II. How does this original experience get broken into two sides? How does the distinction arise between *things* which *are* experienced and a *subject* which *has* these experiences; between an external and an internal? Since the activity is all there is, it is obvious the separation must arise because of something *in* the activity itself. The activity becomes divided; various elements in it conflict with each other. The activity of the organism as a whole is split into minor activities which oppose each other. While the organism so far as the eye is concerned is experiencing the apple, the hand and the mouth are not. This contradiction in the activity of the organism breaks up the existing vague unity of consciousness and sets the various factors over against each other. The seeing and tasting of the apple are no longer bound up together, and accordingly the qualities of color and taste are distinguished in consciousness. Each is freed from the vague whole of which it was formerly a member. At the same time, since the unity satisfies, while the divided activity does not, there arises a contrast between the unity or whole as "ideal" and the separate factors as "actual." *The unity, the complete activity is now identified with the Self. The distinguished elements or conditions, set over against one another and against the whole, are identified as the Not-self.*

What, in reality, is a division *within self or the world of reality* (the experience), this division consisting in such conflict of elements as prevents their complete cooperation, is translated into a separation *between the self and reality.* Then the opposition which exists *within* the self as active experiencing, is made into a resistance which the "self" meets from *without.*

Experience is divided into an internal element and an external. The internal stands for the unity, the external for the separation and conflict. The eating of the apple, which is now only ideal because of the division between the various organic activities of seeing, touching and tasting, represents the side of the self; while that which is "actual" (the qualities of color, hardness and sweetness in their distinctness) stands for the external, the "world."

What is only a *mobile* distinction within the self or reality (the active experiencing) is frozen into a *rigid* separation; a distinction having value only with reference to the state in which action is at a given time—the tension of its factors—is treated as if it were a permanent line of division in the structure of things.

III. The complete cor-relation between the two sides may thus be stated. The ideal side or "self" (in the limited sense which that term now has) is only the unity of the various diverse elements; the eating of the apple is only the whole into which the seeing, the touching, the tasting, etc., enter as constituent elements. It cannot be really opposed to them as if it were a different kind of reality. On the other hand, the actual side (the "reality" in the narrow sense which that term gets when the diverse elements are opposed to the unified activity) is itself the outcome of a unity, is that unity broken up, and passes into a further unity.

It is this latter point which we have now to illustrate. Take again the complete experience involved in eating the apple. At another time the child sees it and the organism so far as the eye is concerned goes through the same activity as before. But not being able to walk, the child does not get the activity of handling, touching, putting in its mouth, etc., which it had before. The result, as already indicated, is *analysis*. The obstruction in the activity of the whole organism shakes the different elements loose, as it were. It marks them off into distinct qualities. They come into consciousness on their own account, instead of being absorbed in the total outcome. Just as soon as these diverse elements are again fully related to each other the total experience, the unity of the self, is again attained. *The complete connection of the elements of the "not-me," of the external, is the wider self and the wider reality.* This reality or self has, it should be noticed, more meaning than the previous unity. While the various qualities are no longer separately in consciousness, the new unity, based upon their complete inter-relation, is not vague and undefined, like the first unity, but enriched in significance by the values of the various constituting elements as these have been brought out. The self is thus only the *synthesis* of the elements which taken in their separateness are the not-self.

IV. The division of the original experience into two opposed sides of the internal or ideal and the external or actual is not an ultimate thing. It is only the *means* through which the unity gets fullness of definition; it is, that is to say, the means through which action realizes its full value.

V. Summing up; through conflict of the various elements entering into an entire activity of the organism, the various elements are opposed to one another, and the activity is analysed into various diverse factors. These various distinct conditions taken in their separateness, that is, in their distinction from the entire activity, are

(1) The external world. It is "external" because, as divided activity, it seems to oppose the self, or the unity.

(2) They are facts, *facta,* things done. As against the unity of the self, which is now something to be attained, to *be* done, the various distinct elements represent what *has* been done. They are the analysis, the distinct realizing in consciousness, of previous activity.

(3) They are the things *known.* The unity is, by its very nature, action. In falling out of this total activity and being set in opposition to it, the distinct qualities, while in reality themselves minor or partial activities, seem to be inaction. They are simply *present* to consciousness; they are *before* it. Their having existence as distinguished from one another and from the "self" is precisely what we mean by knowledge.

(4) They are the multiple, manifold or diverse element. This is implied, of course, in the fact they are the analysis of the unity.

(5) They are the *sensory* elements as against the rational. That is, as separated they are referred to the sense, while their relations or coordinations are referred to reason. (This point will be illustrated when we come to the psychological statement.)

On the other hand, the unity of the activity, *as opposed to the different factors which constitute it,* is 1, internal; 2, ideal; 3, volitional as against cognitive; 4, synthetic or total; 5, rational or conceptual.

Problem: Trace out the correlative character of the two sides, following it through each of these five oppositions.

Questions: What is an object like a book to a child at first, *i.e.,* before he has learned to read? How does different and additional meaning come to attach to it? What is the difference between a child's idea of a ball and its definition as mass in motion by a scientific man? What does meaning *mean*? If it is so practical in its origin, how does it ever become so indifferent, so much *merely* intellectual? How does a lever, for example, cease to be simply a certain activity, and become a mere thing which, of course, *may* be used, but yet has a meaning independent of any use? Does this change have itself any practical value?

The relation of knowledge and action may be illustrated by an invention. With the invention, the activity evidently comes first; this activity being conscious only as to its net outcome, not as to its constituent factors. Friction within the activity prevents this net outcome being reached; a division into different elements results. Only when the savage cannot satisfy his hunger as it arises, is he conscious of the different characters of seed, soil and atmosphere. The postponement of the complete and direct activity is the same as the inharmonious adjustment, the rubbing together, of the various elements in it. This mutual resistance, or the activity in its *direct* course arrested, constitutes knowledge. This knowledge, however, in calling attention to the various factors of the activity in their separateness, calls attention also to their *relations* to one another and thus *points* the way to a further reunion. The activity checked in its direct onward course turns in upon itself and by a close examination of its own conditions attains its end. This end, for reasons already explained, has more value or meaning than would have had the original end, if directly obtained. The indirect or mediate course gives the outcome an *intellectual,* as distinct from a merely emotional value. Knowledge, in other words, is, as disintegration and accompanying arrest of activity, a *report* or account of that activity; as readjustment of the distinguished factors to one another, it is the *project* or *ideal* of further activity; i.e., knowledge on its analytic side is reference to past action which it registers in its distinct conditions, thus objectifying it; on its synthetic side, it is reference to future or purposed activity, which it states as harmony or unity of the distinguished conditions, thus *subjecting* (rendering into its value for the self) the objective. The original activity is relatively subjective-objective in that the two sides are not differentiated; the final activity is again subjective-objective. It is subjective because it has completely mastered the separated elements, reducing them to their unity, their value for the self; it is objective because it contains and expresses the consciously distinguished conditions of action.

A simple illustration of the process is found in the operation of a bank: the activity at first goes on as complex and (so far as consciousness is concerned) undifferentiated activity; that is, while the various acts of receiving and paying out are going on, and these in many different ways, there is no distinct consciousness of the real nature or value of each, because it is not *placed* in the whole. The possible or actual oppositions in these various activities (that is the need of adjusting them to each other so that they will form a harmonious movement) makes it necessary to arrest the ongoing activity; it is turned back upon itself; account or stock of the activity is taken. This registration or statement of activity in its constituting factors is knowledge. On the other hand, this knowledge, if it adequately defines each element, gives also its relations to the others: synthesis. This relating of the various elements shows the direction the business is taking; it gives guidance to the banking business. The report of the business, taken simply as report, gives the objective; the relating of the reported factors so as to get the direction of the business, so as to be able to continue the activity, is the subjective side; it gives the ideal. It will be seen that only during the transition points is there any separation of subject and object; only when the activity is disintegrating in order to get an integration on the basis of a larger number of distinguished factors. The opposition of internal and external, instead of being a fixed and permanent division, is just this *tension* in the re-forming activity between the factors needing to be readjusted. The external stands for the resistance to the reformation; the internal for the growing movement together. In the banking business, for example, at a critical period collections become difficult and it is hard to negotiate securities. Thus elements bound up in the previous activity are now distinctly realized in consciousness; they are freed from the vague whole in which they were previously contained; for unless these difficulties were *implied* in former activity, they would never become explicit. These separate conditions are thus the record or history, the registration of activity. They tell us what the activity all the time was. Their distinct appearance coincides with the arrest of the ongoing activity due to the friction in it. At the same time these different elements form the basis of further action; they are the conditions which have to be adjusted to one another in order that business may continue. They are the material of the action; they are "objective" to it, in other words. Now the movements which will unite them is at first the plan, the conception, the project, ideal, of the business. That is, the conditions in their growing, but not attained, unity are the subjective side. The realized unity is again subjective-objective.

N.B. 1. It is through resistance, difficulty, in our activities that we are brought to consciousness. The educational significance of this fact? 2. The place of unity and difference, of analysis and synthesis in all knowledge. 3. The implicit and explicit. 4. The relation of fact and meaning to each other. 5. The immediate and the mediate.

History of Education

STANDPOINT OF COURSE

The course is intended to give teachers, parents and others interested in correct educational theory and practice some knowledge of the conditions under which our present educational system has grown up; of the origin of the principles that are used to explain and justify it, and of the various projects and controversies for directing its future improvement and reform. No attempt is made accordingly to convey historical information simply for the sake of the information. The ultimate end is practical, better insight into the present; for it is believed that no teacher can do the best possible with present conditions and tendencies without knowing something of how they came to be. Since educational practice and theory have always been connected with social institutions and aims, types of social life and theory are selected for emphasis, and details that do not connect themselves with typical problems, and movements, are ignored.

METHOD

Directions to Students.

1. Aim to work systematically. Lay out your work in advance so as to economize your spare hours. Aim to read some every day, and to read an hour and a half a day upon the average.

2. Keep a note-book, making brief digests of the main points in what you read, and noting your difficulties.

3. Do not aim to understand by first memorizing, but rather to remember by means of first understanding. Think out the mean-

[First published by the School of Liberal Arts and Sciences for Non-Residents, New York, N.Y., 1907–8; Sections I–IV are extant.]

ing of what you read. In particular, be quick to note the points of likeness and difference of the past and the present.

4. Required papers; the questions for these will be intended in the main to test the student's comprehension of what he has read, and to assist him in organizing his own thinking. Questions will be asked from time to time, however, bearing upon the student's knowledge of the subject-matter of the text.

5. Observe carefully in all the exercises the following directions; violation of them may occasion the total rejection of the student's paper:

6. Write your name, the title of the course, and the number of the section upon each sheet of your report.

7. Write with ink (or typewriter) upon one side of the paper only.

8. Make answers as brief and concise as is consistent with clearness.

REFERENCES

Texts.

Monroe, Paul, *A Brief Course in the History of Education.*

Davidson, Thomas, *A History of Education.*

These books both cover the entire field, and supplement each other nicely.

Monroe, Paul, *Source Book of the History of Education.*

This gives quotations from the original authorities. It thus brings the student in first-hand contact with the great minds that have discussed education without the intervening interpretation of others; and in giving the student a chance to form his own judgment gives him also an opportunity to check the ideas of the authors of the text-books by his own. Unfortunately it only covers the Greek and Roman periods.

Davidson, Thomas, *Aristotle and Ancient Educational Ideals.*

This gives both an account and an interpretation not merely of Aristotle, but of the whole course of Greek education.

Adamson, J. W., *Pioneers of Modern Education.*

A very scholarly and careful account of the most influential of the earlier writers who helped form the educational theory of to-day.

Quick, R. H., *Educational Reformers.*

This is a standard work upon those writers of the modern period who have most actively urged educational reform, written with reference to showing the origin of points still at issue between educational conservatives and reformers.

Optional Readings.

In addition to these, the School will supply at cost the following books for optional supplementary readings. No required work will be based upon these books, but some students may like to have them in their libraries as means of extending their reading on special points.

De Garmo, Charles, *Herbart.*

Important for the life and teaching of the most important German theorist of the nineteenth century.

Hinsdale, B. A., *Horace Mann and the Common School Revival in the United States.*

An excellent account of the most important single movement in elementary education in the United States in the nineteenth century.

Hughes, T., *Loyola and the Educational System of the Jesuits.*

A clear and sympathetic account of the best organized educational movement among Roman Catholics since the Reformation.

Laurie, S. S., *Rise and Constitution of the Universities.*

Especially useful for the mediaeval and early modern periods.

Laurie, S. S., *Historical Survey of Pre-Christian Education.*

Especially full for the peoples and races of antiquity, which are only touched lightly by our main texts.

Monroe, Paul, *Text-Book in the History of Education.*

This book is by the same author as the *Brief Course,* and gives a fuller treatment.

West, A. F., *Alcuin and the Rise of the Christian Schools.*

Important for the early mediaeval period.

Woodward, W. H., *Vittorino da Feltre and Other Humanist Educators.*

An excellent account of the first and greatest of the Renaissance Italian educators.

Woodward, W. H., *Studies in Education during the Age of the Renaissance.*

By the same author as the preceding, but covering the entire Renaissance.

Williams, S. G., *The History of Ancient Education; The History of Mediaeval Education; The History of Modern Education.*

A good synopsis of the whole period.

TOPICS

This course consists of twenty-four sections.

I. Nature and Value of History of Education. Savage and Barbarian Education.
II. Types of Social Life and Education: (1) Chinese and (2) Greek.
III. Early Greek Education; the Civic Type.
IV. The "Wise Men" and Socrates: Intellectual Instruction.
V. Plato: Philosophic Basis and Aim of Education.
VI. Aristotle: Scientific Analysis of Education.
VII. Roman Education: Training for Public Life.
VIII. Hellenistic and Early Christian Education: Training for Life beyond the State.
IX. Early Middle Ages: Preservation of Learning and Virtue.
X. Later Middle Ages: the Organization of Knowledge and Conduct. Training for Professions.
XI. The Revival of Learning in Italy. Classic Learning and the Development of Individuality.
XII. The Revival of Learning in Germany and England.
XIII. The Protestant Reformation and the Beginnings of Universal Education.
XIV. The Catholic Counter-Reformation: the Organization of Methods of Discipline and Instruction.
XV–XVI–XVII–XVIII. The Origin of Conflicting Modern Aims and Methods of Education. The Reformers of the Seventeenth Century.
XIX–XX–XXI. The Reformers of the Eighteenth Century. Human Perfectibility and the Child.
XXII–XXIII–XXIV. Nineteenth Century Tendencies: The Application of Science and Philosophy to Education.

Section I

NATURE AND VALUE OF HISTORY OF
EDUCATION. SAVAGE EDUCATION

Specific Directions.

The assignments are:

Monroe, *A Brief Course in the History of Education,* Chap. I.

Davidson, *A History of Education,* pp. 14–41, 45–74.

a. First read this as you would read any book in which you are interested to get its general drift.

b. Then turn to the "Aids" and read the text in more detail, keeping in mind the suggestive questions, especially III–VI.

c. Then look at all the "Required Questions," then consult the text again as much as is needed in order to make the questions and their relations to the text clear to you.

d. Then formulate your written replies independently. If not satisfied with the result, turn to the text again and write again.

Aids to Study and Suggestive Questions.

I. What is the value of a study of the history of education?

1. Its general culture value, irrespective of whether the student is a teacher or not. Suppose all records of the present were lost except an account of our schools, their means of support, their curricula and their methods; how much could the future historian tell about

a. The moral beliefs and ideals of the present?

b. Our scientific knowledge?

c. Our political institutions?

Could you tell from a full account of the educational system of a foreign people whether that people was aristocratic or democratic? Whether it was far advanced in the arts of manufacture and commerce? Whether it was warlike or peaceful? Whether it was predominantly artistic, religious or industrial in its habits of mind? In what esteem children were held? Its intellectual advancement?

2. Its special value to the teacher.

a. Can present practices be understood without a knowledge of their origin and growth? Does the principle of habit tend to keep up practices after their original use has been outgrown? Can you mention any such survivals in our present schools? Would a knowledge of the origin of these practices help us to criticize them and to get rid of them, if no longer useful? Think of an example. If a primary teacher, would you feel freer in your work if you knew under what circumstances different methods of teaching reading had developed? When arithmetic ceased to be exclusively a subject for higher education and was taught to little children and why it was?

b. Can present theories be discussed intelligently and their worth judged apart from a knowledge of their earlier history? Does lack of such knowledge tend to make teachers too dogmatic in laying down and too passive in receiving statements of educational principles?

c. Do you know under what social and industrial conditions Slöyd originated? In what sort of a language the alphabet and syllabic method of teaching reading began? What people first made foreign languages a part of their curriculum and why? What peoples have laid the most stress on imitation in giving instruction? Whether the introduction of the Arabic notation made any difference in methods of teaching arithmetic? The state of learning and civilization in which verbal symbols have been most prominent? In which study of objects at first hand has been insisted upon? The conditions under which memorizing and thinking for one's self have respectively been especially emphasized? The parts played by philanthropy, by business interests and by political causes in developing modern public education? Would it make any practical difference to you if you did? What?

d. Teachers are told to go from the "concrete to the abstract." Have the words had the same meaning at all periods? What causes have been influential in fixing their present meaning? Was a ghost any less concrete to a savage than a physical thing? (See Monroe, p. 5.) Are names any less concrete to savages than the things to which they belong? (Davidson, p. 19.) Teachers are told to "follow nature." Did "Nature" have the same meaning to a savage, to Aristotle, to the Stoics, to Rousseau, to Spencer? Do those who argue for and against this maxim always give the term the same meaning?

II. An educated person is sometimes spoken of as a "lettered" man; the uneducated are called "illiterate." What light does the first chapter of Monroe throw upon this? (See also Davidson, pp. 51–53.) Have you met persons educated in school who were less competent and intelligent than those with little schooling? Where did the latter get their education? What did it consist of? How important a part of education do the present boy and girl get in school and out of school? What are the advantages of each? What are the differences between the education got out of school by a city child and a country child? What light do these questions throw upon primitive education?

III. What is the essential characteristic of education, said (in the first paragraph of Monroe) to be the same in the most primitive and the most advanced societies? What is the advantage of studying the primitive form?

IV. What do our authors mean by the difference between the method of imitation and the method of instruction?

V. What do you gather from our authors as to the importance of tradition and records, oral and written, for social life and education? (See Davidson, *History of Education*, pp. 28, 29, 37, 39, 51–53, 59, etc.) Can an individual learn or teach without memory? Can a community learn or teach if it has no traditional beliefs and ideas? What is the effect of purely oral tradition? Of the vocation of writing? Of printing?

VI. Note in Davidson, *History of Education*, the distinction (p. 13) of the four stages of historic development and the corresponding four types of education. Attempt to systematize your knowledge of the history of education about these four conceptions.

VII. There are many interesting historic details in Davidson which do not bear directly on our topic of study. Study the different peoples spoken of *comparatively*, noting especially points of likeness and difference in (*a*) occupations of life (nomadic, agricultural and political), (*b*) political institutions—how they were governed, (*c*) religious beliefs—position of priesthood, (*d*) literary and scientific traditions in songs, stories, sacred writings, etc. *These four things are always the chief influences upon educational systems.*

VIII. What do you gather as to the bearing of different habits and customs of living upon education—i.e., as to principles of educational aims and method in a people who only hunted and fished, compared with one that had agriculture and domestic animals, or one that could work metals and manufacture? (See, for example, Davidson, *A History of Education,* pp. 21, 25–28, 33, 34. Bear this point in mind in succeeding lessons.)

Questions for Your Report.

Q.1. What do you expect to get, from the standpoint of general culture, from a study of the history of education? (Employ the suggestions given under heading I of *Aids,* etc., in answering this question; it is not expected that each question suggested will receive a reply, but that the net result of your thinking will be given.)

Q.2. What do you hope to get as a *teacher?* (See the previous note.)

Q.3. What is the effect of the type of social life anywhere existing and the type of education given? What is the effect of education upon the existing type of social life?

Q.4. Name all the elements you can think of in our own life whose continued existence is dependent upon education.

Q.5. Enumerate the different methods (kinds of schools and also agencies outside of schools, like magazines and sermons) by which this education is secured.

Q.6. State Monroe's view on the theoretical and the practical elements in early education. Would you consider instruction given the young in the legends and traditions of their tribe theoretical or practical instruction, or both, and why?

Q.7. Why should names at first seem to have magic power? Is there still any tendency to almost worship words and printed symbols? Illustrate your answer.

Q.8. State the differences between savage and barbarian education, illustrating the latter by either the Hindoos or Babylonians.

Q.9. What were the respective functions of the mother, the father and the priest or religious authority in the barbarian education of the young? How does this compare with present conditions?

Q.10. (*a*) What is the importance of imitation and custom in education? What sorts of things may at present best be learned by these methods? (*b*) What is the limitation of these principles— that is, where do they fail or come short? Can they secure progress? Can they secure an investigating and inventive habit of mind? If not, what supplement do they require?

Q.11. Mention the points, either in the text or in the questions, which give you most difficulty.

N.B.—This last question is optional. An answer to it will enable the instructor to be of more help to you. Of the first six questions, select and answer any five. Make your answers concise and definite. The chief benefit of the course is to be got from reading and study. Hence, it is not necessary to write essays in reply to questions. Long and vague answers will not enable the instructor to make corrections and give assistance as effectively as will pointed and brief ones. Trying to make the latter kind of answers will also be of the greatest benefit to the mental habits of the student.

Supplementary References for Optional Readings.

Laurie, S. S., *Pre-Christian Education;* pp. 1–8, history of education in general; pp. 11–48, Egyptian; pp. 65–100, Hebrew; pp. 155–177, Hindoo; pp. 178–195, Persian. (Laurie gives additional references at the end of each section.)

Monroe, Paul, *Text-Book in the History of Education.*

Section II

TYPES OF EDUCATION: CHINESE AND GREEK

Specific Directions.

The assigned readings are:

Monroe, *A Brief Course in the History of Education,* Chaps. II and III to p. 33.

Davidson, *Aristotle and the Ancient Educational Ideals,* pp. 1–37.

Davidson, *A History of Education,* pp. 41–45 and 86–95.

This section offers little difficulty and may well be completed within a week or ten days.

Read and study the references on Chinese education before reading those on Greek education. In beginning the latter topic, read first in a general way without detailed study the reference in Davidson's *Aristotle;* also in a general way the reference in Monroe's *History;* then study each more carefully, comparing their statements with each other. In your reading observe the suggestions made in the general directions accompanying Section I. Complete your study before attempting to answer the required questions; but if you have difficulty with them read the texts again to see what light they throw on the matter.

Aids and Suggestive Questions.

The purpose of this Section is to put side by side two contrasting types of educational practice which correspond to two contrasting types of social life. This contrast serves to bring out certain points, which apply to all educational systems; such as (1) the intimate connection between the educational methods of any people and their general social life—domestic, industrial and political; (2) the importance of the traditional literature and history of a people as a way of maintaining the type of character necessary to conserve the national type of social life; (3) the important differences between the education of a people whose tendencies are to preserve the past and that of a people whose life is progressive, permitting change.

By keeping in mind the general statements just made, the student will find that he will be less likely to be retarded by the length of the passages to be read or to have his attention distracted by the multitude of details. While the latter will be found suggestive and should be thoughtfully read, they need not receive the same careful study as the portions that bear on the above topics.

The following questions are designed to assist the student in getting hold of these more fundamental points:

CHINESE EDUCATION

I. What characteristics are attributed to Chinese life as a social type? (Note Monroe, *H. E.*, pp. 23–25.)

II. What was the importance of the moral element in education? What kind of morality was aimed at? What differences do you find between this kind of morality and that held in esteem in our own country?

III. Why were certain literary writings held so important? How does this differ from the importance attached to the Bible in our own country? Would you regard as just a comparison between the Chinese use of literature in education and the American use of Greek and Latin in higher education? Why not?

IV. What are the good points involved in the fundamental importance attached to the family? (See Monroe, p. 13.) What is the meaning of *piety* in Greek and Roman thought? (Consult dictionary if necessary.) What reasons can you give for ancestor worship having played a part in the development of almost all religions? Do you regard as just the criticisms sometimes made of American life that it thinks too much of the present and the future and not enough of the past and our dependence upon it; also that it does not sufficiently emphasize respect and reverence for elders and for parental authority? What are the weak points in attaching so much importance to the family idea as do the Chinese?

V. Every educational system should be studied from three standpoints: First, the school as an institution having its own organization; secondly, the curriculum, or subject-matter of education; thirdly, the method of instruction. The student may profitably select, put together and condense the discussion of the text under these three heads:

(1) For the school as an institution see especially Monroe, pp. 15–17.

(2) For subject-matter or course of study see Monroe, pp. 11–15.

(3) For method see Monroe, p. 18.

VI. Granted the aim of Chinese education, the preservation of the past without change, what impression do you get concerning the thoroughness and efficiency of the Chinese method of realizing this aim?

VII. How far should any educational system—say our own—have for its purpose the conservative one: that of maintaining the past social order? Is it possible on this basis to develop individuality? Is individuality more a matter of outward act or of power to think, invent and discover for one's self? Can power to think be trained without developing initiative, invention and independence?

GREEK EDUCATION

The aim in this Section is to help the student put himself at the general Greek standpoint and compare the latter with the Chinese. The contrast between the two should not be carried so far as to ignore the like elements, such as the controlling ethical aim and the importance attached to literary masterpieces.

VIII. In the reference to D. it would be well to begin careful study with the third chapter. The statement of the three elements involved is so clear that nothing need be added. In Chapter IV the attitude of the Greeks toward slaves, women, outsiders and industrial and commercial pursuits should be noticed. To the statement made regarding the governing and the governed element it should be added that the Greek mind instinctively transferred this notion also to individual character. He thought of the soul as the union of desire and appetites needing to be ruled, and of reasons which ruled them. This involved the idea of self-control, and thus of freedom rather than control by coercion or external custom. With this idea should be compared what is said in the first chapter of D. regarding the Greek reverence for the ideas of measure, proportion and harmony. Self-control is identical with the idea of a sort of musical harmony of the various elements in character. It is intermediate between unregulated license on the one hand and external pressure on the other.

IX. In Chapter V note first (pp. 98 and 99) the important part played by participation in public affairs in the education of a Greek citizen. Contrast this idea of participation in current community life with the Chinese idea of conformity to the past. Note also the brief but excellent summary of the various geographical facts and historical events that conditioned the development of the great Greek people. The fact that the Greeks originated practically nothing in the strict sense of that word, but borrowed the beginnings of science, art and letters from Egypt, Phoenicia, Persia, etc., shows the important step in human history taken when the rule of custom is broken away from. These other peoples at one time had made an advance far beyond that of the Greeks of the same time; but in their cases science and art were so bound up with fixed and traditional beliefs and methods of doing things that progress was very slow, consisting mainly in accumulation; moreover, errors and useless lumber were also accumulated. The Greeks had the power to select what commended itself to reason and useful ends out of this combined treasure-house and old-lumber house. They changed what had been simply an accumulation into a method for future use. They thus started Europe on the path which it has pursued since the day of the Greeks. They changed progress from an accidental result into a principle of behavior.

X. Study M.'s account with reference to its points of agreement with D.'s. Note particularly the formula on p. 28, "the organization of society for the development of various aspects of personality." Can any higher ideal of education be found than a balance of complete individual development and complete participation in community life? In how many ways, according to the author, did the Greeks endeavor to secure the development of personality? In which of these respects was the Greek ideal inferior to that of Christianity? In which was it superior? What were the chief defects in the Greek realization of their own ideals?

XI. The brief study made of the education depicted by Homer is chiefly of importance not because of this historical period itself, but because of the part which the *Iliad* and the *Odyssey* played in the education of children and youth in the later Greek period. Homeric literature was almost what the Bible has been in certain periods of Christian education, with the marked difference that, like the books of Confucius for the Chinese, it was an outgrowth of their own life, so that a study of it was an introduction not merely into individual and social morality and into religion, but also into their own history. Add to this the strictly literary and aesthetic training involved in the fact that the Homeric poems have never been surpassed as works of literary art, and we get some idea of the many-sidedness of their educational influence, and also of why some of the later educational reformers, like Plato, were so anxious to limit and reduce the place occupied by the Homeric poems in education.

XII. The twofold ideals of a "speaker of words" and a "doer of deeds" presented at the very outset the permanent element in Greek education. (1) Importance was attached to speech because of its connection with thought and reason on the one hand, and on the other with social life—with ability to persuade and to counsel others and to learn from them. (Note what is quoted in this connection on p. 27 of Monroe's *Source Book* by Pericles regarding the importance of discussion as preparation for action.) (2) The conception of a "doer of deeds" connects itself with the importance in Greek education of the development and training of the body—a point upon which Greek education laid more emphasis than any other people known to history. Barbarian people have trained it for purposes of war; the Athenian Greeks so as to make it a better instrument of thought and emotion.

Questions for Your Report.

Compare and contrast Chinese and Greek education with respect to the following three points:

Q.1. Emphasis upon the moral element in education, and the sort of virtues aimed at in each.

Q.2. The importance of literature in the educational scheme of each.

Q.3. The ideal concerning the relation of the individual to social life held in view by each.

Q.4. Write a brief essay of from four to five hundred words stating what the school system of to-day might learn to advantage from either the Chinese or the Greek type of education, or both.

Q.5. Give an account of the examination system of the Chinese.

Q.6. Describe the education of the Homeric period.

Q.7. What factors in Greek life make it possible to say (see Davidson, *History*, p. 86) that "nothing moves in this world which is not Greek in its origin"?

Q.8. What are the main differences between the civic type of education and the savage and barbarian?

Supplementary References for Optional Reading.

Laurie, *Pre-Christian Education*—Chinese Education, pp. 103–152; General standpoint of Greek Education, pp. 196–226.

Monroe, *Text-Book.*

Section III

EARLY GREEK EDUCATION: CIVIC TYPE

Texts.

Monroe, *Source Book,* pp. 15–24.

Davidson, *Aristotle,* pp. 41–50.

Printed extracts from Gardner's *Manual of Greek Antiquities* (see p. 6, this Section).

Davidson, *Aristotle,* pp. 60–92.

Monroe, *Source Book,* pp. 31, 32, and 24–31.

Read the references in this order. The first two refer to Spartan education, all of the latter to Athenian education. In this study we are fortunate in being able to refer in part to original authorities and not merely to the interpretations of others. The student should, so far as possible, form his own judgments of the basis of the extracts from the sources and compare his own interpretations with those of Davidson.

Aids to Study and Suggestive Questions.

The type of education discussed in this exercise is called "civic," because of the thorough-going association of educational ideals, subject-matter and methods with community life.

The unit of Greek social life was the city-state. This community was small enough so that practically all free citizens were acquainted with one another. Generally it was an aristocratic republic, but with the democratic factor, the populace, gaining more and more power. They became pure, not representative democracies. Every citizen might take part in the legislative and judicial proceedings and might be drawn by lot to serve in an administrative position. Religion; art, in the acting of dramas, reciting of poems, in architecture and sculpture; games, athletic exercises, were all public, not private matters. Since commerce and industrial pursuits were despised by the Greeks, all free citizens of noble birth had plenty of leisure to engage in this public and sociable existence. If one looks at the plan of a Greek dwelling-house, he sees that it is adapted simply for eating and sleeping, so far as men are concerned, and beyond that for the household activities of the women.

It is impossible to understand the character of Greek education without keeping in mind the contrast of the Greek city with both the great and more or less despotic empires of antiquity and with the modern state which is so large in extent and so filled with specialized and private activities. Greek education was free as compared with other ancient types; it was public in its subject-matter and aims as compared with modern education; religion and art, as well as business affairs and home life, have now become mainly private matters. Athenian education, in particular, like Athenian life, was comparatively narrow and simple, but deep and concentrated. The citizen and the man were one, and hence the training of the man was the training of the citizen.

SPARTAN EDUCATION

The extract from Lycurgus greatly idealizes Spartan life. Its best aspects are put forward and its evil ones ignored or glossed over. The chapters from Davidson giving many of the same points put them in juster perspective. Three points may be specially noticed in the extract: (1) the survival of barbarian and even savage customs; (2) the subordination of private interests and initiative to public control; (3) the prominence of the military and warlike aims.

Sparta was always hostile to any such development of culture as was found in the Ionian portions of Greece, whether in Asia Minor or Italy or Athens. It regarded any high degree of culture as incompatible both with military efficiency and with the required subordination of the individual to public control.

ATHENIAN EDUCATION

The extracts from Gardner put one in possession of the outlying facts regarding (1) subject-matter or curriculum; (2) the administration of schools and the status of teachers, and (3) the division of education into three consecutive courses which compare fairly well, as Davidson points out, with our modern division into elementary, secondary and higher. The account of Davidson is so clear and simple that little need be suggested. In reading what is said about the important role of literature, it should be noted that there were at that time no sciences, no foreign languages, and no history even of their own people, save that found in literature. The perfection both in variety and form of Greek literature should also be borne in mind. It may fairly be said that if education were to be exclusively literary (on the intellectual side) a Greek city-state was better situated with reference to materials of education than any other people has ever been. The association of various styles of poetry—which it should be remembered were generally heard, not read—with music and frequently with gymnastics (dancing) should be noted. Only when these things are borne in mind can the great emphasis laid by the Greek authors upon rhythm and harmony be understood. Rhythm and harmony in their artistic aspects were never separated from their moral qualities in the Greek mind. Read, for example, *Source Book*, pp. 32, 222–231. This last extract is indeed from a writer who lived at a period much later, namely Plato, but what he says represents fairly enough the spirit of the best Greek education at that time. The reader will, of course, also note how the moral aim binds together the intellectual literary education and the physical (gymnastic) education, since the latter was to enable the individual to take his part in the festivals of peace and in the combats of war.

In the extract from Protagoras, the supremacy of the moral aims comes out very clearly; also the importance attached to persuasion in making the individual appreciate the value of acts and institutions; also the three stages in education together with the fact that political life—knowledge of the laws—was conceived as a form of education—or, otherwise put, that the function of life of the community is itself an educative one, in rounding out the life of the citizen.

Read the extracts from Pericles in the *Source Book* carefully with reference to getting all the material that bears on the following points: (1) The freedom of Athenian life; (2) the all-round development of personality; (3) the importance attached to the intellectual element—discussion, persuasion, etc.—in reference to action; (4) the thoroughly public character of life. In reading the extracts it is well to bear in mind that certain portions of them were intended to point a contrast between Athenian and Spartan ideals. The reference (*Source Book*, p. 25) to ancestors may be contrasted with the same notion as found in the Chinese, and also in our own times. The reference in the *Source Book*, p. 28, to Athens as "The School of Greece" brings out again the extent to which the Athenians conceived not only that education was for the sake of community life but also that community life was for the sake of the full development or education of the individual.

(*Selections from Gardner and Jevons's* Manual of Greek Antiquities *regarding Greek Education* [*Athenian*].)

NURSERY AND PRIMARY EDUCATION

"Until their seventh year boys and girls remained together in the nursery, watched and tended by mother and nurse. The girls, whose childhood lasted longer than that of the boys, amused themselves with dolls, of which many survive made of clay and painted, with arms and legs so fastened on with string as to be easily movable. The boys had go-carts and figures of soldiers and animals of the same material. Children of all times have rejoiced in the ball, the hoop and the whipping top. The swing was also a favourite plaything. The illustrious Archytas condescended to invent the child's rattle. Strepsiades in the *Clouds* relates with pride how his son Pheidippides when quite a little fellow had a mechanical turn; moulded houses and ships, made go-carts of leather, and frogs out of pomegranate rind. It was very easy for children to mould wax or clay, and if we might judge from the rudeness of many figures which have come down to us, we should find in them the work of childish hands. There were also plenty of social games, which the girls practised in their rooms, the lads in the streets. The general character of these was not one of vigorous competition or athletic exercise. A number game was a usual one with children. It was played with pieces of money or other small objects of which one player took a handful and the other guessed whether the number so taken was odd or even. Children also threw nuts as marbles are thrown with us to fall into a marked space. There were a few more boyish games such as that called by us 'French and English,' where two parties of boys pulled at the two ends of a rope; but no contest of skill for children like the modern football or cricket. If we may judge from the reliefs on the tombs, Greek children were very fond of animals and commonly made pets of them. Greek nurses were fond of frightening and amusing their charges with tales. Certain hobgoblins were specially kept for nursery use. The extraordinary richness of Greek legend and mythology must have supplied story-tellers with an endless stock of material. Both Plato and Aristotle would gladly have seen society take in hand the subject of nurses' tales, and work them to a more moral end; and it is easy to understand that there was very much in Greek mythology unfit for children to hear. Beast tales like those of Aesop were much in vogue.

"In regard to education in Greece, it must first be observed that it was a thing entirely of Greek invention. Almost all other civilized peoples have been largely influenced in education by the example of foreign nations, but in Greece we reach the very origin of all that can in the modern sense of the word be called *bringing up;* and the greatest philosophers and artists had in some cases an undeniable influence on its character. It was also directed to a consciously chosen end, the production of citizens worthy of the state, who would carry on in the future the best life of past ages."

PUBLIC ASPECT OF SCHOOL ADMINISTRATION

"It is not very easy to determine how far any education was compulsory at Athens. On the one hand, the laws of Solon seemed to have enjoined upon every father the duty of educating his sons. Plato speaks of the laws as commanding instruction with music and gymnastics. But, on the other hand, the only sanction to these laws of which we hear is the provision that a child whom his parents have neglected to educate was not bound to maintain them in old age.

"There were in Athens magistrates, who were appointed to inspect schools; but it is very improbable that they looked beyond mere outward order and propriety, or in any way controlled the course of study. In matters of outward decency, no doubt the regulations were strict. Aeschines speaks of laws regulating the hours of attendance of school, and fixing a limit to the number of pupils. He also declares that it was illegal to open schools before sunrise, or keep them open after sunset, no doubt in order that the boys might go to and fro by daylight. And we are even told that it was forbidden under pain of death for grown men to visit the schools; but a law of this kind can hardly have been kept. So long as sanitary and other regulations were observed, any one seems to have been at liberty to open a school, and his intellectual qualifications were regarded as the concern of himself and the parents of his pupils."

THE POSITION OF THE TEACHER

"It must be confessed that there was in Greece little of that love and confidence between teacher and scholar which has become in England, since Dr. Arnold's days, at least theoretically universal. Xenophon in the *Anabasis* says of Clearchus, 'he had no tact, but was severe and harsh; so that the relation of soldiers to him was like that of boys to a master; they did not follow him for love and good-will.' At a later age Lucian gives no pleasanter impression: 'Who ever came away from a feast weeping as we see boys coming from school? Or who was ever seen to go to a feast so sulkily as boys going to school?'

"The status of the teacher naturally varied, as with us, according to circumstances; but the tendency of the Greeks was to despise those who in any way taught for money, and to put them on a level with artisans. Naturally those who were most despised were the elementary teachers. The pay of these elementary teachers was no doubt very low, though we have no indication of its exact amount. Boarding-schools were not known among the Greeks. The time of school probably comprised the hours of light. Of course, the instructors in the higher branches of learning received a far higher rate of pay and more consideration, though even to them belonged the stigma, indelible to the Greek mind, of working for hire."

TEACHING READING

"Of the course pursued in teaching to read, Dionysius of Halicarnassus gives us an exact idea. 'First,' he says, 'we learn the names of the letters, then their shape and force. After that we join them into syllables and words. Then we learn about the component parts of sentences, nouns, verbs, and particles. Then we begin to read, slowly at first and by syllables.'" It will be noticed that this is the beginning of the alphabet and syllable method. But it should also be noted that Greek was written practically phonetically, and that there were irregularities in it. The same method is still universally employed in teaching Italian children to read—which language is also practically phonetic as written.

"In the above-mentioned process of forming letters into syllables, we know from a terra-cotta tablet that children were taught to repeat strings of similarly ending syllables like *ar, gar, mar,* etc., probably chanting them in classes. As soon as the boys could read, they were put upon the poems of Homer and Hesiod, and the moral writings of Theognis, Solon and the rest."

Questions for Your Report.

Q.1. Point out how the ideal of power in war influenced the Spartan methods of education.

Q.2. What points do you find in the selection from Pericles in which he appears to be praising the Athenian ideals as higher than the Spartan? (The book may be used in answering this question.)

Q.3. Describe the education of the "family period" in the life of the child.

Q.4. How did the Greek schoolboy spend his day? What was a pedagogue?

Q.5. Describe the physical education of the Athenian boy.

Q.6. Why was their literary and intellectual education called music?

Q.7. What was the relation between the study of literature and moral training?

Q.8. Describe briefly the period called by Davidson the "college" period.

Q.9. State the things in Greek education which justify the statement that it was social in subject-matter, purpose and method.

Q.10. What subjects enter into the course of study to-day that were lacking in the Greek? Why were they absent?

Supplementary References for Optional Readings.
   Laurie, *Pre-Christian Education;* pp. 228–248, "Spartan Education"; pp. 248–282, "Athenian Education."
   Monroe, *Text-Book.*

Section IV

THE "WISE MEN" AND SOCRATES; INTELLECTUAL EDUCATION

Texts.
   Monroe, *Source Book,* Chap. III, The New Greek Education, pp. 51–116, 117–119.
   Monroe, *History,* pp. 52–63.
   Davidson, *Aristotle,* pp. 93–113.

Aids to Study and Suggestive Questions.
   I. Read first introductory portion of the *Source Book,* pp. 51–66, in a general way, noting the following points:

(1) What is said about the growth of individualism in the fifth and fourth centuries B.C. (pp. 51–54. This is amplified in Monroe's *History* and in Davidson).

(2) The account given of each of the four sources later quoted (pp. 54–58).

(3) The effect of the general intellectual changes upon education (pp. 58–66).

II. Read the extract from Aristophanes, rereading in connection with it pp. 55, 56. Much in this quotation is, of course, intended purely for comedy and is not strictly relevant. The following points bearing on the intellectual movement may be noticed:

(1) The hits at the various new scientific ideas regarding astronomy, etc.; for example, on pp. 67, 69, 71, 87. It should be borne in mind that the sun, moon and heavenly bodies generally were associated in the Greek mind with religious practices and ideas, so that new ideas about them were regarded as irreligious; Anaxagoras, for example, who had taught that the sun was of the same material as the earth, was banished from Athens for atheism. "Science" itself was naturally of a somewhat speculative character and lent itself easily to ridicule and caricature.

(2) Notice the hits at mere cleverness in talking and arguing; as, for example, the bottom of p. 72 and top of p. 75.

(3) Note the charges against the philosophers of attempting to unsettle and overthrow ethical ideas; for example, pp. 80 and 90.

(4) Note the charge of encouraging practices among the young which undermined their morality and thereby destroyed the traditional virtues of the Greek people, pp. 82–86 (the account in Davidson, pp. 99–104, may be compared with this). In reading it may be noticed that all the ridicule is not directed at the new teachers. The old, conservative type comes in incidentally for ridicule.

III. The first quotation from Isocrates may be read rapidly; the only passages of particular importance are (1) the attacks on the pretentiousness and the greediness of the sophists (pp. 91, 92) and (2) the effort to describe the kind of literary subjects that may properly be taught (p. 92). The second quotation from him also may be read casually to the bottom of p. 103. The latter portion is significant as an attempt to justify the great usefulness of training in literature. This is identified with philosophy— the love of wisdom and goodness—and is distinguished from speculation about nature and from logical training in disputation, both of which are spoken of contemptuously (p. 107). The passage at the top of p. 107 regarding speech that it is "the power which has civilised human life" might almost be taken as a motto of this new educational movement.

IV. The quotation from Plato really makes the transition from the topic of this section to that of the next. The most significant things in it are (1) the analogy of education to the nurture of plants; the idea of growth depending on right environment, an idea which has never disappeared from the theory of education since Plato's time; and (2) the attack upon the perverting and corrupting influence of the existing social environment of Athens, and the consequent necessity of complete reform.

V. It is difficult either from extracts or from other accounts of the sophists to get an adequate idea of the full force of the intellectual and educational movements represented by them. They present for the first time in the history of Europe a class of professional teachers separate from other interests and callings; they were the first who made a business of teaching for the sake of intellectual results. Schools in the modern sense, that is as institutions for the conveying of instruction and the training of the intellect, begin with them. Their importance for education, then, cannot be realized by comparing them with present-day conditions, but only by contrasting them with what went before. Up to this time knowledge and skill had been distinctly community affairs, bound up with the customs and aims of particular localities. The sophists freed knowledge and training in various forms of skill from their traditional setting, and claimed ability to impart them on a theoretical basis, as an intellectual technique. This doubtless hastened the disintegration of social life which was going on, but for the most part the sophistic movement was an effect rather than a cause of this social change. Monroe's account of the sophists is correct, so far as it goes, but the statement that their purposes were wholly individualistic (p. 63) is an exaggeration, and Davidson's statements are mostly exaggerated on this subject. Many of the sophists were what would now be termed humanists; aiming, by teaching literature and other social studies, to make the Greek states more conscious of their common language, literature and religion, and thereby to bring them into more friendly relations with each other. (Note, for example, what Isocrates says about the bearing of his work upon the politics "of all Hellas," p. 98 and again p. 100.) Even the saying that "Man is the measure of all things" was probably not meant in an individualistic sense, but rather was intended to emphasize the value of culture and civilization of humanity as against barbarism and animal nature.

Summing up, the sophists

(1) Were the first to aim systematically and professionally at general intellectual training.

(2) To introduce literature as an object of study; not merely as means to moral training, but as an end in itself.

(3) To introduce the rudiments of geometry, astronomy, and forms of physical knowledge.

(4) To attempt to train effective speakers and writers, involving the theory of persuasion and argument, and thus introducing the topic of logic.

(5) To call attention to the training in the arts relating to statesmanship and thus introducing the topics of political science and political economy.

(6) Great numbers of treatises were written at this time upon all the arts, as, for example, agriculture, weaving, dyeing, medical treatment, training of horses, fighting in heavy and light armor, tactics, etc.

Thus there was an attempt to work out on a basis of intellectual principle a sort of encyclopedia of the various arts of human life.

Whatever, therefore, may be urged against the individual sophists or even against the moral effects of the sophistic movement as a whole, they have fundamental significance for education in the fact that they originated for civilization the *ideals,* and, in their first crude form, much of the material of modern intellectual training and discipline. Upon the whole, the best way to get the meaning of the term "sophist" is to translate it "professional educator."

VI. Upon Socrates, compare what is said in Monroe's *History,* pp. 60–63, and Monroe's *Source Book,* pp. 118–120, and in Davidson, pp. 107–111.

Nothing is known absolutely at first hand regarding Socrates. He was regarded by the average Greek of his own time as one of the sophists and was finally put to death on the stock charges brought against all sophists, of denying the gods of the state and of corrupting the youth. The following points marked him off, however, from the other sophists:

(1) He was an Athenian devoted to his own state, not a cosmopolitan and traveling teacher.

(2) He took no pay, claiming that improvement of others was a sufficient reward.

(3) He employed the conversational method, method of dialogue or question and answer (the technical term "dialectics" comes from the same word as "dialogue"), not the method of lecture or harangue. According to him, the dialogue method was intellectually and morally better than the lecture method because (*a*) its aim was social, mutual improvement, not merely dogmatic instruction or refutation of another; (*b*) it involved search and inquiry, and thus the modest claim of being "a lover of wisdom" (philo-sopher) and not the pretentious claim of being already wise or a sophist; (*c*) the search for truth through conversation, or question and answer, implied underlying principles and aims common to both parties, which, if they could be brought to light, would furnish the universal standard of truth, remove all controversy and bring the parties to one mind and one mode of action.

(4) The method of Socrates involved the following points: First, bringing about a consciousness of ignorance by making one aware of inconsistencies and self-contradictions in his existing beliefs and opinions. Second, the clearing up and defining of ideas. Socrates seems to have been the first to insist upon the necessity of definitions as fundamental to all thinking in order that one might know just what he meant and stick to it. Third, the development in detail of the consequences and bearings of the ideas formulated in the definitions—the method which ever since the time of Socrates has been called "the developing method."

(5) The essential significance of Socrates is that he restored to the intellectual movement the moral basis and purpose which other sophists had left out in their interest in knowledge for its own sake. Socrates stood deliberately for the attempt to combine in education the moral values of community life with the intellectual methods of free inquiry. He held that virtue is the end of education, while only through inquiry and reflection is it possible to attain to virtue. Thus, like the sophists, he marks the end of the dominance of local customs in human life; the substitution of

intelligence for tradition. But, unlike them, he insists that it is because intelligence is the necessary foundation of moral life that it is of supreme importance. Because he was the first man clearly to conceive the necessity of the union of intellectual training and moral aims in education and because he suffered death for the loyalty with which he held to this conviction, Socrates may fairly be regarded as the patron saint of teachers.

Questions for Your Report.

Q.1. What historical changes brought about the changes in education?

Q.2. In response to what demands did the sophists arise?

Q.3. Why did the words "sophistic" and "sophistry" (see dictionary, if necessary) get a bad meaning?

Q.4. What changes were finally effected in the subject-matter of education?

Q.5. What changes in the methods of teaching?

Q.6. What similarities were there between their educational problem and that of the present day in our own country?

Q.7. What was the belief of Socrates regarding the relation of knowledge and virtue? How did this affect his idea of education?

Q.8. Why did Aristophanes attack the sophists and Socrates?

Q.9. Do Davidson and Monroe interpret this period differently? In what respects? Which seems to be nearer the truth?

Q.10. To what extent is individualism encouraged to-day in the schools you know best? Is it too much or too little encouraged in your opinion?

Supplementary References for Optional Readings.

Grote, *History of Greece,* on the sophists.

Mahaffy, *Old Greek Education.*

Wilkins, *National Education in Greece.*

Psychology for Teachers

This course is designed to supply a knowledge of the principles of human nature in its intellectual, emotional and moral workings with reference to the needs of the teacher. It is assumed that these needs require a knowledge of the human mind in its growth and development; of the conditions, physical and social, which are helpful or harmful to right growth; and of mental operations and processes rather than states and results. Hence the mode of treatment is genetic or developing, or dynamic.

METHOD

Explanation.

This course consists of twenty sections. Each section is divided into three parts: (1) Directions for study. This assigns the portions of the texts to be read, or tells *what* is to be studied. (2) Aids and suggestive questions in studying. This part endeavors to show the student *how* to study. (3) Test questions. Answers to these are to be written and sent in for the information of the instructor, and as a basis for his corrections, criticisms and further guidance of the pupil.

Directions to Students.

1. In psychology more than in almost any other subject, real progress depends upon the use the student makes of his own experience and memory. Use the texts as *aids in directing* your own observations of others and yourself, your recollections of your

[First published by the School of Liberal Arts and Sciences for Non-Residents, New York, N.Y., 1907–8; Sections I, III–VII are extant.]

past experiences, and your thought about them, but not as a substitute for these things. Only in the first Section is it necessary to depend exclusively upon the authority of others.

2. Read systematically; lay out your time in advance; it is much better to read a little every day than to save up a large amount of reading for some one spare time. Use the longer periods at your command, however, to organize your subject-matter, and to write your required papers. An average of an hour and a half a day should be given if possible. To complete the course in a year a Section should be covered every two weeks. When the student cannot command much free time it would be better to arrange in advance to take a longer time for each Section.

3. Form the habit of thinking while you read, rather than of trying to memorize. Take care of your understanding of the subject, and your memory will take care of itself. This understanding will be helped by keeping a note-book systematically. Write in it an analysis of the subject; notes of points not understood; observations and experiences of your own that illustrate or seem to refute statements in the texts.

4. Required papers. The questions asked are intended primarily to assist and test the student's thought and comprehension, only secondarily his memory. Occasionally more set questions (in the nature of an examination on the text) will be sent out. The student's note-book may also be required in order to test the thoroughness of study.

5. Observe carefully in all the exercises the following directions; violation of them may occasion the total rejection of the student's paper:

6. Write your name, the title of the course and the number of the Section upon each sheet.

7. Write with ink (or typewriter) upon one side of the paper only.

8. Make answers as brief and concise as is consistent with clearness.

REFERENCES

Texts.
Angell, J. R., *Psychology.* Referred to as A.
Thorndike, E. L., *Elements of Psychology.* Referred to as Th.
  Angell's and Thorndike's Psychologies are both standard

and recent texts, embodying what is more sure and least controversial in the present condition of the subject. They both emphasize the dynamic and functional aspects of the human mind. Differing in their arrangement of topics, they admirably supplement each other. The illustrations in Thorndike are excellent. The "exercises" at the end of each chapter are concrete and practical, and are of even more value to a correspondence student than to one in personal contact with a teacher. The student should use them constantly to check his study. The arrangement in Angell is very orderly and systematic and the language as clear as the technicalities of the subject will permit. Somewhat more difficult than Thorndike, it affords a more complete and advanced knowledge of the subject.

Thorndike, E. L., *The Human Nature Club*. Referred to as *H.N.C.*

A sketchy and popular book, but reliable, and may generally be used in connection with each Section to gain an introductory bird's-eye view of the topic. Questions are rarely based upon it.

Optional Readings.

In addition to these, the School will supply at cost the following books for optional supplementary readings. No required work will be based upon these books, but some students may like to have them in their libraries as means of extending their reading on special points:

Höffding, H., *Outlines of Psychology*.

A translation of a work for somewhat advanced students by an eminent Danish psychologist.

James, William, *Psychology*.

An abbreviated edition of Professor James' large two-volume work on the *Principles of Psychology*, which is the most important single contribution to the subject.

Morgan, C. L., *Psychology for Teachers*.

While somewhat lacking in detail and in reference to concrete school conditions, this book is a suggestive statement of some important general principles.

Stout, G. F., *Groundwork of Psychology*.

A clear account by an eminent English psychologist of the subject-matter of psychology, with emphasis upon the active factors.

Titchener, E. B., *An Outline of Psychology.*
An especially clear work in analysis, and strong upon the experimental side.

TOPICS

     I. The Relation of Physical and Mental Action.
    II. General Aspects of Mental Action.
   III. The Instincts and Impulses.
   IV. The Emotions.
    V. The Beginnings of Will.
   VI. Habit and Association.
  VII. Attention.
 VIII. Discrimination.
   IX. The Senses and Sensation.
    X. Recognition and Observation.
   XI. Perception of Space and Time.
  XII. Imagination and Imagery.
 XIII. Memory.
 XIV. The Nature of Thought.
  XV. The Processes of Reasoning.
 XVI. The Affections.
XVII. The Developed Will.
XVIII. Character.
 XIX. The Self or Personality.
  XX. Psychology and Training.

Section I

THE PHYSICAL BASIS OF MENTAL ACTION

Specific Directions.

The assigned readings are (in this order): Th., *H.N.C.,* pp. 7–19; Th., *Psychology,* pp. 120–162; A., pp. 11–46. The subject is a difficult and complicated one, but the first reference gives all that is indispensable, and should be read thoroughly first. The two other references may be postponed, and read only in connection with the "Aids" which follow.

Aids and Suggestive Questions.

I. What evidence is there of general connection between mental and and physical activities? Read Th., p. 120, and A., pp. 11–14. Compare the statements with your own observation and experience.

II. What is the general *structure* of the nervous system? Read Th., chap. IX, studying especially the pictures, which are unusually good. Connect your study with the idea of the neurone (A., p. 15) and of the system as the sum of all neurones. If necessary, get rid of any previous idea you may have of there being any fundamental difference between "cells" and "fibers."

III. What are the *functions* of this structure? Just what do you understand by structure and function? (Consult the dictionary, if needed.) What is the significance of the sensory, the motor, the associative functions, respectively? Is the difference between animals and man *primarily* in the first two or in the last? (Read the discussion in A., pp. 38–43, noting especially the statement near the top of p. 42. Compare with Th., p. 149.)

IV. What is the physical basis of "learning by experience"? Read Th., p. 146, on modifiability.

V. Keeping in mind the general statement about the purpose of the nervous system (*H.N.C.*, p. 19, note; Th., pp. 161–162; A., pp. 14 and 20), think out the different sorts of adaptation required when features in the environment are permanent and regular, and when they are variable and novel; and the connection with this of the chief portions of the system, viz., (*a*) the spinal cord (A., pp. 24–27); (*b*) portions between the spinal cord and cerebrum (A., pp. 28–32); and (*c*) the cerebrum (A., p. 32).[1]

VI. What is the difference, on the physical side, between (i) adaptation to surrounding temperature; (ii) adaptation of dodging to ward off a blow, and (iii) adaptation through planning a method to ward off some danger likely to happen in the future? What are the sensory, the motor and the associative features of each case? What about the respective importance of previous *modification* in each case?[2]

1. Do not be confused by the anatomical details, but keep in mind the general problem of adjustment just mentioned.
2. This question may be used to organize your knowledge of the whole topic, and also as a test to see how clearly you understand the matter. If the answer to this question is fairly clear, the object of Section I has been attained.

Questions for Your Report.

The profit of the course lies primarily in your own reading, observing, thinking, only secondarily in the writing of answers. Make your answers as concise and definite as possible. Vague and diffuse writing confuses the student and leaves the instructor less able to give needed correction and assistance.

Q.1. Give examples from your own experience of the close connection between mental and physical action.

Q.2. Show by some illustrative case (real or imaginary) how knowledge of the physical condition of a pupil is helpful to the teacher.

Q.3. What bearing does the conception that the purpose of the nervous system is adaptation of conduct to its conditions have upon education? Consider under three heads: (i) sense-training; (ii) motor-training; (iii) intellectual training. What *kind* of intellectual training violates this principle?

Q.4. Mention all the kinds of motor-training the child gets out of school. The kinds that he gets in school.

Q.5. Judging from this one topic or section, of what use do you think a knowledge of psychology will be to a teacher? Why?

Q.6. Mention the points that you have had the most difficulty in grasping and understanding.

Q.7. After reading the exercises in Th., pp. 177–183, write out an account of the results you get in some one (any one) of the experiments there given.

Section III

REFLEX ACTION AND INSTINCTIVE ACTIVITY

Texts.

Angell, *Psychology,* Chaps. XV, XVI.
Thorndike, *Psychology,* Chap. XII.
Review *Human Nature Club,* Chap. II, and Angell, pp. 48, 49.

Aids to Study and Suggestive Questions.

This section is a development of what was presented in the last section regarding "unlearned activities." It takes up in detail the original human native activities. The importance for the educator, whether parent or teacher, of knowledge of the native endowment and equipment of the being to be educated, is obvious. Upon the side of subject-matter, comparatively few suggestions need be given, as the treatment, especially in Angell, Chap. XVI, is straightforward and clear. The following points may, however, require special emphasis:

1. The connection between sensory-motor adjustment (adaptation of response to stimulus) and power of control. Compare Angell, pp. 53, 54. Compare cases in which you have control, with those in which you have not, e.g., running a locomotive, reading Hebrew, etc.

2. The comparative definiteness of instincts in animals and in human young; the extent to which systematic instincts in animals are tendencies in humans; the connection of man's greater power to learn, or make new adaptations.

3. The connection of this greater indefiniteness and also the lesser rapidity in manifestation of instincts (*H.N.C.*, p. 24) in the human young with the greater *helplessness* of the latter, and this in turn with the greater power to acquire new things, to progress beyond fixed limits.

4. Note carefully the principle of the *modifiability* of reflexes and instincts. Compare this with what was said on the subject of plasticity of nervous system in Section I.

5. Compare and contrast the principle of *delayed* instincts with that of transitory or suppressed instincts.

6. Consider thoughtfully the problem presented in A., p. 293 and pp. 295, 296, regarding the preservation within the human being of instincts once useful, but now harmful. As will be brought out below, this suggests one of the most fundamental questions of education.

7. With reference to such a list as is given in A., p. 297, consider yourself and other persons of your acquaintance, with regard to the *relative* strength or predominance of one or other of the instinctive tendencies in different individuals; and the effect of this upon the person as a whole. A. does not perhaps bring out clearly enough the principle of individual variation. Consult upon this point Th., pp. 193–195.

EDUCATIONAL APPLICATIONS

Many groups of problems at once suggest themselves.

I. The questions of the last section should be reviewed. Consider the significance of the kindergarten activities; of so-called kindergarten methods in primary grades; the introduction of sewing, cooking, and manual training; clay modeling; sand-working; school gardens; excursions; painting, drawing; the use of dramatic plays in teaching reading; of building blocks, measuring and weighing in number teaching; laboratory work in science. Have these tendencies in education been considered far enough? Is there still need of making more connection between *intellectual* acquisitions and practical, motor activities? Is it true that present schools appeal, upon the whole, to those in whom abstract intellectual tendencies are strongly marked rather than to those of artistic or executive habit of mind? Give reasons for answer.

II. "Are the present arrangements regarding reading and writing in the schools most likely to err from relying on delayed instincts too soon or from appealing to transitory instincts too late?" (Noted from Thorndike, *Principles of Teaching,* p. 35.)

III. Are there dangers attendant upon precocity—that is, premature development of capacities? Are these dangers attendant upon a child learning quite early to do a *specialized* thing very well? What do you understand by arrested development? Can you think of any instances of it? What were the causes? (Aside from sickness or accident.) Do not, however, look for instances simply among the obviously feeble-minded; almost every one presents arrested development in some direction.

IV. What position is assigned to instinctive tendencies in the statement that "it is the business of teaching to utilize instinctive tendencies for ideal ends"? Do you think this definition of education is true? Do teachers generally act upon this idea? When they do not, what idea of education do they substitute for it?

V. (*a*) What difficulties arise from the fact that the natural expression of some instincts is harmful or morally undesirable—perhaps of all instincts under some conditions? (*b*) How shall the parent or teacher deal with these difficulties? (Study carefully Th., pp. 196–198; the questions on the latter page should be carefully considered.) (*c*) It has been said, "Respect always the original reactions, even when you are seeking to supplant them." Is this possible, or is it self-contradictory? What does it mean when applied, say, to anger, excessive secretiveness? (*d*) What is the relative importance of threats, command, distraction, arranging of conditions beforehand, argument, etc., with respect to se-curing disuse of a bad tendency? What are the objections to the method of crushing out or sheer suppression? (Compare this with the old idea of breaking the will. Consider the conditions which tend to change pugnacity into irritability, into sullenness or into forcefulness of character.)

VI. (a) Make a list of traditional school studies (reading, writ-ing, arithmetic, etc.). Go over the list of instincts (A., p. 297) and see which are utilized by each, which left untouched in the main.

(b) Do the same for music, drawing, painting, clay-modeling.

(c) The same for the various kinds of constructive work and manual training.

VII. Consider the effect of different methods of school disci-pline upon the social and anti-social instincts, i.e., sociability and sympathy on the one side, rivalry, jealousy, envy, etc., on the other. Do traditional methods appeal especially to the motives which divide or which unite people? Can the sociable instinct of communication be utilized or must it be repressed in the interests of silence and quiet? Consider the general effect of great atten-tion to marks, examinations, grading and promotion, writing names on board, urging children to work more quickly or accu-rately than others.

Questions for Your Report.

Q.1. Distinguish reflex action, instinct and acquired habit, giv-ing an instance of each.

Q.2. State briefly the various theories regarding the origin of instinct.

Q.3. Classify the sixteen instincts named in A., p. 297, with reference (a) to which show least and which most accompanying emotional excitement; (b) which are of most and which of least importance intellectually; (c) which are the most and the least important from the standpoint of practical external results.

Q.4. Analyze cases of mischievousness, and show to what pri-mary instincts they go back. Suggest methods by which the in-stinct might be trained to useful ends. Do the same thing for cases of bullying and teasing.

Q.5. Suggest methods of teaching geography which utilize the instinct of curiosity, social sympathy, play and constructiveness.

Q.6. Suggest a method whereby the instinct of rivalry might

be so directed that the individual competes with himself—that is, to improve himself rather than against others.

Q.7. Write out your answer to 5 under Aids to Study.

Q.8. Write out your answer to II under Aids to Study.

Q.9. Write out your answer to V under Aids to Study.

Q.10. Write out your answer to VI under Aids to Study.

Section IV

THE EMOTIONS

Texts.

Thorndike, *Human Nature Club*, Chap. X.

Angell, *Psychology*, Chaps. XVIII, XIX.

Thorndike, *Psychology*, Chap. V.

The chapter in *The Human Nature Club* should be read over in advance to get a general idea of the topic. The two chapters in Angell attempt both a description and an explanation of the emotional facts, and our main study is accordingly based upon them. The chapter in Thorndike's *Psychology* is mainly confined to the classification of the emotions.

Aids to Study and Suggestive Questions.

So far we have been concerned with mental activities, with only incidental reference to the state or frame of mind accompanying them. We here enter upon the study of personal conditions and variations. On one hand, emotion is an act. By anger, for example, we ordinarily mean the readiness and tendency to behave in a certain way. As an act, it may be externally and correctly described by one who has never experienced it. But anger as a condition of mind could be described only when one knows what it feels like to be angry. (In reading the accounts given of the James theory it is particularly important to bear in mind that he is not concerned so much with what emotion is as an act as how it feels to be angered.)

1. The study commences with the act side of emotion. A point to bear in mind is its connection with instincts. Read Angell, pp. 297, 315, and Thorndike, p. 82.

2. The chapter in *The Human Nature Club* introduces the theory of Professor James; in connection with this read Angell's *Psychology*, pp. 317–319. According to this the emotion is the instinctive reaction turned, as it were, outside-in, so that what we feel when we are angry or sad is constituted by the various organic and muscular disturbances which accompany the discharge.

3. Endeavor to connect what is said about the classification of the emotions in Thorndike's Chap. V with the instinctive reactions of the organism. The agreeable is associated with attraction toward the thing; the disagreeable, with reaction away from it. The other two sets, namely excitement and depression, and strain or tension and relief, are obviously connected with organic conditions of activity.

4. Angell, p. 322, brings out the connection of the emotion on its feeling side with consciousness. If the statement on p. 322 be compared with what we earlier had on pp. 50–52, the identity of the principle employed in explaining emotion with that employed in explaining consciousness will be perceived. From this point of view all states of consciousness are emotional. Consider the different ways the same object feels when one is elated or depressed or bored or irritated or frightened or hopeful. Externally there is but one description or account which can be given of a battle, but if one considers the different states of mind in those who have been defeated and those who have won the victory— how different the battle seems to them—one will appreciate how it is the emotions which mark off conditions of consciousness. There is no way in which the student can so well realize what the psychologist means when he talks of "consciousness" as by calling up such experiences as fear, anger, joy, sorrow, embarrassment, love, hate, etc. And while remembering that the external world remains the same, note the difference which these various emotions make in his feelings about them—the way the objects are colored for him. One of the chief values of this section to the student should be to enable him to appreciate better what is meant by consciousness as distinct from object.

5. The same point of view is carried out in greater fullness in Angell, pp. 325–335, where it is shown that the bodily postures and movements that mark off, say, the emotion of anger from that of fear, may be regarded as survivals of acts which were once useful on their own account, and which have now become partial

because interfered with by other tendencies. The emotion is thus a sign of the shock in passing from one kind of activity to another, not compatible with it; of the stress and strain involved in trying to adjust activities in themselves disconnected to one another, or, as in the case of joy and sorrow, of the successful completion or the failure of one activity to overcome conflicting or rival activities. (This should be compared with Wundt's threefold classification.) Emotion is disturbance, agitation, excitement, or connected with it.

6. What is briefly said in Angell, pp. 335, 336, about mood and sentiment is very important and the student should go over his personal experience until he can find plenty of illustrations. The effect of mood upon intellectual and practical activities should be noted; also the effect of dominating types of sentiment upon character. What we mean by disposition is, upon its psychological side, little else than habitual prevailing sentiment.

7. Note carefully all the allusions to the expression of emotions—e.g., Angell, pp. 316, 317, as to anger; p. 320, as to fear; also 329; joy, 324, 333. Then observe others, and see how largely our ability to "read" the character and mood of others is connected with these emotional discharges. Observe pictures, actors, etc., to see what are generally regarded as the typical expressions of the chief emotions. (Darwin's book on the *Expression of Emotions* gives many photographs.) Think of a man as meditative, as astonished, as disgusted, as envious, as jovial, as irritable. What characteristic bodily postures, gestures and states do you call up? Put yourself as nearly as may be in the same postures, etc. Do you feel anything approaching the emotion? How does your state of mind change when you frown severely and purse your lips; when you curl your lips in scorn, when you smile and relax? Do you know anything about the Delsarte system? If so, do you see any connection between it and this psychological teaching? What would be the effect upon a man's disposition of keeping his muscles constantly in tension, screwed up bodily postures, etc.?

8. There is nothing said here directly about the connection of emotions and intellectual life; but the subject is of great importance educationally. When one is sad, is it easy to call up ideas connected with joyful subjects? If they are called up and held before the mind what is the effect on the emotion? What is the in-

tellectual effect of dislike to a teacher or to a subject? Why does one remember most easily what he is most interested in? What emotions are most helpful to the work of teaching? Which are the most hindrance? Can an emotion (like jealousy) be useful so far as learning a lesson is concerned, and yet be harmful to the character? What is the effect of frequently arousing emotions of emulation in a pupil? What conditions are most conducive to arousing curiosity?

Questions for Your Report.

Q.1. Write out your replies to the first ten of the exercises of Thorndike, p. 83.

Q.2. Write out an answer to exercises 15 and 16, Thorndike, p. 84.

Q.3. What differences do you note between the expression of emotions in children and in grown-up people? Give a concrete case in illustration of your reply.

Q.4. (*a*) What is the effect upon an emotion of acting upon it without resistance, that is, of giving way freely to it?

(*b*) What is the effect of trying to subdue or check it by direct effort?

(*c*) What is the effect of affording circumstances which are congenial and produce joyful emotions, upon tasks which otherwise call out disagreeable emotions? Give illustrations in support of your answer, in each of these points.

Q.5. State the James theory of emotions briefly, and give all the objections you have to it, and the difficulties you find in it.

Q.6. Which one of the various classifications of emotions given by Thorndike do you prefer and why?

Q.7. Illustrate Angell's doctrine of "interruption" and "overflow" in the case of at least three emotions.

Q.8. State what you understand by "mood" and by "temperament." Give a description of what you regard as the temperament of some one whom you know.

Q.9. (*a*) Give the result of your thinking and observations regarding the intellectual influence of emotions—that is, their relation to leading facts and ideas.

(*b*) Give your answer to the query as to the conditions most favorable to arousing curiosity.

Q.10. (*a*) Do you think teachers as a rule pay enough attention to the emotional attitudes and reactions of children in the matters of study?

(*b*) Are they as important with respect to study as they are for matters of discipline?

(*c*) What is the effect of being interested or uninterested in a study? What emotions are active when one is interested? Are all emotions which arouse interest of equal value? Which are most so? Which are least so? (Give the reason for your answer in each case.)

Section V

THE BEGINNINGS OF WILL

Texts.
   Thorndike, *Human Nature Club,* Chap. XI.
   Thorndike, *Psychology,* pp. 274–290.
   Angell, *Psychology,* Chap. XX.

Aids to Study and Suggestive Questions.
   1. It will be noted that part of this material reviews the same ground that has been already traversed. Whatever involuntary action involves, it must at least include certain powers which are instinctive; it must include also impulsive tendencies, leanings, drawings in a given direction. The voluntary act, accordingly, includes the material discussed in Section III. It also involves power of controlling movement so that it is a means of realizing some aim or purpose. This takes us back also to what was discussed in Sections I and II. The study, then, appropriately may be commenced with reviewing carefully A., pp. 53–56, on the Beginning of Motor Control. Then read for advanced study pp. 347–352. In order to fix more clearly the points involved, read then in review *H.N.C.,* Chap. III. What A. calls the principle of excess discharge and accidental success with elimination of useless movements, covers precisely the same ground as Th.'s "trial and success" method.
   2. This review material gives us the background of a voluntary act. The voluntary act proper contains, however, necessarily at

least one additional factor, namely, an idea of mental conception, an intention, aim, purpose, plan, etc. This serves as the basis of selecting appropriate movements, and as the principle of their direction or guidance. *H.N.C.*, pp. 127–132, brings out clearly the difference between cases where (1) the mere occurrence of an idea suffices to set in operation a train of acts, an idea calling up a movement just as one movement might call up another movement, and (2) the case of voluntary action proper, where the idea which is to direct the movement has first to be deliberately and intentionally built up. (The first type is frequently called ideo-motor action.) Take the illustrations given by A. on p. 342 and see which are cases of ideo-motor action and which of volition proper. Go over as many of your own acts of the last few hours as you can recall and see in how many cases (1) an idea just occurred to you which you then promptly acted upon; and in how many cases (2) you had first to consider either whether the idea itself was satisfactory or mentally search for the best means of carrying it out. The less thought which is given either to the plan or purpose or to the means for reaching it, the less voluntary is the act—the less is it an act of will. The more we consider before acting what plan is the wise or right one, and the more we consider the best course of action for realizing it, the more truly the act is voluntary.

3. Now read what is said in *H.N.C.*, pp. 132–135, and in A., p. 345, "Attention and Volition," regarding the importance of attention. In the first illustration which A. gives on p. 342, it is clear that a minimum of attention will do; the thought of what is to be done need not occupy the mind more than a fraction of a minute. With the case of "Whether or not to incorporate a certain subject in the text," attention may be occupied a long time, possibly at intervals for days. At important junctures of life a man may have a certain plan under consideration for months before coming to a conclusion. Now if you will go over the illustrations in the text (or still better, the cases which you can call up from your own experience) you will find that the cases where a minimum of attention is sufficient are those in which the idea of a single end is present; while the cases in which long deliberation is required are those in which alternative ideas of results present themselves—ends which are incompatible with each other; so that when one idea starts to pass into action it is prevented from

doing so because a rival idea suggests another mode of behavior. This stress and strain of conflicting ends and purposes gives intense and concentrated attention. Sometimes one of the ends is naturally more agreeable than the others; then we would like to have it pass over immediately into action, but another end seems more reasonable though less pleasant. Here the strain upon attention, the effort to keep the mind on the whole subject, is specially marked. (The conflict may of course come after the end has been settled, and concern the best means of carrying it out, but such conflict is usually less of a strain.)

4. Upon the subject of the mental precursors of voluntary movements, opposing theories seem to be proffered by A. (top of p. 343 to the section of Attention, bottom of p. 345) and Th. (Section 52, pp. 281–284). A., following James, insists that some anticipatory idea or image of the result to be reached must be present as the forerunner of the act. In some cases this idea is that of the act; in other cases that of indirect or remote results of the act. Th. (p. 282) says any mental state whatever may be the antecedent, and again (p. 283) says the doctrine that an idea "of the previous results of a movement" is a necessary antecedent to the movement is a perverse mistake. This conflict of views is partly verbal; for what A. means by "remote effect," as seen in his illustration on pp. 344, 345, regarding the case of an investment, covers ground which Th. does not include under effects at all. By remote feelings (Th., p. 282) Th. means quite direct products of the movement itself, as will be seen from his illustrations; while A. means such indirect and vague things as anticipation of the profit, etc., to be derived—points which certainly could not be reduced to any such definite sensations as Th. has in mind on p. 282. Moreover, A. would not limit the idea of the end to be reached to "some one of the previous results of the movement" in the most literal sense of "previous." The imagination may readapt images of previous results; after, however, allowances have been made for the different meanings given to the words used there still remains the fact that A. insists that some idea of the result to be reached is a necessary antecedent of the voluntary act, while Th. denies it. This difference of opinion gives the student a good opportunity for drawing independently upon his own experiences to settle the matter. Recall and observe as many cases as you can from your own experience and see which view

they bear out. In doing so, be careful to discriminate between the cases where an idea passes into action as soon as it occurs, and the cases where thought is employed about either the means or the end. Take the illustration on the top of p. 284 of Th. Note under which head it should fall. Does a man voluntarily seek food merely because he now feels empty, or because he also recalls the satisfaction which he has had in the past from eating, or does he think of a meal ready and waiting for him somewhere, etc.? Do you find any cases of deliberative action where there is not an anticipation of the future based to some extent upon recollections of the past?

5. What is said about imitation in A., pp. 358–361, should now be compared with what Th. says, pp. 286–289. The subject of imitation is of great educational importance. The questions which the student needs to put to himself are (1) whether imitation is important regarding ends or means? What would become of independence, initiative and genuine choice if one imitated ends as well as means? On the other hand, how long would it take to reach even a comparatively simple end if one did not borrow through imitation suggestions as to the easiest means for realizing the end? Think of the behavior of parents and teachers where they insist that children shall copy, imitate or reproduce their own purposes and aims. What have been the effects? Do such methods strengthen or weaken will power? The further question is whether (2) imitation of means works best when made *conscious;* when it is insisted upon, as by a teacher who says, "Watch me, do it as I do," or when a child, being interested in the end, unconsciously imitates the movements of others in order to reach it.

Questions for Your Report.

Q.1. Answer the 4th exercise on p. 285 of Th.

Q.2. Answer the 2d exercise bottom of p. 289 of Th.

Q.3. Answer the 5th exercise on p. 290 of Th.

Q.4. What risks are run by the parent or teacher who relies mainly upon arguing and proving?

Q.5. Write a description of a case of your own experience in which *deliberation* is prominent.

Q.6. One in which *desire* is prominent.

Q.7. One in which *sense of effort* or *strain* is prominent.

Q.8. Write an account of a pupil's learning to write to illustrate the principle of development from random to controlled movements.

Q.9. Supposing you have a student who is averse to the study of arithmetic, in what ways can you operate upon him to get him to *will* to study that subject? Can you make a direct appeal to his will; that is, tell him he must will to study?

Section VI

HABIT AND ASSOCIATION

Texts.

Thorndike, *Human Nature Club,* Chap. XII.

Angell, *Psychology,* pp. 52–63 (for habit) and pp. 89, 90 and pp. 170–176 (for association).

Thorndike, *Psychology,* p. 16 and Chap. XIII and pp. 238–255.

It will be noted that A. separates the discussion of habit and association, taking up the latter in connection with succession of imagery, while Th. discusses the general principle in connection with habit and the succession of images and ideas in a separate chapter. Habit and association are practically the same; the association of ideas is a special application and development.

Aids and Suggestive Questions.

A. *Habit.* Note that the psychologist uses the term "habit" in a sense which is both broader and more technical than the ordinary meaning. (Consult a dictionary.) In its very popular use, habits sometimes mean *objectionable* tendencies which have a strong hold on a man, e.g., swearing, drinking. The psychologist uses it not only for useful outer abilities, like singing, walking, talking, typewriting, accurate shooting, etc., but also for *regular* intellectual and emotional tendencies; e.g., Darwin's habits of thought were different from Agassiz'; his habits of feeling different from those of Tennyson. It is a term meant to cover either the inward or outward tendencies which lie between inborn aptitudes and powers (native connections) such as we considered in

Sections III and IV, and *voluntary* activities such as we studied in the last Section. The native tendencies through acts which are more or less voluntary become habits; voluntary acts by exercise and repetition become habits. The psychologist also uses the term to express the *strengthened* tendency due to even one experience to act in a similar way the next time even if it is not regular or established. The material about Habit in A. and Th. may be organized under three heads: (1) Description of Habit; (2) Explanation of its Origin; (3) Results.

1. *Description.* The chief traits of a habitual activity, whether internal or external, are (*a*) uniformity, regularity; (*b*) ease, facility, and (*c*) active tendency or propensity. Reversing the order when an activity has become habitual, we (*c*) naturally incline towards it, any stimulus tends to set it going; (*b*) we engage in it with little strain, effort or difficulty, and (*a*) the resulting performance is well organized; one expression of habit is much like another, the underlying power is so well systematized. All of these tendencies combine to increase the spontaneity, automatism and unconsciousness of habitual factors of action. (Review what was said in Section II about the connection of consciousness with novel elements and with difficulty or friction in adjustment.) Habits thus tend to relapse to a stage much like instincts. Instincts have been called habits acquired by the race; habits instincts acquired by the individual.

2. *Explanation of Origin.* Th. gives an excellent summary of the important factors (p. 205, *Psych.*); viz., inborn connection, frequency of exercise, and selection on basis of satisfaction. The element of "stamping," confirming, deepening through satisfaction is fundamental and clearly brought out on pp. 202, 203. (This of course is the same principle as the "trial and success" method discussed in Section V.) *The most ordinary mistake among teachers and parents is over-emphasizing repetition or frequency* and neglecting the importance of the *native tendency* as a basis, and the importance of *successful achievement* as a test for selection and elimination.

3. *Results.* The three points spoken of in the description are of course important results. But the chief consequence is that certain activities and parts of activities become capable of effective execution without *thought* and hence free conscious thought for attention to *new and more difficult* things. (*H.N.C.,* pp. 140,

141; A., p. 58; Th., pp. 304, 305.) The general principle is that habit should apply to the *means* of our actions, but not to our *ends,* which should be settled by conscious thought. "*Habit is a good servant but a bad master.*"

B. *Association.* Some aspects of association, those touched upon by A., pp. 170–176, and Th., pp. 238–255, will be considered again later in connection with other topics, and may be passed over lightly here. It is important, however, to see that the process of association of ideas is only a development out of the principle of habit. When a succession of ideas goes through the mind, like February 22d, Washington, cherry tree, truthfulness, Weems (originator of the story), reliability of story, etc., each idea is a *response* to the prior one along certain lines which are settled by habit *plus* other circumstances, such as the present state of interest, recent experiences, etc. Th., pp. 205–213, brings out the points very well. Compare carefully the laws given on p. 207 with pp. 242–245, and pick out the similar points.

Questions for Your Report.

Q.1. Show how a habit affects *what* we think and *how* we think as well as our acts. Use a concrete illustration.

Q.2. (*a*) Give an instance of "absent-mindedness," and show its connection with the principle of habit. (*b*) Show how it illustrates that "habit is a bad master."

Q.3. (*a*) Rousseau said the only habit he would have a pupil form before the age of ten or eleven was the habit of having no habits. Criticize this statement and show also the element of truth in it. (*b*) What do you understand by a *flexible* habit?

Q.4. Answer Exercise 3 on p. 213 of Th.

Q.5. Answer Exercise 4 on p. 213 of Th.

Q.6. Answer Exercise 6 on pp. 213, 214 of Th.

Q.7. Discuss the *ethical* side of habit.

Q.8. Can a habit be too automatic—for example, the habit of adding figures without thinking?

Q.9. Supposing a habit is thoroughly acquired but under conditions which are disagreeable (e.g., a student learns to read Latin from fear of punishment). What is the effect?

Q.10. Give a full sketch of the experience of forming some habit which you have recently acquired.

Section VII

ATTENTION

Texts.
    Thorndike, *Human Nature Club,* Chap. VI.
    Thorndike, *Psychology,* pp. 97–107, paragraph on function
        of attention, p. 118 and pp. 309–314.
    Angell, *Psychology,* pp. 64–86.

Aids and Suggestive Questions.
    Habit and Attention have been said to be the *two poles* of
mental life. Think of as many distinctions between them as you
can; for instance, extent of consciousness and unconsciousness;
automatic character; ease or difficulty. What is the effect of attention in formation of habits? Is it better to form a habit by a large
number of repetitions with little attention; or by concentrating
attention so as to reduce the number of repetitions to the lowest
possible number? Supposing a child has the habit of spelling a
word wrong. Is it best to break the habit by having him spell the
word correctly a large number of times, or by his getting *once* a
very clear and vivid perception of the word? What are the connections between this topic and what was said in the last section
about the importance of perception of success and error in forming habits? What is the effect of habit upon attention? Do habits
tend to fix the direction of attention? Can we attend where we
have no habits at all? Do we attend where our habits are thoroughly formed? Why do people sometimes do things very well as
long as they do not attend to them, and then become clumsy
when they think of them—like walking a straight line? Why is it
difficult for an ordinary person to walk on a plank high in the air,
when he could walk the same plank on the ground with no
trouble? Formulate the results of your consideration of this topic
of the relation of habit and attention upon the basis of the relation of the *old* and the *new* to each other in attention. Why
doesn't the miller hear the noise of his mill? Why are we more
likely to notice that a clock in our room has stopped than to hear
it ticking? What things most attract the attention of children in
the schoolroom of the first grade? in the sixth? in the last year of

high school? Why? You have now been employed in exercising attention with respect to the subject of attention. Go over your thoughts upon this subject, and see what conclusions they lead you to concerning attention. Remember that you have the same material for formulating its laws as has any one else, except those who experiment with apparatus.

Special topics to be reflected upon carefully after having read the texts and thought out the general connections of habit and attention are:

1. *Fixity and movement* of attention. What does fixing or concentrating attention mean? Does it mean excluding mental change? (See A., p. 78.) What does alertness of attention mean? Can a person be concentrated and alert at the same time? How would he show each? What is the trouble with "quiet," "bright" pupils who never get anywhere in particular? Can pupils be *too* responsive? Have children who were inert and dull in school become celebrated afterwards? How do you account for such cases?

2. Voluntary and involuntary attention. Which is primary? Why does A. make three divisions? What is the effect of sense of strain in voluntary attention? What is the effect of telling children to pay attention when they have no idea of their own to what to pay attention? *With* what does any one pay attention? With some faculty by sheer will-power or by special habits and past experiences?

3. The topic of native and acquired attention (Th., pp. 101–103) is important and should be mastered. Does it have any connection with the topic of voluntary and involuntary attention?

4. Focus and Selection. Is there any difference between the principles that attention is focal and that it is selective? Does the first relate to its condition *at any one time,* and the second to the *succession* of the fields of attention?

5. Attention and Inattention. Is there any such thing as an inattentive pupil? What does inattention mean? Is there any difference between inattention and scattered or diffused attention?

6. Attention and Movement. Read *carefully* A., pp. 82, 83. Why are children more likely to be attentive when they are making a kite than when they are studying grammatical definitions? In the Elmira Reformatory boys whose attention could not be got to their school lessons were given gymnastics and manual

training, and finally they acquired more power of concentration. How do you explain this?

The topic of attention is perhaps the single topic of the most importance to the teacher. It is hoped that each teacher will take plenty of time to observe the workings of attention in himself and in others.

Questions for Your Report.

Q.1. (*a*) Show by an illustration how things are clear in the degree we attend to them. (*b*) Why does attention make things clearer?

Q.2. (*a*) What do you mean by scatter-brained? (*b*) What do you mean by dull or stupid? (*c*) Give at least three causes why pupils may be *habitually* inattentive to their lessons. (*d*) Give three causes why pupils usually attentive may be inattentive at a particular lesson. (Use observations you have actually made.)

Q.3. (*a*) What happens in a pupil's mind when he is told to "pay attention"; what is the immediate effect? What is the lasting effect? (*b*) Mention three better ways of securing attention.

Q.4. Give an account of some experience showing how involuntary attention passes into voluntary and voluntary attention passes into involuntary.

Q.5. Answer Exercise 1 on pp. 105, 106 of Th., giving all three heads, and analyzing cases "g" and "h" in some detail.

Q.6. Compare three pupils you know (or other persons) as to (*a*) the *extent* of their attentive grasp—the amount each can take in at once; (*b*) the *continuity* of their attention; (*c*) the sort of things that best catch and hold their attention. Make the description as lifelike and concrete as possible; and select contrasting types.

Educational Lectures before
Brigham Young Academy

1. How the Mind Learns

It is a special pleasure for me to be with you, for a few years ago I met, at another place, quite a number of those who are here to-day. I had the pleasure of becoming acquainted with the President of your Institution in classes in the University of Michigan; and quite unexpectedly to myself, I also found a number of other familiar faces here. I have, in fact, a good many friends around me to-day and do not feel at all that I am among strangers.

I am going to speak in these afternoon lectures on psychological topics in their bearing upon education. I shall take up a number of points familiar to you, and attempt to show how they are related to the intellectual development of the mind, and especially to that development of the mind which is undertaken by the teacher in the schoolroom. This afternoon I wish to make a sort of general survey of the whole field, taking up the question of how the mind learns. If there is a single process of learning, or of mind growth, such as there is a process of plant growth, a knowledge of that process and of the laws which govern it ought to be of the same help to the teacher that the knowledge of how a plant gets its food and adds to its structure helps the scientific gardener or farmer.

Since we are, I suppose, mostly teachers, we have a special interest in the process of learning; and of course the process of learning and that of teaching go together, just as do buying and selling. No one can buy unless someone sells, and no one can teach unless someone else is learning. I think you will recognize that, as a matter of fact, we can teach only when someone else is learning, just as we can sell only when someone else is buying.

[First published in *White and Blue* (Provo City, Utah), vol. 5, no. 2, 1 November 1901, pp. 5–9, 12–14. These ten lectures were delivered 17–21 June 1901.]

Now, that it is the mind which learns is of course no longer a question, and we are learning all the time. Children are learning from morning till night apart from their formal instruction in the schoolroom; and I will at once take up the question in a larger way of how the mind learns when it does not have any intention of doing so, when it gets knowledge by a sort of natural accumulation. Certainly the baby does not have any intention of learning during the first few years of its existence, and yet it is a question whether at any time of our lives we learn so much and so rapidly as we do during these first two or three years. It may be said that we learn in an unconscious way and without any set purpose to learn at all.

One definition of the term education, based on its etymology, is that it means, as you know, a drawing out. I think it is generally considered now to mean a leading forth. At all events we shall find, if we think a moment, that a child does not learn much by being drawn out by others; it learns rather through the overflow of its own activities. The child learns, not because the mind is like a piece of blank paper, to which it is sometimes compared, nor like a waxed tablet on which the natural world makes impressions. The people who said those things had evidently never watched babies much. Instead of being passive and waiting for things to impress them, children are usually so active, so overflowing with energy of all sorts, that much of the difficulty parents have with them is not to draw out their activities but rather to keep some of them in. They are so very active indeed that a good deal of their restlessness goes by the name of mischief or naughtiness.

A little child, when awake, is always busy. If we analyze this tendency we shall find that the mind, acting through the medium of the body, is all the time seeking for something. For instance, the child seems always hungry for physical food. In that respect he is certainly not a blank piece of paper. On the contrary his hunger is an active thing, so active that it causes him to search eagerly for food. Now the child's eyes, his ears, his fingers, his nose are just as hungry as his stomach. Children naturally hunger for what gives health, for what makes up life; for form, for color, for sound, and especially for handling things and doing something with them.

These forms of hunger, these appetites in the child, we call instincts. The child is born with a number of native tendencies, instincts, or impulses, which do not fail to unfold themselves if there is any chance at all. Unless absolutely repressed, they are bound to make themselves known. We call them instincts because the child does not know what he is going to do with them; he wants to use his eyes, for instance, but he does not know what for. He does not know what he is going to get by using them. These impulses make the child investigate, inquire, experiment. If we take the child from a year to two and a half years of age, we know that from the moment he is awake, he is reaching for this and that, crumpling paper, playing with things, trying to hold things. If there is a door with a knob, he will take hold of it; if there is a brush at hand, he will try to brush with it; he will take hold of a pencil and move his little hands round and round without any conscious set purpose at all—without being aware that by doing all these he is learning—that is, becoming acquainted with the world.

Now the two or three main points that I want to make in connection with the active energies, instincts, or impulses, I have already stated in brief. The thing to bear in mind is that they are instincts, and as instincts they are original. The next thing to remember is that they will assert themselves if they get any chance at all. They are spontaneous. They are bound to make themselves known. The child is not waiting passively to take in experience. He is looking for experiences, and in every moment of his waking life, he shows this original and spontaneous eagerness to get more experience, and become acquainted with the world of things and of people about him. The parent or teacher does not therefore have to originate these activities, does not have to implant them, they are already implanted in the child's makeup. What the teacher or parent has to do, is just to supply proper objects and surroundings upon which these impulses may assert themselves, so that the child may get the most out of them.

The child supplies the hunger but he does not supply the food. And just so the child has the active impulses or instincts to see as much as he can, hear as much as he can, and do as much as he can. But those instincts must be wisely supplemented in the matter of providing the material—the instrumentalities, through which they may express themselves. By a sort of spontaneous instinct, the wise parent does generally so guide the child; does meet these needs of the child by giving objects of various sorts, such as things to play with; and while playthings are rather to be despised as they are now regarded, it is necessary to give some kind of objects for the child to handle. Playthings supply him with the material through which his own active powers can express themselves, precisely as food is a thing necessary to satisfy the physical appetite of hunger.

Proceeding with my theme, the first question I would ask is whether, as we go from this same unconscious, informal kind of learning to the learning which goes on in the school—whether there are not found, even there, intellectual tendencies, hunger, or appetites which, while they do not assert themselves in such an uproariously active manner as they do before the school age, are yet awake, alive, alert, and looking for their food supply. If this be true, then the business of the teacher is not so much to rouse those activities, or "draw them out," as to supply the proper nutriment—the intellectual and spiritual food for these tendencies to feed upon.

In this connection we may ask whether there is not a marked difference between the schoolroom where attention is naturally alert and active, where there is manifested a wide-awake disposition and a pleasant atmosphere, and the school where there is constant repression and stimulation by the teacher; and whether the difference is not always in favor of the natural method. In the first school, it is recognized that children have the instincts, and that the business of the teacher is to encourage and stimulate these tendencies mainly by furnishing the material whereby they can build themselves up. In the second school, the working hypothesis is a sort of theological doctrine of total depravity, as if children were assumed to have no natural instincts or desire to learn, and consequently that everything they get must be poured in or hammered in from the outside. I sometimes think that the word "drill" is made to stand for this process—the process of driving knowledge into the children, or hammering it in from without. A child does not really learn by any such external driving, or filling, or hammering. He learns rather by the expression of his own impulses. The material for growth is supplied from without, and that is all. The tendency to activity must come from within.

Our next consideration must be that these instincts and impulses are very largely motor in character. They express themselves through the muscles. The mental activity of the child shows itself in physical form to a very considerable degree, and the physical form is motor. Physical activity is a very important and indispensable feature of mental life. It is not, as is often imagined, just a sort of accompaniment that goes on irrelevantly with mind activity; it is a vital part of the very process of learning. Psychologists are just beginning to recognize how one-sided was the old psychology which laid all the emphasis on sensation.

You see this book or this watch; you get certain sensations. Since Pestalozzi's time it has been recognized that it is not enough to learn words; sensation or sense perception must be called into play in order really to see and hear. The recognition of this truth marked a very great advance in education; and it may be stated that we are on the point of an equally great advance in recognizing the fact that sensation is just one-half the circle; the other half is the movement. For instance, even in getting a sensation of color from the watch—getting the idea of color and brightness and form—movement has to come into play. Of course with grown people there is not much movement, simply a turning of the eye; but even that little goes to show that the mind is active. The mind is never inactive or passive in the presence of sensation. The loving eye, the inclined head, the caressing hand, are all signs of the alertness of the mind; all physical activities indicate that the mind is already active and going out to catch ideas.

We know from the structure of the brain that the organs of sensation are very closely connected with the organs of movement, which shows that there is no sensation at all which does not tend to express itself in movement. [A window fell at this point in the lecture.] We heard that sound, for instance. There was a tendency on the part of every one to jump a little or at least turn his head. Why? Because sensation does not stand alone as sensation merely, it is the beginning of a movement which would investigate, would explore, and find out more about the thing producing the sensation.

Of course grown people have to learn to control a great many of these responses, from the simple fact that they are engaged in a line of sensation of more direct interest to them; and to keep their minds on that they must keep it away from the other. But the little child is open to every sensation and every sensation is a stimulus, a sort of signal, to call out a response or a reaction on his part, and that reaction operates through movement of some part of the body. We get our ideas through the use, very largely, of our hands, our eyes, and our ears. That is the natural mode of learning.

When educational reformers said that is a part of doing, the statement was true in an important sense. That idea has been formulated in this way. No impression without expression. No reception of an idea without counterpart expression. Now in our educational system that is called constructive work. Manual training of various kinds really rests on this principle, that the simple taking in of sense impression is not complete; we must have some tangible reaction of each thought; the impression must be completed in the expression. The impression, or sensation, is only half of the circle. Imagine a circle drawn on the blackboard; on one side is sensation, or impression, representing the mental income; on the other side is expression or movement, representing response to the stimulus in the way of something outgoing. There is or should be always a balance between this income and this outcome.

It is by this way that the child learns before he goes to school; and the same law explains, in schools where there is no active work going on, why so much of the time of the teacher is taken up in keeping the children still. In such a school they are forced to take in learning in the receptive way; either by looking at objects or taking in ideas from the printed page. These ideas naturally call out some response or reaction; and if the pupil does not get a chance to do something with what he is learning the result is artificial expression, which begets nervousness; and that he does not get the full benefit of what he is learning, is only least of the evils. For instance, in the teaching of geography sand and clay are not used simply to give a better illustration of the lesson. Were this the case the teacher might better do the modeling and molding before a class and have it ready to show to the children.

The materials are there mainly because the child thereby gets a chance to do something.

The child has been trying to get the idea through looking at pictures, through reading, listening, or something of that kind, but the impression is vague; if now he is allowed to try to work out that idea, to make something which somehow corresponds to the idea he has in his mind, he naturally gets the outlet or expression corresponding to the impulse.

Instinctively it has been recognized that reading aloud ought not to be simply an exercise to find out whether children pronounce the words or not, neither ought it to be an exercise to enable the teacher to check up whether the child has learned his lesson or not. Reading aloud gives a chance to express the impressions he has taken in; and when you find the pupil reading in a way that we term natural, or that we might term spiritual—reading that does not proceed in a sing-song way—you will find that the teacher, without any conscious knowledge perhaps of the psychology of the matter but simply because she is a good teacher, has given the children a chance to express themselves, to give out what they have taken in; for in no other way is there the natural completion of the circle. Such reading is a good thing. Through its means there comes to the pupil a sense of satisfaction with this work; but when the mental operation is chopped right through in the middle, interest is soon killed through the medium of mind stultification.

Another way of formulating the true mental operation might be, no instruction without construction; the instruction being what is taken in, and the construction being what is given out. Young children ought especially to have a certain amount of active reading and singing. As they get older the construction can be more intellectual in character. This does not mean that the child should review what he has taken in simply that the teacher may find out how much he has taken in. That is not a natural process. It is not the way the little child learns. It is not the way adults learn—storing in things and taking them out without change or modification, just for show.

Suppose you talk to another grown person and you get the idea that he is just repeating. You at once lose interest in the conversation and set him down as either stupid or conceited, as one who is trying to show off. The person you like to talk to is the person who, when he gives things out, constructs what he has taken in; who puts something of himself in, something of his own spontaneity, something of his own originality, so that the facts, as he gives them out, acquire a flavor of originality. Of course the facts are not changed, but he has used them in a constructive way, turned them over somehow in his own mind.

Every exercise can be made a constructive exercise—can be made to yield intellectual expression; but this cannot be done when the teacher gives lessons with a view to seeing how much the child can take in and give back again. Questions asked in a way different from the rote-fashion, make the child put together two or three apparently unrelated facts. We should have the principle of expression going along with that of impression, the construction completing the instruction. This is the natural way for the mind to learn; this is the way the mind learns when there is no set intention of learning, when we accumulate ideas and facts and acquire ability and skill without meaning to do so.

A good many people have attained to unusual knowledge and ability with very little schooling. You all know people whose intellectual ability and store of information you have very great respect for, yet whose schooling has been very limited. On the other hand, most of us know people who have had a very wide schooling, but whose judgment we do not care for. The difference between these two classes of people leads us to conclude that the first class, owing to circumstances, had to do something with everything they learned, so that even if their original capital was not very large, they were continually forced to apply what they got in order to do anything and get ahead. The new thing learned they turned over, invested it, and got good interest on it. They gave expression to all their impressions. A very little will sometimes go a good way, if it is the right kind of a little; on the other hand if the mind, sponge-like, simply soaks up information, it is likely to get water-logged. If it does anything at all in expression, it will be simply to give what has been taken in.

I think too often responses are simply repetitions. The textbook is studied and the child expected to give back the information just as it was taken in. We all know the evils that come from this mechanical squeezing out process, for we all hear it preached again and again. My only point is to try to put before you psychologically the fact that impression is only one-half of natural mental activity; that the necessity of knowing the meaning of what is taken in, is the reason that this reciting does so little to build up the child proper.

Sometimes it is helpful to look at the matter from a physiological side; for it is often easier to understand a matter if put in physical terms than if put in mental terms. If we could look into each other's brains, we should find sensory nerves leading from the eye, the ear, and all other organs of the body, to the nerve centres in the brain; and we should find the energy so communicated, making a disturbance there. On the other side, we should find nerve channels leading back to the muscles so as to get up movement. It is unnatural, from the very construction of the body, to think sensation and stimulus should terminate in the brain. Suppose a reservoir with water constantly running into it; there must be pipes leading out in order to maintain an equilibrium. The comparison fails in one particular. There is no dam, so to speak, in the brain between the impressions received and the reaction set up.

Of course, as the child gets older reactions are very much dulled. They also become very much more complicated. For instance, a man may study medicine for two or three years without practice; but it is found that medical students do better the more quickly they are put through some kind of expression. The same truth is practically recognized in law schools. They have mock courts, so that the young lawyer may get the practice necessary to make the law lessons his own. I suppose many of you have had the experience of never really understanding a thing while studying it; perhaps you studied arithmetic from four to six years and had a sort of knowledge of it. You taught it one year and now you cannot forget if you try. In teaching it, you got the expression. You had to give out what you took in, and by so doing you made it part of yourself.

The real value of the laboratory method comes in here. It is not really that a person can discover truths over again, truths which took some of the greatest geniuses of the world years and years of patient toil to discover; but the mere handling of the thing, the mere going through the operation originally gone through with in finding that truth, gives a natural outlet of expression which makes the idea his own.

I need not point out, of course, that if it were not that the mind is so organized, there could be no particular moral value to education. Learning, therefore, becomes part of ourselves only through the medium of conduct, and so leads to character.

I need not dwell longer on the possibilities of the recitation. We all know that if children can work out with their hands the idea taken in, they know they know it better. I have seen children drilled and drilled on two and two make four, until they were not quite sure they knew it, and might well be suspicious of the fact; for, if it were true, why make so much fuss about it? We do not keep the children a month on the fact that snow is white. The child finds out naturally that snow is white. Too much stress is often laid upon the drilling side of impression study. Very often a little constructive work, such as building with blocks or playing with dominoes, will accomplish in a minute what a month of mechanical drilling will fail to do. My point is that if we would spend more time in giving the children use for their ideas, we should not have to spend so much time in trying to drill the idea.

The third point is that these various tendencies, these instincts or original powers of which I have been speaking, ripen consecutively, and in their time they are very powerful. If you are much acquainted with babies, you have found that you cannot keep the child's hands off of things. His whole being seems to be dominated by a terrible desire to get hold of things. He simply has to handle and pull at them. This handling instinct has ripened. The month before, it was not so active. Months after, it is not so active.

The child's instinct to walk, to get on his feet, comes at another time. There are cases on record when the child walked when it wanted to without any practice,—just got right up when it wanted something. The mechanism had been ripening and when the time came it went off. Months before and after, this walking instinct was not nearly so urgent.

Then there is the time for learning to talk. The child wants to repeat all the sounds he hears and make all the noises he heard over again, imitate the words he hears, and two or three years almost is given up to getting his vocabulary and then the instinct or power lessens somewhat. The mind passes on to something else. As the child gets older it is very difficult to point out the dominant activities. We cannot see them so easily as we can earlier, but they are there to a certain extent. The time to strike is while the iron is hot. There is a time when the child learns reading and writing easily and thoroughly. I think the recognition of these periods is one of the great advantages that are to come from child study in the future. We do not at present know so much about successive development as we should like to. We can get at it definitely alone, say of children from one to five. In this period we can practically map out the ages of strongest tendencies. We cannot do it yet between the age of six and twelve. This is the study to which every teacher can contribute. Find out what the children are thinking about and talking about outside of school, the kind of thinking they want to do, what games they are playing, why their activities are passing from one thing to another, and watch the development of these spontaneous activities.

We can get better work from children during the maximum of power, or along the line of least resistance than across grain, as many of us now do. We find that the tendency of the child to collect is very strong at a certain year. This can be developed into certain forms of nature study. The collecting instinct, which is at first just a blind instinct, could be taken advantage of in gathering nature specimens not for scientific study in the sense of very much analysis, but rather to get acquainted with these things.

One of the best professors of English says the children ought to be personally introduced to trees and flowers, and I suppose also to familiar rocks and animals, just as they are to people, so that they may know them just as they do people by being introduced in the social world. There is a time when this instinct is at its height. Then it is that the child should get acquainted with all these things. I am inclined to think that there is an instinct for long division; a time when children take very much more interest in doing problems than at any other time. The thing does not appeal to them after that time, there is not enough to it, it bores them, and you want to put them onto something else.

There is also a time when children like to work out puzzles. You generally find that children like to do sums at various times, puzzling them out when this puzzle instinct is at its maximum. If we could teach long division just at this right time and get the child interested in working out things without much meaning, we have succeeded in adjusting the power and skill to manipulate intellectual things to better results. When the child first comes to school we should conduct our studies very much more to finding out the direction of activity by giving the child just the kind of thought that he wants, and at a time when his appetite is naturally asserting itself. He thus learns much more and with keen interest, and consequently assimilates more thoroughly than when we fire at him with a loaded shotgun all kinds of facts, in the hope that with a long-range fire something will stick. That is really what our teachers are doing now, loading the curriculum with all kinds of studies, firing them at the child, and trusting to kind providence to have some of it stay by him.

As we come to know children better, we shall know what their activities are; we shall be able to substitute a rifle that will go a good deal straighter to the mark; we shall give the intellectual and spiritual nutriment that is particularly needed by the child at that particular stage of his development. We must remember that the mind needs food just as much as the body needs food and that there is something wrong when children do not like to learn, when studies are repulsive to them. The food is not being presented in the shape that they recognize as food. They have these appetites somewhere and it is the business of the teacher to find them.

You go into an audience and ask people to go back over their childhood and pick out the teachers that did the most for them. I think you will find in every case that they will say such and such a teacher waked them up, or such and such a teacher first inspired them. They will put it in different ways. They may have forgotten whether she was a good disciplinarian or not. The mechanical teachers will not be the ones they will speak of; it will be the teachers that roused them, that got hold of them. That means the teacher that found out the mental trait that was uppermost in the pupil, and that succeeded in giving it intellectual nutriment in such a way as to make it grow. The child did not know this trait. The other teachers did not find it out; but through some natural instinct, this particular teacher divined what was going on in that mind and succeeded in making connections.

That is the great object of education. The subject matter and whether to teach this or that is not the point; after all, it is the boys and girls that have to be taught. The subjects are secondary, the children are primary; and the teacher who recognizes these spontaneous activities and wants that are growing up in the child's mind, and knows how to give them material that will stimulate them, is the one that stays by him when all the rest are lost in the fogs of the remote distance.

2. Social Aspects of Education

An acquaintance with the history of educational theory shows that there have been two explanations of the purpose and nature of education. One of these ideas is the social idea. The definition which it offers is that education is the preparation for the social position of life, the preparation of the individual to play his proper part in the community or state of which he is a member. The other is a more individual definition. A formula which is quite familiar to us all is that education is the complete development of all the powers of the individual, intellectual, physical, and moral. Sometimes one definition is offered and sometimes another. In a general way we probably all of us believe in both explanations; and yet without any very clear idea of how one of them—the idea of preparing the individual for playing his part in social life—is to be combined with the other—the idea of the complete development of the individual as an individual.

In Greece, especially in Athens, there was the highest form of expression or realization of the social idea of education; that is, of the idea that the whole object and purport of instruction is to fit men for citizenship in the community to which they belong. Education began with little children and consisted of making them acquainted with the literature and religious classics of their own people. They had no reading books, no writing lessons, no spelling lessons, excepting such as were derived from the study of the history and literature of their own race. We may study the *Iliad* and the *Odyssey* as literary classics, or we may derive from them tales or myths; but to Greek children it was more than literature or more than myth, it was their religion, that they were becoming acquainted with. It was their own history;

[First published in *White and Blue* (Provo City, Utah), vol. 5, no. 3, 28 November 1901, pp. 1–6, and ibid., no. 4, 18 December 1901, pp. 13–16.]

and so all the curriculum, as we might call it, was saturated with the assertions, the history, and the ideals of their own people.

When they became older and took what we might call a high school or college course, it was to initiate them into the duties of citizenship, civil and military. Their geography lessons were mostly about their own country. They looked on the rest of the world as barbarians, and so there was no reason, no sense, for becoming acquainted with the list, the history, or habits of other people. But they studied their own country very carefully. They went on military duty, and in their militia training they made a most careful study of their own regions, the mountains and the mountain passes and places of defense against enemies that might attack them. So they went through their whole course, just being steeped in the civilization and ideas, history and ideals of their own people; the whole thing being concentrated and focused to prepare them for citizenship in their own community with a supreme disregard of all outside life.

We can hardly realize what such intensification of education through limitation meant. We know so well that there is a large world of which we are only a part, and that our history is bound up with the history of other people. We know so well that we occupy simply one portion of the globe surface and are accustomed to study all the other portions and to place our own country in the larger physical whole. We are acquainted with foreign languages, foreign literature; and we branch out and take up studies that do not have any particular bearing upon our own social life—higher branches of science and mathematics; so that we cannot realize what a highly cultivated, intellectual, and artistic people like the Greeks could accomplish simply by taking fifteen or twenty plastic years of childhood and youth, and concentrating everything upon making the individual a citizen of that little community.

There, for instance, was Athens, not so big as hundreds of towns in the United States, with indeed a comparatively small number of free citizens—so small that they could all be personally acquainted with each other—and yet through their peculiar form of education they brought their culture to such a high point of intensification that the whole world still looks back to Greece as the source of many of its most important ideas in science, in philosophy, and in art.

I am not going to follow educational evolution down through the ages. Every successive period of civilization has had to take account of a larger and wider field than did the Greeks. The Romans had to make acquaintance with the Greek language and literature. They had to study a foreign language, and so the study of foreign languages became part of the curriculum; and this made a tremendous difference in the entire aim of education. It meant that it was no longer possible to have what I might call a perfectly indigenous education, an education limited to the history, the literature, and the ideas of one people. It meant that the physical and mental horizon was broadening. It also meant that the course of study was widening to take in things which were outside the range of personal experience and personal contact— things which the individual can have no direct knowledge of; and to take them up in a way more artificial perhaps than the education of the Greeks had been.

During the Middle Ages the barbarous Germanic or European tribes recognized the dependence of their civilization on the art of the Greeks. They had themselves nothing in law, politics, and social organization, which could compare with the ideas and methods worked out by the Greeks and Romans; and they were even more dependent on them for intellectual material.

If we come down to our own day, we shall find, as already intimated, that the intellectual horizon has expanded almost infinitely. We have the world's history to study. We do not speak of our own history, the history of this American people, as the beginning and the end of all history. We cannot even imagine, as the Greeks practically did, that everything began with their own history, and that everything was going to end with them. We know that our forefathers came from other countries, and came with habits and traditions and ideas already fixed. We know, as we gaze back through the centuries, that we are dependent upon people in Palestine, in Greece, and in Rome; people that lived in Europe century after century; and that our civilization has come from these comparatively far-away sources.

On the other side, scientific men have been investigating and exploring until they have made known worlds upon worlds of which the Greeks never dreamed. To them that little peninsula constituted, for all practical, educational, and social purposes, the entire universe. We know about the entire world. All the continents have been explored to their minutiae; the mountain ranges, rivers, and cities have been located; the physical universe has expanded in the direction of astronomy. It is true, they had a certain vague knowledge of the sun, the moon, and some of the planets and constellations; but even these they associated through myths with their own history. When they looked out upon the heavens they felt that, in a way, they owned the stars and the constellations; for did not these represent their own national heroes and illustrate incidents in their lives? The universe came down close to Greece, and to their own social life. Of course they did not know anything of the infinite distance of these things, nor that this world is just one body among many others. They regarded it, of course, as the centre of the universe. Now that the world has expanded to almost infinite dimensions and we know this tremendous universe of worlds, what a small speck we are! And just as the telescope has made known to us this great physical world, so the microscope has revealed to us an equally infinite world of minute things. We have had the great masses of matter broken up into molecules and atoms, and we know what is dependent upon the inter-play of these forces, which are so far beyond the possibility of acquaintance of our senses.

Now, what does all that mean? It means of course that in one way it is not possible to relate the material of education—the things that we study—nearly so closely to the ideals of our present social life, as it was with the Greeks. We have, on our hands, so to speak, this great physical universe, this great social and historical world, which is so far beyond and above us, and of which our own life, our own community, and our own state occupy, comparatively speaking, such a fractional part; and this fact has made the problem of education very much more difficult than it used to be. For, after all, what is the use, morally speaking—and practically speaking—of the study of these things—trying to cover this whole history of the universe, the geological history, the social, political, and industrial history? What is the use of peering into the far-away heavens, and delving down into things that even the microscope cannot see, and that can be constructed only by theory? What, I repeat, is the use of going into all these far-away things, unless they can be brought into some kind of working relation with our present life?

The Greeks, who accomplished so much, did not have to face

that question, because, as I said before, the world they had to study was in a sense their own world; at least they thought it was, and that made it so, so far as their ideals were concerned. Everything they studied touched them, was most intimately bound up with them, so that in studying it, they were really studying themselves. They were just becoming acquainted with the conditions of their own social life so that they could play the part they had to play. But it is very often difficult for us to see how knowledge went on in this globe during geologic ages, back, say, in the carnivorous age; or even of what went on in Egypt and Syria and many other countries during the Middle Ages. What meaning has all that to us after all? What points of contact does it have with our own ideas? How do expressions of thought by ancient and little known peoples fulfil the first definition of preparing for the responsibilities and privileges of our social life? Very little. The aim of it all must therefore be a preparation and cultivation of the powers of the individual; which is equivalent to saying that the purpose of acquaintance with this world, individually extended in space, and of going back indefinitely into that which has been, is not of any particular social use. It is not going to help man play his part in social life, but it makes a development of his own powers. He gets intellectual discipline by studying these things; his mental powers are trained and he gets culture; he gets an enlargement of his horizon; there is less danger of his being narrow, and prejudiced, and hemmed in.

The idea, which has been emphasized by many educational reformers, that after all the end and object of education is this perfection of the powers and capacities of the individual, has, perhaps, more than any other, stagnated intellectually the theory of education; but not perhaps its practice. Practice and social instruction are too important to be overturned by adverse theories. But for a hundred years, perhaps since the time of Rousseau anyway, the idea which theorists have insisted upon is that the aim and object of education is simply to get the harmonious, complete development of all the power of the individual. Now I have tried to put before you the two factors which have to be taken into account in any scheme of education. There certainly has got to be regard for the individual and for the powers and capacities and needs of the individual. It is not likely that history is going backward. The movement of history has been in what I might call a democratic direction; from despotism, from the absolute intellectual and moral subjugation of the man, in the direction of giving more responsibility and freedom to the individual; giving him more power to choose, even more power to make mistakes of his own that he may learn by his own mistakes. It gives him more scope for experimentation, to find out what he is good for and what he can best work at. We know that, politically and intellectually, the development of the world has gone far from despotism in the direction of recognizing the greater claims of the individual; and we know that our education in theory has gone even farther in that direction. In practice also this development has done a good deal in the way of introducing something that can be shown to have direct social utility.

It would be pretty hard for any of us to prove that we are made absolutely better by studying this particular part of geography, or this particular part of history, or this particular part of mathematics. We could show, in a general way, that a knowledge of the elementary branches, such as reading and arithmetic, is necessary for purposes of social intercourse; but we should have difficulty in showing any direct social value in these branches beyond the development and culture of the individual as one factor in society. On the other hand, we certainly should not think much of an education which did not result in training an individual to a proper regard for social considerations, and to the idea of subordinating himself when necessary to the needs and aims of the social life to which he belongs. We should not, for instance, give much for the education which did not impart to the individual a sense of loyalty and devotion, an enthusiasm for the country and state and community to which he belonged. We should regard such education as very defective morally. We should regard it as practically inculcating selfishness, if this complete development we talk about of all the powers did not lead to a better ability to serve the community, and a greater interest in serving it.

Educational ideas and practices, as I have intimated, tend to swing backward and forward, acting and reacting. Now too much stress is laid on the social factor, the rights of the individual not being fully recognized. In many countries the individual is trained to subordinate himself entirely to the state. This was the case in Greece, especially in Sparta, where the individual was trained simply to be a citizen and a soldier, to defend his state, and was not permitted any development of his own independent intellectual life at all. Anon the pendulum swings to the other extreme, and we have a sort of selfish, too individualistic spirit coming into education.

I met, a few weeks ago, an inspector who had been sent by the government of England to examine and report on this particular point, viz., what was being done in the schools of America to cultivate a social spirit. In talking to her about the object of her mission, I was informed that a number of educational leaders in her own country—she mentioned one gentleman in particular— were getting alarmed about the spirit of individualism which had come into English education. It seems that the schools over there put the whole stress practically on getting ahead, training the pupil along individual lines. Their whole system of promotions and rewards tends to hold up that the student is best who can go furtherest ahead. Practically the one ideal that is being put before children in many of the schools is that all depend upon individual success to get on in the world; to make one's way honestly, as far as possible, and without doing any open violence to the rights and claims of others, but yet to get ahead individually. They are not trained, so I gathered from her, to think of the dependence of others upon them—in other words, the necessity of a cooperative life—and she had come to this country to see what the schools here were doing to introduce the spirit of social service and of community life; whether we were making pupils feel that after all the chief office is not simply to accumulate as much learning for themselves as possible nor that the highest purpose of this learning is for individual use in getting ahead. While admitting that the civilization of the Anglo-Saxon race has been individualistic, that civilization, she maintained, has been carried to the opposite extreme of the pendulum; at least the leaders of educational thought seemed to think that it had in England.

We have, at all events, these two factors to harmonize and bring together. From a material standpoint, the fundamental problem is to get the proper development of individuality—the power of thought and action necessary to judge and to choose for oneself, and yet have this power controlled by social exigencies and through the medium of a social spirit. This is a difficult problem, chiefly because in our curriculum we have so much that is remote from anything called for in our present social life. The universe has grown so big—for space and time have been stretched out so tremendously—that it is very difficult to trace any connection between the world of studies and the social matters and interests of the present. And yet, unless we shall find this connection, direct and indirect, there is great danger that we shall be getting the intellectual development of the individual at the expense of the social spirit and the social matters which ought to control it. The question that comes to me is, what are the common connecting elements in society? What is there that can be relied upon to introduce this social spirit? One of the superintendents of the New England schools, Mr. Dutton, wrote a book which he called *Social Phases of Education*. One thing that Mr. Dutton dwells upon is what he calls correlation of the educational forces of the community as one method of introducing this social spirit. He points out the fact that the school is after all only one of the educational agencies; and he deplores the fact that the school, at least in that section of the country, has become isolated from the other agencies with which it ought to be in close connection— the home life, for instance. No one can deny that the home and the family is one of the greatest educational influences. During an educational meeting in Canada a few months ago, at which I was present, the mayor of the city was called upon to make a little speech of welcome to the teachers. In the course of his remarks, he said something which I suppose he intended in good faith, but which struck me as fine irony. Turning to the body of the house he said, "I want to say a few words to the parents. With all the great advances which have been made in the principles of education, and in spite of all that the teachers are doing for the pupils, our schools cannot entirely dispense with the assistance and cooperation of the parents. The parents must help in this work."

Sometimes educational writers have spoken of the work of the school as if what went on there could be almost entirely cut off from what the home and the family have to do in the education of the young. In some sections of the country, at least, there has been a sort of misunderstanding or lack of understanding between the teachers and the parents; the parents, perhaps, laying all the blame for the children's bad habits on the teachers, and the teachers feeling that if they only had the complete management of the children they would get on alright, but as it was what they did was undone by the home influence. If there has not been this jealousy, there has, at least, been a lack of cooperation between the home and the school. Certain it is that one thing which has marked recent advance movements in education is the attempt to break down this isolation of the school from the home.

There are a great many ways in which this movement for correlation appears. In the first place, what we might call home studies are being introduced in the schools. A more dignified name for these studies is Domestic Arts, or Domestic Science. Probably no movement has made more rapid progress in the last ten or fifteen years, taking the schools at large, than the introduction of studies in cooking, sewing, and household management; things that make the children feel that they are learning something in school which connects them with their family life and which enables them to be more useful at home than they otherwise would be. Now that movement certainly represents a recognition on the part of the school that it has certain responsibilities and duties toward the family and the home life, and that it is not enough to take up studies which begin in the school and have nothing to do with the life and pursuits of the child outside. The formation of clubs of various kinds, the organizations of parents and teachers to meet and to discuss points of common interest, has aroused the feeling that the teacher has a responsibility in becoming acquainted with the home life and environments of the child, and, on the other hand, that the parent has a responsibility in becoming acquainted with the school, and that consequently there should be an interchange of suggestion and ideas. I suppose that is another thing which has been going on with multiplying rapidity in the last ten years, but most of all in the last three years. If we had the statistics, we should find that organizations which bring the teachers and parents together are multiplying very rapidly. I will not take time to go over these things one by one, but shall mention a few of them.

One good thing is the cooperation of the library and the school and in many towns there are now public libraries. Many of these libraries have children's rooms in them, and there are systematic ways in which books are to be borrowed for the use of children in connection with the work of the school. Museums and art galleries are being intermingled with the school influence. I do not suppose this is needed so much in communities like yours as it is in many of the eastern communities; because, I take it, from the conditions of life here, all these things are more naturally inter-woven than they are elsewhere. I presume you have not had this isolation of the school, and the school life, and school studies, to contend with as much as we have in many of the communities farther east. At the same time however, there is a tendency in every organization to forget somewhat its relations to other in-stitutions; and too often it devotes its attention too exclusively to what goes on within its own walls. There can be no question, I think, that the school life has lost a great deal of its meaning for children because they cannot see any connection between it and the social life which they are carrying on outside its walls.

Little children are tremendously social beings. They are very dependent upon other people. They have not the experience, nor have they the ability or maturity in any direction to go ahead as individuals. They are dependent upon the suggestions of others, upon the guidance and approbation of others. If you watch chil-dren outside of school, you will see that they cannot do anything without turning to parents or those about them and trying to get interest and approbation for what they are doing. A good deal that makes children hard to care for, that makes them inter-fere so exasperatingly, is simply the intensity of their social spirit. They do not like to be by themselves because they do not feel satisfied with what they are doing, unless others are interested in it too. As they grow older this social spirit naturally leads them to choose boy and girl companions. Under the worst circum-stances, if they are thrown by themselves without judicious guid-ance, they will get up gangs of some sort or other and will thus have a social life of an undesirable kind.

Children are dependent upon social influences, and yet much of the school work has paid no attention to this natural depen-dence. They are often taught to read, write, and spell in a purely individual way; that is, in a way which does not have any social element in it at all. Now language is after all a social pursuit. The reason that a person wants to learn to write is a social reason; viz., that he may communicate with his fellows. Purposes of busi-ness or friendship make it necessary for him to learn to write. Now, if the child could feel, at the time he is learning to write, that this social element is introduced into it, would not his writ-ing mean a good deal more to him than a purely technical exer-cise? The difficulty is that we are always postponing this explanation. We say, "Teach the child to read, write, spell, and figure now; because by and by he will need them in his social life." But any device or invention which should make the child feel they were going to be useful, not simply in the future, but right now, would add to his interest in these studies and enhance their value for him.

I heard a supervisor of primary schools in Boston say that she had visited some grades in the poorer districts and asked the children what they were studying their arithmetic and reading and writing for, what they expected to get out of them. At first they said they had to get their lessons. She said that was not what she meant. What use was it outside the school? They could not for a while make much headway with this question, excepting that by and by they would need them sometimes. They might get to be President of the United States sometime. She explained that what she wanted to know was what they would do with them now. They thought of a good many uses. Some said they lived a good way from school and might get on the wrong car, so they had to read the signs on the streetcars. Others said that their parents were not very well off and they had to watch out for bargain sales. They finally found a good many uses for their reading and writing. But when they came to arithmetic they could not think of much social use, beyond making change when they bought things in the stores, until one boy said he might get arrested for doing something and the police justice would give him a choice between paying a $15.00 fine and serving fifteen days in jail, and he would have to figure it out to see which he had better take. That story is both humorous and pathetic,—rather tragic. A bright lot of boys and girls of ten or eleven years of age, and yet, that was about the first definite answer as to any actual benefit in social life outside of school coming from the pursuit of their studies.

Now I cannot stop to indicate carefully just how this social movement can be introduced. The child can be led to feel the direct social use that he has for reading, writing, and arithmetic; and we must remember that after all language was developed for social purposes. It is a means of social intercourse. By it we get at the ideas of others, and by it we give our own ideas to them. Just think how narrow, how poor, our social life would be if language were cut out; if we had no way of getting at the experience of others. It is by this means that people who have gone before still speak to us; their best thoughts are recorded in history and in literature. It is by the use of language that we get at the experience of others all about us. The child outside of school has the social motive all the time for the study of language; in other words, conversation.

I spoke this afternoon of the importance of using the recitation to make children do more thinking and more inventing. It is equally important to make children introduce the social spirit into the recitation; to make them feel that they have experiences and ideas which are of use to others; that it is not simply a question of reviewing something to see how much they know of learning to speak of it, but that they have something to say to others, and that they may understand what others have to say to them. They can thus be made to see that language is a sort of clearing house for their ideas and experiences. The school is certainly a social realm and the recitation ought to be a social realm; both should be actuated by this feeling of a united exchange of thought and experiences. There is no real school where the social spirit does not prevail. It is not a question as to discipline. Children are not made over by school government of the repressive sort. Children are children and they will always have their faults; will always need to be corrected and looked after; and after all, when there is a feeling of unity of purpose and aim, and a feeling of mutual confidence, there is always a basis, a natural basis, for correcting and straightening out the faults and difficulties that present themselves. This correcting does not have to be done by brute force, or by sheer imposition of a threat of punishment; for in a natural school there is a recognition of mutual natures, a community of interests in keeping things the way they ought to be.

Even arithmetic has been developed for social purposes. People did not originally set to work to invent arithmetic as an abstract science. The practical necessities of life caused men gradually to work it up. The Egyptians developed the beginnings of geometry, for instance, because the river Nile flooded the valley every year and they had to have some way of keeping track of land boundaries. The Assyrian and Babylon civilization originated elementary mathematics for building purposes, to aid in their great architectural development. In Egypt, accounting was developed originally from practical necessities; for keeping track of flocks of sheep and herds of cattle and for making other ordinary exchanges. Even the sciences, or most of them, were developed in the same way; becoming more technical and scientific as the world advanced; and so going back we may trace one study after another to a period where it grew originally out of the actual necessities of social life: physiology and anatomy out of necessities of avoiding and curing diseases; botany out of the needs of the farmer and gardener, and also out of the needs of medicine; mineralogy and geology, out of the interest people had in rocks and stones and metals of various kinds, and the use they made of all these things in their social life.

Many educational philosophers say that the child is, so to speak, a sort of savage originally, and that just as the race goes step by step from the lower to the higher plane, so the child must go through similar stages of evolution. I think that if this idea is carried out too literally it becomes absurd. I once heard a gentleman say that it sounded very nice, it was a beautiful theory, but we wanted to remember that the time-element came in pretty strongly, and that if children have to do, in fifteen or twenty years, what the race has been doing for twenty thousand years, they have got to be in something of a hurry. They have to remember time, especially when they get to staying too long in some of the primitive phases. The thing is rather absurd if we take it too literally; but in a certain sense, the child's original interest in all these studies must be developed gradually, like the race's interest in them.

What is the standpoint for investigating the connection and bearing of the technical and isolated studies of life? So far as these branches are concerned we might accept the statement of the race-development theory. We have separated and segregated them in the most empirical fashion, making one study of reading, one of writing, one of spelling, one of geography, one of science, and so on. That may be all right for a mind with experience and maturity enough to recognize the common background of all these things; but to plunge a child into isolated and segregated studies is a somewhat artificial thing. The unity to the child is to be found in their relation to social life. Consider a little child outside the school—before he goes to school: he is, for instance, studying geography; that is to say, he has to locate his own house and his own street, his father's store, the church, the school-house. This is all natural geography, this knowledge of the streets where live his friends and relatives. If he takes a journey on a railway train, his geography is still further enlarged; and all these additions to his knowledge become part of his social life.

So in the study of literature, stories are told him, and from these stories he gets a knowledge of his parents and grandparents. That is the natural beginning of the knowledge of one's ancestors. All this has a direct social meaning and value to the growing child. As he goes about out of doors he is studying the rudiments of science directly from nature; he is making acquaintance with plants, flowers, trees, rocks, gardening, and all these natural things about him which interest him from a social point of view. He knows that if it rains he cannot play or make a visit. His acquisitions are all prompted by things that he comes in contact with. Now, suddenly to break off all that and make him study school studies, in which he sees no connection with the social life, is to make these studies artificial for him; and this is one reason why so many children take so little interest in their school studies. They feel the artificiality of them and want to break away.

A woman who had been on the Chicago Truant Commission told me that the saddest part of her experience was the fact that in the district she attended the brightest children ran away from school and the duller children remained pretty regularly. The truants were children who had more capacity and ability than it was possible to keep occupied in the school. They lived on the streets in order to get more to do. When compelled to remain in school these runaways would be at the head of their classes in a week or two. I do not suppose that this is a very common phenomenon, but it indicates in a slight degree how emphatic this point is. Methods of education are partly responsible for the lack of interest in the school. Children are introduced too early to many studies, and introduced moreover in such a technical, spliced manner, that they do not feel that these things connect with their everyday life and interest. They do not feel that such studies are a part of their social interests. Somehow they are different from other things. You know there gets to be a sort of feeling that things which are true in school are different from things which are true outside of school. The child does not expect to apply the same standpoint of judgment to facts inside as to facts outside. He has one standpoint at home and outdoors and another standpoint in school.

Perhaps the most extreme case of that is the boy who was asked to explain the circulation of the blood. He said the blood would run up one leg and down the other. That boy, I think, had learned so many things he could not understand, that he had really come to disconnect the legs he had in school and the legs he had out of school. He did not know but that the legs which were studied about in school might be constructed that way.

A few years ago there was a good deal of amusement created by a teacher in Brooklyn publishing extracts from children's examination papers. All kinds of perfectly absurd and impossible ideas came out—ideas that you would think came from a lunatic asylum and not from bright boys and girls. I think the source was not stupidity. The weakness lay in the fact that the studies of the children had been so widely separated from their every-day life. They did not think of using the same kind of sense and judgment inside of school that they did outside. School things were for school purposes, and were different from outside things. At all events you might make a guess. You might come out right and you might be wrong. One thing was about as likely to be true as another.

One way of getting at this defect is of course to make the child realize that the things he gets in school are only a part of the things outside; that the experiences outside of school are not definite enough, and so he needs to take up these things in school in a more systematic way; that after all they are the same things. Show that even geography is the science of the world about us, the science of just the common, ordinary soil, air, sunlight, heat, etc., which are being investigated in the schoolroom. It never occurs, I fear, to many children, to think that geography has anything in it of the outside world. Of course we sometimes make a mistake about the innocence of children.

A boy in one of the New York schools was asked to define geography and said it was the science or study of the earth's surface. He said he had never seen the earth's surface. The teacher began to make him analyze the fact but he stuck to it. "You see," he said, "I have never been outside of the city and have never seen anything but the pavements." He hoped to go sometime to the country and see the earth's surface. In that particular case it was not evidently the fault of the teacher. He had been doing the best that he could. I think there are some children that do not even get as far as that: to know whether or not they have seen the earth's surface.

I will not follow out this line of thought any longer, save to suggest that after all, while the problem of connecting individual development with the social spirit is great enough, we sometimes unnecessarily increase it by isolating school studies, school methods, and school discipline from the experiences, methods, aims, and work outside the school; and to suggest further that one of the great educational tasks of the future is to break down these middle walls or partitions which isolate the school life from the larger life and interests outside; so that what is best and most worthy in the outside life can flow into the schoolroom, circulate through it, and give it such vitality and interest that the children may be able instantly to apply what they learn.

I have repeatedly told the story with which I shall close. The school in Chicago for teaching swimming taught this subject without having pupils go into the water. They were taught all the strokes they might need to make when they should go into the water and were carefully drilled. One young man was asked what happened to him when he got into the water. He answered, "I sank."

We are preparing in the schools for social life and unless there is a social spirit in the school itself and a feeling of contact and connection with the outside world, are we not doing a good deal what this swimming school did? We are taking the children through all the motions of social life but the actual conditions in which they are to perform these motions are not there, and so when the child gets out there is a good deal of a break. I will not say that it is so wide as between the swimming motions in and away from the water; but then these things do not get so closely tested as did the dry air swimming habit. Educators often wonder what becomes of all this material in the nature of training and culture which is being given in the schools. We cannot count on its being there in later life. Now if the school will bring in the social life and social discipline, the training which the child is getting will gradually grow and expand itself, so that when he comes into the larger final responsibility, there will not be the break there is now. Real life will simply be an enlargement, an expansion, of that in which he is already trained.

3.   Imagination

I shall speak in this lecture on the topic of imagination, its uses and means of development. Possibly what I mean by imagination would be clearer if we called it imagery and power of imaging. There is an idea that imagination stands for something quite mysterious and peculiar; that it has to do particularly with inventing things not true, or with the unreal or the fantastic. The imagination which is called into exercise in the school, and of which I wish particularly to speak, is something quite different. It is the power rather of realizing what is not present than of making up anything which is unreal.

The chief point I wish to make is, that imagery in this sense is the chief instrumentality in the pupils' minds upon which the teacher has to rely when dealing with facts and material that is not directly present to their senses. In history, in geography, in literature, and even in arithmetic, a pupil is always having to understand things, to take hold of things, which are not present before his eyes. The question comes, how can anyone get hold of things which are not directly present? The answer is, through this power of imagery, the power of forming mental pictures of whatever is presented. Now there are different kinds of these mental pictures, or images. We are most accustomed to take simply the eye pictures, the visual pictures, as they are called; but we have also auditory images, mental reproductions of sounds and tones; motor images, the images of movements, and touch images, images of the feel of different things.

Suppose you attempt to reproduce to yourself a meeting that you had with some friend yesterday. Some of you will imagine your meeting him on the street, will have no difficulty in seeing

[First published in *White and Blue* (Provo City, Utah), vol. 5, no. 5, 15 January 1902, pp. 11–16, and ibid., no. 6, 1 February 1902, p. 11.]

him as definitely as if he were actually present; will see his form and the color of his face, his hair, and his eyes; you will even see the pattern and color of the clothes he wore, and so on; while there are others here, who, I venture to say, will have a very dim and indistinct picture. They will remember perfectly well that they saw the person and remember what was said; but they will perhaps not be able to form any clear mental picture whatever.

In speaking of this matter I have always noticed that those who do not have these images have very great difficulty in believing that other people have them; and people who do have them wonder that they should be spoken of as unusual. These images now have been studied by psychologists for a very long time. Mr. Galton began the investigation about twenty-five years ago by sending out certain questions among his friends, asking how many could see their breakfast table, and whether they could see the distinctions of light and shade, the places where the sunlight fell, and so on. Could they see the vegetables and the dishes that were on the table? If they saw the table in detail, did they see it all at once or a little piece at a time until they got a picture of the whole thing? He began among his scientific friends; but they laughed at him and told him that only a crazy person could see things present that were not present. He persisted in his investigation, however, and found that a great many people, more than half, had these definite visions, especially among children and among women. Among engineers and architects it was quite common, though not so much among his scientific acquaintances who were pursuing abstract researches. Now if there were a little more time—about a week instead of an hour— I should like to ask who, among those present, can see this morning's breakfast table and see it very definitely all at once. How many saw it all at once? A few. How many saw very little of it? A comparatively small number. How many got the lights and shades? About a quarter of those here.

So we shall find all gradations down to persons who can really hardly picture it at all. Referring to my own case, I have to stop and think of one thing at a time. If I should simply pronounce the letter O, a number of people here would doubtlessly see that letter suspended somewhere here in the air. Is not that true? How many saw it? [A number of hands were raised.] I don't know why, but I did not. Some probably did. In pursuing his investigations further, Galton found that many had number forms. Some, probably not so many as raised their hands before, see numbers before them in space, perhaps arranged in the form of a cross or perhaps in other ways. I should just like to ask how many of you see numbers anywhere before you in space. [There was a show of hands.] Quite a number. Some of them no doubt see the months of the year and days of the week projected into space. It is natural with some people to see visual numbers projected into space.

I knew a woman who had quite a complicated number form. She disliked arithmetic and knew so little about it that she could, with difficulty, make change in a store. She had to pick out the figures used from her number form. Sometimes, it may be often, children who are a little abnormal in school, have one of these number forms. Some people think that, if arranged quite arithmetically such a device is a great help. It is the same way, I presume, with a great many who want to speak an oration or deliver an essay; they probably memorize it by seeing the page before them; others see only the words. I have heard of people who speak from manuscript; that is, they memorize their manuscript, and have to pause mentally and hesitate, when they get to the foot of a page, in order to turn over the page.

To go back now to auditory images. If you will again imagine meeting this friend, while some of you will see him quite clearly, others will hear the conversation; they will not merely remember what the general tenor of it was, but will seem to hear the words of the speaker and hear the peculiar quality and rhythm of the voice and all that. Some of you probably carry music quite easily in your head; so that when you think of music you hear it over again, to a certain extent. I would like to know how many hear over again, mentally, the voices of their friends. [A show of hands.] Quite a number. Of course, in talking about these images I do not mean that the same person will not have both kinds. They may or may not have both visual and auditory images.

Now when we come to motor images, as they are called, the images of movement and touch, it is more difficult to get mental pictures, and so I am sure that not so many would raise their hands as in reference to the other two. Suppose that, without looking at that Sistene Madonna over there, you just think of it. In the first place, you know where it is and I think if you watch yourself very closely you will find a pretty strong instinctive tendency to move your head or your arm in that direction. Though I do not make many gestures, yet as I spoke of the picture I pointed toward it. I had a sort of motor feeling in that direction. Now if you have imaged that picture in your minds I think some of you will probably not only see the figure but feel yourself, to a certain extent, assuming that posture. At least as I now speak of it more particularly, some will feel, for instance, the curve of the arm as it holds the infant. I should like to know if any do get a sensation of that kind. [A show of hands.] Quite a number.

I once asked this question about Millet's picture the *Angelus*. I found that quite a good many in the class felt this tendency to bend over in the reverential posture; and one young woman, whose touch energies were unusually strong, said she could feel the roughness of the clods under her feet. She was a very truthful young woman. She said that one of her cheeks was uncomfortable because she felt the setting sun striking on one side of her face. That, however, is unusual susceptibility to touch images. If you take any person who is using his hands for delicate work, such as drawing or engraving, you will see what a very fine sensitiveness he develops to the distinctions of touch pressure; distinctions which you and I would probably not feel at all. Now, in the experiment we are trying, talking with a friend, you can imagine him putting his hand on your shoulder, and some will probably be able to get a feeling of the weight. Or if you imagine yourself putting your hand on his shoulder you will get the feeling of movement forward in your hand, even if you do not move it at all.

A drawing teacher, who is quite successful in getting good art work from children, told me that if the children first acted out the human figures they were about to draw, they made a more life-like and spirited picture than otherwise. After such acting they had evidently had a sort of feeling or motor image of the position, which aided them in their drawing. As a rule, the child who posed in the class drew a better picture than those who had looked at it.

Now these illustrations will indicate what I mean by imagery, that it is a perfectly definite thing, not a sort of vague mysterious power of making up things or dealing with the unreal and fantastic. In the sense in which I use the term, imagination is a way by which we mentally present to ourselves things that are not present. You know how limited our experience would be if it were confined to what is before our senses. If it were not for this power of imaging, the rest of the world would be blotted out. Even when we remember things we remember through images. I want to emphasize that fact; we have the power of memorizing things only as we image them. Even when we think and reason we employ images.

Geometry is a pretty good example of the power of deductive reasoning, and yet even in geometry the student has to have a figure either on the board or on paper as a sort of mental symbol of the thought. Now by cultivating the habit of visualizing many people can get along without the drawing, simply by making a visual image of it, by seeing it in the mind instead of actually making it. I suppose many good visualists would do better work in geometry if they relied less on the drawing and more on the visual picture or image. So even in abstract reasoning, a person must have an image. Teachers are often surprised to find boys and girls, who, though bright in other subjects and manifesting no lack of mental power and reasoning ability, yet fail to do much in geometry. Very often it will be found to be due simply to lack of imaging power. If they could image the thing, they could reason about it. Because they cannot, there is nothing in their minds to reason about. This is particularly true when the figures get more complicated. Very often to stop and give a little systematic practice in visualizing these figures, and so train the pupil to see these figures, would be of very great assistance in the intellectual work, because it would give the pupil the necessary data to work with. Even though a person may have good reasoning ability, if he has no images of what he is handling or thinking about he has nothing to work with mentally.

Mr. Frank Hall, superintendent of a blind asylum, has had a good deal of occasion to notice the effect upon mental operations and mental habits of inability to see things; and being an unusually thoughtful man, he made a careful study of this mental weakness. Afterwards, in seeing and observing children in a public school, he got hold of the other side of it and has written a very interesting article on "Imagination in Arithmetic."

Imagination and arithmetic seem to be pretty much opposed in the minds of most people. Arithmetic, most people seem to think, is a matter of hard, cold facts, of logical relations. Yet, very often failures in arithmetic are due to lack of proper imaging power on the part of the pupil. Children ought not to deal with symbols unless they can be made to stand for images of some sort or other. It is not, of course, necessary to image, say the number 33, nor is the pupil very likely to do it very distinctly; but it does not follow that it would not be good for little children, if they were dealing with the figures 33, to have geometrical figures, say, cubes for the tens, and smaller blocks for the ones. At all events, when there are many failures, it is often due to lack of imagination.

Nor ought the images given the child to be incongruous. A teacher, for instance, asks the class to give an illustration of the half of three units, or one and one-half. The children are asked to make up a story about that, a problem. One child says, "I had three marbles and gave half of them away, and had one and one-half marbles left." If he were asked if he would be likely to do anything of that kind, he would see the absurdity of it. The mental conditions have not been at all. So it is very often, if you give children something to do with figures they will get out their paper and pencils and figure on it, and perhaps look up to ask if you want them to do the problem by multiplication or addition. They have not stopped to form the picture of what you are talking about. They go at once to manipulating the figures. A superintendent told me that he had once given children, in an apparently bright class in arithmetic, the following problem: "You can load twenty cattle into a car. Each head is worth $20. How long will it take to load the car?" About three-fourths of the children got out their paper and pencils and went to figuring on it. Problems without much sense to them generally catch children. They think that if only there are figures they can do them. A teacher was telling this same superintendent about similar difficulties in her class. He thought he would test the teacher's imaging power. A team was going by just then and he said, "How many feet of lumber do you think there are on that wagon?" She said she could not tell whether there were one hundred thousand or a million! I should not, by the by, like to make a guess myself and have it go on record as to how many feet of lumber can be put on a two-horse wagon.

Children are sometimes asked to find how many yards of carpeting it will take to cover a floor. They begin figuring on the thing without stopping mentally to lay those rolls of carpet down and see just how they go. The difficulty is very often not with the arithmetic part at all; the mistake lies in not stopping to image the conditions with which they are dealing before they start. They do not translate the sentence over into the facts. Now imaging is precisely the power or the instrumentality through which we translate abstract terms and symbols and formulae over into the actual conditions. Very often a child gets mixed up in problems about yards and rods because he has no picture of what a rod is like or what it is, and the lack of certainty which comes about because he does not picture the thing, tells against all his work.

I should like to say, on the other side, that very often in the primary work pupils are kept dealing too long with objects. Teachers have heard that it is not well to begin with abstract formulae too soon; they therefore begin with things, and rightly so, but they continue too long with things. The child should be led to deal as soon as possible with images. I think it would be almost as bad to keep a rod in the room for the child to keep looking at all the time, as it would be for him never to see the rod at all. It is better to deal with the concrete two or three times and after that with its images. In the same way, with the earlier arithmetic, dealing too much of the time with tooth-picks and buttons and a lot of things to represent numerical combination, the child grows so feeble in imagination that he cannot get away from those things. He does not gain as he ought to in power. If he had symbols long enough to get images, and after that dealt only with images, he would be much freer and more independent in his work.

A teacher, who is a very careful observer, said that she often brought up in teachers' meeting this question of imaging power. She had asked the teachers of the fifth and sixth grades how their children took hold of problems that had to deal with the number of sides of a room; say, where the floor is carpeted and the walls and ceiling are papered. This is a problem of how many square yards it will take, and how many sides the pupils would say that the room had. Well, the teachers in those grades said that the tendency was always to say that a room has four sides, and to figure on the basis of four instead of six. She then asked if the children, who had been in the kindergarten,—and had therefore, of course, counted the sides of the cubes over and over again— made this mistake. The answer was, yes. These children would make this same blunder over and over again. Her conclusion was that though they had dealt with the cube for two or three years, they had never been led to form an image of the thing. A bright child ought not to count the faces of the cube more than two or three times before he has a mental picture of the cube. If he happens then to forget how many sides it has he should count them on his mental cube. As the child gets on in school, nobody is going to carry around actual cubes for him to count. If he has an image nobody needs to. Even though he cannot remember, yet if he has the power of imaging that cube, he can count the sides at any time for himself.

The same teacher tried this little puzzle, which is more intellectual than are most puzzles. He asked the pupils in the last four grades to imagine a three-inch cube. They were not allowed to have paper or pencil, but had to rely on their power of visualizing. They were next asked to paint it red all over the outside, then to cut it up into one-inch cubes. How many one-inch cubes would there be? You can see at once that it is one thing to say three times three are nine and three times nine are twenty-seven, and another thing to see that cube split up into three rows with three in each row, an image involving twenty-seven parts. That was the first step. The next was to tell how many of these blocks had paint on four sides? Some pupils could pick out quite a number! How many have paint on three sides? How many have paint on two sides? How many have paint on one side? How many did not have paint on at all?

There are a number of simple exercises of that kind, which cannot be done unless a person can mentally realize and present to himself the conditions. I am spending a good deal of time on this matter of imagination in arithmetic, because if I can convince you that the power of imaging is useful in arithmetic, I have no fear that you will be ready to admit its usefulness in geography, history, and literature and science. When you come to more advanced problems, questions of business arithmetic, banking and things of that kind, you will find that the question is not so much on the numerical side. In the first place pupils haven't the experience of the things they are talking about. They have seen a bank perhaps but do not know what goes on within it. They are talking about notes and discounts, and drafts, but have never seen the actual thing. Even if they have a little experience they seldom have constructive imagination enough to put together the facts about which they are talking.

The difference between one child who has general intelligence and another who can perhaps recite his lessons just as well but does not have the same mental "gumption" or independence, is largely due to a difference in his constructive imagination. Before the brighter child tries to solve a problem, he sets to work to find out what it is about and see the thing mentally. An educator has lately been insisting that we hurry the child too much in the first studies. We give them something, then ask them questions before giving time to assimilate it. A good deal of the confusion children get into is because they have to react too quickly; they should be given a few moments to image what they are talking about. I will now leave the arithmetic side of imagination and go on to the value of the imaging power in some of the other studies.

As I said before, if you admit its value in arithmetic, there ought to be very little difficulty in reasoning the point in other things. Take geography. You are studying about an isthmus, or a cave, or a river, or a lake. What does that mean to the child unless somehow or other he pictures what corresponds to the thing about which he is talking? Geography is almost entirely, one might say, a matter of the cultivation of the imagination, and to a very considerable extent, of the visual imagination. A woman of my acquaintance who has traveled a good deal, especially in Palestine, and whose descriptions are unusually vivid is often asked how she can remember so well things that she has seen. Her reply is that she does not remember them at all. Whenever she wants to talk about any particular place she sees it before her and simply describes what she sees just as if it were actually there. I should be willing to guarantee that I can pick out the people in this room who are naturally good visualists simply by asking them to describe some place. There is hardly anybody whose abstract memory, simply memory, is capable of carrying in mind a complicated landscape, unless he has seen it time and time again and mentally systematized it. On the other hand, if he has a strong visual imagination, he need see it only once; the picture of it stays by him so that in one sense he does not have to remember it at all—he recalls it by power of imagination. All eminent geologists are good visualists. The same thing would have to be true of great geographers. Two people may travel the same ground and have the same original intelligence, and one person will be able to tell very little of what he has seen, because he is defective in his power of visual imagination; the other person may not possess half of his reasoning ability, and yet will beat him all out in remembering and describing what he has seen. But probably the first person may better reproduce episodes, things that have happened, because these he can put more in motor and auditory terms. A person who is not a good visualist need not therefore feel that he has no mind at all.

But to go back to geography. I think there are two propositions which are perfectly simple. One is that the child must have seen what he is talking about or seen something like it, in order to talk intelligently. You would not probably have to spend much time here developing the idea of a mountain. One institute instructor, who went into a hilly district, spent two days in the institute telling the teachers how to develop the idea of a hill! There are other things concerning which the child has to work on the basis of something he sees until he gets a fairly good mental picture. The idea of beginning with the concrete and going to the abstract, might be more helpful by saying that we must begin with sense perception, then work as rapidly as possible to imagination. The value of sense perception is, in the long run, to be found in the assistance it will provide in giving a child material, and data, and tools. If it is geography, he ought to have outdoor excursions in order to get images; he must then learn how to handle these images, how to construct and reconstruct or make them over, in order to realize scenes which have never been actually presented to his senses, but only to his mind's eye.

Even in physical geography imaging power is equally important. A great many children have difficulty in understanding the theory of the winds and ocean currents because they do not image what they are talking about. They do not see the thing. If they could see it they could get the principle very quickly. I should like to make a little digression here and say that the same thing is true in physics. Suppose it is difficult to understand the mechanism of a pump. You often get a fairly bright child who does not seem to make much headway understanding it. I think three times out of four the difficulty is not in his reasoning power, or in his general intellectual ability, but in his lack of imaging power; in other words, in his not seeing what he is talking about. If he could see those things and then see what is happening when the pump handle goes up and down; if he could see where the piston is and where the valve is, he could explain it as well as anybody else. He would merely have to follow the direction of his own images, and simply tell what he sees from step to step. If he sees it consecutively his explanation will be logical.

Take it in history. A good deal of history will remain merely verbal, unless pupils are cultivated in the power to present to themselves the personages and scenes they are talking about. If there were not so much hurry to get over the ground; if more time could be spent on a smaller but more important number of historical events and the children were encouraged and given an opportunity to build up the picture of what they are talking about; or were even made to speak or act it out to a certain extent, using the characters until they got a feeling of what these various people were like, and got moreover the strongest visual image possible of the scenes and physical surroundings in which these things happened,—I think you will agree with me, that even if they did not know so many facts when they got through the history, yet what they did know would be very much more vital to them, much more a part of themselves.

The same way in literature. Very often teachers expect children to appropriate the beauties of a poem and they really don't do it. They naturally wish to please their teacher and often pretend that they do see beauties in it, when in fact it is only a collection of words to them simply because they have not pictured the thing for themselves. Take some simple poem such as is read in the fourth, fifth, and sixth grades, and instead of talking so much about the words used, take pains to see that the children are picturing to themselves one scene after another that is described there; and I think it will not take more than one or two experiments to convince you that literature will mean more to them than it ever did before. Take Whittier's "Snow-Bound" or any of the poems by Longfellow, or Whittier, or Holmes, which we are accustomed to use in the reading lessons in school, and ask fewer questions about the grammatical construction of this and that, or the verbal points, and spend more time simply on having the children see the whole thing.

This reminds me to suggest in passing that it is not well to do what is sometimes done, that is, ask the children too much about their images. You want them to think about the scene but you do not want them thinking about their own images. Teachers have heard something about images and image-making, and stop every few minutes to ask the children about their images; as a result of which, you will see children gazing quite painfully around the room and thinking more about whether the image is there than about the thing itself. It is not necessary to keep talking to children about imagery. It is rather better to suggest the scene and give them time to image it for themselves. Many children are naturally pretty strong visualists. The power is more apt to grow weak as we grow older than to grow strong. I would rather not ask the children too much about their images; instead, have them get up and tell their pictures.

I want to go back once more to the matter of reasoning, because it is generally thought that reasoning has no connection at all with imagery. The ordinary understanding of reasoning is that it is taking two truths and from them drawing a third truth different from the other two. That is a correct, logical statement. It tells what happens when we reason. We do start with two truths and come to the third; but it doesn't tell us how we reason, what is going on in our minds when we start with two truths and arrive at a third. It is a logical, rather than a psychological definition. The teacher is more interested in the psychology of the thing. I would suggest that what really goes on when we reason is that the mind starts with two truths different from each other, then, with what we call reason, these images are manipulated and finally made to run together and blend, so to speak, into another image. When, therefore, we find children having difficulty in understanding and explaining a thing on the logical side, ninety-nine times out of a hundred the best way to correct the fault is not to try to deal with the reasoning directly, but to go back to the images which are the basis of the reasoning. In the majority of cases, if these original images can be made definite and clear, it will be found that the reasoning process will then very largely take care of itself.

[In answer to a question Dr. Dewey said:] It is all wrong to have the children personify everything. If they personify, things themselves do not interfere with them. It is a mistake to think that they will not be interested in things if they are not personified.

4. Periods of Growth

I am going to speak on the periods of growth,—the periods of development—in child life. I suppose Shakespeare was the first person to make a classification of the various ages of man, and I do not know that anyone can improve very well in general on the classification he gave. The crying infant, the schoolboy going so whiningly and unwillingly to school, the youth, the lover, the warrior, the matured man, the judge, and the reminiscent old man living in his past and second infancy, are the seven stages. We might not classify them exactly as Shakespeare did, and yet his classification is scientific as well as finely expressed from a literary point of view.

We have first the period of early infancy, lasting up to the time of the acquisition of speech. On the average this period ends at about the age of thirty months. Then comes the period of later infancy, from this time up to six or seven years. Then we have the period of childhood, up to the age of adolescence, say thirteen or fourteen. This is followed by the period of youth, the end of which is fixed conventionally at between eighteen and twenty-one years. It will not be necessary for us to carry our survey beyond that, because it is within these four periods that the conscious education of man occurs.

While the period of early infancy, two and a half years, does not fall within the period of schooling, there are a number of points in the mental growth of that period which are perhaps worthy of some attention, even from an educational standpoint. Speaking in general, it might be said that the purport or struggle of this early period is to get command of the body as a tool or instrument of the mind. We have to spend our first two or three

[First published in *White and Blue* (Provo City, Utah), vol. 5, no. 6, 1 February 1902, pp. 12–16, and ibid., no. 7, 15 February 1902, pp. 1–4.]

years catching up, so to speak, with our body. We have our eyes, ears, legs, arms, and vocal organs, but we do not know how to use them; and it takes just about all we can do for two or three years to learn to manage these things.

But in learning to manage them we learn a good deal else besides, a good deal more than physical control. We get the beginnings of mental control through tackling this job of managing our physical organs. John Fiske has put a good deal of stress upon what he calls the "significance of prolonged infancy," or delayed infancy—the putting off the period of attaining maturity. He calls attention to the fact that the infancy of the human young is much longer than that of the animal young. Others have since called attention to the fact that the more barbaric the race, the shorter the period of infancy, the greater rapidity with which children mature; and the more civilized the race, the longer this period of relative helplessness or social and industrial dependence. Mr. Fiske emphasized the effect this lingering infancy has on society, calling attention to the fact that the longer children have to be cared for, the longer will parent and child be knit together by ties of affection. His conclusion is that one of the things that have been influential in building up homes filled with the spirit of care and affection is the long period in which the young have to be taken care of.

We certainly know that among animals where the little ones are matured very rapidly, there is very little or no family life. The offspring take care of themselves so quickly that the parents are not held together. The period of helplessness and dependence among children has developed the intellectual as well as the moral qualities of race; the acquirement of prudence, of thrift, and of planning ahead, resulting mainly from the fact the little ones have to be taken care of. So it is that Fiske insists upon the proposition that the helplessness of the infant and the prolongation of infancy, so far from having been a disadvantage or backset to the race, has been a very important factor in the moral and intellectual evolution of society.

There is another side to this question, which I want to speak of for a moment. It is the fact that only through the prolongation of infancy does it become possible to educate the young. Experiments show that as soon as a chick gets out of its shell, it can strike with its head and pick for food with just about as much accuracy as it can at any later period of its life; and that it can often catch insects on the wing the second or third time it tries, and sometimes without any trying, as well as it ever could later on. This is what we call instinct and we know how thoroughly well-formed these instincts are in animals. Contrast for instance the brief time required by the little chick to get control of its organs, with the time it takes the human young to do the same thing. It takes six months at least before the human baby can begin to reach with any degree of certainty at all, to say nothing about catching minute insects on the wing. It takes about six months to get even vague ideas of distance before the baby knows enough to reach for anything. Even after it does begin to reach, it will over-reach and under-reach. It is as likely to reach for something beyond its arm as not. The little chick has the coordination even to a limited degree of accuracy and refinement.

Now we might think this a mistake in nature; that there is a decided advantage on the part of the animal; and that it would be better if the human young started with more ability—with greater capacity along these directions. But if we look a little below the surface we shall see that it is this very capacity with which the animals are born, that limits their development. It is this which locks up, so to speak, their career and sets the bars which they cannot pass over. Just because they have ready made this instinct, which appears from the outset, there is no occasion, no opportunity for growth or development to any great extent. And this, for the reason that there is no motive for further growth. On the other hand, the very dependency of the young; the complete helplessness which makes it necessary for him to acquire all these powers; and, in acquiring them, learn so many other things,—teaches him to struggle—teaches him the meaning of desire and effort and hope, and the use of memory and imagination in planning and constructing.

To be an unlearned being is, in other words, to have an infinite vista of future capacity and development open before one; while to be born with powers ready made and complete, means a limitation, an arrest of capacity. Moreover, it is this helplessness, this fact that all have to be taught which gives the opportunity for variation and therefore for progress. The animal has to do with the same thing in practically the same way, because it is by instinct he goes ahead and operates; very much like a machine. But just because we have to learn things, we can select our means and methods of doing—adapting means to ends; and with such growth,—with the selection and adaptation of means to ends, there comes the capacity, we might almost say the certainty. So whether we look at it from the standpoint of influence upon the parent and society, or from the standpoint of effect on the development of the young themselves, I think we shall come to the conclusion that this fact of helplessness, the long continued period of social dependence during which the child needs the guidance and direction of others, is a thing of exceedingly great importance—of even great moral and spiritual importance. And so it was that I said there is a good deal of meaning in the fact that the child has to learn the use of his physical organs, learn to see, to hear, to walk and to talk. All these things, which are habits with us, which are automatic, which have become second nature, have to be acquired by the child.

There is no doubt that the child is deaf for a very short time at least after birth, and he cannot see objects; perhaps it can begin to distinguish light from darkness, but that is a thing very different from seeing, observing and recognizing things. To see is just as much a habit that has to be acquired as is walking and talking. If I hold up this book, you see it is a book so instantaneously that it does not occur to you there is any mental process, any creative activity required. But that is because you have the power of seeing so thoroughly formed that it goes on automatically. You do not have to use force and will-power to walk; and if it were not for our having little ones among us, and seeing what a struggle they have to learn to walk even, we might think walking, too, were something impressed upon us from without, and not requiring active energy on our part. It is because these things have become a habit on our part that we are not conscious of the activity of thought and attention put into doing them. But the child, when he is really learning to see, to hear, and to walk, is solving problems; he has to investigate, experiment, correct his mistakes, and start over again, in order to do the thing right. The problem is much more complicated than we might think, and it is in dealing with these problems, which to us do not seem to have much intellectual significance, that the child gets the beginning of his mental training; because he has to use his memory and judgment in order to see and hear and walk and talk. In a certain sense he is also getting beginnings of moral discipline in that he is finding out the processes of control. In order to do these things he has to learn to direct his activities to a certain definite end, and I think we should all be very slow in saying that there is no moral value in acquiring this ability to control, even in the use of the physical organs of the body.

When the child can walk and talk, can use words—employing his physical organs to make sounds which are intelligible to others—he has completed what we might call the first epoch of his career, that of early infancy. At the age of two and one-half years, the child, as a rule, will have a pretty good vocabulary. The average child in average surroundings knows six or seven hundred words when he is two and one-half years old. Children vary about this. Some who are bright in other ways are backward about learning to talk. They understand the words. They are mentally learning to put words together very often in their minds before they try them in speaking. I was told of a boy who had absolutely refused to talk until he was about three years old. The parents had heard that children who are backward often begin to talk in a remarkable way. One day as he stood by the window he remarked, "When it rains it is wet." That was a contribution of youthful genius which has been handed down in the family. While the intellectual quality was not up to the expectation of the parents, it was, as you notice, a somewhat complex sentence. These were the first words he ever uttered, and he must have been practicing talking in his mind for some time. For some reason he had not seen fit to bless the world with his discoveries until he made that very scientific observation.

When the child has gained the power to walk and talk he has the ability to enter freely into relations with others, and of course that means the attaining of intellectual and moral freedom, the ability to initiate, the opportunity to try things for himself, and make acquaintance with things and objects on his own account. Walking is, so to speak, a sort of outward symbol of the elementary beginnings of moral freedom; and then there is also the ability to talk, then the great world of social intercourse is open to the child. I should say that just as the essential mark of his first period is making acquaintance with his physical organs, and consequently with the intellectual and moral discipline which go along with the mastery of that problem, so the next period up to the age of six or seven is characterized by the making of fundamental social adjustments. If we stop to think we shall see that the child learns about all the larger social relations between the time of two and one-half and six or seven years of age.

The society with which he comes into relation is not a very large one. It is composed generally of his own immediate family, his relatives, his neighbors, and the few other children who are playmates. But to make the necessary adjustments with those few is after all in a way to make about all the social adaptations. He has to learn politeness, courtesy, the social functions. Then he has to learn the matter of sitting at the table properly, using his knife and fork and spoon properly, observing the social way of asking for food, and saying, "Thank you" and "If you please"—things which are elementary and trivial to us. Perhaps if we think of these things at all, it is with the feeling that they do not amount to much; but for a child they really mean introduction into the social world; for in forming these little habits, he is getting the rudiments of social adaptation. So of course he also has to learn to understand the wishes and ideas of others and accommodate himself to them. He must learn also to take the initiative in certain little things to begin to do for himself and to do things for others. And while his social world is a very miniature one, I think there are very few typical social relations to which the child is not introduced—and introduced moreover in a very intimate and close way—during these years.

If in the earlier period he has been making acquaintance with his body, he is in this period making acquaintance with the people around him. It is now people and his relations to people that are of the utmost interest to him. He has not much intellectual power and intelligence. We do not send him to school to learn things for the sake of learning. If he goes to school at all it is to the kindergarten, where the main thought and idea is that of proper social relations with others. What we want him to learn most of all are the social lessons of kindness, politeness, and ability to do things with others, and to take the lead when it is the time to take the lead. It is accredited by some that the Battle of Waterloo was really won on the playgrounds of Eton and Rugby in the English public schools. This means, of course, that in the social discipline of sports and games the young learn both to follow and to lead. They learn to work together for a common cause; and this community of effort goes back to the period of youth, taking its life out of the personal relations of children with each other and with their parents. The unconscious moral training which children get in making these social adjustments and adaptations, if they live in a favored and happy family environment, is perhaps the deepest moral education which they ever get; an education which goes down to the very fibres of their being and which stays by them when things which they have learned in a semi-conscious and deliberate way pass away. We have, in my opinion, pretty good reasons for supposing that if, during the first seven years of their lives, we could get for all children a perfectly ideal social environment,—one which should bring them into right relations with others and guide properly their thoughts and imaginations, we should succeed in giving them a tremendous start in the right direction. We should form social instincts and habits of helpfulness which would carry them very far in the later years of life.

What might be called the mental side, the really essential feature of this period between the ages of two and a half and six or seven, is the development of fancy or imagination. I spoke a good deal about images and image-making this afternoon, but I wish to follow up that same thought along a little different line here this evening.

When the child gets along to about two years of age, say, he has become acquainted with a good many physical objects, and with the uses to which they are put. The latter idea is the more important. To a little child the object is what he can do with it. Some of the studies made of children have been directed to seeing how they define things. Even older children begin generally by defining objects from the standpoint of the use, function or activity of the thing. Smaller children seem to have no idea of things excepting in terms of their use. A hat is something to be put on, and when the child sees the hat, he puts it on. A doorknob is something to be turned, and if he can get hold of one he will turn it. But having reached this power, his range of capacity is after all rather limited, because he knows simply the local uses of the things which present themselves to his senses. Now it is by the power of imagination, or imagery as I tried to explain it, that the child gets released from the bondage or thralldom of sense perception and begins to build up a larger world.

I saw a little baby once, a bright boy of about three and a half years of age, who happened to see a watch chain hanging in a pendant form. "See the hammock," said he, swinging it back and forth. That expression represented the dawn of imagination in him. If he had seen an actual hammock he would undoubtedly have tried to swing it back and forth. This was simply a watch chain; but it suggested something not present to his senses. Now it is this carrying over of one experience into another which marks the dawn of imagination in children; and consequently marks their emancipation from enslavement to the very limited world of things which can be presented to their senses.

Some brought up a question about children's make-believes. There is no question that this is a marked feature, perhaps the most marked feature of the mental life of children in their third and fourth year. The child gets hold of an acorn cup and plays it is a teacup. He makes believe leaves are plates, and very soon he has a whole teaparty organized. I have never seen a child of three years old who did not go through the form of knocking at the door and coming in and saying, "How do you do?" We all know these little plays and make-believes of childhood. They are part of what makes children so cunning. We always say, "How cute they are!" But we do not always recognize the great intellectual principle involved in these things. I tried to indicate that these make-believes are not, in one sense, the make-believes that we have in fairy tales and myths. The child that makes believe that he is making a call, is doing a real thing after all. The child who lays out his acorn cup and leaves and plays teaparty, is playing something which in itself is perfectly real. He is not going off into the purely unreal world. So it is with most of the make-believes of children. As far as I have noticed normal children, they always make believe the things which they see other people doing. Through imagination and make-believe they are learning to understand their world. The child is not competent to have a real teaparty; he is not competent really to cook the food and set the table and all the rest of it; but by playing these things he gets a certain control over the form of the process and a certain educative knowledge of the elements and factors that enter into it. The child is so immature, so incapable physically and in many respects mentally, that he cannot do the real thing, and cannot therefore get the education that would come by doing the real thing; but by making-believe doing it, he becomes acquainted with the factors and relations involved. This make-believe is a sort of vicarious means by which the child brings home to himself a world of experience too complicated and too difficult to come within the reach of his practical, real powers. The child therefore whose imaginative life is cut short, whose life of make-believe and play is cut short, has, of necessity, an arrested development. These plays are the tendrils by which children reach out in every direction to lay hold of and become acquainted with truths and activities which otherwise they never would come in contact with. It is a wonder the world had to wait so long to recognize the great educational value of these plays and activities of early childhood. To be sure, Plato taught this truth over two thousand years ago; but his words and ideas did not make much impression, and for centuries the plays of childhood were, on the whole, looked upon with a good deal of contempt. They were rather despised as trivial, or at least treated simply as amusement which could be tolerated because children were children and couldn't be expected to do things which could amount to anything, and so were not given credit for value of any sort. It was not until the time of Froebel that it was recognized what a great power—what a necessity in mental and moral growth are the play activities as based upon the child's imagination.

What I have been saying takes it for granted that there is a certain relation between the child's imagination and his play. I wish to emphasize that point a little by saying that the image and the play are simply the inner and the outer side of the same thing. I have referred several times, in a previous talk, to the psychological principle that every thought, idea, or suggestion tends to be acted on at once; tends to find some sort of motor outlet, unless arrested or inhibited by a conflicting image. Now the child's play is about as good an example of that principle as we can find. The moment he has any thought, that moment he wishes to put it into action, and this is where his play comes from. He is taken possession of by his ideas, by his feelings and his fancies; and these at once show themselves in activities. This is the reason that he is always dramatizing, always carrying forth his thoughts into play or other activity.

Whether science gives any light upon the question of stimulating a child's imaginative thought was a question that came up this afternoon. When children's imaginations are stirred and excited beyond the capacity of carrying them out in action in any way, I should be afraid that we are reaching the danger point. I mean that when, from stimulation of the imagination, there results an image that cannot be carried out in some kind of play or game or dramatic make-believe—such, for instance, as to stimulate the child with stories which he does not react on, which do not enter into his playlife—the evil is just as bad for the child as it would be to excite the adult with emotional entertainment and harrowing spectacles which could in no way be related to his character. Stories for children are a very good thing, but sometimes the thing is overdone. They are told one story after another, each one a little more sensational, until the budding imagination is seared and dulled. Parents know that children like the same story over and over again, if it is a good story; and they get new food for imagination out of it time after time. The mere formality of it instead of being monotonous seems to add to its interest for them. Now my point is here: that when the child's imagination is stimulated and excited time after time, he soon gets more images and feelings stirred up than he can possibly act upon. On the other hand, when we see the child putting out his thoughts and feelings in his plays in some way or other, we may be pretty sure there is less danger of immoral or unhealthy results coming in; for the activity takes, on the whole, a helpful channel, and so what might be hurtful if it were penned up inside the child, can be turned off.

Imagination really is the transferring of one experience over into another. I saw a little girl whose doll was all broken to pieces. It had just one leg left, but she took that piece and put it to bed and played with it just as if it were the entire doll. She carried over to a part the experience that was proper to the whole thing. The little child who called the watch chain a hammock and began swinging it, was transferring over the value and meaning of one experience into another and similar one. Now through that vicarious principle—the principle of transfer—the child's world is tremendously enlarged and he learns to get many things in order; and his activities are all, of course, controlled in a very free and plastic way by suggestion and by emotion. You know what the drawings of children are like. If they draw a house the walls are transparent. You see the bed or table or whatever they wish to show. The actual reality of the thing does not count for very much with them. A few months ago, I saw some little children's drawings illustrating Christmas, and in several of them the stockings were so big that they could not be got inside the house at all, and had to be hung outside. From the artistic standpoint, so to speak, of effect and proportion, children have but little interest in the matter, they are guided mainly by their feelings.

One of your number was speaking to me this afternoon, and it happened to be on a subject I thought of touching, viz., children's lies, especially little children's lies. I suppose a good many parents have been shocked, especially with their first born when instead of the moral child they hoped for, they have apparently brought into the world a little infant Satan, who tells lies with remarkable freedom and ease; and not understanding the psychology of the matter, these good people have been very much worried. While, of course, there are kinds of lies which are very serious, even with young children, a great many of these so-called lies should not in any moral sense be considered lies at all from the adult standpoint. They are simply images in the child's plays, and result from inability of the child to distinguish between imagination and fact. Some children are pretty logical from the start and do not have this tendency to imagination. Others, while they think clearly, yet identify themselves so completely with the things they are doing, that they fail to distinguish fact from fiction.

A recent noted writer, in his book of children, quotes the story of a little girl who told her older brother and sister about seeing a snake. The child was very excited about it. They thought she was romancing, however, and asked her if it had a little silver bell tied on its neck. She said that it did, and then they were convinced that the whole thing was made up. In later years she still maintained that she had seen the snake, and that the moment they suggested the little silver bell around its neck she saw that, too, because she was excited. It was only in her own later years that she realized she really had not seen the snake in that way. This is perhaps a somewhat extreme case of the extent of the child's imagination, because it illustrates what may happen when the emotions are intense. The instance of a child's drawing a stocking bigger than the house illustrates better what I mean. In one sense the child knows that the stocking is not bigger than the house, but not from the same standpoint that the adult knows it. And so I am inclined to think that, excepting where the child tells lies to deceive, and we can see that there is something else that is back of the lie, possibly we should not take too seriously a good many of these little stories. Sometimes by dwelling too long on them we hold before the child what he would naturally throw off if left to himself. I am speaking of course of romantic stories that have no bad motive behind them.

Another fact is that the child in this period is at the mercy of suggestion, is controlled by it, and is best corrected by it. The really skillful disciplinarian, whether parent or teacher, learns to govern children for the most part indirectly; that is, by putting some thought or image in their head, and trusting that image or thought to work itself out. By this means the teacher is relieved from the necessity of seeing that the child executes the thing; he just drops the seed and it sprouts into action on its own account. The power of suggestion with children is tremendous. Possibly teachers sometimes use it too much. I sometimes think that teachers almost hypnotize the children with suggestion. But after all, suggestion rightfully used is on the whole the chief instrument of directing the activities of little children.

I once stood watching a little boy running briskly along the street. Presently he stubbed his toe, then fell and hit his head a pretty good crack on the sidewalk. Another boy came by and said, "Did you lose your glasses?" The boy up to this time had not thought anything about his glasses; but now he stopped crying, almost by a miracle you might say, and proceeded to look around for his glasses. It was about as striking an example of the power of suggestion as I have ever seen. It switched off his thoughts into another direction. When he had his mind at rest about his spectacles he had forgotten all about his hurt.

The skillful teacher knows how to use this same principle to keep attention out of undesirable directions, and direct it to working along the right line. In the same connection I should like to say a word about the psychology of too many "don't-to-dothises" and "don't-to-do-thats." We all know practically that a very little negative suggestion works a long way, and there is a very good psychological reason for believing that it works the wrong way. As an illustration: the child is playing quietly enough and the parent says, "Don't climb the tree." The child had not thought of it before, but there is a great deal of suggestion about "climb the tree," and he gets uneasy and finally starts to climb the tree. The only part of a negative suggestion that really operates in the child's mind is the positive part. The negative part really leaves him with a sort of uneasiness to go ahead and do the very thing he has been forbidden to do, or that has been suggested to him not to do; while if he had been given a positive suggestion in another direction he probably would not have done the forbidden thing at all.

A coachman came to confession, and after listening to his sins, the priest asked him if he ever filed the teeth of his master's horse. The man did not know what he meant, so the priest told him that if he did, the horse could not eat the oats and then he could steal and sell them. The next time the man came to the priest the first thing he confessed was that he had filed the teeth of his master's horse.

The purely negative way of dealing with children has very often no other effect than strengthening the force of the forbidden suggestion in their minds. You can say "don't" for a good while and it doesn't really carry much motor power with it. Of course it may be associated with other things that do carry motor power; but the don't itself doesn't go a great way. The moral of this whole matter is to be careful to give the child positive suggestions along positive directions as far as possible. Of course I do not mean that even this principle cannot be carried to the extreme. We have to use judgment; but the emphasis or stress ought to be on the positive rather than on the inhibitive side.

As children get on to six or seven they move less by simple suggestion and images and are more anxious to work at and reach something for themselves. The little child is propelled from behind; as an image comes into his mind he goes ahead and acts it out. He has no purpose, no definite aim or intention, at least not very far ahead; but a change comes at length. Our children cease to be babies, and we begin to feel that they have their own little plans and schemes; and when this time comes they begin to control their activities from in front, so to speak, instead of being propelled from behind.

I saw some children playing "I Spy," at the age of six or seven, and when the person who was "it" called out "coop," about half of these children would start and run for the goal, paying no particular attention to the rules of the game but just trying to get there. They simply had in their minds the image of moving toward the goal and when they got started they just kept on doing it. Other children recognized that there was a definite point to be gained, and they were regulating their activities and taking counsel what they should do.

The ability to forecast some definite result and to direct the intermediate activities so as to lead up to that result, marks the passage, or transit from later infancy to childhood proper. Of course this transition comes gradually. From my putting these things before you in the way I have, you might think the change happened all at once. Of course it does not. It is with children of six or seven years of age that we begin to notice the transition. The make-believe play ceases to take so large a part of their thought, which means that they are not so contented to go on and make-believe. Their plays change to games. A play has no rules, no particular point or end, no aim. Suggestions come one after another to children, and each is played until they tire of it. But when you have a game, like hide-and-seek, you have a certain point that has to be made, a certain result that has to be reached, and consequently the steps toward it have to be regulated. When children therefore begin to substitute games for plays, begin to be more critical, begin to plan ahead, then has the changed attitude fairly come upon them. It is by the practical recognition of this fact that the period of six or seven years has been fixed for the child to go to school. He can now be given tasks, can now assume responsibility for performing certain things that bring definite results. Schooling, that is to say, more conscious instruction, can now profitably begin.

I shall leave our little child at this point this evening, and start him off at this same point to-morrow evening, when I shall give a general discussion of what takes place in his mental growth during the next six or seven years. [See lecture six.]

5.   Attention

I suppose there is no word which has been more honored in the schoolroom than the word attention. It is used so often that it almost becomes, both to teacher and pupils, a byword, a mere command or suggestion, such as "Attention!" "Pay attention!" And with good reason, so far as the idea is concerned; for though the word is possibly a little overworked sometimes, attention really represents the unity of the action of the mind. If the teacher is attentive, or if the children give attention, real attention, to the subject matter, it means that they are giving their minds to it.

We use the terms attention and mind as synonymous. "Mind me" or "Pay attention to me," and "Why don't you give your mind to what I have to say?" convey almost identical ideas. Attention is the mind. At least we come nearer to the truth of the matter by identifying attention with the mind than by considering it separately. Completeness of attention, absorption of attention, concentration of attention, means that the mind is given unreservedly to the matter. It is not so much a testing of the power or faculty of consciousness, as it is consciousness itself in its intensified workings.

Young men pay attention to young women, by which is meant that they care for them, that their minds and thoughts are taken up with them. It is not a particular faculty that is brought into play; their whole being is absorbed in that direction. A mother tends to her infant. The cook tends to the cooking. It means that the whole energy, interest, consciousness, is in that direction. If we therefore get the attention in reality and not the mere form of it in the schoolroom, we really get the absorption of the ego, the

[First published in *White and Blue* (Provo City, Utah), vol. 5, no. 7, 15 February 1902, pp. 4–8, and ibid., no. 8, 1 March 1902, pp. 1–5.]

subject, with its subjects, and the whole universe of values is centered in the particular thing to which the person is giving attention.

Unfortunately, however, there is a schoolroom attention which is a sort of simulation, or imitation of the genuine article. When anybody is absorbed or attentive, there is a certain physical poise, a certain expression of the countenance, a certain bearing of the whole body which indicates that attention is being given. Children instinctively learn to simulate the outward appearance of fervent, even enraptured, attention; and they do so only because they know that the more they have the appearance of attending, the better they can be thinking of something else.

I suppose there are certain children in every schoolroom who are considered by the teachers to be dangerous when they have this rapt and lost look on their faces. The teacher knows from experience that it is a sign of mischief. Sometimes by the way in which attention is asked we unconsciously make hypocrites of school children. We almost insist on their deceiving us by insisting that they put on the form of attention. Now, as a matter of fact, people can attend very well when they are a little relaxed. A child can attend pretty well when he does not look straight at the teacher. He can attend even if he is looking at something else, or playing with a pencil. It takes some judgment, some tact on the part of the teacher to be able to discriminate the signs of genuine attention; and not insist all the time on this external form which the child comes to simulate while he really keeps his mind elsewhere. This truth will perhaps appeal to you from your own experience. Unless you are more fortunate than most people, you have felt yourself wake up just in time to hear your name called or a question asked, and then felt yourself relapse back again into the train of your own thoughts, although you did not for a moment lose the attitude of attention. Simply telling children to give attention does not secure the reality. The word is a very poor substitute for the idea; and when the teacher relies simply on the command, he is very likely cultivating the mere semblance of attention. This brings me to a consideration of the natural, necessary, indispensable conditions, psychologically speaking, of attention.

What attitude must the mind be in? What conditions must be supplied in order that there may be real attention? Very often the word attention rings out across the schoolroom in such a way that one is led to believe attention to be a sort of dark lantern which persons carry around with them to flash now on this thing, now on that; and to conclude that when the command is not heeded it is because pupils do not choose to do so; that to do so or not to do so is purely a material matter, so to speak; in other words that there are really no psychological conditions of giving attention.

It is the teacher who acts on this principle, who does not recognize that there are conditions to be met, that gets the form of attention without the reality. If I were to tell you there is something in this room which is most valuable and were to dwell for a long time on the great value or importance of it to you, saying nothing about its nature or quality, but just talking on in general about it being a most important thing,—and then at a given moment tell you, "One-two-three, start and get that." What would you do? Would you give much attention? Would you try to direct your energy? You would either think you were being made a joke of, or your minds would be confused; you would think that you were expected to do something without any idea what it was.

To tell a child to attend is a good deal the same kind of procedure, unless there is some end at which he is to direct his energy. You would not know how to go to work to look for a thing if you had no idea whether it was a moral, mental, or physical quality. You would have to have some clue of what to look for— something which stands for an end, an object. In other words you must have an image of what you are to do. It is the same with a child in the school. Unless he has some explanation, some anticipation, some mental image, to which he can give attention, it is impossible for him to attend. Really, all the word attention can do for the school is simply to act to give notice that there is going to be something to attend to. It may call off their activities from elsewhere and put them in an expectant attitude. The same effect might be got by striking a bell, or any of a hundred other ways. Used as a command, the word is nothing but a signal that there is going to be something to direct attention to. The first point that I would make about attention is that there must be some end in view, some result to be reached, some image in the child's mind to which he may direct his energies.

Attention is directed toward the future. The cat watches for the mouse, not because she has the mouse and has killed it, but because she is going to have it and going to kill it. So it is of attention. Etymologically, the word implies a reaching forward, or stretching out, as the Germans call it, for something which is ahead. We cannot pay attention to anything which is perfectly familiar, that is to say, to anything which is already in our possession mentally. It is this element of reaching out towards the future, which of course implies some kind of aim or purpose, that is the basis of directing the attention.

It is convenient perhaps, in speaking of attention, to refer to three elements in it, which I shall very briefly call, the "for-what," "to-what," and the "with-what." The "for-what" is the end, the aim, the thing to which the present material or fact points. The "for-what" is not present, it is future. It is the something ahead which we are after; but in order to get at that future something we have to have a present something to which we can attend. In order thus to move from point to point in interest, we have to have some fund of resulted experience, some already formed habits, some apperceptive material—to use the language of psychology—with which to attend to the thing.

Going back to the "to-what," I may remark that there is a great deal of confusion in teaching in regard to its relation to the "for-what." Teachers often think that all that is necessary is to furnish the child with something *to* which to attend. If it is an object lesson, all that needs to be done is to put some object before the child and tell him to attend to it. Or if it be in arithmetic or geography, to point out the lesson and tell the child to study. But the full conditions of attention are not simply that the child have something *to* which to attend; he must also have something *for* which he is to bend his mind—some end that he wishes to reach. When that end is an intellectual end, we call it getting truths; but the difficulty of this general way of putting it is in the implication that there is something in general which is true, and that a pupil can be interested in truth in general,—both untenable ideas.

The truth which can be made to interest a child to get, must be specific, must take the form of a problem in his mind. Such a truth then becomes the "for-what" of his mental quest, and he attends to the subject matter, not as a thing important in and of itself, but as furnishing the material or data to help him reach the end he has in view. The principle might be illustrated by considering the case of a person who is lost in the woods. He has to attend to things about him, but his attention does not begin nor end with these things. Otherwise he might begin to study the kind of trees around him or the formation of the rocks. A hundred things might claim his attention which, so far from helping, would actually hinder his getting home. But if he keeps the "for-what" in mind, he has some basis for a choice of the "to-what" which is likely to assist him. In other words, he will pick out those things which help him get home, and will neglect the other things.

Or you might take another instance which happens to appeal to me just now. If you were going up a mountain without any definite trail, you would have to attend to things about you or you would never get to the top. Keeping the summit in view gives you the basis of attention to those things which serve as guides; should you forget your purpose, you might still attend to the things around you but you would certainly never get to the mountain top. You would perhaps be gazing upon the objects of nature about you, very interesting possibly, but not likely to further the particular point in view. I wish to repeat once more that too often we give the child simply something to attend to without giving him any motive for attention. He is made to study without having any question or problem in his mind; and he does not know when he comes to that which he should be interested in finding out about. Or we might say the only interest he has is just in getting the lesson. He has no intellectual interest in the subject matter to make him keen and on the alert with reference to it.

The good teacher by instinct perhaps more than by conscious knowledge of the underlying principle, tries to arrange her work so that the child's mind at the end of the recitation shall be left in a state of suspense instead of being made to feel that the whole business has been thoroughly gone over, and explained, and understood, and recited upon, and finally laid away on the shelf. She will try to leave questions in the child's mind at the close of the recitation; will leave him with the feeling that there is something more coming quite as interesting, or even more so, than what has been already gone over. The more active, the more positive, and self-assertive that attitude of expectation and inquiry, the more vigorously and intelligently will he go at the further study, because he has something which he wants to find out, and he knows that what is in the book and what he can get from others is going to help him solve this question.

We generally assume that problems and questions belong to arithmetic; but intellectually speaking problems and questions are just as much a necessity in teaching geography or history or even spelling as they are in teaching arithmetic. The child who is not brought into the inquiring attitude, the attitude of having problems which he wishes to find out about, will never get control of his own attention. He may give attention as long as he is under the eye and direction of others, but the moment this pressure is taken off he will not have a motive or stimulus within himself to attend; and so his thoughts are quite likely to go flying off in all kinds of directions. On the other hand, the person who seizes upon ultimate questions will always have an active and alert mind, will always have a basis for directing attention to what is new.

So much for what I have called the "to-what" and the "for-what" in attention, the end or aim, and the material or facts to which we attend in order to reach that end. I fully comprehend that object lessons carried very far, become about as monotonous to children as mere booklearning does. At first they seem necessary in order to stir up interest, but if kept up they lose their fascinating and absorbing quality quite as certainly as do statements in print, that is to say, if the object lesson is presented in a certain way. That way is to neglect bringing into the child's mind the proper motive, before giving the material; just making him attend to the object without any question that he wants to solve.

There was an epidemic of orange object lessons. Oranges were exhibited and analyzed in every institute and then they circulated in the schools. I am so far from Chicago that I can speak of this matter without hurting any feelings. There was no question roused in the children's minds to sort out what they knew from what they did not know, and then come to the orange to answer the question; but the whole object was gone into and exhaustively analyzed: the skin, the color, then the texture of the skin, and so on. After all the external qualities were enumerated and cataloged, the children were directed to the interior of the orange. Now it is probable that nine out of ten of those children had a fairly intimate and somewhat personal acquaintance with the orange already, while they may not have systematized these points and put them down in their minds one by one. But the question is whether they did not get nineteen facts with which they were already familiar for one new fact.

If there is one law of attention more positive than another, it is that we do not attend to familiar things. The only use of attention is to bring things under control, to get hold of them, to master them. If they are already familiar, it is a waste of physical and mental energy to direct our minds to them. Once thoroughly under command, they get more or less habitual, and then more or less unconscious so far as our taking note of the process is concerned. We walk and talk without having to stop and direct our attention to how we do it. If we did stop we should not succeed as well as we do without. Almost anybody can walk straight until he begins to think of doing so. If you try to walk a chalk line you will find it very much harder to do it than if you did not think about it. Directing the attention to the thoroughly familiar thing is very often confusing besides being a senseless step.

To go back to the orange. There is nothing but monotony in forcing the child to give attention to things it already knows, because there is no motive for it. Now I do not myself wish to try to give a model lesson; but I would say the thing could be gone at very much more intelligently by telling the children to tell what they could remember about the orange without looking at it. That would introduce something new, the element of experimentation in forming an image of the orange, and then when everything they did know was exhausted, bring in the object in order to correct the mis-statements made, and answer some question which they themselves could not answer from memory. You can see at once how much more alert, keen, and interested you would be in the orange if you came to it to get an answer to some question you already have in your mind, than if you came without any earthly reason whatever excepting to make an exhaustive and complete inventory of all its qualities. Of course the psychologies are full of illustrations of the fact that we do not attend intellectually to familiar things. We do not hear the ticking of the clock. It is perfectly regular in our room, and unless we are very much interested in the striking of the hours we soon cease to hear the striking. If it stops ticking, then attention is at once on the alert. Psychologists point out that we do not attend to things with which we are familiar, but they do not bring out the principle quite fully enough. The whole object of attention is to bring the new under control, to explore, to inquire, to investigate, to carry the mind out into fields not familiar, to carry forward the states of knowledge, to expand them further into the boundary of mystery and the unknown; hence the entire lack of economy, not to say the lack of sense, in giving attention to what is thoroughly familiar.

Now if we recognize on the other hand that we cannot give attention to anything that is completely unfamiliar, we are brought round to the third division of attention; namely, the "with-which" we attend. Everybody knows how confusing it is to see a large number of entirely new and strange faces at once and to hear many new names, or be set down in a foreign country and hear everybody jabbering, as it seems, a strange language. How confused, how lonely we find ourselves, and how we have to hunt round for some point which is reasonably familiar, at which to begin in order not to get entirely flustered with the strangeness of the scene. This means that while there is no sense in attending to things familiar, there is no possibility of attending to things wholly unfamiliar. We have to have in the mind something that is at least akin to the unfamiliar—a "with-what" to which the new resemblance may be joined. The secret of instruction is very largely that kind of judgment which enables the teacher to present new points in material in such a way that while they seem to be new and thus stir up the mind and arouse it to put forth new energy, are not felt to be so new but that the pupil, hunting over his present store of knowledge, can hit upon something that shall enable him to deal with them.

Arithmetic is one of the ideal subjects for making these gradations between the old and the partly new. Yet there is no subject, perhaps, where this principle is oftener violated. The child is put into fractions, and very often the teacher takes pains to bring before him fractions as an entirely new subject, instead of putting the matter already dealt with in such a way as to bring the child to realize what points of the new are like the things he already knows. Such teachers never think of making a survey of the things already within the pupil's power and then locating in it the one factor which is new; they never realize that because it is new, it needs to be developed by the assistance of what the pupil already knows. The child is plunged into a new field and goes all over it at once. There is a good deal of false breaking up of things in such analysis; but there is another mode of analysis of which we do not have nearly enough: the kind whereby the pupil may, without the teacher's aid, make himself familiar when he tackles a new job; that is to say, by looking the entire field over and finding the point of least resistance, the point to be counted with first. The child reads his arithmetic or grammar over and over again, and trusts to the many times of going over the thing in this wholesale fashion to make it a part of himself, while if he were trained by the teacher to habits of study in his recitation, he soon would learn that there is always one thing which is the first to go at; that there is always a certain amount in the new lesson which he virtually knows, or which is at least very much like what he knows, and therefore that it is wasting energy to spend very much time on that; that the thing on which he centres his attention is the new thing, the one step in advance beyond what he already knows.

Anybody can attain,—I will not say miraculous,—but striking results in intellectual discipline, who learns this simple mental trick of seeking the keyhole of the situation; who breaks up his habit of tackling things at large and wholesale, and learns, when he has anything new, to go at it carefully and find out how much is familiar to him, or reasonably like what is familiar. He thereby discovers wherein lies the difficulty to be mastered and understood, and can concentrate his whole attention on that point, and then go on to the next. It is a law of attention that we do not attend to the familiar, and it is a law that attention wearies or weakens naturally at the point of greatest difficulty, at the point of greatest stress or strain; and the teacher who helps the child to recognize for himself where this point of stress is, so that he may concentrate his attention upon it, is doing a tremendous lot to give him command and control of his own mental faculties, to the end that after a while he can be independent in his work— take the initiative—and not need the continued guidance of the teacher. We attend with the old to the new. That is one reason why it is so absurd to put a certain lesson before the child and tell him to attend to it, and that if he attends he can learn it, when possibly he cannot attend. You might just as well put one of us down in France, who knew not a word of French, and when he said he could not understand it, just tell him to pay attention and listen and he would understand it. The trouble is he has no point of identity, no point of communication. If he could just strike one thing in common, could say this particular word means this one idea, he would have a basis from which to get a mental outlet with which to reach out and get more words and ideas. Until this point of contact is set up between the mind and the object, we can tell a person for a long time to attend, and he will not do it; not because he is naughty and does not want to, but simply because, psychologically, the mental conditions of attention are not there.

One reason why constructive work is so good a training for children is that it introduces them naturally and necessarily to the conditions of giving attention. In the first place there is some result they have to reach. They have to weave their mat, or make their box, or cook their cereal. It does not make any difference what, so that there is something practical to be done, some end to be reached which affords the necessary and indispensable basis for giving attention to the various steps by which they reach it. If he is going to make a box, he has to attend to sawing his wood straight. He has to attend to measuring his wood and getting the right angles. He has to attend to driving nails in right places, and there is a continual demand for attention at every place.

Col. Parker said he never really knew what attention was until he went into a manual training school and saw how absorbed the children became. The psychology of it was that they had something to do which gave them a motive; and the end to be reached being there, they really could not help paying attention, any more than a boy who is interested in baseball can help paying attention to what is happening to the ball. The boy who does not come to be alert, and watch what is happening to the ball, very soon gets put off the playground. The alertness, keeping the eye on the point, is recognized to be the necessity of success. It seems to me that while we cannot at once bring about these same ideal conditions in the schoolroom, we ought to recognize that when there are normal psychological conditions, it is just as inevitable, up to the point of physical fatigue, that a pupil will give attention to what is going on as well as the boy who is interested in the game of baseball, or the young lady who is interested in the parlor social, will give attention to all the forms that enter into that thing. These various forms of manual or constructive work make good educators of attention, because they represent the end to be reached, a point which, from its correctness, can be the more easily grasped by the mind; they make therefore an excellent preparation for the more abstract and intellectual attention with reference to getting intellectual ends; that is, solving problems.

Were I to attempt to make this lecture practical, I should insist on the teacher asking himself three questions in giving a lesson to children. The first would be: have they been supplied, either by past experience or by me, with some unsettled thing, some point which they want to reach but have not reached? In other words, have they been given an aim?

One of the greatest fallacies that pervades the schoolroom is that if only the teacher has the end the child does not need one. The teacher knows the point that is to be gained by learning these facts in geography or history, and so it is thought that by some mysterious process the end in view is going to get into the child's mind. Or the teacher simply says the end to be gained is so and so. Well, you may continue for a whole week to state that so and so is the end or aim of the lesson and it is *not* the end to the child, unless it is the end to him; unless the purpose somehow enters into his own mental operation, all this reminding on the part of the teacher is waste work. The first question therefore is, has the child an aim in moving in this direction; if not, how shall he be given an aim?

The second consideration will be: is the child supplied with the material necessary to help him solve the problem?

Of course, the more the pupil can be made to bring in of that which is not in the textbook, the more he can be made to turn over his own experience and bring in his observations from outside—the more likely is he to come in contact with the problem, which is a real problem to the child, and not simply a school problem. I should like to say on this point that it seems to me teachers often overestimate the necessity of making up problems. There is a pretty fair number of problems that arise within the child's own experience, and the idea that you have to make up questions for the child to wrestle with in order that he may get mental muscle and fibre, is very misleading. It is simply laziness on the part of the teacher. It is much easier to take a puzzle out of a textbook and just tell the child to go ahead and solve that than it is to come into intimate contact with the child's experience and see what things are there which would naturally lend themselves to study in the forms of problems. The second point then is to see that the child is supplied with the material necessary to answer the question that has been raised.

The third consideration will be: what has the child had in his past experience either in or out of school, which will be valuable to him? and how shall the new matter be presented so as to connect most closely with the old?

I used to talk sometimes to teachers about the subject of interest. I found out that the term is getting to be misunderstood. A great many people think that to interest means to make everything easy and amusing, when in reality it means quite the opposite. Give the child a problem; there is no real and genuine interest unless there is something new to be mastered. Natural interest is in getting ahead. There is no question that until the mind is supplied, it wants to get more experience, and so has a natural interest in that direction. I want to say that interest is really just this connection between the new and the old. There is no interest where there is nothing new. There is no interest where it is all new, because there we have no power, no sense of assurance. We have no ability to go ahead. Very often you hear that the boy has no interest in a study, but it is generally because he cannot do anything with it. If you can arouse him to a sense of power, to a realization that he is accomplishing something, you will find that his interest stirs up tremendously. Just to make him feel that there is one point which he has thoroughly mastered for himself will arouse interest. To put it etymologically, interest is that which comes between the subject and object in attention, between what the man has to give and what the object brings. And wherever there is this sense of contact between the old that is already in the mind, and the new which is yet to be mastered, there will not fail to be interest.

I want to say one word or two along another line. We insist very largely in talking about attention, the concentration of attention, the fixity of attention; but it is well to recognize that alertness is just as important as concentration. You know that no one can keep his mind fixed for more than a fraction of a second. If you do, you become hypnotized, get into a state of hypnotic sleep. The mind is made to move and must move from one thing to another. For instance, give attention to this book for a minute; you will find that what you were really doing was to turn from one point in the book to another; while the mind was on the book, it was all the time changing. You thought of its form, its color, its markings, and then something inside the book. If you just try to keep your mind on the book without any change, it is either an impossibility or you will go to sleep. One way to hypnotize is to get people to concentrate their attention fixedly upon a single thing. Concentration of attention does not mean what it is sometimes taken to mean. It does not mean mental paralysis. The mind must be kept moving. If that is the case, how, it may be asked, can there be any concentration at all? By having one end in view. If you have a problem to solve, you do not take one thing after another at random; you select. Concentration is not then an arrest of movement of the mind. The general concentrates his troops not by keeping them still, but by moving them somewhere. He moves his regiments in varying order to some common point, to some destination. It is this movement of our ideas towards a common point that stands for concentration; and there can be no concentration without alertness; without the pupils being on the *qui vive* to take in the new.

A teacher told me a little while ago that they were discussing the various "persons" in grammar when she asked of a particular boy a question of this sort, "If I say, 'we are talking,' what person is it?" He thought a moment and said, "Second person." The class raised their hands and corrected him very promptly. The teacher told him he ought to know better than that; that of course it was the first person. She said afterward that she got to thinking about it, and wondered whether he had not probably had something on his mind; so she asked him what made him say it. He said, "The second person is the person spoken to. Then you said that there were more persons spoken to than speaking." He had done more thinking in all probability to get the wrong answer than the majority of the class had done to get the right answer; and if it had not been that the teacher was more on the alert than the average teacher, and gone back, nothing would ever have come out of that.

Suppose that boy had never been given a chance to justify himself; and suppose such discouragement went on day after day; what would be the effect on his mental attitude and power? Would he not get, unconsciously, at least, the habit of thinking it is not worth while to think things out? He would never be allowed to justify his answers. Reciting would be just a question of saying the right or wrong thing from memory,—or perhaps from peeping in the book. Reciting in this fashion brings no real alertness, though the children may look as though they were intensely interested, raising and shaking their hands, and displaying all the other physical and mental signs. But really if the child has not been given an opportunity to turn the problem over in his mind and tell the reason for the answer; if there is less attention given to finding out why the answer is given than to whether the answer is right or wrong, so that it can be marked,—alertness is bound to be killed, unless the child simply has, by native force, an unusual force of wide-awakeness. Some minds have so much natural vigor that they come through successfully, in spite of the repression and deadening of attention which they get in the schoolroom; but no average boy or girl can stand more than about so much of it.

I would like to suggest in closing then, that we perhaps over-exercise docility—I mean mental docility—in the schoolroom at the expense of mental alertness. It is a little disturbing to have children too much on the alert. They sometimes get off their poise and visitors think they are rambling, and it is so easy to mark them. And so to a large extent, the one great intellectual feature of the school comes to be docility; simply making the mind a blank surface upon which first to impress, then to repeat the ideas of the book and teacher, instead of making it a place of active questioning and cross-examining, both on the part of teacher and children, and thereby keeping the mental movement going on. You will say that there could not be concentration; that the children will bring in all kinds of questions and nothing definite will ever be accomplished. This of course is not so easy as it is simply to hear recitation, as it is to hear simply the words or even the ideas of the textbook given back, and then mark the children or judge how correct they are in the answers they give. It is a much more difficult thing, but things worth much are generally harder than things humdrum and ordinary.

I will close by saying that real, genuine attention means mental movement, not only on the part of the individual but also on the part of the class. It means that ideas come into the class, various persons follow out those ideas, and new points are brought out; and yet the teacher harmonizes it all, combining this play of variety, this expression of different elements, so that it leads consistently and consecutively in a definite direction. Sometime or other, when every child in all of our schools shall recognize that there is a motive for everything worth learning, that there is really a reason and a present reason for learning it, and that he has something to say that is of value to others, there will be such a regeneration of our schools as it is now almost impossible to contemplate, even in our imaginations. When we shall have gained that one necessary thing, then I shall be willing to say that all other things will be. That which deadens school work and makes children shirk it, is simply the lack of a controlling motive, an aim with an assurance of some meaning, some problem on their part. I repeat that when this assurance of ends and aims can be brought into the school as a whole, we shall have an educational regeneration, we shall have a new life in the schoolroom.

6.   Period of Technic

[*Theme of Lecture Four Continued.*]
   I spoke last evening of the first two epochs of growth, the period of earlier and the period of later infancy, bringing the child up to the age of six or seven. In order to get the thread of the course I will review very briefly what I said at the end of the hour last evening; viz., that while the smaller child is moved by suggestion, by feelings and imaginations which he tends to work out according to the interest and importance which they have for him, as he grows older there dawns upon him another spirit, a desire to reach definite results, an attempt to control activities so that they shall tend toward the wished-for result.
   Dr. Harris, in his psycho-educational writings, has indicated these same distinctions by referring to the earlier period as the symbolic period, and to the later one as the conventional period. Now we are not to think that this change from the very plastic attitude, where the child moulds things to suit himself, to the observance of principles of cause and effect, is a sudden and abrupt thing. The child of three or four years who is learning to dress himself, to brush his hair, and to wash himself is getting initiated into principles of cause and effect. He knows he has to do certain things in order to reach a certain definite result; and in much of the kindergarten work during the last few years there is an attempt to get more of a balance between symbolic work and actual constructive work, where some regard has to be paid to morals. Children learn along causal lines, and they really attempt to make little things and make them in a definite way. But on the other hand the child of six or seven still needs a good deal of free play. It is found by experiment that children of seven can

[First published in *White and Blue* (Provo City, Utah), vol. 5, no. 8, 1 March 1902, pp. 5–9, and ibid., no. 9, 15 March 1902, pp. 1–4.]

play many kindergarten plays with more enjoyment and really work them out more intelligently than the kindergarten children themselves. They like store-keeping, for instance, and similar games, working them out and developing them day after day. I repeat, therefore, that we are not to assume that the child suddenly changes wholly from one attitude over to another, but simply that there is a gradual change of the stress or centre of gravity; that in the earlier years the preparation is on the side of free play, with only a fraction of the mind energy given to observations of causal relations, and that gradually the emphasis shifts to the other side.

Last night I called attention to two distinctions between games and plays. In the game there is a definite end, a particular point which the children call the goal. Because there is this definite point to reach, there have to be rules to the game, principles to be observed. There are certain laws laid out, certain formulas, which have to be learned and abided by. Popular psychology has rightly located the age of games as the beginning of strictly school work; work that involves instruction along certain definite lines. Six years likewise is made the legal age, in most of the states, for sending children to school. I am inclined, however, to think, from observations I have made, that the average child of six is nearer the average child of five in his mental and emotional attitude than he is to the child of seven. Changes whereby the child apprehends the more technical things, such as cause and effect relations, are not marked in his development before the age of seven, unless forced upon him. I am quite convinced that we should do better if we made the first year of primary school a larger element of the kindergarten, leaving still prominent the social instincts and play elements, and reducing to a smaller margin the definite and specific instructions given until the next year. These things differ in country and city. I do not know what the practice is in this community.

A few years ago, I was accustomed to meet once a month or so, with a round table of city superintendents in the suburban towns about Chicago. We were discussing number, and it was interesting to find that many of the superintendents had taken the formal instruction in number from the first year of school. A few had it in the fall quarter, some in the spring, but many did not begin until the second grade. The unanimous testimony was that children so treated knew quite as much about number in their third year as did others who had been drilled throughout the first year, and had moreover an interest all the more lively and intelligent from not having had the life and vitality all taken out of it. I mention this as a specific instance of where a large number of intelligent school men found it practical and desirable not to introduce so much formal instruction in the first year of school.

There are doubtless many sub-divisions in the mental growth of the child during this next period—the period between the age of seven and, say thirteen or fourteen—but I wish to speak simply of one. Children seem again to change their attitude about the age of nine or ten. At first they are interested in getting particular results and in getting at the means requisite to such results, in other words, causes. Later on we find them interested in getting the skill necessary to produce the desired results. They have, so to speak, generalized this principle, that in order to get a certain result you must make use of certain means, must do things in a certain way; from which principle they become actively interested in the matter of skill as a thing in itself; whereas up to this time they have been interested in skill, not as a thing in itself, but simply as a means necessary to a particular result. Now the character of their games changes; we find boys especially going over to games where the element of competitive skill becomes more important, where the point of the game is not so much the outcome as the skill; and they exercise a great deal—repeating and practicing over and over in order to get the necessary dexterity.

A greater knowledge of these things would help a good deal in school teaching. We should find it advantageous in teaching for us to postpone mere acquisition of skill until this period; until the child was naturally interested in getting skill. We should thus lighten the work of the sixth, seventh, and eighth year, requiring training for skill only in directions justified directly by results. I might illustrate it by the study of penmanship. If the child six or seven or eight wants to write, it is the thing itself in which he is naturally interested, not accurate writing, but simply writing. Teachers can of course develop an interest in the skill, even at this age, but it hardly comes natural to the child. He is interested rather in expressing the thought. I have often heard children of this age, when told to write a little story or essay, say, "Now, shall we write a lot and tell what we want to, or shall we write just what took place and see how well we can write, and say only a little?" Their own natural interest is rather to say as much as they can, not caring much about the form and quality of the execution. Not so at a later period; there comes then to be a basis for interest in the skill and perfection of the handwriting, apart from the thought to be conveyed; the same thing is true in number and to a certain extent in reading. You will often see children of nine or ten asking for hard sums; they sometimes actually like long rows of figures because they find a pleasure in testing themselves on things that are hard.

The same change comes about quite clearly in drawing. So far as I have noticed, children of seven or eight are, in the matter of drawing, a good deal in the attitude of children of five or six; they do not care much whether pictures resemble reality or not. Their drawing naturally is illustrative drawing, not an accurate reproduction of objects. Children do not draw the apple that is placed before them: they draw an apple that they have the thought or the feeling of,—an apple in their mind; and unless they are watched very closely, they will draw their stock apple, their mental apple, so to speak. We all know how conventional are their trees,—just a line up and down and little branches sticking out,—and how box-like are their houses. When they get to be about nine or ten, children are apt to lose interest in purely imaginative drawing, because they feel that it is likely to be laughed at. Before that time they take no thought about it at all. Boys and girls also give up some of their childish play at this time. They feel that there is not enough cause and effect in this to command the respect of other people. Many children who have drawn naturally and freely up to this time, begin to lose interest unless they are introduced to the proper technic of the art. And I wish to say in passing that technical art for schools,—and this period from ten to thirteen or fourteen is particularly the age for acquiring the technic of various subjects, the technic of writing, of reading, of drawing, of number, and so on,—is no other than the art of acquiring skill as skill; that is to say, the art of acquiring the best, most effective, and most economical ways of doing things.

Before this the child has been interested in the thing, and the way of doing it has been simply incidental to the thing itself; but now there is this gradual change of attitude, this transaction whereby he gets to be more and more interested in the way of doing things; and the teacher will do well to take advantage of this new interest children have in doing things in the best way. The difficulty in our education—music is a very good example— is that the child is introduced to technic too early. Children are set playing the five finger exercises and scales over and over again, without having any musical thought or ideal or result to reach. A young woman once told me about her art education. She said students went to a famous art school full of ideals, full of artistic thoughts; but their teachers said they could not do this, nor do that, it was too ambitious for them. So they were put on pure exercises in technic and kept on that kind of work for about two years. In the third year they were allowed to construct something, but by that time they had as a rule been so drilled in the mere dress of ideas that they had ceased to have ideas to express. The same thing often happens in music and singing. The pupil is so much drilled in the technic, apart from the music or the song which completes the musical whole, that by the time he has practiced long enough to attain musical efficiency, he is no longer interested in playing anything. His musical feelings have been killed outright, unless he has much genius.

I have been very much interested from a psychological stand-point in watching the change which has come into the teaching of music in Chicago, during the last ten years. It is a good illus-tration of the psychological principle under discussion. They are beginning to let children try themes or musical wholes from the very first lesson, and then give them their technic incidentally. If a child wants to sing a song or wants to play a little tune on the piano, he must, in order to do that well, learn certain things that pupils ten years ago used to be drilled on. The fact that the chil-dren under such a stimulus voluntarily do their practicing, and are interested in doing it from this very feeling that it leads to some definite purpose of their own, is sufficient explanation of the much more rapid progress made even in the skill and technic of the thing.

The same changes are coming about in the drawing instruc-tion. I can remember when drawing was introduced into the schools of New England, the exact look of the drawing board, and the kind of exercises. Originally it was a very beautiful scheme. As all drawings are made with lines, there are but straight lines and curved lines, and by proper combination of straight and curved lines you can draw anything. So our first lessons were to make dots and then we made straight lines connecting these dots, first horizontal and then perpendicular lines. We next put these horizontal and perpendicular lines together and made little crosses; then drew diagonal lines this way and that way, and put them together into squares; we then made a few curves, and if a pupil survived that process, he was allowed to go on and draw pictures somewhere up in the high school. Theoretically it was a very nice scheme. All pictures certainly are made by straight lines and curves. Therefore teach pupils first to make straight lines and curves and they will know how to put them together and make pictures. Logically, I repeat, it was a beautiful scheme, but psychologically these drawing books were not worth the paper on which they were printed. A few natural born artists may have survived, but nobody really learned to draw.

Begin where the child is. Let him illustrate the story he has in his mind. And yet, I think that even this idea is carried to an excess; to put it a little more strictly, the method is not of itself an intelligent method. If children are allowed to go on too long making crude pictures, they recognize at last that they have no skill and get disgusted with the whole thing. I am not making a plea for having no technic, but rather for introducing the technic along the line where the child feels he has a use for it in order to reach his end. Even kindergarten pictures can be helped in the matter of technic. The child draws his picture, and the teacher calls attention to this and that and suggests to him indirectly that such was not his own idea, and would he not like to see better how to carry out his idea? He will very soon learn the difference between the foreground and the background, not as points by themselves, but simply as assistants to a more effectual communication of his own thought. The same thing of course applies to writing. The old orthodox method in every subject is to reduce the thing to its different logical elements and then practice the pupil on these logical elements until he has mastered them all, when he was supposed to be able to make the combination. The writing method was just like this drawing method. The letters were analyzed into various lines and typical forms, and we were practiced on these until we were reasonably perfect; we were next allowed to make words and afterwards sentences; and then if anybody had a thought left, he might write a composition to express those thoughts.

Here again the tendency is to reverse the method; to make it a psychological rather than a logical matter; that is, to start from the child's whole—from some idea he is interested in communicating—and train him to use words as helps in expressing the thought that he has. Then also they can introduce the technic, at first incidentally as a mere assistance to the expression of the thought, and finally in the skill for skill's sake, when he learns to recognize the value of exercises purely as practice. Pupils who have thus been given technic as helps to themselves finally become interested in the skill for its own sake, and are willing and even anxious to do technical exercises which, had they been presented at the outset without any such use relation, would have repelled them at every point.

Of course I might go on to state this matter a little more in terms of pedagogical theory as the relations growing out of analysis and synthesis in education. I shall not stop to develop it, except to say that the child must of course begin with the mental whole. He cannot really begin with anything but the whole, whether in reading, writing, drawing, music, or geography. He must have something which satisfies his mind. That does not necessarily mean a physical whole; a theme is a psychological matter, not physical matter. It is whatever comes to the child as complete in itself, so that he can get intellectual and emotional satisfaction out of it. Now the child's first wholes are often impressions, crude and indefinite; and this fact points out the reason why analysis comes to have its place, and gives us a principle for determining when analysis is necessary and valuable. When the child is brought to realize the imperfect and crude character of his original whole he feels the need of a more adequate, more perfect, more definite whole; analysis, in other words, comes in to clear up the vague thing with which he has been struggling, and enables him to locate the point or question that he is dealing with. In a previous lecture on attention, I referred to the principle of concentrating the mind where the point of stress comes in, and letting what is more familiar take care of itself. It is exactly this same principle which controls the use of analysis. The difficulty is that theorists often invent a certain method of analyzing and it is copied without any reference to common sense or the natural limitations of the thing; and so, instead of concentrating the analysis upon the particular part which at the time is not clear to the child, and directing analysis so as to clarify that particular point, absolutely everything in the problem is analyzed. I do not know about your local conditions; but I do know that about twenty years ago there was a wave of analytic teaching which went through the east. That wave is still moving and is stranded upon the beach, so to speak, in a good many schools yet. The child was not allowed to do any sum without analyzing every step. Nobody can distribute his attention over a whole field and have any mind-power left.

The same thing is true in grammar. Analysis of sentences helps pupils realize the force of language, clarifies his ideas about language and the conventional use of language, gives him mastery of the most effective and economic way of communicating thought, and goes back to the mental sources behind the expression of thought in a sentence. Because analysis is good, a child is made to analyze and parse every word in a sentence, familiar and unfamiliar, putting on the same level things already understood with things new and novel, instead of bringing the analysis to bear on the new and difficult part and allowing the rest to remain a natural synthetic whole. To repeat, then, the child begins naturally with the psychic whole. Analysis should come in to clarify and build up the points that are defective and imperfect; but it should not proceed to the point of leaving the child unable to see the woods for the trees. Analysis should not go so far that he cannot put the details back into the whole again. This happens when everything is analyzed to the same extent; in such a case the child practically loses his capacity of seeing the whole.

I heard a college gentleman speak to a college audience on the business man's view of college education. He said he firmly believed in college education, but he would like to tell a few stories. He asked a large business man in Chicago about his experience with the boys who had a college education. He said, "Well, if I want a person to do careful, analytic, routine work, I like to get a high school or college graduate. I know he has been trained to analyze and take care of the details and the parts. But if I want a man to get ahead in business, to make new projects, new constructive inventions, instead of sending for someone who has been trained in school, I send for someone who has been trained in business." His idea was that the excess of analytic work in schools had left people very often with the capacity of analyzing what other people had done, but without the power to go ahead and make constructions themselves. In other words, it made them good critics, but poor constructors and inventors. He raised the question whether this defect, often seen in college-bred people, was not connected with excessive education in tearing things to pieces, unaccompanied by the necessary synthetic or constructive work in projecting and dealing with wholes.

To repeat my point and bring it into a little closer connection with the main topic, I should say that the determining unit of the child's mental life should be the manipulation of means to reach ends or results. This unit of purpose subdivides into two heads: first, where, during his early school life, he is interested chiefly in the result itself, and only incidentally in the way of getting that result; and second, where, during later years, he is more interested in the method of doing the thing in general, than in securing any result in particular, because he feels that if he can master the method he can do any number of these particular things at will.

The moral which I have attempted to draw is the necessity of working from the child's mental whole, crude though it be, toward the end in view, and so communicating or expressing the thought involved as to keeping technic and analysis secondary to it. Another way of stating it is to say that all instructions ought to be so given as to add to his power and to his sense of power. The two things do not necessarily go together. It is not enough to add to his power; his sense of power—the recognition of his own increase of command and control—ought to be coordinately trained. He ought not only to know, but to know that he knows.

I said a few words this afternoon about interest, and I should like to repeat them from this point of view. There is nothing that the strong growing boy and girl is more interested in than increase of power. Children are not interested simply in being entertained: they get sick of it. It is only the spoiled children whose interest tends excessively in that direction. I do not say they do not like a certain amount of pure recreation; they do, of course. But they are interested in this sense of power, if they are normal; and it seems to me that, along this line, teachers can appeal to children's interest without incurring the weaknesses often resulting from special appeals, such, for instance, as softening their mental fibre, causing them to hunt for soft jobs, and, in general, disinclining them for tackling anything that is hard. The interest in power, in the acquisition of skill, is the general interest and can be entertained and appealed to without these evil consequences following. Interest can, of course, be cultivated in very wrong directions; but rightly managed it can be turned in the direction of standing up fairly and squarely and mastering difficulties; not by saying dogmatically, "This thing has got to be done, and you go and do it," but by making them feel the increase in power and consciousness of power which comes with facing a difficulty instead of dodging it. Interest is sometimes presented and practiced upon as if it were a sort of vehicle by which the child could enter and be slipped from one difficulty to another without his knowing it; a sort of carriage with springs and cushions in which he could glide over all difficulties and never really stop to face any of them. Such a smoothing of the way comes from a misconception both of the nature of interest and of the nature of children. Children are children, but they are not the weaklings which they are sometimes taken to be.

I have spoken, I hope, sufficiently about the strong points in the kindergarten; points which in many respects are fundamental to education. But sometimes sentimental ideas get introduced too much into the practice. In one Chicago kindergarten a little child asked the teacher if lions ate people. The teacher said, "Oh, no, lions wouldn't do such wicked things as that. No, lions wouldn't eat dear little children." The child said, "What do lions eat?" "Well, lions eat hay." The idea was that nothing unpleasant or hard or difficult should ever be put before children. This is simply a rather exaggerated illustration of how the idea of interest is sometimes looked upon. The difficulties are to be sugared. Such a view is simply a perversion. Interest really means that the child shall have some end to meet, an end which means something to him, which will call out his powers. There are very few ends worth reaching which do not take some effort to reach; and I think the candid testimony of teachers would be that if children are really interested in reaching an end, instead of putting forth less effort, they will put forth more effort, because they have something in view which calls out their power.

But on the other hand, there are, as I said this afternoon, plenty of obstacles naturally in the way, so that teachers need not lie awake at nights to invent difficulties. There is discipline enough in doing things that need to be done, things which the children recognize the necessity of, so that it is really not necessary nor advisable to give too much time and thought to inventing puzzles and artificial difficulties and obstacles. To hear some people talk about the necessity of discipline and having children trained to work and face difficulties, you would think the world did not have difficulties in it until they invented a few to put before people. There are enough difficulties in anything that is really worth working at to give a child plenty of opportunity to exercise his power of facing and overcoming obstacles.

Now it seems to me that these two things—interest in doing things and skill in doing things—are the main ends we want to reach during the periods of elementary education. I do not mean, of course, that students are not expected to get a certain amount of information. They must cover a certain amount of ground and learn a certain number of facts in order to get hold of the data on which to work. But after all that side—the side of pure knowledge—ought, in my opinion, to be secondary to developing the child's sense of ends and aims which are valuable, and to developing his judgment and strength in adapting and adjusting means in order to reach those ends. In the development of science we have come to place more and more stress on methods, and less and less upon facts by themselves. Scientific men do not usually expect to carry the whole universe of facts in their minds, but they do expect to carry certain methods for finding out facts; and the really scientific man has, generally, these methods well at command. He has to have the necessary amount of information of course to work his methods; but after all the scientist is not made by the amount of information he has acquired, but by his ability to use old truths and find out new truths.

It is only children that we expect to be walking cyclopedias. Adults recognize the value of reference books. We do not expect to remember ourselves all the facts of geography which we try to make children remember. Somebody has said that a "forgettery" is quite as valuable as a memory. Since we cannot remember everything, why not recognize the fact that some things are more worth while than others to remember? Since I have come to be an adult I have learned to doubt whether it is really worth while to remember the name of every river and mountain in Asia, the exact direction in which the river flows, tracing it out as if it were a thing of life and death importance. I have come to be convinced that if I really want to know the direction of that river I can look it up. And there are a great many other things I would rather have a book remember for me.

Grown people, I repeat, trust more and more to methods of finding out things. We want to know where things are to be found and how to use books to get at them, but we do not load down our memory and conscience with the whole universe. I believe we shall come to recognize that the same is true of children. The great thing is to train them to methods of getting to work to solve problems. I suppose it is my own conviction—but it is a conviction—that about two-thirds of the time spent on arithmetic could be saved and devoted to something else. We seem to act on the theory that the child must learn in school all he is going to know in life; and consequently that we must teach him everything that is so and a great many things that are not so, during his school years, instead of training him in certain arithmetical methods. There are not a great many: addition, subtraction, multiplication, division, integers, and then fractions. Who has ever heard of any arithmetic not the outgrowth of these methods? A pupil who has mastered fractions, more than the laws and definitions about fractions, he has a method which will enable him to work out the necessary principles and problems in ratio and percentage; but for fear that something will sometimes come up, and for fear he will miss some element of discipline which we ought to give him, we make out a lot of different cases; and this is supposed to be commercial arithmetic. But the business man does not use any of that at all. The child is given them because he is expected to be prepared for business life, but if it is pointed out to a teacher or text-book maker that these things are not really in use, he says they are included just for the discipline involved. I notice that when no sensible reason can be given for a procedure, somebody says it is necessary for discipline.

My point is this. We could get better results if we laid more stress on training the child in methods of doing things, and made that the primary thing. I suppose that if some earthquake were to blot out all the scientific books in the world, and yet leave the scientists with their methods of investigation, it would not be an irredeemable catastrophe. Persons could utilize those methods. That is the difference between modern civilization, especially western civilization, and that of ancient times and of the Orient. You take the Chinese of to-day, and they think they have to learn and hold in memory every fact about the universe. The reason the Anglo-Saxon civilization is superior is that we have learned to get methods and so can get particular results when we want them. We have introduced this idea into our education up to a certain point, but I do not think we have carried it far enough. This thought did not occur to me until just a few years ago when I got to thinking about geometry. It occurred to me that there are really not so many methods in geometry after all. This thought had never been suggested to me when I was a student. Every proposition seemed to stand on its own legs and had to come out as if there were an independent proposition. It seems to me I should have got my geometry a good deal more easily if I had known that there were only about so many methods, and that I might go to those systematically, trying one method after another. I suppose eventually some writer of textbooks will be daring enough, instead of filling up his book with all the problems he or others have been able to invent, to try to bring the child to recognize the methods, and classify a lot of these problems merely as particular cases in the developing of the methods.

The period between seven and fourteen is the time above all to get command of skill, of technic. This truth is recognized of course in our excessive curriculum of studies, only too often they are presented topsy-turvy. We do not recognize that the conscious command of the method must grow originally out of the child's conception of definite aims and results. There are two theories about this matter, as there usually are about every matter. Some insist that the child ought to begin by making something whole. Others say the child does not have ability enough to make a whole, that he has to be trained in principles or elements before he can make combinations. One person says, "Let the child make something and get the skill through the process of making." Someone on the other side replies, "You have to show the child how to hold a pen before you can teach him to write." "No," is the rejoinder, "You can teach him to hold a pen as part of the process." This is the gist of the discussion in a nutshell. It applies to writing, reading, grammar, drawing, music, as well as to manual training. Upon the whole our schools in the past have been conducted under the idea that children must have all the technical exercises first and then the method. Let the child begin by trying to do something, by getting at the thing, object, or result; and then his training on the side of skill necessary to reach this result will come along with the doing, and will seem real, instead of mechanical or routine. This divergence in practice results from a difference between the two conceptions of education. One regards education merely as a preparation for the future. The child is going to use certain operations, hence he must be trained now to get the skill. The other regards the child as being educated through present experiences, and that he must get skill out of and along with such experience; and furthermore the skill and power he gets must find present and immediate application.

I heard a class discussing this matter of education for something a good way off, in other words, the value of the respective theories of preparation. I am not going over it all, but will allude to the one matter of procrastination. It is not in human command, when you are not going to do anything with a certain power for two, three, four, or five years, to feel that certain things are of pressing interest; so the habit of putting off is largely the natural product of this artificial preparation far away in the future. Making a child go at a thing on the basis of the immediate value and worth of the thing could never induce this mental vice. While in the earlier years the child gets only general values and relations established, it is what we call the elementary school period which ought to give him a fundamental initiation into the methods of reaching results; and results, let us add, which are results to the child, not merely to the teacher; and results to the child mean something in his present life, something immediate, not a vague something in the future.

7. Habit

The subject of habit has been discussed so many times and is so familiar that it is, perhaps, not a very attractive topic; nor do I know that I can add anything to it beyond what you have already heard. At the same time, however, a consideration of the subject will enable me to present, in a little different light, some of the psychological principles that I have spoken of in connection with my other lectures. I suppose that in spite of the dryness of the topic, no subject has been more widely discussed, nor is there any point upon which more extreme views have been taken, than regarding the value of forming habits in education. One view says, that character itself consists of habits, and since the object of education is to make character, the object of education can be stated as consisting in the formation of habits. We all know how much of the time of the schoolroom is actually spent in the formation of certain habits: punctuality, obedience, conformity to certain rules, reading, writing, the use of figures, and so on.

At the other extreme we have the idea of Rousseau, who said that the only habit he would have his ideal pupil form, was the habit of not forming habits at all; that he would do everything possible to keep the activities of this pupil from getting into habits. Now when we have such extreme views we have a paradox that is worth examination. Why do some consider the formation of habits to be the end of education while others— among whom are Rousseau and some of the reformers ahead of him—have so low an opinion, such contempt, you might say, for habits that they would take pains to eliminate them from the

[First published in *White and Blue* (Provo City, Utah), vol. 5, no. 9, 15 March 1902, pp. 4–9, and ibid., no. 10, 28 March 1902, pp. 1–3.]

process of instruction? There is an old saying that habits are good servants but poor masters. Those who consider habits important in education doubtless think of habits as the organized instrumentalities through which the mind carries out its various ideas. To have habits is to have a body of servants at command who take the orders of the mind and lie in wait about us until we have arrived at the decision, until we have formed our plan, and take upon themselves the performance of the choice which is arrived at. They take upon themselves the execution of the plan, thus sparing the higher activities of the mind from the details of performance and execution, relieving those higher aspects of the mind, so that they may again go on to devote themselves to reflection and deliberation on matters not yet settled.

On the other hand when Rousseau and those who follow him say that they would minimize the formation of habits in education, I suppose they are thinking of habits becoming so fixed that they run us instead of our running them. Habit in any act is a sort of routine or groove in which the mind works. It marks a channel in which the activity goes on almost unconsciously or automatically. Now habits can be formed in such ways as to limit choice, to limit deliberation, reflection, and investigation. There is such a thing as becoming a slave to habits, becoming a creature of routine. We may get our habits formed in such ways that they limit us; that we cannot go on thinking new thoughts, or change our modes of action when we ought to change; cannot switch off onto any other track because we have worn the ruts so deep that once in them we stay there. Habits then are good servants but poor masters. That arouses the question of how it is that habits can be servants? Putting it the other way, what are the methods of the schoolroom which tend to fix habits in such a way that they limit and so arrest our growth and shut in our individuality? What are the dangers in habit formation that we ought to be on our guard against? You hear it very frequently stated that habits are formed by repetition. Indeed that may be taken as the common statement of the formation of habits. In order to give a little emphasis to my point, so that you may realize what I am getting at, I wish to state that repetition comes after habits are formed. We do not form habits, ordinarily, because we repeat, but we repeat because we have formed habits. A habit formed simply by repetition is very likely to be the undesirable sort of habit—that which is likely to be our master instead of being our servant.

I heard a gentleman once lecturing on the formation of habits by animals. He told this story to indicate the way in which habits are formed through repetition. He said a friend of his had a fine dog who was kept shut up inside a high fence. There was a gate with a latch on it and the pup was always trying to get out. One day he accidentally struck the latch, the gate came open, and he got out. The next day the pup was trying the gate and hit the latch again, and this time it did not take him so long to get the gate open. Day after day the dog struck the latch a little quicker, until finally he went straight to the latch, opened the gate, and got out whenever he pleased. The lecturer said this was a good illustration of the way in which a habit is formed: merely by repetition of an act originally performed accidentally and without any intention or purpose.

Now it was thinking about that story which led me to question the theory that habits are formed through repetition. I made up another formula to take the place of that one. It is this: that habits are formed through success and not through repetition. If that dog had repeated the actions of the first day he would very likely have been in that pen yet. He would have just gone on doing the whole thing over and over again. He wouldn't ever have formed the habit of going straight to the latch, opening the gate, and getting out. The first activities of the child, as well as of the dog, contain a great many superfluous activities. When we first start to do anything we make many more movements than are necessary. The pupil who is learning to write twists his body, squints his face, sticks his tongue out, and moves all the muscles of the body; and when gradually he has learned, motor activity is restricted to the one channel that is most effective. It takes time to learn to eliminate all this superfluous activity and send the nerve current out only to those muscles of the arm and fingers which are concerned in the writing. To the extent that he limits motor activity, to that extent he is free to think about what he is going to write. On the other hand the beginner is so occupied with the mere movement itself that he has no consciousness left for anything else.

The point is, if we went on repeating original performances

we should form no habit at all, or else we should form a very awkward one. We really form habits by eliminating the excessive activity of our first attempt, and emphasizing that particular activity which leads in the direction we want to go. Everybody who has tried learning to ride a bicycle has a good instance of such elimination and emphasis. Take some habit you have acquired since you can remember. You know you began in a state of confusion. When you got on a bicycle you made a good deal too hard work of it; you went through many unnecessary motions and got in your way. A child beginning to write screws up his body and gets between himself and his end. So it is in the formation of all habits. Selection must come before repetition, and continues to have more prominence than repetition.

What is the basis of this selection? Success. One movement of the dog was more successful than the others. What he hit the latch with—his nose or his paws—became the most prominent sensation, for thereby he got what he wanted. The sensation corresponding with the movement which was successful gained in importance at the expense of all the rest. The sense or image of the one activity which succeeded left a sort of percept in the dog's consciousness, and it was from this percept that he started the next day. It was through the building up of that consciousness—that sense of the successful activity—and the eliminating of all the others that he finally got the habit.

I should like to ask you to put that statement over from the dog to the child who is learning a habit, and see if exactly the same principle does not hold there; then ask yourself whether our school practices are not vitiated by overrating the relative importance of repetition and not emphasizing the importance of getting a clear and definite consciousness of the right way of doing the thing. That is what I mean by saying that success, not repetition, is the true principle in the formation of habits. The one activity which really accomplishes something, and which leaves the child with a sense that he has accomplished something, and also with the idea of how he accomplished it, is worth a hundred humdrum routine repetitions in forming the habit.

I said the other day that I have seen children drilled on two and two make four until I am sure they were suspicious about the things being true. This is an example of habit formed by repetition instead of through a sense of the relations of numbers. I heard a teacher say the other day that when a child she could remember perfectly well all of the multiplication table except seven times eight. She was a good psychologist by nature, and had said to herself, "I mustn't fool about that thing any longer but must learn it." Instead of repeating over and over again seven times eight equal fifty-six, she just wrote it once and then looked at it hard and said to herself that she was never going to think about it again, but was going to get it this time once for all. Although but a comparatively small child, she had the sense to realize that the proper way to get the number habit is to get the attention so thoroughly concentrated that there is a mental grasp of the thing to be learned, and then one complete intense experience obviates repetition.

All of us have heard about meaningless repetition in religion. We have altogether too much of this same memory or voice repetition in our schoolrooms. About three-fourths of the repetition, I should say, is not intrinsically necessary, or if necessary it is so simply because we do not have the conditions so adjusted that the child does it right the first time. If he did, and his interest was at white heat, we should find that the amount of repetition necessary to transform it into a habit would be greatly reduced. But we act on the principle that the child has to do it a whole lot of times anyway, and so it does not make much difference if he doesn't give more than about one-sixteenth of his attention the first time: by and by the thing will grow in him simply by sheer mechanical repetition.

Now see the waste of valuable time that there is in trying to form habits by repetition. In addition to this waste there is failure to train the child's concentration; but even this is not the worst evil. Habits so formed become our masters instead of our servants. They are inflexible and inelastic simply because there is little or no mind in them. You all know of children,—possibly you have had the experience yourself,—who have learned the multiplication table by saying it over and over again; and if they want to know what seven times nine are, they have to go through the whole performance until they get to the place they want. Such habits are necessarily mechanical.

Now there is a sense in which habits ought to be mechanical, indeed the object of having habits at all is nothing more or less than to have a sort of machine that will take care of our ideas and execute them for us without our having to think of it. The danger lies in the habit's becoming mechanical to the extent of fixing our ends for us. The absent-minded man goes on walking simply because he has got started. The habit, instead of carrying out his end, furnishes him with his ends. Too often we find children who have acquired the habits of reading, writing, and figuring, and yet cannot use these habits, cannot apply them. They are not flexible instruments which they can adapt to their purposes here and there. Their thoughts as well as their outward activities go along certain routine grooves.

Thus it is that habits become a sort of grade of mentality. They mark an actual limitation of mental growth. I think it is because Rousseau had seen those results that he went so far as to say that the only habit he would have formed would be the habit of not forming habits. There is a lack of independence because there is no power to adapt the habit. Growth means that we get into new stations. We push out our horizon and get into new surroundings. Now if we are going to be capable of dealing with those new surroundings, we must be able to change our habits. We cannot do anything excepting with our habits. Habits are our tools and if we haven't our kit of tools with us we are certainly helpless. These tools ought to be so readily adjustable that they will operate not only the immediate purpose to which we have become habituated, but the new ends and aims that may come to us.

I think there is often too much stress laid upon mere information. Ideas too often become perfectly automatic. For instance, in arithmetic it is thought the child must know his number combinations so that he can say them without thinking. The child so trained will go faster than one who has not been, but will make more errors. Suppose he has a long column of figures to add. He has been trained not to think at all, or perhaps he gets to thinking of something else, and then the errors creep in. Haven't you found that so? Your consciousness gets off entirely and so you make errors and blunders you wouldn't make if you could get at it with a minimum of effort and yet with enough effort to keep your mind on it. Children would undoubtedly be slower than they are in doing their sums, but they would be more accurate. An inaccurate arithmetical combination is hardly a desirable thing. That there is some advantage in doing things quickly whether right or wrong is absurd. One essential of any operation of course is that it shall be absolutely accurate, and this takes a certain amount of attention. We can attend only with habits or powers already at hand, with what is already reasonably mastered and familiar to us.

Speaking of habits you can put it the other way: habits ought to be formed with and through attention; not by mechanical repetition but by concentrating our consciousness upon things that bring about our success in any given case. The child must be left with a clear, positive, vivid—vivid in the real sense means alive, that which is vital with the living—sense of the way in which he achieved that which he was struggling for. Anybody with a very little experience can go into the third or fourth grade and by hearing the pupils read five minutes tell how they were taught to read. There will perhaps be a certain mechanical execution in reading. It may be very accurate, the words may be pronounced correctly, and there may be few vicious faults; but it is all inactive, there is no real life, no individuality, no feeling. You know that the child is not putting out his mental tentacles and identifying himself with what he is reading. When you get such results you can be as sure as if you had them from the first day, that they have been taught to read by repetition.

I am not going to speak of those points in habit which are most commonly dwelt upon, because I take it for granted that they are already reasonably familiar to you. I have but one more thought, really, on this theme beside the one that habit is to be formed through success—perhaps two more. I ought to say a word more on this one before I go on to the other. What is the substitute for repetition? Where does repetition come in? Repetition comes in afterward, because the habit is formed. But you say there must be a certain amount of repetition in forming the habit. Of course, for while there are cases where the first impression would be so intense and vivid as to fix the habit indelibly, that is not the rule. Generally we have to have a certain amount of repetition. What then can keep it from becoming mechanical? It is this: Keep it from being pure repetition. Repetition with variation. There is a difference between practice and repetition, application and repetition. Simply to say over and over again, and day after day, "two and two equals four" is purely mechanical repetition. But to give the child opportunity to use the knowledge, creating a variety of problems that he cannot solve without falling back on the acquired truth—that is practice. This is all the positive value of repetition without any of the danger of the thing becoming purely mechanical.

Now there is nothing worth learning to which this same principle does not hold. But it takes more ingenuity on the part of the teacher to invent or suggest a situation that is a little different than previous ones. And the evil results of rote teaching have crept in from this very fad: That it is easier to do the same thing over and over again than to give the problem just that variation which shall compel the child to use what he has already learned, instead of making a mechanical application of it.

The question of the value and necessity of drill is an old one. Of course drill is simply this mechanical repetition which is supposed to be necessary for the sake of fixing a necessary habit. Drill is just a common name for this formation of habit through repetition. The difference between intelligent drill and unintelligent drill, which latter leaves the mind passive, is that one does not contain the element of variety and the other does. Exercise is the idea that I would substitute for the idea of drill; having the child say what he has to say, under slightly different circumstances. If the circumstances be changed and he is given a chance to say what he knows in these changed circumstances, there is no danger of repetition being overdone, but the moment the new element drops out, and the child is still kept going over and over without modification that which he has already had, that moment you are of necessity shutting out growth. The mind cannot stand still; if it does not go forward it goes backward. There is no middle termination. Mind must be either progressing or else fossilizing, getting shut up into a shell of its own making, or of the school's making.

I said I had one other point. That is that the natural source of habit is some instinct or impulse which the child had. If you heard my first talk, go back for a moment to the idea of the original equipment of impulses which are striving to fulfill themselves. Now the most necessary and the most valuable habits are merely the systematic organization, classification, and arrangement of these original impulses. That is, the habit has its wellspring within our own makeup. It is not something which is forced on from without. It is possible to teach reading in such a way that it is nothing but a drilled-in accomplishment whereas the child's reading habit ought to be simply the organizing, and getting command of his original language instincts and impulses. I take it that since the human race has developed all the principles of mathematics, there must be inherent in human nature the mathematical instinct or impulse; and it ought to be possible for the child to reproduce these number relations, not by having them forced upon him from without, but by having them developed from within. Habits are simply the organization of one's natural powers and tendencies—powers which are native but imperfect. This being so, there is no danger of habit being a limitation of freedom, if it is built up in the proper way.

To go back again to the two kinds of reading. You hear children in one schoolroom reading naturally,—we might as well use the term spiritually. They are reading with thought and feeling. In another schoolroom they are reading mechanically. The spiritual reading is an organization of the child's own self. It is not external to him, it is the manifestation of his own spirit and being. The reading is simply the leafage and flowering of his own spirit. The other, or mechanical reading, is something which has been fastened on to the child by some external cause. Even though it be a necessary thing, such reading is, in a certain sense, a limitation because it has been impressed upon him from outside himself.

We all know the kind of people we like and admire. They are the people whose thoughts and ideas we feel to be expressions of themselves. We know that they are genuine and sincere; and even if they haven't the same measure of ability in certain technical lines as other people, there is a certain guarantee for their thoughts and ideas, because they are an outgrowth of themselves. With some people we do not know how much comes from themselves and how much is second-handed. Now the only way to prevent this second-hand, and therefore more or less artificial expression of ideas, is to see to it, in the school as well as elsewhere, that the development of habit becomes nothing more nor less than the organization of the instincts and impulses which are ordinary to the nature of the being himself; instead of simply taking it for granted that all these school subjects are external and artificial, and have therefore to be injected into the child from without.

I shall now leave this topic of habit with these two thoughts. The first is that the habit should be built up on the basis of success, on the basis of the selection of what marks achievement and accomplishment; and that the element of repetition should be secondary, and might in fact better be called exercise, use, or application of the selected operation. The second thought is, that while proper habits are built upon success or achievement, and not upon repetition, they are built out of natural instincts.

I will give one more definite illustration of that last point. Take the habit of speaking or using articulate language. Somebody suggested the other day that the child is not born with the ability to speak. He gets ability in language only through contact with others. Now it would follow from this idea that language is something that is conferred upon him, or injected into him, or fastened upon him, by others. Quite the contrary. The child does have a certain definite tendency toward language. He makes noises and sounds of various kinds; but if he does not come into proper relations with others, nothing will ever come of his special tendency. It will remain in the inarticulate state. He has the impulse to listen and to hear the speech of others, and through the adjustment, coordination, harmonizing, and organizing of these original, natural tendencies, which would not amount to anything if left alone, he finally comes to the capacity of articulate speech. He never would have got it simply from his own impulses, and he never would have got it certainly from without. There is no kind of inoculation or vaccination by which the ability to speak can be injected from one consciousness into another. It has to be growth from within; a growth which consists in taking each of these original tendencies and organizing them constructively along certain lines until they are changed into positive power. So it is with the child in all other directions. Too often we do not want him to operate on the plane of his own instinctive tendencies: because we regard his instincts as low and crude we will not have anything to do with them, but take our own thoughts and tendencies which are far in advance of his, and thrust them upon the child. To the extent that we succeed, he becomes an automaton. If we would leave the child as natural as we found him, we must make connections with his own impulses and lead them forth and outward in order to get anywhere.

There is a topic closely allied to habit upon which I will now say a few words in closing. It is imitation. What is the proper place of imitation in forming habits? I think you will see the connection of what I have just been saying. Imitation may be treated as a means of impressing the methods and activities of another. The child may be taught his reading and writing and number simply by imitation; that is, as the teacher does it or as the textbook gives him a model. His activities are then confined to reproducing, to copying or imitating the model given him. Now when imitation is handled in that way it becomes a limitation, an arrest of individuality, and leads to a servile and selfish personality. It makes no difference how good your personality may be, you have no moral right to impose it by sheer imitation upon another; because it never becomes a part of him, but rather a limitation.

On the other hand, it is possible to use imitation so as to wake the other person up and increase his powers, instead of leading him simply to copy yours. This happens when the teacher does not merely say to the child, "Now just copy that, just do as I do and you will be alright," but rather does the thing in his more perfect way, simply to give the child a clearer image, a higher ideal, an added stimulus or word of encouragement, to work it out for himself. When the teacher supplies the child with an end instead of a means he is limiting the child's rightful intellectual and moral growth. But when he says to the little one, "Here is the thing, do it somewhat like this," and proceeds to set the example in such a way as to arouse in him the want, the desire, the inspiration, of doing it, then the imitation, so called, instead of being servile and mechanical becomes a means of realizing and organizing the child's own powers.

The thing, for instance, comes in again in learning to read. I do not know whether the method is in vogue here, it is in our part of the country, especially in dealing with foreign children. They cannot pronounce the combination "th" very clearly. They say "dis" and "dat" instead of "this" and "that," and so the teacher tells the child to put his muscles just so and then copy her exaggerated vocal action. They finally get so they can say "*this*," "*that*" [the lecturer here imitated the overdone vocalization], and go on in that way to the end of their days. You can tell by hearing them say these and similar words that they were mechanically impressed upon them. They never get any individuality or spirituality into these words, because they were impressed upon them as fixed models, and so prevented any real organic connection or assimilation.

The same way in singing. Of course the teacher can sing and invites the children to copy her singing as a model; but if they really copy, the life of the song goes out. Singing may be given so as to inspire, suggest, arouse, and stimulate; and in that case the imitation, if it may be so called, serves as a model in getting a better expression or manifestation of their powers; powers which might otherwise continue locked up inside themselves. It is not always easy to put the distinction in words; but there is a kind of imitation where the teacher simply supplies the end and says, "Do as I do, my end is your end, and you just copy and reproduce that." There is another way where if the teacher, instead of furnishing the model for slavish imitation, helps bring the child to a consciousness of himself, shows him what his capabilities are, what may be the outcome of powers latent within himself. Such a model stimulates him to put forth these powers; and whenever he gets a result which is his own, no matter if he does have it through the suggestion and assistance of the teacher, you may be sure that the model has not been an external one, but rather the awakening or heightening of his own image or ideal.

While habit then is the most mechanical part of our mental makeup; while it is that part of us which, when properly developed, represents the line of our unconscious thought, reflection and choice,—it is serviceable to us only as it has been developed out of freedom; only as it is the organization into power of our inherent capacities and tendencies. Even the oyster grows its own shell. The shell is a shell truly enough, and in a certain sense it confines and limits the oyster, but even as a shell it is the development, the manifestation, you might say, of the powers of the oyster itself. Are not children at least equal to the oyster? And if the oyster is capable of creating what shall assist its life development, shall not the child be counted capable of organizing from within, habits—even mechanical habits—in such a way that they shall always remain an outward token of the inward personality, and be flexible enough to respond to the further needs of that personality? Under no other condition can habits become assistants to progress, instead of its limitations.

8.   Social Value of Courses

One of the favored terms in recent educational theory is correlation or concentration. Various terms are used to convey the idea, but probably the term correlation is used oftener than any other. Both the idea and the term were introduced from Germany. The fundamental notion, as developed by Herbart and his followers, is that our conduct is the expression of our ideas and therefore the way to control our conduct is by correlating ideas. If we acquire ideas that are independent in the sense of being unrelated there will of necessity be a lack of unity in character; and instead of our conduct being a single organized chain, we shall, so to speak, have as many modes of conduct as we have different groups of ideas. If therefore we are to have an organized unity of character we must see to it that all our ideas are carefully interwoven so that each shall supplement or sustain the other. The more perfectly we thus connect our ideas, the more unified and harmonious and therefore the more effective and efficient will be our character.

Now I am not going to discuss this particular theory, which the Herbartians give as the basis of their educational scheme, further than simply to indicate briefly how the notion came into our pedagogical theory. Herbartians maintain that, for instance, to teach arithmetic as an isolated subject tends to give an unrelated group of ideas which influence conduct in one particular way; the effect is, consequently, to fractionize character and conduct. Hence they worked out a scheme of correlation which has figured in many German schools. Literature, especially the great classic literature that has been developed in various epochs of the race, was made the centre of the curriculum. Out of it or around

[First published in *White and Blue* (Provo City, Utah), vol. 5, no. 10, 28 March 1902, pp. 3–9, and ibid., no. 11, 15 April 1902, p. 1.]

it is developed instruction in other subjects. Of course the history would grow out of it very naturally, number and science less naturally perhaps. Now there is no question in my mind that very great good has come from this method of correlation in the schools both of Germany and of this country, wherever the notion has been adopted and carried out. There is, without doubt, a great gain in interest and effectiveness when, instead of isolating and dividing subjects, we weave them together as far as possible into an organic whole.

The particular mode of correlation advocated by the Herbartians does not however strike me as successful. The theory seems better than the execution. In working out, it runs quite easily into artificiality. There is, for instance, in the German schools, a course of religious history running parallel with secular history. For one or more years the history of Israel is chosen, and the great classic literature which goes along with it. My objection is not to that particular study, but to the way other studies are made to group around it. In arithmetic the artificiality seems especially glaring. German school children get arithmetic by adding, dividing, multiplying, and subtracting the Twelve Tribes, and by dealing numerically with the various incidents of history, the number of people engaged in battle, the number of miles in Palestine from this point to that, and so on. The idea of welding together into an organic whole various phases of instruction is clear enough, but I doubt whether, from a psychological standpoint, these number ideas are really infused and interwoven into the actual content of instruction any more than if the arithmetic were made a completely isolated study.

It seems to me a little artificial also when you come to science. Many teachers in this country, if they wish to give a lesson on the pine tree in the lower grades, introduce, possibly, it by a fable of the discontented fir tree; or if they are going to have the children study a flower, lead up to it through a poem about the flower. The idea is that they cannot go at the thing directly, but must always introduce it through correlation with literature. My objection is this: that while literature is a very admirable study and a very necessary study, it is not after all the natural centre out of which other experiences radiate. It is not the way the child gets his experience out of school. He does not first have a piece of literature presented to him and then go into the fields, or farm, or kitchen, and have his experiences expand and grow out of it; and it is because the literature does not occupy the central position in outdoor life, that it seems hardly fitted to occupy that position in school life.

Generalizing this matter a little, one cannot escape the conviction that Herbartians are simply correlating studies with each other, not connecting them with life and the life experiences of the child. I do not doubt that it is better to connect studies with each other than to have studies purely isolated; but I think it better to connect studies with the thing which is not a study; with the activity, the feelings, the emotion, the ideas of life which the child is living all the time outside of school. Very often there are fifty things in the child's out-of-door experience which would illustrate the particular point which the teacher is holding before the class, but instead of taking one of those things she turns around and says, "Don't you remember we took up such and such a point day before yesterday?" The whole aim seems to be simply to connect the new point with school facts or ideas, instead of making the connection directly with experiences out of school.

My point here is that the various social experiences of the child are the natural medium in which his ideas grow up and flourish; and consequently whatever correlation is worth attempting in the schools—for like other good ideas it can be carried too far— should be made directly with the child's experience. If we get a school fact connected to-day with this general trend of his experience, another to-morrow, another the next day, these school ideas may not be directly correlated with each other, but they are all being built into and developed out of the more general field of social life.

Now I am not going to follow out this line of thought further than to introduce a sort of philosophy of the studies which make up the school curriculum, and of their correlation in the general tenor of life's experience. As a sort of working hypothesis which you may develop for yourselves, I suggest a three-fold classification of the various studies, operations, and rights of the school. It is based on correlation with the general phases of social life. I put first those activities which are not so much studies in the technical sense, but they are direct modes of social existence. A few illustrations will make my meaning a good deal clearer than does the general formulation which I have been giving.

Here then is language, which is essentially a social instinct. I am aware that most writers on educational pedagogics say that language is a mode of expressing thought. Language is primarily a social agency, a means of expression which has been developed for purposes of communication. It is the social instinct, not the logical instinct, which lies back of language. The child does not talk because he is manipulating logical thoughts; he talks because he is a social being, because whenever he gets a thing he wants to give it out to someone else. It is rare that you will find an adult, much less a child, who is so selfish that he does not wish to communicate his feelings, ideas, and experiences to others. If the piety of man can be made to praise God, the vanity of the child is a very good inducement to praise himself. But vanity, after all, is a social instinct though it should not be cultivated too far. Even this desire of the child to talk for the sake of showing off, or at least making other people recognize he is there, can be turned to good account in teaching the child to get command of his own thoughts and experiences, and to state them clearly and forcibly so that they will commend themselves to others. Now we do not call this talking instinct a study, and yet we make no mistake in suggesting that conversation is or should be the basis of the recitation.

As I have elsewhere said the recitation ought to be a sort of clearing house where the children get the power to give out their ideas and enrich them. Dr. Harris has dwelt on the fact that there is a good deal of difference between spiritual and material wealth. Material wealth exists to be divided, while spiritual wealth by its very nature exists to be multiplied. There are no limits to the number of people who can know an idea, share an emotion, or be impressed by a beautiful landscape. Somebody said that our assurance of the truth of an idea is multiplied when some other mind accepts it also. We none of us feel easy with an idea so long as it is limited to ourselves. We really appropriate it fully only when we give it out. Language then is one of the activities which fall in the first groove.

Manual training in its less technical form is another example of it. The child does not build with his blocks for the sake of getting the fact or the principle, he plays for the sake of building. But in doing that he learns something. Smaller children, so far as I have noticed, do not cook for the sake of learning to cook, for the sake of making a scientific study of the chemistry of foods and the proper method of treating them; they cook for the fun of cooking. It is the occupation that absorbs them. Of course from the teacher's standpoint children go to school to learn certain facts; but after all there is more than that. From the child's standpoint interest comes from the opportunity to express what appeals to him, and the facts that he learns are secondary. I am speaking of elementary, not of secondary or college education. So there are a variety of similar operations and activities, as exemplified in the kindergarten, and primary school, that are not, at least from the child's standpoint, to be classified as studies, but rather as modes of expression or occupation. I think occupation-work is as good a descriptive term as can be given to these activities, the peculiarities of which are that they only follow out the child's own end, but many of them, as I have already said, recapitulate the social relations surrounding him.

I will confine my remarks on this immediate topic to the manual and industrial activities of various kinds: woodwork, ironwork, cooking, weaving, and things of that sort. The first interest of mankind must be in getting a living, for without that they can do nothing else. Mankind must therefore be primarily interested in these industries for the sake of civilization. Now if these operations were made part of the curriculum, they would give the child a chance to reflect from within the school the social interests and activities of the home. For it makes no difference how simple the home is, if it is really a healthy, wholesome home, there is the spirit of work there, and work which is directed toward material ends. There are educational theorists who despise what they term the material phase of life; and in attempting to get culture and refinement they often draw a line between spirit and matter which is not drawn in the universe itself. I have heard the material things of life objected to in the schoolroom on the ground that they are too utilitarian. But it seems to me a fair presumption that so long as the thoughts and energies of so large a part of mankind are directed to these things, we cannot afford to ignore them in the school. Since the majority of mankind have a great deal of their time and attention directed toward producing, buying and selling either directly or indirectly, I think the school ought to deal with these things if for no other purpose than to idealize them, and introduce the social element into them. The lessons themselves need not be material, because the subject matter is material; it is the spirit in which they are given which makes them material or spiritual. Because a man is occupied with material things in building, and so on, it does not follow that his soul is confined to the material or physical things. Of course conscience can be degraded to that level; but on the other hand this occupation can be elevated and spiritualized to the extent that he recognizes the laws he is following to be the laws of the universe which he must abide and follow out, if he would complete his work. He may also be elevated by recognizing the social significance of what he is doing; for certainly anybody who does honest work is doing something more than a selfish thing. Nor is it necessary for him to think he is doing it simply for love of humanity; he may get his pay and yet if he is doing something which the world wants done, he is rendering social service; and the recognition of this fact may give dignity to his life.

It seems to me that since activities of this sort take up so large a part of the energy and aims of mankind; since their thoughts, their plans, their feelings, and their interests cluster so largely about these activities,—it is a moral duty that the school have at least enough of these things to teach the children what they mean, and arouse their sympathies for those engaged in these operations. Because a man is a carpenter or a woman a cook, it does not follow that they see the scientific and social factors involved in that service. They may be doing it in a servile way. Plato defined a slave as one who was expressing the ideas of others. That is what a slave really is. A person who is doing a thing not from any interior volition, but only as he is compelled by the thought of others which he neither understands nor appreciates, is not free. The school ought therefore to treat these things, not merely as helps in getting a living, but as things that need to be refined by introducing workmen who will recognize in them the elements of truth and of law, and whose gaze will be so broadened that they shall see the social service they are rendering. Of course in our present system of civilization, with our great factories and all that, the labor problem is getting to be a very serious problem. I do not suppose education alone can solve it. It will take a great many other agencies as well to straighten out all the questions that we are finding ourselves in. But one thing education can do and ought to do: that is to give the working man a sense of what he is doing, so that his conscience shall not be hardened down to the mere material comprehension of his work. A person who is attending a machine is working along the line of great scientific principles and laws. Now if he knows the laws embodied in that machine he certainly is going to do his work in a spirit different from what he would if he knows absolutely nothing about it. The average working man of to-day knows little of the history of his own line of activity, where it came from and how it came to be what it is. He does not even know the business as a whole, for his mental access is confined to a single part of it. Neither does he know what becomes of the products he makes or what their real use is.

Here is a duty of the educator. My point is that this first group of studies, which are hardly studies in the technical sense, have a great social significance. On the one hand they are simply the natural expression of the child's socialized instincts. On the other hand they can be developed to the extent of introducing the child into the scientific and social values involved in occupations which he must shortly follow for a livelihood. For instance, I have seen a very simple series of exercises in weaving worked out for children between the ages of six and twelve, where, in connection with the textile work, they got a sort of panorama of the historical progress of the world in that direction: beginning with the uncleaned wool of the sheep, and finding out what had to be done with it to cleanse it; then what had to be done with it before machines were invented in order to get that wool into yarn (it is surprising to see what excellent yarn little children of six or seven would succeed in spinning with their fingers, or from simple devices such as the savage tribes still use); then going on to weave this yarn into simple forms, using the looms which are still actually in use by uncivilized people; next taking the more complicated devices, those which involve hand and foot power, and getting an insight into conditions of colonial civilization in this country and the methods of spinning and weaving of the sixteenth or seventeenth century. (In their carpenter work, boys can make these looms. I have seen looms and spinning wheels which the children themselves made. I saw the other day a very good reel which a boy of twelve had invented in order to reel several skeins of yarn at the same time. I do not suppose he could patent it, but so far as he was concerned it was an invention which he had worked out with his own head.) At a later period, they took up the factory modes of production by steam or some other forms of mechanical energies.

There then is a course of manual and industrial work which illustrates what I mean by saying that these industries can be made a good deal more of than mere manual labor. They can be made to teach a broader view of the evolution of civilization down the avenues of history. Through them children can be made to trace the historical steps in many of the arts of civilization. The schools of which I spoke have also made some study of the evolution of machinery, or the development on the scientific side of economy in the application of energy. But I have spoken long enough on this first group of studies—studies that constitute in one way or another what we know as the kindergarten and the various forms of busy work which are coming more and more into the elementary schools. I judge from what little I have seen in this state that you are already far advanced in that direction; also that people in this state are naturally more sympathetic perhaps with this industrial work as a factor in education, and that consequently there is less of a pull in getting it introduced than in some of our older communities.

Such an attitude is only the proper recognition of the value of pioneer life. Everybody knows the true character, the intelligence and great force of mind, which were developed throughout this whole country in our own pioneer days, through having to wrestle with these problems, bring the forces of nature under control, and adapt them to human needs. We do not want our children to feel too much the hard pressure of that kind of experience; we do not want to have their lives weighed down by the burden of passing literally through such another economic struggle. But by means of these exercises in the schoolroom, which are from a certain standpoint play to the children, there is yet an opportunity for the child to get, mentally at least, something of the discipline and culture which come from working out these problems in actual life. From a social standpoint the purpose of this first group is simply to bring samples of past social activity into the schoolroom, to broaden the child's horizon, and refine his thoughts regarding them.

The second group of studies are those which give background to the social life. Among them I would put history and geography, and include in geography nature study in its various forms. It requires no great argument to see that history, so far as it can be taught in our schools, is a social record, and that it gives the background of our present social life. That proposition is so simple that it must be its own comment; yet if history were always taught in that way it would make a great difference both in the material and in the method of teaching. We should take the emphasis away from the military side. We should still have to deal with the history of some of the errors; but we should not spend three-fourths of the time, as used to be done, on the various campaigns, for instance, in United States history. There has been great improvement made in that respect. In the history that I got, practically the whole stress was laid on the military campaigns. I do not think that aspect of history develops the social instincts very much. The political aspect should be relegated to the secondary schools. We should get our history down to a human basis, finding out how people lived, and how they came to live as they did—I mean the common people—the difficulties they were laboring under, the struggles they had to make, the victories they won—not the military victories so much as the human victories,—the artistic advances, the educational movements, and the moral and religious conquests. School history ought to be a sort of object lesson in sociology. Abstract sociology is a difficult study, but history gives it a sort of crude, yet dramatic form whereby the child can appreciate through his feelings, if not intellectually, the play of forces which make human life what it is. Through history taught in that way he can get the sublimer side of the methods of social organization. I think that it is the only basis on which we can justify the teaching of history in the schools. If it is made simply a matter of learning what is past and gone, it is better to let the dead bury their dead. But if we can make of history a sort of moral telescope through which to view the conditions of past social life, we really make it part of the present, since through what has been we become the better able to understand what is.

I cannot stop, as I should like, to go into the matter of geography as a social background, but I will simply indicate how I think the thing should work out. The old definition of geography was something like this: The science of the earth as the home of man. Now if you take the last half of that definition, the earth as the home of man, you will see that geography is a social study, a study of the social background, a study of the theatre of life; and I think we get the culture value, the human value of geography just in the degree that it is taught with reference to its bearing upon human life.

Environments do not, of course, entirely make history. It would be absurd to say that the Greeks were made what they were by the physical characteristics of the country in which they lived; but it is equally absurd to deny that the physical environment has a very important influence upon social life. We do not live in a void, we live on the earth; and what we do is controlled by the kind of earth we live on. What we do depends largely on the conditions under which we live. We are compelled to adapt our activities so as to bring them into line with our environment. The material with which geography deals comes to have great psychic significance as it is being taken up into consciousness; and it seems to me that the elementary sciences ought to be taught very largely from this standpoint in order that the interest in plants and animals shall be associated with the human interest. There is a very great field to look at from here. The child cannot possibly study all the plants and animals, why not therefore restrict his zoology to those which have had an influence on man's social activities? If, for instance, you were going to study trees from the standpoint of certain laws, and you want to get a scientific lesson, it seems to me it would be quite as well to take the rubber tree; for thereby the products of the tree, the influence and effect of rubber upon the social life of the past and the present, can be taken up and followed on.

It is an old principle in pedagogy that we ought to begin with the concrete and go to the abstract; but it is fallacy to suppose that the thing is all in the mind simply because it is a physical whole. We do not begin with the concrete simply because we comprehend the physical fact. To be concrete an object must have a certain social contact; for example, if I were giving a lesson in mineralogy as a part of nature study, and therefore a part of geography, I should choose minerals which have been associated with some industry or occupation whose influence can be traced in social life. It takes a certain amount of contact to make anything really concrete. That is how I would get around the tendency to personify nature. What led to the personification of natural objects was the recognition that the child is not greatly taken up with the physical thing as a thing, but only as the human element mingled with it. Personifying first began in terms of human life. The need that the teachers were trying to meet was, I take it, perfectly genuine; but the method was artificial. The child is not necessarily more interested in the cow because it is referred to as "Mrs. Cow." The cow is a friend of the child already and is familiar. I think it can be said that the cow is a part of the social experience of the child, that he has a sense of it as part of a social whole, and that social feeling radiates out and extends from it. If we introduce our elementary sciences from this standpoint—the standpoint of their connection with human needs, activities, powers, and modes of control, we shall get from them the maximum interest for the child, and therefore the maximum value to him.

The specialist has left his trail over all these things. Now I have profound respect for the specialist,—I should not want to run down my own calling,—but the specialist should remain where he belongs,—in the special field. Whenever specialist results are introduced into education they ought to be taken out of their special technicalities and turned over into terms of our common life, or the life of our social experience. As to the scientist, he will naturally go into the high school where students will be sufficiently advanced to follow technical methods; but the child in the grades ought not to know that he is studying zoology or botany. The very moment you put one of those labels on the study you isolate it. He ought simply to be made to realize that he is getting acquainted with the world. It makes no difference what the fact is, it is just a part of this one common world, and therefore merely a sign of our life and relations to each other. My second group of studies will thus include geography and all the elementary phases of nature study and science.

That leaves for the third group of studies in the curriculum, the instrumentalities, agencies, or social technic, so to speak; reach-

ing the more advanced forms of reading, writing, spelling, arithmetic, studies in short which deal with symbols and forms. Now
these are social just as much as is the manual training or the
history and geography; but they are not so directly or immediately
social. The first group of studies that I spoke of are directly social.
The second are just one stage removed. They are the background
of social life. The third are a little further removed. They are the
technic, as I say, of social communication, of social intercourse,
and therefore they also should be taught on the social basis and
with a social motive. If anyone questions that these various studies are social, although they are more technical in form, he should
think what our life would be if we were cut off from these things;
how we should be united, for instance, with those that have gone
before us without those various forms and symbols on which history rests. It is through language, through symbols in one way or
another, that men have recorded their discoveries, their thoughts
and ideas; and by learning the language which they used, we get
initiated into their thoughts and experiences.

This is in a certain way the mastery of human nature. In one
way everyone is shut off from everyone else. We have, for instance, no access to each other's consciousness, should we choose
to be silent; and yet through the medium of my voice you somehow or another are enabled to participate in my consciousness;
and my consciousness is enabled to expand and enlarge until it
gets into the community with yours; so that my consciousness—
while it is individual—is also social, because it has taken to itself
an indefinite number of thoughts and suggestions coming from
everyone in all ages. In a very literal sense, we are what people
hundreds and thousands of years ago have thought and done;
and it is become a part of us through this mastery of language,
this mastery of symbols. Now when we neglect grammar, which
has a strong social value in these language studies, and treat it
merely as a form of technical skill with which to get at other human elements, we lose the science of language. Reading lessons
by a similar neglect become so trivial that they cannot by any
possibility come into living contact with social life. For a while
the child can keep up his interest in the reading through a sense
of increase in power; but a living interest is born only when the
social value of reading is recognized. And so with all other lessons we do not always formulate the principles underlying this

social contact, but we certainly recognize them in a tacit way, and through such recognition has come an advance in the kind of reading matter, the introduction of literature of a higher quality, the introduction of wholes, and an appreciation of the fact that even the beginning language lesson shall have some idea be- hind it.

This matter of socializing technical studies may be summed up under two heads. On the one hand, we want to make the child capable of appreciating things in the life and experience of others. We want to make him receptive. It takes a great deal of activity to be receptive, to be sympathetic with others, to be appreciative. It is far from being a passive thing. We want to make the child so receptive that he can come into living contact with everything in others. All this is one side. On the other side we want to make him capable of giving out, not only social appreciation and participation, but social effectiveness. We want to make him both a participator and a contributor socially; and the ultimate philosophy of education, it seems to me, will so arrange and correlate these studies, that they shall become social instruments for reaching these two ends: for making the child more receptive, more open, more appreciative, so that he shall participate in the doings of others with as few walls of prejudice around him as possible; and on the other side making him a positive contributor to the life and experience of others. That is our ideal. It is far ahead of us, but so much the better for that. It gives us something to work upon. When we can arrange our studies from the standpoint of agencies for enlarging and deep- ening the range of our individuality, and for sharing in the life and experience of others, I think we shall all agree not only that ethics and morals will have been planted in the schoolroom, but that they will have grown up and flowered and borne fruit.

9. Memory and Judgment

My friends have been so kind in taking me about this morning that my ideas, I am afraid, are not in very good shape for presentation. I shall therefore have to ask you to draw on your imagination as to what I should have said had I had the opportunity to prepare myself. [The forenoon had been devoted to a horseback ride up Rock Canyon and the heights east of Provo.]

The topics, memory and judgment, are a little unusual; and you may think I have joined together things somewhat separate. I shall give part of my time to memory and part to judgment. While they are distinct topics they are closely related, both by way of contrast and by way of similarity. There is a way of treating memory which puts it in sharp distinction, almost in antagonism, with judgment; and there is another way whereby memory becomes simply the materials which the judgment has to use, and judgment becomes, so to speak, the flowering of memory. And yet, to a certain extent, I shall have to treat the two topics independent of each other. You may remember in one of Mr. Pickwick's stories the person had to write an essay on Chinese metaphysics. He first read up on China, next on metaphysics, then mixed up the two subjects.

You know the old idea of assuming that mental powers are isolated faculties; so there was a single faculty of memory. There is a good deal more reason, psychologists concede, in simply distinguishing and classifying all the faculties under the one head of consciousness. We know to-day that there are a great many forms of memory and a great many stages in the development of memory; and that it is anything but a single power which can be

[First published in *White and Blue* (Provo City, Utah), vol. 5, no. 11, 15 April 1902, pp. 2–9.]

labeled with just one name. It seems to be necessary, therefore, to call your attention to some of the various phases and stages which make up memory.

In the first place there is what some German writers have termed organic or physiological memory. As one writer has expressed it, the scar is in a certain sense the memory of the wound or the cut. So also the creases that get into a pair of gloves or shoes after we get thoroughly used to them and they get used to us, might be called a sort of organic memory. This is of course the principle of habit which I discussed yesterday. There are a great many things which we get so used to that they become almost a part of ourselves, and yet we do not think of describing them by the term memory. We hardly seem to remember these things, they are so much a part of ourselves. We wear creases, so to speak, in our minds, from the way we are continually using them just as we wear creases in gloves and shoes. And there can be no doubt that organic memory, which we get simply by our more or less unconscious accommodation to surroundings, is quite fundamental in the development of the more conscious phases of memory. In general, we use the term memory only for conscious reproductions or recognitions. Even there, however, there are a great many subdivisions to be made. I shall endeavor not to go into too many of them; but one of them, important for the educator, is illustrated very well by a fact which Dr. Hardy told me at the Asylum the other day. Friends and former acquaintances of patients, who perhaps have not seen them for ten or fifteen years, would go away after a few minutes' conversation and say what remarkable memories these people had. Patients will remember things they did when they were children, recall quite trivial incidents, and their memory seems unusually bright. Visitors, however, do not appreciate the fact that these feats were merely examples of memory revived in the minds of patients by seeing their old associates, and that half an hour afterwards they might forget, unless specially reminded that visitors had been there at all, and would perhaps not think of these incidents again until these same people came up and stirred up the reminiscences over again.

While there are many technical definitions of memory, the little fact to which I have called attention points out a distinction which is important for the educator; a distinction dependent upon external association and suggestion. The memory on which this distinction hinges might be called a reminiscent memory. When such a memory gets started it unravels yard after yard of matter which has been connected by what the psychologists call the law of contiguity, or association in space and in time. You know the woman in Shakespeare's *Romeo and Juliet,* who cannot even finish a sentence. She thinks of one thing and then of another until you cannot tell even what she started to say; or if you happen to have read *Nicholas Nickleby,* you will remember how Mrs. Nickleby unravels those tales of memory, not connected by idea or thought, but by some mere incidental circumstance or experience.

Now over against that, we have the memory which we call recollecting or remembering. Many of our words have in them a good deal of honest, straightforward psychology. Those people in the Asylum were not exactly remembering anything, they were simply getting an external jog and so went on reminiscencing. Remembering is membering or joining things together again; that is, taking facts of our experience and putting them together to make a living organized whole. The term remembering brings up that idea very clearly. Genuine remembering involves control over our past experiences. Reminiscencing, on the other hand— this going over a lot of more or less trivial incidents just in the way they originally happened, without any sorting of them out, without classifying, without putting any perspective into them— requires little or no control. Now, as you will undoubtedly infer from what I said about habit, I believe it possible to train memory in the wrong way, as well as in the right way. Do what we may to develop memory we are really training only this power of reminiscencing; making the mind dependent upon external associations so that the skein of experience shall unwind in exactly the way it was wound up. I illustrated that the other day by the memory of the multiplication table, fixed through mere repetition, and by the memory which has to begin at the beginning and go over the whole web of facts to get at some particular point. I dare say there are many of us who learn the alphabet so mechanically if we were asked suddenly whether the letter J came before the letter Q we should have to go over a number of letters in order to find out. We haven't the thing so we can recollect it; we have to unwind the earlier numbers of the series to trace out the thing wanted. Things memorized in that way do not really become individual parts of our working capital, because they do not become individual parts of ourselves. I do not doubt that, while I have apparently forgotten most of the geography I studied when a boy yet if somebody should start me off and get my chain of associations running just right, I should soon get off a good deal about boundaries, surfaces, rivers, and so on that I cannot say anything about just now. It is really no part of my intellectual acquirements just because it was mechanically memorized, never in a really systematic way. You can see what I am going to come to by and by: viz., that remembering is very close to thinking, while memorizing has very little to do with judgment, and is even to a certain extent antagonistic to judgment.

Another point I wish to call your attention to is the varieties of memory. Psychologists are pretty well agreed now that instead of having memory we have memories. We have a distinct memory of every distinct line of facts, or truths. You very often hear a person say, "I have such a poor memory," whereas, unless he is actually going imbecile, or is on the verge of paresis of one sort or other, he probably does not know himself what he is saying. What he means, of course, is that he has a poor memory in a certain direction. You will hardly find anybody who hasn't a good memory in some direction or other. He may forget this kind of facts, but he will remember the other. He may forget people's names but will remember faces. He may forget both and remember episodes that happened in connection with them. He may forget names and faces, dates and stories, but will remember abstract ideas. He will remember intellectual formulas and things of that sort.

Our memories become developed a good deal according to our occupations. Of course the tendency works the other way also,— we select our occupation partly by our ability to remember. We choose our vocations according to the native quality of our memory to a certain extent. On the other hand after we get to working in a certain line we develop a memory in that direction; and unless we take care to keep ourselves balanced, we forget in other ways. The success of the politician depends more or less on his cultivating himself in that particular line. You would not expect a man to obtain any success as a historian who did not have a good memory for dates and things chronological. Now a man may have a very good memory in one particular and have a poor one in others. There is a certain amount of comfort in that, especially as people grow older. They think their memory is failing them entirely, when it is really a case of specializing on their part.

To make this topic specific and more directly applicable to school work, there are many kinds of memories connected with the mental images spoken of the other day. We tend to remember things in our favorite line of imagery. I alluded to this fact in answer to a question about spelling. One person's memory will be of the visual appearance of the word. He will memorize most easily by fixing his eye on the column, another will remember it reading aloud, while another person will have a purely physical or motor remembrance. You know there are people who actually get hoarse just in thinking. It is a moral fact. Instead of visualizing they are saying the words over in order to get those little motor clues; and if they keep it up for several hours there is often a severe physical or mental strain. A preacher of my acquaintance always memorized his sermons before he preached them. He had difficulty in pronouncing certain combinations and had to practice on them when he wished to memorize them. When he preached he had a certain mental stutter when he got to that point, because he had memorized the words by means of his motor faculty.

Another person gets his spelling most easily by sound. He wants to hear it and fixes his attention on the sound. A man who cannot read fast, but who is very intelligent, told me he had to read slowly, in order that he might mentally hear the thought. He had to get the auditory image and if he read too fast, the sounds became blurred into each other. It is safe to say he would have remembered what he was reading in auditory sounds. A student told me that whenever she heard a lecture by one of her college professors she was always writing, not with pencil, but with the tip of her tongue on the roof of her mouth; but if he talked fast she could not make the whole mental chain there, and consequently could not follow the lecture any longer. She had never observed this peculiarity until she had begun the psychological study of imagery. There again would be an example of the motor memory. Now my point is that the child does not remember or memorize by the general power or faculty of memory; he does his translating over into some of these groups of images. And while I agree perfectly with the statement made here the other day, that poor spelling is due to poor observation—that is, visual or auditory observation—defective memory is after all a question of defective attention or of not attending in the right way.

This leads me to mention a principle which Mr. James has dwelt on in his writings, that the best way to train memory—I am speaking more of memorizing than remembering—is through original observation. Of course it is the same principle I spoke of in respect to habit yesterday, that instead of trusting to mechanical repetition we ought to trust more to acting out our consciousness of the matter to be made habitual. So here, if the boy has a column of words in spelling and he gets at it merely by repeating them over and over, his attention is not fixed. There is not enough mental activity to occupy his mind; for it is a psychological impossibility to keep the mind five minutes on a mere repetition of words. It goes off on something else. But if the boy is a visualist and if he is trained to look at the column of words carefully and intensely he can by one or two rapid glances do more in the way of memorizing than by ten or fifteen minutes of listless repetition.

All of you are doubtless acquainted with Mr. Speer's work on arithmetic; but Mr. Speer's educational theories are themselves merely a part of a large scheme of sense training. In his school in Chicago he has greatly improved this matter of spelling simply by rapid exercises in observation. All of which is a practical demonstration of the principle that if we take care of the original comprehension, the original grasping of the thing, memory will take care of itself. If we grasp it readily it becomes a part of us, we assimilate it, and cannot help remembering it. You all have had certain experiences which, though they happened only once, will haunt you till your dying day. You know every detail of them and can live them over again with sometimes too much intensity; even the cares, the sorrows, and the joys incident to them come back, because the thing meant so much to you at the time. And yet all this has happened simply through having had the experience once.

I once made an experiment with a child's picture book in which the pictures were unusually artistic. Somebody had made a study of old costumes of the Middle Ages and had costumed Little Boy Blue and Little Bo Peep in these old gowns, and in old forms of caps, and hats, and shoes, and hosiery; and there were quite a variety of forms and colors. I gave the class six of these pictures allowing them just half a minute to look at each, and simply telling them to observe them carefully. Then I asked the class to write down what each of the figures had on his head, and what he had on his feet, objects which, as I have said, were quite original and distinctive in character. The visualists did that very accurately and correctly. I had not told them what I was going to ask, had not told them to memorize anything. But they saw those things again in their mind and wrote off what they saw. I made a little scale of percentage of accuracy. The visualists had about 80 per cent; and those who were not visualists had about 30 or 35 per cent, and had very hard work to do anything with them at all. I gave them a half dozen more pictures and told them in advance I was going to do this same thing again and this time wanted them to impress it on their memories and write it. The second time the visualists didn't do so well; but the others did better, because they knew what to look for and had taken pains to repeat to themselves and impress it on their minds. This time the visualists could not give their whole attention to seeing the thing; they got distracted by thinking that they had to memorize. This is a striking instance of how we get in our own way. By thinking we have to memorize, we do not go at the thing with the same intensity as if we were only thinking of the subject matter. After all, the best training of the memory is rather that which says: "I am going to cultivate my power of observation; I am going to observe vividly so as to comprehend this thing correctly; I am going to understand it and understand it so thoroughly that I shall assimilate it." Then we make the thing a part of ourselves. Then this organic memory, this unconscious assimilation comes to our rescue and helps us out. Of course the other moral is that we want to make allowances for a variety of degrees and kinds of memory among children. There is a tendency, as I have already indicated, to carry principles that are all right too far. Recognizing this fact we should seek to balance them.

In the matter of learning to read there occasionally is a rage for word method. The method is a visual method. Words seen on the board are learned readily by the visualists, but persons of auditory or motor types are at a disadvantage. Then some teacher makes great progress with phonic matter, in which all the words are analyzed into their sounds, and reading is taught on that basis. That is an auditory method. That is of value to the ear just as the word method is of value to the eye. In this the ear-minded will get on well, and the visual-minded will be more or less at a discount. We ought to remember the variety of minds; and any method of teaching reading ought to appeal to the eye memory, to the auditory memory, and also to the motor memory. You have to make allowances for the variety of types of mind which you are pretty sure to have in the schools. The majority may be average for a pretty fair combination, but you will have some on the border line, who will memorize much better in one set of terms than in another.

Of course it is impossible to speak of memory and remembering without making some allusion to association of ideas. Everybody brings himself up with a sort of start sometimes and thinks, "How did I get to thinking about this?" and trace it back and find a chain of suggestions which have come one after another from some first idea; and then that which seemed so peculiar at first becomes perfectly simple and natural. Some of you may have heard of the man who traveled through his country giving memory lessons, or teaching, as he claimed, the instantaneous art of never forgetting. He charged the sum of five shillings and five pence. His method was all based on this principle. He appropriated it from somebody else and made a sort of secret out of it. He simply systematized this matter of association of ideas. If I had a blackboard here, I could easily write down a line of twenty words; and if I had not told you I was talking about the subject of memory or did not really ask you to memorize those words at all, I would be willing to guarantee that nine out of ten of you would repeat the whole list accurately, with practically no errors and practically no suggestions from me.

Let me, for instance, put down the word "tub," and then "wash," and ask you if there is association by similarity, or contiguity; after "wash" I put the word "clean," and you will see that this association is of similarity. Then go on from the word "clean" to the word "snow," a combination of similarity, and take it then from "snow" to "hail," and from "hail" to "lightning," and from "lightning" to "electricity," and from "electricity" to "telephone," and from "telephone" to "bell," and from "bell" to "church." Now if I were to go on like that most of you could repeat that list without an error, simply because there is a natural association, either by the principle of contiguity or similarity of these terms, and so this instantaneous art, this secret of never forgetting, that Mr. ——— got wealthy on, was in fact only a systematic method of following out these ideas in a consecutive way a good many disorderly suggestions of this kind.

In a discussion before I came here to-day, the point came up as to how the associations were to be directed and drilled so as to be helpful. I wish I could answer the question, because I do not know of any question that has more in it from a moral as well as intellectual point of view. When you stop to think of it, we use our wills not every minute nor every five minutes but only at certain junctions so to speak, in our stream of consciousness. We start to think about a certain thing and then the association of ideas takes it up and carries it on. The mental machinery begins to operate and it seems sometimes that the ego is simply a spectator. Then the will comes in and stops that and we start off on another. The coloring of our thoughts and imaginations is determined very largely by this automatic play of association.

"As a man thinketh in his heart, so is he." That kind of thinking seems very often a consecutive play of one line of images. Certain more or less habitual trains of suggestions come into thought. Now it is the inner life of which our character is made, very largely. "As a man thinketh in his heart, so is he," because his thoughts are going to be the experience of his usual train of ideas. He cannot systematically entertain any particular line of thought and then act persistently in another direction. Sometime or other these customary trains are going to show themselves, and when a man breaks down in a community, we say, "What a hypocrite he must have been." He must have been constantly deceiving us, living a double life, having one train of thought and another mode of life. But the inner life had to come out. This is the psychological explanation of a great many of the sudden falls that shock a community. People whom we have taken to be ordinary and commonplace often do very striking and heroic things, because while their inner life has never been given an opportunity, their thoughts were in the right direction, and when the crises came their real selves came out in some great deed.

So I wish the person who is to answer that question as to how best to control one's customary trains of thoughts or imagery would appear among us, for he would do a great deal for our mental and moral hygiene. I can answer the question only by going back to the principle of attention. We cannot control every link of association. "No man can add a cubit to his stature by taking thought," and no man can tell what he is going to think by taking thought. Our thoughts surprise us and are governed by themselves. What we can do, is to concentrate our attention on a particular starting point; we can shut out the wrong thought as soon as it shows itself and entertain and cultivate the right one. Somebody has said that a right start is more than half the journey; and in this matter of associations it is a good deal more than true. The right start is nine-tenths of the journey. Of course the difficulty is that the people get in the habit of saying, "Although I think this thing, and feel it, and indulge myself, I will never do anything of this sort; I shall go on in a straightforward, honest, pure way. This thinking is all inside my consciousness and therefore does not hurt anybody," forgetting the fact that they are setting in line trains of internal action which will finally show itself in external action. The law which controls the association of ideas is this law of the motor power of an idea. With a little child the idea, or image, tends to show itself in action. That is the reason the child is so plastic to suggestion. The reason he plays so much is because he cannot entertain an idea as an idea, save as he puts it forth. With grown people the path gets complicated. The idea goes through a long train of other ideas. Association involves many links of intermediate ideas. With a child there are but two links, the idea and the idea passed into action. As our life grows complex it stretches out and gets a lot of intermediate links and thoughts, constituting a train or association of ideas. But none the less an original, primary idea with the adult has started for its outcome in action,—is headed for that last step, the act,—just as certainly as in the case of the child. The intermediate case has been lengthened, but the law of relation between the image or idea and the action is just as sure in one case as in the other. Hence the necessity of controlling, through the concentration of original attention, the train of these ideas.

I have only a few moments left to consider judgment; but as I suggested, there is a very little difference between remembering and judging. There is a very great difference between memorizing, or reminiscencing, and judging; but when we come to remember a thing, putting together the various parts of our experience so as to make an orderly whole with proper perspective, we are practically judging and cultivating our faculty of judgment. I heard a man who was illiterate as those things are counted, give a definition of judgment which I have borne in mind since. It seemed to strike the nail on the head. "Judgment is a sense of the relative values of things." That is the difference between judgment and pure memory. Memory accumulates but it does not sort out and appreciate or put a price on things. A man of judgment has on hand a great stock of accumulated facts and can use them to advantage because he knows their relative value. He has put a price on all the ideas constituting his information.

As a student of mine said to me recently, "Memory is not knowledge; it is a half-way house to knowledge, a candidate for knowledge"; by knowledge meaning judgment, wisdom, understanding of the matter. As long as a thing is only in memory we have it there to look at, to inspect, to consider, to reflect upon. It is material to know more of, but not yet knowledge, wisdom or judgment. And so the wise teacher, while bearing in mind the necessity of training the memory, will always remember that memory is not the goal. We do not memorize things for the sake of memory, or even for the sake of memorizing, but merely that we may have on hand a suitable lot of candidates for judgment. When we get into difficult positions we need a good many suggestions to select from; and the man who has not observed widely and memorized sufficiently, will not have the data for wise judgment.

Now, as I said the other day, the "forgettery" is also important. If we are wise, we forget things that do not become part of our judgment; we leave behind things that are not candidates for use and profit. We need not burden ourselves by carrying around a great lumber house. We occasionally meet a man who prides himself on his good memory, and thank the Lord that we are not cumbered down like him with all the rags and tags we have ever studied. We feel instinctively that he is lost in this mass of material which he has accumulated. The last thing we should do would be to go to him for advice. We might go to him for information as we go to a dictionary; but as for the rest we look upon him as a kind of handy repository, a mere encyclopaedia of useful information. A man can have a good judgment who hasn't a good memory along certain lines,—that is to say, a memorizing memory; but he must be on the alert, when he sees a fact that is in his line, to reach out his mental tentacles, appropriate it, and make it a part of himself. My image of the mind is a sort of biological thing with arms or tentacles reaching out everywhere, and when they get appropriate food, just fastening down upon it. We take into the mind a good many things which we do not assimilate at the time. The geologist has to be on the lookout for a lot of things which he does not completely assimilate; but they stay in his sub-consciousness until by and by when he gets the clue to them, they are sorted out, arranged, and classified into knowledge. You know how in a chemical experiment a drop of acid is sometimes put into a glass of clear liquid when all of a sudden crystals appear and everything takes shape and order. While the wrong kind of memorizing is a sort of scrap bag into which everything has been stuffed, the right kind is this liquid in which many things have been dissolved and which when the right moment comes, assumes the form and classification needed for judgment. We talk about intuitions and the necessity of having quick and therefore decisive judgment. The right training of the memory is that which gives us the material for our intuition. The crisis comes along and the man responds with a quickly formed thought or plan of action.

There is therefore no dividing line, no middle wall or partition between the right kind of memory and judgment. Judgment is simply the terminus, the natural depot or station where the goods of memory are finally delivered. Memory is judgment in the process of making, and judgment is memory completed and defined. Memory is the food that is taken into the stomach but not thoroughly digested and circulated; judgment is the food in complete circulation,—in the process of being put just where it is wanted. If the brain needs it to think with, it is there. Memory gradually works the food over and over until it becomes part of our mental circulation so that the right plan and conception comes up when we need it. Therein lies the value of experience. There is a good deal of dispute among philosophers as to the relative value of experience and reason. One school says everything must come from experience. The other school says, No, it is reason or intuition that gives us our best and highest thoughts. Experience is disorderly; it deals simply with the mass of particulars not yet classified. Experience is reason in its earlier stage, in its solvent or uncrystallized condition; judgment is that experience arranged, organized, thoroughly digested, worked up into power. A student in one of my classes this spring was around visiting schools with reference to this particular point, the training of judgment. He went to four or five schools—it would not do to tell this in Chicago—and found only one case where judgment was being appealed to in all the schools he visited,—one case where the student was asked to weigh the fact and put a value on the material so as to arrive at the conclusion for himself. The rest of the exercises consisted in reciting the material which had been memorized.

We ought not to forget in our education the relative value of these things. While memory is a necessity, it has educative value only as it accumulates candidates or materials for judgment. There ought to be just as many questions to every recitation devoted to whether the student has been considering the question, as there are questions devoted to seeing if he has memorized the ideas. In so far as this is done, we not only find a better training of judgment but a better training of memory. It is of no use to learn things unless we can get at them when we want them; unless we can get them out of our storehouse. The training of memory independent of judgment does not give us such control. We want to get hold of an idea not only so that it shall be in mind, but so that we can get it *out;* and the only way we can get it out is to be continually exercising our judgment with reference to it. Mere verbal memorizing is not resorted to as much as it once was; but we have improved a good deal more in our theory than in our practice. What I have tried to put before you is the need of giving memory its place and finding out what that place is. Memory comes into education just in the degree that it gives the materials to be organized, remodeled, and classified in the process of judgment.

10. Some Elements of Character

I am going to speak this evening on some elements in character, considered from a psychological point of view. You understand, of course, that I do not expect to cover the whole field of moral education in an evening's talk. Some phases of the subject I shall make no attempt to touch at all. I once knew a gentleman who used to preface his remarks by stating that he hoped his audience would understand that he did not deny a thing simply because he did not say it, and that there were other things which, if he had more time, he might say beside what he did say. In touching upon the subject of moral education, I should like to make that same disclaimer. I am going to confine my remarks to those phases of character-forming which lend themselves most easily to statements, and which perhaps are commonly overlooked.

When we say that the end of education is the formation of character, it is, I think, at least desirable that we should have some sort of psychological analysis of this term. What then are the factors which make up character from an analytic point of view? For our purposes I think those factors may be stated under three heads; in other words, into the traditional classification of consciousness into the executive or doing side, the feeling or affective side, and the intellectual side. I am talking now about character, not general morality. In the kind of character that we wish formed by education we want something more than a simple moral passibility, or even more than a freedom from evil tendencies. We want something that is wider and deeper than what some people understand by the term moral. There are people who identify goodness with good intentions, with merely

[First published in *White and Blue* (Provo City, Utah), vol. 5, no. 12, 1 May 1902, pp. 1–8.]

meaning well in general. Well, you all know the place that is said to be paved with good intentions, and I suppose the reason they got there is that nobody ever acted on them and so they got pushed downward. The goodness that consists simply in just meaning well, just having a sort of general respect for the moral law at a respectful distance, is not the sort of morality we want. As has been well said, it is not enough to be good, people ought to be good for something; and that is the kind of character we want to build in our education. And so I say that character is quite a complicated thing and involves the development of the executive powers, of the feelings, and of the intellect.

I spoke a few moments this afternoon on the subject of judgment, and I am not going to repeat therefore much on this side of character. I will merely recall briefly some things I said; viz., that judgment is a constituent of character. It is our sense of relative values or perspective: a sort of scale by which we can appreciate the relative worth and significance of things; and as I tried to indicate this afternoon, simply storing facts and principles in the memory, no matter how important they are, does not of necessity affect judgment and therefore does not necessarily affect character. It is only the knowledge which passes over into wisdom, the information which passes over into our ability to reflect and estimate, that becomes part of our character. Now we certainly want our boys and girls to leave school with some sort of developed power of judgment, of ability to put two and two together, and to pick out the two and two that ought to go together; for when we come to practical life it is not merely knowing that two and two make four which counts, it is putting together this two with that other two; in other words, the ability to size things up at their right value.

A Frenchman said the chief value of an education was the sense it gave one of not being imposed upon. That is a negative way of putting it. Putting it positively it is the sense of liberation, the sense of command and control of ourselves by our own thoughts which frees us from the necessity of being merely hangers-on or dependents. I wish there were some way by which this thought could be made a little more specific, so that every teacher might realize the difference between simple accumulation of facts and this active turning over of the facts until they become part of mental power or the ability to judge. In this world we are all of us called to be judges; if not to sit formally in the seat of justice and pass upon misdemeanors and crimes, straightening out local quarrels, to pass judgment upon the social, political, and economic matters with which we have to deal day by day. Through judging, we get above the mere routine of habit; through judging, we get above being mere imitators, copiers, and followers of others; through judging, we get above caprice, above mere random activity, and sit in the seat of judgment, having within ourselves a measuring rod which we can apply to every variety of facts as they come up. From the intellectual point of view that is certainly the one thing above all others which schooling ought to make secure. Ability to judge is character on its intellectual side.

Some people, like Herbert Spencer, have said that you should not expect moral results from education; that education does not improve morality,—it is not expected to train a saint in the essential difference between accumulating information and doing right; that to do the right brings in something entirely different. It seems to me that statement ought to be put the other way. We ought to say that nothing is education unless it does affect character; that this accumulation of facts, even if it results in making the memory good and the man very learned, is not after all educative, unless it goes over into judgment; that is, unless it creates this sense of relative value, knowing the sense of things of most worth and the circumstances under which one value should be chosen and another rejected. I shall now leave the intellectual side of character, because, in speaking of attention and judgment I have virtually gone over it already in one form or another.

I want to go back to the volitional or will element in character; or, to avoid misconceptions that sometimes gather about the term will, the executive power, or power of carrying out our ideas. So there has got to be some active interest, some native momentum in the character to insure the carrying out of judgment in action. We talk about taking the will for the deed and very often excuse a child for certain things, saying, "Well, he meant right, he did not intend to do this evil thing." If there is any sense in what we say, we probably mean that he did go so far as he could, that he had within his consciousness a good intention, and that so far as his capacity and ability were concerned he did put forth activity; but owing to outside circumstances, over which he had no control, the result did not become obvious. In other words, he did perform a deed, and it was simply the things outside of himself which prevented that deed from coming to its full fruition.

If you stop to think of it, a man really acts when he makes a choice. We speak sometimes as if there could be choice of execution without performance; as if a man could make up his mind to do something sometime in the future. My experience is that you need to look out for a man who makes up his mind to do something by and by. He is deceiving himself and is really putting off the choice. A man who actually chooses begins to act from that very moment. You decide now to go to New York next year and proceed to act this year. How do I reconcile these two statements? Of course during this year you do not begin to go to New York, but you begin to do things differently from what you would if you had not made this choice. The choice goes out into action at once and expresses itself somehow or other in conduct.

This conception, that we can choose to do things by and by and not begin now, is responsible I think for a great deal of moral mischief. Of course the bearing of the delusion here is that the tendency may ruin his executive compliance with any thought. No judgment is complete until it is rounded up to a conclusion. That conclusion is a choice. We build up the mind too much artificially and talk about the intellect being here and the will there, just as if a man's intellect could go one way and his will another. When a man's intellect or judgment does not effectuate in action, it is because he did not quite get there with his thinking. He never really comprehended his thoughts or his ideas; his judgment did not come to a conclusion. If it had, his will also would have come to a decision. Judgment and choice are only sides of the same matter viewed from slightly different standpoints. There is only one mental reality in the case.

Now how are we going to train this executive power? If we follow the traditional education, just think how little scope or opportunity of any sort is provided to educate this tendency to carry forth things into conduct. How little opportunity there is given for any function whose effect is to maintain the natural assertive force of our impulses. I do not like the word impulse very well because it suggests something spasmodic, and to many minds something selfish. What I mean is this tendency within us to find some kind of active expression. The child goes to school, and instead of being encouraged in the direction of executiveness, he is met mainly by the demand for inhibition, "Sit still," "Don't be restless," "Don't talk," "Don't do that," "Don't do the other thing," "Just sit still and take in the ideas of the book"— these are the commands dinged into him upon the slightest sign of restlessness. Now that is a most successful way to dwarf and kill executive power and reduce the child as nearly as possible to a state of immobility. It may train his capacity for taking in the thoughts and ideas of others, and may in a way give him a certain training of memory, and even a sort of intellectual culture; but in order really to train his executive power he must be given room for experimentation, opportunity for the use of judgment in selection, and freedom to act upon the basis of that selection.

Everybody is prone to mistakes. The child is going to make more than other people because he is a child. The child cannot have the same scope, the same freedom of choice, the experimental effort to act out his choice that a grown person has. All that goes without saying. But you cannot train his judgment or executive power by putting him into a groove and keeping him there. He must have a chance to do even if he does wrong,—even if it be only to find out the real difference between the right and the wrong. Suppose I say to you that X equals seventeen. What does it mean to you? Absolutely nothing, it is pure nonsense; and yet if you had worked out the thought, the equation might mean a great deal to you. What is the difference between my telling you that X equals seventeen and your working out the equation? The result, so far as the answer goes, is precisely the same; but in the one case you have worked it out, and the whole meaning of the process goes over into the result. Some one has said that if God gave him truth in one hand and the search for truth in the other, he would take the search for truth. He might have added, however, that the truth given to him would not be true because he would not know what it meant. The child needs vigorous training of his executive power, and unless he has a chance to work things out for himself within reasonable limits, he does not get it. You cannot train his power of will merely by training him to be docile in his observance of the thoughts and experiences of other people. Now I know that many teachers think otherwise. They imagine the child is getting a very good training of his will by negatively shutting out all ideas leading away from his task and holding himself down by force of will, to his lesson. Perhaps he is. But is that the kind of will power we are anxious to obtain? If so, what sort of society or community life are we trying to educate our children for? Is it for Egypt, for China, for the Roman Empire, or for the America of to-day? After our children leave school, do we want them to show their will power simply by ability to catch and hold the thoughts, words, and ideas of others, or do we want them to show their will power by American independence which stands for native constructive and executive power?

I take it for granted that we want the latter. How can we get it? Only when the child gets outside school, unless we give him some provision for exercising it in school. There are so many children to look after in the school, however, that there would be chaos if you attempted very much of this individual sort of will training. Nor would the difficulty be altogether in the schoolroom; for it is true to a certain extent that education within the school cannot be forwarded any faster than the educational ideas of the community at large. We have to educate everybody together, parents and school boards as well as children. And the reason educational reforms break down sometimes, is because the teacher imagines he can make them inside the school walls without the change of public things about him. The school cannot get very much ahead of the public. This means that it is everybody's business not merely to see for himself that a given reform is necessary, but to try to bring the public to see that it is.

Now if one thing is more certain than another it is that the American people believe in education. If they can really be persuaded that a thing is right and necessary in education, they will make all the sacrifices necessary to provide for it. On the other hand no matter how favorable the conditions, a great deal depends upon the spirit of the teacher. One teacher will say the conditions are so bad that there is no use trying this, that, or the other, and of course if he is so convinced the reform will not be tried. Another teacher working under the same limitations will transform the whole spirit of the school: for reforms first of all are matters of the spirit. There are certain forms of construction and experimentation which cannot be carried out without adequate material,—something in the way of a scientific laboratory to explore and find out things with; but there isn't any school which does not have out doors, and therefore opportunity to encourage children to bring in not only objects but experiences.

Every recitation can be made an exercise in executive power by seeing to it that students state not merely what they have learned by the efforts of the teacher but what they themselves have worked out and found to be true and the reasons therefor. Such mental performance is at least preparation for the more positive performance in action. Because we cannot get all we want, is no reason for us not starting in the right direction. It seems to me we tend to think of our ideals as something far off into the future, rather than as guides indicating the direction of the line of progress. When people get in the habit of talking about their ideals as far off, they soon begin thinking they will never get there anyway and so there is no use in trying. The ideal, as I take it, is always really the very next step; and there are no limitations so absolute that one step forward cannot be taken. Nor have I ever found that the first step did not lead to another just ahead.

I once heard a man say that he had struggled a good deal with the appetite for drink; he had never been a drunkard, but he drank more than was comfortable for his own moral respect. He felt somewhat enslaved to the habit and kept trying to make up his mind to quit, but could not quit. Finally he read something in a book that struck him as a good idea. This was that he should not try to make progress toward some definite goal, but strive to move in the right direction. After that, he had no difficulty at all; instead of struggling for something afar off, he just took the next right step and so his temptation and enslavement to drink passed away from him. The only thing to do is to do it, and not just try. I know that when matters of reform come up, the natural feeling among teachers is that their conditions are different; if they had better equipments and smaller classes they might do something; but under existing conditions they cannot. Well, there is at least always a choice between the mere passive method of treating children and the method which appeals to their judgment, and holds them responsible for acting on that judgment.

You will not get the impression, as I find teachers do sometimes, that this individual training of the will means a sort of lawless freedom in the schoolroom; I take it that the reason the human race is continually progressing in freedom is because freedom and responsibility necessarily go together. The real question in the schoolroom is how much freedom can children stand? We have no right to give them too much, because they are only children and therefore lack experience. The reason for giving them freedom is not just for the sake of the freedom; it is to be found in the fact that only through freedom can we develop responsibility. There is a good deal of school discipline which is simply a scheme for relieving children of responsibility; and when I see teachers promoted because of mistaken admiration for such school government, I think that the public money is paid to men for carrying the entire burden of the school themselves and leaving the children barbarians and savages—unable to face any responsibility of life when it comes. One of the teachers in Boston had been thus promoted and her discipline was the pride of the town. When she fell sick, they had to put a substitute teacher in her place. She stayed there one day, then said she would beg to be excused from that place. They used up a teacher a day for two weeks, until this teacher could get back to those children. She had the government but the children had not. When the pressure had been taken off, the children, not having undergone self-discipline, found themselves and all about them at sea. We need not assume, therefore, that will-training means that children must do just as they please in order to gain the power of initiative or self-control. It means the giving of freedom up to the limit of the responsibility that children are able to assume. We have no more right to burden them with too much liberty than to take it all away.

As for the matter of training the feelings in their relation to character, the Anglo-Saxon races have the habit of scoffing at the Latin races for what they regard as their levity and lack of seriousness in their moral attitude towards the world. It is a good thing sometimes to turn matters around and look at ourselves. The judgment which the Latin races pass upon the Anglo-Saxon is that they are hard, angular, and without the delicate susceptibility to attend to the needs of others; that they set up their mark and go at it roughshod, regardless of the feelings of others. If we call them light and frivolous, they call us hard, and coarse, and brutal. And it is a fact, that in their educational systems, both in the school and in the family, there is much more attention paid to the training of feelings, especially in this matter of delicacy, or response to the state of mind of others. The chief value of art in its various forms—music, painting, drawing— crude though the work of the child may be, is that this is about the only way in which we can get into direct contact with the feelings, so as to train this delicate and somewhat subtle and refined appreciation of things. Somebody quoted to me within a day or two a saying of someone, that a child who had not been brought to a consciousness of beauty had lost the best part of his education. No matter what else he had learned, unless he had learned to appreciate the beauties of the world about him, he had lost a most serious thing. What is it really that he has lost? I think it is this delicacy, this refined responsiveness to things about him. You really cannot make up to the child for his failure to hear music in the first few years of his life. This unconsciousness of the adult to his surroundings and to the atmosphere of song, of art, of beauty, comes from not having the consciousness awakened at a time when it could best have been attuned to these things.

There is also the other side of this training of the feelings or emotions which I wish to speak about. There is a sort of direct training of the emotions which is of very doubtful value; very dangerous indeed, and leading to sentimentalism in one form or another. To try deliberately to stir up a child's feelings or emotions, when the natural and proper occasion for producing them unconsciously is not there, is, I think, to take very great risks. The feelings, in a certain sense, are the deepest things in a person's character, and the most private. No one has any business, wilfully and deliberately, to enter into the secret places of another's consciousness and try to stir up certain feelings. We excuse ourselves on the ground that they are good feelings which we want to arouse. Why not then really surround the child with the proper influences—the influences which would inevitably call out these feelings, instead of going at him with a sort of moral gimlet to put these emotions on exhibition? We make hypocrites of children by forcing feelings on them prematurely. I heard a woman say that her chief objection to novels at an early age was that it acquainted children with human affections, such as love between the sexes, before they got to it in their own lives and experiences; and so it aroused a sort of affection or artificial consciousness in that direction which robbed the reality, when they got to it, of its full force and meaning. The natural development of the affections was, so she maintained, arrested because they had been externally drawn in that direction before they were ripe. So also to expect a little child to have certain religious emotions which require a depth and range of experience utterly out of his possibility, is simply to prevent and distort the child. If we get him started in the right direction for having experience in the more serious responsibilities of life, there will be time enough later to have these deeper religious feelings. I do not believe he can have the reality of the more fundamental ones before that.

I do not know whether you have had the fad out here of making children appreciate the beauties of literature. They are not allowed to read a poem for the story and the rhythm—for which the child enjoys the thing,—but they have to stop and analyze the beauty. I am exaggerating somewhat, but I have to in order that you may better understand what I mean. We are just trying to stir up the emotional activities of the mind. Children like to please grown people if they can, and so draw out this great appreciation which even they are expected to have. The thing is not only unreal at the time but it really prevents the deeper appreciation that would come later on. I do not think that, as a rule, our deeper emotional lives develop until the period of adolescence. There are very good reasons for this belief if this were the place or time to go into it. The child has emotions of course. He loves, and gets mad, is frightened, and hopeful. He has these positive and personal sentiments or emotional attitudes, but the deeper emotions, moral and aesthetic, hardly develop before the period of adolescence. When we train the child prematurely in these emotions, we are very likely to hinder his fuller development later.

I can remember when I was a little boy, being sent out to look at the beautiful sunset. Now there is a way of calling attention to the beauties of nature which makes one more on the lookout for these things, and there is another way of expecting one to bring forth a kind of a gush of emotion, which, however, does not always gush. I always remember this particular instance when I was sent to look at the beautiful sunset. I could feel a strain all over my being trying to get hold of that sunset. I wished to please the person that sent me there and did the best I could; and the best I could do was to feel that it was a very nice thing, but what was there to make such a fuss about? We are doing this very thing, not only with the aesthetic emotions but very often with the moral and religious emotions, when we expect the feeling without the background to which these feelings naturally attach. Feelings are the tune of our experiences, and to try to get that tune without the actual experience is to set to work systematically to build up unrealities. The unconscious influence of the environment is the most natural way to cultivate these feelings in the child. There is such a thing as giving him plenty of good literature to appreciate and enjoy without expecting him to analyze and know in just what way he had those feelings.

When we were singing the "Star Spangled Banner" I was reminded of an article, which many of you may have seen in *McClure's Monthly,* about someone who went around and had the children write down the words that they thought were in certain songs which they had learned through the year. One wrote down for "America," "Land where the Pilgrims pried." That child builded better than he knew, trying to bring forth an exhibition of the proper kind of feeling on the proper kind of occasion. There is a certain undesirable moral introspection which comes with the attempt to cultivate the feelings directly. And yet, as I hope to have made clear from what I said before, I consider this training of the feelings one of the most important parts of the training of character, but one of the phases, upon the whole, which has been most neglected. We put a great deal of attention on giving the child facts, and there has been a disposition to look down upon art, especially the aesthetic art, and to regard it as a sort of luxury which does not come in until absolutely everything else has been taught. You know the man who said if you gave him the luxuries of life he could get along without the necessities. If we had more luxuries in education we could possibly get along with fewer of those things which have been considered fundamental necessities. I am not saying this to depreciate the great importance of the training which appeals to the feelings, but simply to indicate that we get the best training of the emotions by the proper kind of environment and by seeing that the child has the proper kind of experience, and then letting him manage his feelings as he naturally will, and not by going at him directly and saying, "Now, don't you feel this or feel that?" and similar methods of that sort.

The three great factors in the formation of character are first good judgment, or the sense of the values of things about us; second the executive disposition, or tendency not to stop with intentions, but to be positive, self-assertive, and have a reasonable amount of aggressiveness in one's make-up. I think it was Jackson who said he had only contempt for the man who could not get angry. We do not want to cultivate the habit of getting angry; but there is a certain kind of assertiveness, of positive aggressiveness, in hanging to an idea and not being contented until we have made the effort to put it into execution which is necessary to character; and the third factor is that delicate susceptibility of feelings which shall give poise to this executive tendency which in itself is likely to be a little hard and inconsiderate.

Now, if we look at the changes that have taken place in the spirit of education during the last fifty years, I do not see how we can help facing the future in any other spirit than that of optimism and courage. Fifty years ago there was hardly the sign of any one of these factors of character-training in our schools. There was hardly the sign of the artistic spirit in any of its forms; not a sign of constructive or manual training work in any of its forms. There was not a sign of direct acquaintance with nature or the beauties and truths of nature. There was practically nothing but the bare dealing with the symbols and forms of knowledge. Now that we see this great spirit which is coming to the schools, to the extent that it already seems at home and part of the new life and necessary equipment of the schoolroom, I think we may be perfectly sure that everything regarded important and desirable is going to be worked out in the future, and very much nearer in the future than we dare to anticipate. Revolutions, it is said, never go backward. Progressive movements never go backward. When they get started they accumulate momentum as they go; and the first we know, everybody is convinced that the thing is important and desirable, and it is done. We feel that we are on the threshold of a period when we shall recognize the complexity of matters that enter into character. We are going to move our materials and methods and see to it that our schools really become homes for the training and building up of men and women who are both noble and beautiful in the make-up of their own personalities.

Unpublished Writings

The Historical Method in Ethics

The remarks of my paper have arisen in connection with the course I am giving at present, where I am dealing with the historical development of conduct, and which has led from this to a consideration of the possibility of a science of morality. I have naturally arrived at the foregone conclusion that there is a science of morality possible, and I have further concluded that the condition of a scientific treatment of morality is in the use of a universal method; in other words, that it is only by a historical method that matters of moral conduct can take the form of a science. It seems to me there are positive data which consist of practices and beliefs and ideals or aspirations,—that is, a body of fact which is in existence just as much as are the facts with which the sciences of meteorology or physics deal. My thesis is that it is only by using an historical method that we can put these facts in that sort of order or get them under control so as to consider them scientific. There are one or two objections.

One is that no science of morality is possible because morality deals with what ought to be, and science deals with facts that are, that science is by its nature descriptive and explanation only grows out of description, and that obligation, the ought, is something the nature of which eludes description. It is not a fact or event. It is not a phenomenon. The objection seems to me much more specious than sound. I should dispose of it briefly by saying that there are ought facts just as much as there are is facts. It seems to me almost a verbal catch to say that you cannot have a science of what ought to be because what ought to be is not, but

[Address delivered to the Philosophical Club, University of Chicago, 4 December 1901. Typescript, not typed by Dewey, in the Joseph Ratner/John Dewey Papers, Box 44, folder 7, Special Collections, Morris Library, Southern Illinois University at Carbondale, and in the Henry Waldgrave Stuart Papers, Stanford University Libraries, Stanford, Calif.]

simply ought to be. It is a fact that the human race presents to itself certain relations in terms of obligation just as much as it presents other facts to itself in terms of heat or electricity or light, and there is a perfectly definite body of these facts. Some things are regarded as ought facts by some, and others are so regarded by other people. Now, we may say that moral ideals are unrealized or utterly unrealizable; none the less, the ideals are facts; they exist as facts, and they influence other facts. There are efforts put forth to realize them or put forth in relation to them. There is a struggle, and there is at least a varying measure of failure and success in reaching them. It is those things which give us a positive and definite body of data. In fact, it is difficult to deal with the objection because it is difficult to get the force of it. It seems almost a catch to say that because your facts relate to obligations that they therefore relate to something which are not facts and therefore cannot be discussed scientifically.

An objection of another sort not so often stated as presupposed is that morally the facts are so individual that they escape scientific description and analysis and explanation. In popular phraseology we have the idea of the rights of the private conscience and the sacred character of conscience; or, as stated in religious language, a man's conscience is a thing between him and his God. It is so peculiar and unique individually that the facts of it do not come within the sphere of scientific treatment. This seems to me a peculiar sort of egoism. Romanticism is egoism wherever it shows itself, whether in literature or puritanical morality or in some sort of consciousness. It may be gotten around by calling to mind that, if our own ego and moral affairs are of such great importance, so are everyone else's.

An adequate discussion of what science is would take up a whole evening, but perhaps a standpoint may be suggested which, even if not agreed to, will serve to make the rest of the discussion a little more intelligible. I mean by science a definite control of our interpretation of facts, that is, some kind of method for regulating the meaning that we assign to facts, or a method of controlling the judgments that we form. These are flexible definitions, but necessarily so. Aristotle said that science was relative to the body of facts that are being dealt with. In so far as in any of these subjects we get a definite method of regulating the judgments that we pass and discriminate them, in so far we have science.

This is what I mean by the control of interpretation: the process of control, the intellectual attitude that we take, and consequently the meaning that we assign to these facts. Control of judgment leads to control of the experience itself, and intellectual control tends to pass over into particular control. If we know how to pass right judgments, for instance on electrical data, we are pretty sure also to be able to control our experiences that have to do with those things. In so far as we know how to assign meanings to facts and objects, there is a presumption that we will be able to secure also those values or meanings that we want and to avoid those which we do not want. I mention that because it suggests that, if we can control our final judgments, it would not stop at that point with simply a better interpretation of the facts themselves, but from analogy at least we should expect that the control would extend itself into a control of experience itself. The confusion that exists at present, for instance, in the interpretation of conduct I suppose no one would deny has a tendency to confuse action and conduct. If, therefore, we could clarify our judgment of conduct, it would give us a guidance to the actual conduct itself. If it is possible to control our interpretation of our moral experience, to get some kind of technique, some kind of method into the way in which we pass judgment on acts, conduct, or character, the question comes up, where shall we look for that method? If we attempt to rule out all the methods that seem to us unsatisfactory I would not agree to the main point. I do not see how any amount of direct inspection of moral facts will enable us to control our judgment in any way, though it may be a preliminary step in that direction. The simple fact is that we take this direct inspection and direct reflection upon us. As they now present themselves we are dealing with judgments that are already formed. We are committed necessarily by all the judgments that we have previously passed, and we may incidentally get rid by more systematic observation and reflection and comparison of some of the inconsistent elements in these judgments, so modify them and make them cohere with each other. After all, our standard remains in judgments that we have already formed. We do not get beyond simply rendering those judgments more consistent with each other. We do not get back of the process itself. It is exactly the same as if we tried to make physical science simply by comparing all the observations that had already been made, extending them somewhat, and then sorting out and classifying them. It was a preliminary step in science, but the standard still remained the judgments that had already been passed, while what was wanted was to get away from these judgments to reform them, to change the process. On the other hand, we cannot dissect these moral facts. We cannot bring reagents to bear upon them. The methods of physical experiments are clearly not available.

Now, if neither direct inspection nor reflection upon our moral observations is possible, it suggests at least by way of elimination that we try the historical method. The idea that I shall try to bring out is that the historical method does do for data which exists in our miscellaneous experience what the experimental method does for physical facts. The historical and the experimental methods are identical, not in their outward relation, but their ultimate logical factors and logical aims. I shall go so far as to try to show that the experimental method is itself a form of the historical method, as well as the method applied in the only way in which it is available to these conscious data.

The business of experimentation is to define any given fact by stating exhaustively the conditions of its origin, the conditions under which that fact appears. All the conquests that have been made for human knowledge by the experimental method have been made simply by sticking to that very simple proposition. We will go behind the given fact to see what the conditions are which are necessary to the appearance of that fact. There are words which are always used by everyone, as well as by scientific men and by writers on logic which convey that idea, although the words are frequently used without seeing all that is understood in them. We say we are dealing with facts or with consequences, and we are trying to refer the consequences to their antecedents or the effects to their causes. By this we mean that we are interested in discussing the fact from the standpoint of its appearance in a time series. Science is not at all interested in facts in themselves as facts. It has nothing to do with that question. It is interested in the facts taken in relation to the historical antecedents, that is, the conditions which have to present themselves in order that this fact may show itself; though, if that proposition regarding the nature of experimentation is correct, at least we will be prepared to admit that in some more or less general sense the historical method is the correct one.

We might say that in physical experimentation we are making history and the reason that the experiment has its value is precisely because we are making the history; consequently the sequence is under control, while in history we read an account of an experiment that has been already tried. There of course is the less degree of certainty, the greater degree of complexity in the problem on the historical side. What we call history we do not make when we come to deal with it scientifically. We have to read it back into the terms of the antecedent and consequent which is therefore much less under direct control than when we can go ahead and make the history ourselves, as every scientist does in the laboratory. Experimental science is essentially then genetic science and the scientific value of the experimentation consists in the fact that the method pursued is genetic. Physics and chemistry give us pure history, so far as the experiment furnishes its ideals. When we analyze water, and say that water is H_2O of course it is that, simply from the standpoint of science; it is not really that; it is a liquid, a thing which we drink.

If I had time I should like to try to show why it is that we do not recognize commonly the historical character and the genetic character of the physical sciences. The obvious distinction will occur to you at once in what we are accustomed to call history; not merely the particular sequence is of importance, but the entire context in which that finds itself. In the physical sciences we are accustomed to think of particular sets of antecedents and consequents recurring at any particular point in the whole series. Not only do we have these pieces or samples of water appearing when proper historical conditions have been present, but we have them occurring and recurring at any point, theoretically speaking any place in the entire series. Now, it is not true that a certain piece of water shows itself more than once, any more than it is true that George Washington or Napoleon Bonaparte show themselves more than once. It is always individual water. Now, any water which is not an abstraction is truly here but once. It can come at only one point in the historical series. It is unique. When it is there, it is there for the first time, just as if it were a special creation made by the deity, and when it is gone it does not come back. When we get water again it is another water, so far as its existence is concerned. Existences in the physical side are just as unique and just as individual as those of persons and acts. Where the difference does come in is that the meaning is not unique. On the physical side, one piece or one sample of water is just as good as another, provided it is water. It serves the same purpose. It has the same value. It is only on the side of meaning that this interchange takes place, not on the side of existence. Water from the nearest faucet will slake our thirst just as well as water from the Pierian spring. If the water had anything to say about it, it would make just the same objection to being regarded as simply universal and reappearing at any point as an historical character would.

Now, the next point in my argument, to carry this comparison a little further, is to try to show that experimentation is historical in character, but that in the progress of the experiment we have two factors in the employment of the historical method in moral matters. All scientific matters go back to isolation and accumulation. The scientist must first isolate the fact that he wants to deal with, so that he can ignore a large number of other facts with which it is physically in juxtaposition. He has got to simplify conditions to such an extent that he will be able to identify exactly what he is dealing with, and rule out a lot of complications, a lot of surrounding facts which to immediate observation are common sense, are connected with the fact,—are a part of it. If he is going to make an analysis of water he must be sure he is dealing with pure water, in order that he may control all the various facts that enter into the experiment. A large part of the technique of the science consists simply in being sure that no factors are operating there except those which we have recognized and intend to be operating there. We cannot get this exclusive knowledge of the conditions under which a fact shows itself excepting as we can put in the facts that we want there and put out the things that we do not want there. On the historical side we get our parallel with that in the primitive phenomena. The earlier the fact shows itself, the farther back we can trace it in the historical series, the more we escape the complications with which all moral facts are overlaid as they present themselves to us. The earlier terms of the historical series have the value of presenting the phenomenon in question in something like reduction to its lowest terms, to the minimum of meaning and of content attaching to it, and so far as I can see, by going back and back we get the phenomenon reduced,—we get it stated in its lowest terms. Speaking again relatively, we carry it over from one subject to another and get it laid bare, we get it isolated. Some one has said that the value of evolution is that it takes the lid off of the universe. It uncovers the crust,—the complications which from our present standpoint have grown up everywhere. The genetic method, using the term in its ordinary sense, gives us the analysis exactly comparable to the isolation and separation which we find in experimental science.

The ideal of the physical scientist is, after he has gotten a number of simple conditions and knows what the effect of each of these is, to proceed cumulatively, to put them together. He proceeds to build up synthetically more and more complex structures; on the one hand, he tries to isolate and then put together the things which have been isolated, and build up again a complexity which differs from the original complexity which was presented to the mind because it has been through this process of conscious disintegration and of conscious reconstruction. The first time the fact was given to us we could not control it. So far as we realized it, we had to know what it was, and what it was like, because we made the fact, and it would be a pity if we could not know something about the objects of our own manufacture, and through this combination and interacting analysis and synthesis we change the present static facts of our experience into complicated facts that have been brought about through a series of steps of our own, and we get in control of these facts just because we have passed through that process of demonstration and re-creating of our own. It is the later steps of the historical period that give us this cumulative force. If we can trace a relation clear back, we get it into its simplest form, and then the problem is to see how it worked itself out, to see how it shows itself in more complex environs in a high degree of civilization and culture, where of course the problem is more complicated. There seems to me no difference in the essential logic of the case. It is a process of unraveling on one side; but going back to the most primitive materials available, we can see how these unraveled threads are woven together until finally we get back to today, and the civilization of today, and the moral civilization of today, and moral ideals and practices and conduct, and have gotten facts which we can look at although not made by us individually in this case, but made by others who had like ourselves received them, since they had been made by a long experiment which has been going on for centuries and in which humanity as a whole has had its share.

Through the history we get our present data which are so confusing, so real. We see them in relation to a process, and thereby can know how to place them. We have got a control. We have found out under what situation people came to regard a certain act as of value and as desirable, and by following it through its subsequent history we get a test of it. We get knowledge along three lines. (1) What was the situation which called forth a certain moral reaction, whether in the way of an ideal or practice? What was the setting, the situation which arose, which was the stimulus to this moral conception or practice? (2) Did it function adequately in that situation? Did it meet the requirements which called it forth? Was it simply a blind or unsuccessful reaction, or was it an adequate reaction?

Having historically taken to pieces and put together again our present moral situation, we can carry over the result of that judgment into our present interpretation and to some extent into our present practice, in so far as the same situation persists, or a situation which in its more important phases is the same. In so far as the situation has changed or modified itself, the necessity of some change in the reaction takes place. Or, we can go further. It is the knowledge of the moralizing process that is important, not simply the knowledge in itself, though sometimes things were gotten at by a mere accumulation of those bare facts, which, however, would not take anybody very far; but if we have the whole social and economic situation that called them out and the reaction they had upon their control of their environment and control of their own life, we get an insight into the moral process and thus can view the present situation to see what the processes are which are at work.

I will close with two points more on the philosophical side of the whole matter. The value of the earlier event in time is really one of method, one of giving us insight into the later conditions. The material fallacy is transforming this superior logical value into an ontological value, considering the earlier in time the cause and such more real things as reality, what comes later, more complex and more spiritual and accordingly only an inferior degree of existence or to some extent illusory. It is this tendency to degrade the latter terms of the series to the reality of the earlier that causes the ordinary opposition to the application of evolutionary method. The material point of view realizes the value of getting all things to their simplest terms; for instance, from a logical scientific point of view, taking primitive ideas has certain advantages. The material point of view takes abstractions as if they were real facts, some superior absolute value in the way of existence belonging to a thing because it came earlier. Should the cause have primary existence in its own right? I cannot see that things are any better because they come earlier in time. All we know about a thing called cause or antecedent is what comes after. We would not be able to make an intelligent statement about it. It is only by seeing and knowing its consequences that we can get any meaning from it as a cause. This conception, that if we only knew perfectly say the original nebula or the other things from which the whole physical universe has descended, we could have prophesied everything that has happened since, is a purely tautological statement. The only way we could have had a knowledge of it in the beginning is by knowing what came after it and what came out of it. Take the relation of hydrogen to water. We know that water is made of hydrogen and oxygen, but we would not know one single thing about hydrogen if we did not know the thing which it made. The whole proposition is a reciprocal one. And so when the materialist (in a rather wide sense) says that because our present morality has grown up out of savage morality, and that it is therefore nothing but savage morality shifted around and dressed up by a little different association, he is confusing these matters of superior values with the super-ontological values and contradicts his actual argument.

It is that which made the ordinary ethical writer object to applying this at all. He says this deprives them of all their real value and meaning. It puts the cart before the horse. It does not explain but simply explains away by reducing all to their simplest form. If that was what the historical method really did, this objection would be well founded. The idealist falls into exactly the same error from the other end. He assumes that the last thing has a superior and a finer value, and that everything that has gone before has to be interpreted as a sort of half-baked inadequate attempt to get what we have now gotten. The significant thing is the process of moralization and that process shows itself both in primitive morality and in such morals as we have now. There is no more finality attaching to our present stock of ethical conceptions. The only thing that does have finality is the relation between the process, between a situation, and a certain way of looking at that situation which exists now and all the time.

Knowledge and Existence

I. A Realistic Theory of Their Relation

It is a great gain in the discussion of any problem when simplification can be introduced; energy hitherto wasted is conserved from dissipation and, at the same time, the simplification reveals the exact point upon which energy may be fruitfully concentrated. Professor Woodbridge's treatment of the relation of knowledge to existence seems to possess many of the traits of a far-reaching simplification of this sort. In brief, the position is this: Things, existences, objects, facts,[1] are just what they are out of knowledge and in knowledge. Nevertheless knowledge adds something: viz., known objects qua known *mean* certain other objects. Smoke has itself, independent of its being known, a certain constitution and properties. When smoke is known, these remain just what they were, but there is added the further property of standing as a sign—say of fire. Smoke results from fire irrespective of the knowledge relation; but that smoke indicates (*means*) fire is as much a function of the knowledge relation as its density, color, etc., are a function of its physical relations. In this view, moreover, consciousness, mind, etc., are neither things, essences, stuffs, 'end-terms,' nor mere illusory epiphenomena: they are names for the existence of precisely this added relation of meaning among things.

It would be a grateful task to point out the numerous and

---

1. Later we may see reasons for differentiating these terms. At present, they are used indifferently.

[Typescript, not typed by Dewey, in the John Dewey Papers, Box 51, folder 14, Special Collections, Morris Library, Southern Illinois University at Carbondale, ca. 1909. For Frederick J. E. Woodbridge's article to which this is a reply, see this volume, Appendix 5.]

profound simplifications involved in acceptance of this point of view—the problems eliminated as factitious, the genuine problems that are defined and concentrated. But my office here is the more ungrateful one of a sceptical questioner. My questions relate however not to the truth or falsity of any particular proposition, but to the logical relations existing among them.

The propositions are (1) Knowledge is a meaning-relation. (2) Things that enter into knowledge remain the same that they were out of it—save, of course, the assumption of the meaning-relation. (3) Consciousness and the meaning-relation are coextensive, denotatively and connotatively.

I. If we start from the first and third we seem obliged to deny the second: which does not imply however the assertion of the contrary, but only the meaninglessness of any proposition either way. For if all knowledge is meaning-relation *and* this relation is coextensive with 'consciousness' in every way, it does not seem possible to make any reference to or raise any question about objects 'out of knowledge,' whether like or unlike. II. If we start with the second and the third, in combination, the first becomes impossible; or if we try to combine the second and the first, we find it necessary to restate the second. For the possibility of upholding the second seems to depend upon holding that knowledge is not a meaning-relation, but direct prehension or intuition of what already exists, while the doctrine that knowledge is meaning-relation indicates that the objects or facts which express its outcome have undergone radical change as respects the "things" that assumed the meaning-relation.

I. As to the consistency of the doctrine of the inclusiveness of the meaning-relation (or its identification with "consciousness"), with the notion of any reference beyond "consciousness." Here, the antinomy that presents itself is this: Thesis—Unless there is reference of the meaning-relation beyond itself (involving of course the elements *qua* elements in this relation), there is no knowledge. Antithesis—But if 'consciousness' is coextensive, in denotation and connotation, with this relation no such reference is possible. Let us recur to the smoke-fire instance. Unless the smoke has characteristics that are independent of its meaning fire, and unless the fire has characteristics independent of its being meant by smoke and unless *connection between these characteristics* is involved in smoke meaning fire, there is no such thing as smoke *meaning* fire. Probably the simplest way to appreciate these considerations is to refer to the possibility of a situation in which two things are co-present simply by way of suggestion. Smoke may *suggest* fire with no *belief* in fire beyond its being suggested—as it may suggest a face. The fire thus suggested and not believed in may suggest hell without any belief in hell. In this case, neither the fire suggesting nor the hell suggested has any implications whatsoever beyond the situation. There is no knowledge, because there *is* no meaning-relation. There is only a suggestive relation in virtue of which certain things are co-present. Generalizing all "consciousness" reduces itself to such bare co-presence of "associated" elements, the elements having no reference beyond the bare fact of their association.

My intention is not at all to show that since there *are* such situations, the view that consciousness is equivalent to a meaning-relation is incorrect. I use this matter of suggestion-relation only as a hypothetical illustration to enforce the proposition that it can be said that S *means* P, only when both S and P have implications outside this S - P situation.

So far, we are only in line with Professor Woodbridge's teaching as to things outside of the meaning-relation that are presupposed by it. But now let us consider the other proposition: The significance relation is denotatively and connotatively the equivalent of consciousness. On this basis, what is meant by the reference to things outside of this relation? How is it possible even to refer to them? And yet if it is not possible to refer to them, there *is* no meaning-relation, no knowledge. Prior to the question, then, whether entering 'consciousness' *alters* in any way things as they exist outside of 'consciousness' is the question *whether* upon the basis of the identification of 'consciousness' with knowledge as defined, *any reference to such outside things is possible?*

This difficulty has been felt by others, notably by Professor Bode. In reply, Professor Woodbridge has said: "It is not the 'awareness' of a fact that makes the fact a fact of a particular kind in consciousness; it is that in its own right. The simple existence of the fact in consciousness appears to be all that is involved in 'awareness of the fact as fact.' But let the fact mean something and its meaning appears to be identical with

'awareness of it as meaning something.'"[2] We have here a peculiar situation. Professor Woodbridge gives as a resolution of a
difficulty a proposition that seems to me to state the difficulty. If
we invert the second sentence—and the proposition seems to
intend equivalence—it reads "all that is involved in 'awareness
of the fact as fact' is precisely the simple existence of the fact
in consciousness." In other words there is no reference beyond
'consciousness.' To say a fact exists is to say it exists in consciousness; and this (as we have seen) involves the substitution of bare existential co-presence for a meaning-relation, and
hence the denial of knowledge as defined. Or putting the matter
the other way, the second and the third sentences quoted have,
on the basis of Professor Woodbridge's identification of consciousness and meaning-relation, exactly the same force,—while
to be a solution of the difficulty urged they should have a different force, i.e., put the matters referred to on a different footing.
The expression "the simple existence of the fact in consciousness" means, by definition, existence in a meaning-relation and
so is exactly equivalent to the expression (in the third sentence)
"let the fact mean something." Hence, the only awareness of the
fact possible *is* the awareness of it as meaning something which
in turn we are aware of only as meant. And this, as we have
already seen, is the destruction of the meaning-relation itself.
This contradiction is surely the *reductio ad absurdum* of one of
the premises from which it follows: viz., either that knowledge is
a meaning-relation or that knowledge and 'consciousness' are
coextensive.

II. Let us check up this result by trying the first and second
propositions in combination. Knowledge is a meaning-relation
between things which are the same 'in' as 'out' of the relation.
Here the alternatives of the dilemma are: If it can be intelligently
asserted that things are the same without as within the meaning-
relation, then knowledge is direct prehension of fact, and the
existence of a meaning-relation is a token of deficiency of fact
and hence of knowledge. Or, on the other hand, if the meaning-
relation is genuine, not illusory, and if it identifies knowledge,
then "things" are transformed by assuming it.

(1) Says Professor Woodbridge (article cited, page 397 [this

2. *Psychological Review*, November, 1908, p. 398 [this volume, p. 543].

volume, p. 543]), "Take the water again. When it is unknown—meaning thereby when it is not an object in consciousness—is it lacking in particular chemical and physical properties? Does it take on these properties—or lose them—only in consciousness? If it can have properties both in consciousness and out of it, there is no necessity of adding anything to them to make them just those properties when they are in consciousness." This seems to state exactly the difficulty. The water and its properties referred to as fact are known; they are defined. They are known moreover as the outcome of long scientific inquiry. History shows that many different and incompatible properties have been attributed to the constitution of water, that much has been taken for water that is not H_2O; hence not what has been taken to be water, but "real water," as we say, water which is known to be a certain thing with certain properties, must be referred to by the proposition. Hence the force of the passage quoted would seem to be that objects *qua* objects (as distinct from what they are from time to time taken to be), facts *qua* facts (as distinct from our opinions about them), do not change in passing from one knowledge relation to another. Of unknowable objects there would be no sense in saying that they remain the same in and out of the knowledge situation; and of what objects *seem* to be, the statement is obviously false. Just *their* change in "knowledge" convinces us that they are not 'real' objects with properties changeable only by new physical relations. But upon this line of argument, there is no reference to objects passing into a knowledge-relation absolutely, but only to those passing from one knowledge-relation to another. Knowledge in this case is precisely the recognition and definition of fact as fact. As respects the meaning-relation then, we are either asking the contradictory question of whether entering a knowledge-situation alters what we already know objects to be; or else we are indicating that it is *through* this relation, or its fulfilment—actual or indicated—that things *are* objects and facts with their unchanged constitution for further knowledge.[3]

3. It is tempting here to raise some side issues. The view that the contrast is between *one* partial meaning-relation and a whole system of such relations leads of course to rationalistic or objective idealism. This view would claim that in Mr. Woodbridge's argument there is a confusion of 'being in knowledge'—i.e., being in the related system of mutual implications or the perfect

But why, in any case, should it be supposed that if things gain or lose properties upon entering the meaning-relation, these 'properties' are of the same type as the chemical and physical properties they present *when* known? One who accepts neither Professor Woodbridge's logic nor that of idealism might contend that all knowledge *qua* knowledge involves reference to 'things' totally outside the knowledge situation as such, and yet hold (and for that *very* reason) that *objects* and *facts* denote that which *satisfies* or fulfils the conditions of the knowledge or meaning situation. It might hold that knowledge transformed 'existences,' but that it transformed them into 'objects and facts' possessing properties unalterable for any other knowledge situation, so that, if subsequent alteration is found to be necessary, that alteration proves that we have not 'knowledge' but error. Such a theory would protest as much as does Professor Woodbridge against the gain or loss of properties *of* objects or facts through the assumption of the knowledge relation.

In no case, if knowledge means meaning-relationships, could the doctrine that "things" are transformed into "facts or objects" by entering it be termed *subjectivism,* for we are perfectly familiar, in the objective region (as in the case of all organic events), with modification of *previous* relations by supervention of a new one, and hence with a *qualitative* change of the elements in the relation.

(2) I now propose to examine the situation from the other side. We now accept and ask for the logical consequences of the doctrine that an object or fact enters into the knowledge situation in such fashion that it *is,* and hence (by definition) is *known* to be, in the knowledge situation that which it is outside. We seem at once to be enmeshed in a net of cross-threads. If an object is

---

all-inclusive judgment—and being present 'in consciousness,' that is in a fleeting, fragmentary apprehension of this total system. It would insist that his argument turns on confusing two senses of 'knowledge': knowledge as a scientific, or logically ordered, system in which alone do "objects" exist *as* objects (or with necessary, or uniform and universal characters) with 'knowledge' as a personal event—the fragmentary reproduction in finite conditions of the total system. It would point out that the possibility of maintaining the reference beyond itself of 'consciousness' (and hence of escaping 'subjectivism') depends upon precisely the implication in the fragmentary knowing or consciousness of the total system of judgment as its intent and standard. Compare, for instance, the doctrine of 'inner and outer meaning' in Professor Royce.

already (i.e., outside of the knowledge situation) completely qualified as fact or object, and if it then enters without any change into the significance-relation, how is it possible for it to *signify* anything? It *is*, and it would seem as if knowledge were just apprehension, seizure, of what is, not *one* thing meaning *another* thing. But if a thing outside does enter *as* signifying something else beside itself, then it would seem as if it had to be *different from the object of knowledge*, for the latter is not fixed till the signifying situation is terminated and is out of the way. For example, smoke means fire; water means quenching thirst. *What* smoke? First alternative: Why the smoke-*of*-the-fire, of course; just as it is thirst-quenching water which means quenching. But in this case 'means' is a senseless word, 'is' is the only word to be used; we simply have prehension of a fact as it is, without any significance-relation. Second alternative: The smoke which *means* fire is not *yet* determined as smoke-of-the-fire; hence it can be said genuinely to mean it. But in this case, since the *fact*, the *object* is by definition precisely smoke-of-the-fire, the real object did not *enter* in its reality the significance relation, but rather *issues*—in consciousness—from it. In any case, if knowledge refers to the object which concludes and terminates the meaning-relation, this relation is not knowledge; while if it refers to the thing that first presents itself as meaning something, that thing is transformed.[4]

Before we consider farther whether (on this view) the change suffered is merely quantitative, simply a shrinkage of extent, or is qualitative, we have to face the probable reply that while the fact as cosmic fact has undergone change, it has not undergone change by virtue of entering into the meaning-relation, but by virtue of coming into relation to the organism, the organism being itself a fact of the same order as the fire-smoke fact, and hence capable of being related to it as any one fact is to any other fact. Hence, it may be argued, the fact which actually enters the knowledge situation—the visible, odorous related set of qualities called smoke—is precisely the fact as it really is. The argument is plausible; with respect to its import upon the physiological

---

4. It is of course this logical alternative which leads some to the view that what *enters* (*qua* entering) knowledge is only appearance; while reality is what issues (or would issue) with respect to perfect knowledge.

argument for idealism it is, in my judgment, conclusive. But its bearings upon the idealistic notion of consciousness as an existential stuff, entity or force are not at all the same as its bearings upon the definition of consciousness as significance relation. What is required by the theory of the entrance of the "fact" without change is that the 'smoke' should enter 'consciousness' *as* smoke-of-fire-having-come-into-relation-with-a-percipient-organism. What the argument has shown is that relation-to-an-organism is part of the fact; what was required to be shown is that the fact as thus constituted enters unchanged into 'consciousness.' Now the fact as known is not only lacking in this relation as part of its apprehended content, but the argument assumes that it is lacking—for it attempts an explanation of *why* it is lacking. The more the argument proves that this relation-to-organism enters into the constitution of the fact, the more difficulty it has to account for this fact not being what presents itself in 'consciousness.' The fact so constituted appears in 'consciousness' only as the termination and fulfillment of meaning-relations. We have the same alternatives as before: Either the thing entered as it really was and then the object in which the meaning-relation terminates is its transformation; or the conclusion presents the real fact and then the real fact was altered in entering the relation.

We come now to the question of the character of the transformation involved in the assumption of a meaning-relation. Is it quantitative only? If so, it may be argued that a mere disappearance of some elements leaving others unchanged is not to be termed, save sophistically, an alteration. This contention seems to me just. But *is* the change a merely quantitative one? If we know 'this' to *be* smoke is there any possibility of a relation of significance? Does not the fact of its being smoke already contain as part of itself an apprehended relation to fire? Can the smoke-of-fire be said, intelligibly, to mean fire? If *this* is already characterized *as* water, is there any possibility of its *meaning* quenching thirst? Isn't that a property of, or a related element in, water?

The proposition "water means or implies quenching thirst" is not to be identified with the judgment that '*this* water will quench thirst'—the force of the proposition about water in general is that one *meaning* implies another meaning; or else it is that certain attributes actually coexist in the constitution of some object. In the latter case there is of course no *meaning-relation* at all; there is a fact apprehended in its constitution as fact. Or in the first alternative, the proposition 'this water means quenching thirst' contains no meaning-relation, provided 'this' and 'water' are already identical. We have mere tautology so far as statement is concerned; we have just a single prehended fact so far as *knowledge* is concerned. But if 'this' is not already identified as water, then the situation must be described as of this sort: this, *if* it means water, means quenching thirst. The question is as to the meaning of 'this'; and that question is a genuine question *only when the character of 'this' is uncertain or indeterminate.* The 'this' gains determinate character,[5] moreover, only through the fulfilment of the meaning-relation. If the possibility indicated is accepted and 'this' is drunk, and it quenches thirst, *then* this *is* water. Or else it poisons, and was not water; or else, it does not quench, and the thing meant was not thirst; or else, since it does not quench thirst, either water or thirst, or both, have a different character from what I took them to have. But upon any of these alternatives the 'thing' meaning and the 'thing' meant are *qualitatively* different in the meaning-relation—*qua* in it—from what they are out of it:—for they are in it only in virtue of their lack of character or determination.

I have put the argument, for brevity, categorically. Of course, its force here is purely hypothetical. It is simply a development of the implications of the propositions that the meaning-relation is genuine, and that it identifies and defines knowledge (instead of knowledge being recognition of the given constitution of fact or object). *If* the meaning-relation is genuine and genuinely identifies knowledge, then qualitative transformation is implied in knowledge.

For completeness' sake, we refer again to an alternative already disposed of: 'This' *is* already (independently of entering the meaning situation) of a problematic and indeterminate character, and its entering the meaning-relation only exposes it for what it already is. Hence there is no alteration. In this case, however, 'this' is characterized already by the meaning-

5. Of course, the argument does not require the *this* to be totally indeterminate in character, but only as respects that in virtue of which it is in the meaning-relation.

relation, for the problematic and indeterminate quality of 'this' is precisely with respect to a determination of meaning. Knowledge is not accordingly identical with the meaning-relation, but it merely lights it up as it already exists. In short, if we force Professor Woodbridge's logic to its conclusion, the conclusion seems to be that the meaning-relation and the constitution of facts and objects with their spatial and time relations stand on the same level, and must be served with the same sauce. Either the meaning-relation is already a part of the fact outside of knowledge, and hence knowledge is not a meaning-relation; or the thing meaning and the thing meant have their quality in the meaning-relation, and hence are *not* to be identified, *either* with the objects and facts in which the relation finally terminates, *or* with 'things' qua not-entering into the knowledge situation.

This concludes the detailed examination. It may however be rejoined that the whole criticism overlooks the primary fact in the view of Professor Woodbridge. It may be said with reference to my first difficulty that it is precisely the situation itself which is either merely 'suggestive' or of the 'meaning' type; and that only by overlooking this essential portion of the doctrine has the dilemma or supposed antinomy been created. Similarly, it may be said, that what the situation actually *is,* is one in which things constituted-as-the-same-out-of-knowledge-as-in-it mean one another; and that it is only the arbitrary assumption that consciousness changes what enters it that introduces any of the difficulties that have been urged.

This rejoinder, if made, merely gives another illustration of the fundamental dilemma. The rejoinder means that the situation already *is* that sort of a situation apart from 'consciousness' and that knowledge or 'consciousness' is just the awareness of such a situation as already existing; or else it does not mean this. If it does mean this, then the meaning-relation exists apart from knowledge and 'consciousness,' and they are not to be defined as its equivalents. We surrender the view that knowledge is a meaning-relationship. If it does not mean this, knowledge *is* a meaning-relationship, then we do not *know* that the situation is of the kind indicated; it just *is* of that kind as a conscious situation. The situation as such is not *knowledge* at all, but just an existent empirical—or 'consciousness'—situation. This of course is logically fatal to the proposed simplification, for it abandons the statement that "consciousness" and knowledge are coextensive, either denotatively or connotatively. It assumes that knowledge is a peculiar, qualitative relationship in or between the constituents of a situation, which as a situation is not knowledge at all. Realistically speaking, there is no more reason why the conscious situation should not *be* and yet not be known than why any other thing should not be without being known. At bottom, it seems to me a survival of idealism to suppose that the existence of an empirical situation (or if you please of an experience or of a 'consciousness') is the same as knowledge of that existence. But, in any case, if for the situation to exist and to be known is the same thing, we have surrendered the contention that knowledge is a meaning-relation, for the proposition is not that the situation *means* so and so, but that it *is* so and so.[6]

Finally, I restate my difficulties in a dogmatic way, hoping, however, that this summary will be interpreted in the light of what precedes, instead of having a ready-made meaning read into it. Knowledge seems to be employed in a three-fold fashion: First, a direct presence, intuition one might say, or prehension of

6. There is, of course, *another* situation possible to which the proposition that the situation of this-meaning-smoke-fire itself means so and so properly applies. The situation of smoke-meaning-fire *is* genuinely known, according to the definition of knowledge as meaning-relation. This consideration has some interesting implications, such as (a) Professor Woodbridge's own discussion, or Dr. Bode's, or this paper are illustrations of the possibility noted. That is, it is only from the standpoint of *logic* that the situation in which S means P can be said to be *known;* apart from such reflection, it just exists. (b) Logic, or any branch of philosophy, since it is a form of knowledge, is not an endeavor to show what knowledge *is* but what knowledge *means.* As the only way to have smoke is to have it, and as the only way to have it when wanted, is to have such control of other things as to be able to produce it, so the only way to realize what knowledge *is* is by knowing—by recourse to the actual empirical situation. But the question of what knowledge—or the meaning-relation—itself *means* is nonetheless an intelligent and, under some circumstances, an important question. The recognition of what knowledge means may help, for example, to produce the existence of knowledge when wanted; it is clearly necessary to a discussion of the relation of science to life; it carries with it the possibility of differentiating philosophy from science, etc. (c) The situation in which the meaning of knowledge is discussed is not itself, as situation, knowledge. As situation it just exists, or is "experience." (d) This is the proper meaning, as I understand it, of appeal to 'experience' as final in philosophy and in science. It indicates the proper sense of the term 'immediate experience,' i.e., not a contrast to 'mediate experience,' or thought, but something which overlies both mediate experience, that which can be set over against it and the distinction and relation of the two. At least, this is the only sense in which I have used the term 'immediate experience,' while critics of that doctrine have always interpreted it to mean a cognitive distinction; in which sense, it yields absurdities, naturally and inevitably.

things as just what they are as prehended; second, something involving inference, 'thought' (judgment in the ordinary, non-technical, sense of the term), the meaning-relation; the third, this meaning-relation transcended and completed, an assurance which is rational, grounded, an insight which is not merely there but which can explain and maintain itself when challenged—knowledge as science. The term object has a similar "triguous" meaning. In the first sense, it denotes existence irrespective of value or validity; in the second, it denotes *data,* crude material, as selective determinations of *existence* for the sake of their interpretation or valuation in reference to meaning; in the third, it denotes *valid object, fact* which is secure, which satisfies the conditions of knowledge. These distinctions seem to me both genuine and significant; fallacy arises only when they are so identified that the description of one is carried over into an account of another. The problems of properly stating their distinctions from and connections with one another are *the* problems of a logical, as distinct from epistemological or psychological theory of knowledge. These problems are genuine, not factitious. They have been frequently rendered factitious through entanglement with irrelevant psychological or cosmological materials. But they stand forth all the more clearly when these irrelevant trappings are stripped off. Any simplification which does not recognize *all* the factors involved in all the problems cannot endure, for it will surely call out a reaction by reason of the elements overlooked—and lead probably to an equally one-sided insistence upon them, and a consequent swing of the pendulum in the opposite direction. And a realistic theory which itself rests upon the fundamental postulate of idealism—the identification of conscious experience or 'consciousness' with knowledge—offers a peculiar provocative to an idealistic reaction.

In short, the impact of this paper is not particularly upon the special theory examined—that of Professor Woodbridge. By its simplicity, conciseness, and thorough-going character, his theory lends itself to discussion of the ultimate logical issues involved. But as compared with other theories of the relation of knowledge to existence, it sins, if it sins at all, only by its clearness and conciseness—by the completeness with which it has rid itself of irrelevant cosmological and psychological

trappings and left the logical issues stripped naked to vision. The fundamen-
[p. 30 missing] versus states of consciousness, it generated epistemology. Meantime the logical question which is fundamental persists; and its fruitful analysis and resolution is hindered by distraction of attention to ontological and epistemological questions which would themselves mostly vanish into thin air, if the logical problem were faced and solved;—or which, if the logical problem were found to be insoluble, would quietly be laid away on the shelf as themselves therefore insoluble.

All the purely psychological presuppositions regarding 'sentiency' and 'thought' can be stripped away from both the subjective and objective types of idealism; and those theories still have serious claims, as typical methods of dealing with the *logical* problem of the relation of knowledge to existence. The subjective type is then found to select the alternative noted early in this paper: the reduction of knowledge to bare copresence or conjunction of existential elements; the objective type is found to select an alternative mentioned later: the assumption that 'real'—as distinct from 'phenomenal'—existence is the content of an absolutely completed system of meaning-relations, and that reference to this system is intended in every (fragmentary) human knowledge. The instrumental or functional theory of knowledge sketched in the *Studies in Logical Theory* was intended to indicate, through criticism of both of these types of theory, considered as logical types, another type of theory which should deal more effectively with the problems at issue. Almost without exception, the theory has been treated as a rather complicated—probably over-elaborated and hence obscure—method of treating questions which being in themselves either cosmological or psychological or both may be approached better more directly. In this paper I have tried to indicate that the danger under which current 'realism' labors in its logical method is that of denying, by ignoring, certain fundamental logical problems. In a subsequent paper, I hope to come back to the question of idealistic theories of the relation of knowledge and existence, and show that in them also the logical problem is fundamental, and that they also restate, instead of solving, the difficulties they are supposed to deal with.

Some Thoughts concerning Religion

Not long ago, Christians justified Christianity on the ground of its uniqueness, on the ground of its contrast with other religions, on the ground that it was true religion and they were religions falsely so-called. Other religions (save Judaism, which was regarded as Christianity in preparation or in prophetic types) were possibly inventions and insinuations of diabolic powers, possibly creations of fallen human nature, and evidences of its lost estate, possibly corrupted reminiscences of an original divine revelation. But in any case, this contrast with Christianity as the one true religion was the characteristic thing about them.

The more enlightened apologists of to-day have changed all this. We pride ourselves, morally, on having outgrown the intolerance of such a view; intellectually, upon having attained a more historic and impartial attitude. Christianity is defended to-day on the ground of the universality of religion and on the ground that Christianity expresses most adequately the motives and aspirations that dimly and feebly are operative in even the most superstitious of beliefs and cults. Fetishism, animism, idol-worship, sacrifice and ritual taboo are employed not so much as evidences of false religion in contrast with a true, but rather as testimonies to the universality of the religious instinct or the religious need. The dialectic demonstration by Hegel of Christianity as "absolute religion" paved the way for this mode of conception even among anti-Hegelians; evolutionary and historic methods are supposed to warrant it independently of any philosophic doctrine.

[Address delivered to the Philosophical Club, Columbia University, New York, N.Y., 17 March 1910. Typescript, not typed by Dewey, in New York Philosophical Club Papers, Rare Book and Manuscript Library, Butler Library, Columbia University.]

I advert to this situation not for the sake of directly discussing it, but because it suggests to my mind not only a loss of intensity on the part of traditional religious convictions, but also loss of a certain intellectual clarity and simplicity. More explicitly, in listening to various discussions on religion, both in and out of this club, I have detected (or at least I have seemed to myself to detect) a certain confusion between a consideration of religion on historic grounds and a consideration on ideal grounds; a confusion of the *de facto* and the *de jure,* an attempt to decide what religion is and should be for the present and for the coming generation on the basis of what has been. I have felt, putting the matter more technically, some confusion between efforts to set forth the universality of the religious need and attitude in terms of what have passed for religions, and conceptions of universality in the sense of what certain persons regard it as desirable to have become more general and more fundamental. It may not be true that religion is to be defined in terms of the contrast of Christianity with Paganism, and yet it may be true that it is to be defined—or anticipated—in terms of contrast with historic religions, Christianity included. It may be true that certain phenomena (psychological, social, ethical, or metaphysical) have "universally" attended religions in the past, and yet that *these* "universalities" have little to do with any religious attitude or conviction which we should wish to become universal. It may be true that religion has *not* been universal in any sense, and yet it be true that there is a certain quality, disposition, or attitude which it is desirable to have universal—in the sense of as widespread as possible—an attitude which might properly be called religious. At all events, it is some of the connotations of these suggestions which I wish to discuss.

II

One point that is characteristic in what for short I may call the developmental definition of religion is the insistence upon the gradual evolution to the point of explicitness of the ethical factor:—traits that had a physical or magical meaning in the lower religions have taken on moral signification in the higher and later, so that we must suppose this factor will become dominant in the future. Well, is this an evolution, or is it a revolution? Is this change one that emphasizes or that ignores genuine historic continuity? Is there any conceivable dissolution of continuity more radical than a change from non-moral to moral as a defining trait? Now can we describe or define religion by means of the common denominator method if we admit this transition from the non-moral to the moral? I confess the attempt to conceive the *proper* universality of religion on the basis of a survey of historic religious phenomena which at the same time emphasizes the historic evolution as one from the non-ethical to the ethical seems to me self-stultifying. I recall with interest the ardor with which in one discussion that I heard, the historians scouted the idea that religion had anything to do with morals. There was nothing, they declared with emphasis, with which the religions that had come under their observation had less to do with than morals! As I listened I was perplexed, for it seemed to me they were correct, and it also seemed to me that those who pointed out the constantly increasing explicitness of the moral factor in religions were also correct. The only way out of this confusion which I have found is to admit frankly that we are not dealing here with lower and higher "stages" of the same phenomenon, and that we must frankly make our choice between two criteria. We must either take the traits characteristic of the non-ethical religious phenomena as furnishing the materials out of which to construct our conception; or we must cut loose, and say that we decide (however arbitrarily) that nothing is worthy to be called religion save a somewhat profound qualification of our moral attitude, so that it is only by a somewhat doubtful courtesy of language that the greater part of historic "religions" and that which we now propound as the "religion" of to-day and to-morrow can *both* be called religions.

III

It is perhaps pertinent to note that those who attempt to justify the religious attitude by its universality in the past do not agree either as to the criterion for this universality or as to the characteristic structures and forms in which it is found expressed. Some seek it by the psychological road. Of those who seek it by this path, some find its exhibition in a special "instinct" that drives out upon the unknown or the infinite, or upon the vaguely felt welfare of the race as against that of the individual. Others with the same general type of criterion, emphasize certain emotions, wavering between that of fear running into awe and reverence, and that of communion and kinship, or some juxtaposition of the two emotions. Others emphasize the sense of luck, of chance, of fortune, amid the uncertain vicissitude of life. Others again look not to a universal instinct or emotional reaction, but to some universal need.

There are others (not so numerous perhaps, but nevertheless others) who hold that any attempt to find universality by *any* psychological road is doomed to self-stultification—the universal must be objective, and objectively necessary. They look for universality upon the side of a relationship, quite independent of any instinct or emotion (though possibly having its own specific emotional accompaniment) that necessarily exists between man and the universe. Some would hold (any realist would be bound to hold) that this universal relation might exist and yet many individuals be unconscious of it, so that the universality of religion would be compatible with many individuals being non-religious,—and even, possibly, being none the worse on that account. This relation may be variously conceived; as that of the finite to the infinite, as that of intelligence to a world which cannot be rationalized, as that of necessary ignorance and consequent faith, to a world which even though itself intelligent can never be mastered by our intelligence. I have no mind to use these diversities between and among the psychological and the metaphysical criteria of universality as proof of the futility of the search for any existential universal. I am willing to admit the possibility of some reconciliation of them; or that the progress of knowledge will dispel erroneous attempts and substantiate the truth of some one method. I think, however, these diversities are evidence of the difficulty of the situation, and that they require greater attention than they have received. I wish especially to call attention to the difficulty of reconciling any one of the conceptions with historical facts on one side and with the justification of religion as a present and future fact on the other side. If we start with the concept of awe and adoration, it is perhaps possible to adjust the wholesale human sacrifices of say the

Peruvians to this notion. If we start with those of kinship and communion, we may bring the organized temple prostitution and the licensed promiscuous intercourse of some Asiatic cults under the rubric. But just where are we as to the import of any religion that we at present wish to recommend and justify? Again many (seemingly a growing number) of historic scholars are inclined to take the view that historically magic is a much more widespread and significant trait of religion than has been hitherto recognized. The belief that there is diffused in all things a sort of wonderful energy—a kind of electric charge as it were—which has both a baneful and a beneficial effect on human destiny, with which certain individuals may by certain practices get in to sympathetic relations so as to control it for personal or social ends—this belief is thought by some scholars to be the root fact of all so-called natural religions. That this belief may have some points of contact with both the psychological and the metaphysical definition of religion is obvious. It may even be regarded as symbolically prophetic of a profoundly ethical fact—the practices in question may turn out to be certain attitudes and passions of the soul, and the advantages to be attained may turn out certain profound moral ameliorations. But again I do not see how the universality and presumptive validity of religions is furthered by assimilating the magical and the ethical types of relationship to each other. We may take one type or the other as the measure of our conception of religion. Can we possibly take both?

It is indeed an interesting problem to determine the psychological and the social phenomena that have characterized or determined historical religions. To discover the types of emotional attitudes that various historic religions have appealed to and nourished is a legitimate field. It is conceivable that future study will justify a reduction of accompanying psychological phenomena to one or two fundamental themes upon which seeming diversities are merely variations—though it seems more likely that farther study will reveal a greater diversity of psychological motive and reaction than we have as yet supposed to exist. But even with successful reduction and simplification, is it to be supposed that any more light is thrown upon the proper nature and validity of religion than is thrown upon the science of today and tomorrow by a study of its forerunners in alchemy and astrology?

IV

I must, of course, pay my respects to evolution and the continuity of history. As my readers are doubtless already acutely aware, I am denying the necessity of conceiving and defining present religion in terms of its evolution out of past religions, and am upholding the futility of such a method of claiming *validity* for religion. But to deny that any possible future religion can be, strictly speaking, an evolution from past religions is not to deny that future religion will be an evolution. There are other things than prior religions, we may remind ourselves, out of which a future religion may evolve. We are not limited to supposing that a proper religion is an emancipation of some religious factor which has been all the time latent, in past cults and creeds, although loaded down with all kinds of extraneous and harmful accretions. The root of the religious attitude of the future may lie immensely more in an improved state of science and of politics than in what have been termed religions. Doubtless there are certain constants, roughly speaking, in human nature. Doubtless these constants in their interaction with the natural and social environments have naturally produced, among other things, religions. But it would seem as if the "universal" was to be sought in these interactions rather than in any one isolated strain, psychological or metaphysical. If so, the democracy and the science, the art of to-day may be immensely more prophetic of the religion which we would have spread in the future than any phenomena we seek to isolate under the caption of religious phenomena.

Obviously what I have said is not a confession of religious faith. But it may properly be added that it is not necessarily a confession of irreligion. About as universal a fact as there is, is the fact of individuality itself. It is noteworthy that up to the present toleration has been a negative rather than a positive idea. We have learned to put up with what seem to us erroneous divergencies and eccentricities of belief (even when we conceive them more or less harmful) partly because we want others to bear with our own idiosyncracies, and partly because we have learned that the method of intolerance does not pay, socially. Practically, in matters of religious belief, these attitudes have carried us a very long way. But we have hardly adjusted our emotions and ideas to the practical change. More has been said about the sacredness of individual belief than has been deeply affirmed. If I were making a more positive search for something universal to be called religious, I should be inclined to look towards the uncoerced and untutored attitude of the individual as his natural instincts and his matured experience coalesce in a certain serious temper regarding the things of life. If religion is not more universal or widespread than it is, I am inclined to believe that to a considerable extent this is due to the age-long tendency of some people to tell other people what religion is or ought to be. Externally Protestantism seems to be a historic episode of revolt; perhaps its deeper and more permanent meaning is carried in the suggested intrinsic individualism.

V

It may facilitate discussion if I sum up in certain questions, though of course I have no wish to limit discussion by formulating these questions.

1. Does the search for and discovery of a common factor (whether psychological or objective) in past religious phenomena establish

(a) a presumption in favor of the religious attitude? If so, how?

(b) Does it shed definite light upon the nature of what persons to-day should be encouraged to cherish as religion? If so, how?

2. If we abandon this sort of method for conceiving and justifying religion, what other method remains?

Tolstoi's Art

Literary art of the dramatic sort—and Tolstoi's art is vividly dramatic—and philosophy have a common point of departure, even though they go such different ways that their goals are at the antipodes. They both begin in a sense of the contradictions of life: conflicts between its purposes and the conditions of existence under which these purposes must be achieved. The first element in the equipment of a dramatist is a keen and direct perception of the ironies of men's aims and endeavors. If the dramatist later turns philosopher, if that is he begins to reflect upon the contradictions that observation has revealed, and tries to find some theoretic solution,—solution by universal principle instead of in the movement of a particular situation to its natural destiny—he has at least one great advantage. Having first seen the problem in the concrete, in the entanglements of human beings in perplexities that vitally concern them, his method and his conclusion within the sphere of abstract reflection are likely to retain a reality and a force of appeal that do not belong to theories that begin as well as end with generalities.

Tolstoi's method, even in his most abstract treatises—and he has written a number of abstract treatises, like "Life" and "Power and Liberty"—is that of the dramatic artist. He did not start out from general principles or from purely intellectual difficulties. Some actual and individualized happening, involving the suffering and joy of some actual human being, struck him, impressing him so deeply that it stayed by him, and tortured him till he discovered a *general* reason for a whole class of failures and perplexities.

[Typescript in the John Dewey Papers, Box 60, folder 29, Special Collections, Morris Library, Southern Illinois University at Carbondale, ca. 1910–11.]

The whole of Tolstoi's philosophy of government, of crime and the further crime of its violent punishment, starts, for example, with a vivid and unforgettable scene, observed almost by accident, a guillotining in Paris. "I gasped and realized in every fiber of my being that all the arguments which I had hitherto heard upon capital punishment were wickedly false; . . . and there was I, by my silence and my non-interference, an aider, an abetter and a participator in the sin." Again his whole philosophy of society upon its industrial side, had an equally concrete and personal origin. He went to visit the slums, being uneasy in his wealth and idle luxury and moved to do something to relieve misery. But when he got to the slums, the eye and emotion of the artist showed him that the problem was concrete, not abstract. He really, not merely conventionally, *saw* the individual human beings: "the scolding old women, the light-hearted old men, and the sliding boys. . . . I now realized for the first time in my life . . . that they must somehow fill up the rest of the twenty-four hours of every day, a whole life of which I had never even dreamed before. I realized now . . . that these people beside the mere need of food and shelter must live through the rest of every day of their lives just as other people have to do; must get angry and be dull while appearing to be light-hearted or be sad or merry. And now for the first time I was aware that it was not a matter of feeding a thousand beings like a thousand sheep, but that each of the thousand was just such another man as myself."

Certain situations haunted Tolstoi as anomalies, as contradictions, as gratuitously unnecessary. If one is not content to accept them as regrettable indeed, but nevertheless inevitable, one must be led to try to account for them. And Tolstoi's speedy conclusion was that while certain sufferings are inevitable, the really serious evils do *not* flow from anything in the nature of things or in the nature of life; they are all due to false conceptions of the meaning of life, to false philosophies in short. And so he was naturally led to a search for the true conception of life which if generally entertained would put an end to these miseries that contradict the meaning of life; and also to describing the various kinds of false philosophies whose prevalence is responsible for the evils of the existing situation; or which just formulate and justify, and thereby continue it. I mention first some of the false theories. One is the belief that the evils are inevitable, because due to the free will of man, the doctrine of free will being an invention according to Tolstoi of theologians and experts in criminal law. But man's freedom is not found in the relation of his will to his acts, but in the relation of his reason to the *meaning* of his acts. Activity, the actual doing of things, proceeds from the energy of the universe itself not from will in its fancied isolation. Man is free either to recognize or not recognize the law of this energy, the direction in which it is proceeding, the end toward which it is making. Man is truly free and hence happy only when he recognizes this law and identifies himself with it, makes the law of the universe his own law. Man, he says, is like a horse drawing a wagon which is itself drawn by others. Go on he must in any case; he is not free to stop nor to draw the wagon at his own caprice. But he can either draw freely, or unwillingly and then be pushed on; that is to say, he may recognize the end of the activity as his own end, and so be in an attitude of peace and joy in the performance of his tasks, or he may isolate his consciousness, his own wish and purpose and so be in a state of opposition, of struggle condemned in advance to failure, and hence to discontent and misery.

Almost everybody has got disgusted with the futility of the discussion of free will, and hence I am afraid that my brief statement of Tolstoi's attitude will suffer from that polite indifference with which all references to the matter have come to be received. But in the case of Tolstoi, the underlying idea, whether we call it free will and necessity or call it something else, is absolutely essential to the understanding of his philosophy of life in general and of his attitude towards special attempts at economic and political reform in particular. The latter point is simpler, even if secondary, and so may be mentioned first. In a letter addressed to the Liberals with reference to their agitation for a representative form of government in Russia, he said, "True, the rights, the powers of a member of Parliament are greater than those of a plain man, and it seems accordingly as if much could be accomplished by using these rights. But the hitch is that in order to obtain these greater rights one has to abandon part of one's rights as a man." Other passages of his writings make it clearer what he means, and that it is not a part but the essence of man as man that is abandoned. After describing the mass of evils that exist in the world, he says, "What can I do against all this ocean?

Why should I express my opinion? Why should I even have one? So leaving the most powerful of all the weapons—thought and its expression—that move the world, almost everybody resorts to the weapon of social activity, not observing that every social activity is based on the very foundations against which one must fight, so that in entering upon the resort to methods of social reform, one has first of all to make some concession, to deviate from the truth. . . . There is but one adequate weapon in our possession, the consciousness and expression of truth, and that we refuse to use." In other words, there is literally but one thing needful; the change in the attitude of consciousness, of thought, the turning away from a false notion of the object and law of life to a true one; till this radical or moral revolution has been effected, every practical and overt step at reform, economic or political, is infected with the principle of evil, and hence is bound to turn out badly. On the other hand, given the adequate recognition of the nature of life, and all other things will follow as matter of course in due season. All or nothing, is Tolstoi's philosophy, and upon the truth or falsity of this division rests the truth or falsity of Tolstoi's philosophy. And "All" means the willing adoption of the law and aim of life as presented by reason or thought as the law and aim of individual existence; "Nothing" means the self-contradiction, the predestined failure and hence misery of everything short of this.

Just what, then, is this universal law and aim? Every one would recognize I suppose that action is not free in the building of a house, and that failure and unhappiness result in the degree in which activity proceeds on the basis that it is free. Except in the degree in which the end is necessary, in which a house is *really* needed, and except in the degree in which one willingly observes the necessary laws of nature in the building of the house, the work is a relative failure. Now the first principle of Tolstoi's philosophy is that life as a whole, both as respects the necessity of its end and as respects the necessity of the means of accomplishing this end, comes under exactly the same necessary laws, laws which man cannot change or deceive, any more than in the case of building the house. The difference—and this is the source of the unhappiness and contradictions of life—is that everybody practically recognizes that the successful building of a house is dependent upon the recognition of natural laws and conditions, and that this recognition depends upon our consciousness, our thought, having first studied out these laws, while practically nobody recognizes that there are laws as fixed in themselves whose discovery and acknowledgment is our primary business in the case of building of the house of life.

With respect to the meaning of life, that is, the attainment of good or happiness, man still acts under the guidance of an illusory consciousness, which because it is illusory inevitably leads him astray—that is, to misery. The essence of this false theory is that life, or existence, is an individual thing, with an individual aim: that the self which the senses reveal and which manifests itself through the bodily appetites, a self which as thus expressed, is separate, is real. This is isolation of self as the root of belief in free will and is the illusory consciousness, from which all the evils of life proceed. (This, of course, is the point of greatest contact between Tolstoi and oriental thought, especially Buddhistic.) (This way of conceiving life is itself the basic philosophy and what we call, conventionally, philosophies are only more elaborate formulations and attempts at justification of this original philosophy.) Elaborations of the primitive illusion constitute philosophies and theologies, and fall, roughly speaking, into two groups, which Tolstoi picturesquely calls that of the Pharisees and that of the Scribes. The former is the theory of life which has universally become the creed of ecclesiastical organizations. Its essence is that *this* life and *this* world are inherently evil, or at least so evil that man has no right to expect happiness here; this life being something to be suffered as a painful discipline for the sake of the enduring happiness of a life still to come. This doctrine means then that the ultimate moral principles (which are also as we have seen the sole ultimate metaphysical principles) do not really apply here and now. It also means that the underlying philosophy is self-centered; it is the personal life, the personal existence which is to be eternally perpetuated as the condition and residence of true happiness. It would be impossible to say which of these two conceptions Tolstoi finds more false. The doctrine that the law of life is not really the law of life as it actually is here and now, that the discovery of this law is a matter of "faith" or the acceptance of a doctrine or dogma and thus totally beyond the scope of reason—instead of the essence of reason being the search for and discovery of this law—is the reason that men in general make no systematic attempt to live here and now according to the teachings of Buddha, Confucius, Socrates, Jesus and Epictetus and others who have used their reason to discern the true law of life, and also accept the miseries of our present economic and political order as necessary, or even as having a positive value in leading men to place their thoughts upon a next life. Upon the other hand, the emphasis upon a life after death, the doctrine of resuscitation as Tolstoi contemptuously calls it, is proof that the professed representatives of the true philosophers have absolutely perverted the teachings of their professed masters, reverting to the illusory consciousness that happiness or the good is something connected with a separate, individual self.

By the doctrines of the Scribes, Tolstoi means all the modern philosophies of all schools, which have reacted against the supernatural philosophy of life but have attempted to find a substitute in an examination of the world, physically considered, as it is made known in the natural sciences, or else logically intellectually considered. We may perhaps without doing violence to Tolstoi's thought cite Spencer and Comte as types of the first, Hegel as a representative of the second. It is not easy to state briefly and accurately the attitude of Tolstoi toward science, though it is simple and in some respects identical as he himself recognizes, with that of Plato. Its very simplicity gets in the way of our understanding it. It is that primary science consists of knowing the laws in terms of its end or object, and then proceeding to study things on the basis of their relation to the final object. But if one does not first know the object, intellect is totally without a guide in all its other studies. And this is just the fallacy of all scientific philosophies so called. As a result what now passes for science is either an attempt to justify the existing order of life—as the social sciences—or a collection of trivialities without reference to the guidance of life and the happiness of the masses—the physical sciences. Tolstoi makes use of the metaphor of a miller and his mill for grinding grain. For a while this miller fixes his attention on the product, on the quality of the flour that issues; with respect to this he watches, adjusts and repairs all the parts of his mill. His knowing has an object and consequently his knowledge is ordered. But after a while he gets interested in the mechanism of grinding; he forgets the object, the product, entirely. He is thus brought to the conclusion that the secret of the mill is in the dam and the river. And finally so infatuated is he with the discovery that the river is the source of his power that he proclaims that the river *is* the mill. Meantime the mill as the source of flour is neglected. In this parable Tolstoi conveys his two main ideas. It is a primary principle of Tolstoi—which he applies to history as well as to nature—that the facts—the things which may be studied—are literally infinite, innumerable. Hence they of themselves give no clue either to what should be selected for study—and selection there must be—or of the order of their arrangement or importance. Hence there finally arises the exact inversion of the true order; the miller says the river is the mill, the "scientific philosopher" says life is an arrangement of purely physical energies. And since he too must go by what is physical and sensible, he too succumbs to the illusion that life is something separate and isolated. The other absurdity of scientific philosophy is that it takes what is remote, what is less sure, and substitutes it for what is truly certain and the closest to us of all things. A part of Tolstoi's ironic vision is that he sees scientific inquiries hastening away from what is most sure, what is absolutely certain, to what is very remote, to what is purely abstract and hypothetical, and then calling the latter science—genuine, rational certainty. The thing that is indubitably certain about life is that it is a struggle away from suffering, from evil, and towards joy, towards good, happiness. But fears and hates, hopes and loves, joys and miseries—this is just the thing that scientists and philosophers both leave out of account. And in leaving it out of account, they not only deprive their intellectual inquiries of all point and order, but they also ignore the most certain of all things in behalf of what is remote and inferential. "However much one may assure and instruct a man that all real existence is an idea, that matter is made up of atoms, that the essence of life is will or physical energy, etc., one cannot thereby explain to a being with pains, pleasures, hopes, fears, his position in the world."

The essence of true philosophy is then simply the recognition of the testimony of rational consciousness regarding the happiness of man and the conditions of its attainment; and this is simply the repudiation of the illusory, or sense consciousness of separate or individual existence: the recognition once for all that happiness resides in identification of individual aim and effort with that of all living beings. For the positive demonstration of this truth, Tolstoi appeals in part to the teachings of the great teachers of the race, but more especially to the sincere, the honest conviction of every man in the moments when he is honest with himself. "At bottom," he virtually says, "you already know all this as well as I if you have thought upon life at all; you know also all the ingenious and insincere devices you have for concealing from yourself your own acknowledgement of this truth; you know that you spend a large part of your time in activities whose underlying motive is but to distract yourself from your recognition of this truth and the responsibilities to which it engages you. But the crowning absurdity is that while your wish as the wish of every man is to be happy, you decline to take the one simple way which you already know is the only way in which you can find happiness." Thus it is that Tolstoi's demonstration of his main thesis, if we may call it such, is negative; it consists once more in pointing out in vivid and cumulative detail all the miseries that come to men here and now in their search for happiness as long as they take happiness to be something connected with their own personal existence and consciousness of this existence, instead of proceeding from the renunciation of all such private and severed existence. These ironies of search for individual happiness in a life every step of which is a step towards its own annihilation, or death; this search for happiness of an exclusive ego every act of which brings defeat because it involves conflict with others who are just as much exclusive egos bent on their own exclusive happiness as we; of search for happiness in getting power and possessions every item of which is a challenge to others to get them away from us into their own control and every item of which takes us a little further way from the natural and healthy sources of enjoying life—these ironies of a self-centered life which Tolstoi first portrayed dramatically in his fiction, he afterwards proclaims as a preacher and a prophet. There is no such break between his literary, or artistic career and his moral as is often represented. In his later life he but makes articulate the moral of all his earlier literary work. As I said at the outset his theories are but the generalized statements of his own vivid perceptions of life as it dramatically goes on.

In conclusion, I would point out that while Tolstoi is fundamentally a mystic and an ascetic—or teacher of renunciation—he differs very radically from most of those with whom we are familiar as mystics and ascetics. He differs from most mystics in his absolute conviction that the road to the final good—the losing of one's separate personality in the life of all—is to be attained by reason and is to be exemplified in a life of concrete relations to nature and to other people. He differs from the ascetic in his absolute conviction that happiness is the only good and end of life and that renunciation is simply the logical condition of attaining true happiness, being indeed only the renunciation of the self-contradictory ways of trying to be happy.

It would be impossible to exaggerate his reliance upon reason and rational knowledge, and his contempt for faith in the conventional sense of that term. Of the doctrine that the teaching of Jesus has reference to a future life instead of to the conditions of getting happiness here he says: "It is a doctrine that the only true life is only in faith, that is in imagination, that is in lunacy. . . . Only a conviction that reality does not exist and the nonexistent is alone real could lead to the surprising contradiction that the doctrine of Jesus is true but is not the rational principle of this life." At times he even goes so far as to say that the chief real purpose of individual endeavor is to improve reason so that it may apprehend the meaning of life in all its details more accurately and fully. "We are accustomed," he says, "to consider moral doctrine as an insipid and monotonous affair, in which there can be nothing new. In reality human life with all its complicated and varied actions—even those that seem to have nothing to do with morals, political activity, endeavor in the sciences, the arts, commerce—has no other object than to elucidate moral truths more and more, and to confirm, simplify and make them more accessible to all. I recollect once while walking a street in Moscow I saw a man come out and examine the flagstones attentively; then choosing one of them he sat down by it and began to rub and scrape it vigorously. 'What is he doing with the pavement?' I wondered. Coming close I discovered that he was a butcher's boy and was sharpening his knife on the stones. He was not thinking concerning the stones even when examining them; he was merely sharpening his knife in order that he might cut meat; to me it had seemed that he was doing something to the pavement. In the same way, mankind seems to be occupied with commerce, treaties, wars, sciences, arts; and yet only one thing is important for them and they do only that—they are elucidating the moral laws by which they live."

We usually associate the doctrine that this life is evil with the doctrine of complete renunciation, with the Buddhistic theory of illusion and Nirvana and so on. There are many striking likenesses, as well as equally marked differences between Tolstoi and Rousseau. Among the likenesses is an extraordinary sensitiveness to the feelings, the joys and sufferings of all sentient creatures. If in some sense Rousseau is the discoverer of democracy as a social idea, not merely as a governmental arrangement, it is because Rousseau had such a vivid perception that whatever the differences of men in social rank, political power and in culture, they are alike in their power to feel, in their sensitiveness to misery and happiness, and that by the side of this fundamental likeness all differences are trivial and superficial. Capacity for sympathy with the pain and pleasure of others is, fortunately, among the commonest of human endowments; capacity for abstract reflection is not infrequent; but capacity to reflect widely and deeply on the basis of and in terms of this sympathetic sensitiveness to the weal and woe of others is perhaps the rarest of gifts: so rare that its occurrence is as good a definition of genius as any we are likely to find. And this gift, Tolstoi, like Rousseau, had in extraordinary measure. Through this sensitiveness he was saved, even in his most extreme reactions against society as it is and life as it is usually lived, from the abstractions or aberrations of most moralists—making duty or a good character by itself, instead of actual concrete good, or happiness, an end in itself.

I have said nothing directly regarding my announced subject: the connection of Tolstoi with the thought of his time. From one point of view, there is no more to say under this caption than fell, in the history of Ireland, within the famous chapter on snakes. Tolstoi is, at every turn, an opponent of what is most characteristic in contemporary thought. Yet without artificial forcing there are very genuine connections. They are not, however, in the solutions proffered but in the apprehension of problems. It is not too much to say that all the significant philosophy of the latter half of the nineteenth century is preoccupied with essentially the problems which Tolstoi felt so keenly. The first and fundamental is the relation of theory and practice, of knowledge and conduct. And as respects this point Tolstoi, like so many other practical moralists, anticipated the teachings of one of the popular philosophic isms of the day. He teaches that man knows, in the full and intimate sense of knowledge, only what he does; that belief in principles that are not carried into behavior is incomplete and insincere. He teaches also, in common with this ism, that practical purposes and ends furnish the motive of all knowledge, and the only ground for selection and arrangement of facts inquired into.

For at least a hundred years professed philosophy has been increasingly perplexed with two great questions: How are the results and methods of modern science, bound up with a purely mechanical view of the world, compatible with man's moral interests, that proclaim the supremacy of purpose and thought? And how is the increasing preoccupation of man with the things of the material world, the multiplication and cheapening of commodities that relate to the senses and to the appetites, related to man's ideal interests, what somewhat indefinitely we call his "spiritual interests"? Even from the side of abstract and technical philosophy there are two seeming contradictions or antinomies: Man's increasing intellectual command over nature—in his science—seems to reveal mankind absolutely caught and helpless within a vast unrelenting mechanism which goes its way without reference to human value or care for human purpose; Man's command over the means of life, his industrial conquest, seems only to have sharpened prior existing social inequities, to have led to devotion to the *means* of life at the expense of its serious and significant ends—a noble, free and happy life in which all men participate on something like equal terms. Now the relation of Tolstoi to modern thought may fairly be said to be that he puts modern thought up against these problems with absolute severity, as problems that are not merely intellectual and technical—problems of a class of men labelled thinkers—but problems with whose right solution the welfare of man, individual and social, is absolutely bound up. I do not imagine that his own solutions will satisfy many: they are too much on the

All or Nothing basis; they make too absolute a separation between sense and reason, between the physical and the moral, between the individual self and humanity. But the intensity, the sincerity with which Tolstoi proclaimed and lived the reality of the *problems* make him a figure that the thought of today must absolutely reckon with.

The Meaning and Progress of Morality

Considering the topic of the morning, I am afraid that
my first statement may be a disappointing one, namely, that in
the strict sense of the term, there has been no evolution of morality. I do not mean by this that moral practices and beliefs have
stood still, or that, in the words of the older school, "Morality is
eternal and immutable"; I mean rather that there have been so
many varying lines of development in moral belief and practices,
that it is not easy for us with our present knowledge, in fact, it is
not possible to pick out or to identify any one single, steady, consecutive line of evolution in morals; that is, we cannot find any
one unified, consecutive trend of events, such as we find in the
plant world or in the animal world, or even in the development
of our solar system. Now the reason I think is quite obvious
upon reflection. Our moral life is an exceedingly complex thing
and it is influenced by a great many different independent forces.
It is what the mathematician might call the function of a great
number of independent, variable moral practices. Mankind, for
example, has always been influenced by political organization.
The kind of social organization that has existed at a certain time,
has reflected itself in the morals of a clan, of a despotic empire, of
a city, state and of a large democracy, is always different, because
the social conditions, the political demands and regulations are
different. Again, of course, legal procedure has had a very great
influence upon morals, because one of the businesses of the law
has been to define what men could do and what they could not
do, to make a list, a schedule of offenses and of the penalties for
offenses. Now while legality and morality are never the same

[Address delivered at Mount Morris Baptist Church, New York, N.Y., 17
December 1911. Stenographic report in Dewey VFM 88, Special Collections,
Morris Library, Southern Illinois University at Carbondale.]

thing, history shows that men's moral conceptions have always been influenced and have sometimes been modeled after their legal ideas and practices in industry, trade, commerce.

The industrial, economic life of men is another thing that has profoundly influenced their moral conceptions, as certain virtues, like thrift, industry and prudence, have been almost a direct product of certain conditions of industrial life. Perseverance and patience, as virtues, have always thrived among people where the industrial element—agricultural, especially—was very strong.

It is obvious that men's moral ideas have been very closely influenced, have been very dependent upon their religious conceptions and upon their scientific knowledge and ideas.

Now, not to go farther, we have at least four important lines of human interest and activity which have influenced the moral history of mankind, and these four influences have not been parallel; sometimes one has been uppermost and the others backward, and so we do not find a steady, uniform course of development. For example, so far as the connection between morals and science, the free play of man's intelligence and man's intellectual life is concerned, so far as the connection of morals with a somewhat narrow but intense form of social organization is concerned, we should be hard put to equal the achievements of Greek life at its best practice in Athens; but so far as morality was connected with and dependent upon industry and commerce and a wide net-work of peaceable relations, so far also as it was dependent upon well established and well ascertained methods of legal procedure, we should find Athenian morality quite backward. On the other hand, some of the great empires, especially some of the Oriental empires, have been distinctly advanced in all matters of morality that have to do with commercial integrity, with the making and keeping of promises, carrying out of contracts. In the Babylonian Empire, for instance, to be a clever trader was almost synonymous with being more or less of a liar. We all know how high the standard of commercial morality is in the great Empire of China.

Upon the whole again, in the Mediaeval period there was, upon the religious side, a great sensitiveness of emotions to certain forms of distinctively ethical value, but we all know that there was a backwardness in the matter of science, of the play of intelligence, of industry and commerce and certain other forms.

Now because these various forces which have modified the moral history of mankind have not proceeded parallel with each other, because one has been uppermost and then another, the fortunes of morality have been distinctly checked. It has had its ups and downs; one phase of morals has been almost, perhaps, at its culmination, when another has been in very backward condition. Under these circumstances, about all one can do is to pick out certain of the larger features of the moral history of mankind, where, upon the whole, we can be sure that there has been a fairly steady, uniform movement in one direction. That is where after all these various forces, political, legal, economic, religious and scientific, have modified each other and have reenforced each other, so that there has been a certain convergence of direction.

Now the first great achievement in moral history that I shall mention has been the widening, the extension of the field, of the area of human beings between whom moral relations exist. In the enlarging and expansion of the field of human beings who recognize that they have moral responsibility and moral rights in respect to each other, the first knowledge of mankind—what we call primitive man, though even then he probably was quite advanced in his career—the unit of organization is the clan, a group of persons supposed to have the closest kind of blood kinship with each other, consisting at the most of only a few hundred people. Now within that narrow clan, bound together by these blood ties, there were many moral duties and responsibilities which were very sharply marked out, but beyond this very narrow limit, there were practically no moral relationships, no ethical obligations whatsoever recognized on the outside, for the stranger, the foreigner, the alien was presumably an enemy, and if not an enemy, he was a person toward whom they were morally and ethically indifferent; no duties of honesty, of regard for life, of chastity, no duties whatsoever, excepting hospitality under certain peculiar conditions, was the stranger or foreigner entitled to.

Now, as we trace the history of mankind, we find the scope of this field enlarging, until now in theory at least, the field of moral relations is as broad as humanity itself and has been influenced undoubtedly by the stoic philosophy of the Roman poet who said that he esteemed nothing human foreign to himself. He was expressing at one of the earliest times in history an idea which it had taken long centuries, long millennial periods of human struggle to work out, and even then of course the statement was more or less a conventional one, a literary phrase rather than the statement of an actuality, for the larger part of mankind was still distinctly foreign and alien even to the most advanced moralist of the Roman Empire; and even to-day, while theoretically we recognize the brotherhood of all mankind, or the fact that moral duties and relations exist wherever human beings come together, no matter what their differences of race, economic condition or religion, we still know that we are dealing with an ideal something that we hope for, that we cherish and hope will come into existence, rather than a fact, for our international relations. Our struggle for peace, our struggle against war shows as a matter of fact that we do not yet recognize the same rules of morality as binding towards other people that we acknowledge in our relations to our own people. We are living a sort of enlarged clan morality still.

Many moral relations cease or may cease at a moment's notice to large numbers of people outside of our own kin, and of course our morality is still affected by partisan considerations, by distinctions as to social status, economic classes, and so on. Not to dwell upon the incomplete, inadequate features of the situation, it is true that there has been steady development, something we may call evolution in this direction, in the enlarging and widening of the field within which ethical relationships are acknowledged, and to a considerable extent are acted upon.

Now along with that, in the second place, there has been a substitution of a more uniform, impersonal standard and ideal of action. When it was said that God was no respecter of persons, there was a marked, an extraordinary advance which had taken place in human history, over all the earlier Gods. Jehovah himself, as reflected in a large part of the Old Testament, was distinctly a respecter of persons, of groups, of nations; He had his own selected people in whose fortunes He was interested, and He had another standard of judgment for them than that displayed towards other people. Now here, as so often, the logical conception simply marked, in somewhat vague and projected form, the ordinary ethical conception, and we find, at the beginning of the earlier stages of human history that there were as many different moral codes, as many different standards and as many different ways of applying these standards as there were different social groups. Even in what we now regard, perhaps, as distinctively the dawn of our own civilization upon the Teutonic side, we find, for example, penalties for wrongdoing very definitely graded according to the social status of the one who is offending and the one who is offended; for a peasant or a low class person to offend in any way against the person or the property of a nobleman was a most serious offense; for the nobleman to offend against his equal was a serious offense, but for him to offend against a serf or a slave was a comparatively trivial, negligible offense. It would be absolutely impossible, even if I had a great many hours at command, to begin to recite the inequalities, the inequities, or the distinctions made for persons and for all kinds of circumstances and conditions that appear to us purely arbitrary. In the long history of humanity, the advance of what we call justice, the advance of what we call equity, is primarily this—the recognition that there is a single standard of judgment, a single basis of rights and of duties, with respect to which all individuals, no matter what their class or condition, are equal; that all persons are to be served, in other words, alike, morally speaking. I will not stop here to cite or recite how far we have still come short, in many ways, of practicing this idea, but at all events, we have the idea, and we are sensitive, as the people in the past, in the period of history mentioned were not sensitive; we are sensitive to our deviations from the idea of the single, uniform, all-embracing standard for judging and treating mankind; we are uneasy about it, and we are taking more or less tentative and faltering steps to get away from these inequities.

In the third place, the history of human morals shows continually a larger part played by intelligence, played by man's best judgment, working by the best methods that it can employ in judging human actions and in forming its schedule of the things that it regards as virtues, as desirable, and the things that it regards as vices and to be reprehended. I do not know how to put before you, in a moment, this progress along the line of the importance attached to intelligence, but perhaps the best way to do it is negatively by indicating some of the many, many ways in the past history of men's moral thought in which it would seem as if anything but intelligence, anything but judgment and reflection had been employed to determine the rights and the wrongs, the goods and the bads of human action.

In the early history and the middle, and to some extent even the later history of the moral ideas and practices, mankind was bound up, in a most entangled way, with things which most people to-day frankly call superstition, and even their better ideas that we should pick out as most akin to our own best moral ideas to-day were not free; they were not put forth on their own grounds to win assent and consent for what they were, but they found their sanction, their motives, their justification in the most irrational kind of consideration. The fact of taboo, the fact that some individuals, or certain classes of individuals, could put a sort of spell on objects or on persons, and make them in some way sacred and holy, endowed with certain magical powers which would bring evil to anybody that touched them, was for long ages of human history probably the chief motive in securing regard sometimes for personal life and in almost all cases for property or personal belongings. The sacredness or stability of property among certain savage peoples otherwise not far advanced has often been noted, and without any wish to in any way derogate from the moral standard, these people seemed to be, in many respects, quite superior to men of to-day. In fact, property could be left anywhere, almost, and then found again when wanted. A careful study has shown this was because a certain taboo or magic spell had been put upon these things and people feared to touch them because of the magical curse or spell that would follow them, if they in any way came near or even put a finger upon this property. Now for ages it would seem as if the chief moral influence sanctioned, the motive operating upon mankind had been taboos or semi-magic spells of various kinds rather than a principle or idea which would commend itself to the enlightened intelligence; consequently a great deal of the moral energy of mankind, the intellectual, practical energy of mankind was diverted into all kinds of perfectly useless and irrational channels. It would sometimes seem as if the barbarous races, those who did not advance very far, had the best of it as compared with certain other peoples who had made a further advance, because these more barbarous peoples were at least left free from all of those rules and fears and rights and cults that had grown up in connection with these magic and quasi-magic notions. When this conception, that morality or things of morals, matters of right and wrong, of good and evil, were things of a metaphysical character, which could be reposed in things and which were contagious and infectious, working by some sort of spiritual, unknown means and rules, there grew up the most elaborate codes of activity, in which moral interests centered, complicated rituals and cults for avoiding all kinds of impurity or contact with any of these infections, and equally elaborate cults for purifying by all kinds of symbolic and semi-magical means the results from any possible infection. These things really engaged, to an incredible extent, the activities of very large numbers of people, especially those people who prided themselves on being the superior class, morally, spiritually and scientifically. It was the lower classes, who had to make a living and had to make enough living so that these other people also might have a living, who are doing ninety-nine one-hundredths of the useful work of life. It is impossible to conceive of the extent to which the actual progress of mankind has been kept back by this deviation of intellectual and moral practices. In contrast to this, one can conceive of what is meant by speaking of the advance in morals along the greater regard for intelligence and for man's best judgment in determining the consequences of conduct and of intelligently using what we can find out about the consequences of conduct, the natural, inevitable and social consequences, and use that factor in determining the right and wrong; only in that way can we see what great moral advance has been made.

This leads me to my last and fourth point along which the moral advance has been marked, namely, a freeing of the powers of the individual. We often think, and for a long time it was the only way to think, of the savage as a man who is perfectly free, who is not in any bonds or under any rules or laws at all, but one who does just exactly as he likes. As a matter of fact, the larger part of his life is enmeshed with all kinds of taboos and fixed regulations; the individual had no private property, for example, in the sense of anything which he could dispose of or sell or part with; he had no individual rights whatever; the rights he had were simply because he was a member of a certain family, or of a certain caste, or of a certain social class.

The history of political liberty and the history of the growth of economic freedom, the evolution of slavery, of serfdom, and the reduction of the actual operations and depressions that come with great industrial inequalities, even when there is, legally speaking, no slavery—these great advances on the political and the economic side have reflected themselves in a greater regard for individual capacity in every form. The conception for anything approaching universal education is an extremely modern conception, hardly over one hundred years old, and as an actively operating idea, not even one hundred years old. Now, no such ideal as this one of universal education would be conceivable, were it not that we have come to have respect and a reverence for all kinds of individual capacities simply because they are capacities of some human being.

It is often said, and said truly that the older codes of morality, put in the form of "do this or that thing" or, "do not do this or that thing," evolved certain actions, external over-actions, which were enjoyed, and as long as these external things were done, it made no especial difference what the attitude, what the capacity or the frame of mind of the individual in doing them. We are much more wary and cautious than we used to be about prescribing a definite code of external prohibitions and of external injunctions to perform just this and that task. We confine ourselves largely to simply enjoining and forbidding some of the coarser aspects of conduct, without which society could not hold itself together at all, but we are much more sensitive and much more eager about the things that have to do with the individual capacities and individual attitude towards life, that each may make the most of himself. On the other hand, we should see to it that opportunities are provided every individual, so that he may make the most of himself. All that goes with the development of the notion of democracy, which, as a social and a moral ideal, has marked one of the most fundamental and important lines of moral progress, for this democracy as a moral ideal becomes essentially a matter of respect and reverence for the capacities of the individual, because there is something unique in him not found in others, and for that very reason, all the more precious and all the more reason why the individual should have the opportunity to make the most of himself.

It is possible, to go back to my first point, that this comparative lateness of the development of a sense of individuality and of what goes with that is largely accountable for the checkered, the up and down career and fortunes of the moral history of mankind; at all events, it shows us the point of view from which the evolution of morality, the future possible evolution, is to be conceived. With the rights of the conception of evolution, many people have seized upon it as if evolution furnished a sort of big automobile, which was carrying the world and carrying the human race on, anyway, to a certain destiny, as if evolution marked out a certain predestined force; that we were riding upon it and riding forward inevitably to a better and better condition. The notion has been used to sanctify, as it were, a great deal of very cheap and very harmful optimism about what was going on and what was sure to go on morally.

Now with this deepening sense of the individual we come to realize more and more after all that it is not any force which we call evolution which is going to bring any further development of morals that we shall have, but it is rather certain attitudes in human nature itself that we have to depend upon instead of this impersonal, external force. We have to rely upon human intelligence and we have to rely upon good faith, good faith as to ourselves, sincerity, and the equal attribution of good faith to other people, even when they are doing things that we do not exactly understand because of their individuality; and we have to rely upon what is very close to that, the growth of sympathy. It is the freeing of these powers of intelligence, of the attribution of good faith wherever possible, and the development of sympathetic regard, the freeing of these forces which has been after all the net outcome of the human development of morals up to this time; for their future more vital and more energetic activity we will have to depend upon the evolution of future mankind.

Some Connexions of Science and Philosophy

Science, like the school-master, is abroad. It is dangerous to raise any question of the extent of its ranging, lest one
thereby proclaim that one is not one's self abroad, but is living in
a retired corner. Yet as philosophy was of old but love of wisdom
not its possession, so it is possible to-day that philosophy is
neither an analysis nor a synthesis of science, but a questioning
of its uses—its relations—in life. Not that I mean to raise the
jejune question as to whether science is of use and if so of what
use, but to indicate that whatever science is or is not, and whatever its contents are and are not, living is for man a broader
affair than knowing; and that hence it is for life, and not for
knowledge, to say what is the place of knowledge in that life; none
the less for it to say, even if it cannot tell truly without knowledge.

There has never been a time since philosophy began when it
was not defined either as a comprehensive synthesis of all science, or as a criticism, rectification and extension of the partial
and hence distorted conceptions of the special sciences or as an
analysis of these conceptions and of the methods that attend
them with a view to discovering the ultimate traits of existence. I
shall not here refer to the fact that it is not obvious how a philosophy that professes to be built exclusively upon science is to
learn from science itself to which one of these three structures to
devote itself. Neither shall I now point out what an elastic and
accommodating term science has shown itself through the ages,
from the dialectically won insight of Plato, the theology of the
middle ages, seventeenth century astronomy, to the mathematical physics of today.

Such remarks are possibly but carping, and in any case are but

[Typescript in the John Dewey Papers, Box 52, folder 1, Special Collections,
Morris Library, Southern Illinois University at Carbondale, ca. 1911–12.]

symptoms of a more significant matter. The philosophies that purport to be built upon science both take advantage of and repudiate the struggles—the very human struggles—that have gone to the making of science; they prize the jewels of human belief that have been mined, but the efforts involved in the mind and the aims involved in regarding them as jewels are treated as part of the rubbish and debris that has been got rid of in the mining operations. And in making science, like the Moral Will of Kant, a jewel in its own behalf, apart from the lives that it illumines, these philosophies also tend to make science, like the Kantian goodness, an empty and a futile thing.

For it was man and not science that educated man into becoming a scientific man; and it is man, not science, that commends and eulogizes science. It is no part of the business of science to anoint itself with priestly unctions or to issue testimonials to itself. The more the importance of science is insisted upon, the more is implied a context of an experience proceeding from and terminating in irrational life sufferings, struggles and trials. A philosophy will have enough to learn from science and enough to do with it that frankly takes for its task the business of making as articulate as possible the ties that connect the methods and results of science with blind human effort, defeat and achievement. It will doubtless be called upon, among other things, to analyze, to synthesize and to criticize various scientific conceptions. But these operations will not be carried on in the interest of science or in the presumptuous expectation of extending or rectifying or supplementing science in its own sense and direction, but with a view to promoting a freer and more facile give-and-take of intercourse between science and a humanity whose chief concern is to make a living that is worth while.

Perhaps I trench upon a field from which I have already warned myself away when I say that the very conception of a single, self-enclosed somewhat called Science is largely a superstition. The vitality of this superstition is a tribute at once to the power of words to dominate thinking, and to the capacity of a unified emotional response and interest to insinuate itself into objective facts and speciously confer upon them their own quality of inclusiveness and exclusiveness. It is easier consciously to ridicule Plato than to cease being his unconscious disciples; and I know of no philosophy more certain to be suffused with per-

sonal emotional reactions than one which professes itself to
be a colorless objectivism—as witness the attitude of adoration,
partly pedantic and partly barbaric, of our Neo-Realism to that
Platonic entity which they have baptized Science.

I quote from a recent utterance of an anthropological authority
of the very first rank a testimony all the more valuable, because
not made with any philosophic issue in view.

I believe it is a mistake to assume that the interpretation
made by each civilized individual is a complete logical process. We associate a phenomenon with a number of known
facts, the interpretations of which are assumed as known,
and we are satisfied with the reduction of a new fact to these
previously known facts. For instance, if the average individual hears of the explosion of a previously unknown chemical,
he is satisfied to reason that certain materials are known to
have the property of exploding under proper conditions, and
that consequently the unknown substance has the same
quality. On the whole I do not think that we should try to
argue still further, and really try to give a full explanation of
the causes of the explosion.

The difference in the mode of thought of primitive man
and that of civilized man seems to consist largely in the
difference of character of the traditional material with which
the new perception associates itself. The instruction given to
the child of primitive man is not based on centuries of experimentation, but consists of the crude experience of generations. When a new experience enters the mind of primitive
man, the same process which we observe among civilized
man brings about an entirely different series of associations,
and therefore results in a different type of explanation. A
sudden explosion will associate itself in his mind, perhaps,
with tales which he has heard in regard to the mythical
history of the world, and consequently will be accompanied
by superstitious fear. When we recognize that neither among
civilized men nor among primitive men the average individual carries to completion the attempt at causal explanation of
phenomena, but carries it only so far as to amalgamate it
with other previously known facts, we recognize that the
result of the whole process depends entirely upon the character of the traditional material. . . .

In scientific inquiries we should always be clear in our own minds of the fact that we always embody a number of hypotheses and theories in our explanations, and that we do not carry the analysis of any given phenomenon to completion. In fact, if we were to do so, progress would hardly be possible, because every phenomenon would require an endless amount of time for thorough treatment. We are only too apt, however, to forget entirely the general, and for most of us purely traditional, theoretical basis which is the foundation of our reasoning, and to assume that the result of our reasoning is absolute truth. In this we commit the same error that is committed, and has been committed, by all the less civilized peoples.

It would be just neither to Dr. Boas, the writer of these lines[1] nor to my own purpose in citing them to give the impression that their object is to create scepticism concerning the value of science, or to suggest that, after all, the differences between our scientific traditions and the myths of early man are insignificant as compared with an underlying identity. Professor Boas's motive is to show that the difference between primitive beliefs and those of contemporary civilized man is due not to differences of inherent mental structure and capacity but to the cultural medium in which individuals think and act. My own purpose is simply to emphasize the fact that there is such a medium, and that science itself, even in its own internal intellectual content reflects it. In some sense, science is a function of this cultural medium. It reacts upon environing social life, and by this reaction gradually transforms the latter. But the context can no more be excluded and science remain, than a man can lift himself without a physical leverage beyond himself.

Hence the arbitrary nature and the almost arid tendency of the philosophies (or parts of philosophies) that purport to build upon science alone. Take such portions of the philosophies of Aristotle, Descartes and Spencer as claim to analyze or else to systematize and extend the well established results of science. What do we find? The most valuable and permanent parts of their ideas? Rather material which is exceedingly important as symptomatic of the social spirit and imaginative temper of the

1. *The Mind of Primitive Man,* 202–206.

day, but material whose intrinsic intellectual value is outworn and trivial compared with remarks these same writers make when they frankly give their interpretation of some attitude of life or their estimate of the value of some standing tendency of human nature.

Science is science. It is corrected by more science. Equally it is extended and built out by scientific men using scientific methods, not by philosophic syntheses however comprehensive, nor by definitions however acute. The results of such extensions and excavations may not, to be sure, turn out to be science; but neither will they turn out to be philosophy. They will only turn out to be poor science. That a philosopher may make respectable contributions to a science is a likely enough supposition, and one to which history has given some confirmation. His philosophic antecedents may count as an asset, as well as a liability, in making the contribution. But they operate pedagogically, so to speak, not philosophically; they help or hinder just as part of the intellectual equipment brought into play.

Of course, the same is true, mutatis mutandis, of the scientific man turned philosopher. He may try to combine into larger intellectual wholes the results of highly specialized sciences; he may even engage in the more dubious task of arriving at a "completely unified knowledge." But the outcome is either a contribution to one of the special sciences, or to creating a hyphenated science (like astro-physics, physiological-psychology, etc.) that springs up to cover the gaps left in a prior conventional divisioning of the field—or else, again, to the mythology of science, an interesting department to which Sir Isaac Newton as well as Plato has paid tribute. And again he may say something of immense importance for philosophy—something that he would not have said without his scientific training. But here, again, his science operates in making him more sensitive to some human predicament, not enclosed within the mesh of a science.

I do not know whether it is necessary to disclaim the intention of minimizing the importance of science for philosophy, but it is generally safe to assume misunderstanding, actual or latent, in any discussion in or about philosophy. So I shall point out a number of points of contact and cross-fertilization of science and philosophy. In the first place, philosophy can and does render a service of criticism to science. But it is capable of performing this purging service just because there is so much in science that is not scientific in origin and which persists without scientific sanction. It is not difficult to find cases where notions that originated within philosophy have been taken up by some science, and have become influential there. There was the notion, for example, of the fixity of species with its long role in the sciences of life. The notion was familiar, of course, to common sense and had an immense amount of familiar observation to sustain it. But it was definitely formulated within philosophy, explained and justified on general philosophic grounds. Moreover, it was criticized as a piece of philosophic apparatus, in its form of the separation and fixity of conceptions, before it received critical examination in biologic science. I could pick out in contemporary psychologies, psychologies that are ultra-scientific in temper, many survivals of a conception of consciousness, of conscious process and state, that originated within philosophy for the purposes of philosophy. And philosophy to-day, in some of its representatives at least, is much more critical of these conceptions than the average working scientific psychologist shows much disposition to be.

Some of these ideas persist among the sciences, I believe, simply because they are of so little importance there—because their significance is hardly more than verbal. Almost every student of philosophy has had occasion to note and sometimes to marvel at the equanimity with which scientific men tolerate as part of their nominal equipment ideas that seem to be anachronisms, ideas that a little reflection would throw into the discard as quite inconsistent with scientifically established facts. In most cases, the explanation, I fancy, is quite simple. These ideas do not actually function, and it is easier to let them alone and devote the time thus saved to some research. Scientific men generally, in fact, stigmatize as "metaphysical" those of their brethren who show any disposition to get excited over such of their current notions as do not directly affect the conduct of experimental inquiry.

But, as has been already suggested, the sciences also carry along with them foreign ideas that are not innocuously imbedded—like boulders from another stratum. There are some ideas picked up and assigned scientific standing that do harm; they conventionalize and restrict inquiry. They direct it into unfertile fields and favor a misconception of the results reached in fruitful fields. Naturally we cannot tell offhand just what and where they are in the science of today. But even mathematics has only very recently got around to substituting a scientific determination of an axiom for the old popular "self-evident truth." The biological sciences on account of their recentness are probably quite infested with unfortunate borrowings and transfers. Almost any critical person could pick out in the still newer social sciences highly influential ideas which are at least subject to arrest as suspicious characters, intellectual vagabonds without legitimate means of support.

Now when the philosopher deals with such concepts he is quite on his own ground. Frequently, indeed, he is occupying himself with the products of prior philosophic industry when he considers such notions. The outcome of his examination may have a liberating effect upon science: not because the ideas dealt with are categories of science—not even because they are categories of unscience, but because his examination may place the ideas in their proper universe of discourse, and by putting them in their own social context relieve science of an incubus.

The criticizing work of philosophy need not terminate abruptly at this point. Various terms characteristic of scientific inquiry are also employed in other callings of life. A comparison of the meanings they possess in these different contexts may well be illuminating, and at times is necessary as a policing against ambiguities. If, however, one determines the meanings of such a term as cause in science and in practical affairs, there is no sense in concluding that the scientific conception is *the* conception to which that of daily life must be made to square. The conclusion is that the scientific notion is the meaning of causation for purposes of knowledge and that the practical fact is the fact for purposes of practice. Beyond the clarification that may come from such a distinction, the criticism may be of further value, for the distinction of meanings puts in condensed and more manageable form the general question of the relation that science bears to practical occupations.

To my mind such considerations as these exhaust the scope of one of the conventionally proper things to say about the relations of science and philosophy: namely, that each special science presupposes, assumes without inquiry, some special conception or group of conceptions, building itself thereon. Philosophy then comes in—so it is said—to examine and criticize these uncritical assumptions, having the further task of organizing the purged conceptions into an intellectual system. Without such a work, we are told, the sciences indeed may get on very well as specialized pursuits, but after all get on only by begging their own premises which remain unsanctioned and obnoxiously open to sceptical queries. I waive the miracle that the sciences should be able to get on so well if they really were using ideas which are not clearly understood and which are without adequate justification. I shall take the simpler method of dogmatic denial and dogmatic assertion. I do not believe this orthodox view has anything to commend it save the ease with which it may be uttered.

Geometry does not take an unexamined notion of space as its basis and then rear its scientific superstructure. Geometry takes certain facts and their qualities as its starting point and then arrives at its conception of space by dealing with these facts. Its conception of space is a highly critical result and a highly systematized one. It would be truer to say that the system of geometry *is* the critical and organized conception of space than to say that geometry is derived from or is built upon some hastily snatched notion which remains at the end still unexamined as to its inner meaning and ultimate validity. From the standpoint of knowledge, of intellectual inquiry, testing and organization, the science of geometry says all there is to say about the notion of space, instead of leaving it over for a philosopher to say the fundamental things about it. If the philosopher suspects that in the *current* system of geometry there are unexamined and unsystematized notions, his sole recourse is to criticize the current geometrical results and improve the science—in short, engage in the very business the geometers are themselves endlessly engaged in. When the philosopher takes it upon himself to regard the conceptions of space, time, energy, matter, motion with which the sciences deal as untested, haphazard notions which it is his privilege to sanction and arrange, the chances are about n to one that the result will be neither science nor philosophy.

The kernel of truth in the orthodox view lies in the two points already noted. The sciences after all still retain some infiltration of popular traditions, prior philosophic or theological enterprises with respect to which philosophy may have a purging work to do. The facts that are employed in arriving at the scientific conception appear in other contexts than that of science. Space qualities function, for example, esthetically, as well as mathematically. Motion and force are qualities of effort as well as terms of knowledge. To compare the respective ways in which the same facts are utilized in their different contexts for different purposes may well be an important part of the philosophic undertaking. But only confusion arises when this task is regarded as either a rectification or an extension, from the standpoint of knowledge, of the scientific conception. The confusion and the resulting scandal to intelligence are as great whether we pit the scientific definition of motion against the practical, the vital, qualities (of which, after all, it is the intellectual definition), denying the reality of their existence because they are not the same as the scientific content, or assign to the scientific result a low intellectual place because it isn't the same as the vital qualities themselves. Why should time for example present itself in exactly the same form in mathematical physics and in the context of waiting for Roosevelt to make up his mind whether or no to become a candidate for the presidency? Finding that time presents different traits in the two contexts why insist that one presentation is alone the real one, and the other an imitation or a make-belief? The obvious fact seems to be that in the region of knowledge, for the purposes of science, the scientific conception is the *only* conception; and in the sphere of action and esthetic appreciation where qualities are the essentials, quality is the *only* quality. Accept this point of view, and we shall have done with the idea that philosophy must revise or sanction a scientific idea.

Unless the forest has disappeared in the trees, it will be apparent that what I am trying to say is that philosophy is not concerned at all with science *as* science, and that when it ventures in that direction the result, unless overruled by a special providence, is poor science. But something positive is implied in this negation. Philosophy is concerned with the places where science touches life, the points at which it borrows and at which it lends, where it is generated and where it operates. There are vital, there are constructive interactions of the practice of knowing with other concerns of our common life. These nodal points, these junctures, give philosophy its problems. History teems with examples of ideas first worked out and made at home in industry and commerce that found their way into science for its animation and direction. Take, for instance, the origins of mechanical science. Greek inquiry made some marvellous advances in the direction of modern scientific methods. The human body was held in high esteem; physiology and medicine flourished. The stars retained the dignity of their divine elevation; astronomy made headway. There has almost always been a close, probably a logical, connexion between the literary-dialectical method and pure mathematics; geometry was elaborated. But the Greek gentleman felt himself demeaned by contact with the productive crafts and their tools. The problems, the fruitful suggestions, the means, the physical appliances of experimentation were thus excluded save in exceptional cases. But as the arts developed in less aristocratic neighborhoods, and the artisan became a social figure of greater dignity, experimental and mechanical science became inevitable. The questions, the technique, the apparatus of its inquiry were all evolved in the control of nature brought about by industries aiming to satisfy the needs of daily life. The logic of Descartes and Bacon were but halting attempts to transcribe the operations of the once despised mechanic into the language of science.

The biological conception of evolution affords another instance. Today the layman can hardly read with understanding the contributions that are making. But the earlier hours of this idea of evolution were spent in the company of political idealists proclaiming the indefinite perfectibility of man, and of social interpreters trying to resist the dissolving tendencies of a purely individualistic rationalism by conceiving history as the progressive development of one continuous whole—humanity. It is also pertinent to note that Malthus's theory of population was the chief document in the reaction against this optimistic perfectionism, and that Malthus was still sufficiently imbued with deistic piety to wish to justify the scantiness of the board which nature set for her own children on the ground that this niggardliness was a needed providential spur to work and to invention—the sources of human progress. It is all the more pertinent because Darwin has recorded his personal indebtedness to this doctrine of political economy for his conceptions of struggle for existence, selection and survival, as keys to understanding the origin of species.

Science is itself a vast cooperative social endeavor, impossible save where conditions make possible the dividing of tasks and the bringing together of the distributed results. Without the modern appliances for publication and exchange and intercourse modern science would be an idle dream. In more ways than one it is the offspring of the industrial revolution as in more ways than one it is its parent. For science gives as well as takes. What is called the conflict of science and religion is not a conflict of two abstractions, two Platonic entities, but of social groups and forces. In spite of what literary critics say, literature is written by men and women and not by imagination and abstract faculties, and men and women are subject to the influences of their times. No matter what coop an artist may build to shut himself in (and it is generally the critics not the productive artist that build and label these coops) his work is inwrought with scientific influences. Not that he does or should post himself upon the last scientific discovery before he writes, much less that he should write with the latest novelty of science upon his penpoint (the scientific romance being a strong contender with the historic romance for ineptitude), but that the life which solicits him, that presents to him the problem life puts to life, has itself sucked avidly in the differences in belief and practice that science makes.

One more instance and these illustrations conclude. Under the influence of certain vested, institutionalized traditions, the relation of science and morals has been conceived in a negative spirit, as a matter of protective insurance. How shall we save some scrap of freedom, of the ideal, of responsibility, from the devastating influence of the conceptions of natural science? This way of feeling and putting the question is, however, itself a mark of a social life in which science has made little headway, and where the procedure of intelligence is not thought of as openminded inquiry, competently fitted out with the needed apparatus, but as the dialectical elaboration of antithetical concepts—an eternal intellectual law suit. What is now beginning to show as the significant point of contact of modern science with our moral life is the carrying over into behavior, individual and collective, of the way of thinking, of questioning and testing characteristic of experimental inquiries into natural events. For the most part moral standards are still thought of as dogmatically, as rigidly, as if the inductive conception of law and its importance as a tool of inquiry had never been heard of, or else, in irritated reaction against the unreasonable and external constraint of any morality dogmatically conceived, there is a recourse to a deification of individual inclination, that again completely ignores the discovery in science of a method of intelligence that is watchful, exacting and obeying no law but that of its own end.

It is not too much to say that the philosophy of a period always focusses in the science of the time. Whatever of significance and scope seems to some to be lost in refusing to philosophy license to burrow below science or to round out its ragged edges is more than made up for by holding philosophy to its own business of reinterpreting human concerns in the light of the advances in the method and outcome of intelligence that we call science. Housekeepers become in time acutely conscious of the extremely limited number of animals that may be drawn upon for food. Persons experienced in the larger economy of life become aware of the small number of interests that make it up and of their comparative stability—almost monotony. Left to themselves they change but little, or change as do sand dunes on a wind swept shore. The forms gave way to one another with great rapidity, but the "more they are different, the more they are the same."

Significant differences in politics, morals, religion, art, industry are all due to changes in the temper and outlook of the imagination. Were we gifted with capacity of observation but lacking in the community of mind due to intercourse, what a drearily monotonous scene the actions of our fellow beings would present! We have just so many muscles and there are just so many combinations and coordinations possible—more, indeed, than the number of motions that may be made by a horse's legs but hardly enough more to take account of. But these external movements are fraught with meanings that vary, that grow, that take on hue after hue of idea and shade after shade of discrimination. Intelligence, reflection, knowledge permeate them, and each act is uniquely alive with import. I do not think the case is markedly different with those massed motions of mankind that constitute our government, our loves and hates, our rites and cults, our business. It is their penetration by the discoveries and the adventures of intelligence, the hypotheses and the conclusions of science, that confers upon them significance of contour and of movement. No wonder that the eternal symbol of intelligence is light. But the value of light for man is the visibility, the splendor, and the variegated color it confers upon things that are not light. So the significance of science is what it does for things that are not science. To speculate upon this significance, to clarify it, to promote the educational intercourse so as to help embody this significance in the actual practice of living will give philosophy quite enough to do.

Brief Studies in Realism III

I

The new realism agrees with a number of independent tendencies in modern thought in turning away from the "category" of things and attributes to that of elements and relations. I have no doubt of the advantages that have accrued to logic and to various branches of philosophy from this change of attitude. It brings with it certain difficulties, however, and one of these difficulties I propose to specify here. On this basis, just what is the status of a "complex"? A complex is, I take it, the equivalent of the old-fashioned "thing." What is the warrant for accepting, believing or knowing, the existence of any particular complex? What is the warrant, put more objectively, for its individuality? A tree or a rock, for example, is analyzed into a number of relations obtaining among a number of simples. When we have so analyzed it, is it possible to recover the tree or the rock at all? The difficulty is an old and familiar one in discussions. The scientific resolution of the tree and the rock breaks down the seeming spatial and temporal isolation of the thing—its sundering from other things and its seeming self-centred reference. The tree as a complex of related elements includes elements and relations of soil, air, light, etc. Nor does it seem possible to draw a definitive line, theoretically, as to where these elements and relations leave off. We seem caught in a network of a maelstrom.[1]

1. I think it probable that the difficulty I have in mind is exemplified on a large scale in Leibniz. Compare his insistence, on one hand, upon the purely simple which is, since simple, windowless, unaffected by anything else and incapable

[Typescript in the John Dewey Papers, Box 51, folder 16, Special Collections, Morris Library, Southern Illinois University at Carbondale, ca. 1912–13.]

The other difficulty is not *ad hominem,* but resides in the matter of the conception. As I look out of my window and see houses, trees, fountains, lampposts and bricks, grass and posts, it is evident that some of the things seen—the manufactured articles—owe their individualized existence to their being embodiments of human ends. But admitting this, the ends so involved are not mine; in seeing them I do not consciously share a will to make bricks and posts and girders and chimneys. Why then should they present this individuality in my perception? It seems somewhat forced to say that there is something in my present *conscious* purpose or conscious intention which marks them off. Take a natural object—a stone. My use of it as one, in throwing it or building with it, is calculated to insist upon its unity, and may well be the agency through which its individuality is experientially enforced. But it seems equally true to say

---

of affecting anything else and, on the other hand, upon universal harmony and the systematic character of the universe.

The most familiar way of disposing of the difficulty is, of course, to refer the individualization and qualification of an indifferent and homogenously ramifying material to the operation of "consciousness" in the act of apprehension. The realist, of course, is precluded from falling back upon this explanation. But it is somewhat striking that, up to the present, he has paid so little attention to this particular phase of the subjectivism of rival theories of knowledge. So far, it would seem, he has been content to utilize the common sense belief in things in his theory of perceptual apprehension and the relation-element conception in his theory of conceptual apprehension. But it is precisely the incompatibility of these two theories that constitutes the difficulty with which we are dealing. The existence of errors in detail or special illusions and hallucinations is a small matter for the realist to cope with compared with the characteristic individualization, external and internal, of all subject-matter whatsoever save that resulting from conceptual analysis.

More recently the practical and purposive element in "consciousness" has been appealed to in explanation of the facts of individualization. Bergson with his theory of the parcelling, carving and sundering of a homogenous matter in the interests of action has of late given special prominence to this view. So far as this theory interprets purpose and practice (or behavior) in terms of consciousness, it is of course a mode of explanation as obnoxious to the new realist as reference to the role of consciousness in apprehension. But criticism and rejection of the theory only makes it the more incumbent upon him to supply a genuinely realistic theory of the nature of individualized things. And reference to behavior at least has one advantage over the reference to the psychology of apprehension: Behavior is not merely psychical or a mere matter of "consciousness" although intelligent behavior involves awareness and conscious aim: a difference which gives the "behavior" explanation as we shall see shortly a different status from the "apprehension" explanation.

that I throw it or build with it because of the character it already possesses. We do not pick out a handful of air to throw.[2] In order that natural objects may serve as means for the execution of our purposes they must have a character fitting them for that service. Even though it be true that we apprehend things as externally sundered and qualitatively identified only in so far as they are employed as means in a scheme of behavior—a doctrine which seems to be much better psychology than the doctrine of fusion of sensations with associated images—or even were it true that ultimately their individuality means that they *are* means in a scheme of behavior, it is not the conscious intention to use them as such which makes them means. They must be fitted on their own account to be means. In short, a thoroughgoing pragmatism (using this ambiguous term to denote reference to systems of behavior as the ultimate universe of philosophic discourse) cannot play fast and loose with the notion that things *are* means; if they *are*, then that is *what* they are in their own right.

The line of argument so far seems to be good realism. But it only intensifies, it does not relieve, the difficulty of reconciling a realistic philosophy of things with the doctrine that all existence, as well as all subsistence *is* an affair of elements and their relations. The more thoroughgoing the realism, the more impossible does the latter scheme appear as a metaphysics of existence. The resolution of existence into related elements is precisely the theory which makes it necessary to regard concrete natural things and events as complexes which are subjectively determined, parcellings out of reality due to "consciousness," whether in conscious perceptions or in conscious intentions. The failure of some of the new realists to recognize this situation, is due I think to the fact that they have so largely taken their point of departure from subsistents, from the realm of subsistence. In this realm, the difficulty does not present itself, because the individual or complex is a class, or a complex of correspondences between classes. Where the entities dealt with *are* classes, the metaphysics of the thing in question—its own nature—is wholly congruous with knowledge of it as a complex of related

2. Compare Dr. Boodin's article on "Do Things Exist?" *Journal of Philosophy, Psychology and Scientific Methods*, Jan. 4, 1912.

elements. But to call natural things and events classes, requires one to invoke a principle of conscious subjectivity (either in apprehension or use) for the arbitrary external sundering and inherent qualification. If the existent tree or existent rock *is* a class, it is a class which involves, directly and indirectly, all the elements and all the relations of the physical world; i.e., it *is,* existentially, that world. Nor can the difficulty be avoided by saying that "consciousness" operates merely to pick out or select a portion of the whole. For the characteristic of the thing—the tree or the stone—is that it does not present itself as merely a quantitatively small part of a larger homogenous whole[3]—but as itself a *thing,* a qualitatively characterized individual. From the standpoint of a thoroughgoing metaphysic of related elements, this is an illusion. To admit the possibility of "consciousness" being responsible for this illusion is, as already pointed out, to create a difficulty for a realistic theory of knowledge compared with which the occasional occurrence of specific illusions is a matter of slight moment. It is to cast aspersion upon the whole scope of perceptual experience. In doing so it provides idealism with one of its chief weapons, for, of course, it gives opportunity for idealism to reply that in acknowledging that this individualization is the work of "consciousness" (whether intellectualistic or voluntaristic) and in holding that "consciousness" *really* constitutes existence it is rescuing real things from the limbo of illusion into which realism has thrown them.

II

My main purpose is fulfilled in calling attention to the difficulty. I shall supplement the discussion, however, with propounding a rival hypothesis regarding the metaphysics of things, asking the reader to note that the validity of this hypothesis is a matter wholly independent of the seriousness of the difficulty pointed out. My hypothesis may be all wrong, but the incom-

---

3. Compare my article on "Perception and Organic Action," *Journal of Philosophy, Psychology and Scientific Methods,* Nov. 21, 1912 [*Middle Works* 7:3–29].

patibility of the metaphysics of related elements with the facts regarding things remains.

We are not held to a dilemma of a choice between the old metaphysics of substances and attributes and a universe of related elements. In fact, the former is but a step in the direction of the latter, and the dialectic superiority of the latter is due to the fact that it makes explicit the logic already operative in the former. Things may *be* integrated systems of *behavior; centerings* of energies. Such a view does justice to their external sundering and intrinsic identification, while at the same time it does not commit us to a rigid separation of things from each other. These centred systems of behavior interact; they have the maximum of individuality with reference to their centering, while they overlap and vaguely pass into one another at the points of their maximum interaction with other things. From the standpoint of a realistic empiricism, such combinations of strict individualization with loose and varying peripheral demarcation are the commonest of affairs, and their genuineness is not to be disputed on grounds of dialectic incompatibility of centredness and complication with extrinsic systems of action.

Human behavior, intelligent or purposive behavior, would then *be* simply one system of integrated behavior—just the one, namely, which it is. There is nothing either inherently incredible or objectionably "subjectivistic"[4] in holding that other systems might most completely exhibit their own characters as integrated and differentiated factors within this system of behavior. Such a position would enable us to do justice to all the *facts* urged in support of the conclusion that individuality is accentuated by (or even in some sense connected with) such systems of intelligent behavior, without our being forced to conclude that a "consciousness" or "mind" defined in antithesis to "objects" and the "world" is responsible for this individuality.[5] One can say "the only key we have to reality is what reality must be taken as in the progressive realization of the purposes of human nature."[6]

4. The real meaning of the term subject would simply be such a characteristic system of existent behavior.
5. Individuality here and elsewhere is used purely denotatively to designate such things as *a* tree or *a* stone.
6. Boodin, article cited, p. 14.

III

It will be urged, I suppose, that such a view comes into conflict with the findings of science which treats objects, through its mathematical analysis, as complexes of related elements; as propositions, or the subject-matter of propositions. It is not open to a realist, however, to urge this objection. Apart from the point (belonging to the strategy, so to say, of philosophic 'isms) that in the past this view has always been an open door to objective idealisms, it involves that wholesale discrediting of perception which has already been indicated. Dialectically, it involves peculiar difficulties of its own, which I will not go into here further than to say that they are of the nature of the Platonic difficulties regarding the presence of the universal in the particular, the combination of particular and universal of essence and existence, to make physical things: How can elements and relations drawn respectively from the realms of existence and subsistence unite in constituting specific things and events? But, supposing all these difficulties got over, it surely is not open to a realism which holds that both science and perception "know" things directly as they are to employ science to annul the metaphysical validity of perception with its presence of individualized things.

Accordingly I advance, with equal summariness, another hypothesis. Science is concerned with the interaction of these individualized systems of behavior with one another; it is not concerned with their existence or structure *as such*. It is always *about* them, and about them with respect to their mutual influences, in furthering or retarding one another. Being concerned, therefore, wholly with relativities, not with individualities, it naturally falls into the schema of elements and relations, and views things simply from the standpoint of correspondences and substitutions. This is not a deformation of the actual existences. It only becomes such when it is presented as an exhaustive metaphysics of existence.

And, to carry the hypothesis one point further into the speculative, since we as living beings are primarily concerned with the human system of behaviors individual and social, in which natural things and events enter and upon whose cooperation the success of the human systems depends, it is wholly natural that science should be from the standpoint of and in the interests of the successful regulation of the human systems. That is to say, it is concerned with the mutual interactions of the physical systems of action with respect ultimately to their efficiency as factors in the human career.

I have presented these points simply as hypotheses and in highly summary form. They seem to me, however, to be in accord with the evidence of the case, and to present the only hopeful method of doing justice both to what are ordinarily called "objective" and "subjective" considerations—the only method which does not give a power and scope to the socalled subjective which, in the very midst of realistic systems, always calls out an idealistic movement.

A Working Method in Social Psychology

A moderate degree of acquaintance with recent socio-logical literature shows that at least five different sets of problems have been discussed having supposedly some connection with the topic of social psychology. To a certain extent these different problems have been discussed by different writers, with quite distinct and independent aims. To a certain extent, however, they have overlapped even in the same writer; and there has been a more or less unconscious transition from one group to another, with resulting confusion. As preliminary to an attempt to delimit the field of social psychology, and to plot a chart of its activities, it may be well to discriminate somewhat precisely these different types of discussion.

The first takes well-known social phenomena and employs psychological considerations whenever these are found likely to assist in the interpretation of the facts in question. It may be a question of language; it may be a matter of myth, or magic, or religious cult; it may be a matter of blood feud, or of exogamous marriage; it may be a question of the character of property ownership or political authority. The investigator dealing with the problem is led to the conclusion that a certain phase or bulk of the facts, greater or less as the case may be in different instances, has a distinctively psychological origin. Naturally he then draws upon the best psychological theory accessible to him. Here is psychology general or analytic psychology, frankly recognized as such, and employed to assist in the statement, explanation and classification of sociological facts.

In the second place, we have attempts to account for and deal with mental phenomena which are experienced in common by a

[Typescript in the John Dewey Manuscript Collection, Rare Book and Manuscript Library, Butler Library, Columbia University, New York, N.Y., ca. 1920(?).]

considerable number of people. An extreme case is the crowd or mob spirit. Another instance (if one is permitted to assume against certain French writers that this *is* another instance and not just a case of mob spirit) is public opinion viewed as a *de facto* matter: as simply meaning that a very considerable number of people hold the same view so as to be led to common action. To many writers the psychology (generally that of sympathy, contagion, imitation or communication) which accounts for the common content of belief and purpose in different persons in a given social group, is social psychology. The existence, nature and mechanism of an identical or homogeneous content is the problem of social psychology.

In the third place, there is consciousness of common interests, purposes: such an awareness of the common weal or woe as materially modifies the action of the individual in whom the consciousness is found. Facts belonging to this group, while occasionally confused with those spoken of under the second head, are readily enough marked off. There is an obvious distinction between simply holding the same idea that another holds (whether consciously or not), and employing reference to social well-being as the standard by which one consciously tries the ideas which one accepts, and the aims that one sets up. I may believe with a number of my fellows that "protection" is absolutely indispensable, or that a certain method of baptism is necessary. This is a matter of what I call the common content. But a reformer may be practically the only individual who, at a given time, accepts a given principle and yet his state of mind be thoroughly socialized because he has been brought to his belief by considerations of social well-being. In this sense, 'social consciousness' takes on inevitably something of an ethical meaning; social consciousness stands more or less over against individual consciousness, the latter having a somewhat distinctly egoistic or selfish reference. Some writers have proceeded more or less definitely on the basis that the problem of social psychology is that of thoughts and feelings having as their object or focus of attachment general social welfare.

Fourthly, the influence exercised upon a given individual by the social medium in which he lives has attracted the attention of some investigators. They have endeavored to account for a given system of individual opinions and purposes in terms of the social medium in which it forms. They have occupied themselves with the mechanism by which the individual's feelings, judgments and intentions have been socially elaborated. There is clearly some point of connection here with the second set of problems in so far as these structures involve a common content, and I think some writers have passed quite unconsciously from one sphere to the other—to the detriment of their work. For the problem in the two cases is different. In one it is the existence of the common content *as common* that defines the investigation; in the other, it is a matter of explaining under what social influences a given individual A B, or a given set of individuals M N, come to hold certain concrete ideas—and habits—which in their totality constitute such and such a type of character. Why and how does the city dweller differ from the country resident? What makes the difference in the type of interests and ideals of the inhabitant of Massachusetts and South Carolina? Under what social conditions is this man a burglar and the other man a speculator, and the third a physician? While these are questions about individuals, or groups of individuals, they are clearly social questions—questions of describing and explaining certain social types and figures. It is the individual as a social individual that is under consideration—not the individual in his psychical mechanism, but as a concrete personality with a concrete equipment of habits, plans and ideas. Undoubtedly psychology may be useful as a method in solving this type of problem; but some writers have apparently been misled (because it is an individual that is under examination) into thinking that the results obtained are of a distinctively psychological character.

Finally there is the delicate and subtle matter of explaining the mental process as such in terms of that social situation which stimulates and motivates it. For example, the sensation as a psychical event, as distinct from a given content or quality, would hardly come within the purview of social psychology in any of the four previous types of problems. It belongs to social psychology under this fifth caption, in so far as it can be shown that a social medium evokes and determines the sensation considered as a type of mental attitude or operation. The actual structure of sense-perceptions that make up the working equipment of a savage, or a civilized American of the 19th century, belong to the fourth class of problems; but the keenness and alertness of sense perception in the savage, the particular quality of the act of perceiving, the role it plays in the whole *psychical* life, is a different sort of question. Scientifically we can abstract from the actual experience the aspect of content, and that of mode or form. Hence if confusion is easy between this point of view and that of our fourth head, discrimination is also easy. There it was a question of explaining certain concrete and definite mental contents through reference to other contents of the same sort already existing. Here it is not a question of any particular idea, plan or habit, but rather of the typical psychical attitudes and operations involved in them. It is not a question of explaining them by reference to similar attitudes on the part of other individuals, but rather by connecting them with the structure and movement of the social situation in which they appear. It is one thing to account for the acceptance by a given Chinaman of a certain set of traditional ideas; it is another to account for the Chinaman's habit of relying upon authority in memorized forms, instead of employing initiative in thinking out things for himself. In problems of the fourth sort, we are interested in the statement of the behavior and ideas current in a given individual or group of individuals, essentially a social matter. Under the present head, we are concerned with the existence of a certain psychical type, a certain mental pattern, form or schema—and this is essentially a psychological matter.[1]

If we now contrast the first with the fifth of our sets of problems, we shall find that we have reversed our point of view. In the first, the point was to explain certain social phenomena through reference to well established principles of psychology—such as the association of ideas, the formation of visual images, the value of symbols in directing intellectual processes, etc. Under our last head, the problems that come up have to do with explaining psychical processes by reference to social situations. The distinction between these two extremes is then sufficiently well marked. The direct interest in the first case is sociological; in the last case, it is immediately psychological. But what with the three intervening terms? How shall we group them?

1. My article on the "Interpretation of Savage Mind" in the *Psychological Review* for May 1902 [*Middle Works* 2:39–52], may be referred to as exemplifying in more detail what is meant by a mental type or pattern.

These intervening terms, be it recalled, (1) the existence of common contents; (2) the existence of conscious social references in the ideas and feelings entertained by an individual and the acts performed by him; (3) and the complex system of ideas and modes of behavior current in an individual, or a group of individuals, so far as these require to be socially explained.

Without surrendering for a moment the necessity of clear distinction between these various groups of problems in order to prevent confusion, I yet hold that all these affairs fall into line as phases of a common investigation which from the methodological standpoint may well be termed social psychology. To show how and why this is true may afford a fitting introduction to the discussion of the working standpoint in method of such a science.

In the first place I shall point out that the problem of certain institutional forms of religion, politics, economics, etc., is practically identical with the problem of the actual beliefs and customs current in a given group of individuals in so far as an explanation of either is attempted, which involves the use of psychological conceptions; and accordingly the first and the fourth of our original heads resolve themselves naturally into each other. In both we have ultimately the same facts. In one case the facts are considered more institutionally and objectively; in the other case more personally and from within. It is clearly the same reality we are concerned with whether we investigate the body of myths obtained in a given Indian tribe, or consider the persons of that tribe in so far as they accept and are influenced by these legends. In the first case we give for the time being a sort of tentative existence to the myths, neglecting for scientific convenience the fact that after all they are only part of the intellectual and emotional equipment of that group of individuals who believe in them and report them. In the latter case we take account of the myths as actually phenomena of the experience, religious, aesthetic, scientific, etc., of this group. The latter point of view simply takes the facts at a somewhat lower level: it recognizes that "institutions" have no existence except in terms of the concrete interests, emotions, and systems of conduct that prevail in a given set of associated persons. As a matter of scientific division of labor, the first point of view is that appropriate to the philologist when he occupies himself with the linguistic phenomena of a given group; to the comparative religionist when he is investigating myths, rites, cults, dogmas, etc.; to the student of jurisprudence concerned with the system of rights and duties that obtain in a community—in short to the specialist, preoccupied with description and explanation of a given set of social phenomena. The other point of view, that which refers the institutional phase to the concrete habits of action and opinion that are found among the individuals of a group, then attempting to explain them by reference to the social medium, is the attitude appropriate to the general ethnologist. He must accept his particular phase largely at the hands of the specialist; he is concerned thereafter with them in their interrelations as parts—more or less loosely bound together—of the common and more comprehensive body of experience.

If this virtual identity of subject matter be borne in mind, it should also be clear that the problem of the conscious reference to social well-being as an operating motive in determining the individual's opinions and behavior, is simply a more special instance of a phase of personal equipment which requires social explanation. It is an instance in which the social aspect is so obvious and striking as to have misled some into thinking that here alone is to be found a distinctively social fact. In truth what we have here is an additional exponent of sociability. While in detail it affords one of the most interesting and important of all the sociological problems, in principle it stands upon the same level with any way of thinking or acting which is socially generated and conditioned. The prevalence of a certain religious cult in a given group of individuals would clearly be a fact falling under our fourth type of problems. We may find, however, as one phenomenon among others in the operation of that cult, that it regards certain other ideas and practices as merely private or personal and accordingly reprobates them and tries to suppress them—this happens for instance in some communities with magic, which in others is tolerated as a legitimate part of the socially accepted religious phenomena. In the latter case the religious facts requiring explanation are loaded with an additional element of significance—that of being felt and conceived as common or distinctly associational in kind. The nature of this annexing of conscious social reference; the origin of the distinction between the public and private significance; the bearing of the distinction between public and private, upon not only the details of the cult itself, but upon say other social phenomena, domestic and political:—all these are points needing investigation. But after all they only supply additional characteristic qualities of those personal experiences and equipments which need explanation in the light of their social context. An institution is social because of its working, because of its effects, what it actually accomplishes. Explicit consciousness of the importance and necessity of these results reacts of course into the institution itself; it calls out a new set of emotions and ideas which in turn modify the practical workings and the actual results. Yet the institution in order to acquire social value does not wait upon the rise of such distinctive conscious reference. The distinction is quite analogous to that of a spectator who is aesthetically enjoying a picture, as compared with another spectator who in addition to his enjoyment is reflexly conscious of its aesthetic origin and nature; and who accordingly to a greater or less degree controls his attitude of appreciation by reference to aesthetic norms. What we have here is simply an additional complication which supervenes within the aesthetic fact—not any radical difference of kind.

So far as method is concerned, the significance of that particular type of social phenomena which is accompanied by specific ideas and emotions, serving as conscious indices of social value, is two-fold. In the first place (as already indicated) it marks transition from the social sphere into the socio-ethical. In the second place it suggests and almost compels express recourse to the psychological point of view. As stated at the outset, the sociologist may go to psychology at any point where he finds psychological data and methods likely to be of use to him. When he is dealing with [*missing text*] where the social quality [*missing text*] simply on the part of the investigator, but on the part of those actually experiencing them), psychology becomes of almost inevitable resort.

Problems of Contemporary Philosophy: The Problem of Experience

Friends, fellow students: When I arranged with Mr. Bohn last Spring to give these three lectures on philosophical subjects, I didn't realize that there would be as much need to be philosophical when the lectures began as there is now. However, philosophy proper has perhaps got a good ways away from the conception of being philosophical, which was philosophy taught how to grin and bear it and understand the trouble of life, an idea, I suppose, that came down from the old stoic philosophy.

In speaking of the problem of experience the first question I want to raise is what difference does it actually make whether one holds a philosophy based on experience, one holds the theory of knowledge and of conduct, personal conduct, social relationship based on experience, or whether one holds a theory of these things based on something else beside experience? What is the human bearing of the issue itself? Does it make, would it make, any actual difference in the conduct of life if people in general held to a philosophy of experience or they held to some other philosophy? I'm ready to discuss this before I take up anything about what experience itself is.

Now the first point that I want to make is that there is a very practical human bearing in this issue as to whether one has a philosophy based on experience or one based on something else. And the first aspect of the difference that it makes may be brought out, indicated, by a reference to the English thinker John Locke, who wrote in the latter part of the seventeenth century. His chief work was published right after the English revolution, when the Stuarts were finally overthrown in 1688. He was one of

[Lecture at Rand School of Social Science, New York, N.Y., 8 March 1933. Microfilm of stenographic report in Tamiment Collection 13, Reel 45, #121, New York University, New York, N.Y.]

the first of the modern thinkers to insist that all our beliefs, scientific and moral, political, should be based on experience. Now he contrasted his philosophy of experience with another philosophy that had a good deal of vogue. A good many adherents at his time had believed in innate ideas, principles, standards, ideals, which were not acquired through the processes of living through our experience, but that the mind brought with it, which were therefore deeper than all experience, more fundamental, more sure, more commanding than any idea, any belief or principle that is derived from our actual experience. Now he gave various reasons attacking the theory of these innate ideas, which included all kinds of moral, intellectual, philosophical principles, some of which were purely theoretical. But the practical one, the one that indicates the bearing of philosophy of experience upon other things, was the statement that if the people believed in these innate ideas, then all kinds of prejudices, notions which were instilled early in life, so early that people didn't know later how they came by them, would seem to have this sanction of being inherent in the mind and therefore would not be subject to any examination or criticism. He then went on to say that it would give a man or a class of men very great authority, very great influence and very great power over the beliefs and conduct of other people . . . or that group were the ones to instill in the minds of people these beliefs and these standards; standards, principles, which could not possibly be examined because they came from such a higher source that they were exempt from all examination in the light of our actual experience.

Now he struck there a very real note which one finds running through the history of thought, especially for reasons I'll speak of later, the history of modern thought, about why this problem of experience, its issue of having a philosophy based on experience or on something else, is important. In those books that John Morley wrote about the great French thinkers of the eighteenth century, one on Rousseau, another on Voltaire, another on Diderot and the Encyclopedists, Morley points out and history justifies his remark that these empirical thinkers that did hold to experience as the source and the authority for our beliefs, had been very uniformly on the liberal side of political and social questions, and those that held to innate ideas, a priori principles, those which don't come to us through actual experience, had been with practical uniformity on the conservative side, reactionary side in all questions of government.

Now for reasons that I think are particularly obvious and will state a little better later, I just want now to call your attention to that fact—that it has been that the belief in standards or ideas which are not derived from experience, therefore which can't be tested by experience, has been all through the ages a very powerful instrument, one may say a very powerful weapon, in the hands of those people who are in power, who had social control in their hands; that, in effect, it was comparatively easy for them to say that the standards and principles which are represented in the existing political and social order, existing type of government, are eternal in their nature; that they are necessary and universal and therefore not to be questioned. John Locke, in one of his essays, made perhaps a statement that is rather extreme when he said that our minds like our churches and temples have in them certain figures by which they are ultimately governed, that final authority, the final source of man's actions, their ideas, their ideals; and that therefore to be able to dictate to others through the medium of ideas that are superior to experience, that come from some source higher than experience, is ultimately really the power to regulate man's action.

Now that perhaps is a little extreme. Man's conduct governs perhaps, governs relatively more by habit and less by simple ideas than Locke thought, but there is enough truth in that we are controlled enough by our thought and ideas, certainly, that Locke was right in saying it's no mean power and authority that a person has if he can get into the minds of other people that the ideas and principles which he represents come from a superior source.

Putting it a little somewhat the other way, the fundamental authorities through church, religious organizations, have always held that their fundamental ideas and standards were essentially supernatural, that they were superempirical, and therefore men simply had to bow before those principles and not just their practical judgment or their convictions that were derived from an experience with the world, with one another, to bring to bear on those ideas. That is the most specific issue which is at stake in this matter of a philosophy of experience versus some other kind of philosophy, technically, generally, transcendental philosophy, that is, a philosophy coming from some source that transcends or goes beyond anything in actual experience.

There is another reason which is not so definite but which is equally important, perhaps in the long run more and more. That is, these other philosophies, which taking human history as a whole have had more influence in controlling people's beliefs and their institutions and conduct than ideas based on philosophy of experience, have led people to, well, to depreciate experience, to make light of the actual possibilities of experience. I want to break that sentence up into two parts. One is that this issue is important, I repeat, because the mass of people through the whole of recorded history have not accepted actually in their conduct a philosophy of experience. They have accepted standards and ideas which cling to, claim to have, an authority and a sanction beyond experience. And the other point is, I repeat, that because of that they have not esteemed actual experience very highly, or put it the other way around, they have put their chief attention and attached chief importance to things that cling to, belong to, realms that were beyond our actual experience here on earth.

The reference I made a moment ago to the influence, power, of supernatural ideas, that is, ideals claiming supernatural authority, standards of criteria to measure values by, claims to have come from revelation, from a source higher than experience, therefore possesses great thought . . . had we all know this great influence upon man all through history. Now the effect of that I repeat is to have made people think that those values and those standards were of greater importance than anything in experience; and in my judgment one reason that our actual experience hasn't been any better than it has, the fact that actual human experience has been a good deal of a mess and human experience is still a good deal of a mess, is that so many people have been taught to believe and have come to believe that the remedy is to be found outside of experience, that there isn't much use in relying on experience anyway, that experience is incapable of giving us any great values to work by, that experience isn't capable of setting up methods which will really guide people effectually.

I don't want to dwell unduly, but I do like to call your attention to this point; the very great probability that one reason that the human race, humanity, hasn't got out of experience more than it has is this fact that it has been taught to look elsewhere for supreme values and for supreme guidance to conduct. Of course a greater and greater number of people are questioning that point of view today, and don't regard it as very modern, or uptodate, to hold it. But mankind as a whole, I repeat, through the course of history has been habituated to that; and so there has been a disparagement, this lack of esteem for experience and this lack of serious thought and attention to what we might make out of experience, if we took that experience as our only ultimate guide to action. Those are the two great reasons why this problem of philosophy of experience is of human significance, generally significant and not merely of technical philosophical significance and importance.

Now coming to the history of philosophic thought itself I would say that there have been three main stages in the development of thought regarding the matter of experience. The first of those notions about experience comes to us from the great philosophies of ancient Greece, of ancient Athens: great philosophers of the fifth century before the Christian era, Plato, and his pupil, but not exactly disciple, Aristotle. The philosophical tradition of something higher than experience, something having a greater authority than anything in experience, was formulated (I don't say originated, but formulated) in a systematic way and was justified by argument in this period of Greek thought and then found its way into the whole tradition of the western world. We must remember that the philosophy which was dominant in Europe for centuries and still influences that of the Catholic church was based, as far as possible, upon the teachings of Aristotle. And so not just through professors' teachings and writings, and universities, but through the church itself for centuries through the Middle Ages and a period preceding it, ideals became a part of the common intellectual stock of trade of the European world without any conscious knowledge of these great philosophers themselves and to . . . America's(?) . . . certain extent also is true of Jewish philosophy of this period, combination of Aristotle or Plato with the Old Testament, much as the Christian theologians, Catholic theologians, made one between Christians and these old people.

Now we come to the particular point. They identified experience and the knowledge that comes from experience essentially with custom, with habit, with things that have been found to work pretty well and therefore are adopted because they become usual and customary. Also, people did not know any cause or reason for it. When it is said today that up to very recently medicine was a purely empirical science and not a rational science or that the architects and masons of the Middle Ages built their cathedrals empirically and not on the basis of scientific engineering knowledge, it is still that meaning of experience that we have in mind. It is illustrated in an anecdote of James' *Psychology,* of a passenger in a railroad train. When the railroad car still had stoves that burned wood, one in each car (anybody here except myself old enough to remember the kind of passenger cars?), a passenger complained when the train was stopped, of the stove smoking and filling the car with disagreeable fumes and the brakeman said, "Well, it will stop just as soon as the train starts," and the other person asked, "Why will it?" "It *always* does." Now that is empirical knowledge in the sense in which the Greek philosophers formulated experience and empiricism. Doctors used certain remedies just as they use quinine for malaria. They didn't know why it worked but it did, just like the brakeman and his stove. It always has, almost always, and so it will probably cure you. Or the average carpenter will build his house. Actually of course he had to obey certain laws of physics, gravitation, of strength of material, laws of stress and strain, and so on, but after all he didn't know because he understood those principles and causes. People by cut and tried methods, trial and accident and success and failure, had found that they built up certain habits and on the whole those habits gave the desired result. Well, that was experience there, and these great Greek philosophers made a sharp contrast between that and sciences.

Science was higher than experience because it involved a knowledge of the causes and the reasons which brought about these things. Now you know the Greeks originated our scientific mathematics, especially geometry, and up to very recently the geometry we still study in high schools was called Euclidean from this old Greek geometer, who lived in just about this period when Plato was writing his philosophy. And so they held geometry up as a rational science that they said doesn't depend upon custom or upon experience at all. There are certain axiomatic eternal truths—we still call these axioms—that meant self-evident truths, not realized from experience. Experience could only give us these principles which are generally true. They are not necessarily so, since truth, true science, like geometry, appealed purely to reason and dealt with the rational principles which were above and beyond experience. Now so far as Greek experience was concerned, there was a lot of truth in that distinction. Their experience, practical experience, was based on custom, that is, habit; that is, on tradition that had been worked out through the process of slow selection and passed on from one individual to another and therefore it was quite natural, one might almost say quite proper, that they cannot imagine any kind of experience which would ascertain the real causes for things and the real reasons for things.

The result was that they had two levels: the higher level of rational science which gave us eternal universal necessary truths which were found in science and which ought to govern man's moral behavior, ought to control human institutions; and the lower level of the experience of the average man, of the carpenter and the shoemaker and even the physician and all the other people who just did the best they could, utilizing the customs and ideas, beliefs, that had been handed down to them from the past. Now to anticipate a later point, they could not imagine these truths of science; not only couldn't they imagine them being generated or produced by experience, but they couldn't imagine them being embodied in experience. They thought of these two levels as necessarily forever separate and isolated from each other. And to make a jump, to save time, down to the modern period, what we know now is that the understanding of scientific causes, of the principles of things, is actually capable of being embodied in everyday experience. We know that, because we have a technology or the technique by which these truths of science, that is to say, understanding of cause, relationship of cause and effect, are actually applied. I don't see how anybody could have ever invented the electric light merely by following experience in the general sense of experience, that is, the more or less accidental occurrences, habits and customs of the past. But when men developed a scientific understanding of the laws of electricity, of cause and effect in relation to light and electricity, the causal laws of the conservation and transformation of energy (one form of energy is transformable into another), then it was possible for people to deliberately invent such things as electric lights, the telephone and all of the other inventions which now are a part of the daily experience of everybody. The Greeks had no theory or system of invention and of technology and therefore they could not close the gap between these, between these scientific truths and the average daily experience of the mass of people in ordinary life. We have got this great system of controlled methods, techniques of invention, which enable us to live ordinary experience, live higher than the plane of habit and custom that accidentally had been hit upon in the past. That is the reason that experience can mean something today very different from what it meant to the Greeks.

Now there is another very important conclusion from that, which I would like to point out, though I don't stop to dwell upon it now. That is that while we have acted on this fact that it is possible to carry over scientific truths, thoughts and principles, the understanding of causal relations into experience (everyday experience in the physical field and illustrated by the electric light, the telephone, the dynamo, the internal combustion engine on the motor car, even the steam engine on the locomotive), we have not as yet found any way of discovering, or at least of applying when discovered, the social truths and principles making them carry over into everyday experience the way in which scientific truths in the physical field, the field of the natural sciences, are brought down through suitable technology into everyday human experience in this other field.

Well, there came on Greek civilization, which was more or less swamped, and covered a good many centuries of history. All northern Europe you know, outside of the Mediterranean Basin, was inhabited by barbarians. Finally these barbarians overran Rome, Italy and the higher culture of Greece which was already some good deal diluted in the Roman Empire. It was still further swamped. And yet it remained as a higher culture, and it was preserved by the church and by other authorities and was looked up to by the barbarians throughout Europe, and rightly so, as being something higher than their own experience. Now that is a very significant fact in human history, that here you have barbarians, not savages, but people on a barbarian level of civilization, contrasted with this very much higher grade of civilization of Greece and Rome, superimposing upon the people through the authority of the church and the state these principles which did not grow out of the actual experience of people. So the whole European situation came to be of a kind which confirmed this idea of a higher set of truths and standards beyond the experience of everyday life. They had, one might say, if they are going to become really civilized—regain the level which had belonged to the earlier civilization—they had to accept these things coming to them from the outside, something they had to struggle to live up to, and the authority of the church and the state naturally took advantage of that situation. Well finally Europe became relatively civilized.

Now we have a period that is known as the revival of learning, the Renaissance, when the leaders of European civilization began again to think for themselves and to speak their own experience and not merely look back to that of Palestine in religion and Greece in science and philosophy, and of Rome in law, government and politics, as something higher and superior to anything in their own experience. And then you've got a revival again of the appeal to experience as the ultimate source of anything that is entitled to belief as the ultimate authority in all matters of conduct, personal and social.

Francis Bacon stands out, as a contemporary of the Elizabethan age, as a great thinker, because he is a typical representative of this new appeal. He said we are the real ancients. The people we call the ancients and that we have been looking up to, they really were the youths of civilization; we are older than they are because we have all of the intervening experience and wisdom, and with a certain independence we should find our own methods for discovering truths instead of taking them on the authority of the past, something outside our experience.

And then we come to Locke, to whom I referred earlier, and his point of view, and there I want to go back just for a moment to this point of his liberalism. He had more influence on Thomas Jefferson and people that drew up our Declaration of Independence and so on, than any other individual, and in a way the democratic principles as they evolved in this country and later in France were very closely connected with the later development of this appeal to experience and the ultimate thing. Every individual has experience. He may not have this higher reason; he doesn't have these innate ideas—no one has that—but every individual has experience and, if he is normal, certain good sense, judgment, to utilize that experience, and therefore we ought to build our social institutions on appeal to the experience of the average person and his needs, requirements, instead of upon this authority supposedly coming from outside superior powers.

He also is greatly interested in the principle of toleration. You know the seventeenth century was the century of great religious wars, of clashes there in England that had been the wars—conflict between the Catholics and the Protestants; and then the Protestants got into civil wars among themselves, more or less Church of England on one side, and Presbyterians, representing another policy in government and not merely in religion; and then the Independent Baptists, Congregationalists, Puritans, and so on, and Cromwell having still another; and these people quarreling and actually fighting among themselves. And so Locke said, now a great deal of this comes because people are a great deal bothered and troubled about things beyond experience. You can't prove anything of these things; you can't disprove, because they are outside of experience. If people will stick to experience and the lessons of experience they will stick to things which are possible for them to verify and prove and they will have very much more tolerance and respect for each other. In other words, in fact he said the civil wars and troubles come because people are asserting on supposed authority higher than experience these things which lie outside of the scope of experience. And the people will come down to periods and places; they will have a toleration, regard for each other which will make them respect each other and save them from constant friction, antagonism with each other.

Now the French in the eighteenth century took up this conception of Locke, that all our knowledge and ideas come from experience, and they took certain things that he said and carried them much further than he did, the French being a more logical people, more given to following principles to their logical conclusion. And Locke said the mind is a piece of blank paper and experience writes everything on it through contact with the outside, what we call the environment; some of these French thinkers said, if that is so, then education can be omnipotent. If the mind of every individual at birth is a blank and if all beliefs, standards, are built through experience, then by controlling the environment, especially the social environment, the political environment, you can impress any kind of beliefs and develop any kind of conduct you please and thus remake the world. And this idea, the possibility of indefinite progess, the idea of the perfectability of man, of people, would get away from ignorance and superstition and from tyranny and despotic institutions. That from freedom of thought and enlightenment and good political institutions you could create a new race of individuals was the somewhat extreme conclusion that these French thinkers built up out of the development of this philosophy of experience of Locke; and while of course it was actually economic troubles and distress that brought on the French Revolution, yet this idea of the possibility of building a new civilization and the building of a new type of humanity creating a new world of human beings came into the French Revolution, gave it ardor and enthusiasm very likely—a development by the French of this older philosophy of experience. And thus again in the general liberal ideas and more especially the development of democratic ideas in France following that in this country, which was more influenced by John Locke than by any other one thinker, this democratic faith was also linked up with underlying conceptions of philosophy of experience.

It seemed to me that, perhaps to be more useful, to point out its larger bearing on the issue, probably it would be necessary to go into details concerning the third notion about the nature of experience. When I come to the third, however, I said there were three periods, stages of the idea. When I come to this which is the more recent, almost contemporary, aspect of the philosophy of experience, it does become necessary to go somewhat more into technical detail: this conception of Locke's emphasis, as I've already indicated, on the passivity of the mind, that experience comes to us from without, that experience is a sum of the impressions which objects and people outside made upon the mind. Locke was so afraid of giving the mind any innate ideas or principles that he tended to go to the opposite extreme and made it purely passive and receptive. Now that idea that I have just indicated, extreme as it was and faulty as it was, that fundamental idea yet nevertheless did play a part, as I've just indicated, as an instrument of attack upon superstition and upon traditional and despotic institutions. The general principle was that laid down once more by Locke. If our beliefs, even the over-complicated ones, those that have great, a greatest weight with us, are built up by experience, then we can go back over experience and pick them to pieces; we can show exactly where these ideas came from. And naturally those who used that method showed that a lot of the ideas, creeds, standards of governing people, instead of coming from a very high source, came from a very earthly one, that they came from self-interest of people in power or that they'd grown accidentally. And they accepted them merely because they happened to get established in some earlier period in history. So this empirical method used to analyze prevailing ideas was a very powerful instrument of criticism and disillusionment, of disintegration, and that time created an action against the philosophy of experience, at least against the philosophy in that form, that experience is something where we are purely passive and we receive impressions from without, and that these are built up through associations in a more complex form.

There were two great sources of reaction, and of the development into the third form of philosophy of experience. One is the development of biology, which showed that the human organism with which the mind is connected isn't a purely passive thing. Anybody who sees a baby ought almost to have known that experience wasn't a purely passive thing; this theory held as it was—anyone who has observed how outreaching and active the babies are would have known that experience wasn't purely a passive thing. Really, it took a more scientific development of biology and physiology to bring out the significance of that fact for a theory of experience. Or to put it more specifically: not to go back to the old theory of innate ideas, but to show that experience is what it is because of a motor element and active elements and not merely because of a sensory element—that even the eye or the ear, if you take a more static organ, is not merely passive, it is a motor organ, an active organ; you throw the hand and so on. That scientific factor is more and more bringing about the new concept of experience and recognition of the motor outgrowing active element within experience itself. The other is more complex and associated with the fact that the earlier type of empiricism, that represented by Locke and Helvétius and like eighteenth century philosophers, was much more powerful in criticism, in destruction, intellectual destruction, than it was in construction, than in building up new ideas. It was very powerful as an instrument of man's passion, of release from old traditions and superstitions, but when it came to telling what should take their place, it did not have anything like the same power.

Well, the further story takes me over into the subject of next week, "The Problem of Thought." That is, where does thought come in? And it was that power of thought and of thinking which was overlooked and neglected by this theory of experience as simply an accumulation of impressions and sensations made popular by Locke in the beginning, and his friends particularly, his friends and followers. And so I will continue this story of, carry the story of experience over into what I call the third stage in connection with the discussion of the next hour, which will deal with the place of thinking, of intelligence, in experience, why it has the place there, how it has the place, how because of that, experience can become active, productive, creative, and not merely passive and receptive.

Methods in Philosophy and the Sciences

I have shown my sympathy with the anti-authoritarian, libertarian campaign by departing from the subject which was assigned to me. I am not going to attempt to give a program, perhaps this is as near as I will come to the subject. What I am going to say may perhaps be construed without too much torturing as a statement of some conditions that any program along the lines indicated would have to meet. I can start in discussing these conditions by stating that the problem with which I am going to concern myself was stated in the last point of Sidney Hook's paper: The relative failure of those who accept the standpoint of experience and the experimental method to develop a method adequately and explicitly for use in the various aspects of the social subjects, and not having thoroughly developed it, of course a failure to adapt and apply it consistently in the groundwork of both subjects. In other words, I think the primary condition that has to be met in forming a program is to accept the responsibility for simplicity, cooperative awareness of the fundamental importance of the problem of method and attempt to develop explicitly and cooperatively the essential structure of such a non-authoritative, non-transcendental, empirical method.

If I may refer to something which I said some time ago in a speech, liberals were so conscious of the suppressive, corruptive and harmful work of the institutions which represented and embodied authority, that they tended quite naturally, almost inevitably, to look askance upon the principles of authority itself. But if we take authority, what seems to me in the legitimate sense, the need for some principle of guidance in formation of

[Paper read at The Conference on Methods in Philosophy and the Sciences, New School for Social Research, New York, N.Y., 22–23 May 1937. Stenographic report in the Horace M. Kallen Papers, folder 95, Yivo Institute for Jewish Research, New York, N.Y.]

belief and action, the absence of authority means chaos and confusion, and that is what, as Dr. Hook has just said, just works back into the hands of authoritarians, because a great mass of people will not put up indefinitely with the absence of any kind of principles in their beliefs and actions. So it seems to me that the problem is that of recognition first of method as the source of authority for any non-dogmatic movement, and secondly, the adequate development of a method which has sufficient claim to be taken as authority so as to be able to be self-creative, self-developing in its application. There are exceptions of course of some good forms of authoritarianism that we regard as good over against those that we consider bad. Of course we don't put it to ourselves exactly that way, but when we see claims to authoritative power active and perhaps gaining power, it is a very natural human tendency to set up another authoritative power over and against them. And so again I emphasize the fact that I see no way fundamentally in the long run to meet the claims of authoritarianism of different forms, excepting in the development of scientific method. Not in itself of course is it developed, but with special references to its use in the various social lines of inquiry and particularly, to anticipate a point which I shall touch upon briefly at the close, as a kind of method on which there is a need for hypotheses, alternative possibilities. As far as I can see, it is the only ultimate protection against dogmatism. Even the physical sciences, in spite of the fact that formation of multiple hypotheses is a part of the technique, possibly suffered from a kind of Newtonian orthodoxy that practically speaking made certain alternatives impermissible. It has possibly been true there was hardly any ground for making them during that period, but certainly the atmosphere for a long time was discouraging. Yet we know that when another type of physical hypothesis was admitted as legitimate it was developed.

Now, speaking not of sciences, but of popular beliefs, creeds, conceptions, ideas, in the social fields, I think we all agree that there is much free play in considering alternatives. It is not merely the open partisanship that we find in politicians and the overt sectarianism in religious creeds and so on; but it is even more significant and potentially harmful, an unconscious, undeveloped partisanship which works against even the willingness to consider the possibility of any line of thought or action that hasn't gotten some previous satisfaction. I liked very much what Dr. Kallen said about the two continents without connecting it up with the conference. All dogmatism is by its nature an economy of scarcity, scarcity in forming a hypothesis and entertaining alternative ideas. Any liberal creed, on the other hand, must be an economy of abundance in a freedom of developing hypotheses. I am in a little dilemma on the one hand, if I don't give any illustration, my remarks are rather formal, and if I do, the illustration may take attention away from the principle. But I want to illustrate along the line of Sidney Hook without holding him responsible for the interpretation. Marx has made us very familiar with the idea that every economic, legal and political order develops its own internal contradictions and that those contradictions ultimately do away with the system, and lead on to something else. Well, about that fact, I am not very enthusiastic about using the word contradiction. That, it seems to me, requires more propositions than actual social conditions—but that is a minor point; that any regime does develop a lot of internal conflicts and discrepancies, and that they tend gradually or suddenly to modify the system, and finally bring about another, seems to me good historical sense. But possibly under the influence of Hegel this dialectic is interpreted orthodoxly as very rigid. This is just one thesis and an anti-thesis, and one fundamental contradiction.

Well, now, that seems to me an illustration of an economy of scarcity in thinking and in social and political matters. It seems to me that at least there is a possibility, a chance that there are a lot of discrepant forces, not just one contradiction, a number of forces and contradictions that are pulling in different directions, and therefore we are obliged to consider a number of possibilities regarding the method in which these conflicts of forces and conditions will work out.

Well, I want to go on from that to say, to put it first in a way that might chance to contradict, that the great weakness of historical liberalism, or liberal temper, using that word for short, is that there has been a tendency merely to develop alternative possibilities and stop short with setting them up, a sort of falling in love with the prospect of an economy of abundance, or on the negative side, a failure to consider the conditions under which decisions not only are objective but are this under these alternative possibilities. Now, if we consider the physical field in which scientific method is better developed, we find that they begin with setting up alternative hypotheses. But that is only a beginning. It isn't thought to be a nice lovely spectacle to look at, but it is a way of defining a problem and a way of indicating the activities that will have to be carried out in order to solve the problem. In other words it is the freedom of conditions, it is location and description of the conditions of activities that are to be carried out which will end sooner or later, perhaps sooner, perhaps later, and enable a positive decision to be made with respect to that particular set of alternatives.

Now this earlier period of liberalism, it seems to me, was a period when this which we think of as a survey of alternative possibilities, and as he has suggested at least indirectly, liberals were a little too much inclined to take their personal emancipations and the sense of liberation that they got from their personal emancipations from dogmatism as being an end in itself instead of an invitation and a very urgent invitation to go on and do something about it. And that it seems to me gave liberalism its milk and water reputation and changed intellectual tolerance, which is a positive fact, namely this freedom in the formation of ideas and hypotheses, into a moral attitude. "Well, most anything may be true, and it is a lovely world to have a great variety of scenery, and therefore, let's not get much excited about anything in particular." And in that way this whole conception does not appear to be in any way aggressive social reform.

Now, coming more definitely to the social subject matter, there are two which seem to me to be main lines for programs and experiments. One of them, of course, is the conceptual formalism or formalistic rationalism. I am not going to dwell on that. Looking about I don't believe there is a great deal of literature in these fields. It seems to me the movement, especially by the younger men, is very definitely away from the older conceptual orthodoxies in political economy, politics and law. But in the reaction from that, it seems to me that the tendency is to call blind empiricism,—which thinks that the task of social inquiry is fulfilled by collecting, classifying and pigeon-holing, sometimes quite literally in safety deposit vaults, a sufficient number of facts,—a sort of worship of fact-finding. Well, of course as against the older conceptual method, or any scientific method, fact-finding is a necessary condition, but hardly a sufficient one technically, as in the social sciences. Very little technique is as yet important matter to tell what a fact is or to enable us to recognize the social fragment when we see one. Some one says you are developing the technique of identifying facts. We can make a fact out of most anything, even the most turbulent kind of material. I say the rationalism school was quite right in holding the bare facts. I announce that the bare facts are not even self-identified, that we have to have some kind of conceptual structure of ideas which will organize and serve as instruments of locating. But I think these rationalistic schools were completely and terribly wrong, terrible in their consequences and not realizing that this organization has two ideas and conceptions and can be brought about only as the ideas are employed operationally, by which I mean to direct actual activity that cannot be effective except in a pseudo matter, by ideas really as such, that is, apart from their instigating and directing certain lines of action. That leads me to suggest that one condition of the development of this program is that of considering the type of ideas that have some operational form, that is, that we act upon, that really makes some kind of social difference and a difference of a type that can be discriminated, and that is significant. Now, that leads me to say, as far as I can see, the fundamental cause for the great outburst of mere fact-finding in the social disciplines is the failure to state social problems in terms of what the man in the street or people outside the range of science could call social problems. To the ordinary man a social problem is some trouble, some experience, discrepancy, conflict, need in actual conditions—war is a problem to a great many people, a great social problem. Inability to get enough to eat is a social problem, and the difficulty that farmers are under of getting prices for their crops that will enable them to make a living is what they call a social problem.

Now it seems to me that a good deal of what are called social problems in a technical social sense are self-set problems. A Ph.D. student—I don't say a member of a faculty, but a Ph.D.— thinks his own show would make a nice problem, so it becomes a research problem, it becomes a problem for a hundred people, while it hasn't anything to do with any problem that demands action and organized action for its solution. Well, then what is there to do excepting fact-finding? In other words, I don't think

that fact-finding is out—it merely is a type of intellectual mis-
sile—I think it is a necessary consequence of any procedure that
fails to relate the social problems to problems of action, problems that can only be settled by action, and that fails, therefore,
to form the ideas and hypotheses, to collect the kinds of facts
that are relevant to problems of action.

What I am going to quote isn't specially relevant, but I don't
like to lose any opportunity to advertise this little booklet of
Lancelot Hogben, *The Retreat from Reason*—it costs one shill-
ing, worth a good deal more than that. In his discussion (and his
retreat from reason is the retreat, the same thing we are discussing here today, not from reason in the rationalistic sense but
retreat from intelligence), the retreat from reason is the penalty
we are paying for an inherent dichotomy in the way we educate
people. The training of the statesman and the man of letters gives
him no provision of the technical forces which are shaping the
society in which he lives. The education of the scientists and the
technicians leaves them indifferent to the social consequences of
their own activities.

Well, excepting that this is covered in terms of education, that
is exactly the same point that I am trying to make. The actual
leaders, rulers, of society, the people who are most influential
(newspaper people, maybe, and members of Congress, cabinet
and whatever other officers), certainly don't bother a great deal,
in spite of the temporary brain trust, about ideas and ideolo-
gies and methods that are worked out intellectually. On the
other hand, the intellectual, the scientific man, that is nominally
concerned with that field, hasn't shown any very great acute
consciousness of social barriers of their inquiry or any great
response for relating their inquiries to the actual social problems.
It isn't of course a collection of facts, it isn't necessary, but there
is a very great difference between merely collecting facts and
taking a problem that is socially felt already and then inquiring
what kind of facts would enable us really to develop operationally with that problem and then set to work where you can
get those plans.

Well, now, one thing more, or maybe two. There is another
aspect of a good deal of the work done in the social sciences
which seems to me also to be the direct consequence of this association of work and the methods of work from the actual social

problems in the ordinary, non-Pickwickian sense of social problems and the conducting of inquiry with relation to the determination of social policy, which of course is practically what I've been saying. Now it is easy to understand why people in the social sciences have taken that field. Pressure for partisanship is so great that the chastity and virginity of intellectual activity has been best protected by a policy of isolation more or less monastic, withdrawal, keeping away from any practical problem, in which it has been fairly easy to maintain impartiality and scientific attitudes.

But there is another point, the tendency to take the concept of physical sciences ex post facto into the social field of the meaning of the scientific method. Of course I don't need to say that scientific method has been more completely and adequately developed in the mathematical and physical field. Therefore those sciences have an enormous prestige. It might be factitious but fundamentally very damaging. Then there results the idea that in order to be scientific, investigation in economics, sociology, or whatever, needs merely the general treatises of scientific method which is doubtlessly applied in the other sciences, or else they aren't being scientific. Well, that again seems to me to be a natural result, not merely of the prestige of the physical field but even more from this dissociation of inquiry from the problems of social action and the formation of social problems. Let me put it this way, if social subject matter does have any distinctive features, distinctive as over against that of physical subject matter, how is that fact going to be discovered and how (or what) is a distinctive characteristic going to be authentically discovered? Well, I don't see but one way. You can't do it by speculative discussion to point out certain differences, positive differences in a positive social subject matter, purely argumentatively, dialectically. But somebody else can come back on the other side. But if the thing is inquiry in the social subjects as related to social policies and social acts, then it seems to me that the distinctive features of social subject matter over against physical are bound to come out and come out very strongly, and you will have a condition for the utilizing of the material and techniques of the physical sciences in the social field, but without having to surrender the autonomy of the social subjects too. I anticipate the kind of result that I think would have been an argumentative matter but is a fact in the physical sciences. I appear on the ground and say that is the only way we have of defining what is physical, which is by definition and description external to human culture. But when we come to social subject matter we are mixed up in it and it is mixed up in us, and if you think we can get social science by just getting off and looking at it and writing down what we see, that is incorrect. That is the essential characteristic of the social subject matter, and it attempts in the interest of scientific purity and chastity to eliminate all value judgments from the social sciences. And this seems to me the surest way of not merely sterilizing the human interest in it but in the end of just getting pseudo-facts and not the real facts themselves. Well, that last point is the point I mentioned first.

In accordance with cooperation and conversion among the workers in the different social fields, of course the philosopher can't tell the student of law and of economics and sociology and politics what techniques of inquiry he is going to employ. Those things have to be developed like all techniques by those who are doing the work and within the field of the work itself. But the last time I had any opportunity, some weeks ago, to think about any philosophical problem, I was speaking on the unity of man and you will forgive me therefore if I go back to the last philosophic thoughts and say the economic man isn't so popular as he once was, in the phraseology at least. I am not altogether sure whether he has actively disappeared from thinking, but in a certain way we have the economic man, and we have the political man, and we have the legal man and we have the psychological man, and perhaps the hardest to locate is the man; but still we have it, the moral man, the political man, the primitive man, the biological man, and the historic man, and so forth.

Now we all know that specialization is absolutely necessary. But I do not see how the social sciences can have the social effect that I presume they ought to have, and I do not see still more how they can become a good army, more than a fighting weapon, against authoritarianism unless they somehow can develop, I will say, a more conscious cooperation; but more conversion of the methods used and of the conclusions made, which make certain greater unity of methods and consequently, a greater mutual agreement between the conclusions of the subject specialization, is necessary. But it is a queer thing that the last thing about a worker in any special field is that he feels no responsibility for checking up and coordinating the results in one field with the results in the other. So having dodged, as successfully as I could, the question of laying down the program, I would say that it seems to me that the essence of the program on the practical side is this matter of greater mutual understanding, greater consideration of points where there is possible unity of method and result, translatability between the workers in the different social fields—and I am not setting up any special plea for philosophy there, because from my own point of view, philosophy as well as psychology is ultimately one of the fields of social inquiry.

Between Two Worlds

Not even the wisest and most far-seeing of men could have predicted—or even roughly anticipated—only fifty years ago the course which events have actually taken. Idealists dreamed their dreams. Their visions when viewed in the light of what has taken place are mostly remarkable for presenting almost the blank opposite of what has happened. Waves that now appear to have been only the surface were treated as if they were irresistible tides. Hardheaded realists do not make a better showing. Those who supposed they were realists were in fact but reaping an immediate harvest of personal advantage. Their preoccupation with that narrow concern contributed mightily to creation of the present state of affairs.

When I look about to find a symbol of their unwisdom I think of the reckless exploitation of natural resources that marks our history. Our forefathers proceeded as if the fertility of our soil were unexhaustible; as if mines and forests were eternally self-renewing. Spent soils, burntover forests, depleted oilwells, fished-out waters are part of the price paid. Even now we are hardly more than half-awake to the consequences of the policy of neglecting the future in order to make the most possible out of the immediate present. The symbol is defective, however, in that the waste mentioned was of material things, for there was also waste of human values. As two wars in a generation, the second more deadly than the first, amply prove there was also tragic neglect of the things upon which human happiness depends.

Both idealists and realists were too much intoxicated by the new resources which for the first time in human history were at

[Address delivered at the Winter Institute of Arts and Sciences, University of Miami, Coral Gables, Fla., 20 March 1944. Typescript in Special Collections, Otto G. Richter Library, University of Miami.]

their disposal, to look ahead and prepare for the new world that was being born. The intoxication of him whom I have called the idealist was generous. Beholding a future which science and the industrial conquest of the energies of nature was making possible, he thought and acted as if some natural law of inevitable progress were bound to bring all the better possibilities to realization. The one whom I have called the realist was intoxicated by ability to enjoy the goods which the new science and the new industry had brought into the world.

Both alike failed to see that the new forces demanded new methods and new purposes unless they were to all but devour the mankind which produced them. They easily found excuses for their failure. The forces that were operating were so new that they did not have the material upon which to base foresight of their consequences. We of the present day do not have their excuse. The only attitude today which is genuinely realistic is one which sees that we are living in a moving world, one changing at a rate unknown to all previous history. What we call the present is nothing stable. It is but the pivot on which changes turn. And instead of the changes being regulated by some impersonal law of necessary progress and evolution, we and what we as human beings plan and strive to execute is a necessary factor in giving direction to what will happen. In a genuine sense we are creators of the future world.

Science, technology, industrial conquest of nature, are not impersonal forces going their own way independently of us. They are what we human beings do with them and make out of them. Every one knows that tools, machinery, the apparatus of scientific discovery, were invented and constructed by human beings in the course of setting their knowledge at work. What we have failed to see is that the direction in which they move after they have been invented along with the social consequences they produce, are equally a human matter and a human responsibility. Discussions of the possibility and the desirability of human planning are too often oblivious of the fact that refusal to do the best we can in the way of planning is abdication of a responsibility that events have imposed upon us.

I believe that an outline of the things we need most to think about and to plan for may be derived from noting where the beliefs and hopes and methods of men say fifty years ago, or in the nineties, went estray. Politically it was the common belief that the future of democracy was practically assured; that it was certain that the course of events in no very long time would overthrow despotic rulers in all countries. There was also the expectation that the cause of peace among nations was reasonably assured; that war was bound to disappear, along with other relics of barbarism, because of advance in civilization. In the third place, while there was no expectation of the speedy complete abolition of poverty, there was general belief that its dire forms would disappear, and that an enduring era of prosperity would enlarge the extent of the middle class, so as gradually to do away with extremes of wealth and poverty.

It is unnecessary to dwell upon the tragic disappointments these three hopes have undergone in less than fifty years. Instead of steady growth of democracy, the world has seen the rise of dictatorships. And what is even more significant, they have owed their rise in large measure to popular belief that they could accomplish more for the mass of the people than would or could democratic institutions. Two world wars, infinitely more extensive and destructive than anything prior history has to show, have reduced expectation of permanent peace almost to the status of a dream. Economically and industrially, the memory of long years of depression and unemployment, requiring governmental intervention on a large scale, is still vividly with us.

From the vantage point of the present, it is not hard to see how and why the reversals occurred. Men relied upon the growing interdependence of the peoples of the earth to bring about steady advance in the desired direction. Commerce, industry, growth of the means of communication between countries physically far apart, did in fact produce interdependence. As Mr. Willkie recently reminded us, we now live in what to all intents and purposes is One World. Distance, the isolating and divisive power of seas and vast spaces, has been overcome. Steamship and ocean cables began a work which radio and airplane have carried through. For good or bad, we are now and henceforth more like close neighbors in a crowded city than like the widely separate peoples in which our grandparents carried on their affairs in government and industry. The mistake was not in looking forward to a time of interdependence. It lay in supposing that the breaking down of physical barriers, the mere bringing of peoples into closer physical contact, would automatically create *moral* unification.

The debit side of interdependence is more in evidence now than any credit side. An interdependence which is the product simply of industrial production and commercial exchange has turned out to be mainly a creation of new points of friction and extension of old sore spots. Rivalry and competition in industry and in nationalistic ambitions has extended to become deadly competition in all the means of destruction. We cannot pick up a daily paper in which the word "global" does not remind us of the new situation in which we live physically, but without the intellectual, the educational, the moral preparation that might enable us to cope with the problems it thrusts upon us.

Three-quarters of a century ago Abraham Lincoln said that a nation could not endure half-slave and half-free. Today it is true that a civilization cannot endure when physical energies, electricity, light, chemical reaction, physical materials, iron, coal, oil, the atmosphere itself, are brought under a physical control that has revolutionized the face of the globe, while the ideas and ideals that rule us are still largely those of a pre-scientific, pre-industrial, pre-technological age. One can understand, even when one does not sympathize, the home-sickness of political isolationists for return to the conditions of a simpler stage. The trouble is that they want something which is physically impossible, even were it desirable in the abstract. The really dangerous people are the intellectual and educational isolationists who urge us in morals, education, and philosophy, yes even in religion, to shut our minds to the new forces now active in the world and live upon shreds of beliefs that were formed in and that belong to ages that are past and gone. There is today but one genuine conservatism and one genuine realism. Realism is to face the realities of the present world; conservatism consists in planning and carrying out the new measures and policies in educational, political and moral action which will take account of and keep pace with the physical changes hurrying us into an unknown future.

One does not have to argue to prove the existence of global physical conditions. It is enough to point to the war in which this country along with almost every country of the globe is engaged. But the fact that it is war which provides the evidence is also proof of absence of moral unification. It points to the nature of the scope, the immensity and the intensity, of the task which lies ahead of us. It points to the futility of all thinking, planning and practical effort that is not global in reach. As yet these things are still largely local, provincial. Politically, our beliefs and standards are nationalistic, not global. Something that is wholly unreal in the present state of the world called national sovereignty is appealed to and employed as if it had significance.

Beyond paying taxes and engaging in some useful kind of volunteer effort, most of us who are here this evening are not taking part physically in the present war. We do share, and share deeply, in the psychological and moral conditions that have produced this war, and which, if they are allowed their way, will produce the next and still more destructive one. At least this is true as far as we are actuated by ideas and policies that were generated during the period of formation of independent and irresponsible nations, each claiming ultimate unlimited sovereignty for itself. Patriotism then took on a shape and color which were fitted to formation of peoples who touched one another only at their remote edges. To persist in that kind of patriotism when actual forces, like the radio and press and equally like the bomb that spreads death and leaves rubble where there once were cities, are doing away with old boundaries is the road to national disaster, with little assurance that by the time of the next war, our own towns and homes will be as physically exempt as in the present one.

The old world began to melt away in the fifteenth century because of the discovery, exploration and exploitation of new lands. The known civilized world had not previously extended far beyond the Mediterranean Basin even physically; the beliefs and institutions which controlled that world culturally and morally were exclusively the product of the countries, Egypt, Palestine, Greece, Rome, that form that Basin. We owe an immense debt to the contributions made by these countries. But the movement of expansion that had its beginning in the fifteenth century did a great deal more than merely enlarge the physical boundaries of the civilized world. While that was the direct effect of the expansive movement, the new sciences of nature and the new modes of technological invention and production, the rapid spread of commerce, all that goes by the name of the industrial revolution, were its indirect consequences. In the long run they were its important result.

The old astronomy with its finite bounded cosmos, having the earth as its fixed centre, corresponds closely to the limited area of the old area civilization. The physical science throughout this whole earlier period, lasting thousands of years, regarded fixity, changelessness, as the highest principle, the very measure of perfection. Change was taken to be proof of defect and imperfection. The revolution in astronomy, the work of Kepler and Copernicus, opened up a new and unbounded vista, which was the effect and counterpart of the human and geographical expansion that was going on. Revolution in physics and chemistry, and then in the science of plants and animals, put change in the place that had been held by fixity. Time and temporal things encroached upon what had been supposed to be eternal.

The latter part of the nineteenth century and the first decades of the twentieth century are but the physical completion of the expansive movement which for four centuries had been first encroaching upon and then breaking down the walls that kept the peoples of the earth separate and divided.

I say the *physical* completion. For the institutions and basic beliefs of mankind continued for the most part to be those which were created in and suited to the indefinitely longer period of confinement and restriction in which moral and intellectual stability were identified with absence of change. Literally, we are now living between two worlds, and the responsibility placed upon us is that of creating the intellectual and moral attitudes that will support institutions, international and domestic, political, educational and cultural, that correspond to the physical revolution which has taken place; and whose consequences are so largely negative just because of the absence of corresponding institutional change. We cannot indeed understand the present and prepare for the future without knowledge of the past. But it is ignorance of the past, not knowledge of it, which fails to take account of its most outstanding features, namely, the accelerated rate of change and the causes which have produced it:—the new science and the new technology.

The present crisis, which is the manifestation of great physical change combined with absence of corresponding moral and institutional change, goes deep as well as extends far and wide.

There are no traditions which are not challenged or shaken in some respect. The passing away of the geographical, the physical, barriers, which have kept peoples and races and cultures divided for by far the greater extent of human history, has gone far enough to create confusion, uncertainty, and open and widespread conflict. But the intellectual and moral consequences of inbred isolation remain. Rivalry, suspicion, fear and mutual hatred are the fruit. War between nations externally and racial and class antagonisms internally are the visible and tangible manifestation of the disturbance.

If one looks back upon what we call the Victorian Age one finds that the prevailing temper was one of hope. Commerce and intercommunication were automatically going to bring peoples into harmony with one another. It was forgotten that the human factor in the situation was the psychological outlook and the moral disposition that were bred in thousands and thousands of years of ingrowing isolation, and that without radical alteration in this human factor physical and external contact and interaction could, as I have said, be for the most part only an occasion of new friction and extension of old antagonisms.

The positive aspect of the crisis is that mankind in facing a new situation has a new responsibility imposed upon it—a responsibility that leaves nothing untouched. The men who engaged earlier in social philosophizing looked upon the changes that were going on as a process of natural evolution in the direction of greater harmony, cooperation, peace, and increase of opportunity and freedom for all. The present crisis teaches us the folly and futility of trusting to what is called nature, outside of human nature, to a policy of let alone and laissez-faire. But it can also teach us that a revolutionary change in the conditions under which life goes requires a corresponding transformation in our own dispositions and attitudes—one which will substitute looking to the future rather than the past and planning for passive acquiescence; the planning combines cooperative effort in every field, international and domestic, cultural, political, economic, for the isolationism which is an individualism as destructive, as it is impossible, under present conditions.

It is of course much easier to state in general terms the necessity for psychological and moral change than it is to give a bill of particulars. But we may find at least a clue to the direction in which we should move by noting the immense part that has been played by science in production of the present human worldwide situation. It is the basic source of the discoveries and the inventions which are changing the face of the earth. In the last century there was general belief that the advance in science meant advance in general enlightenment that in turn would be the cause of general social advance. This belief was an integral part of the optimistic belief in automatic evolution of which I have spoken. Just now pessimism tends to replace optimism as far as science is concerned.

We are told, and from many and influential quarters, that undue faith in science has been our undoing. We are told that the rise of natural science has invaded and depressed the humane and humanistic values that are rightfully supreme; that it has strengthened materialistic interests and subordinated ideal moral ends and principles. In putting naturalism in the place of supernaturalism, it has led men we are told to immense exaggeration of what is worldly and thus removed the only effective check upon unbridled selfishness. The return to the past which is now being urged upon us has for one of its mainsprings a return to a supernaturalism which puts science and human intelligence in permanent subjection to external authority.

No one who is both observant and candid can deny that things are out of balance. War, economic instability, and the attacks made upon democratic and popular institutions tell the tale. But with respect to science, as to other things, the lesson of the present crisis is the impossibility of going backward and the necessity for going forward. It is a striking fact that the new science began with things that are the furthest away from man, the stars. Gradually, the new ways of employing intelligence to observe and to test were extended to the things of physics and chemistry, and then, to some extent, to living things. But the great opposition aroused by efforts to extend science to the study of life is multiplied indefinitely when it comes to man and distinctively human affairs. The nearer we approach what is human, the greater the resistance to the use of those methods of intelligent observation, report and test that have revolutionized our physical understanding.

There is no doubt that the present crisis is one of disturbed balance between materialistic and moral values. But the lesson to be learned is not the need of arbitrary subjection of scientific inquiry to external authority, but the opposite: The need of systematic application of directed intelligence in discovery of the solid facts of human relationships. A civilization cannot endure in which inquiry is free with respect to knowledge of physical things but is enslaved when it comes to understanding of man and his affairs.

The actual alternative to use of that method of intelligence, which is called science, is use of a mixture of exhortation and with reliance upon traditions, habits, institutions, which were adjusted to bygone conditions, but whose use now is sure to promote confusion and conflict—since they are the outward expression of inner confusion and conflict. This sort of internal division promotes the use of force wielded by external dictatorial authority to try to establish the unity without which after all a society cannot endure. From this point of view, the rise of Fascism and Naziism is no accident.

We too suffer from lack of balance, though it has not gone anything like as far. It is seen, for example, in the attitude commonly taken toward planning. There is not a large industrial enterprise that does not owe success in its own field to systematic planning, based upon study of events carried on by a staff of experts. But in the human field, in social and political matters, planning is ridiculed as impracticable and even as offensive to the spirit of our institutions. We can hardly listen to a political speech or read a newspaper editorial without hearing or seeing social planning referred to as starry-eyed idealism. Yet absence of planning is both the manifestation of the lack of balance between the physical and the moral conditions of our life and is an active promotion of that drifting which leaves us at the mercy of conditions. For planning is everywhere, in little and great things alike, a necessary condition of direction and regulation.

We do not have to search far to discover how the policy of drift—if it can be called a policy to use our intelligence only *after* an emergency has come upon us—conduces to confusion. Consider the high price in human suffering and loss that we have paid for our unwillingness to learn in the field of international relations the lesson which the First World War would seem to have fairly flung in our face. If we had submitted it to examination we should have seen in it a demonstration, more convincing than a demonstration in a laboratory of physical science, of the social disunion and conflict, which has been created by physical science isolated from understanding of human affairs and relationships. While physically speaking the world has been for untold years the spherical body our geography textbooks tell about, it has not been round in a human sense for much more than fifty years. Yet we go on trusting to a combination of luck, outworn tradition and temporary improvisations to meet the problems the new methods of science and technology have forced upon us.

The hope for harmony and peaceful cooperation which animated nineteenth century thought has been rudely challenged. The cause of democracy has been violently assaulted, not just in words but in facts that speak louder than words. What claimed to be the wave of the future swept out of existence institutions of self-government in many countries and replaced them by dictatorships imposed from above. In some European countries events seemed to justify the assertion that democracy belonged to the historic past, and that the only way to overcome the self-seeking and class divisions that inhered (so it was said) in "liberal" societies was rule from above. This rule was to do away with the evils of democratic individualism by imposing total union:—A union that compelled not just unity in action but identity of belief in every phase of life, religious, moral, political, economic. This totalitarianism was enforced by suppression of freedom of inquiry, speech, the press, and assemblage, even for religious purposes. The concentration camp replaced meeting for free discussion. Toleration of diversity of belief and choice of party and creed was said to be a disease of democracy to be excised by radical social surgery.

It is impossible to imagine a more complete denial of the democratic principle of E Pluribus Unum, of unity out of diversity, than is presented by totalitarianism. For toleration in democracy is more than merely putting up with or "standing" diversity of belief, while permitting experimentation with ideas. It is grounded in the belief that the social and moral unity to be achieved by free cooperative discussion is deeper, more solid and more secure than that which can be attained by any kind of external imposition.

The reaction against democracy teaches, however, the same lesson that is taught by the rise of hostility and conflict in the field of international relations. The new situation which has been created by the new methods of science and technology does not demand surrender of democracy on the ground that it fosters an individualism which undermines unity and saps the strength which comes from unity, putting all on the same dead level irrespective of difference in talent. But it does demand reconsideration of the forms and techniques which developed in and were appropriate to this country in a pioneer period. It demands a reconsideration of the nature of individuality and the means by which it can be made secure under present conditions.

The kind of individualism that developed when the natural resources of the country were practically untapped and when there was open opportunity for all to reap the rewards of initiative and enterprise, is not suited to an era in which natural resources have been appropriated and often monopolized, and in which working equality of opportunity easily becomes a byeword with which to cover up inequality bred by vast differences in wealth. The ideals and aims of democracy are the same today that they were in the pioneer era of our country. To suppose, however, that they can be realized by just the same methods, institutions and attitudes that operated in pioneer times is another case of trusting to chance and to the blind uncontrolled working of natural forces to promote the freedom, equality and fraternity that are the enduring goals of democracy.

To speak in more concrete terms, the ideas that are to be entertained and put into practice regarding the function and methods of government have to undergo a great change from those of the earlier period of the Republic. When democracy was new, it stood over against governments that were oppressive and that assumed inequality of classes as the natural and proper state of mankind. The vast open range of free opportunity in this country blended with jealous suspicion of governmental power. The possibilities of democracy as positive and constructive *Self-*government were unrealized and untested. There was no background of experience by which to create a concrete image of a society in which governors and governed were one and the same body, having identical interests.

There is no doubt as to need for continued vigilance. Too easily, as history proves, do the interests of officials become separate from those of the mass of the people. The holding of office then becomes through corruption and oppression a source of private gain. But that fact does not mean such a minimizing of governmental action as is equivalent to political abdication. This conception of individualism is an invitation to totalitarian government as a cure. Viewed intelligently and realistically, we find that a new positive responsibility is imposed. Just as genuinely peaceful relations among nations cannot be secured save by systematic intelligent study, foresight and planning, so with democracy within a nation. The development of procedures and techniques, legal, political, economic, which will foster and sustain equal freedom for all, instead of irresponsible freedom for a few and constraint and depression for the many, is the outstanding social problem of our age. It requires the kind of vigilance which is positively expressed in study, planning, experimentation, to establish institutions which will make equality of opportunity and hence freedom realities for all—not slogans to be manipulated by a class for its one separate interest.

I cannot conclude without saying a few words about the bearing of what has been said upon the prospects and opportunities of youth now growing into maturity. I think there is something new and indicative of the new world into which we are entering in thinking of the young as the guardians of the future. In the past they have been regarded as passive vessels to be filled with traditions formed in the past; as receptive clay to be molded into conformity with customary institutions. The problem of looking to the future instead of to the past, of studying the present to find opportunities for shaping the future through intelligent planning and experimentation, is something new. It is an attitude which is still inchoate. But it exists in sufficient measure to affect seriously our thinking and our action regarding youth and education:— Not just the education given in the schools (though it includes that) but the wider education gained more or less unconsciously in the family, the neighborhood, the playground, by listening to radios and reading newspapers, and above all by association with others.

The problem of so educating youth that they will be effective creators of the future—for it is only through creative acts that they can be its guardians—is a tremendously difficult one. The one certain thing about the future is its uncertainty, just as the only thing which is constant is change. Moreover, nothing could be more unfair than to place upon the young the responsibility for undoing the mistakes of their elders. Nor do I have in mind the absurd notion that the young shall be engaged in endless and futile peering into the future. The best possible preparation for any future is the development of certain attitudes in the present. When change is as rapid and as extensive as it now is, this applies with double force. What is wanted in the way of preparation for the future is that the young be so educated and aware that they are living in a world of change and realization that continued change is inevitable, and that they come to possess some kind of chart of the directions in which change is taking place.

Possession of an open mind is a necessary part of the disposition that can deal effectively with change; but too much of traditional education, especially in the school and other set forms of instruction, tends to create the closed mind—and the closed mind is that which is shut to realization of change and cannot cope with it. The open mind is not one which says in effect "Come right in; there is no one home at home." It is something active and positive. The open mind is the mark of those who have (in all their special learning) learned the eagerness to go on learning and the ability to make this desire a reality. The one precious thing that can be acquired in school or anywhere else is just this constant desire and ability. The most serious defect in our schools and other set forms of instruction is that instead of making learning to be an active ongoing process, they identify it with what is called scholarship and scholarship with ownership of fact and principles acquired with a minimum of active personal observation and stored away in memory. Learning is treated as acquisition of what is stored up in textbooks or is told them by others, and the kind of passive possession which can be tested by examinations. The next effect shapes the mind to look backward; to rob it of power to see and judge what is actually going on around us. There will be almost a revolution in school education when study and learning are treated not as acquisition of what others know but as development of capital to be invested in eager alertness in observing and judging the conditions under which one lives. Yet until this happens, we shall be ill-prepared to deal with a world whose outstanding trait is change.

Learning as eagerness to learn, learning how to learn, includes of course learning use of books. But men who learn use of telescopes and microscopes do not learn to look *at* them. They learn to look *through* them so as better to see other things, and the things they learn to see are the things that exist and act in the common world around them, whether stars in heaven, insects that harm plants, or the chemical changes going on all the time in things, but which without the aid of these devices go unseen. The facts of physiology are not in books. They are in our own bodies, and in the transactions carried on by the organs of the body with the air we breathe, the water we drink, the food we eat. Without knowing how to use books our ability to get at and understand actual facts would be reduced almost to zero. But the usual course is to treat what is in books as an end in themselves instead of means of creating ability to see and judge things which are outside of books.

When men were living in a relatively fixed world, in conditions that changed so slowly that they did not seem to change at all, what was learned from books was a natural supplement to what was learned from life. Living in a world that is changing and that is bound to go on changing whether we like it or not, demands subordination of what is acquired from books. Continued use of scholastic aims and methods that suited the world that no longer exists tends to fixations and to swallowing things whole; to allowing others speaking dogmatically and with external authority to form our judgments and dictate our opinions. These are the things that create the closed mind, and the closed mind is that which incapacitates us to cope with the new conditions which change is sure to bring upon us. In the field of science discovery rules. In the field of industry, invention is supreme. In the field of school instruction, they lag far behind. Even at the present there is an active movement to shut out the moderate progress that has been made by enstating acquisition of what was known or believed in the past as the supreme educational need. In so far as this movement succeeds it will increase the lack of balance that now exists between dispositions and habits that are the result of education and the conditions of the world in which the products of education have to operate. Whether we like it or not we are deeply involved in a complex of new forces which are so new that we have not as yet the ability to direct their course.

Two alternatives present themselves in education. One is to continue to tread the paths that have been worn by scholastic tradition and institutionalized habit. The other alternative is whole-hearted recognition that the schools are a vital part of the moving and changing scene, sharing in movement and having the responsibility of preparing the youth who are guardians and shapers of the future to play their part in forming a free, just and worthy social order. In case we adopt and energetically pursue this course, we shall be able to face the scene of change with hope and courage—traits which are the proper and the just heritage of youth.

The Future of Philosophy

Professor Edman is responsible for the title of my talk. The title is more vivid than any I would have thought of. He tells me that he heard me talk on this subject five years ago. Fortunately, I have forgotten what I said at that time. I had more hopes five years ago than I have now. My fears have increased within the last five years, and my fears have more to do with what I have to say than my hopes.

I shall begin by stating briefly the standpoint from which I see philosophy—the business of philosophy, that with which philosophy is concerned. I think that from my standpoint, the poorest idea about philosophy is that it is a theory about "being," as the Greeks called it, or about "reality," as so much of modern philosophy has assumed that philosophy was. As I may suggest later, one of the incidental positive advantages of the present retreat of philosophy is that it's becoming recently clear that philosophy hasn't made any great success in dealing with "reality." And there is hope that it may take some more human standpoint to deal with.

My standpoint is that philosophy deals with cultural problems, using culture in the broad sense which the anthropologists have made clear to us—dealing with the patterns of human relationships. It includes such subjects as language, religion, industry, politics, fine arts, in so far as there is a common pattern running through them, rather than as so many separate and independent things. The principal task of philosophy is to get below the turmoil that is particularly conspicuous in times of rapid cul-

[Address delivered to the Graduate Department of Philosophy, Columbia University, New York, N.Y., 13 November 1947. Stenographic report in the John Dewey Papers, Box 55, folder 5, Special Collections, Morris Library, Southern Illinois University at Carbondale.]

tural change, to get behind what appears on the surface, to get to the soil in which a given culture has its roots. The business of philosophy is the relation that man has to the world in which he lives, as far as both man and the world are affected by culture, which is very much more than is usually thought.

There wasn't any "physical world" for a very long time, or anything called "physics" as a subject matter as at present. It was only when human culture had developed to a certain point that physics became a distinctive subject matter. A lot of things had to be stripped off—animistic things. The world was previously seen through human eyes in terms of human customs, desires, and fears. It wasn't til the beginning of modern science (the sixteenth century) that a world distinctively physical came into recognized acknowledged existence. This is merely an illustration of the transforming power of culture, in this broad sense of raw material.

Because the business of philosophy is with the relations that exist between man and his world, as both are affected by culture, the problems of philosophy change as the world in which man lives changes. An example is the increased knowledge in our time of machines, technology, etc. The problems of philosophy, therefore, are simply bound to change, although there may be some underlying structures that remain throughout the changes. Therefore, the history of philosophy still has to be written. It needs to be seen and reported in terms of the distinctive features of culture. There is a sort of formalistic recognition of this fact in present histories—they are divided into sections on ancient, medieval, and modern philosophy, western and oriental philosophy. These serve as certain headings for the material. But they are not carried out in the details of philosophical systems.

I come now to my hopes and fears. The hope for philosophy is that those who engage in philosophy professionally will recognize that we are at the end of one historical epoch and at the beginning of another. The teacher and student should attempt to tell what sort of change is taking place. In all events, this recognition of changes, of ages, of epochs in the world's history isn't an invention of mine. Every history formally recognizes division into ages. We are approaching a change from one period to another; we are undergoing the same kind of change, as a change, that happened when the medieval period lost its hold on the people's beliefs and activities. We recognize this now as the beginning of a new epoch. This new epoch is largely the consequence of the new natural science, which began about the sixteenth century with Galileo and Newton, as the applications of that science revolutionized men's ways of living and their relations to each other. These have created the characteristics of modern culture and its essential problems.

The more destructive features are more prominent than the more constructive phases. For a while, no survey of the world was presented without some reference to the fission of the atom. We see now that this is significant because it is a symbol of the changes that have been going on in science.

There's no secret in the fact that physical aspects of scientific inquiry and their applications have very far outrun inquiry into human subject matter—economics, politics, and morality. This over-weighting on one side gives the clue to what should be hoped for in a further development of philosophy. The philosophers of the sixteenth and seventeenth centuries may have thought they were dealing with the theory of reality, but they were actually forwarding the new natural science. They were engaged in criticizing science as it had come down in the Middle Ages from Aristotle. They were presenting the necessity for a different kind of cosmology. In the eighteenth century, especially in France during the Enlightenment, and to some extent in England, philosophers attempted to do something of the same kind in human and social subjects, but the materials and tools were lacking. They got rid of many things, but their constructive activities never amounted to so much. I think that now we have potentially the intellectual resources that would enable philosophy to do something of the same kind for the forwarding of human and social subjects. The older physical science, after stripping away the animistic survivals, had no concern with human problems. This science was about little lumps of matter which were separated from one another, existing in external space and time, which were themselves separated from each other and from everything that happened. Physical science has nearly demolished that point of view. The material of the physical world is such that, through the increasing applications in physiology and biology, it isn't so fixedly set over against human concerns as it used to be. Science itself has got rid of matter, in the old sense. But this does not mean that matter has become a background to be related to human concerns, which could not happen as long as the Newtonian view prevailed.

There are many obstacles in realizing the hope I speak of. One very serious obstacle is the state of the world now, which is so fearful, so frightful, in the literal sense of the word, that it's very hard to face. The tendency is to look to some unreal solution to its problems which is essentially reactionary—going back to the ideas of Greek or medieval times, or in philosophy to adopt a method of escape because we don't seem to be able to handle the actual problems, which, if we are at the beginning of a new epoch, would probably take centuries to work out effectively.

The most discouraging thing in philosophy is neo-scholastic formalism, which also happened in the Middle Ages. It is form today for its own sake, in so many cases. A form of forms, not forms of subject matter. But the subject matter is so chaotic and confused today in the world that it is difficult to handle. This is how I would explain this retreat from work in the facts of human life into purely formal issues—I hesitate to call them issues because nothing ever issues except more form! It's harmless for everyone except philosophers. This retreat accounts for the growing disinterest of the general public in the problems of philosophy.

Totalitarianism, the attempt to find a complete set of blueprints that will settle every question, is another form of reaction, and a much more dangerous form. We have seen this in fascism and now today, in my opinion, in bolshevism.

It takes considerable courage to see into the present situation. To see it through will be the work of a long period. But the hope for philosophy will be that it will take part in the initiation of movements that will be carried through by human activity.

The first step is to see as frankly as possible the kind of world that we are living in and that which is likely to come. We should at least turn our eyes toward it and face it even if we can't do much with our hands and muscles about it. But what we should not do is to spin a lot of webs to operate as screens to keep us from seeing the reality of the situation. In this respect, formalism may be a hopeful sign. It may be the beginning of a general recognition that philosophers weren't getting anywhere dealing with matter at large, as with some ultimate entity. This reaction might be the opening of a more serious attempt to face the cultural problems of today. Science has done away with so many of the dualisms of the last few centuries, mind and matter, the individual and society, etc. These are simply echoes that once had a vitality because of cultural conditions. We are growing out of these. We need to have an idea of a systematic kind of what we might grow into.

Philosophy can't settle these issues any better than seventeenth century philosophy could settle problems of physics, but today philosophers can analyze problems and present hypotheses that might gain enough currency and influence to serve so that they could be tested by the only final method of testing, which is practical activity. (Applause.)

One thing more, and that is—you who are students really have as great an opportunity as any students of any subject ever had at any time, but it will take a lot of patience, a lot of courage, and, if I may say so, considerable guts!

What *Is* Democracy?

At no time in the past has the world faced as many and as serious problems as at the present time. For at no past time has the world in which man lives been so extended and so complicated in its interconnected parts. This statement is made, however, not for its own sake but as an introduction to the aspect of the world's problems that will be here considered. The recent historical scene would have been regarded as impossible not more than half a century ago. For at that time the progressive triumph of democracy, both as an idea of political philosophy and as a political fact, seemed fairly assured. Of late years its very existence has been so challenged that its fate seemed to hang in the balance and even now its future is far from settled. The first attack made upon it was open, unconcealed. The military assault of Japan, Italy, and Germany and their satellites was attended and supported by the ever-repeated charge that the democratic ideal had outlived its usefulness, and that new and different order was urgently required.

The nations that made the military attack suffered a crushing defeat. The present state of the world proves, without need for extended argument, that the underlying ground of social, economic, and political principles is far from being crushed. The struggle between democratic beliefs as they have been understood and put into practice in the past is more overt and acute than before or during the military conflict. The question "What *is* Democracy?" is not in the existing state of the world's affairs an academic question. Nor at present is it a matter of defending democratic principles and policies against attack by those who openly, avowedly, treated them with complete scorn. The

[Typescript in the John Dewey Papers, Box 55, folder 3, Special Collections, Morris Library, Southern Illinois University at Carbondale, ca. 1946(?).]

conflict is now between two radically different, completely opposed, systems each of which claims to be faithful to the cause of democracy.

A conflict which is of direct practical importance to hundreds of millions of people and upon which the issue of world-wide war or peace may depend is not a theoretical question to be settled by the arguments of political scientists. One of the national states which was an ally of the states that represent democracy as it has been traditionally understood and practiced now engages in an attack upon the latter which is both ideological and diplomatic and which, by common consent, might pass into strife of armed forces. For it accuses the traditionally democratic peoples of the West in Europe and America of betraying the cause of democracy and holds itself up as representing in its policies and principles the fulfillment of the democratic idea now misrepresented and betrayed by peoples who profess democracy but who fail to carry it into practice in one very important part of human relationships.

That part is, of course, that of human relations as they are affected by the economic order, by the conditions under which industry and finance are conducted. However, I do not intend to discuss the conflict as if its focus and centre is primarily located in the matter of economic policies. It is my belief, for instance, that economic policies have been in the past the weakest aspect of traditional western democracies. Nor do I propose to defend these democracies on the ground that each one of them, not excluding the United States which has perhaps been the country the most attached to an "individualistic" economic order, is actively modifying *in its own behalf* its traditional economic system. The fact that "capitalism" is so far from being a rigidly fixed system that in fact it is in almost a fluid state is pertinent to some of the charges brought against this and other western democracies but not to the issue I am discussing;—namely, what is the centre and the foundation of the democratic idea and policies?

This centre and base is, in my judgment, thrown into clear and impressive relief by the fact that the nation from which the assaults now proceed has taken over and improved upon the general totalitarian philosophy and practice, one species of which it was actively fighting only a few years ago—and which in fact is historically continuous with the anti-democratic history of its own political past. For this totalitarianism reveals with startling clearness that the central issue is that of respect for freedom of intelligence versus disrespect for it so great as to amount to its effective denial and suppression when it stands, even passively, in the way of political-economic totalitarian policy.

That no professedly democratic country has in the past been without flaw in its devotion to freedom of intelligence as carried out in freedom of the various ways in which it is publicly manifested is of course true. In my own country, for example, its Bill of Rights inserted there by the efforts of our first great and typical Democrat, Thomas Jefferson, is a guarantee of freedom of speech, writing, publication, and assembly for discussion, with respect to all public issues. Moreover, the Supreme Court of the Federation was charged in effect with ability to declare null and void all laws passed by the political units of the Federation which infringed upon the working effectiveness of this guaranteed freedom of intelligence in operation. As I have suggested, we have not always lived up in times of trouble and stress to this guarantee. But it is true that the idea is so embodied not just in the written legal Constitution of the country but in the hearts and minds of the people that every period of reaction has called out a successful period of protest and restoration.

This last remark is not made for the purpose of defense much less of a boast. It is made to indicate that this principle of respect for free intelligence in action goes so deep and extends so far that it has to be continually re-asserted and re-invigorated as conditions change. It is so far from being self-executing that in every period of crisis it has to be actively fought for though, happily, so far not by recourse to arms. The present assault made by a state in the interest of policies executed by totalitarian methods of violent (as well as ideological opposition) suppression of any departure in press, literature, public assembly, even private conversations, and even conduct of physical and biological inquiries, from officially established totalitarian doctrines, points to maintenance of free intelligence in public operation as the focal issue in the various problems of intelligence.

Another great American democrat, Abraham Lincoln, left as his heritage the statement that democracy is Government of, for, and *by* the people. I have italicized the preposition "by" because government cannot possibly be by the people save when and where the freedom of intelligence is publicly and actively supported. It is debatable whether it can for any long period be *for* the people and not for a governing clique or bureaucracy save where the rights of public discussion and criticism are held inviolate. Revolutionary periods, of which from a world-wide point of view the present is one, tend toward a concentration of power. The concentration claims for itself that it is in the best interests of the people at large. At the outset, that may be the case in fact. But nothing is more certain than unless its movement is attended by scrupulous attentive observance of the principle of freedom of intelligence in action it will rapidly degenerate into the rule of a small section, maintained by use of force, in its own special interest. It is for this reason that it is so peculiarly, almost uniquely, important at the present time not to be distracted into allowing any issue, no matter how useful in itself, to displace freedom of intelligence in public communication by means of speech, publication in daily and weekly press, in books, in public assemblies, in scientific inquiry, as the centre and burning focus of democracy. Nothing will be more fatal in the end than surrender and compromise on this point. Now, more than ever, it is urgently necessary to hold it in steady view as the heart from which flows the life-blood of democracy.

I should not close without definite recal of the fact that it was the pioneers of freedom of thought and speech in France in the eighteenth century, who in spite of every sort of interference by those professing to speak in the name of moral authority and social stability made that century the period of The Éclaircissement, The Enlightenment, out of which has issued all that is best and truest in the democratic spirit first in the civilization of the West and now in promise if not yet in execution of the entire world. If the peoples who have behind them and still with them the living tradition of supreme and steady regard for freedom of intelligence in operation in all channels of communication now live up to their heritage, they, we, shall issue from the present crisis with purification of the life-blood of democracy. In surmounting the cruel trials of the present crisis we shall have opened the way to a nobler, because freer, manifestation of the human spirit.

Education for a New and Better World

There has probably never been a time in all history when the world was as disturbed as it is today. For one thing however troubled the world has been in the past, it was smaller; there wasn't so much of a world to be pulled in different directions and in doubt both about where it *is* going and where it should go. There was a time when men sailed on ponds and lakes. The waters might be agitated; those who were caught in the storm were badly troubled; perhaps they perished. But after all the shock was local. Today we are on a trackless sea; and there are no merely local storms. For good or for evil we are bound together:—That no one lives to himself is not a moral precept any longer; it is a literal statement of a terrifying fact. Whether it will always remain terrifying, or whether it can be transformed into a promise of a new and better world is perhaps the most unsettled and most uncertain of all the disturbing things of the world in which we now live. What we are going to do with the power put at our disposal by the broken atom and what it is going to do with us, whether it is to be used for destruction or for creation confronts us as a symbol of our present world-wide state.

I sometimes think that we people of the older generation should be ashamed to look the younger generation in the face in view of the kind of world we are turning over to them in which to live. It seems at times as if all the responsibilities we had shirked, all the opportunities we had missed, as well as all the mistakes we have made were the chief heritage we are bequeathing to those who come after us and who have to live in the world we are passing on to them. But nothing can deprive the young of the in-

[Typescript in the John Dewey Papers, Box 54, folder 8, Special Collections, Morris Library, Southern Illinois University at Carbondale.]

alienable gift of youth, and of the vigor and the fresh outlook that are a part of that g[ift.] In a way the world begins over again as every new generation enters the field. The scene about them is a challenge to courage and to energy. And it is especially at the present time a challenge to patience and endurance, to fortitude and resolution. We are at one of the turning points in history. As our most beloved American said at a crisis in our own history we shall either greatly win or meanly lose. The only thing that in the end can be fatal is the cowardice that refuses to make a choice as to the kind of world we want to live in and that withdraws from a struggle to bring it in existence.

Amid all the disturbances and uncertainties there is one thing which is constant and which is the same everywhere. There has never been a time in history when education had the importance in shaping the life of the future that it has now. That means that there was never a time when the direction taken by the ideas and ideals, the choices and efforts of the young, had the importance they have now. It was never as plain as it is now that schooling is at most but a part of education; that education includes everything that shapes what men really believe, what they most desire, what they are loyal to; the purposes for which they strive and for which they are willing to sacrifice. Schooling is important but its work hardly goes beyond furnishing the tools, the instruments, with which to strive for realization of the deep affections of the heart and the steadfast and informed aims of the head. Youth have now to take a greater part in their own education than ever before; education is nothing less than the making of character and of mind and the prime question is whether the young are going to have their characters and minds made for them by outside pressures or they are going to have an active share themselves in the making of the world in which they will live. And if I may quote a saying of another great American at a critical time, "the only thing we have to fear is fear." Man still has it in his power to shape his own destiny. Just now he is disturbed and embarrassed not because of weakness but because he is temporarily so overpowered by what he has accomplished in a short time that he hasn't time yet to learn what to do with them.

It is this fact that gives special point to the question whether the youth of the world are to take an active part in the formation of their own minds or characters, or whether they are to be putty to be shaped and moulded by those who arrogate to themselves the possession of the understanding and other means of creating the future. It is an aid when one is in a fog or in the dark to see where the ways part; one can then at least choose the direction in which he moves ahead. I have been reading recently the official instructions issued by the educational authorities of a great and powerful nation to the teachers of that country regarding the intellectual and moral treatment of the youth who are put in their charge. A typical passage reads: "A morally educated individual is one who in his own conduct subordinates his own interests to the service of his Motherland and his people. Such service presupposes wrath and hatred toward the enemies of the Motherland." One may properly admire subordination of personal interests to the interests of the community. But when one finds that it has to be based on wrath and hatred and upon constant inculcation of the belief that one's own community is already the "leader of all mankind," "the most advanced of all mankind," that their own political leader "is the leader of the workers of the entire world," and one finds how every detail of teaching, discipline, every sport, is systematically organized for production of a single pattern of thought and action, which is protected by a steel armor of intolerance and hatred against everything else, one may combine admiration for the thoroughness with which every possible device and resource is brought into the service of education as a means of shaping society, with profound doubt and disbelief regarding the kind of society that can be formed by suppression of every idea, every impulse, every desire, every outside aspiration and purpose that departs from a pattern formed and imposed from above.

However, I am not so much concerned here to express complete repudiation of the controlling end and ideal of this scheme for my own country and for myself as I am to indicate the parting of the ways of human life which is so extreme that choice between them decides the direction in which education and youth will now move and what sort of a human world will exist in the future.

The more we respect the faith which totalitarian nations put in the power of education to give direction to people in a confused and distracted world, the more we are bound to inquire what sort of a world will result if there is success in moulding men and women into a single pattern based upon a single set of principles assumed to embody final truth, the whole defended and protected by cultivation of hatred and wrath against everything that does not conform and that makes a supreme virtue out of the extreme use of violence and even systematic misrepresentation that are justified when they are used in behalf of *the* higher morality. And in asking this, we shall if we are intelligent, ask what is the alternative course and policy for education. If we are as serious, as earnest, as devoted to using education to extend and deepen the realization of a free life as the rulers of totalitarian societies are to use it for production of the fixed predetermined type of life they are set upon, what shall *we* try to do, what shall our guiding principles be? These are large questions; too large to be answered offhand and too large for any of us to be able to answer except by means of long continued cooperative work.

But a few things we can be sure of. We can be sure that the world's need for a fuller and deeper free life cannot be achieved by merely persisting in even the best of the democratic institutions and practices of the past. New occasions and conditions teach new duties. The only way in which the burning zeal, the ardor, which once animated, directed the efforts of freedom-loving peoples can be rekindled, and by which to attain a devotion and energy matching that manifested by those who would save the world by imposition of a single fixed pattern, is to know we cannot live off or upon the past no matter how fine its victories. Freedom of life is not something that can be preserved. It is something that has to be created and recreated. The more marked the change in conditions, the more urgent the need for change in the practices by which genuine free life can be attained. The change in world conditions in the last half-century alone is greater than all previous human history. Here is the challenge to courage, imagination, vital energy. For after all fear is not our only enemy. Complacence and passivity stand in our way. We need faith, but faith in ourselves and the possibility of our making a better because freer world can be nourished into enduring strength only as we put faith in intelligence. Invention has done wonders in the material world. Discovery and invention are akin to the spirit of youth. The technical and industrial matters' continual movement into the new and the use of all methods for exploring the new as we move in are the most marked features of the modern world. The open opportunity and the open task is now to use our vast scientific and technical resources for discovery and invention of the ever-growing new in the things that are human. Imposition of fixed principles may have temporary appeal and may give temporary relief. In the long run—and perhaps not so very long—it marks the road to collision and explosion. Man is bewildered but not so bewildered as to find for long security in chains.

Comment on Recent Criticisms of Some Points in Moral and Logical Theory

A variety of circumstances have made it virtually impossible for me to take proper account of criticisms passed upon one or another aspect of my philosophical views. In the present paper two recent instances of criticism are selected for comment because their respective subjects occupy a central position in the theory of *method* underlying my views on all philosophical topics thereby determining the type of conclusions reached. For this reason, the present discussion will, I hope, be seen to have an important bearing much beyond the limits of the especial points taken up for explicit consideration.

The first matter discussed has to do with a point that is focal in the theory of morals as I have dealt with that subject in my writings. The particular criticism which is the occasion of these present comments is found in recent writings of Dr. Morton G. White. They are concerned (with respect to their bearing upon my ethical views) with the *method* by means of which valid—in commonly accepted language, *objectively* sound—conclusions are to be attained regarding what is good, right, morally obligatory, etc., in human conduct. The special point, as distinct from method in general, which is involved is the distinction made in my writings between that which is desir*ed,* a *de facto* matter, and what is desir*able;* that is, in my treatment, what *de jure should* or *ought* to be desired. The specific criticisms made by Dr. White already have been so amply and so adequately dealt with by Dr. Sidney Hook on the base of an extensive and critically accurate knowledge of my writings that I have only as concerns the particular views criticized to refer interested

[Typescript in the John Dewey Papers, Box 59, folder 5, Special Collections, Morris Library, Southern Illinois University at Carbondale, ca. 1950.]

persons to Dr. Hook's discussion and express my deep and grateful appreciation.[1]

Since the point about to be discussed concerns the question of method of knowing and of reaching conclusions it covers ground not included in Dr. Hook's discussion as it was not directly pertinent to the phase of Dr. White's criticisms to which he replied. Accordingly I cannot claim his assent to what I am going to say though I hope it will be found by him to agree with his own position on the subject under consideration. The methodological philosophical issue involved in Dr. White's criticism of the distinction of *kinds* or type of judgment (propositional statement if one prefers) between "X is desir*ed*" and "X is desir*able*" comes out most clearly in a passage (p. 206 of his essay) in which Dr. Hook engages in a brief consideration of "one variant" of Dr. White's criticism to the effect that "knowledge of the causes and consequences of our desire and of what is desired does not make the desired desirable unless . . . we can get back to some rock-bottom *desirable in itself*."

The words I have taken the liberty of italicizing bring out very clearly the fundamental difference between the methodological position of Dr. White and my own. I do not wish to attach adjectives to Dr. White's position with respect to method which he might wish to repudiate, although it is evident to me that dependence upon that which is "desirable in itself," that is in complete independence of and isolation from investigation of the existential context of "conditions and consequences," involves the assumption of what has been known in ethics as the method of *Intuition* and in epistemology as the necessity of the *A priori* to warrant the validity of statements made on empirical grounds. At all events, I can and do take this reference to this dependence upon the "desirable *in itself*" as the only ground upon which a valid distinction can be made the *de facto* "desired" and the *de jure* "desirable" as a highly significant indication of the methodological ground for my emphasis upon investigation of condi-

1. The article by Dr. Hook in the recent symposium volume edited by him, *John Dewey: Philosopher of Science and Freedom*, is entitled "The Desirable and Emotive in Dewey's Ethics" (pp. 194–216) with a running page heading "Dewey's Ethical Theory." The part of the essay dealing with Dr. White's criticism will be found on pp. 200–207.

tions and consequences as the only way by which valid statements about the desirable can be reached. That is to say the general philosophical bearing and import of reference to conditions and consequences is to bring ethical knowings and what are to be the ethically known out of the domain of absolutes and as far as concerns *method* identify the method of philosophical inquiry in general and moral inquiries in particular with that now pursued as matter of course in scientific and technological matter: indeed in *all non*-philosophical matters. I do not question, of course, the personal right of Dr. White to take the position which as I see it is an heritage from times when scientific method as now practiced did not exist and when the rational as distinct from the observational had to be invoked to guarantee the validity of beliefs and statements. But I am entitled in my own behalf to point out that the method employed in making the distinction between the *de facto* desired and the *de jure* desirable is simply the method pursued in all sciences which conduct inquiries intended to find out what is *fact*—"*objective*" fact to indulge in a pleonasm—and in distinction from what is taken to be fact apart from systematic inquiry into "conditions and consequences."

This last expression brings the present discussion to Dr. White's assertion that my distinction depends upon my having "generated a normative or *de jure* proposition by performing a suitable operation on merely *de facto* propositions." Am I guilty of reaching my distinction in the way here set forth I am certainly to be accused of depending upon a variety of intellectual magic. The statement as made completely neglects however the conditions which in my actual account provide an "operation" with a claim to be "suitable." In the first place, the operation is performed not *on* propositions but *with* them, by means of them; and in the second place the propositions *with* which the "desirable" is determined as normative or *de jure*, in distinction from *de facto* propositions regarding things desired *de facto*, are the outcomes of systematically conducted investigations, in distinction from propositions casually picked up; and in the third place the "conditions and consequences" involved are not just so many cases of *de facto* desireds. The inquiries involved have to do with an actually existent situation in which something needs to be done; which is of a kind in which *not* doing anything may be, in its consequences, the most fatal sort of doing—as when by-standers stand idly by and allow a wounded man to bleed to death.

I hope that even Dr. White would admit that the inquiries by which the proposition "the whale is a fish" were transformed into the statement "the whale is warmblooded" (and hence *not* a fish) did not consist of operations performed on any propositions but upon systematic deliberately conducted examination of the antecedent conditions and the subsequent consequences of a whole set of activities characteristic of the behavior of whales. Dr. White's reduction of the desirable to that which is desired "under normal conditions" is wholly satisfactory to me provided the literally terrible ambivalence in normal is cleared away— which I do not find he even tries to do. "Normal" in the sense of what happens usually, on the average, etc., is certainly *de facto*. The statement that "X is objectively red" is not, if "objective" has any distinctive import, of that kind. "Normal" conditions in the latter case have normative force; the conditions in question are not those of a majority or even the total number of cases in which X appears red. They are conditions instituted by contin- ued experimental inquiries conducted for a definite end-in-view. When this fact is recognized, I welcome the formal or method- ological identification of the statement "X is desirable" with "X is objectively red," for if "objective" has any distinctive *relevant* sense in the latter proposition, that sense, like that of "normal" as having any relevance to the point at issue in the phrase "nor- mal conditions," is itself intrinsically normative or *de jure*. I wel- come Dr. White's identification when its direction is completely reversed. *All* scientifically grounded propositions, those reached by inquiry satisfying the conditions imposed by what the word "scientific" names and stands for, are normative propositions; exactly as, for a final example, "X is *objectively* red" signifies that the case in question fulfills, satisfies the conditions that are constituted by a definitive standard of a certain number of waves of a certain spatial length occurring in a specified unit of time. There are *de facto* and empirical propositions having to do with what has existed and with what now is observed to exist. State- ments that a given thing is *desired*, whether once or a million of times, are of this *de facto* kind or variety. The statement that a thing is desirable, that it should be desired, is *de facto* with respect not to what has existed or now exists but in reference to the activity which is required to bring it into existence. It too is an empirical proposition but only as "empirical" in this case is identical with the *experimentally* determined. Unfortunately, or perhaps fortunately, "normal" conditions for and of an experiment that yields a warranted conclusion do not lie around nor force themselves upon us. They are obtained by undertaking the kind of activities which the best available knowledge at the time informs us *should be* tried in order to find out their specific consequences in and for further knowing.

Pedagogy:—Memorandum

If the work undertaken and planned in psychology and ethics is to be what it should be, it is highly important that it be closely related to work in pedagogy. Even if the opportunity for a department in pedagogy were not (as it is in my judgment) the most promising of any now offered to a University—especially in the west—it is a practical necessity in order to give practical illustrations of checks upon the work in Psychology and Ethics.

On the other hand, the work thus far done in Pedagogy in this country has been comparatively useless; it has been mechanical and vague because separated from psychology and social ethics, or else an artificial deduction from a purely deductive psychology. Ethics and Psychology are to Pedagogy, rightly undertaken, what the theoretical study of scientific principles is to work in a laboratory. Both suffer equally from division. Even in Europe they have not except at Jena begun to realise the possibilities of work in education. It is possible to go much further in this country than even at Jena, because in the absence of central official organization here, the tendency to turn to the University for the guidance there got from the Government is strong and growing every day.

It is my honest and firm conviction that the American University which first sees rightly the existing situation in education and acts upon the possibilities involved, will by that very fact command the entire University situation. I also firmly and honestly believe that Chicago is the most ripe place in America for undertaking this work.

[Mimeograph memorandum (1894?) to President William Rainey Harper, Presidents' Papers, 1899–1925, Special Collections, the Joseph Regenstein Library, University of Chicago.]

Details

1. An educational museum, that is, collections of apparatus, charts, books illustrating teaching of subjects; plans, architecture, etc., of schools, etc., etc.

2. A staff, at first of two or three, ultimately of five or six specialists in various directions and at the same time with personal knowledge of public school work. This staff to divide their time between visiting schools, reporting on their work, giving them suggestions, etc., and lecturing in the University on methods of teaching in their particular branch.

a. This will bring University into direct contact with preparatory schools. The advantages of this do not need to be stated. Even such an occasional visiting of schools by a committee, a day or two at a time, in Michigan, has turned students greatly in that direction; besides, it has given the University a hold on the school curriculum. If such results have been got in this unsystematic way, we might be hopeful as to the results of regular organization.

b. It would ensure real and practical teaching in methods. The present tendencies in University chairs of pedagogy to vague and unrelated theorizing would be made impossible.

c. Advanced students could be taken out on the visits and study educational conditions at first hand.

d. The University would get into such connection with the schools as to be able to recommend teachers more directly and systematically and thus not only afford an outlet for its teachers, but get a direct supervision over and control of school methods.

3. A practice or experimental school, such as now exist at Jena and Columbia, extending ultimately from kindergarten clear up.

The need of this is self-evident. As to its cost, it could be started in a small way, and with no expense to the University, being officially unconnected, yet with the encouragement of the University authorities and under the control of the department of philosophy. As it grew, it could finally be officially assimilated to the University.

This is the ultimate flower of the whole scheme. Existing Universities and even Normal Schools are simply training individual teachers. The advance will come by joining this to a direct reaction upon and readjustment of the existing school.

The Russian School System

THE CHAIRMAN: *To many of us here this evening, this is an occasion not only of intellectual interest but of a very deep and personal interest. We have come, on the one hand, to hear important news and interpretations of Russia. We have also come to welcome a beloved teacher and colleague and neighbor and citizen and friend.*

We are aware, of course, that to present him in a mere setting of our local interests would be a bad case of myopia, and would distort the whole perspective. As I said the other day, in presenting Mr. Dewey as a philosopher, no institution, no university, no community, and I might even go so far as to say no nation, has an exclusive claim on him.

If we were to attempt to press that claim there would be, as I said, protests all along the line, from China and Japan, and from Mexico and South America, and from Turkey and Russia; even some of the more backward peoples, such as members of the United States Senate (laughter), and the members of the English Parliament are showing some signs of recognizing his world-wide citizenship.

In presenting him this evening as an educator, all of this holds with increased force. It was not as a technical philosopher, but as a philosophical educator that Mr. Dewey came to have the world for his parish. It was his Essays in Experimental Logic *and his volume on* Leibnitz, *and his* Experience and Nature, *and that little yellow book called* School and Society, *which was translated into French and German and Spanish and Chinese and Japanese and Turkish and Czechish.*

In spite of illustrious precedence to the contrary from Plato

[Address delivered at Leon Mandel Hall, University of Chicago, 21 February 1929. Stenographic report in the Anita McCormick Blaine Papers, State Historical Society of Wisconsin, Madison.]

*down, there are still people who think if you talk of a man as a
philosopher and an educationalist that you are accusing him of
leading a double life. And they are usually quite sure that they
know which is Dr. Jekyll and which is Mr. Hyde. These people,
of course, usually are those who still cherish the old cloister and
monastic conception of philosophy, what we might call the "sedative" conception of philosophy.*

*Those of us who know Professor Dewey's philosophy know
that it is not sedative; that it is a challenge and a call; that instead
of rendering us insensitive to the ills and sorrows of our ter-
restrial life, it is a call to attack their source, and try to substitute
for them more permanent and more generally distributed goods.
Hence, therefore, the very close connection between such a philosophy and education.*

*I once heard Professor Dewey say—I do not know, but I think
he would still subscribe to it—that the chief justification for philosophy was to be found in what philosophy had to contribute to
a statement of the aims and methods of education.*

*It is therefore, with a good conscience and a glad heart that I
present to you the one and inseparable John Dewey, the educational philosopher, and John Dewey, the philosophical educator.
(Applause.)*

Ladies and Gentlemen: In addition to expressing my great
pleasure at having a renewed relationship with the University of
Chicago, after a period of about a quarter of a century of interruption, I wish on this occasion of the William Vaughn Moody
Lectureship, to state also the great satisfaction that it is to me
that this particular phase of the taking up of old ties should be
connected with the name and memory of my former colleague
and friend. I want also in that to include the satisfaction that it
gives me to be associated in any way with also my old-time
friend, Mrs. Vaughn Moody.

The problem of trying to give in a short time any picture of
Russian education possesses almost insuperable difficulty; and
almost every time I attempt to speak of it, I am amazed at my
own rashness in attempting a task which is practically impossible
of execution, for Russia is a very large country—I need not remind you—one larger than the United States.

I have a Russian friend in New York who said, fortunately perhaps for our relations—this was before I had ever been to Russia, but I had talked about it—he said: "I have been in the United States ten years, and I know the English language pretty well, and I have had pretty wide contacts, but I would not venture to attempt to make any general statements about the United States." Here I find myself, with no knowledge of the language, the Russian language, and after a very short stay there, attempting something which, as he said, seemed to him a matter of very great temerity, as he would not think of undertaking it about this country, where he had lived for ten years. My excuse, if any is needed, is that the educational situation there is such an enormously interesting one, and it presents so many features which, if not novel taking them separately one by one, are certainly novel taken in their union, in their combination, in their synthesis; that there is really something new being contributed to the world in educational ideals, educational theory, and also educational practice; and—something of which I am sure—if they are successful in the generation that is coming in carrying the development further, will be something from which the whole world will be glad to learn educationally.

The large part of the difficulty of giving anything like an adequate account, or even one coherent enough to be interesting, regarding education, is the fact that in the whole principle and idea they are trying to break down the traditional isolation of the school from life outside the school, and to make the school activities dovetail at every point into the social, political, economic, cultural life without. Therefore, to apprehend, grasp the nature of the school system in its real significance, one really ought to have a considerable initiation, preparatory initiation with reference to the social conditions, tendencies, problems and aims of Russian life itself. Not merely the small time at my disposal but my own ignorance forbids me from going into that matter.

In the short time that I was there, I had no contact with politicians or economists; no time for anything, opportunity for anything but contact with pupils and teachers and the various lines of cultural activity. And so I saw but one side of Russian life, and that in my own opinion the brighter and more hopeful side of the Russian situation.

I am, however, going to refer to one element in the background which I think has a good deal to do with the ideals, methods of the present school system. A few weeks ago, after my return, I was reading the memoirs of the French Ambassador at the Court of what was first St. Petersburg, then Petrograd, now Leningrad; a man who had been there some time, was there during the outbreak of the war, and who remained after the Kerensky revolution. And his memoirs are very largely, practically exclusively, in the form of a diary, giving the news taken day by day; a very cultivated, intelligent, trained observer, with that lucidity of statement and detachment of powers of observation which are so characteristic of the Frenchman.

The particular extract from him that I want to read is something that he jotted down in his diary on the 2nd of June 1915. The date is somewhat important, because that meant that the war was then less than a year old, which is very significant in connection with what I am going to read. His account is an account of an interview with a man who at that time was a great industrialist, capitalist, manager of men and materials in Russia. And here is what this man said less than a year after the outbreak of the war.

The days of Tsarism are numbered. The Tsarism is lost, lost beyond hope. But Tsarism is the very framework of Russia, and the sole point of unity for the nation. Revolution is now inevitable. It is only waiting for a favourable opportunity. An opportunity will come. It doesn't make any difference how, what starts it. But a revolution isn't the worst peril threatening Russia, for a revolution strictly speaking is only the substitution of one political system for another by violence. A revolution can be of great benefit to a country, if it can reconstruct after having destroyed.

But with us a revolution can only be destructive, because the educated class is only a tiny minority without organization, political experience, or contact with the masses. To my mind that is the greatest crime of Tsarism; it will not tolerate any centre of political life and activity outside its own bureaucracy. When this goes down in revolution, the whole Russian State will dissolve. Undoubtedly it will be the intellectuals and the bourgeois who will give the signal for the revolution, thinking they're saving Russia; but from the bourgeois revolution, we shall at once descend to the working class revolution; soon after to the peasant revolution, and then will begin the most frightful anarchy, interminable anarchy—ten years at least of complete chaos.

Anyone who reads this book, written by a rather conservative and exceedingly skilful observer, will get a picture of the continuous disorganization and disintegration of all Russian life, in its political, economic, as well as its military features, going on progressively through the war. And when you have such a statement as this, when the war has been going on only a year, I think the greatest wonder is that the country held together and continued to fight at all for as long a period as it did.

I think anyone who takes into account such statements of the background as come here from an observer who, if he was prejudiced at all, was prejudiced on the conservative side, will get a point of view from which to understand the Russian revolution, which is absolutely impossible to get if we take merely what happened in 1917, and in the immediately succeeding year. This understanding would not lead one to justify or apologize for everything that was done, but he would see it as historically speaking, humanly speaking, almost inevitable.

There was just one point where this prophecy is in error, and that is in assuming that the period of chaos and anarchy would continue for at least ten years. The one thing that this great Russian millionaire and industrialist did not see was that there was a group, and particularly a man like Lenine, where there was sufficient will to power and sufficient discipline, at least to bring order, external order, and internal tranquility out of the situation, in a very much shorter time.

With that we have to remember the historic, not simply the lack of political experience, training of any sort, on the part of the masses of the people, but also the historic passivity of the Russians. If you know Russian history, you know that practically every change in Russia has come to Russia from without, and in a way has been passively received by the people, though in time they have made it over to suit themselves.

But there is not a single thing in their political system, their military system, their educational system up to the last few years, their economic activities, their religion and so on, art, that did not come to them from without. In that sense they are almost

unique in not having an active development of indigenous institutions coming out of the people themselves.

In saying this, of course I recognize that gradually they made
over what they took from without, and adapted it to their own
conditions. But there was a passivity, as well as lack of experience, which made it very easy for them to lend themselves to the
rule of a comparatively small minority, as long as that minority
could give the country the peace, the order, the tranquility that it
needed to recover from the very devastating years of the great
war, from the equally devastating years of civil war, and the
criminal blockade which followed.

It is impossible for one who has not been there to realize what
the suffering, misery, starvation, chaos of the people was, that
has been produced by this period of war, external as well as internal, added to the foreign blockade when the population was
already starving from lack of food. And this is not merely a part
of the general background, but it has to do with the educational
activities undertaken even in the hardest years by the new regime, as soon as it came into power.

It is an old story that every great revolution of recent times has
been accompanied by very large educational reform. We have
the same story for China. We have it in Turkey. We have it in
Mexico. We have on a smaller scale the fact that public, popular
education in Great Britain followed the Reform Bill. So that one
of the statesmen said: "We now have to educate our new masters," the newly enfranchised population. With the overthrow of
the Napoleonic regime in France in 1870 and '71, there was a
complete reformation of the educational system there. So it was
natural to expect that some kind of an educational movement
would follow. But the particular form and direction which that
new educational movement took, was, of course, stimulated by
the peculiar character of the new regime and its Socialistic ideals,
and its determination to make the working class, the laboring
class, the supreme element in the formation and control of the
new state.

In the words I quote from a Russian educator belonging to the
Communistic party, typical of the spirit in which this educational
enterprise went on, "The laboring people must themselves build
the structure of their own lives." Without education, without
schooling, any attempt of the working class to build a new social

order, a new structure for their own lives, was obviously absurdly out of the question.

In reading such a small part of Russian educational literature as is available in English, there are certain formulas that reappear. They are a part, as it were, of the slogans of the educational leaders, namely that it is the work of the schools to develop warriors and builders of the new social order. In the words of Lenine, which are often quoted, the business of education is "to lead the entire population toward socialism; to direct the creation of a new social order, the schools must serve as teachers and guides and leaders of the laboring and exploited classes in the work of social reconstruction."

One phase of the new undertaking was what they called "The liquidation of illiteracy." In 1927, sixty-eight per cent according to the available statistics of the Soviet Union was still illiterate. And considering the much greater literacy of the urban population, this meant that at least four out of five of the peasants could neither read nor write. And the rural population is itself eighty per cent, or four out of five, of the entire population.

Now, you can readily see two things. First, that if these people who are trying to create a new social and economic order took their work at all seriously, or thought they had the slightest chance of success, they were compelled by mere force of circumstances to devote enormous attention to the creation of a new educational system. And the other thing equally obvious is the enormous obstacles, the very great difficulties, that they had to contend with.

As for this mere matter of getting rid of adult illiteracy, the campaign went on very actively. Whether one calls it successful or not depends upon how much one expected, and what one thought of the obstacles that had to be met. But by 1927, the latest time to which exact statistics are available, some seven million of adults previously illiterate had got at least the tools of learning. In the whole Soviet Union, about a million and a half of adult illiterates are added to the literate class every year, about a little more than half that number being in Old Russia, Great Russia.

I want to quote again from Lenine, because it gives a little official, formal sanction to this view that they themselves recognize the schools as the central strategic factor in the situation. "The

laboring masses are trained to knowledge because it is indispensable to their victory. Nine-tenths of them recognize that knowledge is the necessary tool in the struggle for freedom; that our
failures are mostly due to lack of education. We must as a matter
of necessity make enlightenment accessible to all." And as they
are fond of saying themselves, exactly as the old regime of the
Czars rested on the ignorance of the masses which made it possible, so the new regime could be possible only by the enlightenment of the masses.

In another speech he said: "An illiterate man is wholly outside
of politics. Before he can be in at all, he must be taught the alphabet. Without at least the knowledge of the alphabet and the ability
to read, there is no politics, only rumors, gossip and superstition."

This attempt to bring reading and writing to the masses, to the
adults, of course is simply one phase of the matter which I refer
to as illustrating the sense that they had of their problem. But
before I go on to the schools proper, I want to say a few more
words about what we would call adult education, what they call
political enlightenment. Civic enlightenment would perhaps be a
better English term, because although political activity in the
narrower sense is part of it, it is somewhat broader than that.

This political enlightenment is a recognized part of the central
system of education. At the head of it is Lenine's widow, who directs the formation and execution of this general policy of adult
education among the people. It is supposed to run through the
whole population. I will speak of it merely as it is found in the
villages because, as I said, that is the important part of Russian
life, numerically and in their occupation.

In the plan every single village is to have a centre, what is
called the village cottage reading room. And in certain centres,
some of the larger villages, they have developed what are called
People's Houses. That is, some have already developed them, and
others plan to develop them. This is to be a sort of social settlement, in our language, for the whole village. The work of teaching adults to read and write is carried on. It is a library centre; a
centre for newspapers, where those who can read have access to
them; where there is somebody to read aloud the newspapers to
those who cannot read, and where in theory, and where the plan
is better carried out, in practice, there are regular meetings for
lectures. It is a forum for discussion, for concerts, all of the
things that would improve the cultural life of the village.

These are under the control of committees, soviets as they call them. The soviet is not a Bolshevist invention. It almost means a committee in the village, something like the old-fashioned New England town meeting. But most any consultation is at least a temporary soviet. When our party was over there, twenty-five or thirty of us going around, the meal hours were somewhat irregular, and there would be a discussion as to what to do next, or when to have our dinner hour. The Russian interpreter would say: "We better have a soviet to settle the matter." (Laughter.) Any discussion almost is a soviet.

These groups that control these cottage reading rooms are supposed to consist of representatives of the more enlightened peasantry, the local doctor, the local teacher; and it is not what we might call a soft snap to be a teacher in Russia at present, because every teacher besides teaching school is expected to engage in some kind of social activity, or politically educative activity outside of school hours, representatives of the cooperatives, of the professional union. There is a cooperative association in practically every village. They are the representatives of the local union, if there is an agricultural experimental station— which has been very much increased; they existed back before the Revolution—and so on.

The methods they officially classify under three heads, agitation, propaganda and teaching. The official definition of agitation as distinct from propaganda is that the appeal is mainly emotional and through the medium of pictures, either verbal pictures or posters, or some kind of graphic reproduction dealing with rather immediate special issues. The corresponding definition of propaganda is that the approach is more intellectual, and that it discusses principles and policies that are more continuous of application. What is left over is called teaching. (Laughter.)

There are about 25,000 of those cottage reading rooms now established. You understand without my saying so, of course, they are very different in quality, some of them rather nominal, perfunctory. Others of them are really active and carrying out the aims. Much depends, of course, upon the local interest and local material.

There are 125,000 adults—this is quite independent of the illiteracy movement—who are engaged in what is called self-education. That is, they follow courses; you cannot call them university extension courses, but more of the type of clubs and classes in our own social settlements. There are some 125,000 adults carrying on self-education either in the cities or country. In view of the much larger rural population, however, it is significant that sixty per cent of these 125,000 are found in the cities and only forty per cent in the country districts. It is also interesting that eighty-five per cent of the city population are engaged in the lines of political study, while in the country districts that figure descends to forty-five per cent. In the country there are fifty-five per cent engaged in what we would call professional education, which really means for the most part studying agriculture and the improvement of local farming and orchards and poultry raising and so on. Now these statistics are not very interesting but it shows the contrast; even now the number of adults carrying on these courses in the city is more than half of the total number, in spite of their having only one-fifth of the population.

That is significant of the very fundamental problem that the present regime has to face. As they recognize, and as all the world knows, the split between the city worker and the peasantry, the interests and needs of the city worker, as the government takes care of them and favors the city workers over against the peasant population and their needs, the relative disadvantage which they are at, that is the greatest internal problem without a doubt which the present regime has to face; and probably, if one can prophesy at all, is the factor which more than anything else will determine the ultimate outcome of the present regime. One could almost use this situation in education as a text from which one could go on to explain a good deal of the whole economic and political problems, the divisions within the Soviet Union at the present time.

I am not going to say much about the formal organization of the school system. It is a nine year system, instead of a twelve year system like ours, with two supplementary years in what they call technical, more specialized schools, of which not the most important perhaps, but the most urgent at the present time, are the pedagogical technical high schools that are giving teacher training, normal training. There are one hundred and ninety-two to two hundred now of these altogether, not in all Russia but in Russia proper.

As you know, the Soviet Union is a federation, of which what we usually think of as Russia is only one part, and even that does not include southern Russia or the part of Russia towards Poland, which have their own independent governments, and their own independent educational systems. I mean within the whole, they have their own autonomous governments like our state governments.

By their paper program, they do not expect to have universal compulsory education until 1933, and even then it will be simply for the first grade of the nine years, namely a four year school. Personally, I doubt very much whether they will be able to carry out their plan for uniform compulsory education for even as short a period as four years, as early as 1933, because of the enormous obstacles they have to face. I will not go into that, but I do not think that their failure to do that, if they do fail, and it seems to me they are almost bound to, will be any cause for permanent discouragement.

The point certainly more interesting to a general audience, or anyway to people at large, is the general spirit of the schools. Of course I did not understand Russian, but there were certain words repeated often enough, so that they impressed themselves even on dull ears like mine. The words we seemed to hear often enough, and that came out oftener in the translations were: "Collectives," "Communistic," as one might expect, "Co-operative" and then "Ideology" and "Culture."

I doubt if any discussion of a general nature could go on for fifteen minutes in Russia without the introduction of the word ideology, the ideology of the bourgeois and the ideology of Russia, and the ideology of the Bolshevist; the ideology of the working class, and so on. One can only sort of pick up just the meaning of it. It is of course the whole mental system and attitude, their prevailing psychology, their mentality, the ideas, the emotions that make themselves operative. Well, the general aim of this school system is not merely then to create literacy, and get a background for citizenship able to participate actively in the government, but to create ideology appropriate to a social order in which the interests of the working class are the supreme interests.

This frequent introduction of the word "culture," "cultivation," was to me in many ways the most surprising of the experiences, contacts which I had. I had a picture of Marxian socialism as practically exclusively devoted to economic reform, revolution, or economic deformation, whatever your point of view may happen to be; to concentrate on the purely economic and merely materialistic features, especially as they call themselves always materialists. It therefore was surprising, something of a shock, to find that they talked so much more about the necessity of the spread of culture and cultivation, and the fact that the economic revolution was to provide the necessary basis, so that all of the community might have a share in culture, in science, and all the various forms of art and all the kinds of civilized contact that make life worth while for everybody.

One gets a sort of topsy-turvy, dizzy feeling when he finds this situation in a country that acknowledges itself to be very backward—as Lenine himself put it, in a condition of semi-Asiatic barbarism—reproaching one's own country for lack of culture or cultivation, because as they say or believe, our cultivation is so largely restricted to the class which is favorably placed. They say that no nation, and only with great difficulty can any individual be really a cultivated man, unless he is interested in sharing his cultural advantages with everybody. In my opinion, this is the noblest, finest spirit, most highly idealistic element in the situation. Though in saying that, I do not mean to imply, of course, that it is the whole of the situation.

One day we were visiting a colony eight or ten miles out of Moscow. We had been going through the shops. We came out, and one of the members of our party who knows Russian called attention to a sign: "Workmen, unite for the defense of your country." Then there was an appeal for contribution of funds to an airplane factory, development of new airplanes for military purposes, of course, for which the popular name is, "The Soviet Answer to Chamberlain." They capitalize Chamberlain at every possible opportunity. I suppose every new religion has to have a devil as well as a god, and so beside Lenine for their god, they tend to settle upon Chamberlain as the diabolical element in the international situation.

There was a very fine specimen of workman standing outside, a magnificent one, wielding a big sledge-hammer; and I took the liberty of going up to him and taking hold of his arms, I said— my friend translating—"You seem to have done your share preparing for the defense of your country." And then he wanted to know who we were and where we were from and so on. He was told.

Then he delivered a very eloquent oration, not an educational oration, one with real spirit, fire, standing by his anvil, with his sledge-hammer still in his hand. And naturally, at least from their standpoint, naturally it was an appeal to us to go back and promote the revolution to free the workers of our own country. The Russian who was with me said that his language was really remarkable, the range of vocabulary, the accuracy of his grammar and so on. He was a young man of about twenty-three; and not knowing any Russian, I could testify to his freedom and power as an orator.

Well, that suggested to me to say it was rather hard to get workmen to start a revolution when they had their own motor cars and radios and phonographs; and painted as idyllic a picture as I could of the prosperity of the American laboring man. We did not refer to his wife with silk stockings, because that had not become part of our campaign literature at that time; but we did the best we could. (Laughter.)

Well, he had to change his attack a little. "Well, that does not make any difference. You are educators; you are cultivated people, and as cultivated people you cannot be satisfied until all of the people of your community have got the same cultural advantages that you have." He said: "Now here, that is my motor bicycle; that belongs to me. I haven't got a motor car, but I have got that. But," he said, "am I satisfied? No, I can't be satisfied"— and then he pointed to all the other workmen—"until he has got one, he has got one, he has got one. I can't be a cultivated man if I were satisfied before they all have one."

Well, that is a sample coming from a workman of the extent to which this ideal of a cultural end or aim has permeated at least the section of the Bolshevist Republic that is sympathetic with the present regime.

Now this story is not anywhere near complete. I want to tell you what this colony was. It was a colony of juvenile criminals, young men from eighteen to twenty-two or twenty-three who are selected by a committee from the penitentiaries and prisons, taken out there, and various forms of shops and industrial work have been developed. They live there. Not only that, but there is no wall.

It is quite a colony now, five hundred people, and growing every year. It is also now a coeducational colony. (Laughter.)

They now have about forty or fifty women, and they expect to increase the number. They are building new buildings, raising funds. They take them—they are all in prison, you understand; they do not create them for the express purpose (laughter),—and they are enlarging, raising funds, and they expect to have a colony of some two thousand juvenile criminals.

As there are no walls around there, there are no guards at the gates. With a very few exceptions, there are no rules except the laws which this colony of criminals themselves pass. There are a few laws. They must not drink on the premises, but they do go to Moscow, and there is no rule against their drinking, though their getting drunk is very much discouraged. But, as the man at the head of it, a doctor, said to us, "It would be perfectly futile for us to pass rules that they could not drink at all." He said, "We can bring pressure to bear to discourage drunkenness." They have actually killed out, succeeded in eliminating, the use of drugs and dope of all kinds, and you know what that means in a large colony, fairly large colony, of criminals.

The other chief law is, for the first three months they are there, they are on probation, and they cannot leave the grounds without getting permission. There is no guard at the gate. Someone asked him if they did not run away, and the man shrugged his shoulders and said: "Well, when there are no means to use force of any kind to keep them in, I do not know whether you could call it running away or not." Then he finally said that last year, during the whole year, there were three persons who left the institution. He said, "At first we were accused of being very antisocial, because we did not restrain them. We were charged with enabling prisoners to turn loose on the community." He was a man of remarkable calmness and equanimity of spirit, a very wonderful character. And again he shrugged his shoulders and said: "Oh, if they do not go back to a criminal life, it is all right. And if they do go back to a criminal life, the police pick them up and put them back in jail before very long. It does not do much harm." (Laughter.) We asked him if there was any real regulation about the class of criminals they take in. He said, "Well, there is one; we do not take murderers." And then again came the humorous look on his face. "But," he said, "at that, I would not guarantee that we did not have some here." (Laughter.) Now this young man who gave us a lecture on the importance of cultivation was one of these juvenile criminals who had been re-educated under the system of extraordinary freedom.

If anything were needed to add to the picture, it is the fact this school, or colony, rather, was founded by the head of the G.P.U., the old Tcheka; that is the secret police espionage force which is responsible for the coercion of the element in the population that is suspected not to be in sympathy with the present regime. One comes across many contradictions in Russia, but I do not know of any that is more picturesque than the fact that the man who is at the head of the most effective coercive organization had founded a colony for criminals that is based upon the idea of the most complete liberty of any educational reformatory colonies ever found in the world. And the head of this school is absolutely convinced that every criminal is capable of being reformed and restored to a useful social life, unless he is absolutely pathological, and provided the proper social environment can be found for him. There is that union of oppression and coercion on the one hand, and an extraordinary amount of freedom and what we call democracy in certain other respects, running through as far as I could observe a great many phases of Russian life.

The main idea of the Russian school is to centre about the creation of this ideology of the laboring class, which means the idea of labor as the central theme of the school. To develop that idea, to see how they work it out, would take too much time, and involve us in some technicalities. I may say this, however: it is a union of two things—they have taken the psychology and a good deal of the methods of the more advanced, so-called progressive schools, experimental schools, from all the other countries about which they knew anything or could glean anything from literature, the newer schools in Germany particularly, in the Scandinavian countries, and especially in the United States.

Up to 1923, their school system was not very much organized. The main idea was a school with a great deal of freedom for the children, and as much activity as possible, as distinguished from the passive absorption, inculcation methods, pouring-in methods of the old regime.

Then in 1923, they felt the lack of organization, and these were more or less borrowed ideas, also coming I should say from Tolstoy's educational experiment, he indirectly getting it from Rousseau. The thing became more systematized, and was united rather consciously and deliberately with the general social and economic philosophy of Marx and Lenine, so that the activity school became what they called a labor school.

Curiously enough—no, not curiously, perhaps, if you take the Russian background and all into account—the Russians do not idealize work, labor, for its own sake. In fact, they come very close to saying that it is, if not a curse, it is a necessary evil; therefore we want to get it over as soon as we can, and distribute it as equitably as possible, and surround it with as agreeable conditions as possible; insurance against accident, good hygienic conditions, frequent vacations and so on. So when they say labor school, they are very careful to say that the work is not to be an end in itself. It is not the utilitarian product they are after, but rather the training in some form of labor that will be useful to society later, and the cultivation of a sense of the significance, meaning, and the history of labor in the school.

Now, with labor as the centre, they work out in two directions, but perhaps first I had better say how they organize their curriculum. They have attempted to abolish separate subjects entirely. They have reacted very strongly against the curriculum or program organization, geography, history, arithmetic and reading and writing. They attempt to find one theme, one subject in the activity of the pupils, in relation to which they will need some arithmetic, some geography, some nature study. These things will come in gradually; and only as they get up to the high school, to the university, will these various phases of a common subject matter, which they call a complex or a synthesis, be differentiated into school studies.

Well, their centre, this synthetic centre, is some form of human activity in the form of labor. That forms as it were the centre. Then to one side that moves out into the study of nature and natural forces, the beginnings of physical and natural science. On the other side, this study of activities of labor moves out into the study of social life, social organization and institutions, and of history; and of course all interpreted from the labor point of view, as that is understood in the communistic theory of economics.

I just give one instance taken from the fifth year of the school. The central theme of the whole year is the agricultural labor of Russia as a whole. The whole thing works in cycles. In the country, they study the agriculture of their own village in the second year. When they get to the fifth year, they take the agricultural activities of Russia, that is to say, the life of the farmers brought to them by pictures or experience and so on, all through the different districts of that very large country, with its great diversity of climates and soils. They study that, and the activities of cattle raising, of poultry, and some accounts of the methods that are being introduced to reform and improve agriculture, and to introduce large scale farming, instead of small scale farming, and the other projects of the Bolshevist regime in relation to the peasant.

Now, on the natural side they study soils, for instance, a more technical study, with some chemistry of the soils of their own locality; some study of the geography and geology of soils all through the different parts of Russia; study of the climate of their own region in greater detail, with more accurate observations, and records of climates of different parts of Russia. They combine geography, nature study and such experimental science as can be worked in or as their own facilities in the particular school permit them.

Now on the social side they make a more detailed study of the life of the farmers, if it is a country district in their own neighborhood; but more especially they study the history of the farming class, the peasant class in Russia. They go back to the early days of serfdom, the creation of serfdom, the feudalism of Russia; the different efforts to get rid of serfdom; the abolition under the Czar of serfdom; the condition of the peasant after that time; and the land problem leading up, of course, to the revolutions of 1917 and 1918, and the taking over of the land by the peasants; and ending up again with the study of the land policies of the Soviet regime.

I take that just as one picture of how making labor the theme, starting with that as the centre, they work out on one side into the study of nature, and on the other side to social institutions and history. And in principle, this is the official program for greater Russia; officially the program goes through on these lines, the whole scheme.

Now in the centre, labor, there are two controlling ideas; first, that it shall not be a matter of books, of being told by teachers. In theory, though still very far from practice, every school in the country—this is pretty well carried out—has to have a school field, a school garden, if possible, with animals, bees or something, and a flower garden as well as a vegetable one, possibly a small orchard; and the students actually take part, not to become farmers, but to get a background for their more detailed specialized scientific study, and to get the general contact, sympathy, with the farmer's point of view. Then they are supposed to have kitchens, dining rooms, and have some practical experience there as a basis for chemical problems, a study of animal and vegetable foods, their origin, growth and so on. And then shops, which are not however formal manual training courses, which they say is too much like factory work, but self-service, making the necessary repairs of the school; taking care of repairing the furniture; in some cases learning how to take care of their own clothes, cobble their own shoes, make simple apparatus used in the other classes of the schools, material for demonstration purposes and so on. So that they get a certain amount of actual activity in connection with the so-called labor activity side.

Then the other great principle is that what they get that they do not get from their own direct activity they must get by observation, before they go to books; not that they rule out books, but the introduction to every subject must come from their own observation.

There is a very important conclusion that at once follows from that, namely, that no two districts or regions can have exactly the same educational system. It is a decentralized central system. The central system lays down the general principles, but to get observation, contact with local activities and labor, they obviously have to adapt the details of their curriculum to their own local system. The regions have taken over in a very general, wholesale way what they call the project system. Their main criticism is that every problem must take the form of some social, useful work, and useful outside the school; not that it must all be there, but it must head up to some kind of activity that takes them out of the school into their own community, in a way that makes them helpful to the community.

How far they have succeeded in carrying this out, how far they can do it in the future, I do not know; but I think no one can deny that if it is practicable, if it is feasible, it is a very great educational idea; that the school, and the children in the school, shall become socialized, become cooperative by actual participation in useful ways in the actual life of their own community.

I am going to take time to read the classified heads, just the main headings under which this work may go on: first, economic activity, and in detail the sorting of grain. Of course Russian farming is very backward. The mere idea of improving the strains of grain, of picking out good seed and not planting seed that will not germinate, and so on, the destruction of weeds, the disinfecting of grain with formalin, the introduction of new varieties, the renting out of agricultural machinery, which may be found at the school, importing newer and better grades of grain, the planting of trees in deforested regions and so on, all this is an advancement in Russian agriculture. Then there is the going out and talking to peasants about better methods of rotating crops, and all of those things.

To us, it is rather humorous, perhaps, for children from twelve to fifteen or sixteen years of age to go out and instruct their elders in improved agricultural methods, as well as actually engaging in certain jobs that might help things on. But the Russian youth are a very fascinating spectacle to my eye; they are very simple, direct, naive, although with a great deal of confidence, but without any element of freshness, which we would associate with a similar degree of confidence on the part of our own youth. Certainly the more intelligent part of the school population, as I came in contact with them, have been imbued with the idea that they really are capable of engaging in a work of social creation, and they have a certain kind of enthusiasm and directness, confidence in life rather than simply self-confidence, that is very attractive.

In the one country village that I went to, they had an experimental station, not just an experimental school but a station with fifteen different experimental schools in it, under a single head, to work out methods and materials for the rural districts. There were certain boys there very much interested in foreigners, and they followed us around, came and visited us at the place we were staying, and talked to us. Unfortunately, as I said, only two members of our party could talk Russian.

One of these boys had been one of the so-called wild boys, one of the products of the war and the famine, separated from his parents, perhaps the parents dead, perhaps simply separated from them in one of those migrations across the country during the time of famine. He was telling various stories about his experiences, and a Russian friend remarked to him: "Well, you ought to write that up." Thereupon the boy replied, a boy about fifteen, in a very natural, direct way: "Oh, I am writing my autobiography. I have got two chapters done already." (Laughter.) I will say the boy was very attractive; there was nothing conceited or offensive in his reply.

Another boy talking to this same friend said: "I wish you would put down my name in your notebook; and then some time in the future when you go back to America, and you see my name, either because of a book I have written or a picture I have painted, or something I have done, you will remember it was the boy you saw over here." That perhaps was a little more conceited, but it was not offensively so in its manner.

I do not know that I should take any more time to talk about their social-political work, that is the direct political work, engaging in campaigning, not generally political but local soviet elections, getting the peasants out to vote, and talking over the candidates. One of these boys showed me a lot of slogans that he had made for one of these campaigns, banners, mottoes and so forth: public enlightenment; dissemination of information regarding works of art; anti-religious propaganda; fight against superstition and prejudice; agitation and propaganda among homeless children; health and sanitation; popular hygiene work, of which as you know there is very great need in the villages, to say nothing of the towns; propaganda against smoking and drinking; fight against home brew alcohol. (Laughter.)

This liquor question is a very serious question. Before I went away, some of the friends I had met over there said: "I wish you would tell us what your most severe criticism is." Well, you cannot be too harsh with people who have been awfully nice to you, and very friendly, who have made you feel they are really old-time personal friends; but I said, "well, I think liquor is the worst thing I have seen, and your greatest problem over here." And it is a very serious question, both the drunkenness and the whole bootlegging question, not because they have prohibition, but because the manufacture of alcohol is a government monopoly and the prices are very high; and they do what some other people do. (Laughter.)

Then there is regional work, work for regional resources, individual information, wrong paths, aid to needy widows, to widows of the red army, aid to victims of fire, aid to needy pupils and so on, introducing flowers. They are not talking of the flowers which they raise in their school gardens, but for the sick and the harder up portion of the population and so on.

Well, I could go on for a very long time. Just in concluding, I want to say one thing; to refer to these experimental stations, including fourteen different schools, with a selected staff, all engaged in working out materials and methods, which after they are tried out, are submitted to the state council, and then transmitted to other rural schools. There is a similar experimental school for urban districts, connected with factories, in the same way that this is connected with the farmers and peasants, in Moscow, which does the same work for the urban schools. This is for greater Russia. Every province, not merely the greater division, but the smaller division, has its own regional experimental school, to make the local regional adaptations.

Aside from this there are four state supported educational research lines of work. One of these corresponds to what we have in many places, departments of research in connection with the teacher training school. Beside that, there is one engaged in research on the curriculum; another one engaged exclusively with animals; branches in different cities in child, infant, pre-school psychology, or as they call it, "Pedology," because they include the study of physiology and child study. I think they got the word pedology from America, if I remember rightly, from Stanley Hall. And one Russian who came over here evidently came expecting to hear the word pedology on every hand, and he was quite surprised in not hearing it. Also as he came out of the American Consul at Riga, getting his visa (he had his initiation there), a man asked him his profession, and he said he was a pedologist, and the clerk said: "Oh, I know what that is; you are a corn doctor." (Laughter.)

There are two hundred and fifty different workers in this psychological child study department of government supported research alone. And they have published literally hundreds of books for teachers and for parents, relating to various phases of child development, besides thousands of pedagogical articles for periodicals. They held a convention in 1927. There were a thousand delegates from all over Russia; seven different sections, two hundred teachers, two thousand guests besides the thousand regular delegates. That in just this one line.

The other branch, which has four or five lines within itself, is the study of out of school education, in which a Russian who has been in this country, a trained engineer, took back many educational ideas from here, social education, that he obtained from living in the university social settlement of New York City; he is a very active spirit. If I had been able to stay there, I could easily have spent my hour just telling you about that one school. One division is children's inventions. They make a collection of the models of all the inventions the children make, if they work, and systematically encourage them. This is for out of school activity, the encouragement of inventive activities, largely of a mechanical type, among children. They are studying out of school reading; have probably made the most extensive collection of children's literature, and attempted analysis of what makes reading interesting to children, that has been made anywhere in the world.

Of course I have touched on the high spots only, the good spots; many of them more theoretical, or at least qualitative, than carried out as yet to any quantitative extent. But it is not just on paper, though I should give you a very distorted idea if I had conveyed the impression that all of these things are working on any very large scale. But these things are actually there, not simply on paper; and they are to my mind genuinely characteristic of the spirit and the vitality of this new educational movement, which made me say at the outset that if they can get peace, quiet, order, continuous development for a generation, I think that they will have valuable contributions. They have already some valuable contributions, but they will have great contributions to make to the educational systems of the rest of the world, quite independent of any injection of the element of communistic propaganda, for many of these principles, and many of these activities, are capable of being very easily taken out of that particular sentiment.

Now I have been asked whether I was hopeful or depressed or optimistic or pessimistic about the situation and its future. If I may say a word or two in conclusion about the latter part of the problem: About the immediate situation, I am neither hopeful nor depressed, optimistic or pessimistic, simply because I do not know enough about it, and it would take a long residence and a good deal of detail study, to my mind, to form any estimate that is worth the paper it is written on, or the ear strain it takes to listen to anybody's view on the subject, who does not know a great deal more about it than I do. But if one means by that the long run outcome, the outcome for the Russian people, and not simply for a particular faction of the Russian regime, I can only say that I am intensely hopeful, and the reason of course is the Russian people.

It sounds quite trite, but I hope not patronizing, in saying the Russians are a very great people; and it is impossible, to my mind, that a people with the gifts that that people has should not have a very great future, and that they should not succeed in finding their way out of their present difficulties and obstacles; and in the end do something which is not merely significant, but which is something new. That it will be exactly in the line of the expectations of the present leaders, I personally am very doubtful. But I do think that it will be something different socially and economically and politically from what has been worked out in the rest of the world, in the end.

The Russians are a great people. Everybody knows that they are greatly gifted in artistic directions. They are great in music. They are great in dramatic expression, not merely in drama but in acting, and in the whole management of the theatre. I suppose there is no doubt that to-day the Russian theatre leads the world; and not merely their old theatre, which existed of course before the revolution, but that their new dramatic developments, theatrical developments along scenic construction and all that, are some of the most interesting experiments going on in the world. And we all know they are great in fiction, and this artistic temperament is in the people. They do not suffer from the emotional inhibition which the average Anglo-Saxon has, which gives them a certain advantage when it comes to artistic creation.

Not merely that, but they are an unexhausted people; they are a fresh, vigorous, pioneer people. One is more reminded of America, at least the older America, the pioneer America, in Russia than in any other part of the world. Now that was my feeling. I could not trust it exactly, but I happened to meet Mr. Bakmetiev, after I got back. He is the ex-Kerensky ambassador to this country, and of course naturally of no great sympathy with the present regime, and I mentioned that I had that impression of the Russian people. He said it was true, and that history bore it out; that they had that same movement on towards the frontier and conquest of their immediate natural environment that we have had.

The rest of Europe, especially after the war, of course is tired; they are fatigued. They talk about the future of civilization and the downfall of civilization. Now, that is not the spirit in Russia, even of those who are completely opposed to the present regime. It is a spirit of vigor, of freshness, of unexpended natural resources, and of unexpended human resources.

For that reason I for one came away from Russia feeling that their future was a very, very great one, and that they deserved the sympathy, the Russian people deserved the sympathy and the help, whatever can be given them, moral support and so on, intellectual and educational, of the American people. For I really believe that in many respects the type and temper of the two peoples is more similar, at least the old-fashioned American, the pioneer American, than any other two countries in the world at present. (Applause.)

Child Health and Protection

I

Mr. Chairman, and Mr. Chairman; Friends, Delegates, Members of this Regional Conference: The discussions of the White House Conference were limited, very wisely so, in one way, in spite of the very wide ground, comprehensive ground covered. They dealt with the school child, but not exactly with the child in school. That is they did not consider distinctively educational or scholastic problems. They left that aspect of the matter, I take it, to the educators themselves.

The men and women who met almost a year ago to carry on the work of the Conference dealt with school conditions as they affected the general health of the pupils. They called for a health program. They demanded adequate recreational facilities, for school and other children. They pointed out the need of special classes and treatment for defectives, delinquents and sub-normal children; demanded sympathetic and curative treatment; for the boys and girls, the unfortunate ones who had already come under the arm of the law, they emphasized the need of vocational training.

They did not raise—this was left I take it to the educators— the question of the regulation of the regular school program, the daily more or less routine administrative work of the school to the great ends which are laid down in the Children's Charter. This is a task which the educators must take up; and so it is from the standpoint of an educator, speaking to the teachers, edu-

[Address delivered at the Chicago Regional White House Conference on Child Health and Protection, Palmer House, 30–31 October 1931. Stenographic report in the Anita McCormick Blaine Papers, Box 168, State Historical Society of Wisconsin, Madison. For Children's Charter to which Dewey refers, see this volume, Appendix 6.]

cators, administrators in the audience, rather than to those who are social welfare workers in a more technical sense, that I am to speak. The findings of the Conference, the Children's Charter, are to my mind a challenge to the teacher, a challenge which will not be met fully, even if all the specific recommendations of the Conference are carried out by the other welfare bodies. There still is left the question of the contribution of the general work of the school in its studies hour by hour, methods of teaching hour by hour and day by day; methods of discipline for the wholesome development of child life that represents the unifying purpose of the Conference.

Now this is far from the first time that those directly in charge of the schools have had a challenge put up to them from the outside that those on the inside improve the technique of their work and perfect its detail. The larger educational changes usually go back to those outside the school rooms, to those who make the social demands, teachers already being absorbed in their daily task. Now it seems to me that the Charter gives educators a chance for once, perhaps, to reverse this process, and instead of waiting until social forces have spoken imperatively, take the lead in a unifying organizing work. For the aims set forth in the Children's Charter cannot be recognized by special institutions and agencies if these latter are independent and isolated from the general daily work of the school.

The great need is that the entire school, in all its methods, performance and operations day by day be so organized as to promote child welfare in the largest sense of the word.

Take for example the matter of vocational guidance; how can the ideals of proper vocational guidance for all, that are set forth in the charter, be realized without a very considerable change in the traditional subject matter, a greater change than has yet taken place, not in all schools, but in many schools? A curriculum based on traditional subjects cannot wholly cover the vocational tastes of all pupils. It is also absurd, though not so obviously so, to suppose that the lack of the ordinary curriculum to disclose vocational aptitude, tastes and disabilities can be fully made good by adding on a special device, no matter how expert, or merely by tacking on special courses labeled "vocational." The pupils must be brought in their regular work in contact with a sufficient variety of materials to disclose their aptitudes. The material, regular materials must be taught day by day, hour by hour, by methods which will bring to light the pupil's own capacities, weaknesses, tastes, etc. Now, as long as our methods in the school are largely devoted to absorbing information and then finding out in the recitation periods simply how much information pupils have stowed away, what real opportunity is there for anything that goes very deep in the way of vocational guidance, the discovery of aptitude and the direction of it into its proper channel?

Article ten of the Charter reads: "For every child an education which through the discovery and development of his individual abilities prepares him for life, and through training and vocational guidance prepares him for a living which shall give him the maximum of satisfaction." Fine, I say, and fine, you all say. But this ideal, I repeat, cannot be realized simply by instituting a few special devices. The whole work of the school must be brought to bear upon the solution of this great problem.

The same is true of what is set forth in the next article of the Charter: That every child shall have "such teaching and training as will prepare him or her for successful parenthood and the making use of the right of citizenship." This is fundamental, but so fundamental, I think you will all agree with me, that the need cannot be met excepting by an organization of the whole work of the school. And this organization means in many, perhaps the majority of American schools, the reorganization of their traditional studies and methods.

Consider again these health aims, which seem to be very specialized, and more likely to be met by particular means. What Dr. Judd has already told us shows us how such a matter as handwriting has a bearing upon the proper nervous and muscular development of the child. Health is not a special end to be brought about simply by special means. Certain things can be specified on the negative side. We must get rid of bad air, foul air, and the kind of seating that almost forces bad postures of the children. And so we can specify positively ample playgrounds and so on. But health is a certain kind of wholeness of body, and it cannot be made secure excepting by conditions that regularly affect the whole attitude, being of the pupil.

A physician concerned in the mental hygiene movement once told me that he is persuaded that there is the most intimate connection between the general health, in all students he had come in contact with who were colored pupils, well matured, more hardened to resistance, and their emotional attitudes of attraction and repulsion toward their school studies. There is much in our traditional curriculum, and in the method of teaching it, which perhaps not only dulls the mind but depresses bodily vigor, even though there is nothing resulting in the way of illness that would require the attention of physicians. Body as well as mind is often cramped, made more inflexible by the ordinary routine of school work.

And this health, of course, includes mental well being as well as physical. Is there not a great challenge to educators in the fact which has been impressed upon us in recent years that in our hospitals, asylums, public institutions, as many beds are occupied by persons suffering from some degree of mental disorder as from all other forms of disorder put together? If mental disorder, small as well as great, mal-adjustment, goes on growing, and we measure abnormality by statistics about the average person, it looks as if the abnormal people would be the normal ones in another generation. (Laughter.)

I do not wish, of course, to suggest the schools are primarily responsible for the extent of mental disorders among us. They grow much more out of mal-adjustments in family and home relations. But certainly it should be—it might be part of the province of the schools to develop more immunity, more prophylaxis against the development of these mental and moral disorders. And here again special methods, special classes and courses can hardly meet the need. It requires again here a good deal of reorganization if we are to bring about the contribution which the school can make to the wholesome development of child life. The great need is the change in the attitude of the educators towards their regular work.

Dr. Judd referred to one point I want to repeat, the importance of the emotions in the development of normal, mental and physical well being. If the schools are to protect from future instability, it must be very largely by greater attention to the role of the emotional factors in the human development. Our schools have been intellectualizing and, in the narrow sense of the word, over-practical in training for special forms of skill at the expense

of the development of the healthy animal, development of affections, relations of the children to each other and to parents.

I have one more instance of what seems to me the impossibility
of meeting the recommendations of the White House Conference
excepting through an organization of the whole school work.
The Conference emphasized the significance of life outside the
home and the school, the life of children outside home and school;
the relation of children, pupils, to the church, to those different
agencies which deal with the spare time of boys and girls—recreation facilities, moving pictures, theatre and radio, commer-
cialized amusements, libraries, the use of libraries, camps and so
on. The report on this phase of child life terminates with saying
that 40 per cent of the lives of most children and youth is really
spent in spare time activities outside home and school; and that
the spare time, leisure time activities, have the most important
influence on character formation, so that the community should
focus attention upon this phase of child welfare.

There again is a proposition to which we may all give a hearty
amen. But can even this proper care of leisure time of children
outside the school be secured without the cooperation of the
schools themselves? For children, youth, will take to their clubs
or recreation fields, movies, camps and so on, the attitudes, the
mental and moral attitudes, which are formed in the school. So it
makes a very great difference whether we look upon these agencies simply as supplemental work of the school, particularly as
supplementing, in making good the defects of the school work,
correcting their deficiencies and faults, or whether the ideals of
the spare time interests and activities outside the school harmonize and work together with those of the school all the way
through.

Now this is not a purely academic issue, I think. There is one
sentence in the report of the particular committee, Committee G,
which dealt with this matter, I would like to quote. The passage
reads: "Our system of education in general does not stimulate
inventiveness, imagination or initiative. Comparatively little has
been done by the school to train esthetic tastes, which could be a
guide to selection of activities in leisure time."

I am not going to ask just how far that statement is justified,
how far it is not. There is enough truth in it to indicate that un-

less the schools themselves do more to develop inventiveness, imagination, initiative and aesthetic taste, any work of the agencies that deal with the child outside of school will be, to say the least, very greatly hampered.

So from these various instances, which of course might be multiplied by going through the whole of the recommendations found in the Children's Charter, I conclude that the fine, noble purposes set forth in that charter cannot be realized if we break up the incidents which shape the life and character of the pupil into separate, isolated and independent fractions. It is one of our American weaknesses to operate by taking on new things more than by reconstructing from the centre outward. So it seems to me the great lesson which we educators have to learn from the proceedings of that Conference is that if its inspiring aims are to be realized, the regular work of the school in its courses of study, its methods of teaching and discipline, must keep these ends constantly in view. Every boy and girl is an individual, that is an undivided unity, and the unity of personality cannot be reached by treating the boys and girls as if they were simply a bundle of disconnected, unrelated elements, with a particular class of institution separately to take care of each one.

So as the various reports of the Conference close with certain recommendations, advice, I would like to close with a note directed particularly to the teachers among us. First, that we should all study very carefully the report, the recommendations of the various committees of the Child Welfare Conference. Secondly, what is obviously more important than merely getting an intellectual acquaintance with them is that we educators should consider how far the schools themselves might become the central and the unifying agency for realizing the aims which are therein set forth; the integrating element that will keep the purposes from being so split up with a variety of different agencies that in the end we shall not succeed as we might.

The task is a difficult one, but after all it is in line with what the best schools at the present time are all doing. And it seems to me unless the educators take these reports as a challenge, and consider the challenge seriously, there is danger that leadership will pass from the schools and educators into a variety of outside special organizations. While on the other hand, only through the integration of child welfare, social welfare agencies bringing it into the regular work of the school, can the schools do what they really have it in their power to accomplish. (Applause.)

II

Mr. Chairman, Guests, Ladies and Gentlemen: I was at a meeting last winter where my friend and former colleague, James Harvey Robinson, was speaking, and the audience rose as you have kindly risen to greet him. Sitting near him, I heard him mutter to himself, "I am not the national anthem." (Laughter.) What he said under his breath, I take the liberty of saying out loud, though I appreciate your kind appreciation.

You will excuse one of my age, a former resident of Chicago, if on an occasion like this, the mind goes back to ten happy and for him very instructive years spent in this city, and the associations formed at that time, many of which on the personal side have been renewed to-day. They are forced on my memory very pleasantly through the friends that I have associated with at this table this evening. For those memories and associations, I think are quite pertinent to this Regional Conference held here in Chicago at this time.

There are, as everyone who has lived in Chicago and learned to love it knows, there are two sides to Chicago, and the real Chicago is that which is represented in this Conference, represented in this gathering here to-night, rather than in what perhaps attracts most attention in the headlines of the papers through the country. I was thinking as I sat here that in everything but the words "White House," not merely the Regional Conference but the National Conference might well have centered in the City of Chicago. If I mistake not, the first university chair that dealt with social welfare, human welfare and social work as a regular part of the university curriculum was here in the University of Chicago. I do not need to remind this audience of what the Social Settlement in this city has stood for; what Jane Addams and Mary McDowell have stood for; what Miss Lathrop, Miss Grace Abbott have stood for. I think one could say with a great deal of truth that the Children's Bureau, which represents the organized federal work in behalf of the causes in which this Conference is interested, is a spiritual child of the work that originated in the

City of Chicago, and that there is not merely the spiritual descent but even a more literal direct and personal movement from the City of Chicago to this great branch of federal government. So other memories have come into my mind which reinforce me on the appropriateness of the meeting and the significance of this meeting in Chicago to-day.

There is one other thought which has come to my mind, which I am going to venture to present, though it is of that kind of a serious note which is closely connected with depression and suffering, and yet which I know is close to the surface of the consciousness, the feeling hearts of those here, as well as elsewhere in our country to-day. So I may venture to speak of it.

The section of the Children's Charter which Dr. Fishbein read speaks of the right of every child to a home, and to the security which the home, the home alone one may add, can give. And yet to-day we know that from no fault of parents, and from causes beyond the control of physicians, child welfare with regard to homes all about us is crumbling, and the children as well as the parents are losing the security which we have declared in words to be the birthright of the children. We know that hundreds of thousands of children—we do not know the number of hundreds of thousands, and we merely estimate—are suffering physically to-day from defective nutrition caused by the economic condition of the country to-day. The lowest estimate for the number of quarts of milk that are distributed daily in Greater New York to-day, as compared with a few years ago, is one million quarts. Think of what that may mean. It is a real tragedy for the future of these children that are growing up.

We have all of us, all the citizens, and not merely the experts, a double responsibility, a responsibility indeed in all these specific directions that have been mentioned, but also a responsibility that society itself provide for the future of the children who are growing up a more secure opportunity for a safe and useful life than we are demonstrating to-day will be possessed unless something is done about it. We learned from Dr. Fishbein that it is only the last thirty years that we have calculated what the value of a child is to society. Let us hope that, say thirty years from now, when a Conference is held in 1960, that those who are there will be able to say that we have also calculated what the value of a just and humane social order is to the child. (Applause.)

III

Mr. Chairman, Friends: The Chairman, Mr. Bogan, might have at least called on two or three other people, and they might have said something that would arouse an idea in my mind. I haven't even any statistics to give you. (Laughter and Applause.) I am not a specialist or an expert. I ought to be, and have been, listening in a humble way to the instructions that have come to us from the experts. I see there is a screen over here. I wish I had some pictures to show you, but I haven't even got them.

I can tell you, however, of the pleasure it gives me to return from time to time to this great city of Chicago, and not merely see my old friends, but have my enthusiasm, my convictions, and my faith for better development of civic and community life in this country renewed. I think there is no place in the country where there is as much devotion, and as much community and civic interest and action as can be found in this region about the City of Chicago. When I read in the morning paper the number of hold-ups there had been yesterday in four hours, I thought there was need for a good deal of civic energy and enthusiasm, but, as I said last evening in effect, I realize that an organization like this means immensely more for the future than these passing episodes which awake the sensational interest which the steady and cumulative work of people who are represented here in the organizations do not attract, the things of a constructive sort.

I wish above all to congratulate the Committee who organized this Conference. I want particularly to congratulate your Chairman, Mr. Bogan, for the great success of these meetings. I am sure you will all go away with the same feeling which possesses me, that a permanent impress upon the future, a better chance for the children, the neighborhood, the state, ultimately the nation, will develop because of what has been said, heard, thought, the new energy that has been aroused in this series of meetings. Dr. Barnard has told me that some ten or a dozen of these regional meetings had been held and other state meetings planned for, but I am quite sure none has been and none will be more permanently successful, more useful than this meeting which has been held here yesterday and to-day. I thank you all. (Applause.)

American Federation of
Teachers Statement

We desire to record publicly our sense of the important contribution to democracy and education which the Executive Council of the American Federation of Teachers has made by its decision to revoke the charters of the two New York locals. Public education in our country now confronts a difficult situation. On the one hand, it is hard pressed to get the funds required to provide essential educational services for all the children of the nation. On the other hand, it is attacked by powerful groups, which for one reason or another, seek to restrict freedom of teaching in this period of social conflict and transition. We believe that the right kind of teachers' union could do much to strengthen American public education in this twofold struggle for freedom and for adequate financial support.

Unfortunately, the two New York locals, although including in their membership many honest supporters of democracy and education, have been brought under the domination of communist forces which have worked under cover to fashion these organizations into tools for their party purposes. As a result of this communist manipulation and control these locals have lost not only the confidence of organized labor and of large numbers of teachers in the schools and colleges of New York City, but also of the public without whose support the union cannot accomplish anything substantial. Hence, although these locals have done certain desirable specific things, the net effect of their work in the last few years has been to injure, not to strengthen, public education.

By its resolute action in revoking these charters the American

[Typescript, not typed by Dewey, in the John L. Childs Papers, Special Collections, Morris Library, Southern Illinois University at Carbondale, ca. 1941; typescript signed by Dewey.]

Federation of Teachers has opened the way for bona fide teachers' unions in New York City. We hope therefore that friends of democracy and education will not be misled by efforts already under way to confuse thought and to conceal the real issues involved in this situation.

Finally, we welcome this action by the Executive Council as indication that those who believe in democratic *social means* as well as in democracy as *social end* are regaining the initiative not only in the American Federation of Teachers but also in the larger sphere of American life and politics.

John H. Randall's *Our Changing Civilization*

I do not know when I have been so mentally excited as in reading Dr. Randall's *Our Changing Civilization*. It is the most penetrating exposition of the present situation of the Western World that I know of; it sets forth the existing conditions in their causes and sweep of movement. One does not know whether to admire most the extraordinary scholarship which marks the book, the ease with which it is handled, or the power of centering to a unified picture the variety of diverse streams that have entered into making our existing civilization. While Dr. Randall escapes the error of "rationalizing" existing conditions, while indeed he indicates pointedly many of the forms this idealization has taken, his historical grasp leaves us with a solidly constructed picture. The debunking which the book contains is a definite contribution to a positive result and not an end in itself. Any one who wants an understanding of how and why our present civilization is as it is should read this book.

[Typescript in the John H. Randall, Jr., Papers, Rare Book and Manuscript Library, Butler Library, Columbia University, New York, N.Y., 1929.]

Remarks on Richard Welling's *As the Twig Is Bent*

Educators have always heard a great deal about our schools as the bulwark of democracy. Here in *As the Twig Is Bent* is the story of a man who for sixty long years has been an active fighter for reform in our civic and political life. Richard Welling, young at the age of eighty-four, has been a leader in every movement of this kind since he left college. This book is an account of his own life as blended with the history of his country. It gives a dramatic account of the practical experiences that led him to find the schools of the country to be the sole sure source and guarantee of the clean, humane, efficient government for which he had struggled in the many reform movements in which he took part. He also tells, alas, how the failure of the schools to get down to basic democratic practices in their own organization and conduct has retarded creation of that alert intelligent citizenship that understands and knows how to carry on the business of government.

A soldier in two of our wars, Mr. Welling makes it clear that his part in founding and vigorously conducting the National Self-Government Committee is the climax of the persistent, cheerful, always good-humored even gay battle he has steadily maintained to help our country get the kind of citizens who will in turn get the kind of civil servants, administrators, legislators that will establish the kind of government a democracy requires. Educators will learn from this book how abstractions and theories about schools as the basis of democracy can be translated into concrete, practical brass-tack facts. Americans in every walk of life will be buoyed and refreshed by this vital story of a gallant indomitable spirit. It comes at the time when it is needed.

[Typescript in the Richard G. Welling Papers, Rare Books and Manuscripts Division, Astor, Lenox and Tilden Foundations, New York Public Library, New York, N.Y., 1942.]

Memorandum for Mr. Pringle

1. In view of the fact that the general public has little realization of the actual significance of Nazi domination of the daily life of persons who come under its control, I suggest there be a concrete statement of what we are fighting against, in terms of what happens to the average man (and woman) in their daily life wherever Nazi wins. Perhaps a beginning could be made in terms of imagining here in our own country complete control of all newspapers, books, etc.; then of theater, radio, amusements, sports; what would happen in our schools and to our children; churches and priests and pastors; also courts, police and administration of "justice"; all with a picture of the amount of spying, tattling and petty interference involved. Something should be included of course relative to control of industry and labor. People with expert knowledge can give the material. My suggestion is simply that the story be told in terms of what would happen here in this country and the methods by which it would be carried out in terms of the life of the ordinary citizen, man, woman and child, in the various aspects of daily life.

2. The fact that people who want to go about their own affairs, work, play and contacts with others are now living under constant threat from nations whose governments are bent on extension of their ways of life by means of military conquest, and that this menace will hang over us until the axis nations have been defeated and some kind of world organization effected in the postwar period to prevent the rise of militaristic nations, should I think be strongly emphasized. We cannot lead a normal life as long as this state of things continues. Germany's early successes, her continuing strength, and the headstart of Japan prove

[Typescript in the Henry Fowles Pringle Papers, General Correspondence, "D" folder, box 1, Manuscript Division, Library of Congress, Washington, D.C., 1942.]

that peoples who want to engage in the normal activities of living are at a great disadvantage in comparison with nations who have at their disposal all modern technological agencies and resources and who organize these for imposing control and regimentation by conquest. Anything approaching a stalemate (to say nothing of victory by the axis powers) would impose upon us the necessity of changing our way of living so as to be ready at any time to meet the militarized powers, whose strength in war depends upon organized regimentation of every phase of the life of the ordinary man, woman and child. (It is this thing which is new in the world, and which makes the menace of axis powers so much more terrible than the kind of militarism we fought in the first world war. The existence of techniques for regulating every act and almost every thought of every one for a single end is new, and Nazi Germany has demonstrated it is possible to unify and organize these techniques.)

Hence this second point links up with the first. Even if Germany should not actually invade this country nor actually defeat this country and yet should win the war against European nations we should be compelled to adopt increasingly as means of self-defense against further aggression more and more of Nazi methods and would be gradually Nazified, even against our will and perhaps almost without knowing it, in our way of living. Industry, commerce, education, political methods, everything, would be radically altered.

I haven't said anything about war for freedom or for a democratic way of life in the foregoing. But I think the line indicated serves to take these ideas out of the field of generalities into what they concretely mean in the life of the average person.

Tribute to S. J. Woolf

The many readers of Mr. Woolf's reports of interviews with statesmen, writers, and artists are aware of his power to portray in words the salient traits of the ideas of the men who talk to him. Readers know also of his power to convey the intangibles, the atmosphere in which men live and do their work. His reports are remarkably free from the descriptions of petty details in which many interviewers revel. When he describes the surroundings of the man with whom he is dealing, one feels their relevancy to the man and to his work. His capacity to sketch in a few words the background of what a man says, political, literary or whatever, is due to the fact that Mr. Woolf himself comes to the interview with a large and well-informed background. I am sure many who have taken part in these interviews will agree with me that Mr. Woolf's own share in them makes them occasions of agreeable give-and-take.

The features that mark Mr. Woolf's reports are evident in his sketches. They show the same insight into fundamentals, the same power of selection and elimination, the same power of rapid and terse summary. They are valuable records of many traits of contemporary life. But they also evince the essential marks of the genuine artist.

[Typescript in Dewey VFM 80, Special Collections, Morris Library, Southern Illinois University at Carbondale, 1935.]

Statement on Retirement of Frank Becker

I count it a privilege to be invited to have a share in this occasion, for although I am not present physically I am permitted to have the great satisfaction of expressing the regards, the admiration, and the affection for Frank Becker of his one-time teacher, and of one who in spite of much too infrequent personal contacts in the intervening years has cherished not only his memory but a vision of him as a teacher to whom philosophy was living interest and vital concern, not a parlor game nor yet a set of exercises to be performed in a gymnasium for training in abstractions. I share with you, his students and colleagues, the sense of loss that casts its shadow on this evening's gathering. But I also share with you the happy confidence that his work will live on in the hearts and minds of those who have learned with him and from him the very best things that philosophy can convey to anyone, anywhere. From my memory of him as a student and as a human being and from what I have seen of him in our altogether too rare contacts in the passing years, as well as from what I have heard of him from others, I know he has infused his teaching of philosophy with personal qualities which have rendered the subject human and humanly liberating. The qualities of straightforward genuineness united with a friendliness of disposition that is only too rare did not desert him I am sure, when he came to Lehigh as a teacher. While you will miss his direct presence in the class-room in days to come, the radiation of philosophy lifted out of abstractions into vitality as it was imbued with his personality will stay with you. I am happy to join with you in grateful memories of past contacts and in wishing for the

[Typescript in the Theodore T. Lafferty Papers, South Caroliniana Library, University of South Carolina, Columbia, 1950.]

teacher whose psychological and moral ties with you will never be severed all of the good things in his future he so abundantly has earned. To you Professor Frank Becker, Hail and Fare You Well, not in the sense of departure and leaving but for a future which, like the past, will be one of happiness and success because one of service to your fellow-beings.

Addendum
The Value of Historical Christianity

Religion, generally, has had for its aim the uniting of man to some force greater, more permanent, more real, than himself, to some power which underlies nature. Man has ever associated with such a unity the sense of reconciliation and peace, of a value in life which can find no justification save in peace. Man has ever been prone to find this unity with God, either in mere outward rites, dogmas, and events, or in his own consciousness. Teaching once incarnate with personal zeal and inspiration tends to harden into formal dogma. Deeds, once the spontaneous and necessary because the unforced expression of sympathy and devotion, become ceremonial rites without meaning. A community once bound together by common interests and love tends to become an outward ecclesiastical organization. When zeal and inspiration depart and give place to rites the life of the religion has departed. There remains but a skeleton—a source of fear and of bondage. The unity that was to unite man to God has somehow grown into an institution which with its dogmas, rites, sacred events, and sacred books keeps man from coming nearest to his God. The individual who thinks finds these forms all outside of himself. They touch him nowhere. It is either a burden he must bear or a bondage he must shake off. It is a dream imposed on him in his sleep: if he should awake, the dream, and with it his religious faith will vanish. Again, man seeks for that final peace, which only reconciliation with God can give in his own heart. His religion becomes a matter of moods and symptoms which the individual must watch as closely as the valetudinarian watches his bodily symptoms. Religion is reduced to internal ex-

[First published in *Monthly Bulletin* 11 (November 1889): 31–36, from an address delivered 27 October 1889 before the Students' Christian Association of the University of Michigan.]

periences of morbid and health-destroying introspection. The individual must watch his every thought and feeling to see if it please God or no. His life is one vast query. Have I the evidences of salvation? Religious activity becomes sentimentalism. Let the individual now awake to self-consciousness, and he is convinced that the realm of religion is a realm of cant; that there is no reality in it.

If the merely outward form of religion is a skeleton, the merely inward form is a fibreless and sinewless pulp, equally lifeless. It cannot be denied that Christianity has repeatedly assumed one or the other of these unspiritual forms. Whenever this has occurred, scepticism, social and individual has arisen as surely as human consciousness is sure to assert itself against everything which tends to bring it into bondage. But it cannot be denied that the great strength of Christianity has been in its power to overcome these onesided forms and to bind the historical and the internal, personal factors into a vital unity; and to bring the individual nearer to God through the uniting of these forces, in society and in history; and to make the historical expression of Christianity not dead dogma, traditionalism, ceremonialism, that happened 19 centuries ago; but to make this external side itself a manifestation of the unity of man with God, and an influence for its higher realization.

Christianity makes religion a social as well as an historical force, for it has its value in the power it has been to raise men out of their isolated individuality, and bind them into families and nations, and make them capable of higher social attainment in language, art and culture.

Christianity is unique, not in its unlikeness to other religions, but in the greater energy and fruitfulness with which it manifests and fulfills the essential elements of all.

The value of Christianity as an historical force in the world lies in the fact that there is a historical side, that Christianity is a principle which transcends all individualism; a principle which must find outward social expression in the world; and that it is a fact entering into that vast complexity of events we call history.

Men of philosophical tendencies have in the last hundred years repeatedly offered to compromise with the Christian community, expressing their entire willingness to recognize the truth of Christian ideas, if the Christian community would acknowledge Christian truth as only an idea, of which the historical facts are but imperfect symbols.

The Christian body have refused to surrender that which is its heart, but hold that Christianity is not only true as idea, but true also as a historic fact and force.

The historic side of Christianity is the growth it has had in history.

In order to teach and spread Christian truth and bring it home to the world, a certain amount of organization and machinery has been necessary. Christianity as a historical force means this and more. It means what Christ meant when he said, "He that hath seen me hath seen the Father." It means what St. John spoke: "That which was from the beginning, that which we have seen with our eyes; that which we beheld and our hands handled, concerning the Word of Life, declare we unto you."

Surely Christ did not mean that the man who had looked on him with bodily eye had seen the Divine Spirit. Surely St. John did not mean that he had actually seen and touched and heard, physically, the Eternal One—The Spirit of Life that was from the beginning. Both these are tremendous metaphors, the most tremendous and magnificent that have fallen from men's lips. They express in the only language which man can command that God is no remote Being away from the world, that He is no Force which works in physical Nature alone, but that He is an ever present fact in life, in history, and in our social relations. They express the fact that the Divine Spirit has touched our actual life so immediately, so directly and so certainly, that men have seen Him and touched Him. Surely only the vast meaning and reality that lie within the words save them from blasphemy. No, God is neither a far-away Being, nor a mere philosophic conception by which to explain the world. He is the reality of our ordinary relations with one another in life. He is the bond of the family, the bond of society. He is love, the source of all growth, all sacrifice, and all unity. He has touched history, not from without but has made Himself subjected to all the limitations and sufferings of history; identified Himself absolutely with humanity, so that the life of humanity is henceforward not for some term of years, but forever, the Life of God. Who can read the last talks of Jesus with His disciples, as recorded in John's gospel, and not feel that their one burden, surging for expression in all commands, entreaties, encouragements, instructions, revelations, promises and prayers, is that the unity of God and man is perfect, absolute, now, in the Christ who has made men realize the presence of God within them forever, in the Spirit, who shall guide them into all truth, and comfort them with all comfort and make them possessors of all God's riches.

Unless these are mere symbols, or at best experiences to be reached by a few choice spirits, but not the common vantage of man, they must mean that the Spirit of God has entered into history, and that the Spirit is not a mystery working only in miracles, in revivals, etc., but is the intelligence present in all man's science, is his inspiration for whatever is better than himself. Such is the meaning of the historical aspect of Christianity. What is its value in practical life? All men, right-minded and serious, have questioned. What is the purpose, the function of my life, and how shall I fulfill it? There has been but one answer—though in form it has varied from the almost inarticulate babble of childhood in primitive religion, to the clear triumphant utterance of a St. Paul—likeness to God, unity with Him.

How shall this unity be attained? The value of what has been termed the historical force of Christianity lies in the answer that it gives to this question. Union with humanity and humanity's interests, and surrender of individual desire.

Consciousness that the purpose of one's life is to be like God gives no help in the attainment of that likeness so long as it shuts the individual within his own interests. Such consciousness but weighs man down with the feeling of his utter impotency and the entire hopelessness of his case. But man is not thus isolated, and hence he does not have to deal with God face to face, but through the mediator of that corporate humanity of which he is a member, and Jesus, the head. Man thus feels that in his weakness he is strong. It is not that his consciousness of responsibility to God is diminished; not that he feels his individual powerlessness now that he has found shelter in the righteousness of another. It is because he knows that the God who has laid the claim upon him is Himself working *in* and *through* humanity to realize its highest good.

The individual has but to surrender himself to the common interests of humanity in order to be freed from the claim upon him as an individual. He stands no longer isolated, but a member of that humanity whose living spirit is God Himself.

If a man, forgetting the historic force of Christianity; forgetting that God is not some remote supernal being, but a present fact and force in historic and social life, attempts to realize what the words of Jesus, Paul and John mean, without realizing their nature, he will impose upon himself one of two things; either he will decide that the words can have no reality back of them, unless they be exaggerated expressions of experiences of some unusual souls, and will reject them as mere cant, or unconscious self-deceit; or he will attempt to realize their truth in his own experiences and feelings as an individual, which is impossible, for they are not the expressions of the experiences of an individual in his isolated relations to God, but rather of a man who has lost his individuality in his identification with humanity's interests, in the family, in the community, of interest in the better self.

The person who thus attempts to realize these things gradually divorces himself from reality, and begins by living a life of unreality of word, then of thought, and too often finally of deed.

The chief danger after all, in our practical religious life, is the tendency for the religious life to become a sphere by itself, apart from the interests of life and humanity. The healthy religious life knows no separation of the religious from the secular, which has no Sunday or week-day divisions in it, which finds in every daily duty, whether in study or business, or recreation an approach to God as surely and truly as in the retirement of the closet. This frame of mind can never be attained unless we realize that God is in history, is in the social state of life, reconciling men unto Him. He who finds in every true and pure relationship in life a bond of union with God, has his religious life built upon a rock which cannot be shaken by the storms of life, nor undermined by the subtleties of temptation.

Appendixes

Appendix 1
The Revival of the Soul
By H. S. Swift

As paradoxical as the fact may at first sight appear, the ground taken by Dr. John Dewey, in a recent number of the *University*, on the subject of the present marked tendency to seek in psychological research the proof and demonstration of man's spiritual nature and his immortality, is substantially the position which the church with most or all of its leading thinkers has assumed. Doctor Dewey should have spoken to a larger and more general audience than the *University* could possibly afford him, for his words gave expression to a wide-spread sentiment in the church; a sentiment apparently of supercilious indignation that the world should presume to undertake to do what the church has for so long failed in doing—establish a rational basis for faith in the immortality of the race, and reconcile revealed religion with common sense. But despite the opposition of the church and its votaries to this latest and noblest impulse of the liberal mind of the old and new worlds, the search after truth will continue until the proof of man's spiritual nature and grand destiny shall rest on the bases of accurate scientific demonstration.

The most urgent need of the times is this scientific demonstration of the great truths of Christianity, which the church, since the close of the earthly mission of Jesus and his apostles, has but dogmatically asserted, and for the reasonable rejection of which on such evidence, the greater portion of the race has been condemned, as the church would have us believe, either to an eternal or to a mitigated purgatorial damnation! The religious impulse is the highest and most natural impulse of the human mind. In it all men share to a greater or less degree. It is but one manifestation

[First published in *University*, no. 224 (9 January 1886): 19. For Dewey's article to which this is a reply, see this volume, pp. 10–14. For Dewey's further response, see pp. 15–18.]

of the faculty of reason and to meet its requirements religious and philosophical systems must possess perfect rationality, or sooner or later the universal and unerring conscience will refuse to give them credence. The strength of Christianity as taught by Jesus was in its perfect conformity to reason; in the element of sensible demonstration that the great teacher and his immediate followers introduced into their teaching. Without the record of this demonstration the church would have no bases for its creeds. And yet, when Christendom cries out for reconciliation between the tenets of revealed religion, based on this record, and the enlightened conscience of the age, the church throws up her hands in holy horror and utters, in the words of Doctor Dewey, the despairing cry: "There could be no more significant token of the hopelessness and heartlessness of the age than this revival of the soul for scientific and spectacular purposes." The present purpose of the world seems to be to rise above creed and dogma to a pure spiritual religion based on sensible demonstration. It is this quest after truth that the church and Doctor Dewey confound with and name the hopeless and heartless skepticism of the age.

That modern Christianity, as distinguished from the teaching of Jesus, is fast losing its hold on the mind and conscience of men, statistics and observation clearly prove. Of our own country it may safely be asserted that in 1886, out of a population of sixty millions not to exceed ten millions are in active and sympathetic connection with the churches. And why? Not because men are becoming with increasing enlightenment naturally more skeptical, or apathetic to the great questions of human destiny, but because Christian philosophy, under the modern interpretation, fails to satisfy the reason and conscience of men.

The philosophy of Jesus was purely spiritual. The dualism of spirit and matter which ancient philosophy had failed to subdue, he perfectly overcame, and sealed the conquest by demonstration, healing the bodily infirm, casting out evil from men and triumphing over death. And by what means? It is on this rock that the incoming flood-tide of enlightened reason will leave the church unless the helm is put about and the bark floated into deep water. With the advent of the age of reason the miraculous has come to be unconsciously assimilated in the minds of men to the mythological, the miracles of Christ to the oriental myths. And here is manifest the precarious foundation on which the fabric reared by the churches stands. The miracle of the resurrection disapproved, the whole structure falls in interminable ruin. And so it has fallen to the majority of the minds of Christendom. And yet, amid the mists of error and misinterpretation the simple yet sublime structure reared by Jesus on the foundation of a subdued dualism between spirit and nature stands ever and evermore, its lofty spires and towering minarets piercing the clouds of error, gleaming in the sunlight of eternal truth.

If the work of the church is not to fail utterly from this age of the world onward; if men are not to sink again into the degradation of paganism; if Christian civilization is not to fade and fade and disappear, leaving the world in the black darkness of moral night, there must be the revival of the soul that Doctor Dewey so deprecates. The church must go back again—where it has never been since the time of the apostles—to the pure spiritual philosophy taught by Jesus. It must give the recorded words of the great teacher a literal where they have had a metaphorical interpretation. And above all it must, following in the footsteps of its master, seek to establish by practical tangible demonstration the bases of its faith, and to realize the promise, "He that believeth on me, the works that I do shall he do also." Then let us have the revival of the soul. Let the societies for psychical research multiply. Let the metaphysical healers supersede if they can the disciples of materia medica. Let ever the faith-curers pursue their vagaries unmolested, for out of it all must come somewhat of the truth that is to make men free.

Appendix 2
Forms of Art Exhibition
By E. M. Benson

In this introductory FORMS OF ART exhibition a systematic attempt has been made to so relate the art of the past to the present that time and place become secondary to the creative character of the works themselves,—and artists separated by centuries in time and continents in space are found to speak essentially the same language. Common bonds, resulting from basically similar artistic objectives, or social philosophies, or both, unite the work of the artists included in each of the three sections of this exhibition.

In the section devoted to FORMAL AND HUMANIZED VALUES you will find that the dominant emphasis on formal construction in a Coptic tapestry fragment of the fifth century, a Florentine chair of the fifteenth, and an American Indian petroglyph of the nineteenth century does not differ appreciably from the procedure and attitude that produced the early Cubist art of Picasso or Matisse; that the intimate semi-humanized design on a Majolica bowl of the nineteenth century closely approximates in form and feeling the gouache paintings by the American artist, Max Weber; that the fine marriage of structure and humanized seeing in Memling's "Half Figure of the Virgin" also animates, though more sensuously, an Indian sculpture of the second century.

A comparable unanimity of purpose unites the work of the artists included in the SOCIAL COMMENT AND SOCIAL SATIRE section. From the more restrained social comments of Pietro Longhi and Jan Steen we pass on to the pungent satirical allegories of Bosch, the fifteenth century father of "true nightmares"; Breughel who could sting like a tarantula and paint like an angel; Daumier, the sharp thorn in the side of nineteenth century French reaction

[First published in *Forms of Art Exhibition* (Philadelphia: Pennsylvania Museum of Art, 1937). For Dewey's comment, see this volume, pp. 128–29.]

(twenty of his acid sculpture grotesques of the conservative members of the French Chamber of Deputies are included in the exhibition); Hogarth whose dislike for lawmakers was almost as venomous as Daumier's; and such brilliant satirists of our own age as James Ensor, George Grosz, Gropper, and two of America's outstanding social surrealists, Louis Guglielmi and Walter Quirt.

Carl Walters' ceramic animals keep equally friendly company in the PHASES OF FANTASY section with a Tournai tapestry of the fifteenth century, with Persian blueware and Delft animal forms, terra cottas from Russia, Turkey, Mexico, Sgraffito pottery and painted bridal boxes of the Pennsylvania Germans, as well as paintings and prints by Paul Klee, Redon, Bresdin and early Italian and Flemish masters.

This FORMS OF ART exhibition,—the first of a series of experimental exhibitions,—is based on the belief that it is more important to understand what an artist is trying to say and how he says it, than to know when and where it was said. Historical facts may explain many things, but they seldom tell us very much about the one thing in a work of art that is essential to appreciation,—and that is why and how it functions as a work of art; and why artists of all ages, despite minor differences of seeing and feeling, have been moved to express themselves in much the same way. The student, no less than the man in the street, will, I hope, find visual nourishment here, and fresh insight into the ageless continuities of the basic art forms.

Appendix 3
A United Command and the Second Front

We face the immediate threat of a German break-through on the Russian front. If this movement goes far enough, it will cut direct communications between the north and south. The Caucasus and the armies defending it will have contact with the rest of Russia only by long and feeble lines running east of the Caspian. In the meantime, the Germans will be able to move toward the enormously rich oil fields. They can by-pass the gigantic obstacle of the Caucasian mountains. In the face of such grim realities, we must soberly appraise future possibilities.

What power of resistance has the Red Army now? We do not have the full answer. This question immediately reveals the weakness of our present situation and suggests means of remedy. Thus far we have had not one war but two. Great Britain, the United States and others among the United Nations have been conducting one struggle which reaches round the world. On the mighty front stretching more than a thousand miles from north to south, Russia has for more than a year carried on an entirely separate battle. The supplies sent in from Great Britain and America are mere gifts. The responsibility for defense of this decisive sector has rested exclusively on Russian shoulders.

The fate of our entire cause depends on Russian power, but the Allies have little or no idea of the extent of that power. The Russian staff alone knows the answer. Until recently, Moscow refused to supply detailed information. Allied military observers have been given little opportunity to visit the Soviet fronts. This creates an abnormal and dangerous situation. A united war demands unity of command and unity of responsibility. A German

[First published as editorial in *New Leader* 25 (14 July 1942): 1. For Dewey's comment, see this volume, p. 130.]

break-through will force upon us all, including Russia, a common front against a common enemy.

The Nazis are striving to cut the Russian armies in two. If they succeed, it will mean that Soviet forces will be fighting side by side with British troops stationed in the Near East. The Russian battle will thus quickly become part of the general struggle under control of the United Nations War Council. The allocation of troops and supplies for this theatre of war will obviously be the affair of all of the Allies. The tactics and strategy must be the responsibility of the great War Council. The war will perforce become unified.

Since the results of the Russian campaign will fall upon the shoulders of all of the twenty-eight nations involved, it is obvious that it should be carried on with the most effective sort of cooperation that is possible. Against this argument for a United Command, we have the argument that Soviet Russia, under the onslaught of Germany, has been forced to fight on its own front, with its own men and supplies and with its own tactics and strategy. Whatever validity this argument may once have had disappeared long since. Russia and the United Nations cannot now act separately and win this war.

Russia would secure definite and immediate advantages from such a union of control. The question of opening of a second front, for example, is her concern as well as ours. The decisions with regard to this vital problem should be made by a council representing all the great powers and in possession of information from all angles. Russian generalship thus far has proved at least equal to anything displayed by her allies. There is no reason why it should not have its opportunity to make its contribution toward the common cause.

A Unified Command has been postponed too long. It is possible that with it we might have prevented the present tragic situation. But since our division of forces is, in part, responsible for the dangers of the present position, it would be folly to prolong the source of weakness. The destiny of each nation depends upon the fate of the rest. In this total and global war, only a total and global high command can meet the tremendous problems facing the United Nations.

In last week's *New Leader*, Walter Nash, Minister of New

Zealand to the United States, proposed definite machinery for world-wide military operations. As a member of the Pacific War Council, he speaks out of a wealth of experience. He proposes a World War Council on Policy, a World Military Council, and regional councils to conduct operations in the various theatres of war. This week's tragic events on the Russian front, with the vision of future eventualities which they inevitably force upon our imaginations, give powerful support to his proposals.

Appendix 4
Religion at Harvard
By Harold R. Rafton

The breakdown of religious belief, and with it the threatening of moral standards, is a cause of increasing concern. Orthodoxy attributes this breakdown to man's sinfulness; but the Rev. T. R. Ferris, '29, in a recent book [*Religion in the Post-War World*] edited by Dean Sperry of the Divinity School, frankly indicates that the impact of scientific knowledge upon religion has been responsible.

Our danger in having linked supernatural beliefs with moral standards is that the inevitable weakening of one gravely imperils the other. The remedy of endeavoring to place the new wine of modern knowledge into the old bottles of the historic faiths promises little success. I propose to meet the issue squarely by fostering Humanism, a rationalistic religion based on science, centered in man, rejecting supernaturalism but retaining our cherished moral values.

Dean Sperry states in his book that the inclusion of the chapter on Humanism "is a recognition of the fact that outside formal organized churches there is a great body of persons . . . who are idealists and loyal servants of their fellow men, but who find themselves intellectually unable to profess the traditional faith in God." An English bishop, the author adds, furnishes the astounding information "that fifty per cent of the intelligent people of the modern world are humanists!" "These persons," concludes Dean Sperry, "though ecclesiastically unorganized, deserve recognition."

Why, then, should not Harvard pioneer in providing a clergy for this important group? Most of the Divinity School courses appear suited for a Humanist curriculum (to be offered in addi-

[First published in *Harvard Alumni Bulletin* 49 (11 January 1947): 330. For Dewey's reply, see this volume, p. 135.]

tion to the present one). Church History 4b offers a study of "Rationalism." Rationalism—as "the mental attitude which . . . accepts the supremacy of reason and aims at establishing a . . . philosophy and ethics verifiable by experience and independent of all arbitrary assumptions or authority"—should include instruction in the attitude, method, controls, and implications of science. Indeed, it is the core of the present proposal that a Chair of Rationalism be established in the Divinity School, to be held by a well-qualified rationalist, who would supervise the Humanist curriculum.

Instruction or practice in prayer, worship, ritual, or other technique of supernaturalism would have no meaning, being discarded for the scientific approach—controlled observation, experiment, and verifiable experience. The Humanist clergy would have a tremendous potential field of ministry, would preach a religion in harmony with facts as now known, recognizing nature as impersonal and inexorable, fostering cooperation under the realization that man has but himself and his fellow men upon whom to rely.

The concept of universality has ever fascinated mankind. Art, music, literature, philosophy, government, religion—none has achieved this goal; all have possessed group, race, national, or geographic flavor. The Church catholic has never embraced more than a fraction of humanity. Of all arts and disciplines of man, science alone speaks a common tongue. It proceeds from known to unknown by controlled investigation, subjecting itself to the harsh taskmaster of experimental verification. Its technique and manner of thought are alike the world over, its results universally applicable. Its achievements have remade the world both materially and spiritually.

Contrast supernatural religion. It postulates a picture of the unknown upon inadequate and naive concepts of primitive peoples, many times upon pronouncements of mentally unstable individuals, and demands that the known ever conform to this fanciful hypothesis. It does not embarrass its advocates by requiring proof of their pretensions, but falls back on "faith" to buttress unverified assertions. Against new knowledge its more intransigent devotees invoke alleged authority. But "infallible authority," whether of hierarch or book, finds little warmth in the

present climate of world opinion. Its more liberal adherents realize the implications of the new knowledge, yet cling to ancient
forms and catchwords, comforting themselves with "interpretations" which fail to reconcile the manifestly irreconcilable.

Humanism is free from such limitations. It is in harmony with
the new knowledge of science; indeed it *is* science and the scientific method in the field of religion. Thus it is the only religion
that can hope to achieve universality. Small wonder, then, that
"fifty per cent of the intelligent people of the modern world are
humanists"; the real marvel is that the other fifty per cent are not
also humanists! Perhaps Harvard can lead the way, inspired by
her immortal anthem:

> Let not moss-covered Error moor thee at its side,
> As the world on Truth's current glides by;
> Be the herald of Light and the bearer of Love,
> Till the stock of the Puritans die.

Appendix 5
Consciousness and Meaning
By Frederick J. E. Woodbridge

In the interest of better understanding I wish to comment on Professor Bode's discussion in the July issue of the *Psychological Review,* so far as he refers to my own views on the
nature of consciousness.

Professor Bode states the general problem tersely, it seems to
me, when he asks, "When an object becomes known, what is
present that was not present the moment before?" I have attempted to answer that question in one word—"meaning." This
answer may be incorrect or inadequate, but I do not see that it
forces the maker into a dilemma. When objects become known,
they do not—as I am inclined to think—lose any of the properties or relationships they had before. Water does not become
water or cease to be water when I become conscious of it.
But when objects become known, they then mean something.
The water which was water before I was conscious of it and is
still water when I am conscious of it, is now, when I am conscious of it, water meaning something, the quenching of thirst,
for example.

Why, then, does Professor Bode state: "Either a fact upon becoming a fact of consciousness transforms itself from an unknowable something into a relation of meaning or it undergoes
no such transformation. In the former case the distinction between what is consciousness and what is not is inept, since all is
consciousness; while in the latter we have again on our hands the
difficulty that no differentia are furnished whereby a given personal experience is distinguished from other facts." Assuredly
when an unknown fact becomes known, it has changed from an
unknown to a known fact, and to that extent has changed its

[First published in "Discussion," *Psychological Review* 15 (November 1908):
397–98. For Dewey's reply, see this volume, pp. 361–73.]

character. But the question is as Professor Bode has put it, What is present with the known fact which was not present with the unknown fact? Take the water again. When it is unknown—meaning thereby when it is not an object in consciousness—is it lacking in particular chemical and physical properties? Does it take on these properties—or lose them—only in consciousness? If it can have these properties both in consciousness and out of it, there is no necessity of adding anything to them to make them just those properties when they are in consciousness. On the other hand, it seems very difficult to believe that water could mean anything and not be in consciousness; and it seems very natural to believe that if water should come to mean anything it would, by that fact, have entered consciousness.

And now a word about 'awareness,' for one may claim that not only must a fact mean something to be in consciousness, but we must also be 'aware' of the fact as fact and also of the fact as meaning something. I repeat what I have already said, but now in general terms. If a fact has certain properties which it neither acquires nor loses by virtue of its presence in consciousness, it is evidently unnecessary to add anything to those properties to make them the same properties in consciousness that they are when out of it. Consequently it is not necessary to add 'awareness.' That is, it is not the 'awareness' of a fact that makes the fact a fact of a particular kind in consciousness; it is that in its own right. The simple existence of the fact in consciousness appears, therefore, to be all that is involved in 'awareness of the fact as fact.' But let the fact mean something and its meaning appears to be identical with 'awareness of it as meaning something.' Or, to state the situation in the form of a paradox: If objects were in my consciousness, but entirely devoid of meaning, I should not be aware of them. The presence of meaning among the facts is the awareness of them. In short—to drop the paradox—'awareness' is but another term for 'consciousness.'

The position which I have thus briefly outlined seems to me to answer Professor Bode's initial question directly and unambiguously. I do not say it answers it correctly or adequately. That is matter for consideration. But I do not see how it can be reduced to the dilemma he states in the discussion of it.

Appendix 6
The Children's Charter

For every child spiritual and moral training to help him to stand firm under the pressure of life

II. For every child understanding and the guarding of his personality as his most precious right

III. For every child a home and that love and security which a home provides; and for that child who must receive foster care, the nearest substitute for his own home

IV. For every child full preparation for his birth, his mother receiving prenatal, natal, and postnatal care; and the establishment of such protective measures as will make child-bearing safer

V. For every child health protection from birth through adolescence, including: periodical health examinations and, where needed, care of specialists and hospital treatment; regular dental examinations and care of the teeth; protective and preventive measures against communicable diseases; the insuring of pure food, pure milk, and pure water

VI. For every child from birth through adolescence, promotion of health, including health instruction and a health program, wholesome physical and mental recreation, with teachers and leaders adequately trained

[First published in *White House Conference on Child Health and Protection, 1930* (New York: Century Co., 1931), pp. 46–48. For Dewey's address on Child Health and Protection, see this volume, pp. 511–19.]

VII. For every child a dwelling-place safe, sanitary, and wholesome, with reasonable provisions for privacy; free from conditions which tend to thwart his development; and a home environment harmonious and enriching

VIII. For every child a school which is safe from hazards, sanitary, properly equipped, lighted, and ventilated. For younger children nursery schools and kindergartens to supplement home care

IX. For every child a community which recognizes and plans for his needs, protects him against physical dangers, moral hazards, and disease; provides him with safe and wholesome places for play and recreation; and makes provision for his cultural and social needs

X. For every child an education which, through the discovery and development of his individual abilities, prepares him for life; and through training and vocational guidance prepares him for a living which will yield him the maximum of satisfaction

XI. For every child such teaching and training as will prepare him for successful parenthood, home-making, and the rights of citizenship; and, for parents, supplementary training to fit them to deal wisely with the problems of parenthood

XII. For every child education for safety and protection against accidents to which modern conditions subject him—those to which he is directly exposed and those which, through loss or maiming of his parents, affect him indirectly

XIII. For every child who is blind, deaf, crippled, or otherwise physically handicapped, and for the child who is mentally handicapped, such measures as will early discover and diagnose his handicap, provide care and treatment, and so train him that he may become an asset to society rather than a liability. Expenses of these services should be borne publicly where they cannot be privately met

XIV. For every child who is in conflict with society the right to be dealt with intelligently as society's charge, not society's outcast; with the home, the school, the church, the court and the institution when needed, shaped to return him whenever possible to the normal stream of life

XV. For every child the right to grow up in a family with an adequate standard of living and the security of a stable income as the surest safeguard against social handicaps

XVI. For every child protection against labor that stunts

growth, either physical or mental, that limits education, that deprives children of the right of comradeship, of play, and of joy

XVII. For every rural child as satisfactory schooling and health services as for the city child, and an extension to rural families of social, recreational, and cultural facilities

XVIII. To supplement the home and the school in the training of youth, and to return to them those interests of which modern life tends to cheat children, every stimulation and encouragement should be given to the extension and development of the voluntary youth organizations

XIX. To make everywhere available these minimum protections of the health and welfare of children, there should be a district, county, or community organization for health, education, and welfare, with full-time officials, coördinating with a state-wide program which will be responsive to a nation-wide service of general information, statistics, and scientific research. This should include:

(a) Trained, full-time public health officials, with public health nurses, sanitary inspection, and laboratory workers

(b) Available hospital beds

(c) Full-time public welfare service for the relief, aid, and guidance of children in special need due to poverty, misfortune, or behavior difficulties, and for the protection of children from abuse, neglect, exploitation, or moral hazard

FOR EVERY CHILD THESE RIGHTS,
REGARDLESS OF RACE, OR COLOR, OR
SITUATION, WHEREVER HE MAY LIVE UNDER
THE PROTECTION OF THE AMERICAN FLAG

Notes

The following notes, keyed to the page and line numbers of the present edition, explain references to matters not found in standard sources. Full publication information for shortened references appears in the Checklist of Dewey's References.

3.3–4   recent . . . College,] Appointed in 1869, Martineau (1805–1900) resigned his principalship on 24 June 1885 but acted as president of the college for two more years.

3.12–13   reviewed . . . *University*.] See *University*, no. 206 (5 September 1885): 7.

7.3–4   publication . . . ago,] See Edward H. Clarke, *Sex in Education*.

7.12–14   wealthiest . . . pressure] Soon after its organization in 1879, Radcliffe College became known as the Harvard Annex. See Dorothy Elia Howell, *A Century to Celebrate Radcliffe College, 1879–1979* (Cambridge, Mass.: Radcliffe College, 1978).

7.31   female health in colleges.] See *Sixteenth Annual Report of the Bureau of Statistics of Labor,* pp. 473–532.

8.1–2   "Association of Collegiate Alumnae"] Formed in January 1882 with the express purpose, stated in its constitution, to "unite alumnae of different institutions for practical educational work," the ACA merged in 1921 with the Southern Association of College Women to form the American Association of University Women.

8.4   twelve colleges,] Boston University, Cornell University, University of Kansas, Massachusetts Institute of Technology, University of Michigan, Oberlin College, Smith College, Syracuse University, Vassar College, Wellesley College, Wesleyan University, University of Wisconsin.

8.17 Colonel Wright,] Carroll Davidson Wright (1840–1909), economist and statistician. His varied experience included a stint with the 14th New Hampshire Volunteers (of which he became colonel) during the Civil War, and a term in the Massachusetts senate. As U.S. Commissioner of Labor he organized the Bureau of Labor Statistics and stimulated objective research on labor problems. From 1902 until his death he was president of Clark College, Worcester, Mass.

10.3 *Discovery of the Soul*.] See Gustav Jaeger, *Die Entdeckung der Seele*.

11.32–36 who . . . structure,] In his 1874 lecture "Body and Mind," William Kingdon Clifford (1845–79), after posing the question of whether the local universe might not be regarded as a "vast brain," concluded that "the particular organisation of the brain" that results in brain function that runs "parallel to consciousness" was not a characteristic of "the great interplanetary spaces" (*Lectures and Essays*, 2:46).

11.36–37 ended . . . stuff,] In his "On the Nature of Things-in-Themselves," *Lectures and Essays*, 2:72, Clifford stated that "The universe, then, consists entirely of mind-stuff."

12.20 Othello's occupation gone.] Shakespeare, *Othello*, act 3, sc. 3.

12.33 New England woman] Elizabeth Stuart Phelps (1844–1911).

12.34–35 gates ajar,] See Phelps, *The Gates Ajar* (Boston: Fields, Osgood, and Co., 1869).

12.35 beyond the gates,] See Phelps, *Beyond the Gates* (Boston: Houghton, Mifflin and Co., 1883).

12.36–37 article . . . *Review*.] See Phelps, "The Struggle for Immortality."

13.29 "other-worldliness."] See Eliot, "Worldliness and Other-Worldliness."

14.26–27 "Black Crook" sprite,] *The Black Crook*, a theatrical production which combined music and ballet with lavish stage spectacle, opened on 12 September 1866 at Niblo's Garden in New York City. It was an immediate popular success and continued to draw audiences to frequent revivals and road productions into the mid-1890s. The play is considered by many theater historians to have been the progenitor of the

American musical comedy. Charles M. Barras (1820?–73), the play's author, included sprites among the "Immortals" in the cast of characters.

19.3–4   editorial note . . . labor,] See *University*, no. 220 (12 December 1885): 3–4.

19.6   inter-denominational . . . Cincinnati.] Convened by Josiah Strong (1847–1916), minister of the Central Congregational Church of Cincinnati, to implement his conviction that concerted interchurch action was necessary. The preliminary meeting was held 7 December 1885, and the congress concluded 11 December.

29.6   May 4th movement] On 4 May 1919 students in Peking (Beijing) protested against provisions in the Versailles Peace Treaty allowing Japan to retain territory and business interests in Shantung (Shandong) province, which it seized from Germany at the beginning of World War I. The protests sparked popular support throughout China and eventually forced Chinese refusal to sign the Versailles Treaty. See *Middle Works* 11:186–91.

29.7–8   inauguration of Sun Yat-sen] Sun (1866–1925) was elected President Extraordinary of China by the rump parliament at Canton (Guangzhou) in April 1921 and assumed the office on 5 May. Dewey met Sun during his visit to Canton. See *Middle Works* 13:127–29, 135–36.

29.9   seventy-two patriots] On 27 April 1911 the revolutionary forces of Sun Yat-sen, under the command of Huang Hsing, made an unsuccessful attempt to capture Canton to use as a southern base of operations. According to popular tradition, seventy-two of the rebels participating in the revolt died. A month later the Wuchang uprising marked the beginning of the Republican revolution. A memorial to the seventy-two patriots was dedicated on 6 May 1921 in Canton. See *Middle Works* 13:135.

29.10–11   Day . . . Demands.] Early in 1915 the Japanese government submitted to the Peking government of Yüan Shih-k'ai (1859–1916) their twenty-one demands, which involved concessions to Japan in both the political and economic affairs of China. After lengthy negotiations, the Japanese government presented China with an ultimatum on 7 May. On 9 May Yüan acceded to a shortened list of Japan's demands. Both 7 and 9 May were named Days of National Shame, also referred to as National Humiliation Days, to commemorate these events.

30.26   teachers' strike in Peking.] Some 800 teachers of higher education in Peking were on strike during the spring of 1921 over the government's failure to release funds for salaries.

31.1   Cassel Collieries Contract] Agreement drawn up in April 1920 by Major Louis Cassel of Hong Kong and the military government of Kwangtung (Guangdong) province granting extensive coal mining and transportation rights in that province to a British syndicate. See *Middle Works* 13:121–26.

31.2   Kwangsi militarists,] Kwangtung province was occupied and, for the most part, governed by the military leadership of its western neighboring province, Kwangsi (Guangxi), under the leadership of Lu Jung-t'ing (1856–1927) from 1916 until 1920, when Ch'en Chiung-ming's army forced Kwangsi troops out of Kwangtung and Ch'en took office as provincial governor.

31.14–16   Not . . . heard.] Governor Ch'en Chiung-ming ordered the permanent closure of gambling dens in Canton on 1 December 1920. See *Middle Works* 13:129.

31.25–26   Governor Ch'en Chiung-ming] Ch'en (1878–1933) was governor of Kwangtung province from fall 1920 until spring 1922. Dewey met Ch'en during his visit to Canton. For his impressions of Ch'en, see *Middle Works* 13:133–34.

36.4   "cultural block universes"] In his *Pluralistic Universe* (New York: Longmans, Green, and Co., 1909), pp. 76, 310, 328, James speaks of a "block-universe."

39.18–19   recent German critic] In 1908 when he wrote his first critique of pragmatism, "Der Pragmatismus," Ludwig Stein taught philosophy and sociology at the University of Berne and edited the *Archiv für systematische Philosophie*, in which "Der Pragmatismus" appeared.

39.19–22   "Epistemologically, . . . utilitarianism."] Dewey probably translated this himself, since no English translation has been located earlier than 1910.

39n.2–5   "Gewiss . . . Utilitarismus."] In his 1909 *Syllabus: The Pragmatic Movement of Contemporary Thought*, Dewey refers to Stein's "Der Pragmatismus," although Stein's *Phi-*

losophische Strömungen more completely matches Dewey's translation. See *Middle Works* 4:258.

45.19–21   H. G. Wells . . . catastrophe.] See his *Outline of History*, 2:594.

50.3–4   good wine needs no bush.] See *Oxford Dictionary of English Proverbs*, 3d ed., rev. F. P. Wilson (Oxford: At the Clarendon Press, 1970), p. 326, for source of English proverb dating back to John Lydgate, *The Pilgrimage of Man* (ca. 1426), later in Shakespeare, *As You Like It*, epilogue, line 4.

50.25–30   A British critic . . . modern science.] The "British critic" is Bertrand Russell. In 1922 Russell wrote: "I find love of truth obscured in America by commercialism, of which pragmatism is the philosophical expression" ("As a European Radical Sees It," *Freeman* 4 [8 March 1922]: 610). Fourteen years earlier he had written: "Pragmatism, if I have not misunderstood it, is largely a generalisation from the procedure of the inductive sciences" ("Transatlantic 'Truth,'" *Albany Review* 2 [January 1908]: 406–7).

54.20   visit to Russia] Dewey visited the Soviet Union from 2 July to 4 August 1928.

57.3–4   translator] For a discussion of Dewey's relationship with Hoashi Riichiro, see Victor N. Kobayashi, "Japan's Hoashi Riichiro and John Dewey," *Educational Theory* 14 (January 1964): 50–53.

67.2   Mr. Fitzpatrick,] Edward A. Fitzpatrick (1884–1960), executive secretary of the National Conference on Universities and Public Service and editor of its proceedings.

67.12   Mr. McCarthy,] Charles McCarthy (1873–1921), University of Wisconsin, Wisconsin Legislative Library, spoke before Dewey on "The Plan of the Committee on Practical Training for Public Service."

68.39   mayor,] John Purroy Mitchel (1879–1918) called the conference and gave one of four short opening addresses. See *Universities and Public Service: Proceedings of the National Conference on Universities and Public Service* (Madison, Wis.: American Political Science Association, 1914), pp. 19–21.

70.9   Dean Schneider] Herman Schneider (1872–1939), dean, College of Engineering, University of Cincinnati, spoke on "Municipal Universities."

70.23   Mr. Cooke,] Morris L. Cooke (1872–1960), director, Department of Public Works, Philadelphia, spoke on "Co-Operation of the University of Pennsylvania and the Philadelphia Department of Public Works."

71.27   Professor Howe] Frederick C. Howe (1867–1940), commissioner of immigration, New York State, spoke on "A National University in a Democracy."

72.2   Mr. Chairman,] Richard Park (1861–1942), vice-president of the Indiana State Teachers' Association in 1916, served as superintendent of county schools, Sullivan County, Ind., from 1895 to 1941.

86.11   statement of Alvin Johnson] According to a newspaper account of that evening's proceedings, Johnson said of Dewey, "You, John Dewey, and your fellow Greek philosophers are the supreme exorcists of fear." See John Beaufort, "Wide Acclaim Given Famed Philosopher," *Christian Science Monitor,* 22 October 1949, p. 3. For complete statement by Johnson, see "Dewey, the Greek," *New Republic* 121 (31 October 1949): 9.

87.10–11   an old friend in Texas] Clarence Edwin Ayres, then a member of the Department of Economics at the University of Texas in Austin, wrote to Dewey on 11 October 1949: "I'm not going to congratulate you on attaining to the age of ninety, since all a person has to do to do that is live long enough. My congratulations are for marching ahead, regardless of age! That is really something!" Referring to Dewey's ninetieth birthday celebration, Ayres wrote: "I'm not very much of a one for celebrations, and neither are you. What I want to try to do is to keep on marching. So lead on, John Dewey! Here we come!" (John Dewey Papers, Special Collections, Morris Library, Southern Illinois University at Carbondale).

88.4   American Education Fellowship.] Known for most of its thirty-six years (1919–55) as the Progressive Education Association, its name was changed in 1944 to the American Education Fellowship in an attempt to facilitate the broadening of its activities, only to be changed back to the Progressive Education Association in 1953. In 1949 the AEF was headquartered in Urbana, Ill.

88.5   Dr. Benne] Kenneth D. Benne (1908–   ), professor of education and national president of the AEF.

88.20–21   Herbart Society] The National Herbart Society for the Scientific Study of Education was organized in 1895 under the leadership of Charles de Garmo (1849–1934). With the waning of Herbartianism as an educational movement in the U.S., "Herbart" was dropped from the name of the society in 1901. This name was further shortened in 1909 to the National Society for the Study of Education.

88.22–23   McMurrys . . . Harris] Charles A. McMurry (1857–1929), Frank M. McMurry (1862–1936), Charles de Garmo, and William Torrey Harris (1835–1909). See George Dykhuizen, *The Life and Mind of John Dewey* (Carbondale and Edwardsville: Southern Illinois University Press, 1973), pp. 91–92.

88.27   McClure,] Matthew Thompson McClure, Jr. (1883–1964).

89.14   *"The Great Community,"*] See Josiah Royce, *The Hope of the Great Community*.

93.6–7   sequel . . . Man."] On p. xxix of the preface to his *The Idea of God as Affected by Modern Knowledge*, Fiske states that "the present essay must be regarded as a sequel to the 'Destiny of Man.'"

94.31   "Deity" of Paley.] See Paley, *Natural Theology*, esp. chaps. 23–26.

94.32–36   Spencer . . . started.] See Spencer, *First Principles*, esp. Part I, "The Unknowable," secs. 18 and 62.

101.20–22   Laband, . . . prescription."] See Paul Laband, *Das Staatsrecht des Deutschen Reiches*, 4th ed. (Tübingen and Leipzig: J. C. B. Mohr, 1901), p. 173.

103.36–104.6   As . . . force.] On 14 February 1923 Senator William E. Borah (1865–1940) introduced a resolution, modeled on proposals made by Chicago attorney Salmon O. Levinson (1865–1941), calling for the creation of an international legal code outlawing war and the establishment of an international court with compulsory jurisdiction to hear and make judicial decisions in international disputes. See *Middle Works* 15 : xvi.
    On 24 February President Warren G. Harding (1865–1923) conveyed a letter to the Senate from Secretary of State Charles E. Hughes (1862–1948) recommending the adhesion, with reservations, of the U.S. to the special protocol that established the Permanent Court of International Justice at The Hague in 1920 under the aegis of the League of Nations.

121.1–2   Answer . . . Schools?"] *Columbia Alumni News* 9 (15 March 1918): 674, lists Dewey as a member of the Council of National Defense.

125.4   Professor Seligman:] Edwin R. A. Seligman (1861–1939), economist, edited the *Encyclopaedia of the Social Sciences* from 1930 to 1935.

127.3   Mr. Ernst:] Morris L. Ernst (1888–1976), counsel for Mary Ware Dennett (1872–1947).

127.4   pamphlet] *The Sex Side of Life: An Explanation for Young People,* rev. ed. (privately printed by author, 1928).

127.5   objection] Dennett was convicted in 1928 on the charge of sending obscene material through the mails. This conviction was later reversed by the U.S. Circuit Court of Appeals.

128.1   "Forms of Art Exhibition"] Held at the Pennsylvania Museum of Art, Philadelphia, from 24 April to 6 June 1937.

128.11   Mr. Benson] From 1936 to 1953 Emanuel M. Benson (1904–71) was head of the education division at the Pennsylvania Museum of Art, renamed in 1938 the Philadelphia Museum of Art. Howard Greenfeld, in *The Devil and Dr. Barnes* (New York: Viking Penguin, 1987), p. 188, reports that J. Stogdell Stokes, museum president, identified Benson as a former student of Dewey's.

133.1   Dean Alfange] Alfange ran as American Labor party candidate for governor of New York in 1942 against Democrat John J. Bennett, Jr. (1894–1967), and the eventual winner of the election, Republican Thomas E. Dewey (1902–71). Alfange later was vice-chairman of the Liberal party, which Dewey also supported.

134.1   Liberal Party] John L. Childs (1889–1985), Liberal party state chairman, presided over and was one of several speakers to address a Liberal party rally in Madison Square Garden, New York City, on 31 October 1944. He read this statement from a telegram he had received from Dewey.

135.2   Mr. Rafton] Harold Robert Rafton, A.B., chemistry, 1910, Harvard University.

137.20–29   It . . . inflamed.] On 8 June 1949 Representative John S. Wood (1885–1968), chairman of the House Un-American Activities Committee, announced that letters had been sent to seventy-one state boards of education, colleges, and high schools requesting lists of currently used textbooks and supplementary readings along with the names of their authors. These requests were made in response to a petition submitted by the Sons of the American Revolution expressing concern over Communist-inspired content in school and college texts. The letters sparked an immediate protest from educational leaders and journalists of sufficient intensity to force the committee to abandon this line of inquiry.

139.29   Society.] A note following Dewey's statement states that "Dr. Dewey served two terms as 'Chairman' of the Society, from 1903 to 1905."

140.10   Korean affair] On 25 June 1950 Secretary of State Dean Acheson (1893–1971), with presidential authorization, instructed the U.S. representative to the United Nations to convene an emergency session of the Security Council to consider the invasion of North Korean forces into South Korea. At that meeting the Security Council called for a cessation of hostilities and the withdrawal of North Korean forces to the 38th parallel. Two further resolutions adopted on 27 June and 7 July brought about a coordinated international effort to repel the North Korean invasion under the unified command of the U.S.

140.12–13   Manchurian affair.] In September 1931 the Japanese army invaded and subsequently occupied Manchuria, in direct violation of the Covenant of the League of Nations to which Japan, as an original member of the League, was bound. For the next several months the dispute was considered by the League's Council, which proved to be both unable to bring about direct negotiations between Japan and China and unwilling to invoke provisions in the Covenant that allowed for economic sanctions to be brought against aggressor nations. Finally, in early 1932 the dispute was passed to the Assembly, which, after another year of fact-finding and debate, adopted a statement on 24 February 1933 ruling in China's favor.

140.18–19   the charge . . . Communists."] On 9 February 1950 in a speech to the Republican Women's Club of Ohio County in Wheeling, W.Va., Senator Joseph McCarthy (1908–57) was reported to have said that there were 205 Communists working in the State Department. Although in later statements he presented a modified account of the extent and nature of this infiltration, McCarthy continued to press his case and, in response to denials by President Harry S. Truman (1884–1972) and Secretary of State Acheson, accused the Democratic administration of a cover-up. The matter was brought before a subcommittee of the Senate Foreign Relations Committee, chaired by Maryland Senator Millard E. Tydings (1890–1961), especially convened for the purpose of investigating McCarthy's charges. The Tydings investigation failed to quell public fears over the possibility of Communist subversion in high offices of government, leading many Republican congressional candidates to echo McCarthy's charges in the fall congressional elections.

141.1–2   The fact . . . isolationists] Republican criticism of the Truman administration's foreign policy, particularly in Korea, was countered during the 1950 congressional elections with the charge of isolationism against many Republican candidates. Among those Republicans who publicly responded to these charges after the elections were Senators Alexander Wiley (1884–1967) of Wisconsin, H. Alexander Smith (1880–1966) of New Jersey, Robert A. Taft (1889–1953) of Ohio, and Guy G. Gabrielson (1891–1976), chairman of the Republican National Committee (see "Two Key Senators Deny G.O.P. Swing to Isolationism," *New York Times,* 11 November 1950, p. 1, and "Speculation Rises on New Congress," *New York Times,* 12 November 1950, p. 59).

145.5   Laura Bridgman,] Bridgman (1829–89) was the first blind deaf-mute to be successfully educated. Her case gained great popular notoriety in the nineteenth century.

146.1   Clifford Beers] Clifford Whittingham Beers (1876–1943), founder of the mental hygiene movement, sparked a nationwide interest in reforming the treatment of mental illness with his autobiographical study *A Mind That Found Itself* (Garden City, N.Y.: Doubleday and Co., 1908).

146.3   Dr. Welch:] William Henry Welch (1850–1934), eminent pathologist and bacteriologist, served as chairman of the Tribute Committee for Clifford Beers.

148.6–7   Roman . . . you."] This quotation is from the stone marker on the grave of the eighteenth-century architect Sir Christopher Wren (1632–1723), in St. Paul's Cathedral, London. The Latin inscription, written by Wren's son, reads in part: "Lector, si monumentum requiris, circumspice."

154.24–26   Compare . . . coherent.] See Herbert Spencer, *First Principles,* p. 360.

198.31   Delsarte system?] François Delsarte (1811–71) formulated certain principles of esthetics and applied them to the teaching of dramatic expression, e.g., coordinating the voice with the gestures of all parts of the body.

213.5   President of your Institution] Benjamin Cluff, Jr., president of Brigham Young Academy from 1892 to 1903, studied at the University of Michigan from 1886 to 1890. At the time of Dewey's lectures Cluff was on an expedition in South America.

243.13–27   Mr. Galton . . . researches.] Sir Francis Galton (1822–1911), an English scientist who conducted research in a number of areas, reported his discoveries concerning mental imagery in his *Inquiries into Human Faculty and Its Development,* pp. 83–89.

246.33–39   Mr. Frank Hall . . . Arithmetic."] Frank Haven Hall (1841–1911) was superintendent of the Illinois State School for the Blind from 1890 to 1893 and 1898 to 1902. See "Imagination in Arithmetic," pp. 621–28.

255.4–5   ages of man,] Shakespeare, *As You Like It,* act 1, sc. 7.

256.8–9   Fiske . . . infancy,"] See John Fiske, *Outlines of Cosmic Philosophy,* 2:159–60, 160n, 342–43, 360–63; *Excursions of an Evolutionist* (Boston: Houghton, Mifflin and Co., 1899), pp. 315–17; and "The Part Played by Infancy in the Evolution of Man," in *A Century of Science and Other Essays* (Boston: Houghton, Mifflin and Co., 1899), pp. 106–10.

274.31   orange object lessons.] For Francis W. Parker's account of these lessons, see his *Talks on Pedagogics: An Outline of the Theory of Concentration* (New York and Chicago: E. L. Kellogg and Co., 1894), pp. 136–37.

284.13–15   Dr. Harris, . . . period.] William Torrey Harris (1835–1909) explains his distinction between the symbolic and conventional stages of mind in his *Psychological Foundations of Education* (New York: D. Appleton and Co., 1898), pp. 308–15.

291.7–8   wave . . . teaching] Probably a reference to the Grube method of teaching arithmetic, named after its author, August Wilhelm Grube (1816–84), which was widely adopted in the U.S. during the last two decades of the nineteenth century. The beginning student, according to this method, was to learn the numbers 1 through 100 by an exhaustive analysis of each number into its factors.

299.1–2   habits . . . masters.] The quotation "Habit is either the best of servants, or the worst of masters" is attributable to Nathaniel Emmons (1745–1840), New England Congregationalist minister and theologian. See *The New Dictionary of Thoughts* (Standard Book Co., 1957), p. 254.

303.12–15   I . . . habits.] The quotation is from Jean Jacques Rousseau's *Émile*. The original reads: "La seule habitude qu'on doit laisser prendre à l'enfant est de n'en contracter aucune . . ." (*Émile ou de l'education* [Paris: Librairie de Firmin Didot Frères, Fils et Cie., 1860], p. 41).

323.19–22   You . . . subjects.] This episode is found in chap. 51 of Dickens, *The Posthumous Papers of the Pickwick Club, The Works of Charles Dickens* (New York: Peter Fenelon Collier and Son, 1900), 21:364.

324.24–25   Dr. Hardy . . . day.] Milton H. Hardy was medical superintendent of the Utah State Insane Asylum, Provo, from 1896 to 1905.

325.6–8   You . . . say;] Dewey refers here to Juliet's nurse. See, for example, the nurse's calculation of Juliet's age, Shakespeare, *Romeo and Juliet,* act 1, sc. 3.

328.7–10   This . . . observation.] See William James, *Talks to Teachers on Psychology, and to Students on Some of Life's Ideals* (New York: Henry Holt and Co., 1899), pp. 132–33 [*The Works of William James, Talks to Teachers on Psychology, and to Students on Some of Life's Ideals,* ed. Frederick H. Burkhardt, Fredson Bowers, Ignas K. Skrupskelis (Cambridge: Harvard University Press, 1983), pp. 81–82].

328.23–24   Mr. Speer's work on arithmetic;] William W. Speer (1848–1934) was district superintendent of schools in Chicago from 1894 to 1902.

331.22   "As . . . he."] Proverbs 23:7.

332.6–7   "No . . . thought,"] Luke 12:25.

338.14–15   Some . . . education;] See Herbert Spencer, *Social Statics* (New York: D. Appleton and Co., 1865), pp. 378–85.

340.30–32   Some one . . . truth.] The passage is from Gotthold
Ephraim Lessing's *Eine Duplik*. The original reads: "Wenn
Gott in seiner Rechten alle Wahrheit, und in seiner Linken
den einzigen immer regen Trieb nach Wahrheit, obschon mit
dem Zusatz, mich immer und ewig zu irren, verschlossen
hielte, und spräche zu mir: wähle! Ich fiele ihm mit Demuth
in seine Linke, und sagte: Vater gieb! die reine Wahrheit ist ja
doch nur für dich allein!" (*Gotthold Ephraim Lessings Sämt-
liche Schriften* [Leipzig: G. J. Göschen'sche Verlagshandlung,
1897], 13 : 24).

346.13–16   an article, . . . year.] Marion Hill, "The Star Spangled
Banner: Does It Get Weighed? or Yet Wade? Uncertainty of
Many School-Children upon the Subject," *McClure's Maga-
zine* 15 (July 1900): 262–67.

346.29–31   You . . . necessities.] Oliver Wendell Holmes (1809–94)
records the following remark made by "my friend, the Historian": "Give us the luxuries of life, and we will dispense with
its necessaries" (*The Autocrat of the Breakfast Table* [Bos-
ton and New York: Houghton Mifflin Co., 1891], p. 125).
Holmes's friend was John Lothrop Motley (1814–77).

352.37–38   Aristotle . . . with.] See *Metaphysics* 4.2.1003^{b}19–22;
Prior Analytics 1.30.46^{a}19–20.

366n.11   'inner and outer meaning'] See "The Internal and External
Meaning of Ideas," lecture 7 in Josiah Royce's *The World
and the Individual*.

373.35   subsequent paper,] An incomplete holographic document entitled "Knowledge and Existence / I Some Idealistic Conceptions" is in the Dewey Papers, Box 51, folder 14.

374.23–24   Hegel . . . religion"] See Georg Wilhelm Friedrich Hegel's
Vorlesungen über die Philosophie der Religion (Leiden: A. H.
Adriani, 1901), Part III, "Die Absolute Religion."

385.23   Pharisees . . . Scribes.] See Tolstoi's "Life," chaps. 2–5.

386.34–387.5   metaphor . . . neglected.] See ibid., "Introduction,"
pp. 287–89.

395.39–40   Roman poet . . . himself.] Terence, *Heauton Timo-
roumenos*, line 77, quoted by Cicero, *De Officiis*, I, 30.

415n.2–416n.2   Leibniz. . . . universe.] For discussion of texts used by
Dewey in quoting Leibniz, see *Early Works* 1 : lxi–lxv.

429.3–4   Mr. Bohn] William E. Bohn, educational and administrative director of the Rand School of Social Science from 1929 to 1936.

429.5–6   I didn't . . . now.] Two contemporary events may have occasioned this remark. First, Adolf Hitler (1889–1945) came to power on 30 January 1933, and on 5 March, three days before Dewey's lecture, the National Socialists gained a bare majority in the Reichstag. Soon after, the Reichstag gave Hitler sweeping dictatorial powers. Second, Dewey was speaking at the height of the depression, just prior to the "Hundred Days" during which the Franklin D. Roosevelt administration pushed many anti-depression measures through Congress.

430.20–24   He . . . standards;] See *An Essay concerning Human Understanding*, bk. 1, chap. 4, sec. 24.

431.27–30   Locke . . . source.] See preceding note.

434.9   James' *Psychology*,] See James, *The Principles of Psychology*, 2 : 342 [*Works*, 2 : 968].

437.22–24   Francis Bacon . . . ancients.] See *Advancement of Learning*, bk. 1, *The Works of Francis Bacon* (London: Longmans and Co., 1876), 3 : 291. See also *Novum Organum*, LXXXIV, ibid., 4 : 81–82.

449.21   speaking . . . man] Dewey delivered an address to the American College of Physicians at the Jefferson Hotel in St. Louis, Mo., 21 April 1937, with the title "The Unity of Man." See "The Unity of the Human Being," *Later Works* 13 : 323–37.

450.11   inquiry.] Following a discussion of Dewey's and Hook's papers on 22 May 1937, the two men commented briefly. The slightly edited text of Dewey's rebuttal (stenographic report in the Horace M. Kallen Papers, folder 95, Yivo Institute for Jewish Research, New York, N.Y.) is as follows:

I don't think it will take me more than one minute or a minute and a half. Certainly one remark I made can prove correct, and that is, that it is very dangerous to use an illustration because it will attract attention away from the principle. I doubt if you use deep scientific method, but whether I used it or not there is a real point there and one point of view, the finding out what empirical method is, is in itself an empirical question. You observe and see what people do who are recognized to be scientific people in their inquiries; people who get conclusions that are progressively accepted and use methods that I say are self-correcting and self-developing, now become empiricists. I don't know any way to find out what scientific method is excepting to see what scientific people do and not set down some views in advance which is, to venture into the dangerous sea of illustration, as I think the Marxists do; they don't find out what scientific method does by concerning themselves with what scientific people do; they take the least developed field and form a priori. That is just by way of illustration.

The other remark I made I was very much surprised to hear that it wasn't recognized by scientific method, really used in the physical field and according to reports, restricted in the social sciences. There is a large variety of that in the universities. Personally I am very glad to hear it, but it is a promising piece of news. The other remark is that while formerly it was very dangerous, if I had to make one theoretical analysis, I should say that truths are infinitely numerous and there is one way fundamentally of getting at them.

At the conclusion of the afternoon session, Dewey again spoke briefly as follows:

It seems to me, if I may say so, I have here a very [*word missing*] in the use of the term reason. I don't mean this, the historical cause of it which attacks the whole conception of rationalism. Now, as I suggested a little while ago this morning, there is a kind of blind empiricism, a mere collection of facts in all the advanced sciences. Now if you are going to use, when you speak of the necessary reasons for the necessary conceptual structures, I think empiricists give that case away if they deny it, but when they talk about rationalism they are talking about precise intellect of Aristotle and so on. And what I think as empiricists we are saying is that a conceptual structure shall be regarded as hypotheses developed because what they lead up to are regarded as hypotheses and tested by their consequences; when I telegraph a friend that I don't think he is acting reasonably, I don't think I have committed myself to Plato or Hegel, although I have committed myself to the fact that I think he has chosen to use means that won't give him the consequences he is after or that he is using means that will give him different consequences. That is the ordinary commonsense of reason in order to get the ends that you are after. It involves a material kind and an operational kind. If we set up science and experience off against reason when reason means the intellect and elements that comprise intellect, I don't think we get very far.

466.2   Professor Edman] Irwin Edman (1896–1954), student of Dewey's, who became a member of the philosophy department at Columbia University in 1918 and later chairman of the department.

476.7   most beloved American] In his 1 December 1862 annual message to Congress, Abraham Lincoln, referring to the Union, said, "We shall nobly save or meanly lose the last, best hope of earth."

476.32   another great American] From Franklin Roosevelt's First Inaugural Address, 4 March 1933.

485.16   Jena] In the late nineteenth century, the pedagogical seminar at the University of Jena was under the direction of an influential Herbartian theorist, Wilhelm Rein. A practice school was operated in connection with the seminar.

488.24–25   renewed . . . Chicago,] Dewey was at the University of Chicago from 1894 to 1904.

488.26–27   William . . . Lectureship,] The William Vaughn Moody Lecture series was initiated in 1917 with a gift from Harold H. Swift, trustee and, later, chairman of the Board of Trustees of the University of Chicago.

488.29–30   former . . . friend.] Moody (1869–1910) became an instructor in English at the University of Chicago in the autumn of 1895. After a year's leave in 1899–1900, he returned as assistant professor, resigning in 1907 to devote his career to literary production.

490.2–6   French Ambassador . . . revolution.] Maurice Paléologue (1859–1944), last French ambassador to the Russian Court, from 1914 to 1917.
            The name St. Petersburg was changed to Petrograd in 1914, and to Leningrad in 1924.

490.16–17   man . . . Russia.] Aleksei Ivanovich Putilov (1866–1926?).

492.24–26   Reform . . . population.] The Reform Bill of 1867 expanded the British electorate by 938,000 names, nearly doubling its former size. Upon its passage, in an address before the House of Commons, Robert Lowe, a liberal M.P., said, "I believe it will be absolutely necessary that you should prevail on our future masters to learn their letters," which was popularly construed as "We must educate our masters."

492.38–39   "The laboring . . . lives."] See Albert P. Pinkevitch, *The New Education in the Soviet Republic*, p. 152.

493.9–12   "to lead . . . reconstruction."] The translation is taken from Pinkevitch, pp. 151–52.

493.13–14   "The . . . illiteracy."] The campaign against illiteracy began with the creation in 1920 of the All-Russian Extraordinary Commission for the Liquidation of Illiteracy, which was charged with the task of organizing a nationwide educational effort to eliminate illiteracy among all people between eight and fifty. These efforts were redoubled in 1928 with the adoption of a Five-Year Plan that included cultural goals such as the elimination of illiteracy, and the attendant commitment of the Komosol, the Soviet youth movement, to the task.

493.40–494.5   "The laboring . . . to all."] The translation is taken from Pinkevitch, p. 152. For the original see V. I. Lenin, Speech at the First All-Russia Congress on Education, 28 August 1918.

494.10–13   "An illiterate . . . superstition."] The translation is taken from Pinkevitch, p. 376. For the original see V. I. Lenin, "The New Economic Policy and the Tasks of the Political Education Departments," Report to the Second All-Russia Congress of Political Education Departments, 17 October 1921.

494.23   Lenine's widow,] Nadezhda Konstantinovna Krupskaya (1869–1939), a leader in Soviet education during the 1920s. Elizabeth Dewey, in her notes on the 1928 trip to the Soviet Union, reports an interview with Krupskaya on 26 July (Dewey VFM 3, Special Collections, Morris Library, Southern Illinois University at Carbondale).

495.5–6   twenty-five or thirty] For a list of educators in Dewey's party, see "American Educators in Russia," *School and Society* 27 (30 June 1928): 779.

498.12–13   semi-Asiatic barbarism—] Lenin refers to the "semi-Asiatic state of lack of culture from which we have not yet emerged" in his "Pages from a Diary," 2 January 1923, *Selected Works* (New York: International Publishers Co., 1943),

9:487. Pinkevitch, p. 152, also refers to the "semi-Asiatic un-cultured condition in which the proletarian revolution found Russia."

498.22–23   colony . . . Moscow.] Elizabeth Dewey reports visiting the labor commune on 25 July 1928 (Dewey VFM 3). Emily Stein of James Monroe High School, New York City, who traveled with Dewey's party, also describes this visit (see "A Russian Experiment in Criminology," *School and Society* 28 [1928]: 789–92). This commune was probably located at the site of the contemporary town of Dzerzhinskiy, on the Moscow River south of Moscow.

498.29   Chamberlain."] Joseph Austin Chamberlain (1863–1937) was British foreign secretary in 1927 when the Baldwin government broke off diplomatic relations with the Soviet Union.

499.39–500.2   It . . . number.] Emily Stein reports that the population of the commune numbered 170 boys and 15 girls ("Russian Experiment," p. 790). Elizabeth Dewey puts the total population at 170, including 16 girls and "building for 400 more" (Dewey VFM 3).

501.4–5   founded . . . Tcheka;] "Tcheka" (or "Cheka") is an abbreviation of "Chrezvychainaia Komissiia," "Extraordinary Commission." From 1917 to 1922 various local Chekas, the branches of the Soviet secret police, came under the administrative authority of the All-Russian Extraordinary Commission for Fighting Counter-Revolution and Sabotage. In 1922 the secret police were reorganized to form the Gosudarstvennoe Politicheskoe Upravlenie (GPU), State Political Administration.

In 1921 Feliks Admundovich Dzerzhinskiy (1877–1926), then the head of the Cheka (renamed GPU in 1922), was appointed chairman of the All-Russian Central Executive Committee Commission to Improve the Welfare of Children. His efforts in this capacity included the development of settlements and correctional camps for neglected and delinquent children.

501.39–40   Tolstoy's . . . Rousseau.] For three years, 1859 to 1862, Leo Tolstoy (1828–1910) operated an experimental primary school at his estate in Tula Oblast for the education of peasant children from the surrounding villages.

505.28–29   an experimental station,] The rural division of the First Public Education Experiment Station of the People's Com-

missariat for Education was located at the village of Obninsky in Kaluga Oblast, now the town of Obninsk, 106
kilometers southwest of Moscow. The station was headed by
Stanislav Teofilovich Shatskii (1878–1934), a leader in experimental education in the Soviet Union from 1919 to 1932. According to Elizabeth Dewey's notes on the 1928 trip, Dewey
visited Shatskii's station from 21 to 23 July (Dewey VFM 3).
Thomas Woody, also a member of Dewey's party, reports in
New Minds: New Men? (New York: Macmillan Co., 1932),
p. 43, having visited Shatskii at Obninsky in the summer
of 1928.

505.36   wild boys,] A reference to Russian children who were or-
phaned or separated from their parents during World War I,
the Revolution, the Civil War, and the accompanying fam-
ines. These "wild children," or *bezprizornye,* numbered in
the millions in the Soviet Union during the 1920s.

506.6–11   Another . . . here."] This episode is also reported by
Joshua Kunitz, a member of the party of educators who visited the Soviet Union with Dewey. See Kunitz's "Eavesdrop-
ping in Russia," *North American Review* 230 (July 1930): 12.

507.23–24   pedology . . . Hall.] Originally spelled "paidology," this
word was coined in 1892 by Oscar Chrisman, an educational
psychologist. The word first appeared in Chrisman's "The
Hearing of Children," *Pedagogical Seminary* 2 (1892): 439,
ed. G. Stanley Hall. Chrisman was a Fellow at Clark University, studying under Hall's tutelage. For Chrisman's own
account of the coinage, see his "Child-Study, A New Department of Education," *Forum* 16 (February 1894): 728–29.

507.41–508.1   Russian . . . engineer,] Dewey is evidently referring to
Aleksandr Ustinovich Zelenko (1871–1953). After graduat-
ing from Petersburg Institute of Civil Engineering in 1892,
Zelenko started his teaching career, eventually collaborating
with Shatskii (see note for 505.28–29) on early experiments
in progressive education. He studied in the U.S. twice: 1904
to 1905 and 1909 to 1910. After the Bolshevik Revolution
Zelenko taught and conducted research at the Institute of
Methods of Extracurricular Work in Moscow. Elizabeth
Dewey reports visiting Zelenko's laboratory on 16 July 1928
(Dewey VFM 3).

509.18–24   dramatic expression, . . . world.] Elizabeth Dewey reports seeing four plays performed by the Moscow Art The-

atre in Leningrad: Anton Chekhov's *Ivanov* on 4 July 1928, Maxim Gorky's *Lower Depths* on 5 July, and Chekhov's *Cherry Orchard* and *Uncle Vanya* on 6 and 8 July (Dewey VFM 3).

509.33–34   Mr. Bakmetiev,] Two Bakhmet'yevs served as envoys to the U.S. during the Kerensky government: George (? – 1928) and Boris Alexander (1880–1951). Dewey probably refers to the latter, who lived and worked in New York City from 1923 until his death.

511.3   Mr. Chairman, and Mr. Chairman;] H. E. Barnard (1874–1946), director of the White House Conference on Child Health and Protection, and William J. Bogan (1870–1936), Chicago superintendent of schools and chairman of the Chicago Regional White House Conference.

511.5   White House Conference] The White House Conference on Child Health and Protection, called by President Herbert Hoover (1874–1964), assembled in Washington, D.C., 19–22 November 1930.

511.24   Children's Charter.] Drafted by Hoover and revised and adopted by the White House Conference, the Children's Charter outlined nineteen aims for children's welfare to which the conference was committed (see this vol., Appendix 6).

513.29   Dr. Judd] Charles H. Judd (1873–1946) was head of the Department of Education and director of education at the University of Chicago, and served on the Committee on the School Child of the White House Conference.

515.32   Committee G,] Committee on Youth Outside of Home and School, chaired by James E. West (1876–1948).

517.6   James Harvey Robinson,] Robinson (1863–1936) taught history at Columbia University from 1892 to 1919.

517.28–31   first . . . Chicago.] Dewey's reference is unclear. The first courses offered for the training of social workers in Chicago were taught by Graham Taylor (1851–1938) and Charles Richmond Henderson (1848–1915) at the University of Chicago in 1903. During 1904 to 1905 a full-time program in social work was offered. In 1908 Taylor established the Chicago School of Civics and Philanthropy, which remained independent until it merged with the university in 1920. The first endowed chair in social work at the university was not created until 1929, when the Samuel Deutsch Professorship of Public Welfare Administration was given to Sophonisba Breckinridge (1866–1948).

517.32–34   Jane . . . Abbott] Mary E. McDowell (1854–1936), Julia C. Lathrop (1858–1932), and Grace Abbott (1878–1939) all began nationally and internationally prominent careers in social work and philanthropy as resident workers of Hull House, the social settlement founded in 1899 in Chicago by Jane Addams (1860–1935), which Dewey served as a founding trustee. Lathrop served on the Committee on Vocational Guidance and Child Labor of the White House Conference on Child Health and Protection.

517.35   Children's Bureau,] Created by Congress in 1912 to investigate matters pertaining to child welfare. Julia C. Lathrop was the first chief of the Children's Bureau, holding that office until 1921. She was succeeded by Grace Abbott, who held the office until 1934.

518.13   Dr. Fishbein] Morris Fishbein (1889–1976), physician and prolific writer, edited the *Journal of the American Medical Association* from 1924 to 1949.

519.17   read . . . paper] See "36 Holdups in 4 1/2 Hours, Crime Wave Opener," *Chicago Daily Tribune*, 31 October 1931, p. 1.

519.33   Dr. Barnard] See note for 511.3.

523.19   two of our wars,] Spanish-American War and World War I.

524.1   Mr. Pringle] Journalist, historian, and government official who was, in 1942, chief of the Publications Division in the Office of War Information.

526.1   S. J. Woolf] Artist who combined interviews with portraits of prominent persons and published them as newspaper and magazine articles. See his sketch accompanying Edward O. Sisson, "The Significance of John Dewey," *Hawaii Educational Review* 18 (October 1929): 29; and his interviews "John Dewey Surveys the Nation's Ills," *New York Times*, 10 July 1932, p. 9 [*Later Works* 6:408–13]; "A Philosopher's Philosophy," *New York Times Magazine*, 15 October 1939, pp. 5, 17.

531.11–12   "He . . . Father."] John 14:9.

531.13–15   "That . . . you."] 1 John 1:1–13.

Checklist of Dewey's References

This section gives full publication information for each work cited by Dewey. Books in Dewey's personal library (John Dewey Papers, Special Collections, Morris Library, Southern Illinois University at Carbondale) have been listed whenever possible. When Dewey gave page numbers for a reference, the edition has been identified by locating the citation; for other references, the edition listed here is his most likely source by reason of place or date of publication, general accessibility during the period, or evidence from correspondence and other materials.

Adamson, John William. *Pioneers of Modern Education, 1600–1700.* Cambridge: At the University Press, 1905.

Angell, James Rowland. *Psychology.* New York: Henry Holt and Co., 1904.

Barnes, Albert C. *The Art in Painting.* 2d ed., rev. and enl. New York: Harcourt, Brace and Co., 1928.

Boas, Franz. *The Mind of Primitive Man.* New York: Macmillan Co., 1913.

Bode, Boyd H. "Some Recent Definitions of Consciousness." *Psychological Review* 15 (July 1908): 255–64.

Boodin, John E. "Do Things Exist?" *Journal of Philosophy, Psychology and Scientific Methods* 9 (4 January 1912): 5–14.

Clarke, Edward H. *Sex in Education; or, A Fair Chance for the Girls.* Boston: James R. Osgood and Co., 1873.

Clifford, William Kingdon. "On the Nature of Things-in-Themselves." In his *Lectures and Essays,* edited by Leslie Stephen and Sir Frederick Pollock, 2:52–73. London: Macmillan and Co., 1879.

Dakyns, Henry Graham, trans. *The History of Xenophon.* Vol. 1. New York: Tandy-Thomas Co., 1909.

Darwin, Charles. *The Expression of the Emotions in Man and Animals.* New York: D. Appleton and Co., 1898.

Davidson, Thomas. *Aristotle and Ancient Educational Ideals.* New York: Charles Scribner's Sons, 1892.

———. *A History of Education.* New York: Charles Scribner's Sons, 1900.

De Garmo, Charles. *Herbart and the Herbartians*. New York: Charles Scribner's Sons, 1895.

Dewey, John. "Interpretation of Savage Mind." *Psychological Review* 9 (1902): 217–30. [*The Middle Works of John Dewey, 1899–1924,* edited by Jo Ann Boydston, 2:39–52. Carbondale and Edwardsville: Southern Illinois University Press, 1976.]

———. "Perception and Organic Action." *Journal of Philosophy, Psychology and Scientific Methods* 9 (21 November 1912): 645–68. [*Middle Works* 7:3–29.]

Dewey, John, et al. *Studies in Logical Theory*. University of Chicago, The Decennial Publications, 2d ser., vol. 11. Chicago: University of Chicago Press, 1903. [*Middle Works* 2:293–375.]

Dickens, Charles. *The Works of Charles Dickens*. Vols. 11 and 12, *Life and Adventures of Nicholas Nickleby*. New York: Peter Fenelon Collier and Son, 1900.

Dutton, Samuel T. *Social Phases of Education in the School and the Home*. New York: Macmillan Co., 1899.

Eliot, George. "Worldliness and Other-Worldliness: The Poet Young." *Westminster Review* 67 (January 1857): 1–23.

Fiske, John. *The Destiny of Man Viewed in the Light of His Origin*. Boston and New York: Houghton, Mifflin and Co., 1884.

———. *The Idea of God as Affected by Modern Knowledge*. Boston and New York: Houghton, Mifflin and Co., 1885.

———. *Outlines of Cosmic Philosophy*. 2 vols. Boston: Houghton, Mifflin Co., 1874.

Galton, Francis. *Inquiries into Human Faculty and Its Development*. London: Macmillan and Co., 1883.

Gardner, Percy, and Frank Byron Jevons. *A Manual of Greek Antiquities*. London: Charles Griffin and Co., 1898.

Green, Thomas Hill. *Prolegomena to Ethics*. Edited by A. C. Bradley. Oxford: At the Clarendon Press, 1883.

Grote, George. *History of Greece*. Vol. 8. New York: Harper and Brothers, 1872.

Hall, Frank H. "Imagination in Arithmetic." In *National Educational Association Journal of Proceedings and Addresses,* pp. 621–28. Chicago: University of Chicago Press, 1897.

Hegel, Georg Wilhelm Friedrich. *Lectures on the Philosophy of Religion*. Translated by E. B. Spiers and J. Burdon Sanderson. Vols. 2 and 3. London: Kegan Paul, Trench Trubner and Co., 1895.

Hinsdale, B. A. *Horace Mann and the Common School Revival in the United States*. New York: Charles Scribner's Sons, 1898.

Höffding, Harald. *Outlines of Psychology*. London: Macmillan and Co., 1896.

Hogben, Lancelot. *The Retreat from Reason*. London: Watts and Co., 1936.

Hook, Sidney. "The Desirable and Emotive in Dewey's Ethics." In *John Dewey: Philosopher of Science and Freedom*, a symposium edited by Sidney Hook, pp. 194–216. New York: Dial Press, 1950.

Hughes, Thomas. *Loyola and the Educational System of the Jesuits*. New York: Charles Scribner's Sons, 1892.

Jaeger, Gustav. *Die Entdeckung der Seele*. Leipzig: Ernst Günther's Verlag, 1880.

James, William. *The Principles of Psychology*. 2 vols. New York: Henry Holt and Co., 1893.

———. *Psychology*. New York: Henry Holt and Co., 1893.

Jevons, Frank Byron, and Percy Gardner. *A Manual of Greek Antiquities*. London: Charles Griffin and Co., 1898.

Krabbe, Hugo. *The Modern Idea of the State*. Translated by George H. Sabine and Walter J. Shepard. New York: D. Appleton and Co., 1922.

Laurie, S. S. *Historical Survey of Pre-Christian Education*. New York: Longmans, Green, and Co., 1900.

———. *The Rise and Early Constitution of Universities*. New York: D. Appleton and Co., 1886.

Lenin, V. I. *Collected Works*. Vol. 23, 1918–1919. New York: International Publishers, 1926.

Locke, John. *An Essay concerning Human Understanding*. In *The Works of John Locke*, 10th ed., vols. 1–3. London: J. Johnson, 1801.

McKay, Claude. *Selected Poems of Claude McKay*. Edited by Max Eastman. New York: Bookman Associates, 1953.

MacMichael, J. F. *The Anabasis of Xenophon*. 4th ed., rev. London: George Bell; Whittaker and Co., 1851.

Mahaffy, J. P. *Old Greek Education*. New York: Harper and Brothers, 1905.

Martineau, James. *Types of Ethical Theory*. 2 vols. Oxford: At the Clarendon Press, 1885.

Monroe, Paul. *A Brief Course in the History of Education*. New York: Macmillan Co., 1907.

———. *Source Book of the History of Education for the Greek and Roman Period*. New York: Macmillan Co., 1902.

———. *A Text-Book in the History of Education*. New York: Macmillan Co., 1905.

Morgan, C. Lloyd. *Psychology for Teachers*. New York: Charles Scribner's Sons, 1906.

Morley, John. *Diderot and the Encyclopaedists*. New York: Scribner and Welford, 1878.

————. *Rousseau.* 2 vols. London: Macmillan and Co., 1886, 1891.

————. *Voltaire.* London: Macmillan and Co., 1891.

Paléologue, Maurice. *An Ambassador's Memoirs.* Translated by F. A. Holt. Vol. 1. New York: George H. Doran Co., 1925.

Paley, William. *Natural Theology; or, Evidences of the Existence and Attributes of the Deity, Collected from the Appearances of Nature.* Boston: Gould and Lincoln, 1858.

Phelps, Elizabeth Stuart. "The Struggle for Immortality." *North American Review,* no. 331 (June 1884): 554–73.

Pinkevitch, Albert P. *The New Education in the Soviet Republic.* Translated by Nucia Perlmutter. Edited by George S. Counts. New York: John Day Co., 1929.

Pound, Roscoe. *Law and Morals: The McNair Lectures.* Chapel Hill, N.C.: University of North Carolina Press, 1924.

Quick, Robert Hebert. *Essays on Educational Reformers.* New York: D. Appleton and Co., 1890.

Randall, John Herman, Jr. *Our Changing Civilization: How Science and the Machine Are Reconstructing Modern Life.* New York: Frederick A. Stokes Co., 1929.

Roberts, W. Rhys. *Dionysius of Helicarnassus.* London: Macmillan and Co., 1910.

Roosevelt, Theodore. *Theodore Roosevelt: An Autobiography.* New York: Macmillan Co., 1913.

Rousseau, Jean Jacques. *Émile: or, Concerning Education.* Translated by Eleanor Worthington. Boston: D. C. Heath and Co., 1883.

Royce, Josiah. *The Hope of the Great Community.* New York: Macmillan Co., 1916.

————. *The World and the Individual.* First Series: The Four Historical Conceptions of Being. New York: Macmillan Co., 1900.

Sixteenth Annual Report of the Bureau of Statistics of Labor [Massachusetts], August, 1885. Boston: Wright and Potter Printing Co., State Printers, 1885.

Smith, Thomas Vernor. *The Promise of American Politics.* Chicago: University of Chicago Press, 1936.

Spencer, Herbert. *First Principles.* Philadelphia: David McKay, 1867.

Stein, Ludwig. *Philosophische Strömungen der Gegenwart.* Stuttgart: Verlag von Ferdinand Enke, 1908.

————. "Der Pragmatismus." *Archiv für Systematische Philosophie,* n.s. 14 (1908): 1–9, 143–88.

Stout, G. F. *The Groundwork of Psychology.* New York: Hinds and Noble, 1903.

Thorndike, Edward L. *The Elements of Psychology.* New York: A. G. Seiler, 1905.

———. *The Human Nature Club*. New York: Longmans, Green, and Co., 1901.

———. *The Principles of Teaching*. New York: A. G. Seiler, 1906.

Titchener, Edward Bradford. *An Outline of Psychology*. New York: Macmillan Co., 1897.

Tolstoï, N. Lyof. *Power and Liberty*. New York: Thomas Y. Crowell Co., 1888.

———. "Letter to the Liberals." In *Shakespeare, Christian Teaching, Letters*, vol. 12 of *The Complete Works of Lyof N. Tolstoï*, pp. 57–72. New York: Thomas Y. Crowell and Co., 1899.

———. "Life." In *What Is To Be Done? Life*, vol. 10 of *The Complete Works of Lyof N. Tolstoï*, pp. 285–441. New York: Thomas Y. Crowell and Co., 1899.

———. "Patriotism and Christianity." In *Essays, Letters, Miscellanies*, vol. 20 of *The Novels and Other Works of Lyof N. Tolstoï*, pp. 1–62. New York: Thomas Y. Crowell and Co., 1899.

———. "Religion and Morality." In *Shakespeare, Christian Teaching, Letters*, vol. 12 of *The Complete Works of Lyof N. Tolstoï*, pp. 73–98. New York: Thomas Y. Crowell and Co., 1899.

———. "What Is To Be Done?" In *What Is To Be Done? Life*, vol. 10 of *The Complete Works of Lyof N. Tolstoï*, pp. 1–283. New York: Thomas Y. Crowell and Co., 1899.

Welling, Richard. *As the Twig Is Bent*. New York: G. P. Putnam's Sons, 1942.

Wells, H. G. *The Outline of History*. 2 vols. New York: Macmillan Co., 1920.

West, Andrew Fleming. *Alcuin and the Rise of the Christian Schools*. New York: Charles Scribner's Sons, 1892.

White, Morton G. "Value and Obligation in Dewey and Lewis." *Philosophical Review* 58 (July 1949): 321–29.

White House Conference on Child Health and Protection, 1930. New York: Century Co., 1931.

Wilkins, Augustus S. *National Education in Greece*. London: Strahan and Co., 1873.

Williams, Samuel G. *The History of Ancient Education*. Syracuse, N.Y.: C. W. Bardeen, 1903.

———. *The History of Mediaeval Education*. Syracuse, N.Y.: C. W. Bardeen, 1903.

———. *The History of Modern Education*. Syracuse, N.Y.: C. W. Bardeen, 1903.

Willkie, Wendell L. *One World*. New York: Simon and Schuster, 1943.

Woodbridge, Frederick J. E. "Consciousness and Meaning." *Psychological Review* 15 (November 1908): 397–98.

Woodward, William Harrison. *Studies in Education during the Age of the Renaissance, 1400–1600*. Cambridge: At the University Press, 1906.

————. *Vittorino da Feltre and Other Humanist Educators*. Cambridge: At the University Press, 1897.

Index